OXFORD STUDIES IN DEMOCRATIZATION

Series Editor: Laurence Whitehead

....

THE POLITICS OF MEMORY

OXFORD STUDIES IN DEMOCRATIZATION

Series Editor: Laurence Whitehead

....

Oxford Studies in Democratization is a series for scholars and students of comparative politics and related disciplines. Volumes will concentrate on the comparative study of the democratization processes that accompanied the decline and termination of the cold war. The geographical focus of the series will primarily be Latin America, the Caribbean, Southern and Eastern Europe, and relevant experiences in Africa and Asia.

OTHER BOOKS IN THE SERIES

The New Politics of Inequality in Latin America:
Rethinking Participation and Representation.
Douglas A. Chalmers, Carlos M. Vilas, Katherine Roberts Hite, Scott B. Martin, Kerianne Piester, and Monique Segarra

Human Rights and Democratization in Latin America:
Uruguay and Chile
Alexandra Barahona de Brito

Citizenship Rights and Social Movements:
A Comparative and Statistical Analysis
Joe Foweraker and Todd Landman

Regimes, Politics, and Markets:

Democratization and Economic Change in Southern and Eastern Europe
José María Maravall

Democracy Between Consolidation and Crisis in Southern Europe
Leonardo Morlino

The Bases of Party Competition in Eastern Europe:
Social and Ideological Cleavages in Post Communist States
Geoffrey Evans and Stephen Whitefield

The Democratic Developmental State:
Politics and Institutional Design
Marc Robinson and Gordon White

The International Dimensions of Democratization:
Europe and the Americas
Laurence Whitehead

The Legacy of Human Rights Violations in the Southern Cone:
Argentina, Chile and Uruguay
Luis Roniger and Mario Sznajder

The Politics of Memory

Transitional Justice in Democratizing Societies

EDITED BY

ALEXANDRA BARAHONA DE BRITO

CARMEN GONZÁLEZ-ENRÍQUEZ

and

PALOMA AGUILAR

OXFORD
UNIVERSITY PRESS

OXFORD
UNIVERSITY PRESS

Great Clarendon Street, Oxford OX2 6DP

Oxford University Press is a department of the University of Oxford.
It furthers the University's objective of excellence in research, scholarship,
and education by publishing worldwide in

Oxford New York

Athens Auckland Bangkok Bogotá Buenos Aires
Cape Town Chennai Dar es Salaam Delhi Florence Hong Kong Istanbul
Karachi Kolkata Kuala Lumpur Madrid Melbourne Mexico City Mumbai
Nairobi Paris São Paulo Shanghai Singapore Taipei Tokyo Toronto Warsaw

with associated companies in Berlin Ibadan

Oxford is a registered trade mark of Oxford University Press
in the UK and in certain other countries

Published in the United States
by Oxford University Press Inc., New York

First published 2001

British Library Cataloguing in Publication Data

Data available

Library of Congress Cataloging in Publication Data

ISBN 0–19–924080–9
ISBN 0–19–924090–6

1 3 5 7 9 10 8 6 4 2

Typeset by Graphicraft Limited, Hong Kong
Printed in Great Britain
on acid-free paper by
TJ International Ltd
Padstow, Cornwall

Alexandra Barahona de Brito dedicates this book to her parents Carlos and Terry, her sister Marina, her children Carlotta and Afonso, and to Joaquim Paço d'Arcos, a true friend.

Carmen González-Enríquez dedicates this book to her children, Celia and Julio, and her husband, Ignacio.

Paloma Aguilar dedicates this book, as always, to her family, particularly her companion Jesús, her parents, Susa and Ángel, her sister Susana, and this time also her niece, Sonia, the source of unexpected joy and emotions.

Acknowledgements

Alexandra Barahona de Brito would like to thank the Luso-American Development Foundation in Lisbon (FLAD) for a generous Visiting Fellowship grant to carry out the editing and research work for the book in 1999 at the Center of International Studies (CIS) at Princeton University. Thanks are due especially to Fernando Durão, the director of the FLAD, and António Costa Pinto, one of the contributors to this book, for their support for the project. At the CIS, thanks are due to director Michael Doyle and CIS staff Jerri, June and Pat, who most generously made her feel at home. Most especially, she would like to thank Nancy Bermeo, the head of the Southern European Studies programme at the Politics Department, and her lovely family, who extended a warm welcome, consistent support and friendship during the work carried out in Princeton. In addition, she would like to extend special thanks to Laurence Whitehead, who gave the project crucial support in the early stages when it had no institutional support. Finally, she would like to thank Alan Angell, Fernando Pérez, the *illustríssimo* Maurizio Viroli, Astrid Arrarás, Jorge Silva, Bill Smith, David Myhre, Jeremy Adelman Franklim, and Jonathan Allen.

Paloma Aguilar would like to thank all the people who have, over the last three years, been associated with her in the 'Authoritarian Legacies' project of Columbia University in New York. Thanks are due in this context to Nancy Bermeo, Paola Cesarini, Consuelo Cruz, Margaret Graham, Frances Hagopian, Catherine Hite, Edward Malefakis, Leonardo Morlino, Anthony Pereira, and Mark Ungar, as well as to Elizabeth Jelin, Elizabeth Lira, Eric Herschberg, and Alexander Wilde, whom she met in the context of this project. Essential institutional support was received from the Centre for Advanced Studies in Social Science of the Juan March Institute in Madrid, where she has enjoyed excellent intellectual and personal surroundings for the development of her work over the last ten years. Thanks are also due to the Ford Foundation. Carmen González and Paloma Aguilar also thank the Political Science Department of the National University for Distance Education (UNED) in Madrid.

All three editors would like to thank Laurence Whitehead, as director of the 'Studies in Democratization' series at Oxford University Press (OUP), of which this book is a part, as well as Dominic Byatt, Sandra Benko and Amanda Watkins at OUP, for their patience throughout the preparation of the book. We also thank the external readers, whose comments on an early version of the project and some of its chapters were extremely useful for improving its quality. Last but not least, we thank Juan Linz for bringing us together in the first place.

Alexandra Barahona de Brito
Paloma Aguilar
Carmen González-Enríquez

Contents

List of Tables and Figure

Tables

Figure

Abbreviations

AC	Amnesty Committees (South Africa)
ACHR	American Convention on Human Rights
ATCA	Alien Tort Claims Act (USA)
AJD	Association of Democratic Justice (*Asociación Justicia Democrática*) (Spain)
AN	National Audience (*Audiencia Nacional*) (Spain)
ANC	African National Congress
ANEP	National Association of Private Enterprise (Asociasión Nacional de la Empresa Privada)
ANN	New Nation Alliance (*Alianza Nueva Nación*) (Guatemala)
APM	Grandmothers of the Plaza de Mayo (*Abuelas de la Plaza de Mayo*) (Argentina)
ARENA	National Republican Alliance (*Alianza Republicana Nacional*) (El Salvador)
ARENA	National Renovating Alliance (*Aliança Renovadora Nacional*) (Brazil)
ASC	Civil Society Assembly (*Asamblea de la Sociedad Civil*) (Guatemala)
ATE	ETA Anti Terrorism (*Anti Terrorismo ETA*) (Spain)
BIS	Social Investigation Brigade (*Brigada de Investigación Social*) (Spain)
BKP	Bulgarian Communist Party (*Balgarska Comunisticeska Partije*)
BPS	Proceedings and Follow Up Office (*Bureau the Poursuites et Suivies*) (Haiti)
BPS	Political Social Brigade (*Brigada Político Social*) (Spain)
BSP	Bulgarian Socialist Party (*Balgarski Socialisticka Partija*)
BVE	Basque Spanish Battalion (*Batallón Vasco Español*) (Spain)
CBA	Brazilian Amnesty Committees (*Comités de Anistía Brasilieros*)

CCOO	Workers' Commissions (*Comisiones Obreras*) (Spain)
CDR	Romanian Democratic Convention (*Conventia Democratâ Românâ*)
CED	Democratic Electoral Commission (*Comissão Eleitoral Democrática*) (Portugal)
CEH	Historical Clarification Commission (*Comisión de Esclarecimiento Histórico*) (Guatemala)
CESID	Centre for Higher Studies of Research and Defence (*Centro de Estudios Superiores de Investigación y Defensa*) (Spain)
CEUD	Democratic Union Electoral Commission (*Comissão Eleitoral de União Democrática*) (Portugal)
CD	Democratic Convergence (*Convergencia Democrática*) (El Salvador)
CDF	Ciskei Defence Force (South Africa)
CDN	National Defence Council (*Consejo de Defensa Nacional*)
CDS	Social Democratic Centre Party (*Centro Democrático Social*) (Portugal)
CDU	Christian Democratic Party (*Christlich–Demokratische Union*) (Germany)
CFMDP	Commission of Relatives of the Dead and Disappeared (*Comissão dos Familiares dos Mortos e Desaparecidos Políticos*) (Brazil)
CIA	Central Intelligence Agency
CICC	Coalition for an International Criminal Court
CIS	Centre for Sociological Research (*Centro de Investigaciones Sociológicas*) (Spain)
CNJ	National Council of the Judiciary (*Consejo Nacional de la Judicatura*) (El Salvador)
CNRR	National Reparation and Reconciliation Corporation (*Corporación Nacional de Reparación y Reconciliación*) (Chile)
CNT	National Workers' Confederation (*Confederación Nacional de Trabajadores*) (Spain)
CNVR	Truth and Reconciliation Commission (*Comisión Nacional de la Verdad y la Reconciliación*) (Chile)
CODESA	Convention for a Democratic South Africa

COFADEH	Committee of Relatives of the Detained–Disappeared in Honduras (*Comité de Familiares de los Detenidos–Desparecidos en Honduras*)
CONADEH	National Commissioner for Human Rights (*Comisariado Nacional de Derechos Humanos*) (Honduras)
CONADEP	National Commission on the Disappearance of People (*Comisión Nacional sobre la Desparición de Personas*) (Argentina)
CONAVIGUA	National Coordinator of Guatemalan Widows (*Coordinadora National de Viudas de Guatemala*)
COSATU	Confederation of South African Trade Unions
CPPD	Coalition of Parties for Democracy (*Concertación de Partidos por la Democracia*) (Chile)
CR	Council of the Revolution (*Conselho da Revolução*) (Portugal)
CSFA	Supreme Council of the Armed Forces (*Consejo Supremo de las Fuerzas Armadas*)
CSI	Socialist Iberian Convergence (*Convergencia Socialista Ibérica*)
CSVR	Centre for the Study of Violence and Reconciliation
DChN	Christian Democratic Union (*Demotraktycznej Chrzescijansko–Narodowe*) (Poland)
DDR	German Democratic Republic (*Deutsches Demokratische Republic*)
DINA	National Intelligence Directorate (*Dirección de Inteligencia Nacional*) (Chile)
DNI	National Investigations Department (*Departamento Nacional de Investigaciones*) (Honduras)
DPS	Movement for Rights and Freedom (*Dvisenie za Pravata i Svobody*) (Bulgaria)
DVU	German Peoples Union (*Deutche Volksunion*)
EAAF	Argentine Forensic Anthropolgy Team (*Equipo Argentina de Antropología Forense*)
EAFG	Guatemalan Forensic Antropology Team (*Equipo de Antropología Forense de Guatemala*)
ECHR	European Court for Human Rights
EEC	European Economic Community
EECR	East European Constitutional Review
EHRC	European Human Rights Convention
EK	Study Commission for the Assessment of the History and Consequences of the SED

	Dictatorship in Germany (*Enquete Kommission Aufarbeitung von Geschiste und Folgen der SED Diktator in Deutschland*)
ELP	Army for the Liberation of Portugal (*Exército de Libertação de Portugal*)
ESMA	Navy Mechanics School (*Escuela Mecanica Naval*) (Argentina)
ETA	Basque Country and Freedom (*Euskadi Ta Askatasuna*) (Spain)
EU	European Union
FA	Broad Front (*Frente Amplio*) (Uruguay)
FF	Freedom Front (South Africa)
FKgP	Independent Smallholders Party (*Független Kisgazda Földmunkas és Polgári Part*) (Hungary)
FMLN	Farabundo Martí Front for National Liberation (*Frente Farabundo Martí de Liberación Nacional*) (El Salvador)
FP-25	Popular Forces-25 (*Forças Populares*-25) (Portugal)
FPS	Federation of Socialist Parties (*Federación de Partidos Socialistas*) (Spain)
FRMT	Rigoberta Menchú Foundation (*Fundación Rigoberta Menchú Tum*) (Guatemala)
FSB	Security Services (*Federalnaya Sluzhba Bezopsnosti*) (Russia)
FSN	National Salvation Front (*Frontul Salvarii Nationale*) (Romania)
GAL	Anti Terrorist Liberation Groups (*Grupos Anti-terroristas de Liberación*) (Spain)
GAM	Mutual Support Group (*Grupo de Apoyo Mutuo*) (Guatemala)
GARF	State Archive of the Russian Federation (*Gosudarstvennyi Arkhiv Rossiskoy Federatsii*)
GN	National Guard (*Guardia Nacional*) (El Salvador)
GNR	National Republican Guard (*Guarda Republicana Nacional*) (Portugal)
GNU	Government of National Unity (South Africa)
HB	Unity of the People (*Herri Batasuna*) (Basque Country, Spain)
HIJOS	Children in Favour of Identity and Justice Against Forgetting and Silence (*Hijos por la Identidad y Justicia Contral el Olvido y el Silencio*) (Argentina and Uruguay)
HROs	Human Rights Organizations

HRVC	Human Rights Violations Committee (South Africa)
IACHR	Inter American Commission for Human Rights
IAHRC	Inter American Court for Human Rights
ICC	International Criminal Court
ICCPR	International Covenant on Civil and Political Rights
ICTR	International Criminal Tribunal for Rwanda
ICTFY	International Criminal Tribunal for the Former Yugoslavia
IFP	Inkatha Freedom Party (*Iqebu Lenatha Yenkulukelo*) (South Africa)
ILO	International Labour Organization
IMF	International Monetary Fund
IU	United Left (*Izquierda Unida*) (Spain)
JSN	National Salvation Junta (*Junta de Salvação Nacional*) (Portugal)
KAS	Socialist Nationalist Coordinator (*Coordinadora Abertzale Socialista*) (Spain)
KGB	Committee for State Security (*Komitet Gosudásrstvenni Bezopásnosti*) (Soviet Union)
KPSS	Communist Party of the Soviet Union (*Kommunisticheskaya Partiya Sovetskogo Soyuza*)
KSC	Czechoslovak Communist Party (*Kumunisticka Strana Ceskoslovenska*)
LCR	Revolutionary Communist League (*Liga Comunista Revolucionaria*) (Spain)
LP	Portuguese Legion (*Legião Portuguesa*)
LPDP	League for the Rights of People (*Liga por los Derechos del Pueblo*) (Italy)
LPN	National Pacification Law (*Ley de Pacificación Nacional*) (Uruguay)
MDF	Hungarian Democratic Forum (*Magyar Demokrata Fórum*)
MDLP	Democratic Movement for the Liberation of Portugal (*Movimento Democrático para a Libertação de Portugal*)
MDP	Portuguese Democratic Movement (*Movimento Democrático Português*)
MFA	Armed Forces Movement (*Movimento Forças Armadas*) (Portugal)
MIEP	Hungarian Justice and Life Party (*Magyar Igazság és Elet Pártja*)

MINUGUA	United Nations Mission in Guatemala (*Misión de Naciones Unidas en Guatemala*)
MK	The Spear of the Nation (*umKhonto weSizwe*) (South Africa)
MN	National Movement (*Movimiento Nacional*) (Spain)
MP	Public Ministry (*Ministerio Público*)
MPM	Mothers of the Plaza de Mayo (*Madres de la Plaza de Mayo*) (Argentina)
MST	Landless Rural Workers' Movement (*Movimento Sem Terra*) (Brazil)
MSzMP	Hungarian Socialist Party (*Magyar Szocialista Munkás Párt*)
MSzP	Hungarian Socialist Party (*Magyar Szocialista Párt*)
MTP	Movement All for the Fatherland (Movimiento Todos por la Patria) (Argentina)
MVD	Ministry of Internal Affairs (*Ministersvo Vnutrennykh Del*) (Soviet Union)
MYFUDD	Mothers and Relatives of Uruguayans Disappeared in Argentina (*Madres y Familiares de Uruguayos Desaparecidos en Argentina*)
NACLA	North American Congress on Latin America
NATO	North Atlantic Treaty Organization
NE	New Space (*Nuevo Espacio*) (Uruguay)
NGOs	Non-Governmental Organizations
NKVD	People's Commissariat for Internal Affairs (*Narodny Kommisariat Vnutrennikh Del*) (Soviet Union)
NIS	National Intelligence Service (South Africa)
NP	National Party (South Africa)
NSA	National Security Archives (USA)
NU	National Unity (South Africa)
NURA	National Unity and Reconciliation Act (South Africa)
OAB	Brazilian Bar Association (*Ordem dos Advogados Brasileiros*)
OAS	Organization of American States
OAU	Organization of African Unity
ONUSAL	United Nations Observer Mission in El Salvador (*Misión de Observadores de las Naciones Unidas en El Salvador*)

OSCE	Organization for Security and Co-operation in Europe
PAC	Pan Africanist Congress
PACs	Self Defence Civil Patrols (*Patrullas de Auto-Defensa Civil*) (Guatemala)
PB	Blanco Party (*Partido Blanco*) (Uruguay)
PC	Colorado Party (*Partido Colorado*) (Uruguay)
PCE	Communist Party of Spain (*Partido Comunista de España*)
PCE m-l	Marxist-Leninist Communist Party of Spain (*Partido Comunista de España Marxista–Leninista*)
PCP	Portuguese Communist Party (*Partido Comunista Português*)
PCR	Communist Party of Romania (*Partid Comunist din România*)
PDH	Human Rights Ombudsman (*Procuraduria de Derechos Humanos*) (El Salvador and Guatemala)
PDS	Democratic Socialist Party (*Partei des Demokratischen Sozialismus*) (Germany)
PDSH	Democratic Party of Albania (*Partia Demokratike të Shqipërisë*)
PH	Treasury Police (*Policia de Hacienda*) (El Salvador)
PIDE/DGS	International Police for the Defence of the State/General Security Directorate (*Polícia Internacional da Defesa do Estado/Direcção Geral de Segurança*) (Portugal)
PJ	Peronist Party (*Partido Justicialista*)
PMDB	Brazilian Democratic Movement Party (*Partido do Movimento Democrático Brasileiro*)
PN	National Party (*Partido Nacional*) (Uruguay)
PN	National Police (*Policía Nacional*) (El Salvador and Spain)
PNC	National Civilian Police (*Policía Nacional Civil*) (El Salvador and Guatemala)
PNV	Basque Nationalist Party (*Partido Nacionalista Vasco*)
POWs	Prisoners of War
PP	Popular Party (*Partido Popular*) (Portugal and Spain)
PPD	Popular Democratic Party (*Partido Popular Democrático*) (Portugal)

PPS	Albanian Labour Party (*Partia e Punës së Shqipërisë*)
PS	Portuguese Socialist Party (*Partido Socialista Português*)
PSD	Social Democratic Party (*Partido Social Democrata*) (Portugal)
PSL	Polish Peasant Party or Polish People's Party (*Polskie Stronnictwo Ludowe*)
PSM	Socialist Labour Party (*Partidul Socialist Muncitoresc*) (Romania)
PSOE	Spanish Socialist Workers' Party (*Partido Socialista Obrero Español*)
PSSH	Socialist Party of Albania (*Partia Socialiste ë Shqipërisë*)
PT	Workers' Party (Partido dos Trabalhadores) (Brazil)
PUNR	Romanian National Unity Party (*Partidul Unitatii Nationale din România*)
PZPR	Polish Unified Workers Party (*Polska Zjednoczna Partia Robotnicza*)
REMHI	Recovery of Historical Memory Project (*Recuperación de la Memoria Histórica*) (Guatemala)
RN	National Renovation (*Renovación Nacional*) (Chile)
RRC	Reparations and Rehabilitation Committee (South Africa)
RTP	Portuguese Radio Television (*Rádio Televisão Portuguesa*)
SACC	South African Council of Churches
SACP	South African Communist Party
SADF	South African Defence Force
SDH	Under Secretariat for Human Rights (*Sub-Secretaría de Derechos Humanos*) (Argentina)
SDS	Union of Democratic Forces (*Sajuz na Demokratichnite Sili*) (Bulgaria)
SED	Socialist Unity Party (*Sozialistische Einheitspartei Deutchlands*) (E. Germany)
SERPAJ	Peace and Justice Service (*Servicio de Paz y Justicia*) (Argentina, Chile, and Uruguay)
SEPAZ	Peace Secretariat (*Secretariado de Paz*)
SLD	Democratic Left Alliance (*Sojusz Lewicy Demokratycznej*) (Poland)

SPD	German Social Democratic Party (*Sozialdemotratische Partei Deutschland*)
SRI	Romanian Information Service (*Serviciul Roman de Informatii*)
StB	State Secret Security (*Statni Tajna Bezpecnost*) (Czechoslovakia)
SzDSz	Alliance of Free Democrats (*Szabad Demokraták Szövertsége*) (Hungary)
TC	Truth Commission
TFA	Federal Court of Appeals (*Tribunal Federal de Apelaciones*) (Argentina)
TNM	Torture Never Again (*Tortura Nunca Mais*) (Brazil)
TOP	Public Order Tribunal (*Tribunal de Orden Público*) (Spain)
TRC	Truth and Reconciliation Commission
TsK KPPS	Central Committee of the Communist Party of the Soviet Union (*Tsentralnyi Komitet Kommunistiheskoy Partii Sovetskogo Soyuza*)
UC	Civic Union (*Unión Cívica*) (Uruguay)
UCD	Democratic Centre Union (*Unión de Centro Democrático*) (Chile)
UCR	Radical Party (*Unión de Centro Radical*)
UD	Democratic Union (*Unia Demokratyczna*) (Poland)
UDF	United Democratic Front
UDI	Independent Democratic Union (*Unión Democrática Independiente*) (Chile)
UMD	Democratic Military Union (*Unión Militar Democrática*) (Spain)
UK	United Kingdom
UN	United Nations
UN	National Union (*União Nacional*) (Portugal)
UNCAT	United Nations Convention against Torture
UNCHR	United Nations Commission on Human Rights
UNHCHR	United Nations High Commissioner for Human Rights
UNHRC	United Nations Human Rights Committee
UNSC	United Nations Security Council
UPP	Union for Progress (*Unión por el Progreso*) (Chile)
URNG	National Guatemalan Revolutionary Unity (*Unidad Revolucionaria Nacional Guatemalteca*)

USA	United States
USDS	United States Department of State
USSR	Union of Soviet Socialist Republics
ZChN	Christian National Union (*Zjednoczenie Chrzescijansko-Narodowe*) (Poland)
ZERV	Central Office for the Investigation on Government and Unification Criminality (*Zentrale Ermittlungsstelle füe Regierungs und Vereinigungskriminalität*) (Germany)

Contributors

Nanci Adler is a research fellow at the Institute of Russian and East European Studies of the University of Amsterdam. Her publications include *Victims of Soviet Terror: The Story of the Memorial Movement.* (Westport, Conn.: Praeger, 1993), 'Planned Economy and Unplanned Criminality: the Soviet Experience', *International Journal of Comparative and Applied Criminal Justice*, 17 (1993), 189–201; 'Oral History in the Soviet Union: Bearing Witness to a Story that should not Die with the Witnesses', *Tijdschrift voor Theoretische Geschiedenis, Themanummer Rusland*, 19 (1993), 449–56; 'Psychiatry under Tyranny', co-authored with G. O. W. Mueller and M. Ayat, *Current Psychology*, 12 (1993), 3–17; 'Soviet Special Psychiatric Hospitals: Where the System was Criminal and the Inmates were Sane', co-authored with Semyon Gluzman, *British Journal of Psychiatry*, 163 (1993), 713–20; *Vampires Unstaked: National Images, Stereotypes and Myths in East Central Europe*, co-edited (Amsterdam and Oxford: Royal Dutch Academy of Arts and Sciences, 1995); 'Life in the "Big Zone": The Fate of Returnees in the Aftermath of Stalinist Repression', *Europe–Asia Studies*, 51 (January 1999); and *The Great Return: The Gulag Survivor and the Soviet Union* (forthcoming).

Paloma Aguilar is a professor in the Department of Political Science and Administration of the Faculty of Political Science and Sociology at UNED, Madrid. She gained a doctorate in political science and sociology from the same university. She is also a member of the Instituto Juan March (Centre for Advanced Study in Social Sciences, Madrid) and teaches Masters students at the Gutiérrez Mellado University Institute. Her most recent publications are *Memoria y Olvido de la Guerra Civil Española* (Madrid: Alianza Editorial, 1996); 'Collective Memory of the Spanish Civil War: The Case of the Political Amnesty in the Spanish Transition to Democracy', *Democratization*, 4:4 (1997), 88–109; 'The Memory of the Civil War in the Transition to Democracy: The Peculiarity of the Basque Case', in P. Heywood (ed.), *Politics and Policy in Democratic Spain: No Longer Different?* (London: Frank Cass,

1999); 'Agents of Memory: Spanish Civil War Veterans and Disabled Soldiers', in J. Winter and E. Sivan (eds.), *War and Remembrance in the Twentieth Century* (Cambridge: Cambridge University Press, 1999).

Alexandra Barahona de Brito is a Senior Associate Researcher with the Institute for Strategic and International Studies (IEEI) in Lisbon, professor of politics at the Universidade Moderna in Lisbon as well as a freelance researcher. She received a D.Phil. in politics from the University of Oxford (1993) and was a Henry Fund Visiting Scholar at the University of Yale (1992) and a Luso-American Development Foundation (FLAD) Visiting Fellow at the Center of International Studies (CIS) at Princeton University (1999). Her recent publications include 'Passion, Constraint and Fortuna: The Human Rights Challenge to Chilean Democracy', in N. Biggar (ed.), *Burying the Past: Making Peace and Doing Justice after Civil Conflict* (Washington DC: Georgetown University Press, forthcoming); *Human Rights and Democratization in Latin America: Uruguay and Chile*. (Oxford: OUP, 1997); 'The Human Rights Movement and Democratization in Latin America', in P. Phillips and P. Burton (eds.), *Contemporary Latin American Politics*, i. Manchester: MUP, 1999; and 'The Politics of Human Rights in Democratic Brazil: *"A Lei Não Pega"*' (with F. Panizza), *Journal of Democratization*, 1998, for which both authors won a prize.

António Costa Pinto is Professor at the Institute of Social Sciences (ICS) of the University of Lisbon, and teaches European and Portuguese politics at the ISCTE at the University of Lisbon. He has a doctorate from the University Institute in Florence and was a Visiting Professor at the University of Stanford (1993) and at the University of Princeton (1996). He has recently published *Salazar's Dictatorship and European Fascism* (New York: Columbia University Press, 1995) and edited *Modern Portugal* (Palo Alto: SPOSS, 1998). Other publications include *Os Camisas Azuis: Ideologia, Elites e Movimentos Fascistas em Portugal 1914–1945* (Lisbon: Editorial Estampa, 1994); 'Portugal and Spain', in R. Eatwell (ed.), *European Political Cultures: Conflict or Covergence?* with José Manuel Nunes (London: Routledge, 1997); and 'Dealing with the Legacy of Authoritarianism: Political Purge in Portugal's Transition to Democracy (1974–76)', in S. U. Larsen *et al.* (eds.), *Modern Europe after Fascism, 1945–1980s* (New York: SSM–CUP, 1997).

Carmen González Enríquez is a professor at the Department of Political Science and Administration at the Universidad Nacional de Educación a Distancia (UNED) in Madrid. She is author of *Crisis and Change in Eastern Europe: The Hungarian Transition to Democracy* (Madrid: CIS, 1993) and co-author of *Political Transition in Eastern Europe* (Madrid: CEC, 1996). She has also published various articles and chapters in edited books on issues related with Central and East European politics, among them 'Elites and Decommunisation in Postcommunist Europe', in J. Higley, J. Pakulski, and W. Wesolowski (eds.), *Postcommunist Elites and Democracy in Eastern Europe* (London: Macmillan, 1998); 'Electoral Behaviour in Central and Eastern Europe', *Revue d'Etudes Comparatives Est–Ouest*, 3 (1996); 'Electoral Systems and Political Stability in Eastern Europe', *Budapest Papers on Democratic Transition*, 132 (1995). She has also written about political culture and nationalism in Eastern Europe.

JAN WERNER MÜLLER is a fellow of All Souls College, Oxford. He holds a B.Sc. (Econ.) from University College London and a politics M.Phil. from St Antony's College, Oxford. He has been a visiting student at Princeton University and a Visiting Scholar at Columbia University's School of International and Public Affairs. His doctoral thesis is on 'German Intellectuals, Unification and National Identity' and he is currently editing a book on 'Memory and Power in Postwar Europe'. He has published articles on contemporary German history, German intellectual history, nationalism and liberal political theory.

NAOMI ROHT-ARRIAZA is a professor of law at the University of California, Hastings College of Law in San Francisco. She received her J.D. and a Masters in Public Policy from the University of California, Berkeley. She was a Fullbright Senior Scholar in Spain in 1995. She teaches and writes in the area of international human rights law, among others, and is the author of *Impunity and Human Rights in International Law and Practice* (Oxford: OUP, 1995) as well as numerous articles on the subject in legal and international relations journals. She is currently working on a book on the domestic and transnational cases against human rights violators in the Southern Cone of Latin America, including the Pinochet case.

RACHEL SIEDER is lecturer in politics at the Institute of Latin American Studies (ILAS), University of London. She is also a visiting research associate at the Facultad Latinoamericana de Ciencias Sociales (FLACSO) in Guatemala. Her books include

Central America: Fragile Transition (London: Macmillan, 1996) and *Guatemala after the Peace Accords* (London: ILAS, 1998). She has published widely on legal reform, peace processes, and human rights in Central America. Her most recent publications include 'Rethinking Citizenship: Legal Pluralism and Institutional Reform in Guatemala', *Citizenship Studies*, 3:1 (1999); 'Paz, progreso, justicia y honradez: law and citizenship in Alta Verapaz during the regime of Jorge Ubico', *Bulletin of Latin American Research* (forthcoming, 2000); with Jessica Witchell, 'Advancing Indigenous Claims through the Law: Reflections on the Guatemalan Peace Process' in J. Cowan, M. Dembour and R. Wilson (eds.), *Culture and Rights* (Cambridge: CUP, forthcoming); and 'War, Peace and the Politics of Memory in Guatemala', in N. Biggar (ed.), *Burying the Past: Making Peace and Doing Justice after Civil Conflict* (Washington: Georgetown University Press, forthcoming). She is currently working on a book on law and citizenship in Guatemala.

RICHARD A. WILSON is senior lecturer in the School of African and Asian Studies at the University of Sussex and was a visiting research associate at the University of the Witwatersrand in 1995 and 1996–7. He has published extensively on Guatemala, including numerous works on ethnic identification, violence and symbolism, including his monograph *Maya Resurgence in Guatemala: Q'eqchi' Experiences* (Norman, Okla: Oklahoma University Press, 1995) and an edited collection, *Human Rights, Culture and Context: Anthropological Perspectives* (London: Pluto Press, 1997). His forthcoming book on the South African Truth and Reconciliation Commission, based upon eleven months' fieldwork in Johannesburg over a four-year period, examines the concrete effects of national attempts at truth telling and reconciliation in townships at the centre of political violence. This research was funded by two grants from the Economic and Social Research Council (UK).

Introduction

One of the most important political and ethical questions that societies face during a transition from authoritarian or totalitarian to democratic rule is how to deal with legacies of repression. It is often the problem with the greatest potential to destabilize a transitional process. Further, some of the most fundamental issues regarding law, morality, and politics are raised at such times, as societies look back and attempt to understand a collective failure to contain violence, and struggle to find solutions to legacies of violence that may affirm the rule of law and democratic government. Legacies of repression have been dealt with in transitional periods through amnesties, trials or purges, through the establishment of truth commissions, by financial compensation, and with symbolic gestures such as the building of monuments or the proclamation of commemorative days of 'remembering'.

The general aim of this book is to shed light on this aspect of transitional politics. Two broad kinds of transition are covered: those that occur as a result of the collapse of the old regimes or regime forces, as in Portugal, Argentina, Central and Eastern Europe, Russia and Germany after reunification, where collapse was followed by absorption into another state; and those that are negotiated between an incoming democratic elite and an old regime, as in Spain, the Southern Cone of Latin America, Central America, and South Africa. The range of transitional situations covered allows one to see how varying degrees of political, social, and institutional constraints affect the solutions adopted or limit opportunities to deal with the past, and permits a comparative analysis of the variety of policies adopted, establishing links between one and the other.

The book concentrates on the presence—or absence—of three kinds of official or government-sponsored efforts to come to terms with the past: truth commissions, trials and amnesties, and purges. To a lesser extent, it also looks at policies of compensation, restitution, or reparation. At the same time, however, it focuses on unofficial and private initiatives emerging from within society to deal with the past; these are usually promoted by human rights organizations (HROs), churches, political parties, and other civil society organizations. In doing so, it examines a 'politics of memory' whereby societies rework the past in a wider cultural arena, both during the transitions and after official transitional policies have been implemented and even forgotten. Thus, in contrast with other recent books, it does not examine just the 'political decisions made in the immediate aftermath of the transition and directed towards individuals on the basis of what they did or what was done to them under the earlier regime' (Elster, 1998: 14): it also covers unofficial social initiatives and the wider politics of memory, transcending official efforts and extending beyond the initial transitional period.

The book offers three additional contributions to the growing literature on transitional justice. First, it assesses the significance of forms of reckoning with the past for a process of democratization or democratic deepening. It focuses on the extent to which the various policies adopted with respect to retroactive justice have had any repercussions on the way in which democracy functions. It is assumed that policies of truth and justice may not automatically contribute to such a process, and that the links between one and the other are varied and must be explored. It thus contributes to an understanding of some of the dynamic links between democratization and accountability policies. Second, the role of international actors is explored, with the impact of the changing international environment incorporated as a crucial variable of the analysis. Last, but not least, the book presents readers with an extensive bibliographical survey that divides the literature according to the main debates as well as on a country-by-country basis.

Truth and Justice in Periods of Political Change: An Overview

Political justice in transition from one regime to another is not an invention of the twentieth century. The policies of accountability carried out with the return of democrats to Athens in 403 BC after rule of the Thirty Tyrants is a case in point (Elster, 1998: 9–13). However, a brief survey of transitional justice across four continents in the post-Nuremberg age shows that perhaps more notable than the 'genocide and regimes of torture marking this era is the invention of new and distinctive legal forms of response' to such events (Minow, 1998: 1). Indeed, at the start of the new millenium, interest in the politics of blame and atonement has peaked, perhaps as a result of what Soyinka refers to as an 'end of millenium fever of atonement' (1999: 90).

In Europe there have been three waves of transitional truth and justice. The first of these, in the post-Second World War (henceforth 'postwar') period, is considered the predecessor to most modern transitional justice initiatives. In addition to the Nuremberg International Military Tribunal, which tried twenty-four top war criminals, domestic trials were undertaken in Germany and the various countries that had been overrun by the Nazis. These include Austria, Belgium, France, and the Netherlands among Western European countries, as well as various Eastern European nations, where trials of collaborators soon extended to encompass the enemies of the newly emerging Soviet satellite states.

Two cases suffice to demonstrate the extension of the punitive process. In Germany, the trials were not domestic, in so far as they were carried out by the United States, the United Kingdom, France, and the Soviet Union under Allied Control Council Law 10. The USA prosecuted 1,814 and executed 450; the UK 1,085 and 240 respectively; France tried 2,107 and executed 109; and the USSR tried an estimated 10,000. However, the German courts later prosecuted 60,000 between 1947 and 1990, although clemency policies led to the release of most of the convicted. In France about 160,000 cases of collaboration crimes were tried and an estimated 24 per cent were sentenced to imprisonment, 7,000 to death, of which 1,500 were executed (Roht-Arriaza, 1995: 74 and 76). Two amnesty laws were subsequently passed in 1951 and 1953 in an attempt to impose 'normality', but the French are still dealing with the 'Vichy Syndrome' today, in part as a result of the forced silence of the 1950s and 1960s. From this period, various Nazi-related transnational prosecutions have emerged. Among the most notable are the Eichmann trial in Jerusalem, the Barbie and Touvier trials in France, the Priebke trial in Italy, and the indictment of Bousquet and Leguay for deportations under Vichy.

The second wave of transitional justice took place in the southern part of Europe, in Greece, Portugal, and Spain. Each country undertook radically different policies to deal with past repressors and authoritarian elites. In Greece, the Junta Trials of 1974–5 sentenced 24 of the more than 100 men that had led the 1967 coup and the bloody colonels' regime, and some were still serving their sentences at the end of 1996. In addition, about 100,000 civil servants were purged and a few hundred trials for torture took place, but few convictions were secured. In Portugal, there were widespread purges, particularly in 1974–5 when left-wing revolutionary forces and radical military officers held the reins of power, which affected members of the former Salazar New State dictatorship, the effects of which were all subsequently annulled or reversed. Spain, by contrast, opted for amnesty in 1977 and an almost institutionalized 'forgetting' with regard to the Civil War and the ensuing Franco dictatorship. While the experience of the war was very present from the beginning in various unofficial initiatives, these did not cover the dictatorial period.

The third wave began in Latin America in the mid-1980s and extended throughout Eastern Europe, reaching Africa and Asia in the 1990s. In Latin America, transitional truth and justice efforts began with the transitions from dictatorial rule in the Southern Cone in the mid-1980s and carried on well into the 1990s, with the peace processes in the countries of Central America. It was Latin America that gave rise to so-called 'truth commissions'. Argentina (1984) and Chile (1990) officially established commissions that issued truth reports. In Bolivia (1982–3), Uruguay (1985), and Paraguay (1992) the task fell to parliamentary commissions. Non-governmental organizations (NGOs) also undertook investigations in Brazil (1979–85), as well as in Paraguay (1984–90), Uruguay (1986–9), and Bolivia (1990–3), each producing unofficial truth reports.[1]

Only Argentina (1984) and Bolivia (1986–93) carried out officially sponsored trials. In Argentina, the 'Trial of the Century' (1984) involved the nine leaders of the military juntas that governed the country between 1976 and 1983. Presidential pardons (1990–5), however, led to the release of all these men and hundreds of others violators who had been tried by lower courts in private suits. In Bolivia, only the top figures of the short-lived dictatorship of General García Meza (1981–2) were tried, on the initiative of two left-wing parties, various HROs, and civil society organizations. After a seven-year trial, García Meza was finally imprisoned in 1995, along with all the government ministers of the time, eleven paramilitary agents, and the former chief of the Air Force. This was the first time in Latin America's legal history that members of a *de facto* military government had been held accountable for usurping power and violating constitutional norms. In other countries, although there have been no official trials, individuals and HROs have filed suit against repressors, and important convictions have been secured in Argentina since the pardons, as well as in

[1] A truth and justice commission was also established in Ecuador in 1996. However, while charged with investigating the previous 17 years of unresolved human rights violations, it was established not in the transitional period, but long after it.

Chile, Ecuador, and Paraguay. However, a mantle of impunity has covered the overwhelming majority of repressors, with amnesty laws either excluding or limiting the scope of prosecutions in Brazil (1979), Chile (1978), and Uruguay (1989).

A similar emphasis on truth over justice has occurred in Central America and the Caribbean, with the exception of two cases of 'revolutionary' political justice this century. These are the Sandinista trials (1979–81) against members of the Somoza regime after their victory in the revolutionary war, and the trials held by the Castro regime against the pro-Batista elite after 1959. Elsewhere, truth commissions have been the centrepieces of transitional policies. In Guatemala (1994–9) a commission established as part of the peace accords issued an official truth report, while the Catholic Church in conjunction with HROs also produced an unofficial report. In El Salvador (1992–3) the United Nations was the key player and organizer of the truth commission established there, and in Honduras (1990–3) the National Ombudsman Office compiled the truth report in collaboration with local and US-based HROs. Finally, in Haiti a Truth and Justice Commission (1994–6) was appointed by Jean Bertrand Aristide to investigate the violations of the Duvalier dictatorship and the military regime that had ousted him from power in 1991.[2]

Justice has not fared too well in this part of the Americas. Although some military officers have been tried for human rights violations in Honduras, with the first conviction in July 1993 and a further indicting of ten officers in July 1995 for torture and kidnapping, as of April 1998 none had actually been convicted or begun serving sentences. Many of those convicted are fugitives under the protection of the forces. In Nicaragua, the 'second' transition that led to the demise of the Sandinista regime produced no truth telling, and led to the passage of three amnesty laws (1990 and 1991) in the wake of the peace accord. A blanket amnesty was also passed in El Salvador (1992 and 1993), but in Guatemala, the situation is slightly more promising. The latest amnesty law (1996) excludes crimes against humanity and crimes of genocide and does not rule out civil liability, so many HROs are now pressing forward with cases in the Guatemalan national courts. Some justice has already been done. In late 1998, a court found guilty

[2] Following Clinton's unprecedented apology for US support for various dictatorial regimes in Central America, US HROs began to call for the establishment of a US truth commission. See 'Rights: Time for a US Truth Commission', Inter Press Service, 1999.

and sentenced to death three members of a death squad for involvement in a 1982 massacre. In Haiti a Proceedings and Follow Up Office (BPS) was established in 1997 by President Préval; this is still reportedly studying compensation, but to date nothing has come of that effort. Despite the filing of various suits and complaints by victims, the establishment of a bureau of international lawyers, and a special unit within the police by President Aristide to aid those searching for justice for past violations, impunity has been the near absolute rule, with only a handful of convictions.

The Central American peace and transitional justice processes coincided in time roughly with those of central Eastern Europe and unified Germany, in the wake of the collapse of the Soviet Union. Here, transitional justice was characterized by two main policies: purges (or lustration, from the Latin *lustratio*—purifying by sacrifice), and truth through the opening of police files. De-communization or purge laws were passed in Albania (1992), Bulgaria (1992, 1997, 1998), the Czech Republic and Slovakia (1991), Poland (1992, 1997, 1998), Romania (1998), and Hungary (1994, 1996), although these led to actual widespread purges only in Albania, the Czech Republic, and Germany. In Germany, after the opening of the political police records and the creation of a truth commission for their review in 1992, thousands of civil servants, including judges and police officers, were dismissed from service for collaboration. Hungary, Poland, Romania, and Bulgaria have also set up offices to permit the reviewing of secret police files, but with different levels of accessibility for the general public. In Bulgaria, for example, access was greatly restricted for 'national security reasons'.

There have also been a few but highly publicized trials in some of these countries. In Albania various former Communist leaders were tried and sentenced to death or life imprisonment in 1996, but all the sentences were annulled in 1997. Fatos Nano, leader of the former Communist Party, was sentenced to twelve years' imprisonment for embezzlement in a trial denounced by various European institutions as fraudulent, and that sentence too was subsequently annulled. In Bulgaria, former ruler Todor Zhivkov was tried and sentenced for abuses and embezzlement in 1992, but was then acquitted in 1996.Various labour camp officials were also tried, but most were never actually gaoled. In Hungary a law was passed to deal with the repression of 1956, permitting the prosecution of the people accused of shooting civilians during the violent events of that year. However, only two people were convicted according to this law, as application was paralysed by the Constitutional Court because of the absence of procedural norms. In Germany a number of borders guards were tried and convicted for shooting people fleeing from East Germany between 1961 and 1989. Further, in November 1992 former premier Erich Honecker was tried along with five other former high officials. He was indicted for thirteen manslaughter shootings at the Wall, but as he had terminal cancer he was released, thereafter fleeing to Chile, where he died in April 1994. In 1997 Honecker's successor, Egon Krenz, was tried and convicted, along with various other officials, for the 'shoot to kill' policy applied at the border. In Poland efforts to prosecute have been sporadic. General Jaruselski was indicted for ordering the shooting of workers in 1970–1 and other senior officials were charged with the deaths of strikers in 1981–2. Criminal trials proliferated in Romania, but two amnesty laws in 1990 prevented serious prosecution attempts. Apart from the trials of the Ceaucescus and their top aides, most released by 1994, twenty-five police officers and officials were convicted of genocide and later most of these were pardoned; and the executive committee of the Communist Party was convicted in July 1990, but again later all were paroled or released. Notably, these prosecutions affected only those crimes committed during the pre-transitional repression of 1989, as statutes of limitation have prevented the prosecution of earlier communist crimes. Indeed, although nine people were convicted for summary executions in 1981, the case was abandoned in 1994.

Parliamentary or government-sponsored commissions were also set up in some of these countries to investigate the past of former regime officials. The most notable is the German Study Commission (1992–6) for its unprecedented scope and thoroughness, as well as the Gauck Authority established to administer the opening of the Stasi files to the public. Parliamentary commissions were established in Hungary to investigate the events of 1956, in Romania to investigate the December 1989 massacre, and in Poland to determine whether General Jaruzelski should be held accountable for the 1981 coup. In some cases restitution and compensation have also been attempted, relating not only to the period of Communist rule but also to the Second World War. Most countries have passed laws to compensate former political prisoners. In addition, many have passed land restitution laws, while Czechoslovakia also approved a law for the restitution of buildings.[3]

[3] In addition to truth telling and trials in the former Communist countries, another peace process in Europe—the Northern Irish—has given rise to demands by local NGOs for a truth commission to be established on the 'Troubles', in the wake of the 1998 multiparty agreement. Demands for a truth commission have also emerged in Bosnia-Herzegovina.

With the exception of some Baltic states, there has been no comparable process in the new republics of the former Soviet Union. However, the Russian government has undertaken some measures to deal with the past—condemning and admitting to the 'Red Terror' and opening police files. In 1991 the legislature passed a law to rehabilitate former political prisoners and provide compensation for moral and material damages, following a public outcry over a 1988–9 rehabilitation and compensation programme that offered very meagre financial resources for victims. However, screening laws failed to garner support from any major party, and in 1993 a law was passed making it illegal to identify former KGB collaborators. Furthermore, statutes of limitation make prosecution impossible. Rather than accountability for past abuses, Russia's political class, and some civil society organizations in particular, have concentrated on reworking past memories to make sense of current political projects and hopes.

Countries in Africa and Asia have also undertaken efforts to punish past repressors or to tell the truth about past repressive regimes. In Africa commissions of inquiry were established, with greatly varying results, by executives or legislatures in Zimbabwe (1985–), Uganda (1986–), the Chad (1990–2), Ethiopia (1992), South Africa (1995–8), Zambia (1998–), and Nigeria (1999–). Uniquely, in Rwanda four international HROs undertook the truth-telling initiative in 1992–3. In addition, a truth and reconciliation commission is envisaged for Sierra Leone following the internationally brokered peace agreement of July 1998. Trials of former government officials or members of police or military forces have also been held in Burundi, Ethiopia, and Rwanda, among others. In Burundi, in April 1998 there were 10,000 people in gaol awaiting trial for genocide and other gross violations, and by October of that year 250 had been condemned to death. In 1998 Burundians also called for a UN tribunal for their country in the hope of better justice. In Ethiopia the first court hearings accusing forty-four former government officials of gross human rights violations were held in December 1994, the first step in the effort to bring 1,000 Dergue officials to trial for such violations. The first rulings of the International Criminal Tribunal for Rwanda (ICTR) were handed down in September 1998, including former prime minister of the interim government at the time of the genocide, Jean Kambanda, who was sentenced to life imprisonment. By the end of that year the Tribunal had thirty leaders of the genocide in custody in Arusha. In Zambia, furthermore, treason trials are being contemplated for those involved in the October 1997 military coup against the Kenneth Kaunda government.

In some cases, however, peace agreements have explicitly ensured amnesty for violators, as in Sierra Leone (1996 and 1999), Liberia (1997), and Angola, where six amnesties have been passed since 1981. Although two commissions of inquiry were set up to investigate abuses against a particular ethnic group and two families, both the opposition and government forces have resisted accountability. Mostly prosecutions have simply not been possible because of armed conflict, weak judiciaries, and, most importantly, lack of commitment to such a policy. This is the situation in Mozambique, where, despite calls for an accounting for the violations during the civil war (1977–92), both government and opposition have opposed truth telling or prosecutions since the first multiparty elections in 1994 on the grounds that they upset reconciliation. In many of these cases, the role of international brokers has been of crucial importance, and their lack of support for justice has limited the scope for action. Such is the case of Liberia and Sierra Leone, much as in Haiti.

Finally, in Asia, the Philippines (1987) and Sri Lanka (1995–7 and 1998–) have established commissions of inquiry into past human rights abuses, and only Sri Lanka issued truth reports. In January 1998 the government released the reports of the three commissions of inquiry into over 16,742 disappearances during the fifteen-year war between government forces and rebel forces, dating back as far as 1988. In July 1988 a new island-wide commission was established to investigate and report on the 11,000 cases of violations and disappearance left unreported by the prior commissions. In the Philippines, about 1,000 complaints were filed for abuses in 1987–90, but only six convictions were secured. Sri Lanka is also the only country to have tried and sentenced soldiers for past violations, with important convictions secured in 1998 and 1999. In July 1998 the death sentence was applied for the first time to six soldiers and reserve policeman for violations, while some policemen were expelled from the forces and put on leave. South Korea also made incipient moves to deal with the past. Under dictatorial rule between 1948 and 1987, in a period of democratization in 1960–1 legislation was passed to permit the prosecution of past abuses and a purge of the military was planned. However, all measures came to nothing in the face of US opposition and a coup by Major General Park Chung Hee. In 1988 a second attempt was made to deal with the past, leading finally in 1995 to the sentencing of Chung Hee and another top official for corruption. Both were subsequently released and pardons were also granted to twelve former Army generals. There are currently plans to allow for the establishment of a truth commission in the country.

In the late 1990s, the Royal Cambodian government began to advocate internationally administered trials for those responsible for crimes against humanity under the Khmer Rouge (KR) regime of 1975–9. However, in reality, members of the government encouraged members of the KR to defect to the main political parties in the governing coalition. To date, no one connected with the KR crimes has been brought to justice. A UN Draft Plan to the UNSC of July 1999 proposed the creation of a tribunal for the Khmer Rouge and for the arrest of the indicted, but as yet there has been little progress. Most recently, in September 1999, the UN Human Rights Commissioner floated the idea of setting up an international commission of investigation for East Timor, following de-annexation of that territory by Indonesia (AI, 1999a, b, c).

Just as there can be transitions that produce no accountability, so there can be accountability processes that take place where there is no transition to democracy. In some of the African cases referred to above, for example, accountability processes have been undertaken in a context not of a change of *regime* but merely in one of *government*. They have taken place in a continued undemocratic context of ongoing human rights violations and armed conflict. Such is the case of Rwanda. This book is interested in determining the links between modes of accountability for past violations and democratization processes, which means excluding political changes that culminate in new forms of non-democratic rule. Although not all of the countries examined in these books have made clear or steady progress with deepening democracy—Albania and Russia are perhaps the worst in this respect—all of them have that aim, at least nominally. Further, given the desire to 'enter Europe', they are under pressure to do so.

This summary is intended to highlight the extent to which processes of accountability have become a part of the politics of transition to democracy and even of a change of government. However, it does little to reveal the myriad elements that condition such policies in each national context, and moreover it masks the great differences in the process of backward-looking accountability and its outcomes. In the cases of the Philippines and Zimbabwe, for example, no final truth reports were issued and made public. In many cases, most notably Albania in Eastern Europe and many of the African cases, it has been an instrument of power, whereas in other cases it has been concerned with reinforcing the rule of law and complying with democratic and human rights standards. In still other cases, justice has been so badly administered that one wonders whether criminal prosecutions are adequate ways to carry out 'justice'. In Rwanda, for example, by the end of 1998 there were 126,000 people in gaol, most of them charged with genocide, but the absence of lawyers and adequate judicial conditions means that most will languish in gaol for years. These differences have everything to do with context. Thus, one must try to answer 'transition from what?' as well as 'transition to what?' The following section undertakes this task.

What Can be Done about an Authoritarian Past? Limits and Possibilities of Transition Types and Other Variables

Accountability processes are intimately interrelated with the type of transition. The more a transition entails the defeat of the old authoritarian elite and repressors, the wider is the scope for truth and justice policies. By 'transition' is meant the shift from a non-democratic regime type to a democratic one, not merely a change of government or a process of liberalization *within* an authoritarian regime. Without getting into the abundant literature on transition types, which is beyond our specific interests, it is useful to take into account the different scope for action one can find in different transitions according to the peculiar strength correlation of each case.

Transitions by rupture can occur after foreign intervention giving total victory to the occupying forces. These can also be found where there has been a revolutionary or civil war leading to the military defeat of dictatorial forces. One can place the postwar European and Japanese examples into the first category, while Nicaragua in 1979 fits into the second. Bolivia after the García Meza regime offers an example of rupture and collapse following mass mobilization and a military coup against the faction of the armed forces supporting García Meza (Mayorga, 1997: 66). Other kinds of 'rupture' occur when the outgoing regime collapses as a result of a gradual wearing down of internal legitimacy and a loss of control of key power and/or ideological resources. This can happen in a number of ways. It can occur after defeat in an external war, as in post-Falklands Argentina in 1983 and the Greek defeat in the Cyprus war in 1975. It can also occur following revolutionary action by military forces and exhaustion in an external war, as in Portugal, with its prolonged involvement in the colonial wars in Mozambique, Angola, and Guinea Bissau, which was partly prompted by army captains refusing to fight what they saw as a losing war. And it can happen through ideological or imperial collapse, as in Eastern Europe and Russia. In the unique East German case, collapse was accompanied by incorporation, which completely changed the context and nature of accountability policies.

Total defeat invariably means that old repressors have lost their capacity to manœuvre as their political, police, or military vehicles have been totally or almost completely destroyed and cannot be reconstituted. However, in some cases defeat is only partial and/or temporary. The old elite can make a comeback, as their political and repressive vehicles for power are not eliminated, or the new authorities are insufficiently strong to prevent a backlash against accountability. This is what happened in the Philippines, where the demise of the Marcos regime did not lead to the demise of the military forces that supported the dictator, which then subsequently severely restricted the room for manoeuvre in the implementation of truth and justice policies.

At the other end of the spectrum, there are negotiated, 'pacted', reform-oriented transitions. Here the repressors or outgoing regime authorities tend to retain such a measure of power that the new democratizing elite must co-exist and must constantly negotiate change with the old guard. Such is the case in Spain, most of the Latin American and Central American countries, and South Africa. In these instances there is a 'balance of power' of sorts, and the new elite must try to carefully exploit any weaknesses, skilfully taking the opportunity to shift the balance of power in its favour. However, the scope for action is often very limited. For example, Haiti between 1986 and 1990, following the demise of the Duvalier regimes but before the election of Aristide, who took two-thirds of the vote in the first fully free elections in the country's history, is a case in point. During these four years the same military and economic elite that had supported the Duvalier regime backed the new governments in power. Thus, while some low-ranking officers and members of the Duvalier repressive guard, the Tonton Macoutes, were prosecuted or made to leave the country, impunity was the rule. There was neither the scope nor the will to act.

Clearly, this categorization is not exact, as some transitions fall between one extreme and another. Haiti after the Raoul Cedras dictatorship, for example, is a modified version of external defeat, as the international community effectively overthrew the regime to restore the presidency to Aristide. However, this was more like a temporary or partial defeat, in that the military and police forces of the dictatorship were not dismantled with the same thoroughness as were, say, the Nazi power machine in postwar Germany. Similarly, the transitions in Eastern Europe and the former Soviet Union are special cases, as they took place in a context of ideological collapse, imperial demise, and social and economic change, which deprived the Communist elite of pre-existing power resources. Thus, even where former Communist parties, carrying new names, won the first democratic elections and remained in power, the nature of their relations with the state and with national societies had changed entirely. Further, these parties had changed internally, so it is difficult to speak of them as being the same parties. They lost around 90 per cent of their membership, and many tried sincerely to become modern social democratic parties. In other cases such as Russia, the shift has been directed towards a new nationalism and even towards religion. Some of the transitions of Eastern Europe and the former Soviet Union have many elements of the first transition type described above—namely, that of total defeat. This is the case in East Germany, Poland, Czechoslovakia, and Hungary, where the Communist ideology was totally discredited and opposition parties won the first free elections, and old but renewed Communist parties experienced an identity crisis. In other cases however, as in Russia, opposition forces simply did not exist and the collapse of Communist structures was not accompanied by the triumph of democratizing forces. In Eastern Europe there is a gradation of transition types between these two extremes, with Romania and Bulgaria in an intermediate position. The Philippine transition is also hard to categorize. It was not negotiated, but its immediate aftermath looked like that of a negotiated transition between two equally powerful 'sides'.

In any case, the key variable seems to be the relative strength of pro-reform groups emerging from the old regime, moderate opposition, and intransigent groups on both sides, namely the authoritarian elite and radicals within the opposition. Negotiations between these political groups and their relative strength in the transitional processes are crucial variables for understanding when and how retroactive justice measures, such as purges, truth commissions, and trials, are adopted. The politics of memory, such as the symbolic and economic rehabilitation of the victims, the building of monuments and ceremonies, and public recognition of the suffering of the victims, will also depend on this equilibrium.

According to Przeworski, the legacies of dictatorship are particularly difficult to resolve in cases where the transition takes place through negotiations between authoritarian pro-reform groups and the moderate opposition. This is what he calls 'transition by extrication'. In his view, the crucial element to keep in mind is who controls the repressive apparatus during the transition, and the attitude that the armed forces adopt with regard to the previous regime (Przeworski, 1991: 67 ff.). In a subsequent study, Przeworski asks how unarmed civilians can administer justice to those that carry arms. In his view, the protagonists of transition processes must try to reach an agreement, that ensures that rules will never again be violated, and the only way to avoid future human rights violations is to ensure that this pact is sustained by all sides. Such a pact can work, however, only if the political actors capable of violating the agreement feel that it is more beneficial to stick to it, given the sanctions that other sectors will apply if they do not. For this reason, human rights can be sustained only if there is a political balance between the relevant forces (Przeworski, 1995: 16). In the view of Przeworski and other authors, the 'remembering to prevent' strategy is insufficiently dissuasive. Other institutional factors are necessary, if not sufficient, to undertake trials that not only 'teach lessons' but also are dissuasive. Laws must be passed, with reasonable and realistic requirements regarding the burden of proof, and a bureaucracy dedicated to the prosecution of abuse, which is independent of other state powers, must exist. In Przeworski's view, the construction of this kind of institutional capacity is a precondition for efficient dissuasion against state terrorism (1995: 17).

Beyond the Transitional Period: Authoritarian and Long-Term Historical Legacies

Above and beyond the immediate limitations or opportunities that each kind of transition offers, there are other elements that condition the search for truth and justice. The attitudes and beliefs of new leaders and political parties are just as important as institutional settings and laws. As Elster (1998) noted, policies depend not only on constraints, but also on beliefs and values. The impact of this difficult-to-quantify variable cannot be underestimated. With it, 'structural' factors (such as the stranglehold of an unfavourable balance of forces during a transition, often inherited from the authoritarian period, or of historically constituted institutional settings) can be, and sometimes are, partly mitigated.

Leadership and values matter a great deal. If this were not the case, it would be impossible to explain the Chilean case.

Chile experienced the 'transition by extrication' *par excellence* and 'authoritarian enclaves' abound, but it is also the country that, of all the cases assessed in this book, at present has the highest number of top and lower ranking military officers in prison for human rights violations. The nature of leadership is crucial, particularly in countries with presidential systems. Personal loyalties, the nature of political beliefs, and even adherence to Christian notions of either reconciliation or forgiveness can temper and leave indelible marks on the design and aims ascribed to truth and justice policies, shaping their subsequent evolution. In the case of Uruguay, presidential links to the commander-in-chief of the army and a lack of political connection with the groups demanding truth and justice resulted in an antipathy to this cause. In Argentina, the desire for President Menem to dissociate himself from the perceived excesses and failures of the transitional Alfonsín administration and his desire to normalize relations with the military also determined a complete reversal of a previous punitive policy towards past human rights violations. In Chile, by contrast, a presidential connection with an activist Catholic Church and a human rights movement with strong links to the president's party led to an insistence on addressing the past, but also to a policy that emphasized reconciliation above punishment.

The nature of the opposition forces to dictatorial rule also shapes strategies to deal with the past and the values expressed by the policies adopted. If the leading groups in opposition to dictatorship are 'revolutionary' and pursue radical social change rather than reform, as was the case in the early days of the transition in Portugal or in Nicaragua in 1979, they may be less concerned with the rule of law and procedural niceties. An opposition like that in Chile, dominated by Christian Democrats and 'renovated Socialists' with a more pro-reform bent, will have a more cautious and legalistic programme of action. If, on the other hand, the opposition is concerned only with ending the dictatorship, and if there is no strong social pressure for truth or punishment, it may avoid accountability policies altogether in order not to upset negotiations for extrication. This was the case in Brazil in 1985 and in Nicaragua in 1990. A new elite simply may not see the need for reparations, truth, and justice or may even oppose such policies because they are formally or informally allied with outgoing military forces or repressors. The case of El Salvador and Uruguay are examples of this.

The legacies of dictatorship condition the position of actors during the transition. If one of the legacies is the weakness, or even absence, of opposition forces, this may mean that cosmetically renewed dictatorial parties are in place to take power after the old regime collapses. This was the case in Romania, where accountability and truth telling were undertaken only symbolically to satisfy immediate desires for revenge and were then abandoned in order not to threaten the position of former Communist elites wearing 'new clothes'. By contrast, if a strong human rights movement is inherited from the dictatorial period, with a clear and powerful agenda for truth and justice, from a civil society with a tradition of activism and participation, this may immeasurably aid the cause of truth and justice. Such organizations may help to prevent a more cautious elite from legislating 'closure', either by working with it, as in Chile and South Africa, or in opposition to it, as in Argentina in the later years of the Alfonsín administration and the first Menem government. Indeed, such organizations can combine both strategies as they do in Guatemala and El Salvador, and to some extent in Argentina and Chile as well, becoming 'critically engaged', constantly pushing forward the boundaries of governmental efforts, tacitly supporting them, but also maintaining their independence and critical power. These organizations can also help to keep 'memory' alive, even when state authorities resist accountability, as Memorial has singularly done in Russia. Conversely, if civil society remains weak and apathetic or, beyond an immediate desire for 'revenge', indifferent to wider notions of truth and justice, accountability policies may be altogether absent, as in Spain, or put to partisan use by competing elite groups, as in Portugal and many Eastern European cases.

One also needs to examine carefully the role of laws and constitutions, as these will shape the nature of accountability. Indeed, here the legacies of dictatorial rule are crucial. Inherited amnesty laws, as in the case of Brazil and Chile, or constitutional limitations on government action, as in Chile, can stand in the way of accountability. Similarly, institutions matter. Transitions can entail agreements or accords that envision basic reforms that will reduce old repressive structures, but these may not be fulfilled given institutional resistance, or may take a long time to implement or to significantly change institutional attitudes and practices. The Central American countries examined in this book are cases in point. The persistence of some 'authoritarian enclaves' may stand as direct obstacles to the pursuit of truth and justice, or may indirectly do so by reminding a democratizing elite that power is not entirely in their hands. Systematically subjugated or politicized judiciaries, as in those inherited by the regimes of south-eastern

Europe, South Africa, or Chile, can also stand in the way of transitional justice policies, at least until they are reformed. Judiciaries may even be willing to prosecute; but if they lack independence, or are ill equipped and technically unprepared, they may not be able effectively to implement laws to punish human rights violators. The difficulties met by Rwanda in attempting to prosecute people accused of genocide and the need to resort to the assistance of foreign judges and lawyers is a case in point.

There is a sad irony in this. On the one hand, the countries with the weakest democratic traditions and institutions are the least prepared to carry out adequate truth and justice policies. Yet it is exactly in such countries where lies have triumphed the longest, and where repression has lasted the longest and claimed the most victims, that the need for justice and truth is most acute. Conversely, it is often in countries where tolerance for arbitrary rule is lower and repression relatively lighter that conditions for prosecution and truth telling are most favourable. And it is also in these countries that social organizations and political parties are more likely to demand such policies, given the influence of historically constituted political cultures favouring individual rights and the rule of law.

Although the aim of this book is not to examine long-term historical memories and lessons learnt from historical experience, it is important to remember that transitional accountability policies are not born in a vacuum. They are historically grounded and thus peculiar to each country.

For example, a negative historical experience of democratic governance, or failed experiments with political freedom culminating in violence or prolonged civil conflict, may shape policy options to deal with the past. The effect may be to dampen desires to 'test the boundaries of freedom' by challenging authoritarian enclaves and to punish those guilty of violations. Furthermore, if civil conflict has resulted, and both 'sides' have committed atrocities, a transitional political elite may decide that the past is best left in the past. Such is the case of Spain. As Aguilar points out in Chapter 3, fear of a return to chaos inherited from failed experiments with democracy, and shared guilt for abuses during the Civil War that ensued, led the transitional elite and the greater part of civil society to accept and even prefer a blanket amnesty. A weak democratic tradition may also produce a weak or fearful civil society at the moment of transition. Weakness and fear not only can reduce social demands for accountability but also can make transitional justice an elite affair, a façade for battle between new elite and old nomenclature. Such is the experience of many of the Eastern and Central European countries as described by González (Chapter 7).

The issue of fear is also crucial, if harder to pin down. Whether inherited from the dictatorial period or generated by older historical memories, it can act as a strong impediment to challenging those in charge of repressive structures. Adler makes this point in her chapter about Russia (Chapter 9), where the Stalinist Terror has left a deep mark on victims, who fear that speaking out even today is unsafe.

Conversely, a positive historical experience of democracy may mean a faster waning of authoritarian or dictatorial forces, providing wider opportunities for accountability. Further, strong historically constituted judiciaries, which are accustomed to independent action and to the rule of law, are more likely to carry out proper accountability processes. In theory at least, a democratic history will make it more difficult for political justice to generate new injustices, as rule-of-law traditions will generally limit attempts to adopt conceptions of 'collective guilt' or to apply laws retroactively. Such is the case in most of the Latin American countries assessed. This was notably not the case in postwar Europe, given widespread desire for 'revenge', but similar violations of the rule of law occurred with even more frequency in the postwar Eastern European cases, where previous experience of democracy was weaker. It has also been frequent in many of the more recent African cases outlined above.

That the long term matters is clear in historically constituted multi-ethnic nations, which face very specific challenges when designing accountability policies. Examples are Guatemala, described in by Sieder in Chapter 5, or the ethnic Turks in Bulgaria. Here, addressing past injustices can involve special recognition of ethnicity, of special community needs and unique forms of remembering or memory making. In the case of South Africa, dealing with the past has meant dealing with the oppression of a black majority by a white minority. Thus, the issues arising from accountability policies and the criticisms directed at the South African solution have been largely related to failures to 'do justice' to the everyday violent reality of apartheid. In these cases, the crucial challenge is not just to bring about democratic governance in the name of a *demos* that is uncontroversial and well defined, but to define the new *demos*. Thus, nation and state-building exercises are necessary, involving wider challenges to democratization.

Historical 'double' legacies are also important. The German desire to make a 'better job' of political justice in the 1990s was largely conditioned by perceptions that the Nazi legacy had not been properly addressed. A second opportunity to come to terms with the past was therefore not to be lost; *verganenheitsbewaltigung* (overcoming the past) would be replaced by a thorough *aufarbeitung* (working through the past). In Portugal, the double legacy of right-wing authoritarianism under the Salazar New State and of the threat of left-wing authoritarianism during the revolutionary first two years of the transition also produced different responses to the issue of transitional justice. Finally, the presence of a strong Church can also be important. Where there is a Catholic Church, its influence can be negative or positive, depending on its historical links with the military or on the changes wrought by the Second Vatican Council. In Argentina, for example, strong military links and a fiercely conservative reaction to changes in Vatican policy in the 1960s and 1970s meant that the role of the Catholic Church was largely negative. In Chile the reverse was true; here, the Church played a major role in the creation of a strong human rights movement and in making transitional accountability more a matter of truth and 'reconciliation' than of punishment.

Although touching on only some of the relevant historical legacies, this brief outline serves to show how the historical constitution of various aspects of a country's political, social, cultural, and ideological environment should be taken into account when trying to understand how the past is dealt with in transitional moments.

It is not only the *longue dureé* that matters, however. In addition to historical legacies, the nature of transitional truth and justice policies will also be shaped by the more immediate dictatorial legacies. One of these is the duration of the dictatorial period itself. The longer dictatorships last and the more victims they claim, the harder it will be to do justice, rather than take revenge, and to discover the 'truth'. Repressors and victims alike may be long dead, record and archives destroyed, and the facts may therefore be hard to reconstitute. At the same time, it becomes impossible to ensure that all victims are in some way compensated, whether financially or otherwise. Russia and Spain are examples of this dilemma.

The nature of the repression itself will also shape the kinds of policies adopted and their aims. If victims were openly executed, the need for uncovering the 'truth' may not be as important as in cases where repressive actions were clandestine. Latin and Central America's emphasis on truth has been in large part a response to regime denial of the policy of disappearance. Disappearances require responses different from mass and prolonged detainment and torture. The former involves a search for bodies or the confirmation of death by the state to solve pending legal problems for relatives, both of which require a difficult-to-obtain co-operation from repressors. The latter may lead to a greater emphasis on compensation and psychological counselling for social reinsertion. If repression was shallow rather than deep, psychological rather than physical, widespread rather than localized—as is the case of most Eastern European countries—the problem of punishment will be more complex. To use the phrases coined by Tina Rosenberg, 'regimes of criminals' such as those of South America require different solutions to 'criminal regimes', such as those of Eastern Europe (1995a: 400–401). Further, if regime forces are not the only ones responsible for repression, this may change the equation. If armed groups violently opposed the dictatorship and also produced victims, this may weaken the legitimacy of efforts to punish only the government forces.

More immediately, backward-looking accountability policies will also depend on the aims sought. As Elster (1998) points out, once a regime has determined that something has to be done, it must then decide what is to be done. Wrongdoers and victims must be identified, policies to deal with them must be determined, and procedural and practical implementation issues must be established. As motivations and aims differ, so will policies. If stability and accommodation with a powerful authoritarian elite is prized above all, truth *without* justice may be opted for. A victim-oriented approach may produce a more participatory process, such as that found in South Africa. A perpetrator-focused policy may lead to more punitive action, such as purges and trials. Aims of deterrence are likely to produce more retributive policies than the ideal of reconciliation. If both are equally emphasized, this may mean implementing programmes to provide for human rights education in schools and military academies. Clearly, the aims and the different kinds of policy option available cannot be completely separated or differentiated, as they are so intertwined; none the less, differing emphases will produce different allocations of resources and political efforts.

The evolution of accountability processes will vary, as the scope for action may increase or diminish over time, depending on the ability of a new democratic political elite to expand or deepen the new order in political, institutional, social, and ideological terms. The immediate political power of old authoritarian groups may wane and create the illusion of defeat, but in many instances they can reorganize themselves and recoup their power. As González (Chapter 7) shows, the return of former Communists to power has ensured limited purges or trials. Alternatively, old repressors may suffer a temporary setback, but retain a 'hidden' or embedded power, which manifests itself within key institutions such as the judiciary, military or police forces, and other state bureaucracies. Such legacies may take years to eliminate and often stand in the way of backward-looking accountability, as in the case of Brazil described by Barahona de Brito in Chapter 4. The Argentine case analysed in Chapter 4 also illustrates how changing conditions shape and reshape policies over time. The initial weaknesses of the defeated armed forces provided unique opportunities for accountability; yet, arguably overly ambitious policies resulted in a backlash, which led repressors to recover some of their power and accountability policies to shrink back. Yet again, however, later success in placing the military under civilian control generated new possibilities in the search for justice.

Varying levels of military power was not the only variable at play, of course. The evolution of the accountability process was also shaped by success in challenging authoritarian enclaves as a whole. It was further affected by the waxing or waning of human rights activism, by the changing nature, priorities, and values of the judiciary, and by the accumulation of international or regional human rights legal 'obligations' or commitments. The same applies to the ability to reform constitutions to allow for wider margin of action, or to eliminate amnesties. Moreover, if an initial accountability policy led to the creation of institutions specifically designed to address past legacies of one kind or another, then, given the tendency for institutions to gain a dynamic of their own, policies may be given continuity in spite of governmental or social indifference and even hostility. In so far as such actions are institutionally sustained, they may generate new demands and opportunities. Thus, if human rights secretariats or compensation commissions are established, compensation policies may be extended to increasing categories of victims; new suits may then be filed against repressors as new information is dug up by institutions established to determine the fate of victims.

Accountability processes, whether at the moment of transition or beyond, are also crucially shaped by the international context in which they take place. All the chapters in this book show that national actors are decisive in determining how a society confronts its past. None the less, the international or 'global ideological' context has gained increasing importance in shaping national debates and policies. Modern international and national human rights law and practice stem from 1945, but the development of international human rights regimes was stalemated by the onset of the Cold War. The 1970s saw the development of regional and UN human rights systems and monitoring mechanisms. For the first time, human rights criteria were incorporated into national foreign aid, military sales, and trade policies by Western governments. This period also saw the novel emergence of national and transnational non-governmental actors that began to engage in 'moral opposition' to dictatorship, using the language of human rights.

The transitions from authoritarian rule that took place in the 1970s, however, did not benefit from these incipient changes. The continued hegemony of Cold War thinking counteracted the universalizing pretensions of the human rights revolution. The left, still attached to the traditional socialist conception of rights, denigrated the importance of basic human or civil and political rights, focusing on social and economic dimensions. On the right, the desire to defeat 'communist totalitarianism' was such that human rights violations by friendly, anti-Communist authoritarian regimes were tolerated as a necessary evil. At the same time, the universal language of human rights had not yet permeated the discourse of pro-reform, democratic liberals or social democrats. Thus, the issue of transitional justice was not conceived of in terms of human rights at all. In Portugal it was an exercise in 'revolutionary justice'; in Spain 'political justice' was avoided for pragmatic and psychological reasons; and in Greece punishment was conceived in quasi-corporate and constitutional terms—it was the punishment of insubordinate middle-ranking officers by the top brass, for crimes against 'the people' and the constitutional order.

By the late 1980s and early 1990s, when the majority of transitions examined in this book took place, the scenario had changed significantly. Human rights had become a universal language, even if not a universally cherished concept. Even those who rejected the concept of rights had to take on board what was by then a well developed body of international humanitarian and human rights law. Conventions covered not only the classical crimes against humanity in wartime, but also torture and disappearance and other crimes in peacetime. These standards were empowered by the progressive ratification by nation states of the various human rights conventions, and were complemented by the national development of 'political conditionality' in aid and trade relations. At the same time, powerful transnational networks focusing on normative issues created in the 1970s were by then well developed, complementing and pushing forward the work of formal national, regional, and international institutions, as well as boosting the influence of national HROs. By the mid-1990s, organizations such as Amnesty International or the Mothers of the Plaza de Mayo had become household names. In part, this was possible because of the communications revolution, and in part it stemmed from the end of the classical Cold War East–West (as well as, to a lesser degree, North–South) dichotomies. These networks have contributed to a lowering of sovereign barriers and to legitimating the intervention of external actors in national processes of democratization and in the promotion of respect for human rights. Concomitantly, the spread of the values of democratic governance boosted the notion of rights and made universality seem possible for the first time. Thus, in contrast with the debate over transitional justice in the Southern European transitions of the 1970s, in Latin America the discussion was clearly framed in terms of universal human rights.

As Roht-Arriaza shows in Chapter 1, international and regional human rights systems have provided legal and political support against impunity, issuing rulings against amnesties, ordering new investigations into abuses, and influencing national jurisprudence. They have also played a role in brokering peace settlements in Guatemala, El Salvador, Haiti, Cambodia, Liberia, and Bosnia, among others, promoting tribunals, as in the cases of Yugoslavia (1993–) and Rwanda (1997–), drafting amnesties in Haiti and Guatemala, or establishing truth commissions, as in El Salvador and Guatemala. More recently, international pressures have been important in promoting the idea of instituting an international commission of inquiry into the Indonesian genocide in East Timor as well as tribunals to judge those responsible for genocide and mass atrocity in Cambodia and Burundi. Foreign assistance can also be given by non-official transnational organizations such as HROs, providing human resources to implement truth and justice policies. HROs have contributed to legal procedures in Africa, where judiciaries are very poor, mostly as defence attorneys. The Danish section of the ICJ, for example, began in January 1994 to establish a corps of public defenders in Ethiopia to represent former Dergue regime members charged with war crimes. Foreign NGOs also provided legal counsel in Rwandan trials, while the UN Human Rights Centre arranged for foreign lawyers to be involved in the defence in Burundi in 1997.

Unlike European, Asian, and African repressors, those from Latin America have not been subjected to formal international trials. However, the Inter-American human rights system has played a key role in pressuring national governments to take action against repressors. The IAHRC has ruled against the amnesties and pardons in Argentina, Chile, and Uruguay, as contravening international legal obligations. Honduras and Guatemala have also been subjected to landmark IAHRC rulings on past human rights violations. Thus, the role of the regional human rights system has been very important, sometimes complementing or replacing the national courts. Furthermore, in a relatively novel development, they have become the subjects of transnational prosecution efforts, undertaken by national courts in Europe and the United States, with the support of HROs, victims, and their relatives.

The most notable example is the Pinochet case. Its impact cannot be underestimated. In addition to making new international and national jurisprudence, giving impetus to national trial efforts in Chile and Argentina, as well as prosecution efforts in other European countries, including Belgium, Denmark, the Netherlands, Italy, France, Sweden, and the UK, it has put 'tyrants on notice'. Argentine repressors and other former government officials in Chile dare not travel today for fear of being caught in the web of international law suits. Thus, to cite just a few examples, a top aide of the Saddam Hussein regime fled an Austrian hospital to avoid criminal prosecution for genocide of the Kurds in August 1999; Menghistu Haile Mariam, who had been living in Zimbabwe protected by the Robert Mugabe regime, was reportedly looking into possible retirement in North Korea; and former Indonesian dictator Suharto recently cancelled medical treatment in Germany, for fear of being caught in the web of transnational human rights prosecution efforts.[4]

However, while significant, the extent to which international efforts have influenced national accountability processes is still unclear. They contribute to a furthering of human rights standards and can give legitimacy to national prosecution and truth-telling efforts; they can push laggardly national courts and elite groups to support those seeking justice; and they can limit the movements of repressors. Yet such efforts are fraught with difficulties. Transnational prosecutions, for example, are limited by the difficulties in making defendants pay the civil suit damages awarded, actually apprehending violators, and finding the necessary documentary evidence to pursue condemnations. It is also difficult to determine the legitimacy of what is still an incipient practice of 'universal jurisdiction' by third-country courts. A 'decentralized, entrepreneurial vision of

[4] Reed Brody, 'One Year Later: The Pinochet Precedent Puts Tyrants on Notice', *Boston Globe*, 14 Oct. 1999.

international justice' poses problems in terms of consistency, and challenges the basis of negotiated transitions with possibly detrimental effects on social peace. Similarly, international tribunals have been criticized for partiality, for being selective, for the sparseness of prosecutions arising from a lack of international will, and for coming into conflict with national prosecution efforts. As Roht-Arriaza concludes, only 'the combined pressure of HROs, transnational advocacy networks, and the long memories of survivors . . . have goaded states into creating existing mechanisms and rendered them effective'. Thus, whatever the strength of international pressures, the domestic context is still the key to understanding transitional justice processes.

Indeed, last but not least, luck or, as Machiavelli wrote, *fortuna*, has a lot to do with the future of accountability policies, and can sometimes be as powerful a force as good institutions and democratic beliefs, or as authoritarian and longer-term historical legacies in shaping transitional justice. Nothing illustrates this better than the arrest of General Pinochet, although some would add hubris to the *fortuna* potion. This fortuitous event put past human rights violations and impunity right back on to the political agenda in Chile, with potentially far-reaching consequences.

Truth, Justice, and Democracy

Many difficult claims have been made about truth and justice. Truth telling is said to address the social need for knowledge to become acknowledgement. It is said to bring victims back into the fold of society, by recognizing their suffering, providing a form of distributive or social justice, and giving out non-conventional resources such as social awareness, collective memory, solidarity, and the overcoming of low self esteem. Truth has been seen as a form of social empowerment, giving to previously powerless and repressed individuals the possibility of reclaiming their lives and understanding the nature of their subjugation. Some would argue that, while selective forgetting is part of the process of history making, constituting the silences described by Trouillot (1995), forgetting the *meaning* of past events can be like losing a moral compass. Truth has also been seen as a form of 'justice as recognition' acknowledgement or admission. It can further be seen as a form of compensatory justice, in that it restores a sense of justice that had broken down (Allen, 1999).

In addition, deterrence has been often held up as a reason to pursue accountability, on the grounds that speaking out and punishing will prevent the recurrence of atrocities. It is seen as a weapon against oblivion, which can combat 'social amnesia', denial, cover-ups, and various pernicious forms of revisionism, whereby past atrocities are either justified or denied. Official truth commissions have also been valued as centrepieces of 'historical founding projects' that make a symbolic and moral break with a dark past. They can contribute to 'establishing a consensus concerning the intolerable' (Allen, 1999). Trials, on the other hand, have been seen to establish moral principles, and to act as a form of 'political theatre' that provides 'collective lessons in justice'. Thus, both truth commissions and trials are opportunities for myth making that may bind a community, as well as provide a framework to explore meaning of violence and create project for future (Osiel, 1998). Both can become part of a process of education about democracy and the rule of law, and they may even help to re-establish trust in tarnished judiciaries, or other emerging democratic institutions.

It is important to note, however, that this vision of trials and the truth of truth commissions is not uncontested. Official reports can become histories that obscure and render marginal other accounts and narratives of past violations. The totality of repression and its more banal manifestations are often not accounted for. These critiques are especially valid in ethnically divided societies where repressor and repressed are of different groups and have different histories altogether. Trial 'truths' can be partial and can get lost in the morass of juridical and evidentiary detail.

One of the most important claims made is that truth telling can promote reconciliation. This argument has been made most explicitly and famously in the cases of Chile and South Africa, where *ubuntu* or 'recognition of the humanity of the other' has been a password of the process. But what is meant by 'reconciliation'? The term stems from the influence that religious figures have had in the transitions in both these countries, yet it is never clarified. What is the 'rainbow nation' described by Desmond Tutu? Can one 'make whole' what was torn asunder? Was there ever such a 'whole' to begin with? Is it possible to create an epic for a single, consensual 'imagined community?' Individual victims may forgive or even become 'reconciled' with their victimizers, but can a process of this kind be reproduced at the national level? It is highly unlikely. It is likely that old hatreds will persist and that many will not forgive, be they victims or even victimizers who feel that they fought to 'defend the nation' or for some other abstract ideal. Making such claims for truth commissions may lead people to become disappointed when these commissions do not produce the miraculous results they are meant to. It may also prevent them from seeing existing flaws in their new democracies, by creating the illusion of justice and reconciliation.

Rather than talk about reconciliation, it is more appropriate to ask whether accountability processes can contribute to affirming democratic governance. As Allen (1999) argues, reconciliation as unity can mean a lot of things. Unity may be elusive and even undesirable if it is conceived of in a non-democratic way. By contrast, consensus around the need for democracy, for a system of rules, laws, procedures, and values that calls for peaceful coexistence among all kinds of groups, whether friendly or not, is a lower threshold and a more practicable possibility. If reconciliation creates too high expectations, the link between truth, justice, and democratization is also often simply taken for granted. What is the link between the former pursuits and the latter?

The relationship between political justice and democracy is a complex one. As noted elsewhere, it is ironic but probably true that non-democratic successor regimes are better equipped in philosophical and psychological terms to implement more 'comprehensive justice policies, due to limited or non-existent pluralism or a lack of concern with due process' (Barahona de Brito, 1997). Democratic successor regimes, on the other hand, must balance the aim of the most far-reaching policy of truth and justice with a respect for pluralism and the rule of law. It is likely, for example, that in a context of democratic pluralism such policies will be limited. In contrast with a non-democratic elite, a democratizing one has to take into account the view of all parts of the political and social spectrum. Some may demand trial and truth, others may argue for 'forgetting' and 'forgiveness'. Governments will have to find a policy that will usually aggregate preferences rather than express the full wishes of one or another sector (Elster, 1998).

Complying with due process, a fundamental feature under any democratic regime, will also limit justice and even truth. Courts may not be able to legally establish the guilt of people that 'everyone knows' to be culpable. In a democracy there cannot be indiscriminate purges, mass trials that assume collective guilt; these may be 'just', but they debilitate the rule of law. In most cases where such drastic measures are adopted, new injustices are perpetrated. Postwar Belgium, Denmark, France, the Netherlands, and Norway instituted policies for rigorous and far-reaching purges, extra-judicial executions, trials by criminal courts, official executions, and mass gaoling. In all instances, severity and speed were prized over adherence to the rule of law. Standards of collective guilt were adopted, and there were serious procedural irregularities as the courts came under great pressure to sentence people. Retroactive justice was applied in violation of the *nulla poena sine lege* (no punishment without law) principle. Treason, for example, was punished retroactively, and, although the death penalty had been abolished in most of these countries, it was put to use again.

Due process problems also plagued the purges in Eastern Europe in the 1990s, which were condemned by many HROs and international institutions. Speedy and severe responses can be 'just', but complying with due process creates a gap between what is 'just', and 'justice'. Trials may do justice but be unfair. The assumption of collective guilt in the Sandinista trials of the Somoza regime was 'just' but unfair in legal terms. The border guard trials in Germany quite starkly raised some of the same problems with trials. There is the question of the fairness of selecting exemplary cases, as one tries the 'small fish' and lets the 'big fish' get away. There are the problems with due obedience or even obedience to a political order that was legal and suddenly is declared criminal. In addition, statutes of limitation, double jeopardy, and retrospective liability all make legal justice less than just, be it in terms of satisfying victims' demands for justice or in terms of ensuring the rights of defendants. Such problems have led some thinkers to prefer forgetting to exacting punishment. Truth telling may also be limited for similar reasons. In Chile, for example, the names of perpetrators were not included in the truth report to avoid trial by publicity or the assumption of guilt in the absence of formal legal charges. Thus, justice with regard to due process can never be enough, but any other kind of justice will not be affirmative of the type of legality required in a stable democracy.

According to Elster, if one takes into account the basic principle of equality among citizens, the basis of democratic rule, and the fact that it is impossible to try everyone involved in repressive activities at various levels (including enthusiastic participants and the forcibly complicitous), it is fairest to try no one. In his view, one must either punish everyone or no one, and as it is impossible to try every one, no one should be punished or compensated. In addition, he argues that people cannot be held guilty for what they are forced to do. He proposes instead a 'general amnesty' and the abandonment of all attempts to compensate victims (Elster, 1995: 566–8).

Furthermore, newly emerging democracies with weak judiciaries may not be in a position to serve justice effectively, raising the question of whether it should be attempted at all or abandoned for other forms of compensation or retribution. Burundi, Rwanda, and Ethiopia are not democracies, but the problems they have faced with weak judiciaries serve to illustrate the problem. As Walzer (1997) notes, in Rwanda, a country that then had about forty-four defence attorneys and 100,000 Hutu in prison charged with genocide, the prospects for fair and speedy justice are not high. Trials in Burundi and Ethiopia have suffered from similar problems. In Burundi most of the persons held for genocide are Hutu, but most of the lawyers are Tutsi, which has led to claims of the application of an ethnic 'politicized justice'. By April 1998 only 18 per cent of the thousands gaoled had been tried, and prisons set to held 3,000 or so were filled with up to 10,000 inmates. The mortality rate in the prisons was 10 per cent and there were no guarantees of due process.

The relationship between accountability policies and democratic stability is also a complex one, particularly after negotiated transitions. Two Chileans have summed up the positions well. Zalaquett poses the question in terms of a conflict between the ethics of conviction and the ethics of responsibility (1992: 1430), while Garretón (1994) terms it as a conflict between an ethical and symbolic logic and a political logic. The former emphasizes the need to understand the political constraints on justice in order not to risk upsetting the process of democratization, while the latter argues for truth and justice and their link with wider institutional reform, without which democracy will be weaker. It is unclear how far one can go without upsetting the apple cart, in large part because counterfactual hypothetical situations would have to be constructed to prove whether different choices would have produced different outcomes.

However, once whatever has been done is done, what is its effect on the process of democratization or democratic deepening? The term 'consolidation' is deliberately avoided in so far as it implies an 'end state' in which democracy is finally 'all there' and somehow immovable. 'Deepening', on the other hand, or simply 'democratization', implies a process that is never quite finished and may be nonlinear as well as reversible. Thus, rather than becoming consolidated, democracies can be or become more or less deep. What does democratization consist of? The term refers to progress in various political, legal, institutional, cultural ideological, social, and economic arenas that make a minimally functioning democracy more 'democratic'. This is necessarily vague, as there is no recipe for democratization, and each country will require different kinds of policies. However, it is possible to outline some of the elements necessary by looking at what the 'deepest' or most successful democracies have accomplished.

Minimally, democracy means fair and free elections and the regular and peaceful rotation of power. However, such a democracy will be 'shallow' if other elements are not present. Linz and Stepan (1996) insist that democratization does not necessarily improve the quality of life of citizens, or even the quality of democracy itself. They emphasize that there are other kinds of public institution that powerfully influence the daily life of citizens, such as courts, the police, or the armed forces. Those responsible for these institutions are not democratically elected, but they are institutions that none the less work within a legal framework designed by those who are democratically elected. From this one can infer that, if such institutions continue to be enclaves for authoritarian forces, either because of the absence of profound reforms or because of the failure of measures undertaken, the quality of democracy will inevitably be affected.

O'Donnell (1996) has coined terms that have become central to the literature on transitions and democratization, such as 'delegative democracy' or the 'lack of horizontal accountability' to account for the imperfect workings of some recently constituted or reconstituted democracies. In his view, although these cases have a lot in common with classic democracies, such as institutionalized and regular elections, they lack many other important elements. Further, in almost all such cases the institutions are damaged by 'particularism or clientelism', both of which can well be the legacy of preceding authoritarian regimes. This normally means nepotism and corruption as well, problems with accountability resulting from the dilution of the frontiers between the public and the private spheres. In turn, this is directly related with the emergence of 'delegative, rather than representative, notions of political authority' (O'Donnell, 1996: 44). All of this means that there is a lack of control that permits the recreation of old authoritarian practices, a form of politics that favours powerful economic interest groups and the limited exercise of civil liberties. In a more recent book published with Méndez and Pinheiro (Méndez *et al.*, 1999), O'Donnell refers to the 'unrule of law' that exists within parts of the universe of Latin American democracies, which means 'the exclusion of vast sectors from the benefits of democracy'. One of the main factors responsible for this state of affairs is the ill functioning of judiciaries, particularly where the less favoured social groups are concerned, thus affecting 'the quality of our democracies' (Méndez *et al.*, 1999: 221). For O'Donnell, this is partly because 'the judiciaries, and those who lead them, have been particularly resistant to change' (p. 223). The authors of this book agree that 'the recurrent violations of many basic rights in Latin America' is a fact of life (p. 303). For this reason, they embark on a critique of minimalist definitions of democracy that do not allow analysts to capture the impact of institutional defects and extreme inequality and poverty.

Non-democratic 'enclaves' and authoritarian legacies are indicative of shallow democracies and as such must be got rid of. Thus, constitutional or other legal limitations on the exercise of popular sovereignty must be eliminated. Further, there must be effective and independent judiciaries to ensure accountability, and military and police forces must be subordinated to civilian authority and committed to democratic governance. Democracy also implies a minimal degree of effective participation or citizenship. Thus, the more extended citizenship rights are, and, moreover, the more conditions for the effective exercise of those rights are present, the deeper the democracy will be. This is not the place to review the vast literature on 'conditions for democracy', but it is obvious that widespread poverty and inequality may be a major obstacle to 'deepening' democracy. In addition, while the establishment of democratic rule does not mean that all members of political and civil society are 'committed democrats', the more closely non-democratic values, attitudes, and behaviours compete with democratic values, the more likely it is that democracy will be shallow.

What is the role of truth and justice policies in this complex web of requirements and conditions? How do processes of truth and justice contribute to institutional, attitudinal, and political reform? There is no single answer to this question. As the chapters in this book show, in some cases they may make little or no contribution to democratization and in others they may make quite a significant one. Their impact will depend in each case on the constellation of specific national conditions and circumstances. It will depend on how such policies are formulated, and on the level of social interest in, importance and expectations attached to them.

Barahona de Brito has argued that such policies alone have little impact on democratization. When all is said and done, democratization can occur without backward-looking accountability, but it will not happen if wider institutional, political, and social reforms are not implemented. What *is* necessary for democratization are forward-looking institutional reforms to ensure present and future accountability. However, backward-looking truth and justice may contribute to initiating that process by setting in motion a dynamic for wider reforms. Conversely, the kind of obsessive concern with stability that leads some elites to avoid accountability for past abuses may lead to immobility, which halts the social, institutional, and political changes necessary to deepen democracy (Barahona de Brito, 1997: 8). In Chapter 4 below she argues that in Chile the renewed search for truth and justice in the wake of the arrest of General Pinochet has galvanized the courts into action and contributed to improving the image and legitimacy of a tarnished judiciary. It has also put basic reforms on the agenda. Thus, the arrest and the wider search for justice and truth may contribute to deepening democracy. In addition, in so far as this trend is challenging a limited vision of the level of conflict that Chilean society can sustain without attacking democratic stability, it is also helping to widen the scope for reform and a more participatory form of politics. She makes a similar argument for Argentina, but claims that the same is not true for Brazil and Uruguay, for a number of reasons.

Looking at South Africa, Wilson argues both ways. On the one hand, the truth and justice process cannot be viewed as separate from a wider national process of political change. Indeed, elsewhere he has warned against the 'familiar but self deceiving separation of law, human rights, truth commissions and reconciliation from questions of nation-building' (Wilson, 1996: 14). On the other hand, as he shows in Chapter 6 below, the Truth and Reconciliation Commission has acted as a 'liminal' institution, filling in for a judiciary that is weak and corrupted and unable to deal with the demands of transitional truth and justice. In doing so, there is a danger that judicial reform—which is essential for democratization—will be forgotten. Thus, while part of more wide-ranging change and reform to build state power (in this case the judicial branch) and democracy, a truth commission can also dangerously replace necessary reform measures, although only with the passage of time can its impact be gauged. As in the case of Guatemala, South Africa's accountability process has been tied in with nation and citizenship building of an ethnically divided society, where whites persecuted indigenous or black majorities. The links between truth telling and justice and democratization in these cases is therefore somewhat more complex.

The Spanish case confirms the link between avoiding truth and justice and experiencing a delay in reform. In Chapter 3 below Aguilar argues that, while amnesty and institutionalized 'forgetting' may have been appropriate to ensure a peaceful transition, they also placed some obstacles in the way of reform over the medium term and thus slowed down a process of democratic deepening. She draws on similar arguments made about the negotiated transitions in South Africa and Latin America. These indicate that, ironically, the kinds of policy necessary to ensure a peaceful transition are not necessarily the same as those needed to pursue democratization, and that, indeed, one may work against the other over the medium or long term. At the same time, given the peculiarity of the Spanish context, Aguilar argues that Basque separatists have used the permanence of certain institutions and persons related to the past as an excuse to question the whole democratic process. It should be remembered that a large number of the victims of repression under the last years of Franco regime came from this group, given that they had already engaged in terrorist practices. The dangers of unreformed police and military forces, which remain enclaves of authoritarian practices and mentalities, was made clear with the emergence of certain 'dirty war' practices in the late 1970s and early 1980s to deal with Basque terrorism. Even before the establishment of Socialist rule in 1982, extreme right-wing clandestine movements, with the passive and sometimes active support of some police officers, carried out violent attacks in the Basque country with almost total impunity because of the aforementioned connivance of the security forces.

The Russian case presents other lessons. In the absence of any committed elite efforts to deal with the past, social action may be the only thing keeping alive a 'conscience' or 'memory' of the past. Hence the importance attached to the work undertaken by Memorial. In addition, the struggle to ensure that archives remain open is expressive of a desire for accountability of an historically unaccountable elite. Here, justice in terms of punishment is perhaps less relevant than a wider memory politics or truth-telling work. This is so because of the enormity of the atrocities of the Red Terror and the Stalinist period. Russia is still far from being even a minimally functioning democracy, and, unless it understands its past of over seven decades of dictatorship, it is difficult for it to make progress towards deeper democracy. Indeed, as Adler shows in Chapter 9, a return to old myths and loyalties becomes possible and could generate new anti-democratic forces.

Sieder, in her analysis of the Central American cases (Chapter 5), also places a great deal of emphasis on the social dimension. In contrast with the more 'elite' and institutional focus of Barahona de Brito, she shows how a process of truth and justice that involves civil society in a major way can be of crucial importance in breaking down authoritarian power and encouraging a broader, socially rooted process of democratization. Thus, the Guatemalan case is held up as a positive case. By contrast, the Salvadorean, while valuable, was more limited in this broader sense, owing to reduced social engagement.

González, on the other hand, finds that purges and punishment in Eastern Europe had little to do with democratization. Indeed, she argues in Chapter 7 that, where such processes were strongest, they expressed a party political power struggle between the old and new elite. That struggle was not framed in terms of the action necessary to ensure democratization, but was merely part of a naked struggle for power. It is no accident that such should be true in demobilized and apathetic societies. Indeed, as these cases, as well as those concerning Brazil, Salvador, and Uruguay, show, the less social involvement there is in the issue, the less likely that it will be an important part of the politics of democratization.

The East German case is again unique. Here, democracy was ensured by 'incorporation' into what can be considered one of the 'deep' democracies of the world. In this sense, rather than an accounting for the past, it was this absorption of East into West, a shift from the undemocratic side of the Iron Curtain to the area of European democracy, that is bolstered by a tight conditionality that ensures democratization. At the same time, however, Müller shows in Chapter 8 how German awareness of the need to work through the past is part and parcel of conceptions of law, democracy, and citizenship in the country, given the Nazi past. Further, the nature of that accountability process has had an impact on eastern perceptions of German democracy, producing alienation among some former dissidents.

Costa Pinto's chapter on the Portuguese case offers quite a different lesson. Here, the process of democratization only really took off after transitional justice measures had been abandoned. Indeed, this case shows that, where backward-looking accountability is not part of a democratic dynamic but is expressive of a power struggle between actors with ambiguous attitudes towards due process in a context of polarization and mobilization, the links between truth and justice and democracy may be negative.

Thus, there is no clear link between transitional truth and justice and democratization. The relationship depends on whether policies are in themselves democratic and are carried out according to due process, or whether they constitute mere instruments for the accumulation of power or revenge. The answer will differ also according to the level of popular participation and interest in the process. It depends on whether such policies are conceived of as a way to break with an undemocratic past and build a new democracy.

As assessed in the bibliographic survey at the end of this book, the literature is roughly divided into the partisans of 'moral decisions' and those who defend 'practical solutions'. In this book it is felt that there is not a strict causal link between measures of retroactive justice and the nature of a democratic regime. Clearly, certain 'omissions' and 'silences' can contribute to generating disaffection towards a new democratic regime among some social groups, but it is also the case that such silences can help to create consensus solutions that ease the transition to democracy. On the other hand, it is also obvious that lack of political activity in some areas, such as the absence of deep institutional reform, including the absence of institutional purges, can negatively affect the working of key institutions. Such is the case when the forces of law and order behave violently or make use of the threat of a coup, or when judges boycott the application of new laws. None the less, such reform measures can also be implemented later on, after the period of transition is over, with lesser risks for the survival of the system.

Finally, it is also clear that the fact that trials, purges, and truth commissions are undertaken and constituted does not *per se* guarantee a better-quality democracy. The correlation of forces, for sometimes fortuitous reasons such as defeat in war, can lead to the adoption of certain policies, but this does not guarantee that they will be effectively applied or will contribute to deeper democracy. Indeed, there are perverse historical legacies that block the proper functioning of institutions. The roots of such legacies can lie in the remote past, far more distant than a recent authoritarian episode, or may have survived endless memory policies (O'Donnell, 1996).

Memory Making and Democratization

> It is a poor sort of memory that only works backwards.
>
> Lewis Carroll

Official or unofficial transitional truth and justice projects are only the first step towards coming to terms with a traumatic violent past. There is no definitive 'closure', as continued and constantly renewed debate about the Holocaust indicates. As noted elsewhere, 'neither official truth nor justice, however wide-ranging and complete, are miraculous remedies to solve what are deep wounds and sometimes irreconcilable differences' (Barahona de Brito, 1997). Indeed, beneficial as they are for a society engaging in a transition away from violence, illegality, and atrocity, and for the victims in particular, in a number of ways that should not be minimized, both truth telling and trials are limited and problematic. They can be cathartic, but they can also perpetuate conflict. They may create an 'us *v.* them' mentality, perpetuating social conflict, as in the 'game without end' described by Malamud-Goti (1996). Just as the judiciary can serve an immoral order (Dyzenhaus, 1998), courts under a democracy can perpetrate a cycle of vengeance and blame as well as a virtuous cycle of justice. Sometimes it is not clear which wins out. Financial, political, personnel, and time constraints, as well as difficulties in gaining access to information and 'hard evidence', mean that both trials and truth commissions will be selective in the picture they draw and the justice they do. As one observer notes about the German case, 'the maximum that can possibly be done within the constraints of the rule of law and non-retroactivity is way below the minimum that would have to be done in order to reconcile the small but vocal groups of those who have suffered most under the old regime' (Offe, 1993).

Truth commissions and trials can offer only a partial picture of the repressive universe, and the responsibilities for it. This will mean a continued need to produce accounts of the past. They may neither teach nor deter, as criminal acts are not committed for self-benefit, and the criminals will continue to believe they did the right thing and to see themselves as martyrs. Hence there are still contested visions of what happened. Even after the evils of the past are known, some will continue to defend repression and to challenge any 'new consensus' that emerges about the past. They can fail to garner legitimacy, as they may be perceived as victors' justice, too politicized, selective, or retroactive. Most Serbs, for example, have not accepted the legitimacy of the International Criminal Tribunal for the Former Yugoslavia (ICTFY), given that most of the defendants have been Serbs—even though this reflects the reality in terms of proportions of violators on either side, it has been seen as victors' justice. Further, it is not clear that the claims of catharsis, healing, or disclosure are met, as the evidence from different case studies is mixed. As Mamdani (1996) insists, there is a difference between 'political' reconciliation and 'social' reconciliation. The first can be achieved by agreement among elites, but the latter may never be truly complete.

The impossibility of ensuring a perfect process of transitional truth and justice means that the past continues to live in the present, to a greater or lesser extent. Terms emerge to describe the effects of past events on national cultures. Hence the 'Vichy Syndrome', the 'Vietnam complex' in the United States, and the various German terms for working through the past and the guilt of the past, all of which indicate that the past is a disease of sorts, a burden on the present. Thus, even after it has ceased to become a part of the active political agenda, the past can continue to be a source of conflict in the judicial arena and of latent or overt deep-seated social animosities. In some of the countries examined here, political and civil society openly reflects upon and debates the meaning of the past. In others, the past is a ghost avoided by political elites, and they become 'haunted lands'. In still others, there are 'irruptions of memory' and then silence (Wilde, 1999). Sometimes memory politics and the rehabilitation of victims may be delayed. The Japanese apology for the pain caused by its forces during the Second World War was proffered by the Prime Minister only in 1995. Swiss banks, American art museums, and the Catholic Church only began to confront the legacy of the Second World War relatively recently—French bishops, for example, issued the first apology for the silence of the Church over the deportation of over 76,000 Jews from Vichy France only in October 1997. However, the long public absence of memory politics does not mean that memories do not continue to shape social and political action in subtle ways.

On the other hand, memories will be reworked and meanings renewed. Hence the shifting paradigms of Holocaust memory with the passage of time, as well as generational and contextual changes. Memory is part and parcel of cultural production, giving rise to biographies, academic studies, novels, films, and theatre productions, all of which reflect on past events or reinterpret them. Symbolic representations and language are transformed; the phrase 'never again' is a case in point. The politics of memory engenders the politics of commemoration and monument building. Symbolic dates and commemorations become established foci of resistance to the logic of amnesty and forgetting. Struggles are waged over the meaning and 'ownership' of symbols, commemorations, and monuments.

It can be said that the politics of memory is two things. Narrowly conceived, it consists of policies of truth and justice in transition (*official or public memory*); more widely conceived, it is about how a society interprets and appropriates its past, in an ongoing attempt to mould its future (*social memory*). It is not easy to establish links between personal and collective memories, and between the latter and 'identity' and political or social processes, in particular with democratization. Social memory has been linked with the creation of 'imagined communities' (B. Anderson, 1991) and with the construction of a moral order. Myths and memories define the scope and nature of action, reorder reality, and legitimate power holders. They become a part of the process of political socialization, teaching people how to perceive political reality and helping them to assimilate political ideas and opinions. They are transmitted by authority figures, and bring together people living within the boundaries of a state. Historical memories and collective remembrances can be instruments to legitimate discourse, create loyalties, and justify political options. Thus, control over the narrative of the past means control over the construction of narratives for an imagined future. Memory is a struggle over power and who gets to decide the future. What and how societies choose to remember and forget largely determines their future options.[5]

Indeed, memories are constantly revised to suit current identities. As Herf (1997) argues, postwar conservatives in Germany deliberately weakened the memory of the Holocaust and delayed bring the Nazis to justice, with the argument that this would destroy a still fragile democracy. In East Germany, on the other hand, memory of the Holocaust was suppressed to portray the past as a simple battle between good and evil, between Communism and Nazism. It was only in the 1960s that Willy Brandt apologized to the Jews, kneeling before the Warsaw Ghetto Memorial. In Herf's view, the delay in dealing with the Nazi past has contributed to the difficulties of unification of East and West (1997: 6–7, 394). Some historically constituted forms of memory making can be affirmative of democratic values, while others lend themselves to the cultivation of renewed violence. Nationalist violence can be legitimated by memories of golden ages and by the politicization of myths of a 'chosen people': Michael Ignatieff speaks of the 'dreamtime of vengeance. Crimes can never be safely fixed in the historical past; they remain locked in the eternal present, crying out for vengeance' (1997: 15). At other times, the politics of memory can lead to fear of any risk-taking that may be negative to ensure necessary reforms.

Thus, it is necessary to engage in 'an ongoing reflection and critical appropriation of the past'. Simply 'enshrining past suffering in memory alone is as likely to blind one to new injustices and to

[5] For a review of the theoretical literature on collective memory and symbolic politics dealing with the past see Aguilar (1996a: 331–56).

contribute to a narrow obsession with self or narrow group as it is to play a sensitising role or stimulate the moral imagination' (Allen, 1999).

Social memory making, the social and cultural 'politics of memory', is an integral part of the process of building various social, political, or 'collective' identities, which shape the way different social groups view national politics and the goals they wish to pursue for the future. As such, the politics of memory is ultimately revealing about, and relevant to, any political process, including progress towards deeper democracy. Politicians, intellectuals and social actors as a whole have memories and learn from experience. Indeed, 'critical thinking is an exercise of memory' (Almond and Genko, 1997: 513). In this broader sense, the whole of 'transitions' and 'democratization' literature, that on memory politics itself, and even this book and others like it, are part of the politics of memory. They constitute attempts to make sense of the present, to make a critical vision of the present based on an assessment of the past, and thereby to mould a future project. In so far as such efforts are never properly 'finished', it is possible to say that the future of the past remains uncertain.

1

The Role of International Actors in National Accountability Processes

Naomi Roht-Arriaza

Introduction

The response of an incoming government to past crimes and gross violations of human rights will depend primarily on a combination of domestic political, military, and socioeconomic factors. However, international influences and institutions play an increasing role in shaping and affecting these processes. International efforts are in turn shaped partly by the perceived success or failure of domestic attempts to deal with the past. This chapter focuses on three areas in which these mutual influences manifest themselves. First, it examines the impact of international and transnational activity on the work of national courts, truth commissions, reparation schemes, and political discourses about the past. It takes into account that the human rights bodies of the United Nations (UN) and the Organisation of American States (OAS) have produced standards and treaties on which legal cases and political mobilization in several countries have been based. Further, it shows how the transnationalization of human rights activist networks, and the flow of knowledge through those networks, have allowed different countries to learn from one another.

Transnational justice also takes the form of legal actions brought in the national courts of one country against civil or criminal defendants based in another. The most notable example, although by no means the only one, is the attempted Spanish prosecution of former Chilean dictator (1973–90), General Augusto Pinochet Ugarte. These transnational cases raise the second possibility of simultaneous actions in multiple arenas. A third area of influence is the creation of new international institutions for

accountability. The International Criminal Tribunals for the former Yugoslavia (ICTFY) and Rwanda (ICTR) have influenced the shape of domestic prosecutions, and the pending International Criminal Court (ICC) will do so to a much greater degree. Some truth commissions, such as that of El Salvador, have also been created and staffed by international actors. While significant, the extent to which these international efforts have influenced political or social reconstruction within societies is still unclear.

Human Rights Institutions and Norms

The United Nations, and to a lesser degree the OAS, have played a key role in brokering peace settlements or governmental transitions in a number of countries, including Guatemala, El Salvador, Haiti, Cambodia, Liberia, Bosnia, and others. In some of these cases the UN has not been a strong advocate of accountability. In Cambodia, under Chinese and US pressure, the UN originally countenanced a watering down of the language of the peace accords to omit all mention of the need to bring the leaders of the Pol Pot regime to justice or even to forbid them from holding public office. More recently, the UN Office of the Secretary General proposed a mixed national–international tribunal. In Haiti, a joint UN–OAS negotiating team similarly pressured then-President Aristide to accept a blanket amnesty of the military leadership in exchange for his return to office (Roht-Arriaza, 1995). In Liberia also, the UN encouraged a policy of 'forgive and forget' (Clapham and Martin, 1998: 133), while in El Salvador protest against the passage of a sweeping amnesty law after the UN-sponsored truth commission was tardy and weak (Roht-Arriaza, 1995).

On the other hand, in Guatemala UN experts helped draft an amnesty law that was more in accord with international norms. It at least excluded genocide, disappearances, and torture, and required an individualized determination of its applicability. Similarly, the Dayton accords in Bosnia–Herzegovina did not trade away the possibility of prosecutions by international or domestic tribunals. In many instances UN observer or verification missions have strongly protested against impunity, giving international cover and backing to domestic human rights and victims groups. And UN-related bodies such as the Human Rights Committee (UNHRC),[1]

[1] This committee is responsible for interpreting and assessing state compliance with the International Covenant on Civil and Political Rights (ICCPR), which

and the numerous working groups and rapporteurs appointed by the UN Commission on Human Rights (UNCHR), have often denounced the evils of impunity and called for accountability and reparations.

In the Americas, the Inter-American Commission on Human Rights (IACHR)[2] has played a particularly important role in Latin America, providing legal and political support to efforts against impunity. In a series of recommendations, the IACHR has found that amnesties in El Salvador, Chile, Uruguay, and Argentina violate the provisions of the American Convention on Human Rights (ACHR). This is so even if other measures, such as truth commissions or compensation schemes, have been implemented, and even if the purpose of the amnesty laws is national reconciliation.[3]

Such pronouncements by international bodies have given an imprimatur of legitimacy to the efforts of human rights lawyers and advocates and victims' groups to bring perpetrators of past human rights crimes to justice. In various domestic cases, often filed years after the disappearances or killings of political opponents, courts have turned to international treaties and their interpretations by the relevant treaty bodies to justify reopening or continuing investigations. In October 1997, for example, an Argentine court ordered new investigations into crimes committed at the clandestine detainment and torture centre, the Athletic Club, in 1976–7, in order to determine the fate of those who disappeared there (CCCF, 1997).[4] The court cited the ACHR, as interpreted by the IACHR, as imposing duties on the state to ensure rights to bodily integrity, to truth, and to mourn. The right to truth, in

is made up of independent experts nominated by states. The UNCHR, in contrast, is made up of state delegates and oversees general compliance with human rights norms.

[2] The IACHR is composed of independent experts from OAS member states. It monitors compliance with, and interpretation of, the ACHR. For OAS members that are not a party to the Convention, it oversees human rights performance under earlier instruments such as the American Declaration on the Rights and Duties of Man. The Commission has played an important role in the protection of human rights through its on-site visits, its reports, and its responses to individual communications. It can also refer cases to the Inter-American Court on Human Rights (IACHR), when states have accepted its jurisdiction. In the landmark Velásquez-Rodríguez case of 1988, the IACHR established that states have affirmative obligations under the ACHR to investigate, and if warranted to prosecute, those who commit human rights violations. For more information on the Inter-American human rights system, see Shelton (1992) and Buergenthal *et al.* (1986).

[3] For further discussion, see Cassell (1996).

[4] CCCF (1997); for a fuller discussion of the legal theories in these cases, see Roht-Arriaza and Gibson (1998).

particular, created an obligation on the state to provide every means possible to find out what had happened and thereby to provide answers to the families and society. Courts in Chile, Peru, Hungary, and elsewhere have used international treaty provisions to find domestic amnesties or statutes of limitations inapplicable. Others have cited Nuremberg or other international precedents to explain why accountability for past crimes is needed. On the other hand, when courts have dismissed such cases, they have found that these international law provisions are either inapplicable, or overridden by contrary domestic law.

Not only courts and legal advocates have been influenced by and have utilized international norms and experiences on accountability. The design of non-judicial measures, especially truth commissions and reparation schemes, has also been profoundly influenced by learning from earlier efforts elsewhere. The Chilean Truth and Reconciliation Commission (CNVR), for example, received its limited mandate in part because President Aylwin and his advisors had concluded that Chile needed to find a middle path between the earlier Argentine and Uruguayan experiences. Too much could backfire, as in Argentina, and too little was unethical, as the case of Uruguay showed. The Chilean government thus concluded that the pursuit of truth was the minimal ethical response, while 'as much justice as possible' would allow for a sustainable transition policy.

The Chilean model became the subject of discussions among those designing a transition process for South Africa. In a series of conferences and workshops, as well as through electronic communications, activists from Latin America and Eastern Europe helped the South Africans define the truth commission option as a centrepiece of their efforts to deal with the past. But, while building on the Chilean experience, the South Africans also responded to activist critiques of the Chilean option. Thus, unlike in Chile, there would be no amnesty; in addition, hearings would be public, and the names of people accused of perpetrating violations would be made public.

In turn, the new Rwandan government, seeking models to manage the enormous number of potential defendants facing a practically non-existent judiciary, borrowed the South African confession-for-leniency model, replacing amnesty (unthinkable in the wake of the Rwandan genocide) with reduced penalties. The Rwandans also incorporated elements of critique of the South African commission. Unlike South Africa's, their national reconciliation law requires defendants to apologize publicly in addition to admitting their crimes.

A growing transnational human rights advocacy network largely drove this learning process (Keck and Sikkink, 1998). International, regional, and domestic human rights organizations (HROs), associations of victims and family members, scholars, lawyers, and political activists shared information and experiences, framed issues, gave names to the crimes, and suggested solutions (Sieff and Vinjamuri Wright, 1999). Like the dissemination and application of international norms and decisions by domestic courts, there has been a dissemination of non-judicial models from one country to another, largely driven by a human rights network with an increasingly specific anti-impunity agenda.

Transnational Justice: The Pinochet Precedent

Transnational networks help to create the demand for, and shape of, domestic measures to address the past. Human rights activists have also directly used the legal institutions of other countries to effect some degree of justice for past violations in cases where the defendant either resides or may be found outside his home state. Through civil lawsuits aimed at providing compensation to survivors directly from offenders, as well as by instigating criminal investigations, activists have tried to supplement available domestic remedies, and to provide them where none exist. In civil law systems, civil remedies are more likely to be claimed within the context of the criminal action through the institution of the *partie civil*. In these systems private plaintiffs may initiate, and sometimes pursue, a criminal complaint without the co-operation of the state authorities. In the USA, criminal and civil avenues are nearly completely separate, and criminal prosecution requires government participation. To date, the US government has been reluctant to use the criminal law in human rights cases, preferring to denationalize and deport suspected perpetrators. Thus, the main avenue for transnational justice has been a 1793 law, the Alien Tort Claims Act (ATCA), supplemented by the 1992 Torture Victims Protection Act. It provides access to US federal courts in suits by aliens for 'violations of the law of nations' as well as by citizens for torture and summary execution. Cases brought under these laws have included claims for forced disappearance, torture, summary killing, forced labour, genocide, war crimes, arbitrary detention, and severe environmental damage and cultural destruction. They include cases from Ethiopia, Bosnia, Guatemala, Paraguay, Nicaragua, Indonesia, Argentina, Chile, Burma, and the Philippines. Judgments in the hundreds of millions of dollars have been issued in these cases.

The first major ATCA case involved a Paraguayan police chief who was accused of kidnapping and torturing to death the 17-year old son and brother of the plaintiffs.[5] The court found that torture was a tort under the law of nations, and upheld a default judgment against the police chief. Argentine 'Dirty War' (retired) General Suárez-Masón[6] was a defendant in a subsequent case. Similarly, Guatemalan General Gramajo was found liable for torture, summary execution, and causing disappearance.[7] The same happened to Radovan Karadzic, head of the self-proclaimed Bosnian Serb Republic, accused of genocide, war crimes, and other international crimes.[8] Other cases have raised human rights and environmental claims against US corporations operating abroad.[9] Defendants must be present in the United States for a suit to be initiated. In several instances cases have begun when exiles encountered their former torturers on the streets of US cities. In the case of Abebe-Jira *v.* Negewo,[10] for example, an Ethiopian woman encountered her torturer working at the same Atlanta hotel where she worked; in several other cases defendants have been spotted walking down the street. Better known defendants have been served while in the United States attending conferences or academic courses, as in the case of Gramajo and Karadzic.

These cases raise a number of potentially intricate and interesting legal problems, but in practice the biggest obstacle to their more widespread use has been the lack of ability to collect money judgments against defendants. Often, the defendant has left the USA, sometimes having been deported or extradited to their country of origin, and their assets cannot be traced. In many of these cases the defendant does not even appear in court, and a default judgment is entered. The effect is to deny the defendant the ability to visit or reside in the United States, which may be significant, but does not otherwise impede their movements. Owing to problems of sovereign immunity, it is generally not possible to reach beyond the assets of the individual defendant to those of the state, even in

[5] See Filártiga *v.* Peña-Irala, 620 F. 2d 876, 2nd Cir. 1980.

[6] See Fortí *v.* Suárez-Masón, 672 F. Supp. 1531 N.D. Cal, 1987; 694 F. Supp. 707 N.D. Cal. 1988.

[7] See Xuncáz *v.* Gramajo, 199 WL 254818, D. Mass, 1995.

[8] See Doe *v.* Karadzic, 70 F. 3d 232, 2nd Cir. 1995.

[9] See e.g. Doe *v.* Unocal, S. Dist, CA, 1997.

[10] See 72 F. 3d 844, 11th Cir. 1996.

cases where the defendant acted in an official capacity. In the few idiosyncratic cases where plaintiffs have managed to sue the state itself, they have been more successful in collecting significant sums of money. This includes a landmark suit of 1994, when a US court found that the Argentine government could be tried for abuses committed against José Siderman, an Argentine who adopted US citizenship.[11]

There are other drawbacks to ATCA suits. Litigation takes place far from the scene of the alleged violations, in a legal and cultural context usually alien to both plaintiff and defendant. It may be hard to find witnesses or documentary evidence, especially where the acts took place many years before. The lapse of time also raises statute of limitations issues. Courts have dealt with the problem by suspending the statute of limitations period for the time during which the plaintiff was unable to bring suit, either because they could not get jurisdiction over the defendant or because it was impossible to bring suit in the country of origin.

Given these significant drawbacks, why do plaintiffs go to the trouble and expense of bringing such suits? First, it can help them to tell their story, to find out more about what happened to their loved ones, and to confront the defendant with evidence of his or her crimes. In other cases, plaintiffs may want the ability to restrict the defendant's travel, to brand him or her as a criminal, or to influence overseas legal or political processes. The case with the greatest potential impact at home to date has been the class action lawsuit against the estate of Ferdinand Marcos, former dictator of the Philippines. Unlike other cases, the Marcos litigation involved a jury trial and thousands of potential plaintiffs. Again unlike most other cases, the Marcos family had sizeable assets, which could be distributed to victorious plaintiffs. The cases eventually resulted in a multi-million-dollar verdict. HROs in the Philippines helped spread the word to potential claimants and to develop a simple form by which victims of torture or disappearance there could become part of the plaintiff class. The case was front-page news in the Philippines, but the government, while initially supportive, eventually claimed most of the money, and negotiations with plaintiffs lawyers dragged on for years without any compensation paid.[12]

[11] See Siderman *v.* Republic of Argentina (965 F. 2d 699, 9th Cir. 1992, cert. den. 507 US 1017 1993).

[12] For more in-depth discussion of the ATCA, see Stephens *et al.* (1993) and Steinhardt (1995).

In addition to these cases for civil damages, there have been important criminal prosecutions. One of the signal developments of the post-Nuremberg era has been the idea that certain crimes are so heinous that they may be prosecuted by any state that has custody of the offender. This *universal jurisdiction* does not depend on the nationality of either the offender or the victim or on the place where the crime took place. It was applied most spectacularly in the Eichmann case, when former Nazi official Adolf Eichmann was abducted from Argentina for trial in Israel, a state that did not even exist at the time the crimes were committed, on charges of crimes against humanity. More recently, there have been prosecutions of Rwandans in Belgium and Switzerland, and of Bosnian Serbs in Germany, Austria, Switzerland, and Denmark. Other cases have been based on the nationality of victims. Such is the case of the trial *in absentia* of retired Argentine Navy Captain Alfredo Astíz, condemned by a French court on 16 March 1990 to lifelong imprisonment for participation in the torture and disappearance of two French nuns in Buenos Aires in the 1970s.

Indeed, apart from the Bosnian and Rwandan cases, the South American Southern Cone military dictatorships of the 1970s and 1980s have given rise to the latest round of transnational criminal prosecutions. The Spanish cases began when members of the Spanish Union of Progressive Prosecutors (UPF), and later the United Left (IU), filed a complaint in April 1996, accusing members of the Argentine military junta of genocide, terrorism, and other crimes regarding the detention and subsequent disappearance during the 1970s of a number of Spanish citizens who were living in Argentina. Unlike in Italy and France, trials *in absentia* are not allowed, so without defendants in custody there can be no trial stage to the proceedings. Indeed, at the beginning the plaintiffs were unsure whether they ever would reach the trial stage, but thought the investigation worth pursuing anyway. The case was thus filed under Spanish laws allowing public interest organizations, as well as aggrieved individuals, to file criminal complaints even without the backing of, and in this case over the strenuous opposition of, the state prosecutor's office (FN).

Local law allowed prosecutions of non-Spanish citizens for some crimes committed outside Spain, among them genocide, terrorism, and other crimes under international law, subject to universal jurisdiction. It assigned such cases to the National Audience (AN), the Spanish court with jurisdiction over international crimes, where chance assigned Judge Baltazar Garzón to investigate the case.

Garzón was already well known to Spaniards. He had been the investigating magistrate in high-profile cases involving, among others, the Mafia, the separatist group Basque Country and Freedom (ETA), corruption and dirty war allegations against current government ministers, and above all the former Socialist government's support of anti-ETA death squads, the Anti-Terrorist Liberation Groups (GAL). He accepted the complaint, created an investigating team, and sent requests to Argentina for documents and testimony. The Argentine government replied that it considered the case a violation of Argentine sovereignty and would not co-operate, despite a Spanish–Argentine judicial co-operation treaty. Spanish lawyers continued to work in conjunction with the Argentine non-governmental organization the Peace and Justice Service (SERPAJ), and in 1998 the AN issued an international arrest warrant for retired General Galtieri and nine other Argentine officers for crimes committed against Spanish nationals. Warrants subsequently expanded to over a hundred officers. After more than a year of investigations, Judge Garzón issued indictments and arrest warrants against Argentine military officers accused of multiple disappearances, torture, and other crimes committed as part of a systematic plan of genocide and terrorism. Among the accused are members of the military junta, the governor of Tucumán province, Domingo Bussi, lower-level officers who allegedly tortured, and commanders of secret detention camps. The case received its first defendant when retired navy captain Adolfo Scilingo, who confessed to his participation in throwing prisoners alive from aeroplanes into the sea, arrived in Madrid to testify. Scilingo was detained in October 1997, and is now free on bail but unable to leave Spain.

Meanwhile, in May 1996 a criminal suit was brought to the Spanish courts accusing General Pinochet and others of the death of 200 people during Operation Condor. This refers to an operation whereby the Chilean secret police, the DINA, co-ordinated an international repressive campaign across borders in Latin America, Europe and the United States. This second complaint was filed on behalf of Spanish citizens killed, tortured, or disappeared in Chile during the Pinochet regime. The complaint names the original junta members as well as the former head of the secret police and other military officers. Judge Manuel García Castellón accepted this complaint and launched an inquiry, although the two cases were eventually joined within a single investigation under Judge Garzón.

Later, human rights groups received word that General Pinochet was in London for medical treatment. The Chilean plaintiffs asked Judge Garzón to issue an arrest warrant and a request for extradition based on the evidence accumulated in the Chilean cases, and he agreed to do so (Wilson, 1999). Pinochet challenged the extradition request, arguing that he was immune from prosecution both as a lifetime senator and as a former head of state. The claim was eventually appealed to the British House of Lords, which twice decided that immunity did not apply for the crimes in question. However, in the second decision the Lords held that Pinochet could be extradited only for torture and conspiracy to torture committed after 1988, the date on which the UN Convention against Torture (UNCAT) had come into force in the UK. The Lords' ruling vastly reduced the number of charges pending against Pinochet, and Judge Garzón promptly provided the British authorities with information about hundreds of additional torture cases arising after 1988. These include over a thousand disappearances, which were presented on the basis that torture is a constituent element of a forced disappearance, and that the crime continues until the body of the disappeared person is found.

In the months that followed, Pinochet's defence lawyers appealed the decision by the Law Lords and the Chilean government made diplomatic efforts in London and Madrid to attempt to ensure the return of the general to Chile, all without success. In January 2000, however, a medical team examined General Pinochet's health upon request of the British authorities to determine his fitness to stand trial in Spain, and in March, despite appeals by various HROs and the Belgian government, the British Home Secretary decided on the basis of the medical report to allow Pinochet to return home on humanitarian grounds. On 3 March 2000 Pinochet finally returned to Chile after 503 days under house arrest in the UK.

Despite the unsuccessful outcome to the attempted Spanish prosecution, the Chilean and Argentine cases illustrate both the power and some of the dilemmas of transnational justice. They demonstrate the reach and sophistication of transnational advocacy networks on human rights, and their ability to bypass traditional state decision-making channels and the bargains of political elites; they reveal the potential and dangers of a decentralized, entrepreneurial vision of international justice; and they have led to substantive advances in international law, and created widespread ripple effects both within Southern Cone countries and elsewhere. The public interest and private plaintiffs in these cases comprise a number of non-governmental associations of Argentine and Chilean exiles living in Spain, Spanish professional associations, and one Spanish political party, the United Left (IU). These groups worked in broad coalition with human rights lawyers and non-governmental organizations (NGOs), academics, associations of victims and family members, politicians, and journalists across three continents. They have managed, with amazingly little funding, infrastructure, staff, government or private support, to mount cases simultaneously in a number of different European countries, bring witnesses from all over the world, and co-ordinate the sending of documents to the Spanish court. In part, this ability reflects the new capacities engendered by electronic mail and the Internet. It also reflects the inherently decentralized, entrepreneurial nature of transnational litigation. Unlike the interstate tribunals and ICC, these cases require little international consensus from states. This is both their strength and their danger.

From the beginning, the human rights and exile groups debated on the best strategy in these cases. While some wanted to rely strictly on universal jurisdiction and to emphasize the large number of Argentine and Chilean victims, the prevailing view held that to be successful the case had to be sufficiently Spanish-focused to avoid the charge of interference in a far-off, irrelevant dispute. Thus, the initial plaintiffs were Spanish citizens and family and descendants of Spanish citizens killed or disappeared in Argentina, and the case was based both on universal jurisdiction as prescribed in Spanish, not international, law, as well as on the constitutional command that the courts do justice for Spanish citizens. At the same time, a Spanish political party signed on as plaintiff and local groups of lawyers and judges began holding seminars for the judiciary on international human rights and humanitarian law. These efforts made it more difficult to dismiss the cases as irrelevant or unfit for the Spanish courts.

The attitude of the Spanish government has veered between formal recognition of the independence of the judiciary and quiet opposition to the trials. At the beginning, caught in the interregnum between the outgoing Socialist Party (PSOE) and the incoming conservative Popular Party (PP) government led by Prime Minister José María Aznar, the executive ignored the complaints in the expectation that they would be quickly dismissed. As the cases prospered in the courts, they proved embarrassing for the PP government, which reportedly sought to protect Spanish commercial interests in Latin America. The office of the FN, led by a fiercely conservative attorney, doggedly appealed against almost every judicial pronouncement favourable to plaintiffs, although with little success.

The cases have also dealt a blow to the model of negotiated transitions towards democracy as a viable transition strategy, whereby a return to democratic rule was achieved by largely allowing former violators to go unpunished. Whether support for limited democracy constitutes a national 'consensus' favouring military impunity is highly debatable; none the less, these were decisions made by the people's elected representatives. Transnational criminal litigation allows a small group of people, who may have lived outside the country for years, to upset whatever deals have been struck, and to do it years after the deal was agreed to. This entails risks. In the late 1990s, the threat of direct military takeover is probably somewhat remote, but increased political instability can occur. On the other hand, the possibility of external upsets for such transitional 'pacts' may in the long run lead to more solid and inclusive democracies, of the 'high-intensity' rather than the 'low-intensity' sort. It also may provide some deterrent to would-be dictators planning a comfortable retirement or a retreat abroad. On a conceptual/legal level, the cases mark the eclipse of a sovereignty-based vision of international law, and the ascendancy of the human rights paradigm as the limit on state sovereign power. Paradoxically, however, they also reflect the continuing vitality of national institutions and laws and a continuing judicial unwillingness to step beyond the bounds of local law.

The effect of the Pinochet case and others like it on international human rights law cannot be underestimated. Three aspects are particularly salient: the affirmation of extraterritorial jurisdiction despite arguments of sovereignty, at least under narrow circumstances; the denial of immunity to a former head of state; and, in this case, the acceptance of broad definitions of genocide and terrorism by the Spanish courts. Article 23.4 of the Spanish Organic Law of the Judiciary gives courts jurisdiction over non-Spaniards for crimes committed within or outside Spain in a narrow class of categories, including genocide, terrorism, and other crimes proscribed by international treaties to which Spain is a party. The Spanish courts had little trouble with jurisdiction, but it is important to note that it was firmly based in Spanish domestic law, not in any notion of custom or international universal jurisdiction. In a similar vein, the British House of Lords found jurisdiction over the extradition proceeding based on UK law, not directly on international law, whether treaty or customary-law based. Thus, the courts overcame national sovereignty arguments while grounding themselves firmly in sovereign domestic law. These results should make legal activists give priority to the passage of domestic laws enshrining the applicable legal principles.

The British and Spanish courts have addressed different aspects of the issue of immunity for a former head of state. In the first

Law Lords decision of November 1998, the judges found, in a 3–2 vote, that there was no immunity for crimes against humanity. The second decision of March 1999 ratified the first, with a majority of the Law Lords finding that torture, disappearances, and other grave human rights violations could not constitute the kind of official acts to which immunity attaches. Similarly, the Spanish courts decided that domestic amnesties, because they are illegitimate and do not correspond to the requirements of Spanish law, do not give defendants immunity.

Finally, the AN decision in Spain embraces a broad, and controversial, view of the definition of genocide. The conventional view has been that genocide covers only crimes with a specific intent to destroy an ethnic, racial, national, or religious group, with 'national' understood as being akin to ethnic. However, the broader view embraced by the Spanish court focuses on the intent to destroy a group *as such*, based on shared characteristics. The court concludes that those persecuted in the Southern Cone were targeted as a group because they were perceived to deviate from the military view of society as Christian as well as anti-Marxist and to be insufficiently aligned with the peculiar military view of the 'nation'. A similar argument has been made in UN reports and by human rights advocates, but had not been accepted by a court before.

The political and legal impact of these cases within Chile and Argentina has been profound. In both countries, the cases have helped revive demands for domestic trials and an end to impunity. They have revitalized organizations of family members and victims who have arranged the taking of testimony and the travel of witnesses. They have led, indirectly at least, to a political climate in which legislators and judges feel free, for the first time, to repeal amnesty laws and investigate crimes involving high-ranking military officers. This effect has been particularly remarkable in Chile. Pinochet's return to Chile did not lead to reversal in this trend as some feared; this was shown by the May 2000 decision by the Santiago Court of Appeals to allow Pinochet to be stripped of his parliamentary immunity. Everyone agrees that it is unlikely that Pinochet will be tried and sentenced. None the less, the loss of immunity implies a preliminary finding of probable cause that he committed crimes. In addition, the armed forces were finally forced to assume responsibility for the disappeared and have made a commitment to let relatives know where the bodies of the disappeared are to be found through the *Mesa de Diálogo*.

The outcome of criminal suits against Pinochet and others will depend in part on whether the courts are willing to interpret the

Amnesty Law of 1978 to exclude war crimes and crimes against humanity even without the convenient legal figure of 'continuing crime'. That characterization of disappearances, which has allowed most of the cases to proceed so far, will eventually fall away either as the bodies are found or as there is a political agreement to declare the victims dead. There are other cases for which around fifty former military officers are in gaol or under house arrest, some of which may lead to more indictments whether the bodies are found or not; these reflect a new assertiveness of the judiciary, a product of the changed political climate, the 'Garzón example', and the retirement of most of the judges of the military era.

The European cases have also helped revitalise the anti-impunity movement in the Argentine legislature, courts and society. Federal judge María Servini de Cubría is investigating the murder of Chilean General Carlos Prats, killed during Operation Condor in Buenos Aires in the 1970s for opposing the coup. She has asked Judge Garzón in Spain to hand over all relevant documentation to continue the case in Buenos Aires. In June 1998, the federal court of the province of Bahía Blanca also accepted a suit filed by Magistrate Hugo Cañón challenging the constitutionality of the pardons issued by President Menem, and the Supreme Court now has to hear the case. In 1998 the legislature repealed the two laws that had precluded prosecutions. In addition, the legislature passed a new, generous package of reparations, and Socialist members of Congress filed suit against President Menem for violating Argentina's treaty obligations to co-operate with the Spanish courts. Human rights lawyers brought prosecutions against the heads of the military for kidnapping the children of the disappeared, leading to the detention of eight former officers, including junta members (retired) General Jorge Videla and Admiral Emilio Massera, who had been pardoned by President Menem in 1990 for other crimes. At least one defendant in these cases, Jorge Acosta, reportedly came out of hiding and turned himself over to the Argentine court after Judge Garzón in Spain asked Interpol to track him down.

While the child abduction legal strategy had been open to advocates for many years, the Spanish and Italian cases seem to have triggered a new willingness on the part of judges and prosecutors to take national prosecutions forward. Argentine courts have reopened investigations into a number of high-profile disappearance cases, including those involving the Army Mechanics School (ESMA) and the Athletic Club, both notorious centres of detention. While admitting that the due obedience laws may preclude convictions, the courts have held that the families' right to know the truth and to mourn their lost family members requires full investigation. Some of the information brought to light in the Spanish cases has also had political repercussions. Domingo Bussi was accused of official misconduct and almost impeached from his post as governor of the province of Tucumán after evidence regarding his sizeable secret Swiss bank accounts surfaced in the course of the Spanish investigation. Protests also erupted over a presidential promotion of military officers implicated in the Dirty War, and the government was forced to discharge Captain Astíz after he boasted of his role in the Dirty War.

The cases have unleashed a torrent of further litigation in Europe as well. In the case of Argentina, the League for the Rights of Peoples (LPDP) had already initiated international proceedings against violators as early as 1976 in Italy, in conjunction with Argentine exiles in Rome. By 2000 trial was underway on the homicide of six Italian citizens involving seven military officers. Prosecution efforts against Argentine repressors have also been undertaken in Finland, Germany, Honduras, Italy, Spain and, Sweden. In Germany, prosecution efforts were initiated in 1998 and are headed by the Coalition against Impunity formed in March of that year and made up of lawyers', human rights and church-related organizations. In Finland the government has paid lawyers to investigate the fate of Hanna Hietala who disappeared on 22 May 1977, as well as that of two family members. In Sweden, where a contingent of HIJOS, the organization representing the children of the disappeared, is active, Astíz is also wanted for the abduction and murder of Dagmar Hagelin, a 17-year-old student who was disappeared in 1977.

Uruguayan repressors are also the objects of Judge Garzón's investigations. In April 1997 the Central Instructing Court in Spain requested that the Uruguayan government co-operate with its investigations, by calling on various members of the forces involved in the disappearances in Argentina to testify in the courts in Uruguay. At the same time, Garzón called on some victims to testify in Madrid.

As with Argentina and Uruguay, the Pinochet case led to the initiation of various other proceedings, and extradition requests were initiated in Austria, Belgium, Canada, Denmark, France, Germany, Italy, Switzerland, Sweden, and the UK. Of these, Belgium, France, and Switzerland actually requested the extradition of Pinochet. And a new law suit against the former heads of the Guatemalan military, alleging genocide, has been accepted for investigation by the Spanish Audiencia National.

These suits, and efforts in other countries to initiate prosecutions based on Dirty War crimes, increase the pressure on potential defendants, curtail their overseas travel, and provide additional witnesses and testimonies. They also may have a wider deterrent effect. Stories abound of Latin American former military officers who have forgone trips to the United States and Europe for fear of possible indictments against them. In sum, the existence of a credible judicial process abroad, together with the full participation of local HROs in providing evidence for that process, has brought to the forefront of national agendas a set of issues that the governing elites had, apparently successfully, tried to put behind them. Issues of impunity are again at the top of national agendas in both Chile and Argentina, and have resurfaced in Paraguay, Uruguay, and elsewhere. The role of these transnational judicial processes, which, because of their decentralized nature and their reliance on independent judiciaries, largely escape the control of national governments and international institutions, will continue to be key events in an era of institutionalization of international justice.

International Justice: The 'Ad Hoc' Tribunals and the ICC

National and transnational efforts to ensure justice have significant drawbacks and limitations. National justice may be derailed by still-powerful militaries or by an elite seeking to avoid a confrontation or to avoid mention of its own participation in crimes. It may also take the form of vendettas or show trials that undermine legality by denying defendants their rights of due process. Transnational justice depends on the vagaries of national legislation, the ability of victims and HROs to mount a credible case, and the fortuitous location of appropriate defendants. These limitations, together with the confluence of a number of historical and political factors, led in the 1990s to the creation of international institutions associated with the UN that applied international criminal law to individuals.

The idea of an international criminal court that would even-handedly dispense justice in cases of crimes of international concern goes back at least to the aftermath of the Holocaust. However, the Cold War context led states to distrust the ability both of other states and of international bodies to render justice fairly, and the court was abandoned for forty years. Furthermore, diplomats and politicians were often convinced that impunity for dictators and torturers was necessary to encourage them to step down or to make peace. The choice was presented as one between peace and justice, and justice often lost out. NGOs and HROs, overwhelmed with documenting and attempting to end violations, paid little attention to post-conflict accountability.

A combination of circumstances changed this panorama. The end of the Cold War coincided with the outbreak of war in the Balkans and the swift and brutal genocide in Rwanda. The lack of political will to intervene to stop these conflicts led to a consideration of alternative means, chief among them investigative and accountability mechanisms. In addition, the history of impunity in both places appeared causally related to recurrent cycles of violations. At the same time, many of the countries, especially in Latin America, where dictatorships had held sway through the 1980s, returned to elected civilian rule, and massive, systematic violations largely ceased. None the less, the continuing legacy of impunity proved a serious impediment to democratization, and human rights organizations turned their efforts and resources to combating this legacy.

The first result of these changes was the establishment, in the early 1990s, of the ICTFY and the ICTR. These tribunals, created by the UN Security Council (UNSC) under its Chapter VII authority to address threats to international peace and security, share an appellate body and chief prosecutor, as well as similar governing statutes and rules. Both were set up in the wake of bloody conflicts, with a mandate to try individuals accused of genocide, crimes against humanity, and war crimes. Both have primacy over domestic courts, which allows them to remove defendants from national court jurisdiction if they choose. They have tried a number of individuals, produced lengthy decisions, and somewhat changed the political balance of power within Bosnia-Herzegovina and Rwanda, although the extent to which they will have long-term or profound effects in the reconstruction of the two societies is still an open question (Ratner and Abrams, 1997; Morris and Scharf, 1995; Bassiouni and Manikas, 1996).

The two tribunals have faced different issues. The ICTFY was created while the conflict was still ongoing, but began operating fully only over a year later, in part because of early personnel and money shortages. Its biggest concern has been an inability to apprehend defendants and its dependence on the sluggish political will of states to do so. Thus, during the first period of its existence, the Tribunal issued lengthy public indictments of the Bosnian Serb political and military leaders, but could not find the military backing to arrest them despite the fact that they were living quite openly in Bosnia. By 1997 troops led by the North Atlantic Treaty Organization (NATO) had found a new willingness to make some arrests, and major powers were able to exert pressure on Croatia to turn over some defendants and documents. In addition, the ICTFY began issuing secret indictments to improve the chances of apprehending defendants, with the result that several high-ranking officials are now in custody. None the less, of the sixty indicted, the Tribunal had less than half in custody by 1999. Moreover, because of these difficulties, its first two convictions were of low-ranking defendants, leading to criticism that the court was making scapegoats of minor players rather than focusing on the organizers and planners of the conflict.[13]

It is difficult to gauge the effect of the ICTFY within the former Yugoslavia. Within the Bosnian Federation, it has largely supplanted domestic prosecutions. A number of domestic trials had been held early on, but suspicions as to the quality of due process afforded defendants, and their ethnically homogeneous nature, led the Tribunal to intervene. An agreement with the Bosnian government resulted in the establishment of 'rules of the road', whereby the Bosnian government submits for ICTFY screening any war crimes prosecutions that it intends to make, and the case proceeds only if the ICTFY certifies it as 'consistent with international legal standards'. Few prosecutions have met this test. In Croatia and the Bosnian Serb Republic few prosecutions have taken place, and none have affected individuals of the dominant ethnic group. Proposals for a multi-ethnic truth commission have stalled, in part because of the insistence of the ICTFY prosecutor that the role, powers, and relationship of such a commission to the Tribunal be defined beforehand. None the less, the public indictment procedure and the accretion of information through trials have allowed the ICTFY to construct and divulge a coherent historical narrative of the 1992–5 wars.

The political value of the international tribunals within the territory of the former Yugoslavia depends in part on their perception as being impartial and even-handed. Yet Serbs committed most of the atrocities of the Balkan wars and are therefore the majority of the indicted. Although the ICTFY has indicted and convicted both Croats and Muslims, there is still a widespread perception in the Bosnian Serb and Serb communities that the Tribunal is a NATO

[13] Prosecutor *v.* Tadic, Opinion and Judgment no. IT-94-1-T (May 7, 1997); Prosecutor *v.* Ermodovic, IT- 1997, both available at http://www.un.org/icty/english/judgements.

creature and irremediably biased against the Serbs; thus, rather than establishing evidentiary facts beyond dispute, to the extent it is accepted at all, the work of the ITCFY is largely seen as repeating myths and falsehoods created by enemies of the Serbs. Ongoing investigations into massacres in Kosovo, also under ITCFY mandate, may well result in more indictments of Serb forces. Yet, if these indictments are not accompanied by serious investigations into possible war crimes committed by Kosovo Albanians and NATO forces, the Kosovo indictments may again simply reinforce the view in Serbia that the Tribunal is a political instrument. In part, the lack of credibility is simply due to a lack of access to information from and about the Tribunal within the former Yugoslavia as a whole. There is hardly any independent media in the region, and the Tribunal has not developed effective strategies for disseminating its work. Thus, the potentially powerful effect within the former Yugoslavia of hearing and seeing witnesses describe their ordeal, and of seeing formerly powerful warlords in the dock, has been muted.

Indictments against the Bosnian Serb leadership, once there was some indication they would be backed by force, did compel some leaders to assume a lower profile and did divest them of some political and economic power. They may also have played an important role in splitting the leadership and in allowing a new, somewhat less tainted, political class to emerge. Within Serbia and Croatia, the indictments may affect the succession of Miloševic and Tudzman, as the political leadership searches for leaders acceptable to the West. The indictment of Miloševic and the Serb political and military leadership for crimes against humanity and war crimes carried out in Kosovo has changed the political equation both within Serbia and in terms of the status of Miloševic as the interlocutor of choice of the West. Yet the most lasting effect of the ITCFY may be outside Yugoslavia, in developing international law and setting a precedent for future conflicts. For ordinary Serbs, Croats, Bosnians, and now Kosovars, the work of the ITCFY seems still far off and abstract, even if positive.

Rwanda presents a different set of challenges. Unlike the ITCFY, the ICTR has obtained custody of thirty-five of some forty-three persons indicted. Those indicted include major organizers and leaders of the 1994 genocide, who had fled the country after the Tutsi-led Rwandan Patriotic Front took over. A number of trials have resulted in convictions, including the first-ever conviction for genocide by an international court. Instead, the difficulties of the Tribunal have centred on stormy relations with the Rwandan government and ICTR internal organizational difficulties. The Rwandan government has pursued its own trials for genocide and crimes against humanity arising from the genocide, focusing generally on lower-level defendants in Rwanda. As of 1998, over 100,000 people had been detained in Rwanda on genocide-related charges, some 1,100 had been tried, 840 found guilty and at least twenty-two executed.[14] To deal with the volume of cases, the new government created a categorization and plea bargaining scheme, which allowed most defendants to reduce their gaol time in exchange for pleading guilty and apologizing for their role.

Tensions with the ICTR have revolved around the interplay between the domestic and international prosecutions. The Rwandan government has from the start objected to the absence of the death penalty for those convicted by the Tribunal. An anomaly results whereby the leaders and organizers of the genocide, who will tend to be those prosecuted by the ICTR, will end up serving time in a relatively comfortable European gaol, while lesser offenders left to the Rwandan justice system may well be executed. Moreover, the fact that the leaders may get off relatively lightly makes it more difficult to convince victimized constituencies that the plea bargaining scheme for minor offenders is an acceptable trade-off for manageable trials (M. Morris, 1999). An overly harsh plea-bargaining scheme attracts few takers.

Some of the choices made in establishing the Rwanda tribunal also made relationships with the government more difficult. The seat of the court is in Arusha in Tanzania, which makes travel difficult for witnesses and victims, and means that investigators are often in Rwanda for only short periods at a time. Organizational difficulties and mismanagement of the administrative apparatus of the court contributed to long delays in getting it up and running. The first defendants only came to trial over two years after the Tribunal was established. These limitations not only soured relationships with the Rwandan regime, but also led to widespread cynicism within Rwanda about the aims and capacity of the ICTR. As the pace of trials picks up, and especially if many of the leaders of the genocide are among those convicted, that cynicism may dissipate (Cisse, 1998).

Part of the sense of disappointment with the tribunals within both Bosnia and Rwanda may stem more from hyperinflated and unrealistic expectations than from shortcomings in the courts'

[14] Prosecutor *v.* Akayesu, Judgment no. ICTR-96-4-T (Sept. 2, 1998), available at http://www.un.org/ictr/english/judgements.

operations. The judicial process cannot, by itself, create a coherent and shared narrative of complex and contested events, and it will always prosecute too few people for some and too many for others. Trials may be necessary, but they are only one in an array of post-conflict measures, which must also take into account a more systematic construction of facts, redress for victims and survivors and a range of commemoration and reconstruction initiatives. The 'ad hoc' tribunals have helped to change the predominant international discourse about impunity, and have allowed judges, prosecutors, and the defence counsel to garner experiences that will prove invaluable in implementing a permanent criminal court. Their dependence on political actors, however, and the drawbacks and inconsistencies of setting up after-the-fact institutions to deal with some, but not all, massive rights violations, make them inherently limited. Thus, the logical next step is the creation of an International Criminal Court (ICC).

The Statute of the ICC was approved by some 120 states in July 1998. The Court will have jurisdiction to try individuals for genocide, crimes against humanity, certain war crimes, and, once a definition can be agreed on, aggression. Cases may be initiated by states, by the UNSC, and by the prosecutor, this last subject to approval by a panel of judges. Either the country in which the crimes took place or the country of which the offender is a national must consent to the prosecution by becoming a party to the statute or by giving special consent. This jurisdictional scheme is perhaps the greatest limitation of the ICC. It means that a future Pinochet or Saddam Hussein could not be tried for crimes within Chile or Iraq, respectively, without the consent of those countries. Moreover, jurisdiction is limited to acts arising after the treaty establishing the court comes into force.

None the less, several features make ICC prosecutions more likely to have a significant effect within post-conflict societies. From early on, the ICC has been envisioned as a backstop or a complement to national prosecutions. Unlike the two 'ad hoc' tribunals, which have primacy over national courts should they choose to exercise it, the jurisdiction of the ICC is secondary. Under the complementarity provisions of the State, a case is inadmissible when it is 'being investigated or prosecuted by a State which has jurisdiction over it, unless the State is unwilling or unable genuinely to carry out the investigation or prosecution'. Unwillingness is a high hurdle, as it requires proof that proceedings or a decision not to proceed were made for the purpose of shielding the person concerned from criminal responsibility, that there has been unjustified delay, or that the proceedings were or are not being conducted independently or impartially. Given the stringency of the complementarity provisions, the ICC is likely to see little business from states with even minimally working legal systems. For states hoping to avoid prosecution of their nationals by an institution over which they have at best incomplete control, the best way to do so is to investigate and, if warranted, prosecute their nationals in the state's own courts. This creates a powerful incentive to ensure national prosecutions commanded by human rights law, and a set of standards to judge, at least *grosso modo*, the integrity of those prosecutions. It may also result in *domestic* judicial oversight regarding actions by military or government officials previously considered purely discretionary command decisions, as issues such as the proportionality of military attacks are scrutinized.

The preponderance of domestic prosecutions likely to result from the ICC structure eliminates one of the main attractions of an international forum, the potential for both uniform legal development and the existence of a fact-finding body that is representative of the global political and legal systems. It may lead to divergent legal outcomes in different national courts. However, it may also have advantages. National court decisions, adopted in accordance with international principles of due process and in good faith, may help to re-establish principles of rule of law in a domestic context. It may also resonate within a society in a way that far off and difficult to understand Hague tribunal proceedings cannot. Moreover, it is easier for potential defendants to make the case that they are the victims of a foreign or superpower vendetta when the prosecution is not home-grown.

The close link to domestic prosecutions raises a number of difficulties. What, for example, should the ICC do in the wake of a domestic decision to forgo prosecution, or apply an amnesty or a statute of limitations? The ICC does not permit statute of limitations for crimes within its jurisdiction. Yet a national statute of limitations, even if it does not violate explicit treaty commitments, would likely constitute 'unwillingness' to prosecute under the ICC Statute. The amnesty issue is more complex. Despite some attempts during the ICC negotiations to make domestic amnesties preclusive of ICC jurisdiction, states generally agreed that any provision allowing an amnesty to preclude jurisdiction would provide *carte blanche* for perpetrators to exonerate themselves. The Statute is silent on the issue, although an amnesty would seem to qualify as a 'national decision made for the purpose of shielding the person concerned from criminal responsibility' under Article 17. If so, the 'unwillingness' bar would be overcome, and national proceedings would not stop the ICC from assuming jurisdiction. This result is consonant with human rights law, which prohibits amnesties for torture, genocide, crimes against humanity and 'grave breaches'. None the less, a prosecutor could decline prosecution where it is not in the interests of justice, 'taking into account all the circumstances, including the gravity of the crime, the interests of victims, and the age or infirmity of the alleged perpetrator'. In addition, the UNSC could postpone a prosecution indefinitely. It is unclear whether these mechanisms will be used to ratify or to overturn national or international elite decisions to negotiate amnesties with dictators. But, like the ability to undo 'pacts' through transnational litigation, the ability of the ICC to take a case despite domestic attempts at shielding creates uncertainty and thus may deter such deals.

The discretionary decisions of the prosecutor will depend in part on whether he or she has adequate access to the views and positions of victims and their representatives. The concern of the Statute with the ability of victims to participate in court proceedings and to obtain reparations may make intervention by HROs and victims' organizations easier. In this area the ICC goes far beyond previous tribunals. While attempts to incorporate provisions for redress into the 1948 Genocide Convention failed, 'ad hoc' tribunals have allowed for restitution only in cases where the unlawful taking of property was associated with a crime within the court's jurisdiction. Compensation is relegated to actions in a national court 'or other competent bodies'. Early drafts of the ICC Statute lacked any mention of redress, and envisioned few opportunities for survivors to be heard during the proceedings. None the less, during the negotiations the importance of redress and recognition, so central to survivors and human rights advocates, infused the discussions. As a result, Article 75 requires the ICC to 'establish principles relating to reparations to, or in respect of, victims, including restitution, compensation and rehabilitation'. It also calls on the Court to 'determine the scope and extent of any damage, loss and injury to, or in respect of victims and . . . state the principles on which it is acting'. The ICC may order reparations from a convicted person, and may invite representations from victims and other interested parties on reparations issues. A proposal to allow reparations to be paid from states when their officials were found guilty was abandoned because of objections that to do so would overly blur the line between individual and state responsibility. In addition, survivors may address the court at various stages during the proceedings. A Victims and Witnesses unit is to advise the court and the prosecutor on issues of witness protection and other appropriate assistance for witnesses and victims or other persons at risk from witness testimony. This increased attention to the rights and needs of survivors reflects the experience of the 'ad hoc' tribunals, especially with gender-related crimes, as well as the influence of women's and human rights advocates on the treaty drafting process (Akhavan, 1998; Bassiouni, 1998; Ratner and Abrams, 1997; CICC at http://www.cicc.org).

Conclusion

The emerging structure of international justice, then, has at least three distinct, yet interrelated, levels. At the international level, 'ad hoc' tribunals convened by the UNSC may continue to be useful for already existing cases, such as Khmer Rouge atrocities in Cambodia, which have not been prosecuted to date and over which the ICC will not have jurisdiction. Another example might be East Timor, where Indonesian troops from the 1975 annexation onwards, and more recently militias linked to the Indonesian military, committed atrocities and killed large numbers of the population; UN High Commissioner for Human Rights Mary Robinson has suggested that some ad hoc mechanism for accountability might be appropriate in that case as well. Finally, when a minimum of sixty countries ratify the ICC Statute, the Court will become operational.

At the level of foreign or third-party states, extradition or prosecution provisions in international criminal law treaties and the principle of universal jurisdiction will continue to allow for prosecutions when potential defendants are caught outside their home state. Foreign courts may also obtain civil jurisdiction over defendants, through the civil law mechanism of *partie civil* or through the ATCA in the United States. Most cases will be dealt with on the national—or even the local—level, however. In such cases, international oversight is ensured by the implicit threat of ICC jurisdiction and the obligation imposed by human rights law to investigate and prosecute grave violations of human rights and humanitarian law and provide some redress for survivors. At the same time, a host of non-judicial mechanisms, some involving international participation or assistance, will emerge to complement, although not to replace, the judicial process.

The existence of such multiple mechanisms cannot hide the fact that the political will to use them, even in the most egregious cases, is usually sorely lacking. The creation of the ICC will not automatically generate new political will, especially if powerful states like the USA refuse to co-operate with it. It is only the combined pressure of NGOs, transnational advocacy networks, and the long memories of survivors, that have goaded states into creating existing mechanisms and have rendered them effective.

2

Settling Accounts with the Past in a Troubled Transition to Democracy: The Portuguese Case

António Costa Pinto

Introduction

The military coup of 25 April 1974 in Portugal initiated the 'third wave' of democratic transitions in Southern Europe. The transition and subsequent process of democratic consolidation evolved in various stages, each with a corresponding phase of 'transitional truth and justice' initiatives and counter-initiatives.

The first, between 1974 and 1976, was the 'revolutionary' period, comprising the downfall of the regime and the crisis of the state that followed. The period was politically dominated by the left and extreme left, and, crucially, by middle ranking military officers, the 'captains of April', who had led the coup because of their hostility towards a dictatorial regime that would not cease fighting a losing war to retain power over the African colonies. During this period there was a process of 'revolutionary transitional justice', guided by powerful if incoherent notions of social justice. It consisted of a wave of expropriations of private enterprises and land, with agrarian reform, nationalizations, and a thorough, largely a-legal or illegal, purge process. The latter was directed against the former supporters of the regime within the military, the civil service, the courts, the media, universities, the former regime party and state and private business enterprises. Most notoriously, it also punished members of the political police of the old regime, the International Police for the Defence of the State (PIDE), which was later renamed General Security Directorate (DGS).

The revolutionary period of 1974–6 was the most complex phase of the transition, if one considers the transition as the 'fluid and uncertain period in which democratic structures are emerging', but when it is still unclear what kind of regime is to be established (Morlino, 1998: 19). During these two years powerful tensions emerged within Portuguese society, which began to subside only in 1976, when a new constitution was approved and the first legislative and presidential elections were held.

The singularity of this period lies in the nature of military intervention by the captains, a rare if not unique case in the twentieth century. The three-front war waged by the regime in Angola, Mozambique, and Guinea-Bissau from 1961 onwards made them protagonists in the country's political transformation (Pinto, 1999). Unshackled by international pro-democratizing forces, and occurring in the midst of the Cold War, the coup led to a severe crisis of the state aggravated by the uncertainty of the politics of transition and transformation and by the decolonization of what was the last European colonial empire (Maxwell, 1995; MacQueen, 1997). Unlike Spain's *ruptura pactada*, Portugal underwent a transition without negotiations or pacts between the dictatorial elite and opposition forces. But there is no direct causal link between this marked discontinuity and the subsequent process of radicalization: other transitions by rupture did not cause comparable crises of the state (Linz and Stepan, 1997; Alivizatos and Diamandouros, 1997).

The second phase, which evolved between 1976 and 1982, gave rise to a period of 'normalization' and constitutionalization and incipient democratic consolidation. That this process was possible was due to the rise of the more moderate parties, which favoured the establishment of a 'European' style constitutional democracy. Through a series of elite settlements, this phase saw the retreat of the military from power (Graham, 1992). At this time steps were taken to reverse the effects of expropriations, nationalizations, and of the purge process (see Table 2.1).

TABLE 2.1 *Transition Phases and Retroactive Justice in Portugal*

Downfall	Crisis	Consolidation
April 1974– March 1975	March 1975– April 1976	April 1976– October 1982
Legal purges	'Savage' purges	Reintegration

Finally, from 1982 until the present the process of democratic consolidation has proceeded apace, under either Socialist Party (PS) or Social Democratic Party (PSD) dominated governments. The recovery of economic growth after the upheaval of the revolutionary years, accession to the European Economic Community (EEC) in 1986, and the routinization of the democratic politics pushed the process of democratization forward. By the early 1980s most active conflicts over measures of 'political justice' had been resolved. For the most part this latter period has been dominated by the first 'mature' attempts to revisit the past. Indeed, this has been the period of the 'politics of memory' *par excellence*. Various official and private civil society initiatives have evolved, permitting the Portuguese to look back and develop new visions and understandings of the country's unique 'double legacy': that of the authoritarianism of the New State and the subsequent revolutionary period. It has involved the opening of exhibitions, the creation of private foundations undertaking new research about the past, the presentation of new documentary films about the colonial war and the dictatorship, and the events of the revolutionary period.

A Portuguese Settling of Accounts

The mobilization of diversified, anti-dictatorial forces was crucial in the first days after the coup of 1974. It was especially important in the immediate dissolution of the most notorious institutions of the New State, as well as in the occupation of various unions, corporatist organs, and city councils.

The prior existence of a semi-legal and clandestine and diversified opposition to Salazarism, although disconnected from the military officers that led the coup, was of crucial importance. It constituted a political option legitimated by the struggle against dictatorship (Pinto, 1995). The replacement of Salazar by Marcello Caetano in 1968 for reasons of the former's ill health gave rise to a two-year liberalization process, and although this was cut short it allowed for the consolidation of a 'liberal wing' of dissidents opposed to the dictatorship. Thus, despite the surprising action of the captains, there were alternative elites with strong ties to various sectors of civil society, ready to play a leading political role in the process of democratization.

Immediately after the coup, the first government, the National Salvation Junta (JSN), took centre stage. This was composed of moderate high ranking military officers and civilians and the more radical left-wing Armed Forces Movement (MFA) that had led the coup. General António de Spínola, a moderate reformist general who had challenged the war policy of the dictatorship, became president of the JSN. For a part of the military elite and interest organizations, as well as the first provisional government, the objective was to establish a rapid institutionalization of a democratic, and perhaps presidential, regime following the convocation of elections. The formation and legalization of political parties to represent the electorate of the centre–right and right—the Popular Democratic Party (PPD) and the Social Democratic Centre party (CDS)—pointed in this direction. A great effort was made to exclude from these parties any persons associated with the New State and to find party leaders with democratic credentials. Indeed, the CDS, which integrated sectors of Portuguese society that espoused conservative authoritarian values, was on the verge of being declared illegal up until the first elections for the Constituent Assembly on 25 April 1975.

Spínola's reformist project was opposed by the radical elements of the MFA, who were at odds with the conservative top brass over decolonization. In September 1974 Lieutenant Major Otelo Saraiva de Carvalho, a leading figure of the MFA, mobilized against Spínola, leading to the general's removal from power. Between October of that year and March 1975, the MFA gained control of the state apparatus and the military, establishing a left-wing government. The rise of the MFA brought about radical political and social mobilization and a crisis of the state, and explains the inability of moderate elites immediately to impose a rapid process to institutionalize a representative democracy.

A failed coup led by Spínola in March 1975 to recover his position served only to radicalize the MFA government, which proceeded to decree the nationalization of banks, insurance companies, and large-scale enterprises. In the wake of this coup attempt the MFA and the political parties signed a pact in April 1975, whereby a system of dual government was established with the military component represented in the MFA Assembly and the civilians represented by the Constitutional Assembly. The new government was not to last long. By the summer of 1975, remembered as the 'hot summer', Portuguese society was in a state of turmoil. Polarization increased as conservative and right-wing forces mobilized for the first time against the radical mobilization in the cities and in opposition to the left-wing regime project. The country was divided, with the north representing the forces of reaction against the revolutionary project and Lisbon and the south in favour of radical change. Extreme left-wing journalists 'occupied' the Catholic radio station, *Rádio Renascença*, and the newspaper *República*, which up until then had been the mouthpiece of the moderate left, and private properties were occupied in Lisbon (Hammond, 1988; Downs, 1989).

Many analyses of the transition rightly emphasize the powerful 'revitalization of civil society' as a factor leading to the process of radicalization. As Schmitter notes, Portugal underwent 'one of the most intense and widespread mobilisation experiences of any of the neo-democracies' (Schmitter, 1999a: 360). It is too simplistic to consider the 'hot summer' simply as an attempt by the Communist Party (PCP) to impose a new dictatorship with the support of the Soviet Union. Naturally, the democratic political elite made much of this argument in its founding discourse, but this does not provide a full explanation of events. The situation was more complex. Conflict was fed by the development of strong grass-roots political organizations such as the workers' commissions, the growing challenge posed by the extreme left during the crisis, and its influence within the military. The importance of internal divisions within the armed forces in driving these events forward means that they cannot be explained as part of a 'programmed conspiracy'. As one observer of the transition has noted, the crisis of the state created a 'window of opportunity' for the radicalization of social movements (R. D. Muñoz, 1997).

It was in this context of increasing mobilization that, on 25 November 1975, moderate MFA officers organized a successful countercoup that toppled the radicals. The PS and the PSD backed the moderates, leading mobilizations in Lisbon and Oporto. In the provinces to the north of the Tagus River, the hierarchy of the Catholic Church and local notables supported parish-level mobilizations. As elements of the extreme right and right, military officers and civilians alike, began to mobilize, the anti-left offensive became violent. Attacks were made on the offices of the PCP, against the extreme left, and associated unions, and there emerged right-wing terrorist organizations, the Democratic Movement for the Liberation of Portugal (MDLP), and the Army for the Liberation of Portugal (ELP) (Pinto, 1995). At the same time, moderate military officers led by General António Ramalho Eanes signed an agreement with civilians in February 1976. The MFA was purged of the most radical elements and its influence was circumscribed to the so-called Council of the Revolution (CR), which had constitutional oversight. Further, unlike the April 1975 agreement, the formerly powerful PCP and extreme left-wing elements were sidelined, and the moderate parties gained the upper hand. A new constitution was promulgated in April 1976 and elections were held in June of that year, giving General Ramalho Eanes the presidency.

In 1974–5 Portugal experienced significant foreign intervention; this was not only in diplomatic terms, but also affected the formation of political parties and civil society organizations such as unions and interest organizations, and the shaping of the anti-left strategy that evolved over the hot summer of 1975. The Portuguese case was a divisive issue in international organizations, including the North Atlantic Treaty Organisation (NATO), and the EEC; it affected relations between these two organizations and the Communist Bloc countries led by the Soviet Union. By all the evidence, it is clear that in 1974–5 Portugal was an issue of great 'international relevance' (Pridham, 1991). Caught by surprise by the coup, the international community, and the United States in particular, focused on supporting democratic political forces of the centre–left and right in the capital, as well as on intervening in the rapid process of decolonization, particularly in Angola. The same methods deployed to deal with postwar Italy were used in the Portuguese case. The moderate political parties were financed by the US administration, which, together with the international organizations of the European 'political families'—these often mediating the US role—also supported the training of party cadres (Opello, 1991; Mateus, 1997). The impact of foreign aid, however, was limited. It was drowned out by the powerful political and social mobilization led by the left, by an economy strongly marked by a large nationalized sector, and by the flight of capital and of actual members of the economic elite from the country. Thus, it was domestic political factors that played a critical role in allowing the triumph of moderate civilian forces and the final withdrawal of the military from the political arena.

The Purge Process

To understand key dimensions of the process of transitional justice in Portugal and attitudes towards the authoritarian past during the transitional period, it is essential to take into account the transition by rupture and, above all, the concomitant crisis of the state. Initiatives of symbolic rupture with the past and with the elite began to evolve soon after 1974, culminating in the rapid and multi-directional purge movement, or *saneamentos*. Following a quick decision to remove the more visible members of the dictatorial political elite and some conservative military officers, the *saneamentos* began to affect the civil service and the private sector. They became increasingly radical, affecting the lower ranks of the regime bureaucracy, albeit unevenly. Calls for the political police and other repressive bodies to be declared criminal also spread very quickly (Pinto, 1998).

Only a few months after the coup, Portuguese transitional justice was based on a number of contradictory measures in an attempt to punish the authoritarian elites and agents of dictatorial repression. Most of the symbolic and real punitive measures affecting most visible and known regime collaborators were undertaken between 1974 and 1976, before the emergence of a full democratic legitimacy. This was a period marked by the crisis of the state, by the action of powerful social movements, and by military intervention, which shaped social attitudes regarding the settling of accounts with the past in which the judiciary played almost no role.

The 'non-hierarchic' nature of the coup, with the almost immediate intervention of democratic forces and popular mobilization, accentuated the real and symbolic break with the past. Political mobilization in favour of criminalization was encouraged by the brief resistance of the forces most closely associated with repression, such as the political police and the Portuguese Legion (LP), and led to the gaoling of many agents of the former.

The first measures implemented by the JSN, presided over by General Spínola, provided for light and rapid purges affecting only the armed forces, in accordance with MFA programme. Members of the former regime that wished to join Marcello Caetano in exile were immediately sent to the island of Madeira. From there, they were almost immediately allowed to go into exile to Brazil. In this way, the new government avoided the consequences of popular demands for criminal trials that would have arisen had these people remained in Portugal. The political police and the anti-communist militia of the dictatorship, the LP, were immediately disarmed and some of their leaders imprisoned. The single party, the official youth organization, and other regime institutions were also dissolved. The MFA proposed that sixty generals should be placed on reserve, most of whom had publicly declared their support for Marcello Caetano just before the fall of the regime.

The main demand, which was nearly unanimous, was to ensure criminal trials of elements of the political police. Some attempts were made to ensure its survival in the colonies, given the collaboration between the PIDE/DGS and the armed forces, but the organization was ultimately dissolved, with the creation of a commission for its extinction directed by military officers and left-wing civilians. The life of this commission was complicated. There were frequent denunciations of political manipulation by extreme left-wing groups and the PCP. The role of the commission was to prepare criminal proceedings for the trial of former police agents and to co-operate with other purge institutions, given its monopolistic access to the three million or so files kept on individual citizens by the PIDE/DGS. In July 1975, Constitutional Law 8/75 provided for the trial in a military tribunal of members of the political police and government officials directly responsible for repression on the basis of a 'revolutionary legitimacy' referred to in the preamble. The law also provided sentences of two to twelve years, and no statute of limitations was established for criminal proceedings.

The first purge laws led to the retirement of various civil servants and the dismissal of the president and cabinet ministers, as well as of the leaders of the single party and the LP. The clandestine and semi-clandestine opposition, particularly the Portuguese Democratic Movement (MDP), a front organization linked to the PCP, took over local posts at the city council level and removed former regime leaders from their posts. Various regime unions were taken over by workers, who removed former leaders from their posts.

The first public statements by left-wing political parties were generally quite cautious regarding the purges. The PS and the PCP both issued moderate statements. The first purges were spontaneous, arising from strikers calling for purges within businesses. Some professors and bureaucrats in the universities of Lisbon and Coimbra who had collaborated with the former regime were denied access to their faculties by student associations. In response to these movements, the provisional government promulgated the first regulations on public administration purges. Two months after the fall of the old regime, an Inter-ministerial Purge and Reclassification Commission was created. It depended directly on the Council of Ministers and was charged with co-ordinating existing purge commissions and/or creating new ones to cover all the ministries. Decree Law 277 of 25 June 1974 charged it with the scrutiny of behaviour that 'contradicted the post-25 April 1974 established order' (*Diário do Governo*, 1, no. 146: 744). These existing and newly created commissions remained active until 1976, and the legislation governing them was revised several times in order to keep up with the radicalization of the political situation. Decree Law 123 of 11 March 1975 was already referring to the former regime as a 'fascist regime' and subjecting civil servants to purges 'for acts committed during the dictatorship' (*Diário do Governo*, 1, no. 59: 375). That same month, when General Spínola fled the country, an out burst of anti-capitalist sentiment caused a second surge in the purge movement. This second phase affected a new and diffuse category of people.

In February 1975, official reports on the purge process stated that approximately 12,000 people had been either removed from their posts or suspended, either legally or illegally (*O Século*, 27 February 1975). It is estimated that between March and November 1975 the number of removals and suspensions increased significantly: on 25 November of that year, when purges were interrupted, if one takes into consideration all kinds of institutions and sanctions, the number had risen to 20,000.[1]

Various institutions were involved in the purge process. Aside from the measures adopted by the JSN and the MFA immediately after the coup, the PCP and the small but influential parties of the extreme left were the main actors involved. However, purge movements in the private sector and even in the government bureaucracy often escaped party political control. Workers' commissions often called for purges. These were established within businesses independently of the unions, and the PCP shared control of these bodies with the parties of the extreme left. The workers' commissions implemented the great majority of 'savage purges', which the PCP often was unable to control.

Generally speaking, the purge process was not governed by a clear strategy and revealed no coherent pattern, varying greatly from sector to sector. The concept of 'collaborator' also shifted during the pre-constitutional period. In 1974 the first purges were limited by a strict concept of 'collaborationist'. By 1975, however, various types of authoritarian attitudes among the industrial and entrepreneurial elite were considered to be forms of association with the former regime.

The first institution to undergo a purge process was the military, for obvious reasons. Immediately after the coup, the MFA gave General Spínola the above-mentioned list of sixty generals, which the JSN dismissed from active service. The purge of the armed forces was part of the political programme of the MFA, and, against the wishes of General Spínola, the process widened to affect a greater number of officers. The first list was composed of persons deemed to have given political support to Marcello Caetano during a political act in March 1974, on the eve of the coup, directed against the clandestine MFA, Generals Spínola and Costa Gomes.

[1] These numbers are provisional, as they are based on press sources that are almost certainly imprecise and must be confirmed by further research.

In the months that followed the 1974 coup, special military commissions administered the purges demanded by the MFA. By October 1974, 103 navy officers had been purged and 300 officers of all ranks had been removed from their posts (*O Século*, 1 October 1974).[2] Incompetence became the official criterion for removal, as it became impossible to sustain political criteria such as 'collaboration with the old regime', given that the whole defence establishment had collaborated with the New State during the colonial war (Pinto, 1999: 65–98). When General Spínola went into exile after the attempted coup of March 1975, the purge movement was reinforced and the majority of the officers working with him were removed from their posts. The purges also affected the National Republican Guard (GNR), a militarized police body. The CR, the supreme organ of the MFA, instructed with Decree Law 147C of 21 March 1975 that all officers who did not 'obey the principles espoused by the MFA' should be placed in reserve (*Diário do Governo*, 1, no. 62: 430–4).

After the victory of the moderate left within the MFA, the revolutionary left and the PCP were subjected to purges. Sympathizers of these parties within the armed forces were removed from their posts, while others went into exile in Angola and Mozambique, by that time governed by socialist regimes. After the dissolution of the CR, some MFA leaders were also forced to leave the armed forces. The military was the institution where a break with the past was clearest (Maxwell, 1982). A new generation quickly rose to the top ranks of the force as the old elite associated with the New State had been forced to retire. The institutionalization of democracy in Portugal therefore entailed an important change in the life of military officers, and it was here that the impact of the fall of the regime was most sharply felt.

The civil service also underwent a thorough if uneven purge process. The first legislation stated that public servants could be purged for three reasons: non-democratic behaviour in the course of duty after the coup, inability to adapt of the new democratic regime, and incompetence. The maximum penalty was dismissal, and it mostly affected the governmental elite of the dictatorship,

[2] A leading figure of the extreme left of the MFA later divided the purge of the armed forces' into four periods. The first was the initial purge directed by General Spínola and the MFA. The second was the purge for incompetence, which was more institutionalized, slower, and more complex. The third was the purge of right-wing officers in 1975, and the last was the purge of the left after 25 November 1975 (D. Almeida, 1978: 39–43).

those who had collaborated with the political police, the leaders of the LP and the former regime party, and the heads of the censorship commission (*Diário Popular*, 5 September 1974).[3] The purge process was directed by the various commissions and presented to the Inter-ministerial Commission, which ratified the penalty to be applied, in each case implemented by the head of the relevant ministry. New legislation was adopted in March 1975 owing to the protest of the trade unions and the members of the commissions themselves regarding slowness of the bureaucracy, but above all owing to the political context. The new law provided for purges based on individual behaviour before the fall of the regime.

It is difficult to determine how the purges affected the state bureaucracy on a quantitative level. The process evolved differently from ministry to ministry, depending on the level of pressure from the trade unions and the limits imposed by the legislation. According to the global analysis made by the commission that co-ordinated the process, the action of the various ministerial commissions was very uneven, depending on the party to which the minister belonged and the degree of trade union pressure. At the end of 1974, eight months after the coup, about 4,300 public servants had been subjected to a purge process (*O Século*, 27 February 1975). One of the least affected was the Ministry of Justice, particularly magistrates and the political courts of the dictatorship, the 'plenary courts'. A good part of the moderate left elite associated with the PS was made up of lawyers that had participated in the great political trials of the New State, either as the accused or as defence lawyers, particularly of communist activists. At the same time, the Salazarist elite had a large component of law professors, and the regime had always obsessively attempted to legitimate its acts in juridical terms. Both of these elements would lead one to believe that pressure to try the legal elite criminally could be high, but this was not the case. Corporative factors and, above all, the moderation of socialist leaders were important elements counteracting this impetus to purge the legal profession and Ministry of Justice. Additional obstacles, such as the autonomy of the judiciary and the fact that the first ministers did not promote purges, limited the purge of magistrates. In response to public criticism, the Secretary of the Purge Commission of the Ministry of Justice recognized that it was not 'necessary or viable to undertake deeper

[3] Four punitive measures were provided for: transferral with maintenance of status, demotion, suspension for up to three years, and mandatory retirement and resignation.

purges at this point' (*A Capital*, 19 April 1975). Out of a body of 500 magistrates, forty-two judges were submitted to a purge process in 1974–5, most of them for participating in political courts or holding government posts or posts within censorship bodies.[4] Two years later, some of the best known judges that had been dismissed or forcibly retired were re-integrated by the Commission for the Analysis of Purge Proceedings. Two of them were placed on the bench of the Supreme Court of Justice, in the face of protest from the moderate parliamentary left.[5]

The purges undertaken in the Ministry of Labour were more complex, far-reaching and radical. This new ministry succeeded the old Ministry of Corporations and Welfare, which had overseen the gigantic corporatist apparatus of the old regime. A large number of the 'savage' purges were 'legalized' by the inclusion in the purge law not only of people who had maintained a formal relationship with the PIDE/DGS, but also all the persons who had in one way or another collaborated with the political police. In addition, nationalization and the intervention of the state in various private enterprises meant that the majority of forced removals took place in this sector, which was also the one most marked by the anti-capitalism of the social movements.

Purges in the Ministry of Education, and throughout the education system as a whole, were also numerous, particularly in the universities. Famous university professors and schoolteachers, as well as writers, formed a part of the purge commission for this sector.[6] The JSN removed all university deans and directors of faculties from their posts, and various high-ranking members of the Ministry were transferred. In the secondary schools, the more radical actions by the student movement forced the military to intervene to protect the accused. It was in the universities, however, that both legal and savage purges were most thorough, given the very strong pressure exerted by the student movement. Some members of the commissions quickly resigned in protest against the savage purges, which were sometimes undertaken in the absence of any legal proceedings. Students would simply deny some pro-

[4] The purge of institutions that depended on the Ministry of Justice was not very significant: 22 proceedings in the Investigating Police (PJ), 16 affecting public notaries, and 4 prison directors were subjected to compulsory retirement (*A Capital*, 19 April 1975).

[5] See the speech by Socialist deputy Raul Rego in *A Luta*, 9 February 1977.

[6] Examples are Teixeira Ribeiro of the University of Coimbra and Mário Dionísio, an intellectual and writer who resigned some months after being nominated (*A Capital*, 10 January 1975).

fessors entry to the university following assembly votes, although only a small minority of those 'condemned' were ever submitted to legal purge proceedings by the purge commission of the Ministry of Education. The same applied to some schoolteachers suspected of collaborating with the political police. The most radical savage purges took place in the Faculty of Law of the University of Lisbon, where an assembly dominated by a Maoist party decided to purge some members of the Council of State and leaders of the conservative parties, against the will of PCP students.

The repression of the pro-democratic student movement in the final years of the dictatorship, as well as the authoritarian behaviour of many professors, explains some of these 'savage' purges. Legal purge proceedings against professors and education workers were more solidly based on two criteria: holding high-level posts under the dictatorship, or collaborating with repression by the political police by denouncing students and opposition professors. As in the Ministry of Labour, the latter category was the most sought after, and purges affected people in the lower ranks who gave information to the PIDE/DGS. Some professors affected by the purges went into other professional activities and others emigrated to Brazil. When the government introduced the *numerus clausus*, thereby conditioning student access to the state university system, some of the professors who had been removed from their posts became involved in the creation of private universities.

Within the Ministry of Foreign Affairs, the purge process was limited to a few members of the diplomatic corps who had held government posts under the dictatorship. When he was nominated Minister of Foreign Affairs, Mário Soares merely transferred some ambassadors, and the purge commission, although fully constituted, worked only in those consulates where collaboration with the political police had been most notable. This was the case in Brazil and France, for example, countries with large Portuguese immigrant communities, where the consulates had been involved in controlling the activities of political exiles.

In sum, purges of the state apparatus were uneven and limited. Where strong trade union and worker commission pressure was exerted, as in the Ministries of Labour and Education, forced removals were more frequent. Indeed, while reports indicate that most of the people purged belonged to the higher levels of the administration, in these cases lower ranking civil servants were also affected, particularly for collaboration with the political police (*Flama*, 11 April 1975). Long delays in purge proceedings, however, reduced the overall scope of the process and made it possible to undertake the rapid re-integration of various people a few years later. None the less, important changes did occur at the top levels of the state administration. While many were re-integrated between 1976 and 1980, the great majority never regained the strategic posts they had previously held.

It is much harder to assess the break at the local level. On 24 April 1974 there were thousands of people running the 304 municipalities and more than 4,000 parish councils. In the first months following the coup, the JSN and the Ministry of the Interior designated provisional administrative commissions. The nominations legitimated the taking of power of local members of the main democratic opposition parties. The MDP was the main purge agent at the local level. This party had succeeded the Democratic Electoral Commission (CED), which in 1969 had obtained a significant majority in opposition to the Democratic Union Electoral Commission (CEUD), the electoral front linked to the PS and the republicans. The MDP was dominated by the PCP, but also had the support of independents, notables of the local democratic opposition. During the 'hot summer' of 1975, anti-communist action led to the fall of various administrative commissions, which became increasingly isolated in the northern parts of the country. The parties of the centre–right and the PS itself were not well organized in 1974 (Bruneau and McLeod, 1986). They lacked proper party structures and it was only later, during the pre-electoral period, that they began to demand positions at the local level. It is difficult to measure levels of continuity and rupture within the local administration given the absence of studies and data. None the less, it is clear that the relationship between the state and local administrative elites changed significantly during the transition process. Local elections created new opportunities and leadership options, and the establishment of a system of proportional representation called for new political strategies to be adopted (Mozzicafredo, 1991). Furthermore, constitutional law barred all the main figures of the dictatorship from standing as candidates for the first elections.

During the first two years of the transition, the economic elite was hard hit by the process of nationalization and state intervention, as well as by the flight of industrialists and entrepreneurs from the country. Despite attempts to reach an understanding between General Spínola and the leaders of the main economic groups, strike movements and a strong impetus towards state intervention led to the first emigrations. Some of the most important illegal purge processes were also initiated against members of the economic elite, which visibly frightened that class. Already in May 1974, the purge of this elite was the third demand during 149 labour conflicts, and it remained on the top of the list of demands made by workers and strikers throughout the following year (Patriarca, 1999: 141). It was only at the beginning of 1976, with Decree Law 52 of 21 January, that two purge commissions were given legal status and formal competence to deal with the banking and insurance sectors, which had by then been nationalized. These commissions were subordinated to the commission governing purges in the public sector as a whole. Its main role at this point was to reintegrate those who had been subjected to the 'savage' purges without respect for the basic principles of due process (*Diário do Governo*, 1, no. 17: 112–13). The exodus of important members of the economic elite became a common occurrence in 1975, as did the nomination of new managers for the businesses intervened by the state. The 'savage purges' were concentrated in the large enterprises in the industrial area around Lisbon and in the banking and insurance sectors. In the north of the country there were fewer 'savage' purges owing to the relative weakness of the unions and the workers commissions (Durán Muñoz, 1997).

The nationalization strategy aimed to dismantle the large economic groups and to give the state control of the main sectors of the Portuguese economy. Apart from direct nationalization, the state indirectly controlled various businesses for a fixed period. The 1976 Constitution confirmed the nationalization process but reduced the level of intervention. A study allows one to conclude that 19 per cent of industrialists abandoned their posts (2 per cent were purged), and that the purges essentially affected the industrial area in Lisbon and Setúbal, hardly affecting the northern textile sector (Makler, 1983: 251–283). Brazil was the preferred destination of exiles although many returned to Portugal between 1976 and 1980. When Mário Soares as prime minister of the first constitutional government visited Brazil in 1976, he called for the return of the members of the economic elite that had fled the country. Thus, the wave of nationalization, purges, and forced retirements of the pre-constitutional period profoundly affected the entrepreneurial sector. Most of its members were reintegrated between 1976 and 1980, but nationalization caused long-lasting changes in the Portuguese economic system, a key legacy of the transition to democracy.

The relationship between the state and the media also underwent a profound transformation (Maxwell, 1983). The administrative and management bodies of radio and television stations, as well as of the main newspapers, were removed from their posts. Only a few directors of privately owned newspapers, already in the hands of the opposition under the old regime, were able to hang on to their posts. The main purge agents in this sector were journalists and typographers linked to the PCP and organizations of the extreme left, which lost their dominant position towards the end of 1975. The censorship services were purged and dissolved. The official dictatorial press had had a limited circulation, for the most part circumscribed to members of the state bureaucracy. The newspaper of the former regime party, artificially sustained through an official subscription campaign, disappeared immediately after the occupation of its headquarters. The most important proceedings took place against non-official newspapers, where journalists and typographers linked to the left-wing parties controlled the purges. The media as a whole suffered profound changes during the transition process.

The political battle for control over the media had a great impact. The occupation of the Catholic Church radio station by its journalists, and the self-management system instituted thereafter, polarized public opinion. This radio station became an instrument of the extreme left in 1975, until its powerful transmitters were destroyed by a military command. The old newspaper, *República*, met with a similar fate. Of all the dailies, it was the only democratic one that had survived the New State. This paper supported the PS and became self-managed after its old directors resigned in 1975. Until it disappeared in 1976, it was the mouthpiece of the revolutionary left. After the nationalization of various economic groups that had controlled a substantial part of national newspapers, most of the printed press came under state control. Later, during the peak of the process of political radicalization, new papers emerged supported by the moderate left and the parties of the right, which re-employed some of the journalists who had been purged.

In addition to the administratives purge process, in 1974–5 various voluntaristic civil and state mobilization initiatives were also promoted to 'purge' society of the past. Such was the nature of the so-called Cultural Dynamization Campaigns pursued by the MFA with the co-operation of left-wing civilians, and parts of the so-called Student Civic Service. The government also created the so-called Commission of the Black Book of Fascism. This depended on the presidency of the Council of Ministers and was composed of intellectuals and politicians of the republican and socialist left. It had access to the archives of the repressive institutions of the dictatorship and published dozens of books, including primary documentation, which denounced the repressive methods of the regime, its political prisoners, censorship, and the collaboration between economic groups and the political police, among other issues. When it was dissolved in 1991, the aim of the commission was to create a museum of the resistance, but the project has not become a reality to date. Another initiative, more emblematic of the period 1974–5 associated with the political parties, as well as with civil society and popular organizations, was the Humberto Delgado Popular Tribunal. Delgado was a dissident general who had stood as a candidate to the presidential elections in 1958 against Salazar and who had gone into exile not long afterwards.

The Cultural Dynamization Campaigns basically aimed to 'democratize' the rural world. These campaigns were marked by the strong presence of left-wing intellectuals and communists, and consisted of cultural initiatives dedicated to denouncing the repressive past and promoting civic participation. Faced with the resistance of conservatives in the north and the criticism of the moderate parties, which saw the campaigns as a means for the military to create their own propaganda department, the campaigns ceased in the north. They were finally terminated on 25 November 1975, following the dissolution of the Fifth Division, a military department dominated by people linked to the PCP.

The Student Civic Service was the product of two interrelated factors: the inability of the university system to absorb candidates for university education emerging from a rapidly expanding secondary school system, and an ideological climate that celebrated contact between students and 'the people'. During a full school year, then, students worked with local communities in literacy campaigns and other support activities, before entering the university. One such activity, linked to the huge campaign to collect ethnographic materials on popular memory, was to serve as the basis for a museum exhibiting oral and material memories of peasant and worker resistance to the New State (Branco and Oliveira, 1993).

Both the student and cultural dynamization campaigns met with resistance, albeit for different reasons, particularly in the north of the country where conservative notables and priests were particularly suspicious of left-wing initiatives, and where the urban middle classes feared the consequences of students escaping the control of the family. The Cultural Dynamization Campaigns were halted in 1975 and the Ministry of Education abolished the civic service shortly thereafter. The Humberto Delgado Popular Tribunal aimed to deal with the most notorious crime of the political police unsolved since 1965, when the PIDE assassinated

Delgado, one of the most famous opposition figures to the regime in Spain, a few kilometres from the frontier. The crime had always been denied by the dictatorship, and it was one of the most important opposition figures to the regime, Mário Soares, who had become the first lawyer to represent the family of the general. The Tribunal was created after the transition, and aimed to mobilize public opinion to support a trial of those responsible for the assassination, namely PIDE agents who were fleeing from justice at the time. These were finally tried and sentenced *in absentia*.

The Constituent Assembly discussed at length the introduction of principles to make politically criminal the agents of repression and the parties and ideologies associated with the dictatorial past. However, apart from the transitory disposition referring to the trial of members of the political police, the only legal legacy of the transition in terms of punitive measures against the old regime was the inclusion, in the 1976 constitution, of a prohibition against parties based on a 'fascist ideology'. This was kept intact following subsequent constitutional revisions, and in the 1990s, despite criticisms regarding its usefulness, it was not only ratified by the parliament but was even used against a group of the extreme right.

The Dual Legacy Discourse and the Consolidation of Democracy

An official exhibition on the twentieth century in Portugal was inaugurated in November 1999, with the sponsorship of the presidency and the government, to celebrate twenty-five years of Portuguese democracy. Directed at the public at large and students in particular, thousands of Portuguese travelled through the dark passages of Salazarism, through the torture chambers of the political police and corridors lined with photographs of political prisoners, while opposition figures and the pro-democratic press were celebrated. There was a dark threatening corridor dedicated to the colonial war, which ended in a well lit area celebrating the fall of the dictatorship. Significantly, the exhibition ended where democracy began. The turbulent period of the first years of the transition were omitted, represented symbolically by thematic panels which portrayed the process of social and political change that had taken place in the twenty-five years since the fall of the Salazar regime.

It would have been very hard for an official exhibition to deal with the transitional period, given the complex legacy of the first two years of the transition. According to the official discourse of the PS led by Mário Soares and the democratic parties of the centre–right, the period of the consolidation of democracy was one shaped by a 'double legacy': the authoritarianism of the right under the New State, and the authoritarian threat of the left of 1974–5. The moderate elite that dominated the period of consolidation inherited a complex situation in 1975. The military intervention of 25 November marked the beginning of the process of democratic institutionalization. At this time, however, the process was still under the tutelage of the military through the CR, which played the role of a constitutional court until 1982. In the economic sphere, there was a strong recession and salaries were drastically cut, to ensure the implementation of austerity measures after the first Portuguese agreement with the International Monetary Fund (IMF). In the social arena, problems arose associated with the return of hundreds of thousands of refugees from Africa, following the decolonization process.

The official discourse of the first two constitutional governments led by the prime minister, Mário Soares, and by the first democratically elected president, moderate Ramalho Eanes, favoured 'reconciliation' and 'pacification'. The purges were quickly interrupted and were re-evaluated under the pressure of the parties of the right and centre–right, which considered them an excess of the early period of the transition. At the same time, a number of communists, as well as left-wing civilian and military personalities, were removed from office. Many militants of the parties of the extreme left or the PCP were removed from posts in the state bureaucracy and public enterprises.

Active and retired military officers unleashed the terrorist action of the MDLP and ELP, but the organizations were soon dissolved with the return of General Spínola to Portugal. Some of their members were gaoled. For the most part, however, trials dragged on for years and led to vendettas between those affected, given their extensive links with moderate elements during the hot summer of 1975 and promises that their crimes would be forgotten. The repression of the Popular Forces of 25 April (FP-25) was much more complex, and trials of various members of this organization are still pending. Despite this outburst of violence, the climate of political reconciliation predominated in the last years of the 1970s, shaping the way in which the government dealt with the legacy of the dictatorship.

After the 'hunt of the *pides*' (*caça aos pides*), when those who had not fled the country became the object of a witch hunt, members of the (PIDE/DGS) languished in gaol for two years awaiting trial.

The trials were carried out according to the new political ethos of the post-revolutionary phase. Those who had not taken advantage of their parole to emigrate received only light sentences, and people who had good military records from the colonial war received especially benevolent treatment. Although there were demonstrations, and the public criticized the light sentencing, a context of reinforcement of the rule of law and the reaction against the turbulence of 1974–5 ensured that moderation won the day.

At the same time, from 1976 until the first years of the 1980s, steps were taken to reintegrate those who had been purged. New legislation was passed and measures were quickly adopted to normalize the situation in the economic arena, in which the 'savage' purges had been most severe. The government also implemented a series of measures to facilitate the return of exiles and business administrators who had been purged. The new decree law number 471 of 14 June 1976 declared null and void the purges that had violated the laws of the period, namely those led by workers in the private and public sectors for political and ideological reasons (*Diário do Governo*, 1, no. 138: 1332).

While the Labour Ministry revised the purge process, those who had been purged organized themselves with the creation of the 'Pro Integration Movement of the Unjustly Exonerated' (*O Século*, 7 May 1976). The trade union movement carried out several strikes and sporadic occupations against the reintegration of purged elements, particularly in the nationalized public sector. They did not meet with success, however, and the new private press played a key role in defending reintegration (*Jornal Novo*, 31 December 1976).

The purge commissions in the ministries ceased to operate in 1976 and the CR, which took on the role of these commissions as well as the leadership of the Commission for the Extinction of the PIDE/DGS, reinforced legal mechanisms to ensure a process of rehabilitation. The Commission for the Analysis of Purge Appeals, which also depended on the Council, continued to work until the beginning of the 1980s and rehabilitated the majority of people whose cases it reviewed. Dismissal was overwhelmingly replaced by compulsory retirement or simply by integration. All remaining sentences were diminished and often were accompanied by the payment of earnings lost and by the validation of time in office for retirement purposes. If the resistance of trade unions or students was particularly severe, some people were reintegrated but transferred to other institutions, and others simply stayed at home for a few years before returning to their posts. In some universities the return of the *saneados* was delayed until the beginning of the 1980s.

When the CR was abolished, some suits were transferred to the administrative courts, and the Commission for the Extinction of the PIDE/DGS, which by that stage had become a mere caretaker of the gigantic archive of the political police, came under parliamentary aegis. Parliamentary debates regarding the future of the archives were often heated and passionate, with some parties such as the CDS arguing in favour of their destruction. Their incorporation into the national archives and their opening to the public, albeit with temporary restrictions, was not uncontroversial. It was possible owing to the pressure exerted by historians and left-wing politicians.[7]

The impact of the return of right-wing exiles to Portugal and of the press campaigns in favour of those who had been expropriated in 1974–5, coupled with the search for some anti-communist 'military heroes', was hardly noticeable. The process of decolonization, aggravated by the inability to mobilize those returning from Africa, marked the end of an era for the Portuguese radical right. The relatively peaceful process of reintegrating those returning from the former colonies was not merely a consequence of the 'quiet habits' ascribed to the Portuguese, or of state support. It was also a product of the nature of the white community in Africa, for example its relatively recent settlement in the colonies and the concomitant maintenance of family ties in Portugal. Emigration to other countries such as South Africa also diminished the numbers returning and the shock of social absorption.

By the end of the 1970s, the situation no longer favoured the political re-conversion of the 'barons' of the dictatorship and of military figures with populist tendencies, who hoped to make political capital out of their involvement in anti-communist action in the mid-1970s. By that time the military had been removed from the political arena, and the parliamentary parties and their bases of support had been stabilized and consolidated. The abolition of punitive legislation affecting the dictatorial elite and the process of democratic consolidation encouraged some of the leading figures of the old regime to return to Portugal. The last president of the New State, Admiral Américo Tomás, who maintained a 'political silence' until his death, as well as some former ministers, returned. Marcello Caetano refused to return from Brazil, where he died in 1980. None of those returning, however, wanted to associate themselves with a possible rebirth of the radical right, and few of

[7] Information about individual cases can be obtained only with the permission of the person at stake or their descendants, or 50 years after the death of the person concerned.

them joined the democratic parties. Some exceptions prove the rule: Adriano Moreira, former minister for the colonies, developed a political career under the new democracy, becoming a deputy and then the secretary general of the CDS for a short time. Among the Caetano ministerial elite there were a few that became involved in politics again, but the number is insignificant. Veiga Simão, who designed the policy to modernize the school system shortly before the fall of the regime, offers one of the rare examples of a reactivated political career.

By 1985, on the eve of Portugal's accession to the EEC, the heritage of the double legacy was practically extinct. There was no party of the right of parliamentary or electoral significance that represented the old elite or acted as a carrier of authoritarian values inherited from Salazarism. The legacy of state socialism and military guardianship had also disappeared after the successive constitutional reforms. In this now fully democratic period, measures to deal with the past have consisted of two strands of action. On the one hand, there have been legislative attempts to solve matters pending in the arena of compensation and access to former police files, as well as judicial processes dealing with pending trials of post-1975 terrorist forces. On the other hand, there have been official and private initiatives that pertain to a wider 'politics of memory'. Initiatives include changing street names, and the public rehabilitation or honouring of opposition figures, as well as the creation of exhibitions or 'memory sites', and the production of new films and documentaries. Attempts to compensate militants who had fought against the dictatorship were made from the 1970s onwards, but some bills were not even approved by the parliament (*Diário de Notícias*, 16 June 1976). It was only in 1997 that Law 20 of 19 June, passed by the socialist government of António Guterres, compensated opposition militants for their years spent in exile or clandestine activity through the payment of social security benefits and pensions.[8]

According to the law, candidates must prove persecution by reference to the PIDE/DGS archives, which is no easy task. At the beginning of 2000, the right-wing Popular Party (PP) proposed that former Portuguese African colonists be compensated for their material losses, arguing that the way in which post-1974

[8] According to Article 1, this encompasses the time lived abroad, when membership of a political group or political activities undertaken in favour of democracy led to victimization or police persecution impeding normal professional activity and social insertion between 28 May 1926 and 25 April 1974.

governments administered the decolonization process makes the Portuguese state responsible for their losses. The Guterres government has thus far refused to accept this logic, arguing that the post-independence African governments involved are responsible.

As in other transitions to democracy, particularly those of Eastern Europe, for some years the fate of the archives of the repressive institutions of the old regime was a topic of heated debate. Given the nature of the fall of the regime, the military took possession of the PIDE/DGS archives and these survived almost intact—including, more importantly, perhaps, the archives of Salazar himself, which were kept in the headquarters of the Presidency of the Council of Ministers after the dictator died in 1970. This archive, which had been rigorously kept by Salazar, gives a unique account of forty years of Portuguese political life. Both the PIDE/DGS and the Salazar archives were deposited in the national archive. Like other archives of the New State, these are governed by a liberal access law. Important public debates about the archives began in the 1990s, when they were opened to the public. One such debate in 1996, provoked by a former socialist minister who had been a victim of the PIDE/DGS, centred around the return to their original owners or their heirs of letters, photographs, and other materials apprehended by the political police. Although some defended this proposed course of action during the parliamentary debates that ensued, the negative reaction of the majority of historians ensured that the archives remained in the national archive.

The most important matter pending in the judicial system is that of the FP-25 and of Otelo Saraiva de Carvalho. This group was active in the early 1980s, and killed six people in terrorist action designed to 'challenge' the abandonment of the revolution and the evolution of the liberal democratic trend of the period. They are therefore more properly related to the second part of the 'dual legacy' rather than with the process of backward-looking accountability for the crimes of the dictatorship. Former President Mário Soares attempted on various occasions to promote an amnesty for all those implicated in these crimes, the last of which was made on the twenty-fifth anniversary of the revolution. The pardon was extended after Saraiva de Carvalho, who had already completed five years of a sixteen-year sentence between 1984 and 1989, and other members of the group signed a document in 1990 promising to abandon the armed struggle. However, the pardon excluded moral and material damages caused by blood crimes, because of the opposition of the CDS and PSD in parliament. Thus, the trial of the fifty members of the FP-25 and their leader for blood crimes, which entered a new phase at the end of 1999, is still working its way through the courts at the time of writing.

In the wider area of the politics of memory, there have been many initiatives, with a renewed surge of interest in the past with the celebrations of the turn of the century. Under the new 'constitutional' period, democratic institutions were immediately associated with the legacy of political opposition to the dictatorship, and successive presidents awarded opposition figures the Order of Freedom and posthumously rehabilitated many victims of the regime. General Humberto Delgado was awarded military honours posthumously, for example. Other attempts to de-legitimate the authoritarian past symbolically were made with the alteration of national holidays and street names, a process initiated immediately after the fall of the dictatorship. Streets and other public places were renamed after famous opposition figures—republicans, communists, and socialists alike—and Salazar's name was removed from monuments and squares. Most notoriously, the name of the dictator was removed from the first bridge built across the Tagus River, which was renamed after the revolution of April 1974. Statues and sculptures in honour of militants of the clandestine opposition and memorializing 25 April were inaugurated, particularly in the municipalities dominated by the left in the Alentejo. The date of the republican revolution of 5 October 1910, which had never been abolished by the dictatorship, became much more salient. The date of the military coup of 28 May 1926 was replaced by a national holiday celebrating the coup of 25 April 1974, which is considered the founding date of the new democracy.

In Portugal the creation of museums of repression and the dictatorship are notably absent. All such projects presented in the first two years of the transition were abandoned because of a lack of interest within civil society and political parties such as the PS or the PCP, or a lack of enthusiasm on the part of the state. A project to turn the Commission on the Black Book on the Fascist Regime into a Museum of the Resistance failed to garner the support of the centre–right government of Cavaco Silva in 1991. Some modest initiatives were undertaken by city councils run by PS–PCP coalitions, such as the Lisbon council in the 1990s. The so-called Museum of the Republic and Resistance is a case in point. It was only towards the end of the 1990s that private foundations were created with the explicit aim of consolidating the memory of resistance to Salazarism and the transition to democracy. Such is the case of the Mário Soares Foundation, established after the former president retired from active political life. Other more modest initiatives were undertaken mainly by the municipal governments when under PS or PCP rule. From the 1990s onwards, however, such initiatives became more consensual. Examples include the creation of libraries named after resistance fighters to the dictatorship, a project for the establishment of a museum honouring Aristides Sousa Mendes, a Portuguese diplomat who gave thousands of Jews visas when he was a consul in Bordeaux without the permission of the dictatorship, and was dismissed without a pension for disobedience to Salazar.

There are also occasional 'irruptions of memory' (Wilde, 1999) that arise from unresolved cases or new revelations by former regime members. In 1998, for example, the chief of the PIDE/DGS brigade that had murdered Humberto Delgado gave an interview to a Portuguese journalist in which he stated that he regularly travelled to Portugal, although he had been condemned *in absentia* to eight years' imprisonment. He was quickly found in Spain, where he had been living under a false name. A Spanish court blocked his return to Portugal, however, and the Portuguese court that had originally tried him admitted that the statute of limitations applied to his case (*Diário de Notícias*, 26 February 1999).

Finally, in the area of cultural production, documentaries and films on the past have proliferated in the last few years. The state television service, the RTP, and the private television channels have produced a documentary series on the Portuguese twentieth century. It has provided viewers with a critical analysis of many of the most important legacies of the past, including the experience of the colonial war, using old footage, much of it seen for the first time since the period in which it was originally filmed. The maturity and depth of the analysis reflects the long road that Portugal has travelled since 1974 in its attempts to deal with the legacy of authoritarianism.

Conclusion

Portugal and Spain are two paradigmatic cases of transition to democracy in the 1970s. The presence in the former and absence in the latter of transitional justice measures is doubtless linked to the nature of the process of rupture in Portugal and of *ruptura-pactada* in the case of Spain. The Lusitanian movement of symbolic and real punitive measures for crimes of the authoritarian past was an integral part of the crisis of the state in Portugal, and was characterized by the emergence of a dual legitimacy. Although short-lived and diffuse, the punitive process marked a durable break in the political culture of the country's social and political elite.

It was the nature of the transition process, which opened a window of opportunity for the process, that gave the Portuguese social elite the biggest 'scare' that it suffered in the twentieth century. Popular participation in the purge process, unshackled by the framework of due process and driven forward by an active radical left, placed retroactive justice beyond the rule of law. Concomitantly, transitional justice measures were reversed once the moderate elite favouring liberal democracy gained the upper hand.

This dynamic contrasts dramatically with the Latin American cases. In these cases transitional justice has been seen by most observers as a necessary or vital component of a process of democratization; in the Portugal of the 1970s, however, the reverse was true. Democratic consolidation was synonymous with the reversal of punitive measures, rather than with their deepening or extension.

The Portuguese case also serves to highlight the lessons learnt in Eastern Europe. When transitional justice becomes part of the dynamic of a political battle between competing elites, in this case between two different social and political projects, and when the capacity of response of the old dictatorial elite is almost absent, the likelihood that new injustices are perpetrated increases. In such cases, the punishing of past crimes when associated with revolutionary demands for social justice may not be conducive to democratization or to the affirmation of basic democratic values or legality.

The importance of international forces also becomes apparent when examining this case. As with Eastern Europe, the desire and perceived need to enter the 'European family' favoured both the containment of revolutionary forces and the moderate, democratic national project. Illegal purges in this context were inadvisable. At the same time, the Portuguese settling of accounts was not submitted to the same international scrutiny by human rights organizations as in Eastern Europe, where the International Labour Organisation (ILO) and European institutions have criticized the violation of due process involved in the lustration process. Portugal was not shackled by the new human rights ethos found today: rather, it was constrained by a Cold War context, membership of NATO, and the hope of belonging to the European Community.

Paradoxically, while a policy of 'reconciliation' in the wake of a badly administered punitive process may be affirmative of a new democratic legality, it may also contribute to a delayed 'working through' of the past. The Portuguese case would seem to indicate this. The trauma of the revolutionary years 'wiped out' that of the authoritarian period. The degree of polarization generated by these processes meant that it was many years before Portuguese society was able to engage in a more mature 'politics of memory' about the authoritarian dual legacy of right and left.

In Portugal as elsewhere, the dilution of the weight of the authoritarian past has occurred simultaneously with the process of democratic consolidation. Economic growth has transformed the social fabric, diluting or even eliminating the traditional society once governed by Salazar. The affirmation of democracy and the gradual modernization of the state, aided and abetted by European integration, have diluted old points of reference and generated new cleavages. While there are attitudinal vestiges of the past among the political elite and civil society, in contrast with more recent transition processes such as that in Chile, loyalties and debates are no longer dominantly framed by the dichotomies or cleavages generated by the dictatorship or the revolutionary period. The demand for and polarization generated by the punishment of the old elite expired early on in the transition process, becoming a remembered part of the legacy of the past.

3

Justice, Politics, and Memory in the Spanish Transition

Paloma Aguilar

Introduction

When a profound political transformation takes place, successor regimes have to decide what to do with institutions and individuals linked to the previous regime. New political elites 'have had to decide whether leaders of, collaborators with or agents of the former regime should be brought to court or otherwise penalised, and whether and how the victims of the regimes should be rehabilitated and compensated' (Elster, 1998: 7). In Spain, the main civilian and military institutions inherited from the Franco dictatorship were not purged after his death. There were no 'truth commissions' or trials to judge those responsible for deaths, torture, and illegal detentions, which surprised some lucid political analysts (Przeworski, 1988: 101). In light of this, it is important to look into the limits of the 'politics of consensus', the groups excluded from 'national reconciliation', and the repercussions of the absence of such political justice on the consolidation and institutionalization of democracy.[1] The first part of this chapter will outline the particular features of the Spanish case, taking into account the impact of collective memories of the Civil War (1936–9) and the subsequent

I would like to thank Alexandra Barahona de Brito (who translated this chapter from the Spanish), Carmen González, Juan J. Linz, and Jesús Cuéllar for their comments and help.

[1] The Communist Party in exile began to announce a policy of 'national reconciliation' from the second half of the 1950s onwards. It thereby explicitly renounced an armed struggle to topple the regime.

aversion to risk that this traumatic memory produced within Spanish society. The second section considers whether there were any actors that actually called for measures of transitional justice. An analysis of the obstacles that emerged to such policies is also undertaken. Any regime change entails the replacement of previous legal structures with new, in this case democratic, ones. None the less, it is fundamental to understand which of the old structures are reformed and which survive over time and come into conflict with the new democratic legality. The third section, then, assesses the perverse legacies of authoritarian rule inherited by new democracies. The fourth section examines various policies approved to rehabilitate victims and also which measures could not be passed and why. Finally, the concluding section deals with the implications of the whole process for the functioning of Spanish democracy.

Fear, Memory, and Risk Aversion

Spaniards have observed with a mixture of pride and surprise how their transition has become the paradigm of a peaceful transition from an authoritarian to a democratic regime.[2] Other countries in transition have tried to emulate the 'Spanish model'. Members of the political elite of the transition have been invited to international debates, in the hope that their personal experiences may limit the uncertainty usually prevailing during periods of political change. It is understandable why assessments of the Spanish transition have not been more critical. The expectations that arose after three years of civil war and almost forty years of dictatorship were not conducive to an especially optimistic outlook.[3]

[2] The exemplary nature of the transition has been questioned in writings by Vidal-Beneyto (1981), Pons Prades (1987), Morán (1991), Martínez Inglés (1994), and Jaúregui and Menéndez (1995). Almost all these authors refer to the 'elimination', 'abolition', or 'eradication' of the collective memory of Spaniards, question a series of concessions made by the democratic opposition, and evaluate critically the regime that emerged as a result. Lately, some academic work has questioned the process of political change; see e.g. Colomer (1990, 1998), Jaime-Jiménez and Reinares (1998), and Buck (1998).

[3] In this chapter it is argued that learning from past experiences, especially failed ones that are traumatic and tend to provoke more reflection that successful ones, is a key element in the structuring of preferences of political and social actors (Jervis, 1976).

After the death of Franco, the memory of the repeated collapse of social peace,[4] coupled with an uncertainty regarding social attitudes towards the old regime, led some observers to predict the worst. Raymond Carr, a prestigious British expert on Spain, confessed in 1997 that he had feared 'the worst', given the climate of mobilization during the transition, the number of confrontations between demonstrators and the police, and the acts of terrorism committed by both left and right.[5] Spanish observers like Juan Benet also had a pessimistic view of the ability of Spanish society to shift peacefully towards democracy after Francisco Franco died in November 1975 (Benet, 1976: 11). The most pessimistic observers were not representative of the feelings of the majority of people at the time; none the less, levels of uncertainty and fear were very high. Fear was present throughout the transition largely because of a traumatic memory of the Civil War given renewed impetus by fears of a military or right-wing reaction against emerging democratic forces. Analysing a poll of 1979, Linz commented that half of the Basque population perceived significant levels of fear around them at the time (Linz, 1986: 16–17). Other polls of 1975–7 show that peace, order, and stability were top priorities for Spaniards (Aguilar, 1996a: 348–54). Even when 'justice', 'democracy', and 'freedom' got better scores, 'peace' and 'order' were still very positively valued, and this is especially true if we compare Spain with other European countries (Eurobarometer Opinion Polls).

It is fear of conflict that allows one to understand the attitude of the main actors involved in the transition process and the institutional framework established during the period.[6] Many decisions

[4] The four civil wars that took place over the last two centuries, the last one in 1936–9, levels of political and social violence during the Second Republic (1931–6), and, finally, the systematic repression of democratic opposition under Franco (1939–75).

[5] According to Carr, the British television constantly showed images of violent demonstrations in the Basque country throughout the period of the transition, and of brutal police repression that reminded one of the conflict of 1936. These scenes did not, however, reveal the moderation of the majority of society, because 'Spaniards were determined to avoid another civil war' (*El País*, 31 March 1977: 23).

[6] The revolutionary experience in Portugal was another factor contributing to the moderation of Spanish social and political actors. It should also be remembered that the transitions of the 1970s did not take place in an international context as favourable to truth telling and justice as those of the 1980s and 1990s in particular, by which time international law and human rights discourse and practice had become more firmly entrenched in both the national and international spheres.

'adopted during the transitions period were taken with a strong risk aversion (limits on street mobilisation, *the absence of acts of revenge*, the preference for formulas favouring institutional stability)' (Colomer, 1998: 174–5; my italics.)

'Risk aversion' is a fundamental variable studied in game theory (Morrow, 1994: 36; Levy, 1992). As one author notes, when key participants in a negotiation have 'a similar attitude towards risk, the final result will be symmetrical. Nonetheless, if they have different attitudes towards risk, the result will be asymmetrical. More specifically, the more a player is averse to risk, the less he will obtain from a negotiation. The less inclined he is to risk the possibility of disagreement, the more concessions he will make' (Sánchez-Cuenca, 1995: 251). These theories can be applied to the Spanish case, given that the transition was negotiated and the protagonists were Francoist reformists and moderate opposition forces.[7] Sectors of the extreme right and left of the 1970s would have preferred some form of violent confrontation to prevent the establishment of a liberal democracy. In fact, both sides engaged in terrorist acts. The groups least sensitive to the threat of civil conflict, however, were small minorities and essentially were absent from the negotiating process.

If, according to Sánchez-Cuenca, the resources available to each actor determine levels of risk aversion, then in Spain the regime reformists who initiated the process from within the regime had the most power. They forced the moderate opposition to follow their lead on many occasions under threat of being made marginal to the process of political change. This explains the decision of the opposition to make concessions precisely in the areas that most threatened the armed forces. Regime reformists were closest to this group, which had the greatest capacity to subvert the transition.[8] Thus,

> the initial advantage of former Francoists and the final pact with the anti-Franco forces avoided a *calling to account and acts of revenge* against the old authoritarians. The policy of 'national reconciliation' entailed an amnesty for anti-Franco forces and amnesia for pro-Francoists or, in other words, a renunciation of submitting political acts of the past to judicial review (Colomer, 1998: 177; my italics)

[7] From a different point of view, see the study of the impact of fear on politics by Corradi *et al.* (1992).

[8] Most researchers include Spain as an example of Huntington's 'transformation' type of transition (Huntington, 1991: 114) as reformist elites from the Franco regime led the first reforms. For reforms see Colomer (1996).

A curtain was drawn over the past in the name of 'national reconciliation', and it was accepted that acts of institutional violence committed under the dictatorship should go unpunished. In exchange, regime reformists accepted the liberation of all political prisoners, the legalization of the Spanish Communist Party (PCE), and truly free elections in June 1977.[9]

Regardless of varying power resources, actors on both sides were risk-averse. There was widespread fear of a coup that might degenerate into a civil war as in July 1936.[10] This facilitated the negotiation process: 'it did not take long before the threat of an involution encouraged Francoist reformists and opposition groups to co-operate more closely' (Rodríguez, 1997: 492). In such circumstances it is also likely that solutions may be accepted that are not entirely satisfactory to any of the parties involved to avoid the least desirable outcome—in this case, a civil war. Indeed, players may limit their demands beyond what is necessary. In Spain it was only with the passage of time that it has been possible to verify the electoral weakness of the extreme right in the elections of 1977, 1979, 1982, and thereafter, as well as the fragmentation of the armed forces (Agüero, 1995: 179 ff., 191–3, 197). At the time, however, this weakness was not clear. After a second electoral defeat in 1979, the extreme right launched a so-called 'tension strategy' which aimed to destabilize the transition, and consequently political violence became sufficiently commonplace to make the threat of regression credible.[11] The threat of confrontation has to be sufficiently credible for an aversion to conflict to become so widespread that it conditions actors' preferences. In 1975 the memory of the Civil War

[9] For some, this kind of negotiated transition 'contributed to legitimate the new regime in the eyes of many Francoists, by initiating political change while respecting the formal procedures established by the Franco regime itself, thus permitting important Francoist groups to play an active role in the reform process, instead of remaining on the margins as resentful enemies of change or victims of a *political purge*' (Gunther *et al.*, 1986: 43; my italics).

[10] There were various potential risks. The fear of a coup and ensuing widespread conflict affected both sides equally, while the fear of being excluded from negotiations affected those with least resources—the democratic opposition. Regime reformists, however, were very interested in attracting the latter group in order to give democratic legitimacy to their initiatives.

[11] Authors have emphasized ETA terrorism more than terrorist acts by the extreme right. None the less, attacks by the right led to the death of 39 people between 1976 and 1981 (Soto, 1996: 366). Various researchers have documented the infiltration in the 1970s of various international extreme right-wing groups in Spain, as well as the impunity with which they operated during the transition because of police and intelligence services complicity and even involvement (Muñoz, 1982; Rodríguez, 1997; Casals, 1998: esp. 205).

was still alive, although it was a transmitted memory rather than a lived one for most people. However, the violence of the 1970s activated that memory and evoked older conflicts. Memories of the only democratic period, the Second Republic, and its tragic culmination in the Civil War were also resuscitated. Thus, although the Spanish transition is remembered as the peaceful transition *par excellence*,[12] more than 460 violent deaths for political purposes were registered between 1975 and 1980 and about 400 people died in right and left-wing terrorist acts (Reinares, 1990: 390). Of the sixty-three people who died in street demonstrations in the same period, over half were Basques (Adell, 1997). Thus, 'Elite pacts were certainly key to the democratisation of Spain, but these pacts were forged in a situation in which extremism and moderation existed simultaneously. . . . 1976 was also a year of widespread violence and unceasing mobilisation. Scholars have placed so much emphasis on the comparatively peaceful nature of Spain's transition that it is easy to forget its violent elements' (Bermeo, 1997: 309).

The absence of measures of political justice and even of public debate about such measures cannot be explained without taking into account social and political perceptions strongly affected by the traumatic memory of a fratricidal conflict, and an obsessive desire to avoid its repetition. The resulting will to forget helps to explain the choice of a model of reformist political change. Logically, those who claimed to feel less fear—the Basque Nationalists—were also the least inclined to forget (Linz, 1986: 17). They also attached least importance to 'order' and 'peace' in the polls and were more critical of the transition model, precisely because their hopes for a radical break with the past were most intense and their rejection of the dictatorship greatest.[13]

[12] Both critics and supporters of the transition refer to its exemplary characteristics. Colomer, for instance, notes the 'near absence of violence' (1998: 180). For similar views from less critical observers, see Huntington (1991: 194–5); and Gunther *et al.* (1986: 14). Although correct, this view may be a retrospective fallacy in so far as the final success of the process should not lead one to forget the violence it also implied. It is my view that it was possible to activate this memory only because of the various episodes of violence experienced at the time.

[13] 'According to the 1975 FOESSA Report "although nationally 80 per cent agreed with the comment, 'In Spain, the most important thing is to maintain order and peace', in the Basque Country the figure was only 67 per cent." (Aguilar, 1998b: 17–18). In 1985 more than 45 per cent of Spaniards felt that Francoism had been partly positive, while only 20 per cent of Basques agreed with this and more than 55 per cent felt that Francoism had been only negative for Spain. Also in 1985, only 17 per cent of Spaniards stated that they had wanted rapid and radical change after the death of Franco, while 27.5 per cent of Basques said they preferred such a change (Aguilar, 1999d).

The initial weakness of the democratic opposition encouraged it to call for a 'pacted reform' rather than a radical break with the outgoing regime. This strategic shift was well calculated, as 'it is likely that a more abrupt change of regime accompanied by higher levels of disorder and violence would have polarised public opinion' (Gunther *et al.*, 1986: 442). However, the abandonment of the strategy of rupture was also accompanied by the abandonment of certain institutional reforms (at least until the mid-1980s), which, if approved, could have produced a better functioning political system. At the time, however, Spanish society hoped that the Civil War should 'never again' be repeated, and its objective was 'national reconciliation'. All efforts therefore focused on creating an institutional framework that garnered a consensus and thus prevented a repetition of past errors. To this end, political leaders embarked upon a prolonged and tense constituent process. The resulting constitutional text was characterized by its emphasis on governmental stability. It is also important to remember the feeling of collective guilt for the atrocities of the war. This political learning process helps to explain the absence of transitional justice and the passage of a reciprocal amnesty.[14] None of the ideological successors of the parts engaged in that conflict was particularly interested in carefully revising the past.[15]

In retrospect, it seems obvious that there was a break with the past, as Spanish democracy is no doubt consolidated and its legitimacy comparable to that of other European democracies (Montero *et al.*, 1998: 16). Furthermore, the transition itself involved a break with traditional procedures when a political change was at stake. Indeed, this democracy is the only regime in Spain of this century that has not called prior regime leaders to account.[16] The

[14] At the first opposition meeting of groups at home, and in exile held in Munich in 1962, nobody called for measures of political justice.

[15] The Basque Nationalists did not feel the same sense of collective guilt, as their ulterior construction of historical memory turned them into the victims of a war that had nothing to do with them (Aguilar, 1998c).

[16] The Second Republic called politicians of the Primo de Rivera dictatorship to account, as Franco did with the Republicans, and the Primo de Rivera authorities called the regime of the Restoration to account. One of the first measures adopted by Republican authorities was an amnesty for all political prisoners, apart from (unlike the 1977, amnesty) the leaders of the previous dictatorship. They set up a special commission to establish political responsibilities in order subsequently to try crimes related mostly to abuse of power. The commission condemned the King for high treason and presented a report in June 1932, listing the accused and the sentences, which was harshly criticized even by some Republicans (Payne, 1993: 40–42, 69–70, 73 ff.).

aim was to put an end to the historical failure to live harmoniously with the enemy, which had been responsible for two centuries of military *pronunciamientos*, civil wars, dictatorships, and political instability. The transition was so positively evaluated perhaps precisely because of this. Expectations were lower than in most other comparable cases, as Spain had been unable to combine liberty with social harmony until then. This is largely why the process of change became a model peaceful transition, despite the moments of deep tension experienced up until the first democratic elections were held in June 1997 and beyond.

The Scope for Retroactive Justice

Many factors explain why some countries adopt measures of political justice and others do not. The scope for trials, purges, and investigating commissions vary significantly from case to case, not only because of the nature of the transition,[17] but also as a result of other factors. Among these are preceding levels of violence, the nature of the violence and its proximity in time to the transition, the residual strength of authoritarian institutions, the type of activities previously undertaken by the democratic opposition, and the possibility of identifying those responsible for repression.[18] This does not justify a deterministic vision of processes of political change, however. While 'initial structures, including the political structure of the previous authoritarian regime, impose certain limits on the number and availability of alternatives to choose from', 'these structures permit different decisions and can produce different results depending on the initiatives, strategies and luck of the various political actors' (Colomer, 1998: 12).

It is necessary to take into account not only institutional conditioning factors inherited from the outgoing regime, but also the overwhelming desire of Spanish society to see a peaceful and gradual change and even to pretend that it had forgotten the past rather than call anyone to account. Electoral behaviour and opinion polls

[17] According to Huntington, in most of the cases he assesses 'justice was a function of political power. Officials of strong authoritarian regimes that voluntarily ended themselves were not prosecuted; officials of weak authoritarian regimes that collapsed were punished, if they were promptly prosecuted by the new democratic government' (Huntington, 1991: 228).

[18] An added problem is the destruction of most of the empirical evidence, secretly carried out after Franco's death (*El País*, 9 April 1978).

confirm this.[19] As far as the political parties are concerned, the two main coalitions parties of the opposition—the Democratic Junta, led by the PCE, and the Platform for Democratic Convergence, led by the Spanish Socialist Workers Party (PSOE) before its unification in March 1976 as the Democratic Co-ordination—hardly mentioned political justice.[20] The Democratic Junta platform of June 1974 called for 'the restitution of the property' of the workers' movement and 'absolute amnesty', with its main objective to 'ensure a peaceful transition'. A year later the manifesto of the Platform for Democratic Convergence proposed 'the immediate liberation of political prisoners and unionists, and the return of exiles'. A joint communiqué of the Democratic Co-ordinator called for a 'democratic rupture' of a 'peaceful nature' and insisted on the need for amnesty (Chao, 1976: 287–8, 311, 315). All of them called for the constitution of a provisional government and a referendum to choose between a monarchic or republican form of government.

An examination of actual party texts before 1977 gives one a more accurate view of positions regarding retroactive justice. In 1974 the PSOE called for the 'dissolution of all repressive institutions', for the 'devolution of rights to all persons deprived of [them] for political or trade union activities', and for the 'restitution of property expropriated from political and trade union organisations'. In 1975 Iberian Socialist Convergence (CSI), later renamed the Federation of Socialist Parties (FPS), demanded the 'suppression of all laws and institutions inherited from the Franco regime' (Sánchez Navarro, 1998: 159, 161). There was a widespread call to 'dismantle the authoritarian regime', but this meant the introduction of democratic forms and not the expulsion or trial of those guilty of repression. Aside from an amnesty, the suppression of special jurisdictions and the restitution of expropriated trade union and political party property were the other key demands most often repeated by the moderate opposition (F. González and Guerra, 1977: 20–1, 36, 76, 123–4; Carrillo and Sánchez-Montero, 1977: 47–8, 70, 104; Felipe González in Ortzi, 1979: i. 50–1). Private property expropriated with the Law of Political Responsibilities of 1939 was not

[19] On the absence of political debate about retroactive justice and a justification for this, see *El País* (15 December 1976: 8).

[20] This is also true for the authors of *The Urgent Reforms* (Figuero *et al.*, 1976).

immediately dealt with,[21] and measures of retroactive justice were never clearly demanded.[22]

In contrast with the moderate opposition, the extreme left and the radical Basque nationalists refused to join unified opposition platforms and violently rejected the reformist strategy of the majority, sustaining demands abandoned by the other political forces (Ortzi, 1979: ii. 34; Esteve, 1977: 175, 212). The radical Basques called for a generic '*calling to account*' and the 'dissolution of repressive bodies.'[23] On the extreme left, the Party of Work of Spain (PTE) called for 'the nationalisation of the wealth of groups that openly oppose the constituent process', or what it called 'punitive expropriations' (Cruzado, 1977: 263–5). The Revolutionary Communist League (LCR) called for a 'dismantling of the regime and all its institutions and repressive bodies' (Cruzado, 1977: 289; Laiz, 1995: 242–3). The latter returned to these demands with special force after the attempted coup of 1981. The Marxist–Leninist Communist Party of Spain (PCE m-l), one of the most extreme, also demanded the 'formation of a Popular Army and the destruction of the current one' and the 'dissolution and repression of the parties of the oligarchy' (Cruzado, 1977: 308).

It is important to stress that these latter parties not only represented a very small minority, but also defended a revolutionary political project incompatible with the liberal democracy. However, not even they contemplated trials or truth commissions in their programmes. Once the process of transition was over, they questioned the new regime, accusing it of continuity with the dictatorship, and attacking its democratic credentials. In the view of the Basque terrorists, Basque Country and Freedom (ETA), in 1977, 'the government is not democratic, but rather a continuation, reform or mere change of image of the dictatorship' (Laiz, 1995:

[21] This law permitted the expropriation of property of all suspected Republican collaborators. It was only in December 1975 that the administrative sanctions provided for by the law were abolished (Baena and García Madaria, 1982: 315). The exception to the rule is the Basque country, which in October 1984 passed a law on the Reversion of Goods and Rights Expropriated (Law of 30 October 1983, *Boletín Oficial del País Vasco*: 188).

[22] Before the 1977 elections the PCE 'spoke not of dissolution' but of a 'greater reorganization'. The PSOE argued for the 'sanctioning the really repressive elements' (Esteve, 1977: 175, 212).

[23] Muñoz Alonso (1982: 69; my italics). The level of public rejection of police action in the final years of the regime was such that it led to the 'Get them out' ('*Que se vayan*') campaign (Rivera, 1998: 82).

256). In a 1978 'Letter to the Basque People' it advocated 'the expulsion from the Basque Country' of all police forces.[24] Unity of the People (HB), the political arm of ETA which was created in April 1978, rejected the transition to democracy as a form of 'pure continuity with Francoism'.[25]

The Amnesty Law of October 1977, one of the first political measures approved by the new democratic government with the support of a parliamentary majority, achieved two things (Aguilar, 1997b). First, most political prisoners were released, including persons accused of blood crimes. Second, a 'full stop' was approved to prevent the trial of members of the outgoing regime.[26] Most Spaniards are not aware that the Amnesty Law contained two articles that prevented the prosecution of torturers and all those who committed abuses during the dictatorship. They amnestied 'crimes and misdemeanours that the authorities or security officers and agents may have committed as a result or on the occasion of the investigation and prosecution of acts contemplated by this law', as well as 'crimes committed by security officials and agents that violate the rights of persons'. This failed to have a political impact because it was hardly mentioned in parliamentary debates before the approval of the law. Both Congress and the Senate focused almost exclusively on forgetting and pardoning. The most important newspapers of the period also failed to allude to these articles. It was the view of many that 'democratic Spain must from now on look to the future, forget the events and responsibilities of the Civil War and distance itself from forty years of dictatorship . . . A people cannot and must not lack historical memory: but the latter must serve to encourage projects for peaceful future coexistence rather than promote rancour about the past' (*El País*, 15 October 1977: 6). Apart from the right and radical Basque nationalists, which abstained from voting on the law, for all other forces it meant

[24] Ortzi (1979: ii. 10) For the argument used to call for the expulsion of the security forces from the Basque Country see Castells *et al.* (1978: 168). For ETA's totally negative view of the transition, see Mata López (1993: 200–202).

[25] Laiz (1995: 275) For the continuation of torture and continuity of personell, see Forest (1978: 36–37, 44). For the particular case of the feared Political and Social Brigade (BPS), see Jaúregui and Menéndez (1995: 165). The BPS was dissolved in 1977, but most of its members were integrated into other security institutions, especially the state security services (CESID), some of whose members were involved in the 1981 coup attempt and the GAL case.

[26] For a very critical view of this exchange of incorporation and impunity, see Morán (1991: 186–8 and 232). On the role of the UCD and the PSOE in this exchange, see Jáuregui and Menéndez (1995: 29–30).

'turning the page'. It was welcomed even by moderate Basque Nationalists, which praised it for promoting 'forgetting'.[27]

During parliamentary debates, almost all groups praised the law precisely because it was an instrument of 'national reconciliation', intended to 'close the past', 'forget', and start a new phase. Even the Communists boasted of wanting to forget the past and 'bury the dead' and called for an amnesty that excluded no one. This was a product of the perception of the dangers of not amnestying the Francoists. As a Communist parliamentarian commented, 'a year ago it seemed impossible, almost a miracle, to get out of the dictatorship without a serious trauma'. The Socialists also insisted on the need to 'bury and overcome 40 years of dictatorship' and stated that the law declared the Civil War finally over. Xavier Arzalluz, a leader of the Basque Nationalist Party (PNV), insisted repeatedly that it was necessary to forget and that 'the amnesty was from everybody to everybody, a forgetting from everybody for everybody' as 'both sides [had] committed blood crimes'. Francisco Letamendía, a radical Basque militant radical who abstained from voting, was the only one to call for a 'measure to complement the amnesty' to replace 'the security forces inherited from the dictatorship by others dependent upon the autonomous provinces', as a 'psychosis of occupation' persisted in the Basque Country (Ortzi, 1979: i. 10, 49). Finally, the representative of the government party, the Centre Democratic Union (UCD), referred to the 'indispensable, necessary, indeed deeply necessary reconciliation' and the need to overcome the past.[28] Clearly, debates about the amnesty law were shaped by the memory of the Civil War.

The Amnesty Law focused on rehabilitating those serving prison sentences for fighting against an authoritarian regime established after a military victory. It allowed civil servants to recover their jobs and pensions, but did not indemnify either military officers or civil servants for salaries lost after being fired from their jobs. The two articles granting impunity to the Francoists were publicly discussed only much later. Following the Anti-Terrorist Liberation Group (GAL) scandal in the 1990s,[29] the Secretary of Relations of

[27] There were 296 votes in favour, 2 against, and 18 abstentions.

[28] *Diario de Sesiones del Congreso, Sesión Plenaria* (DSC) 24, 14/10/77: 954–974. In the end, the law was approved by 93.3 per cent of the votes, with 5.6 per cent abstaining and 0.6 per cent in opposition.

[29] The GAL is a terrorist group created in the mid-1980s with the support of people in the Ministry of the Interior to exterminate members of ETA. Some of its members were on the extreme right and were linked to certain people of the security services and the police. Some authors consider the group to be an inheritor

the PSOE stated that 'the only full stop law that exists is the one that we, the democrats, passed in October 1977 for the Francoists. That year we decided not to call anyone to account for the 40 years of dictatorial rule so as to achieve reconciliation for once and for all' (*El País*, 6 August 1995: 14). The fact that the law was remembered as a result of the GAL scandal is no accident. Many have indicated that this anti-terrorist group could never have been organized if a purge of the armed forces and the police inherited from Franco had taken place. This is difficult to prove, however. Many other European countries have engaged in 'dirty war' practices without the support of institutions and personnel of former dictatorships.

The human rights violations that took place during the second half of the Franco regime were not comparable to the violence of the 1940s but were nevertheless frequent towards the end of the dictatorship, especially in the Basque Country.[30] There were various cases of torture and illegal detention under the cover of a repressive legislation that, according to the Democratic Justice Association (AJD), was itself violated frequently. This association, which was secretly created in 1971 by a sector of the judiciary opposed to the legal arbitrariness of the Franco regime, denounced government violations of the laws approved by its own regime (Sinova, 1984: ii. 570). It never became a pressure group favouring accountability during the transition. In a document of January 1977, it proposed certain reforms to the government, such as the suppression of the death penalty and of discrimination of all kinds, and the penalization of torture. It also called for the reform of the judiciary and the concomitant elimination of all special jurisdictions, and for the derogation of the anti-terrorist decree law and other laws repressing democratic freedoms. Last but not least, the AJD called for the 'immediate civil court jurisdiction over the police forces' and the 'proclamation of a total amnesty for politically motivated crimes and for *all kinds of government infractions of a similar nature*' (Justicia Democrática, 1978: 310–11; my italics) The Association did not call for retroactive justice: rather, it called for a 'full stop' law and an amnesty for political prisoners.

of other right-wing organizations operating during the transition, e.g. the Basque Spanish Battalion (BVE) and ETA Anti-Terrorism (ATE). Security service connivance with such groups is amply documented; see e.g. Rodríguez (1997: 451).

[30] According to Rivera, of the 36 persons killed by the police in Spain in 1974–5, almost two out of three were Basques (Rivera, 1998: 82). For the much more violent nature of the transition in the Basque Country see Gunther *et al.* (1986: 443).

Despite the undeniably wide-ranging amnesty (it even covered trade union issues such as the obligation to restore jobs to those fired for political reasons), there are two important groups that were excluded from its benefits. This reveals the capacity of the military to defend its corporate interests even against the will of the majority of the political class. The officers that had formed a clandestine group in favour of democracy, the Democratic Military Union (UMD),[31] and former Republican Army combatants, who were defeated in the Civil War and constantly discriminated against by the Franco regime, were not allowed to reintegrate with the armed forces.[32] Pressures from the military were accepted to avoid alienating the army from the political process, particularly as ETA terrorism had peaked since the death of Franco. After the amnesty law was passed, ETA carried out deadly terrorist attacks, so that the prisons were again filled with its members. Fear of a negative military reaction, whose officers were top targets of the terrorists, was apparent throughout the whole process.[33] Indeed, it was necessary to disarm some attempted coups, and high-level army officers did not hesitate to show discontent or even to resign when faced with political measures that they found disagreeable, such as the legalization of the PCE.

Institutional Continuities, or the Legacies of Dictatorship[34]

The possibility of introducing radical reforms during the transition was notably reduced after the referendum on the Law of Political Reform of December 1976 and the signature by the government and the main opposition parties of the Moncloa Pacts in October 1977. The former established a reformist path for political change, while the latter consecrated key rights and provided for reforms of the Penal and Military Justice Codes. The section on the reorganization of the forces of law and order did not mention the elimination,

[31] On the UMD military see e.g. Morales and Celada (1981: 8 ff.).

[32] For the role of the military in preventing an amnesty for the UMD military and former members of the Republican Army, see Busquets, cited in Sinova (1984: ii. 514–15), and Morales and Celada (1981: 11).

[33] According to some authors, the PSOE did not block military promotions of some of the most notorious Francoists in order to avoid military radicalization (Jaúregui and Menéndez, 1995: 196).

[34] The pioneer study on the legacies of Francoism is Malefakis (1982).

purge, or total transformation of security forces.[35] In contrast with various Latin American countries, in Spain the military 'did not feel the need to seek protection *vis-à-vis* possible attempts to punish them for past crimes. A lot of time had gone by since the atrocities of the Civil War and human rights had ceased to be a conflictive issue. Memories of high numbers of victims on both sides of the Civil War acted as an incentive for moderation' (Agüero, 1995: 117–18). There was also fear of possible army reactions.[36] In the absence of social demands for such measures, the already timid opposition proposals were dropped immediately from electoral platforms. As national reconciliation was a priority, nobody contemplated retroactive justice measures. However, fear also prevented actors from proposing the institutional reforms necessary for a better functioning of the democratic system.

One of the most delicate issues in the first years of the transition was not only what to do about the armed institutions inherited from the dictatorship, but also how to prevent them from conditioning the transition process itself. They constituted the most serious challenge to political elites at the time.[37] Persuading the armed forces[38] to accept the democratic process was difficult,

[35] The right-wing Popular Alliance did not participate in the political pacts, but only in the economic ones, which received more public attention. This reflects the climate of the period, which resisted publicizing the measures that dismantled the Franco regime. One of the reforms that had not been undertaken in February 1978 was that pertaining to the Military Code of Justice (*El País*, 25 October 1997: 23): that was undertaken only in September 1980 (Organic Law 9/1980; *Boletín Oficial del Estado* (BOE) 9/1980).

[36] Certainly, memory of the fratricidal conflict helped to foment a spirit of understanding and negotiation. The distance in time of postwar repression served to dissolve certain tensions, given that by the time of Franco's death 70 per cent of the Spanish population had had no direct experience of the Civil War. The greatest number of deaths and prison population was found in Spain from the beginning of the Civil War, in 1936, until 1949. According to the most recent study, there were 120,000 civilian deaths during the war, that is, those killed behind the front lines. To these one must add all those who died in the front, as well as those killed in the postwar period. The final figure is approximately 600,000 victims (Juliá, 1999).

[37] Some authors have focused on the main obstacles facing the democratic forces (Jaime-Jiménez and Reinares, 1998: 172 ff.; Morán, 1991). Although the army played a key role in anti-democratic pressures, it too was weak owing to internal divisions and the absence of an alternative political project (Agüero, 1995: 179 ff.).

[38] On the overwhelming Francoist loyalty of the high command and top officers of the army and intelligence services, see Martínez Inglés (1994: 33–4). For opposition to reform, see Delgado (1996: 16). On how notorious cases of torture by the Guardia Civil and armed police finally galvanized the government into action with reform, see Delgado (1996: 17). On the dissonance between the new democratic society and these forces and their effect on the ETA, see Delgado (1996: 17, 21).

largely because the high command was faithful to the memory of Franco and his political legacy. Indeed, many had fought in the Civil War and their subsequent ideological development, like that of the dictator himself, had been practically non-existent. The coronation of King Juan Carlos I and the continuation in power of the Francoist political elite had calmed the military immediately after the death of Franco. Soon, however, the contradiction between armed institutions inherited almost intact from the Franco period and the new democratic situation became apparent. The police often acted with unnecessary force to repress acts that during the Franco regime had been considered threats to public order. Demonstrations that are unproblematic today frequently ended in serious and sometimes deadly conflicts between the police and demonstrators.[39]

Their loyalty to Franco explains the profound irritation that the armed forces felt regarding three elements that characterized the transition. First, the mobilizations and strikes of the early years annoyed them because the maintenance of public order had been one of the goals most tenaciously pursued by the dictatorship (López Garrido, 1987: 8). Second, they resented calls for territorial autonomy by the nationalist and left-wing parties, as one of the other great Francoist obsessions had been maintaining the unity of Spain at all costs and curtailing any decentralizing political or administrative tendencies.[40] Third, they abhorred terrorist attacks, and particularly those led by ETA, as members of the military were those who suffered the brunt of these attacks.[41] The most recent data from the Ministry of Defence indicates that between 1968 and 1998 almost 60 per cent of ETA victims were members of the police or the army.[42] (The *Guardia Civil* accounted for 25.2 per cent, the National Police for 18.3 per cent, the army for 12.1 per cent, the local police for 2.8 per cent, and Basque Autonomous Police (Ertzaintza) for 1 per cent.)[43]

[39] Jaime-Jiménez and Reinares (1995) have described the bewilderment of the police in the face of the great transformation of the notion of 'public order' under democracy, as well as in the absence of basic institutional reforms.

[40] The latter called for self-determination in the months following the death of Franco.

[41] Conservative forces used continued terrorism to ensure the passage of more repressive legislation. On the negative effect of terrorism on police and military reform, see López Garrido (1987: 16).

[42] Consult site www.mir.es/oris/infoeta/esp. This percentage is notably higher only if one takes into account victims up to 1980.

[43] For figures see also Shabad and Llera (1995: 442). Agüero (1995: 243) also compares victims and whether they are civilian or military.

Apart from the successive attempts to de-politicize the forces (which were barred from political activity of any kind), measures were passed in 1977–1982 to change military symbols and codes of ethics. The reforms carried out under the first Socialist government (1982–1986) were fourfold: symbolic transformations and reforms of (1) military morals and (2) justice, (3) personnel related policies, and (4) other structural measures (Torre, 1996: 293–5, 297–9). Four laws were passed, regarding the Spanish coat of arms, the swearing of allegiance to the flag, ordinances, and the military justice code. The reforms promoted the subordination of the military courts to the civil judiciary, which allowed appeals against sentences by the military tribunals in the Supreme Court. In 1978 the armed police were 'demilitarized', removing the army from police functions it had exercised.

It was however only after the consolidation of democracy, or the failed coup of 1981 and the victory of the PSOE in 1982, that a series of crucial measures were approved.[44] The coup attempt alerted the political class to the anti-democratic tendencies of a good part of the command structure, as well as to the dangers implicit in reforms undertaken by a weak government lacking broad social support.[45] The most profound reform of the security forces was possible only after the PSOE obtained an absolute majority for the first time since 1977. Organic Law 1/1984, which reformed the National Defence Organic Law of 1980, gave civilians control over military and defence matters and promoted the modernization of the army. Measures were passed to reinforce the role of the Ministry of Defence *vis-à-vis* the command of the three branches of the force. The law 'allowed the minister to direct, co-ordinate and control personnel policy in the armed forces and supervise military education',[46] both 'very delicate areas that the military chiefs considered of institutional interest'.[47]

Despite the reforms, the great majority of people linked to the Francoist repressive apparatus continued to work in various state

[44] After the attempted coup, 'only a very modest purge was undertaken' (Buck, 1998: 1619).

[45] All parliamentary parties except the PNV and HB participated in the massive demonstration. The extra-parliamentary left and the anarchist union, CNT, called for a purge (*El País*, 27–28 Feb. 1981).

[46] For the lack of reform in education until recently see López Garrido (1987: 158–159, 163). The first civil–military school of peace and defence studies was established only in 1997 (RDL 1643/1997, 24 Oct. 1997).

[47] See Agüero (1995: 311, 315). For a description by the Ministry of Defence of its own evolution, which takes the reform process right up to 1996, consult www.mde.es/mde/evolu.htm.

institutions. In the case of the police, although important organizational reforms took place that allowed for the elimination of some special police bodies such as the notorious Social Investigation Brigade (BIS),[48] most members were simply moved to other police departments. There was however an effort to ensure that all those who had become particularly notorious for their brutality in the Francoist prisons should have as little visibility as possible in their new posts.[49] In some instances their departure from the police was facilitated by a reduction in the retirement age.[50]

The creation of ETA and the emergence of student and trade union protest during the last years of the regime led to the approval of repressive legislation that counteracted what had been a process of significant political liberalization.[51] The Law of Public Order of 1959, the Decree on Banditry and Terrorism of 1969 (derogated only in 1971), and the Penal and Military Justice Codes had been particularly harsh. These laws permitted the suspension of the civil rights of those suspected of participating in terrorist attacks until 1977 (Royal Decree Law (RDL) 4/1977, *Boletín Oficial del Estado* (BOE) 25/1977). Another key repressive institution was the Tribunals of Public Order (TOP), created in 1963, which processed countless members of the democratic opposition (RDL 2/1977; BOE 4/1977). New courts were created to replace the TOPs in 1977, but they were still charged with processing pending cases in accordance with the pre-existing repressive legislation. At the same time, TOP staff was assigned to other judicial bodies with precedence over other people competing for posts. The rules governing the penal system were also changed in 1977 in order to adapt it to a new 'social reality' and to ensure the greatest possible respect 'for the humanity and legal rights of recluses' (RDL 2273/1977; BOE 210/1977). Some articles of the Penal Code and Law for Criminal

[48] The BPS was responsible for the repression of the democratic forces. It was very much feared, and they did not even respect Francoist legislation (*Justicia Democrática*, 1978: 19).

[49] Pons Prades entitles one of the chapters in his book 'torturers who are still on the loose' (1987: 295 ff.). He cites a letter sent by a group of tortured persons to Felipe González in 1985, which accuses member of the BPS, Jesús Martínez Torres, and an official from the then Interior Ministry, José Barrionuevo, for their suffering and for denying their claims (1987: 296–7). The only book on the BPS is by Batista (1995).

[50] See Jaúregui and Menéndez (1995: 170). It is known that the Ministry of the Interior holds 'a hundred thousand Francoist police files' (Jaúregui and Menéndez, 1995: 183–4). Other archives have been destroyed.

[51] For a study of judicial policy under Franco, see Bastida (1986) and Lanero (1996); for student and worker protest, see Maravall (1978).

Sentencing were also partially derogated (Law 20/1978; BOE 20/1978).

The civil administrative bureaucracy had already undergone some reforms in the preceding two decades. It was left almost intact by the new democracy as, in contrast with the bureaucracies of the former communist regimes, it was considered a legitimate power structure in which forms of recruitment were sufficiently based on merit and efficiency. Perhaps this explains why polls show that a majority of civil servants were openly in favour of democracy.[52] None the less, the provincial headquarters of the National Movement (MN),[53] the single regime party, which were dependent upon the civil governors and were key administrative posts in terms of ideological control and repression at the provincial and local levels, were eliminated. The civil governors were maintained despite their bad reputation in terms of public order. The statutes governing their role were revised only in 1980. Although they retained their powers over public order matters, as well as control over the forces of law and order at the provincial level, they were also charged with 'watching over the rights and freedoms recognized and guaranteed by the Constitution'. It was only years later that the post of civil governor was suppressed completely.

Royal Decree Law abolished the MN and related political bodies on 1 April 1977. However, many of their organs linked to the media, education, culture and sports survived for some time. MN personnel were transferred to other official institutions as civil servants. Most of the women linked to the Female Section of the Falange (about 24,000) were sent without any training to work in public libraries; others, linked to the media section of the MN, were similarly transferred. This caused an outcry among members of the library services, who had obtained their jobs through public competition and complained about discrimination and the lack of qualifications of incoming personnel. In the case of public libraries, the reincorporation of former regime members was not achieved as

[52] There was an overwhelmingly positive attitude of public servants to democracy, political parties, and the way in which the transition was carried out. This is so even among those appointed under the Franco regime, although less so for those over 60; see e.g. a poll carried out in 1983 by the Centre for Sociological Research (CIS) in *Revista Española de Investigaciones Sociológicas* (23) and Beltrán (1985, 1994).

[53] The MN was the only legal party after the end of the Civil War, and its role was to support the regime. The product of a fusion of the Falange and Carlism, the single party became a 'movement' in 1966 and represented the 'communion among Spaniards according to the ideals that gave birth to the Crusade' (*El País*, 2 Apr. 1977: 8).

quietly, because professional complicity was not a factor as it was in the police.[54]

A few analysts have argued that the monarchy is an institutional and personalist legacy of the dictatorship, in so far as King Juan Carlos I was nominated by Franco to be his political successor, while the succession mechanism mandated by the dictator was scrupulously followed. However, Franco could not have predicted that the monarch would be committed to dialogue and to political integration, as his first speech claiming that he was 'the King of all Spaniards' indicated. The importance of the monarchy may have been exaggerated, but it is difficult to understand the transition without taking into account the democratic disposition of the King. He was crucial in the first months following Franco's death, and played an important role in defeating the attempted coup of 23 February 1981.

Finally, there are symbolic matters referred to by Pierre Nora as 'the places of memory' (Nora, 1992). Fearing reprisals from the Allies, Franco considerably watered down the use of fascist symbols after the end of the Second World War.[55] None the less, many of the symbols of Francoism have survived in small cities and villages. Street names have been changed in only a few provinces, the great majority of monuments honouring the Nationalist dead of the Civil War are intact, and it is notable that only in 1995 were coins bearing the effigy of Franco withdrawn from circulation. One of the most visited monuments in Spain is the Valley of the Fallen (Valle de los Caídos), a mausoleum dedicated to victors of the Civil War. The mortal remains of Franco as well as of José Antonio, the founder of the Falange, are buried there. The Arc of Triumph in Madrid remains intact, as do countless monuments of the 1930s and 1940s that perpetuate the discrimination between winners and losers. Only in 1985, ten years after the death of Franco, was a monument discretely inaugurated in the name of 'all' the dead of the Civil War.[56]

[54] For libraries in Valencia and Barcelona see *El País* (24 Feb. 1978; 1 Jun. 1978).

[55] This helps to explain the differences between the attitude of the democratic oppositions in Spain and in Portugal during the transition (apart from the obvious fact that both transitions differed in their very nature): 'the Portuguese regime was seen much more as a fascist regime in the eyes of the opposition. Therefore the purge in Portugal was much more a "*saneamento*" [purge] of fascism, fascist institutions and individual fascists than in Spain' (Larsen, 1998: 1575).

[56] On 22 November 1985, the tenth anniversary of the coronation, a monument was inaugurated in Madrid to all the fallen in the war, a clear attempt to link the monarchy with reconciliation. It stands by a monolith from 1840, which celebrates the heroes of a key historical date in Spain, the 2 May. The inscription says 'Honour to all those who gave their lives for Spain' (*El País*, 12 Nov. 1985: 1, 13).

Private initiatives in this realm were also scarce and hardly ever received support from the state.[57] Perhaps the most significant event was the petition for the return of Picasso's *Guernica* from the US government, which became a form of homage to all the dead of the Civil War, with special emphasis on the Republicans.

What to Do with the Victims of Repression?

It was difficult to compensate many of the victims of the 1940s for their suffering, as many were dead and others exiled. None the less, symbolic reparations, such as acts of moral rehabilitation and public recognition, as well as material reparations such as pensions for the survivors or for the families of the dead, were possible. This dimension of retroactive justice came late and was insufficient in many cases.[58] The need to document facts that had taken place forty years before, coupled with budget restrictions during the first years of the transition, slowed the process of rehabilitation. Further, this kind of legislation is extremely difficult to prepare given that jurisprudence varies widely and tends to produce interminable and complicated documents. Thus, the successive laws, the partial decree pardons, and the 1977 amnesty were insufficient to deal with all the matters associated with rehabilitation. In December 1977 the Communist parliamentary group called for a 'labour amnesty' (*Diario de Sesiones del Congreso* (DSC) 43, 1648–52, 23/12/77). In April 1978 the Socialist group called on the government to deal with the case of teachers from the Republican period whose rights had not been recognized by the amnesty law (DSC 46, 1669–79, 18/4/78; DSC 63, 2155–7, 10/5/78). Similarly, in November 1978 the Socialist group from Cataluña proposed a law to speed up the passage of an amnesty for participants in the Civil War (*Boletín Oficial del Congreso* (BOC), 194, 4171–2,

[57] In January 1978, for example, a series of pantheons for about 200 Republican war dead was made in Aranjuez, financed by public subscription (*El País*, 7 Jan. 1978: 12). The first legal former combatants' associations were formed at this time, which brought together people from both sides of the conflict. Among their aims were '[to] overcome conflict, eradicate violence, promote peace and coexistence and fight for equality of rights of combatants from both sides' (*El País*, 6 Dec. 1978: 16).

[58] Given these difficulties, Elster argues that nothing should be done in order to avoid selective criteria and thereby violate the principle of equality before the law. In his view, victims are also those who had 'opportunities denied to them through the arbitrary or tyrannical behaviour of the authorities. Access to higher education, to good jobs, to travel abroad and other vehicles of self-realisation' (Elster, 1995: 565–7).

30/11/78; *Boletín Oficial de las Cortes Españolas* (BOCE) 1497, 36271–2, 12/4/76). These are only some examples of many initiatives presented to widen the coverage, and increase the efficacy, of the amnesty law in the name of reconciliation.

Another different but related issue was that pertaining to pensions. The first, usually failed, attempts to gain pensions for the vanquished were made under Franco, but the dictator had to die for such legislation to meet with success. Various magistrates of the Francoist courts tried to obtain equal status for the mutilated from the Republican side and to reinstate purged civil servants. In short, they sought to overcome decades of discrimination. Various demands for such measures were made after Franco's death. These included an appeal in favour of the rights of the widows of Republican combatants, and another for the 'application of a pardon on the occasion of the proclamation by His Majesty the King to the former civil servants of the Generality of Cataluña'.[59] A law of October 1984 finally recognized 'the rights and services rendered' by those who were a part of the armed forces or the police during the Civil War (BOE 26/2/84). This did not clear up all pending matters, however. A Decree of March 1976[60] gave pensions to the mutilated from the Republic Army, but not to their widows. Indeed, the decree was approved in order to give some benefits to the war mutilated who had not been allowed to become members of the Order of Mutilated Chevaliers (reserved for Francoists). This leads one to question the reconciliatory aims of the law, as it did not challenge the segregation between winners and losers. On 11 March, the Law for the War Mutilated was also approved,[61] and many forms of discrimination were dealt with. RDL of 6 March 1978 (BOE 678, 7/3/78) solved the situation of soldiers of the Republican Army. Decree Law of 16 November 1978 (BOE, 276, 18/11/78) gave pensions to the 'relatives of those who died as a result of the Civil War'. The preamble to this law was finally explicit: it mentioned that it was 'necessary to ensure the equal treatment for the relatives of those who died as a result of the war in 1936–1939 . . . whose rights to a pension had not yet been recognised'. Various reconciliatory measures were approved even after the passage of the Constitution, such as RDL 43/78 (BOE, 305, 22/12/78), which finally extended economic benefits to those

[59] See: BOCE 1525, 36871–2, 12/8/76. This was attended to in Amnesty Decree 1081/78, 2/5/78, BOE 25.

[60] BOE 84, 7/4/76, complemented by Decree 3025/76 (BOE 9, 11/1/77).

[61] Law 5/76, 11 March 1976 (BOE 63), complemented by Decrees 712/77, 1/4/1977 (BOE 21–22/4/77).

who suffered injury or mutilation. The problem of mutilated Republican combatants merits a study of its own, as the legislation is immense and very complex and the problem is not entirely resolved even today.

Finally, no truth commission was established. Only a few private initiatives were undertaken to investigate the 'truth', permit the filing of suits against individuals or to denounce abuse and torture.[62] The Amnesty Law, however, exonerated all those guilty of such acts, such that the majority of suits were not accepted. The only initiative comparable to a truth commission was a commission of historians established to investigate political responsibilities for the bombing of Guernica. This garnered great public attention throughout the transition period, owing to the great symbolic significance of the bombing immortalized by Picasso's painting; however, it focused more on an event of the Civil War than on the Franco regime itself. One of the first experts' meetings took place in Guernica in April 1977, the fortieth anniversary of the bombing. The historians gathered there committed themselves to clarifying the events and assigning the ultimate responsibility for the bombing. They sent a communiqué to the government signed also by the survivors, which called for the immediate opening of the archives and for a rectification of the regime's version of events—that the inhabitants of Guernica had been the ones to set fire to the city (*El País*, 26 July 1977). The German government agreed to open its military archives and even showed a willingness to build a monument in Guernica (*El País*, 28 September 1977). A year later, the Spanish government decided to allow one of the members of the commission to consult the relevant archives (*El País*, 10–12 February 1977). Similar meetings were held in subsequent years to ascertain 'direct responsibility on both sides for those events' but, given the nature of existing documentation, it has not been possible yet to do so.[63]

Conclusions

There is no agreement among researchers regarding the consequences of amnesty, a policy of national reconciliation, and the

[62] Pons Prades, a former Republican combatant, was the only one to call for the constitution of 400 or 500 local commissions to undertake investigations of events occuring between 1936 and 1975 (1987: 314).

[63] See *El País* (12 and 23–25 Apr. 1978).

concomitant absence of purges, as well as of trials and truth commissions, on democracy. It is not easy to establish causal links between the two, and it is even harder to imagine what might have happened if such measures had been adopted in Spain. Despite the difficulties, some authors have speculated about the impact of the absence or presence of such policies on the nature of democracy. According to some of these, the absence of retroactive justice policies was the product of an unacceptable compromise by opposition forces and has had a negative impact on democracy. For Buck, the dilemmas facing a new regime after authoritarianism can be summarized thus: 'The lesser the seriousness of the crimes and the farther back in time they were committed, the less risky a criminal process will be. On the other hand, in such cases less people will normally demand such a process. This means that the more important it is to deal with the past, the more risky it actually is to do it' (Buck, 1998: 1619). In his view, if a transition is led 'from above', it is likely that the result will be a 'stable but limited' democracy, in which one will normally find 'pockets of undemocratic decision-making'. Thus, Buck criticizes the lack of transparency of Spanish political parties and their tendency to negotiate behind closed doors. He also argues that there is a secretive way of engaging in politics and very little public debate.[64] All this contributes to explain recent corruption scandals as well as the GAL case[65] (Buck, 1998: 1630 ff., 1634). Other authors have linked the GAL case to the absence of purges and the slow reform of the military and police.[66] Indeed, some research demonstrates the survival of people linked to the hard-line sectors of the Franco regime within the security forces under democracy, who were dedicated to the repression of opposition from the end of the 1960s onwards (Medina, 1995; Jaúregui and Menéndez, 1995: 153, 165). However, even the most critical observers have recognized the impossibility of carrying out purges given the absence of alternative candidates trained in anti-terrorist action. The absence of purges can also be explained by terrorist attacks, particularly those by ETA, which increased exponentially after Franco's death and caused great conflict within the military and police forces. In Ballbé's view, a

[64] For limited media diversity resulting from limited transition, see *El País* (26 May 1999: 19).

[65] Faced with accusations by the right of political corruption and involvement in state terrorism, the Socialist government recalled the amnesty and the need to forget the past (*El País*, 14 Oct. 1997).

[66] On the widespread desire to avoid vengeance and confrontation and on the price paid for moderation and the absence of purges, see Colomer (1998: 9, 16–17).

militarized public order has been a constant feature of Spanish life from the beginning of the century and throughout the Franco period, which explains why political elites preparing the 1978 Constitution sought to 'demilitarize and separate the police forces from the armed forces' (Ballbé, 1983: 460, 470). However, limited reform and a persistent authoritarian 'inertia' led public security forces to kill twenty-seven people when dispersing demonstrators between 1975 and 1978. Civil–military jurisdictional conflicts also persisted and were terminated only in 1980 with the reform of the Code of Military Justice.[67] Even then, and notwithstanding the hopes of the writers of the Constitution, the various police forces 'maintained a militarized model', which has no 'equivalent in any other democratic constitutional regime'.[68] Amnesty International reported various cases of torture, and even deaths from torture, at least until the beginning of the 1980s. Although the government gradually adhered to most relevant international treaties against torture and approved national legislation to the same effect,[69] torture was still a common practice at least until the mid-1980s (AI, 1975b, 1977, 1978, 1984, 1985). However, Amnesty International reports also show that this behaviour was found among the police forces of other European countries.

Most authors, however, insist that everything possible in the circumstances was done and that the decision not to revise the past was a good one, symptomatic of the political maturity of the Spaniards. Morlino and Mattei argue that it is not even possible to say that an authoritarian culture has survived in Spain (1998: 1172). For them, in the countries of Southern Europe 'the historical past is definitely over. The old authoritarians make up a tiny group. In addition, with such high percentages of democrats and neo-democrats there are no conceivable alternatives to the present democratic arrangements. The authoritarians do not seem

[67] Even so, the Constitutional Tribunal had to pronounce itself after that, as conflicts still emerged; see Sentence 113/1995 (BOE 184/1995).

[68] For this and the resistance to change within the forces, see Ballbé (1983: 476, 483).

[69] Spain ratified the ICCPR (April 1977), the Convention for the Protection of Human Rights and Fundamental Freedoms (1979), the UN Convention against Torture (UNCAT) and the European Convention on the Prevention of Torture (1987). National legal changes to ensure the protection of fundamental rights and to punish torture are Law 62/1978 (BOE 62/1978), Law 31/1978 (BOE 172/1978), RDL 1201/1981 (BOE 149/1981), Article 15 of the Constitution, and Organic Law 13/1985 (BOE 13/1985). The death penalty has not been carried out in Spain since the death of Franco, although five people were executed just two months before he died (AI, 1979).

to provide a challenge in any sense.' For another observer, 'the restoration of democracy in Spain was almost immediate, and it penetrated society completely' (Buck, 1998: 1630).

The argument put forward in this chapter is that, although there was no viable political alternative, significant legacies of authoritarian political culture remain (Rodríguez Ibáñez, 1987; Torcal, 1995). For example, the fact that at, least until 1987, 15 per cent of the Spanish population had a positive view of the Franco regime is not irrelevant. Other elements of political culture (partly common to Mediterranean societies), such as disaffection and apathy, have also been researched at length (Montero *et al.*, 1998). There was no real discussion of postwar repression during the transition, or even after the consolidation of democracy. None the less, almost all actors were aware at the time of the urgent need to give reparations to those victimized during the first years of the Franco regime. This meant that later repressive episodes, such as those of the 1960s and 1970s, were less visible, as levels of violence and numbers of victims were much lower than had been the case in the 1940s. In the Basque country, however, violence had a higher visibility, given that repression was more severe precisely during the second half of the dictatorship, after ETA began carrying out terrorist attacks. This explains why the absence of retroactive justice was criticized more in the Basque country than elsewhere. Indeed, reservations regarding the nature of the transition process as a whole are much greater in the Basque country, particularly among the Nationalist electorate.[70]

Some researchers view the Spanish transition as 'a model and exemplary, given the low social cost of the path adopted, but one that has paradoxically as a result of its method of timid negotiations, produced a democracy that is mediocre and of inferior quality'. Thus, 'the virtues of the transition have become the vices of democracy' (Colomer, 1998: 10,181). Shapiro makes a similar argument for the South African case. For him, the latter case has been 'identified in the Western press as a model throughout Africa and a symbol of hope for struggling democratisers elsewhere', precisely because of the nature of the process of change. 'Despite considerable violence there was no civil war, no military coup, and the co-operation among the players whose co-operation was needed was

[70] When asked in 1994 if the transition made them proud, less than 50 per cent of Basques said yes but over 80 per cent of the rest of Spaniards answered affirmatively (Aguilar, 1999d: 60). In that article, I argue that continuity in terms of personnel in repressive institutions helps to explain the lower level of legitimacy of democracy among the nationalist Basque electorate.

impressive.' Notwithstanding academic enthusiasm for 'negotiated transitions', Shapiro notes that there are 'serious questions as to whether constitutional orders that emerge from negotiations facilitate democratic politics in the medium term. In particular, South Africa's transitional constitution lacks a system of opposition institutions that any healthy democracy requires.' For him, 'the dynamics of negotiated transitions . . . make it virtually impossible for the principal players to converge on an agreement that includes provision for effective opposition forces in the new democratic order.' He thus concludes that, 'although the interim constitution may well have been the best possible device to end apartheid without a civil war, it should not be replicated in the permanent constitution' (Shapiro, 1996: 175–7).

One of the unwanted consequences of the negotiated transition in Spain is that institutional frameworks designed for periods of change consolidate a way of engaging in politics and avoid open discussion of the most delicate matters that can cause profound cleavages within society. An excessive risk aversion, like that witnessed during the transition, can impose serious limits on accountability.[71] Furthermore, avoiding retroactive justice because the balance of forces after the death of Franco did not permit it (Colomer, 1998: 177) has allowed the political elite to refer abusively to the 'legacy' argument and to blame the authoritarian past for behaviour that is unacceptable under a consolidated democracy.

It is indubitable that Spanish democracy is consolidated and has high levels of social legitimacy. Many of the defects mentioned above as institutional remnants of the dictatorship are also found in other countries for very different reasons. However, I have tried to point out which of the worst aspects of Spanish democracy are at least partly attributable to its authoritarian past and to the fact that it took politicians at least ten years to engage in certain institutional reforms.

[71] On accountability in Spanish politics, see Maravall (1996: 33 ff.).

4

Truth, Justice, Memory, and Democratization in the Southern Cone

Alexandra Barahona de Brito

Introduction

The military dictatorships established in the Southern Cone of Latin America in the late 1960s and early 1970s had a key aim in common: to eliminate internal left-wing subversion and re-establish order. All those opposed to military rule were enemies of the state, to be physically eliminated or politically and socially isolated or silenced by imprisonment, torture, enforced disappearances, or exile. The violence thus unleashed broke the mould of 'traditional' authoritarian repression. It was clandestine and illegal, even according the laws of the dictatorships. It was based on the systematic violation of rights, covered by a protective mantle of official denial and impunity, and facilitated by the subjugation of judicial institutions and manipulation of constitutional legality.[1] Its social impact was devastating, shrinking the public sphere to a bare minimum and paralysing societies in an inertia of fear. Ironically, however, repression was also responsible for initiating a dynamic of opposition. The struggle to defend human rights led to the formation of groups demanding accountability, and played an important role in bringing dictatorships to an end, finally giving societies the opportunity to confront the legacies of repression.

At the moment of transition, two opposing camps faced one another: on the one hand the victims of repression, human rights organizations (HROs), opposition parties, and other social groups

The author would like to thank Paloma Aguilar, Alan Angell, Nancy Bermeo, Carmen González, and Rachel Sieder for their helpful comments.

[1] For repression in the four cases examined, see: CONADEP (1984); Nunca Mais (1985); CNVR (1991) and SERPAJ (1992).

called for 'truth telling', to counteract years of military denial of violations, and for trials of those responsible for abuse, and on the other hand the military and their allies, who were opposed to any 'settling of accounts'. Between these two stood parties and groups that emphasized the need for a balancing act between truth and justice, as well as aims of 'national reconciliation' and a stable process of democratization. Truth and justice policies varied widely from country to country in the region, depending on the balance of forces between the groups supporting one or another of these positions. For the most part, a mantle of impunity has covered former repressors. Continued impunity has prevented victims and relatives from gaining full legal and moral redress. Thus, the issue of retroactive justice has stayed alive in the Southern Cone, well after the transitional period.

This chapter examines how Argentina, Brazil, Chile, and Uruguay have fared with truth and justice since the transition from authoritarian rule. The chapter is divided into four parts. The first examines official policies, or the lack thereof, of the newly inaugurated democracies, and the second looks at how the issue has fared under subsequent democratic governments. While the first section offers more of a 'top-down' institutional assessment, the latter adopts a more 'bottom-up' perspective of how society has pushed forward or challenged official policies adopted in the early transitional period. This dichotomy is somewhat artificial, but it is fair to say that what the judiciary or HROs have been able to do to deal with the past has been largely conditioned by the framework created by the political elite in the first instance. The third section discusses the links between backward-looking accountability and democratization, and the final one considers the impact of the wider 'politics of memory' on that process.

Dealing with the Past in Transition

Punishment and military rebellion in Argentina, 1983–1989

Argentina was the first country to undergo a transition to democracy and the one that undertook the most wide-ranging official policies of truth and justice. The first measure adopted by newly elected President Raúl Alfonsín was to release forty-three political prisoners. In February 1984 a law was passed allowing civil courts to dismiss charges against civilians by military courts, and by the end of the Alfonsín mandate all political detainees had been released. In December 1983 the government also created the National Commission on the Disappearance of People (CONADEP) to investigate the truth about military repression. After nine arduous months, the Commission had gathered more than 50,000 pages of testimony. In 1984 it published the report that came to be known as 'Argentina Never Again' (*Nunca Más*). It confirmed the disappearance of 8,963 people, acknowledged the existence of 340 clandestine torture centres, and listed the names of 1,351 people, including doctors, judges, journalists, bishops, and priests, who had co-operated with repression. In early September 1984 the government established an Under Secretariat for Human Rights (SDH) within the Ministry of the Interior, with a mandate to continue with investigations of all cases not reviewed by the CONADEP.[2] In November the *Nunca Más* report was officially published, and it became an immediate best seller. The time had come for justice.

With Decree Law 158 of December 1983, the government annulled the military's self-amnesty National Pacification Law of April 1983 and provided for the prosecution of the commanders-in-chief of the armed forces and heads of the military juntas by the Supreme Council of the Armed Forces (CSFA).[3] It thus gave the military justice system 'first shot' at judging its peers. It also stipulated that those who had obeyed orders would not be liable to prosecution. The government thereby hoped to limit trials to the commanders of repression.[4]

This was not to be. A last-minute senatorial amendment to the law led to the inclusion of a mechanism that would allow the civilian courts to act in the case of delay or negligence after six months. Further, it excluded 'atrocious and abhorrent acts' from its benefits, creating a loophole for the widening of the prosecutions. In the event, the military courts did not do their job and so placed justice in the hands of the civil courts. Thus, in April 1985, Judge Strassera of the Federal Court of Appeals (TFA) initiated proceedings against the juntas. By December 1985, the nine heads

[2] Since the CONADEP report, the SDH has confirmed about 3,000 new cases, bringing the official number up to 12,000. Amnesty International and other HROs have made estimates as high as 30,000.

[3] In the last days of military rule, a presidential decree also ordered the destruction of documents pertaining to the Dirty War.

[4] According to Norden, the government asked the military to hand in a list of prosecutable officers to thus limit prosecutions and act with the compliance of the armed forces, and it planned to pardon those convicted before the end of the first term in 1989. The military handed in only nine names (Norden, cited in Acuña, 1998).

of the military juntas had been tried and convicted of 709 human rights crimes. The Tribunal heard the testimony of 833 people and produced 3 tonnes of documents and 900 hours of tapes. The sentence of the court was transmitted over radio and television. General Videla and Admiral Massera were condemned to life-long imprisonment, General Viola to seventeen years, Admiral Lambruschini to seven years, and Brigadier Agosti to four and a half years; the remaining accused—General Galtieri, Brigadiers Graffigna and Lami Dozo, and Admiral Anaya—were absolved.

The government hoped that so-called 'Trial of the Century' would constitute the last act of 'justice'. Again, this was not to be. HROs were ready to take their long frustrated search for justice to the civil courts. Item 30 of the TFA sentence against the juntas on 'atrocious and abhorrent acts', moreover, precluded automatic closure of cases in accordance with the provision of Decree 158, which limited responsibility to those who had commanded the repressive apparatus. And the TFA had recommended that other officers involved be investigated in the courts, further widening the universe of 'prosecutables'. By the end of August 1984, HROs had handed in a total of 2,000 cases to the courts. The government faltered; faced with mid-term elections in November, it hesitated to pass any laws favouring impunity. By the year's end a further 1,087 cases had been handed in by the CONADEP. At least 650 of these pertained to military personnel on active duty. Spurred on by the judicial 'obligation to prosecute' principle, the courts began to act. On 30 December 1985 the Supreme Court upheld an Appellate Court ruling against the application of 'due obedience'.

The government now faced a process of calling to account that it could not control or limit, so in April 1986 it tried for the first time to restrict prosecutions. It called on the CSFA to adopt a broad interpretation of due obedience and to speed up all remaining cases with the so-called Instructions to Military Prosecutors. This caused a public uproar and evoked protest marches. The new defence minister, Germán López, was forced to resign, and the TFA took on the case load of the CSFA in June 1986. By then, the relationship between the government and the most famous and vociferous of the HROs, a part of the Mothers of the Plaza de Mayo (MPM), which represented the mothers of the disappeared, had become openly adversarial. Indeed, since the trial demonstrations in favour of justice had become increasingly frequent, placing growing pressure on the executive to allow the courts to proceed. By early December there were an estimated 6,000 cases in the courts involving about 600 officers.

The government then made another attempt to limit the scope of prosecutions. It passed the Law of Statute of Limitations, or Full Stop Law, on 23 December 1986, giving individuals 60 days to present cases to the court.[5] This measure failed on all counts. The public and HROs were not satisfied; 60,000 people had taken to the streets to protest the measure on 19 December. Prosecutions were not limited; instead, the passage of the law produced an unexpected avalanche of new cases, as the courts opted not to take their customary judicial holiday in January and HROs worked overtime to present cases. By the February deadline 300 military officers had been indicted, and the first cases of contempt of court had been heard, relating to officers declining to appear before the judges. The law also failed to quiet military fears: on 16 March 1987 the country was shaken by what was to be the first of a series of military rebellions by the so-called 'painted faces' (*carapintadas*) in opposition to the prosecution of junior officers. The government began to negotiate with the rebels. They quickly laid down their arms, but the price the was high: on 5 June 1987 Congress approved the Law of Due Obedience, which put annulled the effects of Item 30 and confirmed that lower-ranking officers could not be prosecuted.

Why had transitional truth and justice initially been so prominent and forceful? First, the transitional setting was very propitious. Of all the cases considered, Argentina was the country where the military had left power most demoralized and weak as a result of their defeat at the hands of the British in the Falklands/Malvinas War. Thus, in 1983 the victorious Radical Party (UCR) had started out with a wide margin for manoeuvre. It had acted quickly to take advantage of the window of opportunity created by an initial feeling that 'all was possible' in the new, democratic Argentina. The defeat of the Peronist Party (PJ), expressive of a choice of 'integrity' over 'charisma', seemed to herald a widespread public desire for the politics of the rule of law over the politics of emotion and demagoguery associated the predominantly Peronist past (Wynia, 1992: 108). The government was also boosted by a strong judiciary willing to take prosecutions forward and by HROs and a public mostly supportive of truth and justice. Further, while none of the parties had defined policies on how to deal with the past, President Alfonsín was personally committed to addressing the issue. Last but not least, repression had been widespread, atrocious, and was fresh in the memory of all.

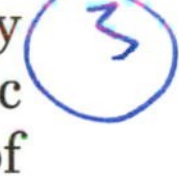

[5] The law was passed with 126 votes in favour, 16 against, and 1 abstention in the Chamber of Deputies, and 25–10 in the Senate.

Why did the government subsequently backtrack? The Alfonsín administration essentially lost control of the policy it designed, miscalculating the level of independence and the commitment of the judiciary to justice, as well as the institutional autonomy of the judicial process, once set in motion. It had also mistakenly calculated that a restriction of prosecution to the junta leaders would be backed by the lower ranks and thus would prevent a serious backlash from what was a weakened military institution. The Full Stop law did not satisfy the rebels, who were discontented with prosecutions, deep budget cuts, and the loss of a sense of mission and honour, and actively pressured what was an increasingly weak and isolated government (Pion-Berlin, 1997: 95–9). Indeed, the human rights issue became enmeshed with an intra-military conflict over who should command the army (Acuña, 1998: 12).

In January and December 1988, two further revolts took place at military barracks.[6] Furthermore, the government did not have a strong, co-operative relationship with HROs. Indeed, a strong alliance between the latter and the political parties opposed to military rule had never been formed. Without ties of loyalty to overcome differences, the powerful movement became a liability. Presidential ambiguity, combined with badly timed or inconsistent efforts to limit justice, further alienated HROs, which immediately counteracted efforts to limit trials, seeking to maximize gains against repressors they feared would get off the hook. Weakened by these challenges, in January 1989 the Alfonsín administration was faced with yet another violent incident, this time an attack against another military barracks, involving a left-wing armed organization, the Movement All for the Fatherland (MTP). This led the government to reverse parts of the National Defence Law of April 1988, with the passage of decrees giving the military a new role in internal security, thus allowing the military to recover partially the ground they had lost since the transition to democracy. Early elections were called soon thereafter.

Alfonsín left power in a climate of insecurity and ungovernability, defeated by a rebellious military, an angry human rights movement, an alienated public suffering from the devastating effects of hyperinflation, and an increasingly vociferous opposition in the legislature. The military would finally get the impunity it clamoured for, but it would have to wait until Alfonsín's successor, Peronist Carlos Menem, came to power.

[6] On rebellions, see Norden (1996).

Amnesty and 'acceptable inaction' in Brazil, 1985–1995

As the military regime in Argentina collapsed in the wake of the Falklands War, a team of church workers in Brazil was engaged in a secret mission, photocopying confidential documents related to the trial of 707 'subversives' by the Supreme Military Tribunal. They were led by Cardinal Paulo Evaristo Arns of the Archdiocese of São Paulo and Jaime Wright, a Presbyterian pastor, and supported by the international organization the World Council of Churches. Between 1979 and 1985, a team of thirty people secretly gathered what was called 'the chocolate' (*o chocolate*), sending the copied papers out of the country for safekeeping, thus laying the groundwork for what was to become a series of volumes of over 5,000 pages.[7] A summarized version was subsequently published by the Catholic Church press and appeared in bookstands on 15 July 1985, nearly six months after the indirect election of civilian president Tancredo Neves of the opposition Brazilian Democratic Movement Party (PMDB). The book reported that all political prisoners had been systematically tortured and that 125 had been disappeared.[8] The so-called *Brasil Nunca Mais* report was an immediate best seller. It acquired 'semi-official' status as a result of to its success (Bronkhorst, 1995) and the groundswell of public opinion contributed to Brazil's decision to sign the Convention against Torture (Minow, 1998: 54).

Neves died before ever taking office, and after the coming to power of his vice-president, José Sarney, no action was taken to address part repression. The past became a part of the governmental agenda only in 1998, under President Henrique Cardoso. How can this absence or 'delay' be explained? First, relatively few people had disappeared, and most of those that had were members of two isolated guerrilla groups rather than prominent members of national parties; what is more, the worst repression had been concentrated in two areas, São Paulo and Araguaia in the state of Pará, and had taken place fifteen years before the transition. Second, Brazilian society is accustomed to high levels of structurally embedded violence, systematic torture, and tolerance for impunity. It is hardly surprising, then, that there was not much protest over the deaths of a few guerrilla fighters in a remote jungle region. Indeed, public and private security forces killed more peasants while protecting landowning interests than political dissidents under military rule:

[7] For a fuller account, see Weschler (1990).

[8] The count has since risen to 339 dead, of which 144 were disappeared.

according to the Landless Rural Workers' Movement (MST), there were 1,188 assassinations between 1964 and 1986 and all but a handful have gone unpunished (Barahona de Brito and Panizza, 1998).

Third, as part of the political opening and 'decompression' announced by the military regime, Congress approved an Amnesty Law, promulgated on 28 August 1979, which led to the release of thousands of political prisoners and the return of many exiles. The military had not wanted to pass an amnesty law, but had been forced to do so under pressure from the amnesty movement launched in February 1978 by organizations such as the Brazilian Amnesty Committees (CBA). The movement called for a wide-ranging, general, and unrestricted amnesty, and was supported by the lawyer's organization (OAB) press association, the bishop's conference, and other social and political groups. The regime finally gave in, but only partly: not all of the political prisoners were released, and members of the security forces were also included in the benefits of the law. This was accepted as a trade-off by the political class: thousands of previously disenfranchised politicians were allowed to re-engage in politics in return for military impunity.

In addition, as in Argentina, no strong coalitions were forged between political parties and non-governmental groups seeking truth and justice for past violations. The OAB, the Justice and Peace commissions of the Catholic Church, the Commission of Relatives of the Dead and Disappeared of the Brazilian Amnesty Committee (CFMDP-CBA), and Torture Never Again (TNM) groups formed in the mid-1980s had not been successful in their search for justice. These groups remained relatively isolated, as their struggle was not the one that mobilized the public against the regime. Rather, the anti-dictatorial struggle centred on an amnesty for political prisoners, on putting an end to the proscriptions that deprived thousands of the right to participate in political life, and, later, on the call for direct elections (*diretas já*) in 1984.

Finally, unlike Argentina, in Brazil there was a high degree of political continuity between the outgoing regime and the successor civilian government led by Sarney. Unlike Trancredo, Sarney was part of the National Renovating Alliance (ARENA), the pro-military party during the dictatorship, and maintained close ties with the intelligence community and the military as a whole, which retained all their prerogatives and a veto capacity over the civilian government. Thus, it was only the commitment to a wider human rights agenda by a president with anti-dictatorial credentials, Fernando Henrique Cardoso, that overcame the up to then 'acceptable inaction' regarding the issue.

Political division and plebiscite in Uruguay, 1985–1989

Although more pronounced than in Brazil, truth and justice were not dominant issues during the transitional electoral campaign that led to the victory of the Colorado Party (PC) and its leader, Julio Maria Sanguinetti, in 1985. The Blanco or National Party (PN) and the left-wing coalition, the Wide Front (FA), although expressing sympathy with accountability, did not consistently or determinedly champion it. The government and the PC initially adopted a *laissez-faire* attitude to truth and justice: Sanguinetti stated that he would not undertake any official policies to ensure justice, but he also promised that he would not prevent individuals from presenting their cases in court. Although ambiguous about truth and justice, the new president emphasized pacification. Thus, on 1 March 1985, the day of his inauguration, Sanguinetti presented a bill to derogate the State Security Law, limit the jurisdiction of the military justice system to pre-1973 levels, and amnesty all political prisoners who had not committed homicides. The bill also provided for the creation of a National Repatriation Commission to receive returning exiles.

The National Pacification Law (LPN) was passed on 8 March after a bitter struggle between the parties. The dispute had ostensibly centred on the release of the political prisoners. While the PB and the FA insisted upon a blanket amnesty, the PC favoured a review of cases by the civilian courts, as some of the prisoners had been involved in terrorist activities. In reality, at stake was the role each party had played in the civil–military transitional negotiations at the Naval Club talks in August 1984, at which a calendar for the transition had been agreed to. Only the PC, the FA, and a small party, the Civic Union (UC), had participated in these talks. Unlike the FA, which had accepted the invitation to negotiate despite the continued proscription of its leader, Líber Seregni, the PN had refused to participate unless its leader, Ferreira Aldunate, then proscribed and in exile, was allowed to represent it at the talks. Given suspicions regarding a possible ‘secret’ agreement favouring impunity, which emerged in the wake of the so-called Naval Club Pact, the FA wanted to show the public that participation in the talks did not mean they were not the ‘true representatives’ of the victims of repression and political prisoners. The PN, on the other hand, claimed that moral status for itself alone; unlike the inconsistent FA, it said, it had not participated in any dubious dealings with the military and its Colorado allies. The PC had no anxieties about claiming any special moral status, but it was angered by what it interpreted as an attempt by the opposition to pre-empt the president's first governmental gesture of pacification. These events, rather than contributing to inter-party unity and cordial relations between the Colorado executive and the opposition-dominated legislature, exacerbated underlying tensions and prepared the ground for future confrontation.

The provisions of the LPN were carried out throughout 1985. On 1 March there had been 338 prisoners in gaol, nine of them military officers that the junta had imprisoned for their disloyalty to the regime; by 15 March all of them had been freed. In April, the CNR was set up to facilitate the return of exiles. It offered medical insurance, housing and financed work projects. Towards the end of the year, in November, the government also passed the Law for the Reintegration of the Exonerated, which permitted the rehabilitation of 10,500 former state employees, and extended retirement benefits to another 6,000.

With the LPN, the government felt it had done its duty with regard to the past. For the HROs and the victims of repression, however, the struggle had only just begun. As early as April 1985, the first cases against military officers had been taken to the courts. The Supreme Military Tribunal immediately stepped in and claimed jurisdiction. The government supported its claim, quickly banishing any remaining doubts as to its position on prosecutions. The judiciary did not take kindly to what it saw as executive encroachment upon its jurisdiction. In June 1986 the Supreme Court ruled in favour of the civil judiciary. By that time the courts were already investigating forty cases of violations involving 180 military and police officers. Sanguinetti responded to this show of independence by openly criticizing the decision of the Supreme Court, but he was unable to put a stop to the judicial process. By December 1986, 734 cases of human rights violations were under investigation and the military had begun to react to investigations, rattling their sabres alarmingly loudly. It was feared that commander-in-chief of the army and Defence Minister General Medina, who had allegedly promised the ranks that he would prevent all prosecutions, would lose his grip over the military. He informed the President that he had decided to keep court summonses issued to a number of his men in his personal safe, thus indicating that a political solution would have to be found in order to avoid military institutional insubordination against the rule of law.

It became clear that the courts could not be prevented from acting if legislation were not passed to prevent further investigations. Between October 1985 and December 1986, three bills were presented in Congress to limit or prevent prosecutions. All failed to pass, given the ambiguity of the PN and the FA, neither of which wished to pay the political price for advocating limits on the pursuit of justice, and the commitment of the majority of the PC to pass a wide-ranging amnesty. Sanguinetti then made a concerted effort to gain the support of one opposition party in Congress, so as to ensure the passage of an amnesty. This was no easy task. Calling for the co-operation of the FA was out of the question, given that its more left-wing radical sectors would not accept any agreement associating them with impunity. Yet persuading the PN was also difficult: why should Ferreira agree to pay the political price of supporting closure when he had not even been present at the Naval Club negotiations? In the end, however, it was precisely his exclusion from the transitional pact that allowed Ferreira to come to an agreement with the PC, in a secret meeting between the President, Medina, and the PN leader. Two days before thirteen officers were due to appear in court (their summonses secretly hidden in Medina's safe), and in the midst of intense interparty recriminations, the PN presented in Congress the so-called Law Derogating the Punitive Capacity of the State (Ley de Caducidad de la Pretension Punitiva del Estado). It stated that, as a result of the *logic of events stemming from the Club Naval Pact* (a pact the PN had not participated in and therefore could not be held responsible for), the state relinquished its capacity to punish human rights violators. On 21 December 1986, the same month that the Argentine Congress finally passed the Full Stop Law, the Caducidad law was approved in the Senate, with the opposition of the FA and minority sectors of the PC and PN.

What explains the Uruguayan failure to pursue officially promoted truth and justice policies? Although the Naval Club Pact had not included explicit assurances of impunity, such an outcome was allegedly arranged between Medina and Sanguinetti. The President's party was the one closest to the military, and its electoral victory did not augur well for a policy that would alienate the armed forces. Nor was the close personal relationship between Sanguinetti and Medina, the key military figure at the Naval Club talks, promising in this regard. Indeed, as tensions within the military mounted over judicial proceedings, Sanguinetti fully supported the military, arguing that Medina would be unable to control the rank and file without an amnesty. Thus, unlike Alfonsín, Sanguinetti evinced a decided preference for burying the past and ensuring accommodation with the military. Interparty divisions did not help either. Although all the parties had expressed support for truth and justice during and immediately after the elections, in the event they were unwilling or unable to take the necessary steps to ensure such an outcome. Sectors within both opposition parties were unwilling to pay the price for laws limiting trials, and, as the PC insisted upon a blanket amnesty, it became impossible to achieve a compromise solution. What is more, the greatest champions of truth and justice, the HROs, had never developed into a strong movement, and after 1985 they became politically isolated and weak, lacking strong links with the parties most committed to truth and justice, the FA and the PN. Finally, as in Brazil, the transition had been negotiated between a still strong military and a cautious civilian opposition. The negotiations had culminated in a pact, and although it did not give the military the guarantees they had initially sought from civilians, it also ensured that there would be no radical rupture with the past. Thus, the military was able to retain a strong capacity to the pressure civilian elite well after the transition.

The Caducidad law did not mark the final episode of Uruguay's struggle for truth and justice. The passage of the law had almost culminated in a gunfight in Congress. This high level of frustration and animosity testified to the failure of the political class to find a satisfactory way to deal with the past, and led to initiatives to deal with the past 'from below'. In March 1986, the Peace and Justice Service (SERPAJ) began to prepare the Uruguayan *Nunca Más* report. It aimed to complement or complete the work of two congressional commissions of 1985 that had investigated disappearances, and another the abduction and disappearance in Argentina of two parliamentarians, respectively. Initially intended to provide evidence for court proceedings, the results of the investigations had not been conclusive, nor had they been officially announced and backed by the government. SERPAJ's initiative also aimed to counteract the dead-end 'investigation' by a military magistrate, which was handed in to the president and had exonerated the military from even any *links* with violations. With the support of various international Church-related and other domestic organizations, SERPAJ gathered data on repression through a random survey of 311 political prisoners. The report took three years to complete and was released on 9 March 1989. It became a national best seller, but its release was overshadowed by the second civil society initiative to deal with the past: a referendum campaign organized to hold a plebiscite to overturn the law, by collecting 25 per cent of registered voter signatures. The campaign was launched in January 1987 by the relatives of the disappeared, the FA, and dissident sectors of the PC and PN, among others. Despite intense pressure from the government and the military as well as conflicts with the PC-dominated Electoral Court, the campaign was a success. However, on 16 April 1989 the Caducidad law was ratified by a narrow majority of 53 per cent of the vote. In Montevideo, the result had been 53 per cent in favour of derogation, but nationwide the result confirmed that Uruguayans, in a climate of threats by military officers and the president, had been persuaded that pursuing justice was tantamount to placing the transition process at stake.[9]

Truth and 'reconciliation' in Chile, 1990–1994

By the time Chile underwent its transition process, it had the benefit of hindsight of the Argentine, Brazilian, and Uruguayan experiences. In 1990 the opposition coalition of Socialist and Christian Democrats, the alliance of parties for democracy (CPPD), won the elections, and President Patricio Aylwin created the multi-partisan Truth and Reconciliation Commission (CNVR) on 24 April.

The Commission worked for nine months, from 9 May 1990 to 9 February 1991, and investigated violations resulting in death or disappearance over 1973–1990, of which it recorded over 3,000, and made various recommendations. The report became an immediate best seller, following in the footsteps of its *Nunca Más* predecessors, and was published as book and serialized by a national newspaper. As in Argentina, it was adopted as the official truth and launched nationwide by a tearful president, who apologized to the victims on behalf of the state. Although the political right and the military did not apologize for the crimes, as a result of the report, for the first time since 1973, they were unable to deny that repression had taken place.

In January 1992, in compliance with recommendations of the report, the government passed a Reparations Law to benefit about 7,000 individuals. In February 1992 it also created the National Reparation and Reconciliation Corporation (CNRR), which legally established the 'inalienable rights' of the relatives to find the disappeared. In addition, it was responsible for drawing up a list of all those to be compensated and administering the process, as well as clarifying the many pending cases the CNVR had not been able to address. Reparations included a monthly 'salary' of US$380 for each family affected by disappearances or deaths resulting from

[9] For a fuller account of the Uruguayan case, see Barahona de Brito (1997).

human rights crimes, and various health and education benefits, as well as exemption from military service for relatives and victims. By September 1992 nearly 80 per cent of eligible families were receiving benefits, and by June 1999 US$95 million had been paid out to the families and direct victims in pensions and education as well as health benefits.[10] In addition, by 31 December 1995 seventy youths had benefited from exemption from military service provision. Furthermore, the CNRR took on another 1,200 cases, most inherited from the CNVR, that remained unresolved, bringing the total number of denunciations to 4,750. Finally, an Office for Return was set up in August 1993 to assist returning exiles, and a Law of the Exonerated was passed extending provisional benefits to 58,000 public-sector employees discharged between 1973 and 1990.

Wider institutional reforms and the search for justice did not meet with such success, however. In March 1990 the so-called Cumplido laws were sent to Congress. They proposed the reform of the Arms Control Law, the State Security Law, the Code of Military Justice, and the Penal Code, and thus the reduction of strong 'authoritarian enclaves' within the legal system. The bills also dealt with the plight of political prisoners through a series of transitory provisions to ensure a review of their cases, retrial, and/or release. The reform measures essentially failed,[11] and the release of the prisoners took almost five years because of right-wing opposition within the legislature.[12] Similarly, the reform of the Organic Law of the armed forces of 27 February 1990 remained untouched and constitutional reform was essentially blocked.

Justice was also fraught with obstacles. In contrast with Alfonsín, Aylwin did not announce an official prosecution policy. The CPPD had been unable to derogate the Amnesty Law, passed by the regime in 1978, covering all security force crimes between 1973 and 1978, even though this had been part of the CPPD electoral platform in 1989. Instead, the President called for justice, 'as far as is possible'. According to what became known as the Aylwin

[10] This figure is very low when compared with the US$900 million paid out to victims by the Argentine state.

[11] At the time of writing, military tribunals retain jurisdiction over crimes committed by member of the armed forces on active duty. Civilian judges still do not have authority to investigate military premises, three of the five members of the military appeals courts are still on active service, and the army general auditor, a ranking general, still sits on the Supreme Court.

[12] On 15 March 1994 six of the last nine prisoners of the dictatorship had their sentences commuted to exile, and in 1995 the three remaining prisoners still awaiting sentencing had their cases reviewed and were released.

Doctrine, he argued that, although the Amnesty Law precluded prosecution of the guilty, it should not prevent an investigation of the facts in order that families might find their dead. However, on 24 August 1990, the Supreme Court unanimously upheld the constitutionality of the Amnesty Law, and between 1990 and 1993 it mostly disregarded the Aylwin Doctrine, sending the great majority of cases presented by relatives to the military courts, where they were closed with a 'preventive' application of the Amnesty Law.

The government faced severe constraints of a constitutional, institutional, and political nature, which explain these failings. Of all the transitions, Chile's was arguably the most restricted, and the country in which the military retained the highest degree of power and legitimacy. Unlike the Uruguayan regime, which had lost a plebiscite for constitutional reform in 1980, the Chilean regime had succeeded in institutionalizing itself through a new constitution, radically transforming the juridical and ideological foundations of the political system. The 1980 Constitution acted like a wall that protected the military, and ensured a step-by-step passage to a 'protected democracy' through various transitional provisions.

After the defeat of General Pinochet in a plebiscite on 5 October 1988, when a narrow majority of 54.71 per cent voted against his staying in power for another eight years, various constitutional reforms were negotiated between the regime and the right-wing and opposition parties; these were submitted to plebiscite and approved. None the less, many restrictive measures were opted by the regime before it left power, and between the electoral campaign of December 1989 and the change of government in March 1990, more 'tie-up' laws (*leyes de amarre*) were passed, further restricting the nascent democracy. Laws were passed that granted security of tenure to civil servants, ensuring that a sweeping change of personnel would not occur. Nine appointed senatorial positions had been created and regime supporters nominated. The Constitutional Tribunal had been 'stacked' to place obstacles in the way of reform. In January 1990, the Organic Constitutional Law of Congress had been passed, forbidding Congress from investigating the old regime and bringing constitutional charges against acts of corruption and treason committed prior to March 1990.

Military autonomy and the 'Pinochet factor'—the popularity of the General, his continued position as commander-in-chief of the armed forces—represented real as well as psychological obstacles to the pursuit of truth and justice. The CPPD had been unable to curtail military institutional autonomy significantly or to force Pinochet to resign. The General had restructured the high command, placing 'unconditionals' in top positions. He had rejected a proposed new law for the armed forces put forward by the coalition in 1989 and presented another law, which came into force on 27 February 1999. The law gave the military full control over its own education, health, salaries, pensions, retirements, and promotions. It allowed the President and Defence Ministry to choose only from a small number nominated by the high command.

In addition, the military remained voting members of the Security Council (COSENA). Each branch of the forces was allowed to designate one of the non-elected senators. Further, the military was automatically entitled to 10 per cent of gross sales of revenue from the state copper company, which meant that its budget was not determined by civilians. Just before the CPPD took power, the intelligence police, the CNI, had been dissolved with no supervision and an estimated 19,000 people had been incorporated into the army intelligence unit. The regime had also altered the electoral law, ensuring the overrepresentation of the right in the legislature through a biased binominal voting system. As a result, the parties of the right, the National Renovation (RN) and the Independent Democratic Union (UDI), had secured 49 of 120 seats in Congress and 16 of the 38 elected seats in the Senate, boosted by the presence of the non-elected senators. As human rights policies required constitutional or other legal reforms, and as the right was unwilling to allow any such changes, many initiatives, such as the derogation of the Amnesty Law, were blocked from the outset.

Furthermore, the judiciary, the Supreme Court in particular, was resistant to both truth and justice. The latter had co-operated extensively with the regime, helping to legitimate it, and feared the criticism directed towards it by the new government. The authoritarian tendencies of the Court were reinforced by the so-called Rosende Law of June 1989, which increased the number of justices favourable to the outgoing regime. Finally, continued terrorist action after 1990 did not favour those seeking to punish human rights violations, as it gave much mileage to military legitimization of anti-subversive activities. The launching of the CNVR report, for example, was most unfortunately obscured and counteracted by the assassination of Jaime Guzmán, the key ideologue of the right and a former adviser to Pinochet, by a terrorist group, the Manuel Rodríguez Popular Front (FPMR).

What there was of success had been possible only because of the unity of the opposition, achieved through successive alliances since the mid-1980s, which had culminated in the formation of the

CPPD. Also important was the elaboration of a high profile and well-defined human rights agenda from 1988 onwards, which contrasts with Argentina and Uruguay. Further, like Alfonsín, Aylwin was committed to an official policy to deal with the past, and announced in March 1990 that dealing with the past and national reconciliation would be key goals of his administration. Unlike in Brazil or Uruguay, moreover, the issue of accountability for past human rights violations was prominent during the transitional elections. All this was largely due to the fact that Chile developed one of the strongest, most durable, and largest human rights movements in Latin America. It had deep links to the CPPD parties, legal associations, think tanks, the Catholic Church, and international NGOs. The long organic relationship between party and human rights activism and the concomitant solidarity between the coalition and the movement was crucial for ensuring that the government did not drop the issue. This relationship stands in marked contrast with that established in the other countries examined.[13] The same is true of the presence of the Socialists within the governing coalition. As one of the main groups of victims of repression, they were fully committed to dealing with the past.

On 28 May 1993 a threatening civil–military confrontation took place. Soldiers of the Army's Special Forces, the Black Berets, surrounded the government palace. The event was widely interpreted as a warning to the government not to pursue human rights trials or to further an investigation of alleged corruption involving Pinochet's son and an army-linked company. The government responded to the pressures by attempting to pass legislation to limit judicial proceedings fear of military discontent. The so-called Aylwin Law failed because of opposition from the Socialists and a general outcry by HROs, but the so-called *Boinazo* effectively limited the already grudging willingness of the courts and the Supreme Court to comply with the Aylwin doctrine. In its wake, the military courts closed fourteen cases for which the Court upheld the application of the Amnesty Law. Although up to 200 cases had been taken to court by June 1993, when Aylwin left power, only two had resulted in convictions.[14]

Despite this setback, unlike the case of Argentina and Uruguay, no legislative measures had been passed to put a stop to judicial proceedings. At the same time, the stage was set for a shift in the

[13] For human rights movement, see Ahumada *et al.* (1989) and Lowden (1996).

[14] Seven officers were sentenced and gaoled. See *Oxford Analytica Daily Brief*, 19 December 1995, and Correa Sutil (1997: 154).

contribution that law would make to the human rights issue. Although the Amnesty Law did not permit the prosecution of crimes committed before 1978, abuses committed after that date were not protected legally. In addition, it was only the pro-regime loyalties of the justices then sitting in the Supreme Court that stood in the way of more progressive interpretations of the Amnesty Law. The longevity of these justices was not indefinite; eventually the CPPD government could appoint new justices, increasing the probabilities for a Court more friendly to the cause of the victims. In addition, as the military had done nothing to reveal the whereabouts of the disappeared, a future application of the Aylwin Doctrine could re-ignite old cases. Thus, the issue was set to reappear on the political agenda under the Frei government after March 1994.[15]

The Ongoing Search for Truth and Justice: National and International Courts and Citizens

As a result of the constraints posed by what were essentially negotiated transitions, the nature of decisions adopted by the executives in each case, as well as the specificity of the political battles that evolved over truth, and in particular over justice, were limited.[16] Thus, the relatives of the victims of repression have continued to seek avenues to vindicate their claims. They have found allies in the judiciary and among political parties, local and provincial authorities, and state institutions, as well as in non-governmental organizations of all kinds. They have also found foreign allies, and have taken legal action beyond national boundaries, action favoured by the legal international and regional human rights commitments adopted by each country since the transition to democracy. The following section examines how the pursuit of truth and justice has fared in each country since the transitional period.

From pardons to punishment in Argentina, 1990–2000

When Menem was elected president on 14 May 1989, he was determined to bury the past. Soon after taking power, he presented the military with a clear-cut trade-off: they would be pardoned

[15] For a fuller account, see Barahona de Brito (1997).

[16] For other accounts of transitional truth and justice, see the Bibliographical Survey at end of book.

for their crimes and for the rebellions of the past, but would not to escape economic austerity or punishment for further revolts against civilian authority. Despite massive protest, Menem issued pardons by decree law in October 1989 and January 1991, which eventually freed all military officers who had been gaoled for human rights violations and involvement in rebellions, the junta leaders, and all former guerrillas.[17] He also quelled the final *carapintada* rebellion of 3 December 1990 and strengthened the general staff of the army, restoring order and hierarchy. The struggle for justice, however, did not stop, for a number of reasons.

First, the powerful human rights movement has remained active, and widespread domestic and international 'name recognition' and solidarity have strengthened it. Sectors within the legislature and the judiciary, as well as journalists, academics, and other professional associations, have co-operated with its continued attempts to seek compensation, find the dead, and bring violators to court. The courts have become key institutional players in the continued search for truth and justice, with some federal judges having adopted the cause of the relatives and pursued cases of past violations with great zeal. As in Chile, the courts were not active in defending rights under the dictatorship, but a purge of the Supreme Court and a change in military jurisdiction, coupled with a climate favouring action against former repressors, galvanized the judicial class into action.

Second, legal 'loopholes' have aided the cause of the relatives. The Due Obedience Law excluded from its benefits those who had assisted or planned the abduction of the children of the disappeared, of which there are an estimated 400. Finding these children, therefore, has been a key area of struggle, led by the Grandmothers of the Plaza de Mayo (MPM). As of October 1998, sixty-one children had been found and returned to their families either spontaneously or after judicial proceedings. In a landmark case of 1998, retired generals Videla, Massera, Nicolaides, and Bignone, along with five lower ranking officers, were charged and gaoled for 194 counts of illegal abduction and adoption of children in seven clandestine centres. These were the first imprisonments since the Alfonsín period, and they marked the reversal of the effects of the presidential pardons of the early 1990s. By June 1999 thirty-two other officers were under investigation for similar crimes, and in

[17] At the time of writing only one carapintada leader, Colonel Seineldín, a former guerrilla leader, plus Gorriarrán Merlo and MTP members who attacked La Tablada, were still awaiting pardon.

January 2000 another nine retired navy officers were arrested for the kidnapping of children.

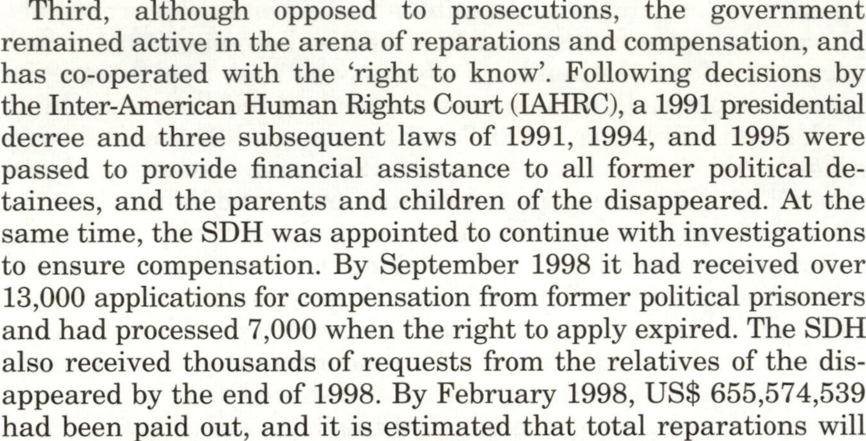

Third, although opposed to prosecutions, the government remained active in the arena of reparations and compensation, and has co-operated with the 'right to know'. Following decisions by the Inter-American Human Rights Court (IAHRC), a 1991 presidential decree and three subsequent laws of 1991, 1994, and 1995 were passed to provide financial assistance to all former political detainees, and the parents and children of the disappeared. At the same time, the SDH was appointed to continue with investigations to ensure compensation. By September 1998 it had received over 13,000 applications for compensation from former political prisoners and had processed 7,000 when the right to apply expired. The SDH also received thousands of requests from the relatives of the disappeared by the end of 1998. By February 1998, US$ 655,574,539 had been paid out, and it is estimated that total reparations will amount to US$750 million by 2000.

The government has also backed the 'right to know', in compliance with an IAHRC 1992 ruling against the pardons. It stated that relatives had a 'right to know' the whereabouts of the disappeared. In 1996 it called on Argentina to accede to investigate their fate and establish a truth commission to that end. Under pressure also from the Grandmothers, in 1992 the government created the National Commission for the Right to Identity, which works with the National Genetic Databank and was crucial in locating some of the missing children. The SDH is also creating a digital bank on the disappeared in an ongoing project, the Programme of Truth and Memory.

Government action has given impetus to action by HROs and other civil society or institutional actors. For example, provincial authorities and the Argentine Forensic Anthropology Team (EAAF) have searched for the disappeared; police, judicial, civil register, and autopsy files, as well as death and burial certificates, have been opened; and federal courts have initiated investigations into the whereabouts of the disappeared. In March 1998, in a landmark decision, an agreement was reached between the UCR and the PJ to derogate both the Full Stop and Due Obedience laws, but excluding any retroactive application. Negotiations were underway at the time of writing to establish a second truth commission, to follow up the work of the CONADEP and systematize all existing information. Meanwhile, in October 1998 the Supreme Court upheld the right of a citizen to have access to government files in order to determine the whereabouts of a relative, confirming

IACHR recommendations in national jurisprudence. Similar decisions have been adopted by federal appeal courts. In May 1999 the Buenos Aires Appeal Court forbade the destruction of archives of the military regime, to permit identification and prosecution in the hands of the CSFA.

International and regional obligations, as well as international diplomatic and regional legal pressures and transnational prosecution efforts, have given impetus to the work of domestic HROs and have weakened the initially adversarial position of the government. The ratification of regional and international human rights instruments does not allow the executive simply to dismiss challenges to the legitimacy of political decisions favouring impunity (Cassell, 1997). Alongside official pressure from the Inter-American Human Rights system, Argentine repressors have come under attack from transnational ad hoc coalitions of victims and relatives.[18] These groups have made use of the national adoption of human rights instruments that counter decisions favouring impunity. Proceedings against or investigations about Argentine repressors have been undertaken in France, Italy, Germany, Honduras, Spain, Sweden, and the USA. Some former military officers have been tried and sentenced *in absentia* and others have international arrest warrants attached to their names. The support of international actors and institutions has been crucial in engendering continued hope to domestic HROs. It has helped to persuade them to continue to dedicate important political and institutional resources to the issue.

Developments within the military and the concomitant change of attitude of the executive have also helped to promote the continued pursuit of justice and truth. There has been a steady stream of confessions, which has constituted a 'breaking of ranks' and produced mutual accusations and mud-slinging among repressors. The most stunning confession was made in 1995, when Navy Captain Scilingo admitted that 1,500–2,000 drugged prisoners had been thrown to their deaths out of planes into the Mar de Plata. This weakened the military, a major source of strength for which is unity and the 'pact of silence'. It also led the commander-in-chief of the army, General Balza, to issue a statement on 24 April that shook the country and military establishments throughout the

[18] Although a part of the permanent networks described by Keck and Sikkink (1998), these coalitions are temporary, formed solely for the purpose of undertaking prosecution efforts. They are ad hoc in so far as they come together as a result of one-off instances of convergence of interest.

Southern Cone. He stated that the Dirty War could not be justified, and that it was 'a crime to violate the national constitution . . . give an immoral order . . . execute an immoral order [and] employ unjust, immoral means to accomplish even a legitimate objective'. This is the first unambiguous institutional apology and rejection of Dirty War methods issued by a Latin American military. Apologizing for and rejecting the methods of the Dirty War has made it difficult for the military to defend past repressors. When Videla was arrested, for example, Balza stated that the general and others like him were no longer active duty officers and therefore were of no concern to the institution (*Pagina 12*, 11 and 19 June 1998).

All this has paved the way for greater executive flexibility regarding the issue. Menem initially defended the military's role in the war against subversion more energetically than the military itself (McSherry, 1997a), and associated protest in the present with past subversion (Feitlowitz, 1998: 172). He agreed to the promotion of officers who are known repressors and threatened to take steps to counteract judicial decisions in favour of punishment or compensation. This position changed over time. After Videla's arrest, for example, Menem stated that he would not issue more pardons and that the problem was a strictly legal one. Although he adamantly opposed the intervention of foreign courts, he continued to adopt this line regarding domestic cases and subsequent arrests, in marked contrast with past cases. The new government of Fernando de la Rua, elected on 20 October 1999, promises to bring a continuation of official compliance with independent court action at home and resistance to transnational prosecution efforts.

Thus, as the UCR returned to power in alliance with the dissident Peronist left, the Socialists, and the Christian Democrats within FREPASO, Argentina had come full circle since the start of the transition process. It would appear that striving for truth and justice is no longer an either–or matter, a contest between justice and stability. Apparently the two can co-exist.

Compromising with compensation in Brazil, 1995–1999

The year of Scilingo's confession was also the year in which the Brazilian executive finally adopted the cause of the relatives of the disappeared. Until Cardoso was elected, the federal executive essentially ignored the relatives. The authorities of various states aided them, however, and the identification of bodies and the search for truth was the main focus of the activities of HROs and relatives' groups. In 1990, after the discovery of the remains of 1,049 bodies buried secretly in a mass grave at a cemetery in São Paulo, the then mayor of that city, Luiza Erundina of the Workers' Party (PT), created a special commission to investigate the remains. Later, a parliamentary commission of inquiry in the municipality of São Paulo and a Commission for the Search of the Political Disappeared in the state legislature (1990–4) were established. State authorities in Rio de Janeiro and Pernambuco also initiated investigations in local cemeteries with TNM groups, legal medicine institutions, anthropologists, the police and EAFF (http://www.eaaf.org.ar/brazil_eng.htm).

One of the first victories of the relatives at the national level was obtaining a presidential order from President Collor de Mello (1990–2) to open police archives. Families had for some time been calling for access to the archives in order to facilitate their search, and their cause was aided by widespread debate about the opening up of police archives in Eastern Europe. In 1990–2 the governors of the states of Paraná and Pernambuco and the federal police of the states of São Paulo and Rio de Janeiro opened police archives. The relatives had also begun to work in 1985, sometimes successfully, to ensure that known repressors would be removed from their posts or would not be promoted; they sent researched biographies of such persons to the press and to municipal, state, and federal authorities.

A new phase in the search for truth was initiated in 1994. In that year, TNM in Rio, Pernambuco, and Minas Gerais and the CFMDP of São Paulo presented presidential electoral candidates with a manifesto calling for the truth regarding the fate of the disappeared, which Cardoso signed. Compared with Collor de Mello and his successor Franco (1992–5), Cardoso showed greater sensitivity regarding the issue, in part because of his background as a liberal left-wing intellectual exiled during the dictatorship. On 4 December 1995 Cardoso passed Law 9140/95, which finally recognized the death of 136 political militants and obliged the government to pay indemnities of between US$100,000 and US$150,000 to each of the families. Between December 1995 and May 1998 compensation was given to survivors in 148 of the 234 cases. In 1998–9 the Commission continued to evaluate requests for, and authorize payment of, indemnities. Following the lead of the national government, in November 1997 the state of Rio Grande do Sul enacted a law providing compensation for persons tortured in the state during the military regime. In 1998 the state of Santa Catarina created a panel to award people tortured for political reasons over 1961–79 compensation of between US$4,400 and US$6,500 (Mierelles Neto, 1996). The decree did not acknowledge the death of fifteen Brazilians in Argentina and Chile or of the 207 persons officially declared dead under the regime. However, it provided for the creation of a Special Commission on Deaths and Disappearances to examine these and other pending cases.

Thus, in contrast with the other three cases, the official policy to deal with past repression has only just begun. Although the measures adopted to deal with the past have been extremely important for the people involved, these initiatives have hardly caused a ripple in the political arena or within civil society at large. Society has remained 'apathetic' about the topic, and 'the struggle of the relatives has been a solitary one' (Hamber, 1997b). Apart from 1995, the year of greatest coverage of this issue since the 1985 publication of *Nunca Mais*, the press has hardly reported on the it. Unlike in Chile, investigative journalism on the matter has also been scarce (Tavares de Almeida e Silva, n.d). This is so for a number of reasons.

First, current human rights violations are so widespread that the import of the past pales when compared with the challenge of dealing with contemporaneous impunity, arguably 'the first national institution' (Nogueira da Silva, 1988: 174). Second, the groups pursuing truth have not received widespread support, and have little power to pressure the government. HROs have largely not adopted an adversarial stance *vis-à-vis* the government. Indeed, in Brazil there has been increasing co-operation between NGOs in general and government in the formulation of human rights, and social and environmental policies since the Rio Summit of 1992. Thus, the tendency has been for the executive to establish direct links with such organizations, allowing them to participate in the policy process. At the same time, Brazilian repressors have not been the objects of transnational prosecution efforts, and, learning from its neighbours, Brazil has been careful to ratify regional human rights instruments with reservations, precisely to exclude the possibility of their retroactive application, as with the 1998 acceptance of IAHRC jurisdiction. What is more, although relatives have complained that Cardoso has tried to 'buy them off' with compensation, at no time has the essential elite settlement that produced an amnesty been questioned (Hamber, 1997b: 4–16). The struggle of the relatives has centred on a search for the truth rather than punishment, and on state recognition of responsibility and compensation for the deaths of the detained–disappeared. It would appear that all actors have accepted the boundaries of the acceptable to the military: compensation was, in the words of Secretary General of the Ministry of Justice Gregori, 'the least that the families can expect and the most that the military accept'. Thus, Brazilian executive commitment finally allowed the formulation of a policy that found the ground between one and the other.

In 1999 the first signs of justice emerged. In March, following a thirteen-year campaign by TMN and various medical associations, disciplinary proceedings were initiated against twenty-six physicians who worked in military prisons and were involved in torture. This has been described as the largest effort to punish doctors since the campaign to criminalize Nazi concentration camp doctors (Larry Rohter, *New York Times*, 11 March 1999). In addition, the Riocentro case of April 1981, when two bombs exploded in a shopping centre full of left-wing concert goers, killing one officer and wounding another, has been reopened. It may yet be that the amnesty will be challenged. However, in contrast with Argentina, the military has remained united and unrepentant. The response of one general to the Riocentro case was to declare that he knew who was guilty but he would never tell a court of law as the action was justified and military secrets are inviolable.

In May 2000, the Human Rights Commission of the Congress launched the first official inquiry into repression and disappearances, and into the murder of former president João Goulart, undertaken in the context of Operation Condor, the co-ordinated repression undertaken by the military regimes of the Southern Cone across borders in the region and beyond. The Ministry of Defense, now headed by a civilian, ordered the military to turn over all documentation on extra-territorial activities undertaken during the dictatorship (CNN, 13 May 2000; 17 May 2000). That same month, the government also announced that it would be compensating the relatives of three Argentine citizens who disappeared in Brazil in 1980 with US$70,270 each, following the Brazilian high court's decision to approve an Argentine request to review classified documents on the three who were disappeared. Despite these advances, it remains to be seen whether any prosecutions will take place. This would require an overturning of the blanket amnesty and firm executive commitment to confront any military resistance to justice. To date this has not been on the cards, but it cannot be ruled out entirely, given the increasing legitimacy of the claims of the relatives and the commitment of the Cardoso government to improve the country's human rights image and record.

The failed search for truth in Uruguay, 1995–1999

In Uruguay the issue of backward-looking accountability became very muted after the 1989 plebiscite, hardly rearing its head under the PN presidency of LaCalle (1990–5). None the less, continued attempts by relatives to locate the bodies of the disappeared were given renewed impetus in 1995, following the Scilingo confession and the institutional apology issued by Balza. Their demands have centred on a 'loophole' in the Caducidad law that, while precluding trials, states that the government is obliged to promote the investigation into the whereabouts of the disappeared, which an updated list now brings to a total of 122. Despite this opening, the search for truth has not been successful, for a number of reasons.

First, the military are resistant to any digging up of the past. In contrast with Argentina, retired and active duty generals are of the same mind and the institution has remained united. The military has continued to act as a political force, publicly imposing limits on any proposed action of search that they perceive to affect their interests. Further, given the very specific nature of repression in Uruguay, the bodies of the disappeared are buried in military installations, which means that, unlike in Argentina, Brazil, and Chile, exhumations cannot be undertaken without a direct confrontation with the military.

Second, in contrast with Brazilian executive indifference and, later, co-operation, in Uruguay there has been only governmental hostility to any initiative to deal with the past. In December 1997, Sanguinetti annulled a ruling by military courts against forty-one officers who had been tried, imprisoned, and expelled from the army under military rule for their political opinions, which enervated the military. For the most part, however, Sanguinetti took sides with the military in very visible ways, and this is really the only measure of redress that has been adopted by the government since the LPN.

Sanguinetti rejected the three most important initiatives proposed to date by the mothers and relatives of the disappeared (MYFUDD), the Catholic Church, and Senator Rafael Michelini, son of the disappeared former congressman, for an exhaustive and impartial investigation into the fate of their disappeared relatives and renewed efforts to locate the bodies. Sanguinetti either stated that the Caducidad law makes further investigations impossible, which is manifestly not the case, or accused those seeking the dead of being 'intolerant' and a threat to democratic values, or simply ignored the proposals, even though all of them have garnered significant popular support (*Brecha* 628, 12 December 1997). So intransigent was the position of the government that it even rejected the possibility of monetary compensation, contesting a judicial decision of October 1998, ordering the government to pay US$1.3 million to the families of twelve torture victims. It also opposed a decision of November 1998, calling on the government to pay the daughter of a man tortured and killed by the military US$100,000 in damages.

It has not helped that the relatives and HROs have not received unified support from the opposition parties. Within Congress, the groups exerting most pressure on the government were New Space (NE), the FA, and the minority groups of the PN and PC. However, these opposition groups have not been able to work in a united and coherent matter, and the traditional parties have merely 'used' the issue in political battle with one another (*Brecha*, 592, 4 April 1997; 18 April 1997; Gatto, 1997). As in Brazil, HROs leading the struggle for truth lack a critical mass of allies in Congress to pursue a coherent and consistent strategy and thus have been unable to overcome military and executive hostility. Further, unlike in Argentina, the only existing 'loophole' has not meant an opening of avenues for judicial action, so that those seeking redress are unable bypass the executive and political class and appeal directly to the courts. The only judicial decision since 1989 calling for the investigation into the disappeared was revoked by the Appeals Court, sent case to the executive, in accordance with Article 3 of the Caducidad Law, and closed. Also in contrast with Argentina, no permanent institutions were created during the transitional period to address the basic needs of the relatives, which might have brought about policy change as a result of an autonomous agenda and action.

Finally, like the Argentine government, the administration in Uruguay has come under diplomatic pressure from various European countries and international organizations. Uruguayan HROs appealed to the IACHR against the Amnesty Law, and both the IACHR (1992 and 1993) and the UN Commission for Human Rights ruled that the government should derogate the Amnesty Law and promote investigations. However, unlike in Argentina, state authorities have ignored both rulings, and, moreover, repressors have escaped transnational prosecution efforts. To conclude, it should not be forgotten that the decision to give up the search for justice was accepted through a democratic vote (the plebiscite), so that its legitimacy cannot be questioned in the same way that a presidential pardon might. Popular support for the truth is high. In 1997 a reported 54 per cent of people polled were in favour of locating the bodies and investigating how they died. Only 14 per cent felt that the Caducidad law had closed the matter, and 10 per cent that further investigations would be dangerous.[19] This support has not been enough to overcome the stalemate that has been in place since the passage of the Amnesty Law. The FA candidate for the presidential elections, Tabaré Vasquez, announced in 1999 that he would pursue a truth policy if elected. However, on 25 November 1999 Jorge Batlle, the conservative Colorado candidate, defeated the left-wing candidate in a second electoral round. It remains to be seen if Batlle is willing to reverse previous Colorado policy on past violations, and break the stalemate. The Uruguayan case stands in contrast with the case of Chile, where various factors and a singular event—the arrest of General Pinochet in London in 1998—served the cause of continued truth and justice in most unexpected ways.[20]

The Frei administration: Chile's unravelling reconciliation, 1994–1999[21]

The pursuit of justice and truth continued in Chile after the election, on 11 December 1993, of President Eduardo Frei who carried 58 per cent of the vote. As he took office in March 1994, the second-time-victorious CPPD faced the same constraints that it had experienced under Aylwin's rule. It retained seventy seats in the Chamber while the right-wing coalition, the Union for Progress (UPP), gained fifty. In the Senate, it held twenty against the right's eighteen seats as a result of the existence of the appointed senators. However, although this president lacked the moral and political commitment to truth that Aylwin had demonstrated, law and *fortuna* opened the door to a wider truth and justice.

In March 1994, fifteen members of the intelligence unit of the Carabineros police, the DICOMCAR, were convicted for the 1985 murder of three militants of the Communist Party (PCCh). As a major human rights organization reported at the time, the verdict 'breached a wall of impunity which held intact for more than 20 years', as a court at last had issued a sentence 'commensurate

[19] Poll carried out by Factum in urban and rural areas, published in *Brecha* 596, 2 May 1997.

[20] The information on Uruguay is from SERPAJ (http://www.serpaj.org.uy/inf96/desapa.htm) and from the press.

[21] A fuller account of the Chilean case can be found in Barahona de Brito (2000b).

with the gravity of a human rights crime' (HRW, 1994a: 18). One of the men indicted was General Rodolfo Stange, director of the Carabineros at the time. President Frei called for his resignation, which led to a backlash from the military and the right. Stange refused to comply, the then minister of the interior, Germán Correa, was forced to step down, and a military court later dismissed the case. Despite this defeat, other cases continued to work their way through the courts. On 30 May 1995 the Supreme Court confirmed the sentence against Contreras and Espinoza. Notwithstanding initial fears of negative military reactions, and the fact that Contreras resisted arrest with the protection of the army for five months, both men were finally imprisoned and are now serving their sentences.

Following the Supreme Court decision on the Contreras case, again under pressure from the right and the military, the government tried to pass legislation to limit prosecutions. In May 1995 the President presented a bill to Congress to allow the courts to suspend all trials in which penal liability had either prescribed or been extinguished by previous legislation. This initiative failed, for the same reasons that had prevented Aylwin from passing any laws to put a stop to prosecutions. In September 1995 the administration presented a package of three laws, linking the human rights issue with various institutional reforms. This proposal failed as well. The right also rejected Frei's proposal that all human rights cases should remain open until the fate of the disappeared had been established. It presented an alternative bill, which proposed that special judges be appointed to resolve all remaining cases; it also empowered special judges definitively to close all cases for which no new information was forthcoming, and stipulated that all cases already in the military courts should remain there. The bill was never passed, given the opposition of the Socialists and the UDI. At this time there were an estimated 600 suits affecting 1,000 military officers in the courts.

The government had hoped to limit the scope of justice. But it had wanted to do so in order to limit conflict and not because it was opposed to justice. Indeed, while it did not actively pursue justice, it supported the search for the disappeared and the work of the courts. In November 1997, for example, President Frei vetoed the promotion of Brigadier Jaime Lepe, a close associate of Pinochet from the DINA, for his involvement in the disappearance of Carmelo Soria. In March 1998 the government announced the creation of a DNA databank to identify the disappeared. Also, the government is acting as co-plaintiff in the trial by an Argentine court of Enrique Arancibia Clavel, a former intelligence agent involved in the assassination of General Carlos Prats and his wife in Buenos Aires in 1974. It has adopted the same position in two other major post-1978 cases.

However, it was not the good will of the executive that shifted the balance in favour of justice: about two years after the government tried to limit justice, that law began to shift in favour of the human rights cause. From 1997–8 onwards, the jurisprudence of the Supreme Court began to show the first signs of cracking in favour of human rights. Even in 1995, divisions had become apparent within the Court. A reform of the Supreme Court revealed that the Court's justices were divided on amnesty cases, with a minority regularly voting against decisions not to apply the Aylwin Doctrine. A later reform of the structure of the Court and the appointment in 1998 of new justices, who took office in 1999, shifted the balance further towards human rights. In short, the Supreme Court began to change its jurisprudence, arguing in major decisions that international law had primacy over the Amnesty Law, and that a disappearance is an ongoing crime until the body is found, which means that it cannot be amnestied until resolved. These decisions have opened the door for future challenges to the legitimacy and sanctity of this legal mechanism for impunity.

There were still some constraints operating, however. On 10 October 1997, following a request by the Military Public Prosecutor, the Supreme Court recommended that the lower courts apply the Amnesty Law to over 100 cases then in the courts. And Chile's democracy seemed as tied up (*amarrada*) as always. On the positive side, on 7 March 1997 the government had managed to change the composition of the Constitutional Tribunal, making it more democratic and facilitating constitutional reform in the future. Further, the last of the commanders involved in the military regime, Navy Commander-in-Chief Jorge Martínez Busch, retired on 11 March 1998. The new commander-in-chief of the army, General Ricardo Izurieta, was widely regarded as a professional, apolitical military officer. On the negative side, although General Pinochet retired on 10 March as commander-in-chief after twenty-five years of heading the army, he took up his lifetime senate position a day later, amidst expression of support from the right, the business community, and the military. The reform of the Organic Law of the armed forces of 27 February 1990 remained on the agenda. Constitutional reform was still to be achieved. Previous attempts made to reform it on 12 January 1993 and 11 April 1996 had failed, and on 17 June 1997 the government was again unsuccessful in passing a reform bill in the Senate to eliminate the designated senators.

For many, it seemed that by the beginning of 1998 the human rights issue was no longer alive. Indeed, what some saw as an unnatural silence prevailed, with an externally or self-imposed censorship ensuring little coverage of the past. Since 1990 two anti-regime newspapers and three weekly magazines have closed. At the same time, Chilean law prevents open coverage of ongoing court cases. Thus, in contrast with Argentina, where an active left-wing press reported on every progress in chamber, in Chile silence reigns until a verdict is reached, diminishing the social impact of ongoing investigations. Censorship is still strong; many books about the past, or touching topics affecting the perceived interest of the old regime, have been censored since 1990. In accordance with the repressive State Security Law of 1958, expressions of criticism of Pinochet and others associated with his rule continued to meet with fines or gaol sentences. Since 1990, an estimated fifteen journalists and eight politicians have been charged under Article 6 (b) of that law.

It would take an unpredictable injection of *fortuna* to truly shake up the political system, shift the balance between passion and constraint, and inject the law with a new energy in favour of human rights. In May 1998 a new criminal suit was brought to the Spanish courts accusing the general and others of the death of 200 people during Operation Condor. This refers to an operation whereby the DINA co-ordinated an international repressive campaign across borders, not only in the Southern Cone but also as far afield as Embassy Row in Washington and Rome. On 3 October the French government denied Pinochet the right to enter the country. Days later, on 16 October 1998, the general was arrested in London, after the Spanish investigating Judge Garzón of the National Audience (AN), the highest court in Spain, issued an arrest warrant for him. On 5 November the AN confirmed Spain's right to judge the general unanimously, and on 10 December 1998 Pinochet was indicted for genocide, terrorism, and torture by Judge Garzón. Meanwhile, in the UK the House of Lords ruled on two occasions, on 25 November 1998 and 24 March 1999, that Pinochet could be extradited, even though the second decision limited the crimes for which he was extraditable. At the time of writing, the British government had decided that the General should not be extradited because of illness and advanced age, and should therefore be sent back home for humanitarian reasons, resulting in Pinochet's return to Chile.[22]

Despite this somewhat anti-climactic resolution by the British government, the arrest altered the human rights scenario in Chile. The courts began to show much greater willingness to try cases. Although the Amnesty Law led to the closure of court cases investigating the 170 disappearances, one-sixth of the total (HRW, 1999a), in 1998–9, five generals, including a former member of the military junta, and approximately thirty active duty and retired officers were arrested and gaoled for human rights crimes. Further, there are an estimated eighty cases pending in the courts, affecting 261 victims.

Spurred on by the work of Spanish prosecutors, in January 1998 a Court of Appeals judge accepted a criminal complaint of genocide against Pinochet by the Communist Party. This was the first time that a court in Chile accepted direct charges against the General. By the end of September 1999 there were forty-three such suits against Pinochet in Chile. Also at that time, the number of generals in gaol had risen to five, a total of twenty-five officers had been tried, dozens more had been summoned, and Supreme Court jurisprudence was clearly favouring the prosecution. At the same time, the government made efforts to pursue a new settlement with regard to the human rights issue, setting up in August 1999 a Dialogue Forum (*Mesade Diálogo*) between representatives of the military and the relatives of the disappeared. Also, for the first time—remarkable in a military institution notable for unity and hierarchic obedience—the 'pact of silence' was broken, with Contreras accusing Pinochet of commanding all acts of DINA repression, and other officers and generals making confessions in the manner of their more unruly Argentine counterparts.

In sum, after a long silence, everyone in Chile was again thinking out loud about past human rights violations and their significance for democracy. The military and the right protested energetically against Pinochet's arrest, and the government also defended the return of the general, arguing that the arrest constituted a violation of sovereignty as well as a threat to Chile's negotiated transition. Can the pursuit of truth and justice have a negative effect

[22] For a full description of this case, see Barahona de Brito (2000a) and Wilson (1999). Since then, proceedings and extradition requests have been initiated in Austria, Belgium, Canada, Denmark, France, Germany, Italy, Switzerland, Sweden, the UK, and the USA, and some have been tried *in absentia*. See Roht-Arriaza in Ch. 1 above.

on democratic consolidation, as these groups have argued? This is the question addressed in the next section of the chapter.

Democratization and Backward-Looking Accountability

Official policies to deal with past violations are not, in and of themselves, necessary to ensure democratic consolidation, as the case of Spain shows. Democratization depends upon a wider process, involving the constitution of effective citizenship through the elimination of authoritarian legacies that both precede and were consolidated by military rule. It means undertaking fundamental, forward-looking institutional reform to promote present and future accountability. This transcends the scope and effect that official policies of retroactive justice may have, even if they can contribute to that reform process. Indeed, the pursuit of backward-looking accountability may be relevant to democratization in so far as it forms a part of such reforms. In the cases examined here, however, it played little or no role in the initial process of institutional reform. During the first transitional period when reform processes were initiated, it is possible to say that wider institutional reform was resisted in so far as governments attempted to link it with backward-looking accountability. In Chile, for example, when it occurred, 'linkage' actually helped to slow down the resolution of important issues; the attempt to link the release of political prisoners with wider judicial reform made both processes more difficult. In Uruguay the issue actually delayed any attempts to carry out wider institutional reform within the military, as the government chose not to deal with reform in a period of so much tension over human rights.

The fact that none of these countries was initially able to undertake, or sustain, wide-ranging policies of accountability indicates that democracy was not consolidated at the time. It is precisely the capacity to try the powerful without provoking a collapse of political regime that strongly indicates that a democracy is strongly rooted. During the transitional period, therefore, these countries practised not the politics of a consolidated democracy, but those of, at best, democratic consolidation and, mostly, of democratic survival. And the policies necessary for survival are more often than not what consolidation requires. Pacts made during transitions, for example, allow for the establishment of democracy with relatively little conflict, but they can also limit the scope for subsequent policies for democratization. Often leaving intact authoritarian strongholds and institutionalized practises, they may limit imaginative and *de facto* capacities for action (Hagopian, 1990).

Since the initial transition period, there has been progress with reform in all four countries in terms of judiciaries, police, and military forces,[23] but none can claim complete success with democratization. Hence the frequent use of terms such as 'delegative' or 'low intensity' democracy (O'Donnell, 1992). Constitutional barriers in Chile, widespread impunity in Argentina and Brazil, and in the latter case poverty—a problem for the constitution of effective citizenship as well as the continued *de facto* if not *de jure* military veto power in Uruguay—show this. None the less, as reform measures have taken root and these democracies have become more self-confident, the scope for trials and truth seems to have widened. And in contrast with the transitional period, in this post-transitional context the struggle for truth and justice may be relevant for democratization. It may be part of a wider struggle to give citizens real power and to render institutions accountable and efficacious, thereby eliminating authoritarian enclaves and democratizing state–society relations. In the case of both Argentina and Chile, such an argument can be convincingly made.

In Argentina, it is arguable that the unwillingness of some groups to let go of the past may have generated a cycle of vengeance and retribution, perpetuating a 'zero sum game' that has always been characteristic of Argentine politics.[24] Some have challenged the legal validity of current judicial action against repressors. The fact that some judges are prosecuting repressors for an 'apology of crime', using restrictive freedom of speech legislation in much the same way that the Chilean right wing has done (only this time to get at men they can not otherwise punish), seems to indicate this.[25] Indeed, some would claim that, from a legal point of view, the new prosecutions are not legitimate, as they establish a form of double jeopardy. However, it is also possible to argue

[23] For continued tutelary role of military, see B. Loveman (1994). For military reform in Argentina, see Pion-Berlin (1997); and Norden (1997). For Brazil, see Hunter (1997). For Uruguay and Chile, see USDS (1985–1999). For police and judicial reform in all cases, see the same.

[24] This is akin to the argument in Malamud-Goti (1996). Huntington (1991: 221) argues even more strongly against trials as producing moral and political chaos.

[25] In December 1998 Captain Astíz was condemned for stating that the military had done what they had done out of pride, machismo, obedience, and love of the fatherland, as well as for calling Balza a 'cretin'. In June 1998 a magistrate cited 'apology of crime' (*apología del crímen*) and called for the detention of Massera for calling the high command 'ridiculous' and some generals 'homosexuals' (*Página 12*, 26 June 1998).

that those pursuing truth and justice may be contributing to an increase in the credibility of the judiciary and in the scope for actions that have been labelled 'destabilizing' and even 'subversive', but which turn out to be a non-threatening part of democratic political life. It should be remembered that Menem often associated 'memory' with subversion, thus 'criminalizing' attempts to make sense of and come to terms with the past. He was criticized for concentrating immense power in the executive and attacking the foundations of judicial independence. And he espoused a restricted vision of democracy, calling for the application of the *ley del palo* (the law of the stick) to control unruly journalists, revealing a limited conception of democratic politics and a lack of respect for fundamental freedoms (Borón, 1991; Larkins, 1998). Furthermore, it is as a result of the continued search for truth and justice that Balza apologized for the Dirty War. And the fact that arrests were made and democracy was not threatened permitted Menem to shift his position and to affirm that there would be no more pardons, and that the judiciary should proceed autonomously during the second half of 1998 and in 1999.

A similarly positive argument can be made in the case of Chile. According to some, the arrest of General Pinochet was a threat to democracy. The arrest unified the right for the first time since the transition and permitted it to mobilize in a way that it had not been able to since the Allende regime. It caused renewed civil–military tensions and tensions within the governing coalition, which, whatever its faults, is the most democratic force in Chilean politics. Yet it can be convincingly argued that the arrest of the General provided opportunities to widen Chile's restricted democracy. Unlike Argentina, in Chile the problem is not so much the need to counteract the *ley de palo*, but the need to struggle to loosen the bonds of the *palo de la ley* (stick of the law). The arrest allowed the governing coalition to pressure the right not only to accept that some efforts should be made to deal with the past, but also to reform the constitution for the first time in years. The new activism of the courts, and particularly the new jurisprudence of the Supreme Court, raised the credibility of a judiciary marked by years of 'collaborationism' with the dictatorship. The idea that Chilean society cannot sustain any degree of conflict without degenerating into chaos, assiduously promoted by the right, was dealt a strong blow. A MORI poll of 2 December 1998, for example, showed that 71 per cent of Chileans felt unaffected by the Pinochet arrest and that 66 per cent did not believe that democracy was in danger. In mid-1998 it was unthinkable that anyone should touch Pinochet; yet he was arrested and Chilean democracy has survived. The General is no longer sacred.

After Pinochet's return to Chile in May 2000, the newly elected president, socialist Ricardo Lagos, indicated that solving the human rights issue remained a key challenge for Chilean democracy and stated that the courts should be allowed to act freely, without political interference. On 23 May, following an appeal by Judge Guzmán, the Santiago Court of Appeals determined in a 13–9 vote that Pinochet could be stripped of parliamentary immunity in order to allow investigations into the notorious Caravan of Death case to go forward. By that time there were 106 criminal charges against Pinochet under the jurisdiction of Judge Guzmán. Although it is unlikely that Pinochet will actually be tried and sentenced, he is far from being the untouchable he was before his arrest. The Right now openly admits that disappearances were a part of a deliberate state policy under his rule, and no one questions of the right of relatives to learn the whereabouts of the disappeared. The also finally produced a military commitment to Dialogue Forum revealing the whereabouts of the bodies of the disappeared (although this is to be done anonymously), which is tantamout to a full admission of institutional responsibility. The air force has even taken the unprecedented step of declining to contest jurisdiction over a trial of some of its former officers.

In all, the continued search for truth and justice may be a factor in breaking down key parts of the authoritarian constitutional order and reducing its constraining influence on democratic development. It may help to counteract the weight of fear and concomitant immobilization of the political system, challenging a narrow version of democracy based on an imposed consensus on the need to subordinate any drive towards deepening citizenship to the need for stability and accommodation with undemocratic institutions and groups.[26]

These gains can be reversed, or not taken advantage of, of course, and other variables come into play that can reverse democratic gain. Further attempts to 'legislate an end of justice' may be made. Pinochet is still defended by many, including the law. Although the basis of an enforced 'reconciliation' and limited *convivencia* as conceived of to date have taken a beating, the CPPD has some way to go to loosen the chains of fear.

Indeed, expanded opportunities offered by more secure democracies for the pursuit of justice and truth does not ensure that such

[26] For a similar view see L. Taylor (1998).

aims will in fact be pursued. As the cases of Brazil and Uruguay show, where those favouring truth and justice are relatively isolated and/or weak, the issue can remain invisible or of little relevance in public debates about democracy. The case of Uruguay is particularly dissatisfying; for if it is not necessary to do anything about the past to consolidate a democracy, is also true that a complete unwillingness to do something is an indication of the failure of democratic leadership. Although President Sanguinetti would probably not agree with this, in the final analysis reliance on a purely instrumental logic is insufficient justification for policies of accountability. Indeed, if one bases the value of truth and justice on the grounds of deterrence and consolidation alone, then, were it to be proved that punishment does not benefit democratization or deter future violations, the apparent 'utility' of past accountability would disappear. As is argued elsewhere, such policies derive their strength and legitimacy from an appeal to more fundamental intuitions about the just treatment of all citizens in a civilized society. Truth telling and trials are about reclaiming history in the face of denial. They allow for a reconstruction of the past and are part of social efforts to reconstruct collective identities and social memory at a critical juncture of a country's political history (Barahona de Brito, 1997).

Seen from a wider social perspective, a single official truth telling is not enough. Indeed, neither official truth nor justice, however wide-ranging and complete, are miraculous remedies to solve what are deep wounds and sometimes irreconcilable differences. The past can continue to be a source of conflict in the judicial system, and of latent or overt painful and deep-seated social animosities. There will still be competing interpretations of the past and intense struggles in the political, social, and cultural arenas concerning memory and its role in the process of democratization. The allies of former torturers will continue to defend them as heroes; and some relatives will not accept any limited action taken by the state on their behalf. Battles will continue over 'who has what rights to determine what should be remembered and how', and over the 'ownership of historical memory' (Jelin, 1998: 25) The following section assesses the significance of this wider politics of memory.

The Politics of Memory and Democratization

The past is still very present in these countries, even when it is not present in the formal political arena. To varying degrees, these societies are still traumatized and fearful. The existence of a parallel world of shadows is constantly brought to light. Victims often see their torturers, and some live with the sensation that tabs are being kept on them. 'Irruptions of memory' occur unexpectedly, holding people to the past (Wilde, 1999). As one Argentine observer notes, 'there is constant vigilance, the certainty of disaster, carnal knowledge of fear, a sense that history never moves on, but circles, raven-like, round and round. And then there is willed amnesia' (Feitlowitz, 1998: xi).

For different groups, coming to terms with the past means different things. For survivors and relatives it means overcoming trauma, fear, and loss; for those once engaged in armed struggle it means rethinking responsibilities; for exiles social reintegration is often a painful process, accompanied by a sense of alienation and even rejection by 'those who stayed'. For young people who did not live the experience of repression directly, 'remembering the past' is about understanding what their parents' generation did to produce such violence, part of a struggle to define positions regarding the imperfect democracies they live in. For the children of the disappeared, the politics of memory may be about recovering the dignity of the ideals that their parents strove for. And repressors, their children, and their allies also have to come to terms with the past and what can often be crippling guilt.

To some extent, all these groups are actively reworking the past. This can be seen in the number of 'memory' books that have become best sellers. In Argentina, weekly instalments of the *Nunca Más* report averaged 200,000 sales a week in 1995–6 and became collectors' items, especially among adolescents. In Chile, a country in which a book that sells two or three editions is a best-seller, Tomás Moulián's *Chile Today: Anatomy of a Myth* (1997), which explores the pact of silence among Chileans from various angles, has sold twenty-four editions. In film, *The Official Story* of 1985 about the missing children in Argentina has achieved cult status, as has *The Battle of Chile*, about the fall of the Allende regime and the first months of the coup, which is a best-selling video in Chile. At other times, however, society rejects writing that seems to bring back too painful memories, as with the play by Ariel Dorfman, *Death and the Maiden*, which has been acclaimed internationally but almost ignored in Chile.

Symbolic representations and language have been transformed as a result of the legacy of repression. The kerchiefs of the Mothers, the phrases 'where are they?' (*¿dónde están?*) and *nunca más*, have the status of icons. Youths in Argentina are appropriating the language originating with torture and secret detention camps, creating new slang and giving rock bands names such as 'Grandfathers of Nothing', 'Collective Amnesty', 'Children's Cemetery', and 'The Kidnappers'. Impunity has led to alternative forms of social sanction and celebration. Several municipalities in Buenos Aires have officially declared former generals and other known repressors *persona non grata* in their areas of jurisdiction. So-called *escraches*, or public acts of 'shaming' or repudiation, in which repressors are located and denounced loudly in public places, are common.

The building of commemorative sculptures and monuments has become one of the most important ways to remember and honour the dead in public. There is the first national monument to the disappeared in the city of La Plata in Argentina, memorials in cemeteries in Rio and São Paulo, a Peace Park and a Wall of Names in Chile, the latter in a former secret detention centre. Struggles are periodically waged, sometimes unsuccessfully, over such 'sites of memory'. In Uruguay, the Punta Carretas prison, which housed thousands of systematically tortured prisoners, has now become a shopping mall, in a way that some view as an 'eloquent testimony to the intimate links between the repressive past and the neoliberal present' (NACLA, 1998: 15).

Symbolic dates and commemorations, such as 24 March and 11 September in Argentina and Chile respectively, have become established foci of resistance to the logic of amnesty and forgetting. Historical memories and collective remembrances are used as instruments to legitimate discourse, create loyalties, and justify political options. In Chile the past became a point of reference for competing candidates for the elections in 2000, part of the language to legitimate or discredit presidential hopefuls.[27]

Thus, even if according to opinion polls the past is not a political or policy priority, the issue of backward-looking accountability is now undeniably a part of the popular and political *imaginario* (imagination). As this indicates, truth and justice policies are only the first act in a play with no final act. There will always be 'contested memories', as well as intense symbolic and cultural–ideological struggles in the political, social, and cultural arenas over memory, because facts are 'never meaningless' or 'created equal' (Trouillot, 1995: 29). The politics of memory about past atrocities will thus become a part of the identity of these countries and their political systems.

[27] Comments by Katie Hite at a round table on the Pinochet case, Princeton University, February 1999.

Conclusions

This chapter has attempted to assess the issue of transitional truth and justice from an institutional and political angle, taking into account the social dimension of the wider politics of memory. It has looked at the formal universe, but also at the dynamic of resistance and accommodation between social and political actors and institutions. The analysis attempts to show that efforts to deal with the past and their significance in the overall politics of the transition to democracy and in the process of democratization are shaped by country-specific historical conditions and developments. More specifically, attempts to deal with the past are shaped by the nature and legacies of repression and authoritarian rule, as well as the nature of the transition process and various political, institutional, and legal factors conditioning the post-transitional period. Among these are the nature of repression itself, the presence and strength of a human rights movement, inherited legal or constitutional limitations, and relations between political parties and HROs. Also important are the degree of executive or party commitment to policies of truth and justice, the unity of democratic parties, the ability of the military to mobilize against any policies of accountability, and the relations between the military and the democratic executive. The attitude of the judiciary to past violations, the presence of a strong legislative right, and the degree to which repression has penetrated the social fabric are other elements to take into account. Furthermore, the way in which the first democratically elected authorities deal with the past, together with the relative strength of the human rights movement in the post-transitional period, sets the agenda for the subsequent evolution of the issue. More specifically, the past remains a source of open conflict if there are loopholes in official policies that preclude full closure or amnesty, and if transnational groups or regional and international human rights bodies challenge national policies favouring impunity.

Finally, the past remains a source of conflict if there are strong HROs that continue to contest official decisions on how to deal with the past, that are strong and have allies in the formal political arena or the courts. Indeed, the relevance of these continued struggles and the levels of conflict they generate vary according to the power of those dedicated to the continued pursuit of justice and their relationship with the formal political arena or the government.

In Argentina, where there is a strong movement allied with parts of the opposition and backed by the courts, the search for justice has been kept alive. In Chile, on the other hand, the human rights movement is strong but, given its historical evolution and nature, its relations with the state and the government forces are more co-operative. Hence the continued search for justice in the courts has not been such a source of conflict in the post-transitional period, and, before the arrest of General Pinochet, the issue had become almost 'invisible', given the absence of open contestation.

In Uruguay the movement is weak and has few committed allies in the political arena. Thus, the past has not figured with any prominence in democratic politics since the passage of the Amnesty Law in 1989. At most, periodic but short-lived conflicts take place between political and social groups calling for the location of the dead and an executive that refuses to carry out its legally established obligation to do so. In Brazil the movement is also weak and relatively isolated, but unlike Uruguay it has been able to co-operate with central and state-level authorities in achieving policies of compensation and 'truth'.

Official policies to deal with the past are not of themselves directly relevant to the process of democratization. What is more, during the first transitional period, truth and justice policies are unrelated to—or may even place obstacles in the way of—wider institutional reform. However, in the post-transitional period, particularly in Argentina and Chile, finding the dead and putting the perpetrators on trial is contributing to deepening essential elements of democratic life. The reverse is also true: barring Uruguay to date the prolongation of democratic politics in each country has helped to widen the scope for retroactive truth and justice. In Argentina, the work of the SED, the institutional military apology, and judicial autonomy have allowed the process to go forward. Among other things, the co-operative links between HROs and a democratic executive in Brazil, as well as the reform of the police force, have produced a compensation policy and access to police files. In Chile constitutional reform proposed by Lagos after failed attempts by Aylwin and Feei may widen the scope for truth and justice. Concomitantly, lack of reform can impede progress with accountability. In Brazil and Uruguay, a still autonomous military can limit or altogether prevent state policies on compensation and the truth.

Whatever the situation, the past has become part of the dynamic of democratic politics. It is part of state–society relations, as HROs fight against or co-operate with state institutions or the government to obtain truth and justice. It is part of the democratic political game between government and opposition in so far as political identities are partially established according to those who supported the old regimes and those who opposed it. Indeed, although the continued pursuit of truth and justice and its links to wider reforms may be difficult to establish across the board, the politics of memory more widely conceived are important for a process of democratization in all four countries.

As noted in the introduction to this book, the politics of memory can be perceived on two different levels. Narrowly conceived, it consists of policies of truth and justice in the transition from dictatorship to democracy. More widely conceived, it is about how a society interprets and appropriates its past in an attempt to mould its future, and as such it is an integral part of any political process, including progress towards deeper democracy. What each society decides to remember and forget largely determines how it projects its future. Never is this more apparent than when countries experience a break with one political system and work towards instituting a new one. The appropriation of history by social and political actors is particularly intense at such moments. History ceases to be the exclusive domain of historians as different social groups engage in a search for meaning, and in the creation of 'memories' and myths about the past to justify their present and future. This process of memory making, the social and cultural politics of memory, are an integral part of a process of building various social, political, or collective identities, which shape the way different social groups view national politics and the goals they wish to pursue in the future. As such, they are ultimately revealing about, and relevant to, the nature of democratic politics in each country. And as such, they are likely to continue for a long time to come.[28] As William Faulkner once wrote, 'the past is never dead; it is not even past.'

[28] See the Introduction to this book for a wider discussion of the politics of memory.

5

War, Peace, and Memory Politics in Central America*

Rachel Sieder

Introduction

During the last two decades, political transition in Latin America has resulted in a balancing act between truth and justice. Official attempts to deal with the past have typically involved commissions of inquiry into past violations of human rights, and amnesty laws providing immunity from prosecution for those responsible for such violations.[1] According to the prevailing orthodoxy, truth telling constitutes a valuable contribution to national reconciliation. Yet legal sanctions against perpetrators are generally rejected because they prejudice the democratic transition. In some instances it is argued that bringing all perpetrators to justice would simply be unworkable in countries where several thousands of the population were directly involved in human rights abuses. By contrast, many human rights activists have argued that, while uncovering the truth can constitute an important form of sanction in itself, it is insufficient to secure democratic governance. From this perspective, investigations without at least some measure of legal accountability and sanction of those responsible means the institutionalization of impunity, with detrimental consequences for strengthening the rule of law.[2]

* My thanks to Paloma Aguilar, Alexandra Barahona de Brito, Carlos Flores, Carmen González, Rachel Holder, and Tracy Ulltveit-Möe for their incisive comments on earlier drafts of this chapter. I also benefited greatly from the opportunities to present and discuss draft versions provided by the Centre for Latin American Studies, Cambridge, and the Institute of Latin American Studies, London.

[1] For a comparative overview of truth commissions see Hayner (1994, 1996a).

[2] See e.g. Pearce and La Rue, in Sieder (1995a), and Méndez (1997b).

With these familiar arguments in mind, this chapter considers the role of 'memory politics'—understood as the combination of official and unofficial attempts to deal with the legacy of past violations—in the struggle for democratization in Central America. Official initiatives can include truth commissions, amnesty dispensations, criminal investigations and prosecutions, and a range of institutional reforms aimed at redressing the previous failure of the state to guarantee human rights. Unofficial initiatives developed by civil society actors to confront the past can include investigations of violations, legal actions, and different kinds of commemorative acts and exercises in collective memory. Memory politics operates at multiple levels and involves a diversity of agents, including local communities, national and international non-governmental human rights organizations (HROs), governments, the media, and, in the case of Central America, the United Nations (UN). However, it is suggested here that its long-term effects in any national context depend on the interaction between official and unofficial efforts to address the legacies of the past.

The experiences of memory politics analysed in this chapter are those of El Salvador, Honduras, and Guatemala, the three Central American countries that during the 1990s undertook official processes of investigating past violations of human rights. The precise nature of memory politics and the impact they have had varied considerably in these three countries. It is suggested here that four interrelated factors are central to explaining differences between the respective national experiences. The first is the specific political and social legacies of human rights abuse in each country, in particular who the victims and the perpetrators were, but also the impact that such violations had on society as a whole. The second concerns the circumstances of the transition from war to peace, specifically the prevailing balance of forces and the trade-off between truth and justice that this engendered in each case. The third is the role of local HROs and civil society in general in the politics of memory, in particular whether and how they supported and/or contested official attempts to deal with the legacy of past violations of human rights. Finally, of particular importance in Central America is the role of international governmental and non-governmental organizations (NGOs) in efforts to uncover the truth about the past and to address the consequences of violations.

The first three sections of this chapter compare the legacies of human rights abuses, the transitional trade-offs between truth and justice, and the role of civil society organizations and international actors in the memory politics of El Salvador, Honduras, and Guatemala. The final section considers the impact of memory politics on the prospects for democracy in these countries. This inevitably raises the complex question of how democratization itself can be assessed. In strictly procedural terms, the shift from an authoritarian regime to an elected civilian government is the most commonly accepted indicator of a democratic transition. However, throughout much of the latter half of the twentieth century, Central America was characterized by the simultaneous existence of electoral politics and military interference. In marked contrast to the Southern Cone, the transition to elected government during the 1980s in El Salvador, Honduras, and Guatemala roughly coincided with the worst period of violations, the consolidation of military power over the state and civil society, and the demobilization of opposition movements. It is suggested here that current prospects for lasting and meaningful democratization depend more crucially on the effective demilitarization of the state and civil society than on electoral competition, particularly in the light of the region's recent history. Demilitarization involves securing formal changes to state institutions, such as the military and the judiciary, in order to subordinate the military to effective civilian control and to secure the rule of law. It also implies the creation of a political culture of citizenship based on principles of universal rights and obligations and the non-violent resolution of conflict. In order to understand processes of democratic consolidation, therefore, we need to combine institutional–political analysis with an examination of the wider social processes involved in the building of citizenship.[3] Although truth-telling initiatives in Central America have rarely resulted in penal sanctions against individuals responsible for violations, it is suggested here that exercises in collective memory have constituted an important variable in the distended and complex processes of demilitarization and citizenship construction.

Authoritarianism and War

Both El Salvador and Guatemala were military-dominated counter-insurgency states long before the counter-insurgency wars that engulfed both countries in the 1980s. Historical legacies of

[3] For democratic consolidation, see Mainwaring *et al.* (1992), Linz and Stepan (1997), Schmitter (1996). None of these discuss Central America. On the importance of bottom-up citizenship construction for democratic consolidation, see Jelin (1995).

widespread socioeconomic inequality, military intervention in politics, and restricted civil and political liberties were common to both countries, and had exacted a high human cost.[4] In Honduras it was not until the 1980s that the violent conflicts besetting the rest of the region began to affect the nature of the military, resulting in the systematic abuse of human rights, albeit on a far lesser scale than that experienced in El Salvador and Guatemala (J. Morris, 1984; Schultz and Sundloff-Schultz, 1996; Sieder, 1995b). The quality and intensity of existing violence was transformed in the latter two countries in the late 1970s and 1980s, when the military targeted the entire civilian population in an all-out war designed to deprive the guerrilla of a rural support base. These counter-insurgency wars took place within a context of increased US involvement in the region following the Sandinistas' successful overthrow of the Somoza dictatorship in Nicaragua in July 1979.[5]

The terror tactics deployed by the military in El Salvador and Guatemala were similar in nature and included selective assassinations and disappearances, systematic torture, rape, massacres, destruction of entire villages, and mass displacement (Danner, 1993; UN Security Council, 1993; HRW, 1990a: 47–48). The greatest number of killings in *El Salvador* occurred between 1978 and 1983, when government forces murdered 42,171 people, close to 1 per cent of the population. In all, a total of some 50,000 people were killed during the civil war (Stanley, 1995: 3), with the overwhelming majority of human rights abuses during the war carried out by the military and security forces. Impunity was supported by the complicity and ineffectiveness of the judiciary, which failed to convict one single military officer for human rights abuses throughout the entire decade.

In *Guatemala*, an all-out war began in 1979 against left-wing and centrist opposition, and many hundreds of students, trade unionists, and community activists were killed or disappeared by paramilitary death squads in the cities. However, the destructive power of the military was most concentrated in the rural areas. Extreme brutality and dislocation of thousands of people characterized army operations.[6] In total, during thirty-six years of

[4] On the military–oligarchic pact in El Salvador, see Baylora (1982), Stanley (1995), Williams and Walters (1997). On Guatemalan politics, see Black (1984), Gleijesis (1991), Handy (1984), Schlesinger and Kinzer (1992).

[5] For increasing levels of US economic and military aid to, see Dunkerley (1994: 145).

[6] On the violence see Falla (1994), Manz (1988), Carmack (1988), and Stoll (1993).

armed conflict over 200,000 people were murdered in Guatemala, including up to 50,000 disappeared persons.[7] Civil society was transformed by the army's coerced integration of the rural indigenous majority into its counter-insurgency design, with negative effects for indigenous cultural and religious practices. Perhaps the most destructive element of the armed conflict was the forced involvement *en masse* of the civilian population in the counter-insurgency violence, through the paramilitary Self Defence Civil Patrols (PACs), organized by the army in every rural community. They numbered some 800,000 men at their height in the mid-1980s and were responsible for numerous grave violations of human rights (PDH, 1994; Popkin, 1996). In Guatemala, state violence effectively divided the civilian population against itself.

Abuses of human rights in *Honduras* were never as widespread as in El Salvador and Guatemala. Although the use of torture and the violation of due process guarantees was common in the early 1980s, those murdered and disappeared by military and paramilitary forces never numbered more than a few hundred. Various guerrilla groups emerged after 1980, but these failed to secure a base of civilian support, and partly because of this, the repressive tactics of the military were never randomly or massively deployed against the civilian population. State violence in the early 1980s was instead targeted at left-wing members of the popular opposition and Salvadoreans suspected of providing logistical support for the guerrillas, the Farabundo Martí Front for National Liberation (FMLN). In the mid-1980s selective assassinations and disappearances by paramilitary death squads became commonplace for the first time in Honduran history, and at least 184 people were disappeared. The widespread use of surveillance and army informants meant that suspicion and fear increasingly characterized civil society. However, the Honduran military clearly never aimed to control society in the same way as their Guatemalan and Salvadorean counterparts, and violations markedly declined in the second half of the decade.

Negotiating the Transition

Official truth-telling initiatives in Central America did not accompany a negotiated transition to elected civilian government, but

[7] One database based on over 37,000 documented cases of murder and disappearance attributed 43 per cent of the violations to the Ríos Montt period of 17 months as *de facto* head of state (see Ball *et al.*, 1999).

rather were part and consequence of the end of the regional and national armed conflicts. Given the decisive influence of the USA in the civil war in El Salvador, policy changes in Washington were of primary importance in securing a relatively swift conclusion to peace negotiations in that country. This was not the case in Guatemala, where the military were far less dependent on external support; here talks dragged on for almost a decade and were finally concluded only in December 1996. The electoral defeat of the Sandinistas in 1990 signalled a further decline of US interest in supporting the Honduran military as a rearguard, which strengthened the position of domestic forces struggling to secure demilitarization of the body politic in that country.

Human rights monitoring groups across the region had long called for an end to impunity and gross violations by military and paramilitary forces, documenting the brutality of the military's counter-insurgency strategies and building important links with international human rights campaigners. In Guatemala, state repression severely restricted the domestic space for human rights monitoring during the early 1980s, forcing these groups to operate from exile. In all three countries, organizations were formed by families of victims of military repression. Given the exceptionally high number of disappeared throughout the region, numbering perhaps as many as 70,000 individuals, effective official investigations had long been a fundamental demand of such organizations. In addition, the fact that a number of Latin American countries, including Argentina, Chile, and Uruguay, had already undergone some kind of official investigation into past violations during the 1980s in the context of their transitions from authoritarian rule provided an important example for campaigners in Central America. The end of the Cold War and the ascendance of an international discourse of human rights lent additional weight to their demands.

El Salvador

The political solution to the armed conflict in El Salvador was a result of the military stalemate between the FMLN and the military. Despite sustained US support throughout the decade, the army was unable to defeat the guerrilla movement, which maintained a large and solid base of civilian support. The corruption and inefficiency of the high command became a focus of discontent for both the United States and the private sector, which by the end of the 1980s had consolidated a political vehicle, the National Republican Alliance (ARENA) party. The turning point was the

November 1989 offensive launched by the FMLN, which questioned the ability of the high command to maintain military control of San Salvador. Two days into the offensive, members of an elite battalion murdered six Jesuit priests, together with their housekeeper and her daughter, which provoked widespread international repudiation.

The armed and security forces were extremely hostile to a negotiated settlement with the FMLN. However, it became increasingly clear to the ARENA government and the Bush administration that negotiations were the only way to end the war, and the USA used its economic leverage over the military to secure such an outcome. The Chapultepec Accords were finally signed on 16 January 1992, following almost three years of negotiations between the government and the FMLN and the efforts of then UN Secretary General Javier Pérez de Cuellar. They set out the conditions for the legal and political incorporation of the FMLN into the national political process, and heralded an unprecedented reduction in the military's institutional and political power. The Accords proposed a number of political and constitutional reforms to demilitarize politics (Karl, 1992; Stahler-Sholk, 1994; Byrne, 1996). Measures included the creation of a civilian police force independent of the military, the abolition of existing security forces and a programme of judicial reform.

The FMLN had argued for investigations into past human rights abuses, while HROs repeatedly called for full investigations and trials. FMLN negotiators initially advocated exemplary trials of the most notorious cases of human rights crimes, to which the government responded by producing a list that included many crimes attributed to the FMLN (Popkin and Bhuta, 1999). Ultimately, the parties accepted a UN proposal to establish a truth commission to investigate violations committed during the war; this was composed of non-nationals, with the power to make legally binding recommendations. The parties also agreed to set up an ad hoc commission composed of three notables from El Salvador to review the human rights records of all high-ranking military officers.

Guatemala

The agreement to create a commission of investigation into past human rights crimes in Guatemala was also secured in the context of peace negotiations, although in very different circumstances. By the mid-1980s, the guerrilla group, the National Guatemalan Revolutionary Unity (URNG), was all but destroyed as a military force, and it came to the negotiating table in a much weaker position than the FMLN. The army considered itself the victor of the war and was not economically dependent on external forces for its survival. In addition, in contrast to the military in El Salvador or Argentina, it had not lost the confidence of the domestic private sector, and in the early 1990s the political elite remained subordinate to the military.[8] The agreements concluded in December 1996 were thus much weaker on the issue of demilitarization than the accords in El Salvador. None the less, formal commitments were secured on the formation of a public security force independent of the military, the reduction of the military budget and its troop strength by a third, a programme of judicial reform, and the demobilization of the PACs (Spence *et al.*, 1998).

The Guatemalan army was initially adamant that there should be no accountability for past violations, and it repeatedly blocked attempts by the URNG to negotiate on this point. However, the Catholic Church, local HROs, and the UN proved central in securing a mandate for an official truth commission. The Catholic Church, whose members had been particularly targeted by military violence in the highlands, was committed to some process of investigation into past violations and had been an important mediator in the peace negotiations since 1987. In addition, civil society organizations gained a unique and formal role in formulating the terms of the peace after 1994. Represented by the Civil Society Assembly (ASC), they were able to make proposals to the URNG and the government negotiating teams on the different topics under discussion.[9] The ASC consistently lobbied for an official investigation into past violations. The agreement for the creation of the UN-sponsored Historical Clarification Commission (CEH) was signed in June 1994 after more than two years during which the army had stalled negotiations.

The remit of the CEH was to investigate violations committed during the armed conflict, clarify the causes and consequences of that conflict, and formulate specific recommendations to prevent future abuses of human rights. However, it was agreed that its

[8] In April 1993 gridlock between the presidency and Congress prompted President Serrano to attempt unsuccessfully the dismissal of Congress and the Supreme Court. This was an important turning point, as civil organizations mobilized against Serrano and the army ultimately backed the ruling of the Constitutional Court against the president, thus upholding the 1985 Constitution. However, the episode also underlined the comparative weakness of the civilian political elite in Guatemala.

[9] Despite the weaknesses of the consultation process, in comparative terms the formal inclusion of civil society organizations in the elaboration of the peace agreements was a distinguishing feature of the Guatemalan process. For a critical view, see Palencia (1997).

recommendations would not have 'legal objectives or effects'. In December 1996 the government and the URNG agreed to a new amnesty law, the Law of National Reconciliation, despite protests from HROs, which had formed an Alliance against Impunity precisely to lobby against such an amnesty. The law protected perpetrators from prosecution and criminal responsibility, but explicitly excluded the internationally proscribed crimes of torture, genocide, and forced disappearance.

Honduras

In Honduras, truth telling and justice were not the result of peace negotiations but rather the outcome of a combination of a gradual process of demilitarization and state reform during the 1990s and the sustained efforts of domestic HROs to ensure accountability. By 1990 the military was increasingly criticized by a wide spectrum of domestic interests including the private sector, which resented its economic privileges and corruption. Civil society also became more vocal in denouncing impunity, particularly after the abduction, rape, and murder of a student by two military officers in 1991. Further, the military suffered a sharp decline in US funding after 1989, a direct consequence of shifting priorities. In the face of such developments, more reform-minded elements within the high command came to favour a gradual and controlled reform of civil–military relations.

A number of institutional reforms facilitated official investigations into past abuses of human rights. In June 1992, in response to increasing criticism of military impunity, President Rafael Callejas (1989–93) created the office of the National Commissioner for Human Rights (CNDH), charged with defending the human rights of individual citizens, as well as a presidential ad hoc commission on police and judicial reform. In April 1993 the latter recommended the abolition of the military-controlled National Investigations Department (DNI) and the establishment of a new state prosecution service, the Public Ministry (MP). Congress approved this in December 1993, thus securing greater autonomy for state prosecution services. The new ministry was responsible for criminal investigation, criminal prosecutions, and guarantees of due process. It came to play an essential role in pursuing those responsible for violations.[10]

[10] Before the establishment of the PM, responsibility for carrying out criminal investigations fell to the prosecuting judge and the military police force.

The Human Rights Commissioner, Leo Valladares, surprised domestic and international opinion by announcing that his new institution would carry out a thorough investigation into the fate of the disappeared. Valladares had close links with national HROs and the Committee of Relatives of the Detained–Disappeared in Honduras (COFADEH), which had long campaigned for investigations and prosecutions. He also received discrete support from staff working at the Truth Commission (TC) in El Salvador, as well as from a number of key international HROs. Despite the 1991 Amnesty Law, which applied to all persons sentenced, tried, or subject to being tried for political and related crimes, Valladares did not rule out the possibility of judicial prosecutions.[11]

Truth and Justice: Gains and Trade-offs

The balance struck between truth telling and justice in attempts to deal with the past has differed widely in El Salvador, Guatemala, and Honduras. In El Salvador the TC report was far-reaching in its revelations, impact, and recommendations, but did not lead to trials or significant reparations of either a moral or material nature. In Guatemala, by contrast, even before the commission began its work, civil society groups had undertaken multiple initiatives to investigate the past, commemorate victims, pursue prosecutions, and work with survivors to try and piece together a social fabric destroyed by violence and war. In February 1999 the CEH recommended the prosecution of those responsible for non-amnestied crimes, including genocide, although this appeared highly improbable. Only in Honduras did state agencies and civil society organizations join forces to bring those responsible for violations to trial and to secure moral and material reparations for their victims, even though the results of these efforts have been far from decisive.

El Salvador

The TC in El Salvador was mandated to investigate major past violations and make recommendations to prevent their future recurrence. During the course of its investigations, it received over 22,000 denunciations, the majority of which referred to extra-

[11] The Amnesty Law of 1991 facilitated the return of former guerrilla members from Nicaragua, Cuba, and the Soviet Union. It followed and superseded the former amnesty decrees of 1987 and 1990.

judicial executions, forced disappearances, and torture. While the Cristiani government exercised considerable pressure for the names of perpetrators not to be made public, commission members interpreted their mandate as requiring the naming of individuals and institutions responsible for violations. They justified the decision by pointing to the minimal possibilities of securing accountability through the highly compromised judicial system. The FMLN backed the policy of full disclosure. The report was published in March 1993 and held the armed forces and paramilitary death squads responsible for more than 85 per cent and the FMLN responsible for some 5 per cent of violations committed since 1980. The Commission also examined thirty-three paradigmatic cases of human rights abuse in detail and indicated the personal involvement of more than forty military officers, including the entire high command. The US government was criticized in the report but, in the light of its direct and extensive involvement in the counter-insurgency war, emerged relatively unscathed. The Bush administration had in fact supported the TC and provided declassified Central Intelligence Agency (CIA) documents, which proved the involvement of high-ranking Salvadorean officers in gross violations.

The TC called for the immediate removal of those military officers named in the report, and recommended that the FMLN commanders identified as responsible for violations should be banned from holding public office for ten years. It also recommended greater civilian oversight of the military, including control over budget and promotions, together with the extensive decentralization and reform of the judiciary. Controversially, it called for resignation of the entire Supreme Court, which was identified as having actively facilitated impunity for the military and death squads. Supreme Court President Mauricio Gutiérrez Castro was singled out for unprofessional conduct in the case of one notorious massacre and for his failure to co-operate with Commission investigations. The TC met with bitter criticism from the right and the military, while the Supreme Court accused it of political bias and of abusing national sovereignty. Under pressure from the right wing of his party, which was furious with the commission's indictment of ARENA founder, Major Roberto d'Aubisson, the president condemned it for failing to meet expectations for national reconciliation. Pressure from the UN and the USA was critical in forcing at least a nominal acceptance of the commission's recommendations by the government.

Five days after the publication of the TC report, a broad general amnesty law was passed, ensuring that none of those named would be tried. The FMLN high command had accepted the need for an amnesty, but had argued for a broad national consensus on its terms. This was not to be, as the right-wing majority in the legislature hastily rushed through the amnesty. The law explicitly extended amnesty to the judiciary, defining a number of violations of due process guarantees as 'political' crimes. It covered civil as well as criminal responsibility, thereby denying victims and their families the right to establish accountability or to seek redress through the courts for abuses committed before January 1992. HROs and the opposition coalition, Democratic Convergence (CD), challenged the law, claiming that a self-decreed amnesty was unconstitutional, but the Supreme Court refused to initiate a review.

A limited and qualified form of sanction was secured through the ad hoc committee, which reviewed the records of 230 officers and in September 1992 recommended the transfer or dismissal of over 100 men, including the entire high command. President Alfredo Cristiani delayed compliance, but his hand was effectively forced by the publication of the TC report in March 1993, which publicly named many of the senior officers the Ad Hoc committee recommended for removal, including Minister of Defence General Emilio Ponce. Following sustained pressure from the UN General Secretary and the Bush administration, which dispatched General Colin Powell to San Salvador, the officers were eventually dismissed. However, far from facing trial, they received full military honours and retained their pension rights, violating the spirit of the Ad Hoc committee recommendations.

In contrast to those implicated in the TC report, many of whom went on to secure lucrative or prestigious posts, the victims of violations and their families received little recompense. The commission called on the government to provide compensation to victims and their relatives and to erect a national monument to bear the names of all those killed in the civil war. However, while a compensation scheme was set up for some relatives of those killed in combat, it did not extend to the relatives of victims of human rights abuses. Cristiani, his successor Armando Calderón Sol, and members of the high command have never publicly acknowledged state responsibility for gross violations of human rights. The FMLN also failed to acknowledge responsibility, and ignored recommendations that the FMLN commanders named should not hold public office. No programmes to benefit those individuals or communities most affected have been proposed by the government. No national monument has been built, and few exhumations have taken place of the multiple mass graves throughout the country. The UN-sponsored exhumation and monument on the site of the El Mozote massacre of 1981, where over 1,000 people were killed, constitutes a rare exception. The profile of HROs, so high during the civil war, markedly declined following the TC, reflecting a relative lack of independence from the revolutionary left and the divisions that beset the latter after the peace settlement. It was also partly a consequence of the massive deployment of the UN Observer Mission in El Salvador (ONUSAL), which effectively relegated national HROs to a marginal position during the critical transition period. Human rights campaigners had a negligible role in determining the terms of the TC and no involvement in its execution; to date, they have not been able to secure compensation for victims.[12]

Honduras

In Honduras, truth telling and attempts to secure justice were framed not by the implementation of a negotiated peace settlement, but rather by a series of local institutional and political developments. On 29 December 1993, just weeks before the inauguration of the newly elected Reina government, Valladares released his report into those disappeared during the early 1980s, *The Facts Speak for Themselves* (HRW, 1994b). In addition to investigating specific cases of disappearance, the report sought to analyse the pattern of violence between 1980 and 1993, noting that extra-judicial executions, arbitrary detention, torture, and lack of due process had also occurred. In the absence of UN support, the report was a much more modest investigating effort than those undertaken in El Salvador and Guatemala. None the less, it signalled the primary responsibility of the military in forced disappearances, attributing responsibility for ninety-nine cases to the military and security forces, and paramilitary death squads. Some thirty-seven disappearances were attributed to the Nicaraguan Contra. The report indicted the judiciary for encouraging a state of impunity. The Washington-based NGO, the National Security Archives (NSA), played a vital role in securing US government documents for the report, which strongly condemned US government involvement in violations as well as those of other foreign actors, particularly Argentine military officers, who were instrumental in the creation of the Contra and training the Honduran military in dirty war techniques.[13]

[12] HROs registered some successes since 1993 in reuniting with their natural families children disappeared or stolen for adoption during the armed conflict. However, no financial compensation or official recognition has been secured for victims.

[13] For an illuminating account of the Argentine role in counter-insurgency in Central America, see Armony (1997).

The Ombudsman's report was less controversial than its Salvadorean precursor. Although the high command was displeased with the findings, only eight military officers were named and the military was not as threatened as its Salvadorean counterparts had been. The Reina government, committed to strengthening the rule of law, welcomed the report. Most members of the administration were on the social–democratic wing of the Liberal Party and were anxious to distance themselves from violations committed under Liberal administrations between 1986 and 1990. In addition, the Commission's recommendation to establish civilian control over public security forces, initially proposed in 1993 by the ad hoc commission on institutional reform, was supported by civilian politicians of both main parties. HROs also endorsed its findings and claimed a moral victory. In comparison with El Salvador, Honduras was far less politically polarized, and the investigation of past human rights abuses, which in any case had occurred on a much lesser scale, did not prove nearly as contentious.

Valladares stated that his report was 'preliminary' and called on the relevant Honduran institutions to fulfil their mandates and uncover the truth about the disappearances, establish criminal responsibility, and prosecute those responsible. According to his interpretation, existing amnesty laws did not prevent criminal prosecutions. Under the leadership of the first attorney general, Edmundo Orellana, the newly created Public Ministry took up the challenge and, through its Human Rights Prosecutors Office, initiated criminal proceedings against several military officers. It also began a programme of exhumations and forensic investigations. On 5 December 1995, a case presented to the courts by an HRO resulted in the former chief of the DNI becoming the first officer to be convicted and imprisoned for violations committed during the 1980s. He was found guilty, along with nine other officers, of taking part in the kidnapping, torture, and attempted murder of six students in 1982. A successful appeal by the military was overturned by the Supreme Court in January 1996. However, attempts to secure further arrests have been largely unsuccessful, and several of the officers charged remain at large and on the military payroll. Many went into hiding in military bases with the tacit support of the high command. Valladares also denounced military officers for systematically destroying files that could provide evidence for future prosecutions. Many within the judiciary and the new government of Carlos Flores Facussé (1998–) remained uneasy about the continued frictions generated by HRO attempts to have military officers arrested and prosecuted. In January 1999 a judge finally halted a case against three military officers also implicated in the 1982 kidnapping, arguing that they were protected by the 1987, 1990, and 1991 amnesty decrees.

Despite the mixed record on securing judicial convictions, the role of national HROs and victims in the official truth-telling process was comparatively greater in Honduras than in El Salvador, something that is itself an important form of compensation. In addition, the report called on the government to set up a fund to provide financial compensation for the families of the disappeared, erect a monument commemorating the victims, and publicly acknowledge the violations committed by the state, which President Reina declared his support for. In February 1996 the first compensation payments were made.[14] HROs welcomed these developments, but reiterated their commitment to securing future convictions of those responsible for violations.

Guatemala

In Guatemala, the official truth commission was preceded by numerous attempts by civil society organizations and local communities to uncover the truth about past abuses and secure some form of compensation and justice. Indeed, the widespread involvement of civil society in memory work is perhaps the most distinguishing feature of the Guatemalan truth-telling process. While this was partly engendered by the peace accords and the political opening provided by the CEH agreement, its main impetus came from a diverse and dynamic human rights movement, which had gained in strength and political independence from the URNG during the 1990s. Culture has also been a factor in the politics of memory. Particularly for indigenous communities, local ritual practices to commemorate the dead have constituted a central feature of collective attempts to deal with trauma and loss. These initiatives have been promoted by many organizations within the heterogeneous Mayan movement that emerged in the wake of the armed conflict.[15]

In contrast to El Salvador and Honduras, the Catholic Church was also decisive in promoting a grass-roots politics of memory. The first extensive report into violations during the armed conflict

[14] In its 1988 Velásquez-Rodríguez ruling, the Inter-American Court of Human Rights (IAHRC) called on Honduras to pay compensation to the victims of disappearances, but official progress has been slow.

[15] On the cultural specificities of loss and trauma in Guatemala, see Zur (1998) and Kaur (1998).

was published not by a quasi-official truth commission, but by the Human Rights Office of the Catholic Archdiocese. The 1998 'Never Again' (*Nunca Más*) report, a product of the Inter-Diocesan project for Recovery of Historical Memory (REMHI), documented atrocities on the basis of over 6,000 testimonies collected in parishes across the country during the course of three years (ODHAG, 1998). It registered over 55,000 victims and more than 25,000 murders, attributing some 80 per cent to state security forces and 9 per cent to the URNG. The REMHI project, originally set up to support the CEH, had intended to go beyond the narrow mandate of the official commission and name individuals responsible for violations. However, fears for the safety of those who had given testimony meant that *Nunca Más* did this in only a very few cases. The military criticized the report for political bias, and many on the right condemned it, accusing the Church of political interests and promoting conflict over reconciliation. Just two days after its publication, the head of REMHI, Catholic bishop Monseñor Juan Gerardi, was bludgeoned to death at his home in Guatemala City in what few doubted was a political murder. Official investigation efforts proved inefficient and inconclusive, despite considerable national and international pressure (F. Goldman, 1999).

The CEH finally published its report, *Guatemala: Memory of Silence*, in February 1999, based on over 8,000 testimonies (UN Security Council, 1999). It included a detailed analysis of paradigmatic cases, and an exhaustive historical analysis of the causes and consequences of the conflict, concluding that political violence in Guatemala was a direct consequence of acute socioeconomic inequalities and a history of racism. The CEH estimated that approximately 200,000 people had been killed or disappeared during the conflict and documented some 658 massacres. In line with its mandate, it attributed responsibility for violations to institutions and not individuals, stating that 93 per cent of all cases investigated were attributable to the military and 3 per cent to the URNG. Despite the considerable support lent to the Commission by the Clinton administration, which provided funds and previously classified documents, the report also signalled US government and CIA involvement in supporting the structures of repression in Guatemala.

The CEH had a relatively weak mandate, but its recommendations were far stronger than initially predicted. Most significantly, it found that between 1981 and 1983 the state had carried out a deliberate policy of genocide against the Mayan population, which commissioners emphasized was not amnestied by the 1996 Law of National Reconciliation. They added that all those found guilty of non-amnestied, internationally proscribed violations should be prosecuted, tried, and punished. The CEH also called for significant restructuring of the military and security forces in line with the reforms mandated in the December 1996 Agreement on the Strengthening of Civilian Power and the Role of the Armed Forces in a Democratic Society, which was part of the peace agreements.[16] Recommendations were far-reaching and included the elaboration of a new military code and doctrine, the abolition of the Presidential General Staff, a reform of military intelligence, and a strengthening of the National Civilian Police (PNC) and purging of any of its members guilty of violations. Additionally, it called on the government to set up an official commission similar to the ad hoc commission in El Salvador to review the history of military officers with the aim of removing those implicated in violations.

The CEH also recommended that the government implement an ambitious programme of compensation, including psychological and economic assistance through a National Reparations Programme to run for not less than ten years, the investigation of the whereabouts of the disappeared, and the location and exhumation of clandestine graves. It called for the establishment of a National Commission for the Search for Disappeared Children to look for children who had disappeared or been illegally adopted or illegally separated from their families during the armed conflict. It further recommended the erection of monuments in memory of those killed, and the official acknowledgement by the state of its responsibility. Finally, it recommended that victims of violations and their direct descendants should be exempt from military service. While many within the UN privately viewed these recommendations as unworkable, prospects for some form of recompense were strengthened by the fact that both the CEH mandate and the 1996 Amnesty Law made explicit reference to the state's obligation to provide compensation.[17] The position of HROs on the issue differed, but most victims' groups continued to insist that it could be no substitute for full disclosure and legal accountability.

Right-wing sectors, including the private-sector organization, the National Association of Private Enterprise (ANEP), criticized the report as biased, but neither the Arzú Yrigoyen government (1995–9) nor the military openly criticized the findings. This was

[16] For more on this agreement, see Spence *et al.* (1998) and Schirmer (1998).

[17] After the signing of the peace agreement the government began to explore compensation (Altolaguirre, 1998). In 1998–9, the governmental Peace Secretariat (SEPAZ) set up pilot projects in three communities affected by the conflict.

in marked contrast to official reactions in El Salvador six years earlier. The fact that two of CEH commissioners were Guatemalan made it harder for the right to level charges of 'foreign intervention' against the UN. In addition, before the publication of the report, President Arzú and Defence Minister General Barrios Celada had publicly acknowledged state participation in past 'excesses' in furtherance of 'national reconciliation'. While this was criticized by HROs as insufficient, it contrasted sharply to developments in El Salvador, where no official sign of contrition has been forthcoming. None the less, the Arzú government rejected most CEH recommendations because they were already being carried out by other institutions as part of the peace implementation. Official truth focused more on the role of the United States in Guatemala relative to that in El Salvador. CEH charges of US involvement were initially met with a curt response from US Ambassador Planty, who insisted that the conflict had been 'between Guatemalans'. However, during a visit to Guatemala in March 1999, US President Clinton set an important precedent by expressing regret at US involvement in violations. The URNG also publicly requested forgiveness, characterizing violations committed by its members as 'excesses' and 'errors'.

Civil society groups were highly active in promoting alternative, 'bottom-up', truth and justice initiatives even before the CEH report was published. From 1993 onwards, dozens of mass graves have been exhumed on the initiative of local communities throughout the country, and a number of local monuments built.[18] Partly because of multiple local initiatives, demands that perpetrators be judicially sanctioned increased. After the publication of the CEH report, HROs vowed to pursue prosecutions for genocide through domestic and international courts against high-ranking military officers, including former heads of state General Lucas García and General Ríos Montt.[19] In March 1999 the victims' organization, the Mutual Support Group (GAM), began consultations with Spanish Judge Garzón, who was responsible for initiating extradition proceedings against former Chilean dictator General Pinochet, and who was threatening to bring charges against thirty-nine military officers in the Guatemalan courts if the government

[18] For one of the best-known cases, see EAFG (1995) and EPICA/CHRLA (1996).

[19] In February 1999 some 165 Guatemalan cases were pending before the IAHRC. In January 1998 the IAHRC ordered the government to pay compensation to the family of Nicholas Chapman Blake, a US journalist murdered by civil patrollers in 1985, and to the victims of a death squad killing (*Central America Report*, 19 February 1999).

failed to respond to CEH recommendations. Working in conjunction with international HROs such as NSA, activists called on the United States to declassify more documents to clarify the whereabouts of the disappeared, and to provide material compensation for the victims of violations.[20] In May 1999, NSA published a confidential Guatemalan military dossier about 182 people who disappeared between 1982 and 1985, which confirmed the murder of ninety-nine, emboldening relatives to press for further disclosure and prosecutions. The military closed ranks, rejecting the dossier as a fake, and maintained that its members should not be tried. In June 1999, in an attempt to defuse rising tension over the issue, the government attempted to broaden the Amnesty Law of 1996 in 'the national interest'. However, it failed to secure the agreement of the left-wing party, the New Nation Alliance (ANN), to revise the amnesty before full implementation of the CEH recommendations.

The following section assesses the impact of memory politics on the prospects for democratization in El Salvador, Honduras, and Guatemala. It considers its impact on institutional and legal reforms to ensure that the basic human rights and obligations of all individuals and groups are respected and enforced, and examines its influence on the construction of a broader culture of citizenship and tolerance.

The Impact of Memory Politics

Democratization in Central America demands an end to longstanding traditions of militarization of the body politic and impunity for the military. In institutional terms, this entails the subordination of the military to a more transparent and accountable civilian authority, together with extensive reform of judicial and public security institutions. However, institutional reforms alone will be insufficient to secure a viable democratic order. The countries discussed have been characterized historically to a greater or lesser extent by what may be termed 'socially constituted authoritarianism',[21] wherein the arbitrary abuse of power and violence have long been seen as acceptable, or at least normal, by a wide range

[20] At the time of Clinton's visit to Guatemala in March 1999, the NSA published previously classified US documents providing further evidence of more direct involvement of the US government in counter-insurgency abuses.

[21] I am grateful to Brandon Hamber for this term.

of political and social actors. Thus, democratization also requires that the political elite should cease to rely on extra-judicial means to protect their interests, and that popular demands find expression through institutional channels—in other words, that conflicts be resolved without recourse to violence or extra-legal means. In turn, this entails fulfilling citizenship aspirations and changing practices throughout civil society 'from the 'bottom-up', and changing the expectations and behaviour of elite groups, which traditionally have considered themselves above the law.

The impact of memory politics on these areas has varied. The nature and extent of legal and institutional reform in El Salvador, Guatemala, and Honduras has been framed by the particularities of each transition process. In some cases memory politics has been of importance in securing changes, in others less so. In terms of citizenship, memory politics has undoubtedly strengthened a sense of rights and entitlement among many formerly marginal and victimized sectors of the population, yet overall effects on elite and non-elite behaviour remain far from clear. However, it is important to recognize that the impact of memory politics on democratic consolidation is not a linear process. Irrespective of the nature of official truth and justice in transition, the ways in which past violations are framed by public memory is an ongoing process that changes from generation to generation, as the cases of Argentina and Chile indicate (see Chapter 4 above). In many senses, the ways in which past violations are remembered within society constitute an indicator of the degree to which political culture has been transformed or democratized. Given the non-lineal nature of memory politics, transitional processes of truth and justice should be understood as a point of departure, rather than of closure. Inquiries into memory in Central America are very recent, and it is therefore impossible to be conclusive about their long-term effects on the prospects for democratic government. Memory politics may resurface in different ways and with differing political and social effects. However, some initial comparisons and observations can be drawn at this stage.

Honduras

In Honduras official attempts to come to terms with past violations of human rights proved to be a critical element in the long and difficult struggle to demilitarize public security and subordinate the military to civilian control. The Valladares report highlighted the militarization of public security forces in the 1980s and signalled their extensive involvement in violations, thereby strengthening the hand of those calling for demilitarization of the police. In September 1995 the legislature approved a constitutional amendment placing the security forces under civilian control. The transfer of power finally occurred in the first months of the Flores Facussé administration. During the Reina presidency, military power and autonomy were also significantly curtailed. Measures included restrictions on military legal jurisdiction and privileges, the removal of several state institutions from military control, the reduction and increased oversight of the military budget, and the replacement of mandatory military service with a voluntary scheme. In January 1999 Congress voted unanimously to ratify a package of constitutional reforms to end forty-one years of military autonomy. With it, the military no longer retained the autonomy to select its supreme commander, determine institutional policy or freely administer its budget. The high command was to be abolished and replaced by an officers' council from which the president would appoint the defence minister. The fifteen constitutional amendments also ended the immunity of military commanders from prosecution (*Central American Report*, 29 January 1999).

This gradual reduction in power of the military was possible in part because of low social polarization, support from most civilian politicians and private-sector actors, and changes in the regional and international environment, which led to a rapid reduction in US support for the military. By the 1990s, a wide range of civil actors had become more vocal, demanding guarantees of basic human rights and accountability. The struggle of HROs for truth and justice was central to this shift. The civilian and the military elite has traditionally been more accommodating of popular demands than its counterparts in El Salvador and Guatemala. Even during the militarization and increased repression of the 1980s, clientelist and patronage linkages continued to mediate relations between the elite and civil organizations. The alliance between official and non-governmental sectors in efforts to investigate the past and prosecute those guilty of gross violations helped to break down the political culture of fear and acquiescence that had prevailed since the early 1980s. President Reina's endorsement of victims' claims in 1995 was highly important in this respect. Compared with El Salvador and Guatemala, the number of those directly affected by military repression was small and the reworking of social memory by victims therefore had a more diffuse impact on society as a whole. For example, monthly demonstrations by the victims' organization COFADEH calling for clarification of the whereabouts of the disappeared were confined to the capital and did not engender widespread organizing throughout rural areas, such as occurred in Guatemala through mass membership organizations such as the National Co-ordinator of Guatemalan Widows (CONAVIGUA). None the less, because of widespread rejection of abuse in a country where recourse to extreme violence constituted the exception rather than the rule, the efforts of Valladares and HROs to uncover the truth were less divisive than similar initiatives elsewhere in the region. They also found sympathy with broad sectors of the population, which were shocked by Valladares's revelations, as they had been unaware of the nature of state-sponsored repression in the early 1980s.

Perhaps most importantly, in the absence of a negotiated peace settlement, the joint efforts of official sectors and HROs to secure truth and justice helped to put issues of state accountability and civil–military relations at the heart of the political agenda throughout the 1990s. Public confidence in the rule of law increased somewhat with judicial reforms such as the creation of the National Commissioner for Human Rights and the MP and reforms to increase the independence of the Supreme Court, together with official attempts to prosecute those guilty of violations and corruption. The credibility and moral authority of new judicial institutions were undoubtedly bolstered by their apparent willingness to challenge long-standing traditions of impunity. None the less, there have been few convictions, and access to justice remains highly uneven and inadequate. In conclusion, the coincidence of diverse political interests within a campaign for truth and justice proved critical to securing far-reaching legal and institutional changes. It also contributed to the development of a more pro-active civil society demanding more transparency and accountability from government and state institutions. However, these developments have not secured democratic consolidation, which remains hampered by weak institutions, deep-rooted traditions of clientelism, and conflicts over resource allocation, although they have improved the relative prospects for strengthening liberal democratic practices and values within the Honduran political system.

El Salvador

In El Salvador, by contrast, the impact of the truth commission on institutional reform and civil society was relatively limited. Members hailed the commission as one of the most far-reaching 'callings to account' in Latin America, but the institutional and legal reforms secured in the transition depended more on the shifting balance of power between ARENA, the FMLN, and the military within the peace negotiations. The TC was important in challenging military impunity and in helping to secure the dismissal of the high command in March 1993. Yet the reduction of military power, the creation of the new civilian National Civil Police (PNC), and judicial reforms were dependent not on truth and justice processes but, again, on the balance of forces among negotiators. The accords mandated the reduction in the size of the military and the demilitarization of public security functions. This involved the abolition of the National Police (PN), the National Guard (GN), and the Treasury Police (PH), which had secured state control over rural areas and were responsible for the worst death squad activities of the early 1980s. They were replaced by the National Civilian Police (PNC), a force with equal quotas of former military and insurgent combatants. International support for the PNC was substantial and ONUSAL played a major role in ensuring human rights training and the development of a new mission for the security forces. These combined changes effectively reduced the capacity for repression of the state.

Judicial reform was, by comparison, more limited. The peace agreements included the restructuring of the Supreme Court, the strengthening of the National Council of the Judiciary (CNJ), an independent body charged with selecting, evaluating, and training judges, and the creation in July 1992 of an Ombudsman (PDH) within the Public Ministry.[22] Despite these advances, the rule of law remains weak. The purge of judges recommended by the TC and the CNJ has been slow and cautious, provision for public legal defence is insufficient, and reform of criminal law and procedures is still pending. In addition, the failure of the judiciary to tackle one of the worst crime waves in the Western Hemisphere has reduced further public confidence in the rule of law. The 1994 election of a new Supreme Court improved its independence, but the controversy in early 1998 over the election of the new Ombudsman demonstrated that judicial posts were still considered political spoils by the parties in Congress.

Memory politics in El Salvador can be understood primarily as a party-dominated process. The main goals of the FMLN during

[22] The PDH has extensive and broad responsibilities for guaranteeing respect for human rights. For a detailed review of judicial reform in El Salvador, see Dodson and Jackson (1997).

the peace negotiations were to secure a reduction in the power of the military and to be included in the formal political arena. Truth and justice initiatives were not essential to either, and the FMLN leadership reasoned that a tougher position on these issues would prejudice the entire peace process. The amnesty law effectively endorsed impunity, and justice for past violations was sacrificed to broader future political considerations. The relative lack of independence of civil society organizations from the FMLN meant that protest was short-lived and of limited impact. After the Supreme Court rejected their petition to declare the amnesty unconstitutional, HROs failed to develop alternative strategies to keep the issue alive. In marked contrast to their direct involvement in the Valladares report, in El Salvador the HROs were kept at arm's length by the UN throughout the TC process, further limiting their influence. After publication of the report, relatives of those killed in the civil war demanded that more should be done, and in February 1998 HROs led an initiative to erect a monument to the victims in San Salvador. Questions of justice and compensation were absent from the political agenda of both left and right. Democratic viability has improved with the legal and institutional changes secured through the peace accords, the end of the historical military–oligarchic alliance, the consolidation of ARENA as the political vehicle of the right, and the incorporation of the FMLN into electoral politics. None the less, civil society was demobilized after the accords, and growing popular disenchantment with the political system is reflected in rising abstention rates—over 60 per cent in the March 1999 presidential elections. While observance of human rights has improved, impunity and violence persists, and the extent to which the political elite is willing to respect judicial independence and the rule of law remains open to question. Advances in building a shared political culture of citizenship in El Salvador therefore remain extremely limited.

Guatemala

Legal and institutional reforms have been far weaker in Guatemala, particularly with respect to curtailing the power of the military, which remains the most powerful political actor in the country. Progress on the one-third cut in troop size and budget signalled in the peace agreements has been uneven, with targets set largely by the army (Schirmer, 1998). The creation of a civilian police force and the removal of responsibility for public security from the military has been similarly mixed. The National Civilian Police

(PNC) hastily set up in January 1997 failed to adequately screen new intakes, leading to criticism that it represented little more than a cosmetic reorganization of a force highly implicated in abuses, corruption, and extortion (Garst, 1997). In addition, the rise in common crime after the end of armed conflict has led to the employment of the army in police patrols and anti-kidnapping operations, raising fears that public security will be re-militarized. Limited institutional reforms notwithstanding, significant advances in demilitarization have occurred, including the abolition of village military commissioners in 1995 and the demobilization of the PACs in 1997, two mechanisms previously central to ensuring military control over rural society. In February 1999 the CEH recommended reforms for the army and a purge of human rights violators. It also called for a new training doctrine, the reform of military intelligence bodies, and the formation of an official commission to review officers' records, to remove those implicated in violations. However, the Arzú government responded that the army was already being reorganized and purged in compliance with the peace accords, thereby ignoring the recommendations.

Many measures for judicial reform were included in the peace agreements.[23] Progress has been made with the establishment of new tribunals in rural departments and the strengthening of the PDH. Community courts are being developed with the aim of incorporating indigenous legal practices, as mandated by the 1995 agreement on indigenous rights, and the UN has supported the training of legal translators. Reforms to the penal procedures code effective in 1994 have entailed a shift to oral proceedings, promoted by foreign donors as a way to secure more expeditious and transparent proceedings. None the less, the judiciary continues to suffer from chronic problems of intimidation, corruption, politicization, lack of adequately trained personnel, and insufficient provision, particularly in the rural areas. State investigation and prosecution services remain highly ineffective and subject to military pressure. High indices of criminality and lack of public confidence in the judiciary, combined with the authoritarian social legacy of counter-insurgency, have resulted in numerous occasions when mobs lynch suspected criminals.[24] More significantly, impunity for violations continues. In the vast majority of cases the military remain immune from prosecution or investigation, even

[23] For more detail on recent changes to the judiciary, see WOLA (1998).

[24] HROs have also raised the possibility that such summary justice may be deliberately provoked in order to justify tougher policies on law and order.

in cases that have gained an international profile, such as the 1998 assassination of Bishop Gerardi.

If memory politics in El Salvador was a party-driven process, in Guatemala it has been led by a broad range of civil society organizations increasingly independent from the former revolutionary left and supported by international NGOs and the UN mission in Guatemala (MINUGUA). HROs have long demanded an end to military impunity. However, in the wake of the armed conflict, perhaps precisely because of the limited nature of institutional and legal changes secured through the peace agreements, they have increasingly challenged military power and impunity though a grass-roots politics of memory. Civil organizations have developed multiple unofficial initiatives to uncover the truth and secure justice for victims. In many cases individuals or civil groups have carried out tasks of legal defence and criminal investigation normally attributable to the state. In the case of the massacre of eleven former refugees by the army at Xamán, Alta Verapaz, in 1995, for example, the Rigoberta Menchú Foundation (FRMT) acted as an auxiliary for the prosecution.[25] The Catholic Church and other HROs have worked exhaustively to meet the demands of local communities to exhume clandestine massacre sites and identify the remains of their relatives.[26] The support of international HROs and forensic anthropologists proved a vital support to these efforts. In addition, many NGOs are working with communities to try to address the mental health problems generated by years of violence, fear, and denial.

In marked contrast to El Salvador, in the ethnically and politically fragmented society of Guatemala grass-roots memory politics has become a central part of the search for new collective identities in the postwar dispensation. Locally organized exhumations or the construction of local monuments have prompted the formation of new transregional communities of survivors, across regions and ethno-linguistic barriers: for example the huge cross built by twenty-eight displaced Q'eqchi'-Maya communities at the village of Sahakok in northern Alta Verapaz in memory of over 900 people killed; or the monument to those massacred in 1982 at Río Negro in Rabinal, Baja Verapaz. This has promoted a new understanding of rights and justice. Through local initiatives in memory, and with

[25] The RVM works with former indigenous refugees.

[26] REMHI identified over 300 mass graves throughout the country, the majority of which have yet to be exhumed. Demand for exhumations far exceeds the capacities of the various forensic teams.

the support of international observers, many rural Mayans have come to reject military domination and to demand their rights to more autonomous, peaceful, and culturally appropriate forms of development. In many cases this has exposed them to threats or violence from former civil patrollers and others. None the less, such initiatives challenge fear and militarization and help people to understand, even if not to come to terms with, the highly localized form of violence that divided families and communities.

Memory politics has empowered many previously marginal sectors, particularly Mayan peasants, and has thereby contributed to the construction of citizenship 'from the bottom up'. However, political and economic elites have given little indication that they are willing to submit themselves to the rule of law and cede historic privileges. Most importantly, impunity for violations persists. There is a danger that popular frustration with the justice system and democracy will increase when expectations for justice are not met. Over the medium term, however, only the combination of pressure from civil society organizations and the international community holds out a prospect of securing the legal and institutional reforms necessary for the minimum conditions for democracy.

In conclusion, then, non-official initiatives in truth and justice have contributed to a strengthened and radicalized civil society in Guatemala although, as historical precedent suggests, this alone cannot guarantee democracy (Yashar, 1997). While the cohesion of civilian parties of the right increased during the 1990s, their capacity to channel popular aspirations and the extent of their independence from the military remain open to question. Since 1995 the political spectrum has widened to include left-wing parties, but their ability to respond to popular demands for accountability remains limited in the face of the continuing power of the military. Significant advances have been made in institutional reform and in building a culture of citizenship since the signing of the peace accords, but changes in the civil–military balance and in elite political culture have been insufficient to guarantee liberal democracy.

Conclusions

Different official trade-offs between truth and justice were reached in all three countries. Official commissions of inquiry into past violations were carried out everywhere, but the claims of victims for compensation and justice met with very different official responses. Only in Honduras did the transitional state support victims' demands for compensation and judicial sanctions against those responsible for violations, and few successful convictions were secured. In Guatemala the state endorsed the notion of compensation but not trials, despite a high degree of mobilization by civil society organizations. In El Salvador official memory politics contributed to the demobilization of civil society and the state provided neither compensation nor justice to victims. The differences outlined here depended on a number of factors, including the impact of violence and armed conflict on political and civil society, the particularities of the transition itself, and the role played by local and international HROs. In El Salvador, where a strong left secured a share in political power and a reduction in the power of the military through the peace negotiations, trade-offs between truth and justice were determined by the political elite, and such questions all but disappeared from the political agenda after 1993. In Guatemala, where the guerrilla movement was defeated and failed to secure significant concessions from the military through peace negotiations, memory politics continues to mobilize a heterogeneous and independent civil society in the wake of the armed conflict.

The experiences of El Salvador and Guatemala also indicate that, while UN involvement guarantees thorough, well funded investigations and a high international profile for the results of truth commission reports, its impact on domestic human rights monitoring can vary. In El Salvador UN operations overshadowed and displaced local HROs, contributing to their demobilization.[27] In its subsequent verification mission in Guatemala, the UN specifically included the strengthening of local civil society organizations as part of its mandate and adjusted its operations accordingly. Analysis of memory politics in Honduras and Guatemala also suggests that strategic collaboration with international NGO counterparts can prove particularly empowering for domestic human rights groups.

Memory politics cannot by itself guarantee a genuinely inclusive and democratic political system. Indeed, there is a danger that popular mobilization around truth and justice issues may give way to widespread disenchantment and frustration if demands for justice and compensation are not met. However, while widespread social mobilization around issues of historical memory and justice is in itself no guarantee that democracy will endure, a memory politics that demobilizes and does not empower civil society cannot bode well for deeper democracy. Again, memory politics is not

[27] For a critical view see Popkin (2000).

lineal, and transitional truth and justice processes should be understood as points of departure rather than points of closure. In none of the countries assessed is the rule of law and liberal democracy consolidated. Rather, to a greater or lesser extent, all three are 'illiberal democracies', where electoral alternation of power coexists with few guarantees of basic civil rights for the majority of the population.[28] Impunity for powerful military and civilian elites persists, and access to justice for the majority of the population is limited. Yet, when supported by the active involvement of civil society, official truth commissions have contributed to the reconstitution of a less authoritarian social order in the wake of civil conflict and state violence.

Across the region memory politics has made important contributions to demilitarizing state and society, challenging traditions of military impunity and political cultures marked by denial, silence, and fear. To the extent that it has emphasized the idea of accountability and the rights and obligations of all groups and individuals within society, it has begun to promote a culture of citizenship. For the victims themselves, the opportunity to give testimony and commemorate their dead has strengthened their self-perception as individuals and communities with rights. In some cases initiatives in memory have contributed to the building of new collective and individual identities in the post-conflict political dispensation, leading to the reconfiguration of 'communities of belonging'. The commemoration of the victims of political violence also implies a symbolic re-valorization and the inclusion of those previously excluded from the national polity, and as such represents an attempt to rework the moral and political community of the nation-state. Officially recognizing the wrongs perpetrated against historically marginal, oppressed, or demonized groups is a necessary first step towards their inclusion as citizens. Exercises in memory politics cannot secure or consolidate democracy, but in the wake of widespread and systematic violations of human rights by the state, they are an essential first step towards its constitution.

[27] On 'illiberal democracies', see Zakaria (1998).

6

Justice and Legitimacy in the South African Transition

Richard A. Wilson

Introduction

New regimes that supersede an authoritarian order do not 'suddenly' have to face the issue of how to deal with human rights violations of the past. Decisions to establish truth commissions and the extent of prosecutions are constrained by events before the accession to power. The parameters of justice are framed by the historical character of authoritarian legality, by the balance of power between bellicose parties, and in concrete pacts reached during negotiations to end armed conflict. Opposition movements are seldom wholly excluded, and instead are often party to decisions on amnesty, truth commissions, and the limits of criminal prosecutions. Thus, the room for manœuvre of postwar regimes is often severely limited, as the boundaries of justice have been set at an earlier stage in the transition.

A common formulation of post-conflict human rights imperatives is that new regimes are torn between a 'political logic', which gives priority to the consolidation of democratic stability, and an 'ethical logic', which urges prosecutions for all offenders (Benomar, 1993). This is sometimes portrayed as a tension between 'revenge' and 'reconciliation', with legal redress identified with the former and truth commissions with the latter. Yet there is only a single logic, where prosecutions and pardons, truth commissions and selective amnesia are locked into in a direct relationship. The criminal justice system and other institutions for addressing past violations such as truth commissions are part of a single process. They both complement and contradict each other, but are never autonomous from one another, nor independent in their implications for the other.

Truth commissions exist to both transcend the limitations of the courts and restore the legitimacy of a tarnished legal system, which can in turn can be directed to occupy the interstices created by the process of truth finding and indemnity for perpetrators.

Race, Nationalism, and Political Violence

There is no one single cause for the massive levels of political violence in the recent history of South Africa (Adam and Moodley, 1993; Kane-Burman, 1993; Thornton, 1990). Reasons for the conflict changed over time as ideological struggles shifted to new terrain and involved changing actors. New conflicts were swept into the path of older ones and fuelled them, while local conflicts escalated when they were linked to national and global ones. Violence emerged from a history of dispossession and extreme social inequality, and the violent protection of a racially divided structure of social and economic privilege. In South Africa social indicators are in line with much of the rest of sub-Saharan Africa, even though the World Bank has classified the country as 'upper-middle income'. It calculates that two-thirds of the black population is poor or 'ultra-poor', and that 61 per cent of children live in poverty. On average, whites earns 9.5 times the income of blacks and live 11.5 years longer (Table 6.1).

Violence is not simply the result of competition over material resources, but was created, expressed, and exacerbated historically by nationalist and racial discourses, which sought to 'naturalize' social inequalities. Forms of scientific racism were widespread in Europe during the period of the modern republic established in 1910, and were internalized by the local white elite administering a neo-colonial racial hierarchy (Dubow, 1995). The dispossession of

TABLE 6.1 *Poverty and Social Exclusion Indicators in South Africa (%)*

	African	White	Coloured and Asian
Population	75	14	11
Income	28	61	11
Infant mortality (per 1,000 live births)	100	10	
Illiteracy (all groups)		54%	

Source: CIIR (1996); World Bank (1996).

Africans is conventionally traced back to the 1913 Land Act, which consolidated the 1902 Treaty of Vereeniging on land and residence, and enabled whites to occupy the best lands and control the lucrative mining industry. In the 1920s a nationalist movement among descendants of Dutch settlers, or Afrikaners, became dominant and led to greater encroachments on to black land ownership. After the Second World War the National Party (NP) became the expression of Afrikaner and then, more generally, white nationalism, and was easily re-elected in whites-only elections for the next four decades. From 1948 onwards the NP pursued a project of racial segregation, *apartheid*, and introduced legislation that progressively denationalized black citizens (Dugard, 1978). This denied Africans rights to own and run businesses and confined them to 13 per cent of the national territory. The cornerstones of apartheid legislation were laid in the 1950s, and by the 1990s 69 per cent of land was owned by 50,000 white farmers or farming companies, out of a total population of 41 million (Trade Union Research Project, cited in CIIR, 1996).

March 1960 was a watershed for modern resistance to authoritarian rule, when the police shot dead 69 protesters against pass laws in Sharpeville. The African National Congress (ANC) initiated its armed struggle with acts of sabotage on a key day in the Afrikaner national calendar, 16 December 1961.[1] State repression and the gaoling of leaders such as Nelson Mandela in the early 1960s led to a lull in resistance, but the late 1970s saw an outburst of popular hostility to the regime, with students in Soweto rioting against the teaching of Afrikaans in 1976. The development of the anti-apartheid movement in the 1980s went from strength to strength in terms of political mobilization and was never systematically crushed by the apartheid security apparatus. Although the ANC was banned and could not formally organize inside the country, and the armed wing of the ANC, Spear of the Nation (MK), never mounted a significant military threat against the state, ANC-aligned trade unions challenged state and elite economic power. The unofficial ANC confederation in the country, the United Democratic Front (UDF), succeeded in 'making the townships ungovernable' through rent boycotts, school boycotts, demonstrations, strikes, and other means.

[1] The ANC was formed in 1912, and is South Africa's oldest political party. It is a broad coalition, which includes forces ranging from the far left (the South African Communist Party), to the centre–right. It is the most popular political party and won nearly two-thirds of the vote in the 1994 elections. It led the Government of National Unity (GNU) until mid-1996, from which time it has ruled alone.

Throughout the 1980s, the main local expressions of the liberation movement were the civic associations, or civics, in the black townships. Civics were formed in the wake of uprisings in townships across the country beginning in June 1976. The Soweto Civic Association was the first civic structure to provide an organizational framework for overt resistance, and subsequent civics were formed in other locations around the country, notably in Port Elizabeth. The civic movement was unified under the UDF in 1983, which provided national co-ordination and promoted the creation of new civics.[2] The latter contributed significantly to weakening the state at the local level and were central to the strategy of creating a mass insurrection. Radicals saw them as expressions of 'people's power', the seeds of a revolutionary state (Shubane and Madiba, 1992). The rise of civics had wide-reaching policy implications for the apartheid regime, which considered black settlements in the white cities only as temporary residential areas. The 'real' black residential areas were to be the separate black 'homelands'. By showing that blacks were in the townships to stay, civics seriously challenged the grand apartheid project to denationalize black South African citizens and make them citizens of weak, corrupt, and dependent homelands, such as the four created—Transkei, Bophutatswana, Venda, and Ciskei.

Despite successive states of emergency beginning in 1985, which transformed many townships into war zones, the anti-apartheid movement managed to survive and even hold on to and politicize its community and trade union bases. Political mobilization in the townships created myriad forms of resistance, which combined with an effective foreign campaign of sanctions that ultimately forced the state to halt apartheid, roll back existing legislation, and consider talks with the enemy. There were also economic incentives to end the war. Because of its human rights record, South Africa was a pariah state, and the white elite desperately sought to be part of the international community to qualify for international aid, credit and investment, bilateral loans, and access to foreign markets for national exports. Exports were hard-hit by international economic sanctions, particularly after the Congress of the United States passed the Comprehensive Anti-Apartheid Act in 1986, which banned South African agricultural products, coal, iron ore,

[2] The UDF subscribed to the ANC Freedom Charter and was the informal national wing of the ANC. It was an umbrella organization made up of approximately 800 organizations, ranging from civic associations, women's groups, and trade unions to sports clubs, and claimed 2 million members.

textiles, and flights from South African Airways (Landsberg, 1994; Manby, 1992). This led sectors of the business community with a more enlightened view of self-interest to recognize that internal war and international isolation were bad for business, and to pressure governments to negotiate with the opposition.

Delegations from the white business elite went to Lusaka, to Zambia in 1986, and to Britain in 1987 to engage in talks with ANC leaders, much to the chagrin of the white minority regime (Atkinson and Friedman, 1994; CIIR, 1996; Friedman, 1993; Shubane and Shaw, 1993; Sparks, 1996). The South African army was embroiled in wars in southern Africa in the 1970s and 1980s, notably in Namibia, Angola, Zimbabwe, and Mozambique, and the defeats it suffered drained military capacity and morale, furthering the aims of the anti-apartheid movement. In the 1980s, the NP knew that involvement in Namibia and Angola, while combating insurrection at home, was not sustainable in the long run, with defence spending running at 15 per cent of an already overstretched budget. Further, the military conscription campaign was in tatters as young white males refused to fight in the bush wars in South Africa and beyond. By the end of the 1980s the armed conflict had reached a stalemate, and neither side could hope to wholly annihilate the other. The ANC realized that any victory would be merely phyrric, as little would remain on which to rebuild a new multiracial society. It was feared that the dominant minority would hold on to their privileges for ever, and parts of the opposition began to consider the possibility of a political settlement.

The NP, which ruled from the white citadel of Pretoria, was neither stable nor secure. In the 1980s many black townships were war zones, where state agents ventured only in armed personnel carriers. Some NP elements knew that sooner or later a political settlement would have to be sought, although they hoped that talks would weaken the ANC and dampen its revolutionary zeal. Initially, they only wanted to tinker with apartheid, to create a system of power-sharing that would entrench white 'minority' rights, ensure an NP veto on the introduction of key legislation, and thereby allow whites to cling to their historical political privileges. Their strategy was to use negotiations to destabilize the ANC politically and undermine its bargaining position through violence. This led to the creation of the so-called 'Third Force' in the black townships, composed of security force personnel, right-wing and non-ANC parties such as the Inkatha Freedom Party (IFP), and allegedly directed by high-ranking ministers in the NP government (S. Ellis, 1998). However, although the NP government was militarily hegemonic, it was politically weak, especially in the majority of townships where civics controlled local government functions.

In contrast with Latin America, the depth and resilience of the political resources commanded by the liberation movement in the late 1980s led to a transition that involved a successful wresting of real control from the former regime, and resulted in profound social and political transformations. It should be remembered that, notwithstanding the central role of civil groups in the peace process, the single most important determinant in the democratization of authoritarian governments beyond the simple technical functioning of liberal institutions is the potency of the political opposition.

The international context was also highly conducive to the peace process. It is difficult to overestimate the importance of the demise of the Soviet Union and the end of the Cold War in undermining fossilized political positions. The global political thaw caused a sea change in the strategies of socialist movements, away from models of a centralized state and the path of armed revolution. The fall of the Berlin Wall challenged the governmental elite to revise its ideological commitment to fighting the 'international communist threat', which justified state repression. The rigid political configuration began to change after the withdrawal of Cuban troops in Angola and an agreement on Namibian independence. In this context, authoritarian regimes across the region came under greater pressure to liberalize. In 1989 the USA informed President de Klerk that he had only a year to end the state of emergency, release political prisoners, and lift the ban on the liberation movement (Landsberg, 1994: 280). In 1990, the ban on the ANC, the Pan Africanist Congress (PAC), and Communist Party (SACP) was finally lifted, and Nelson Mandela was released after twenty-seven years' incarceration on Robben Island.

The Negotiations for a Transition

The start of negotiations did not lead to an immediate reduction in political conflict. Indeed, it led to its intensification, as the looming political settlement crystallized divisions between and within opposing political positions. Right-wingers inside and outside the government resorted to political violence on a number of occasions in order to destroy the peace process. As old state structures crumbled and failed to be replaced, police and soldiers became either ineffectual or dangerous, as they took advantage of the uncertainty to act with impunity. Evidence that the transition bred violence

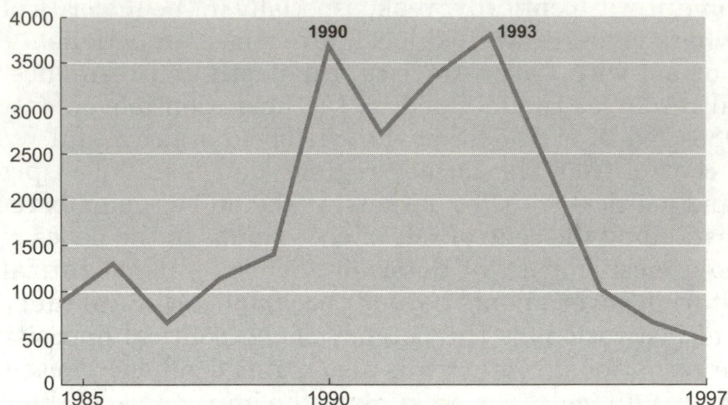

Figure 6.1 *Political Fatalities in South Africa, 1985–1997*

in South Africa is striking (Figure 6.1). Levels of violence surged the year talks began and peaked the year talks ended. In 1990 there were 1,000 fatalities on the 'Reef' around Johannesburg, and in 1991 the number doubled to 2,000 (Shaw, 1994: 182).

In July 1990, political violence exploded in the hitherto relatively calm Transvaal townships following the formation and organization of Inkatha as a political party and the lifting of the ban on liberation parties. The month that talks commenced, there were four days of clashes between ANC and IFP members, which left thirty dead. Within a year, conflict became routine and swept whole communities into a maelstrom of violence. In 1991–2, drive-by shootings, attacks on beer halls and commuter trains, and other acts of retribution became commonplace. The strategy of the Third Force became one of randomized terror; it attacked people not for their political affiliation but simply to create an atmosphere of fear and instability in the townships of the Transvaal. Despite government backing of the Third Force, the government accepted no responsibility for the wave of terror. It referred to the upsurge in killings as the result of primordial inter-ethnic 'black-on-black' animosities. President de Klerk maintained that the 'Zulu IFP' fought the 'Xhosa ANC' out of ethnic hatred going back hundreds of years—even though the ANC had been founded by a Zulu and was preponderantly non-Xhosa.

In contrast to many other negotiated conflicts, the South African government insisted that foreign mediation was unnecessary. In 1991 the ANC insisted that foreign intervention was essential, since it had long enjoyed influence with many European social democratic governments and international bodies. It looked as though the 'go-it-alone' strategy was doomed to failure, as the second Convention for a Democratic South Africa talks (CODESA II) ground to a halt in June 1992. The ANC began to adopt measures outside the negotiating hall to ensure that the process would continue. On 16 June 1992 it mustered rallies and a mass stay-away around the country to pressure the government. ANC mass rallies were overshadowed on 17 June, when IFP hostel dwellers attacked the community of Boipatong in the industrial Vaal region and arbitrarily killed forty-eight residents. There was compelling eye-witness evidence of police and army complicity and even direct involvement in the attack, as residents claimed that IFP members were transported in armed personnel carriers. On 22 June the ANC leadership, under immense pressure from its bases, formally suspended talks with the government. It presented the government with a list of fourteen demands, which had to be met before talks could resume. With the peace process in crisis, it took events outside the negotiating forum to break the political stalemate.

The ANC mobilized its political bases and in so doing gained a leverage that became vital in the transition process and would have major implications for its enhanced ability to deal more thoroughly with past violations after the transition. In conjunction with the Confederation of South African Trades Unions (COSATU), the ANC organized a 'rolling mass action' campaign of huge demonstrations around the country, involving 4 million people. Civic associations called on township residents to continue boycotting rent and mortgage payments to pressure the government to stop the violence and negotiate in good faith (Seekings, 1996). Although numerous offers of international mediation were rebuffed by both parties, an increased international presence in the country, including observers from the United Nations (UN), the European Union (EU), the Organization of African Unity (OAU), and the Commonwealth, somewhat lessened the possibility of violence during marches. Yet the political situation was so highly charged that a tragic confrontation seemed unavoidable. The corrupt homelands, crumbling through historic neglect, were particularly targeted by the mass action campaign. They had continued to bar the ANC and prevent free political organizing. On 7 September 1992 the Ciskei Defence Force (CDF), led by the corrupt military leader Oupa Gqozo, fired on unarmed ANC demonstrators marching in Bisho, killing twenty-eight people.

The Bisho killings, the demonstration of increasingly massive support for the ANC throughout the country, and the inability of President de Klerk to suppress the campaign gave renewed impetus to the negotiations. On 26 September 1992 de Klerk and Mandela signed a settlement on violence and conditions for restarting talks, the Record of Understanding. This was the critical moment when the balance of power in the transition shifted away from the NP regime to the ANC negotiators. Up to that point the NP had been in control, but after the Understanding it realized that the process had taken a course of its own and that the ANC was now setting the agenda. The NP was forced into significant concessions; most importantly, it left its main political partner, the IFP, out in the cold as it sought to ensure a position for itself in the emerging structure of power. Liberal constitutional ideas began to gain a stronghold over power sharing and 'minority rights' for whites. At the same time, an awareness of the limitations of mass action ultimately led activists, the ANC, and the SACP to oppose an insurrection to seize power, which left radicals in the ranks of both parties on the margin, and reinforced the tendency towards compromise and negotiation.

At this point there was greater unanimity of purpose between the ANC and NP, and informal repression became less of a threat to the talks. A negotiated settlement was finally reached in November 1993, leading to the first non-racial elections in South African history and to the establishment in April 1994 of a Government of National Unity (GNU), run by the ANC but including high-ranking NP ministers such as Pik Botha and de F. W. Klerk.

Negotiating an Amnesty

The negotiations leading to the new South African political dispensation were among the most participatory and democratic seen in any transition from authoritarian rule. Even in CODESA I and II, political parties and civil groups had already intervened and advanced their agenda. The political system of the new South Africa and its economic structure were all hotly debated. The issue of amnesty for human rights offenders was the least subject to open discussion, and was decided by a direct political deal between the NP and the ANC. This is typical of a general pattern. The area of justice in transition is the one in which civil groups are usually the least effective in shaping the course of the talks, and where the two main protagonists in the conflict act most expediently to protect their interests. It is one of the most elitist questions of all the issues in transitional negotiations, and the one in which leaders are most likely to reach a deal over the heads of ordinary people.

Part of the reason for this is structural: amnesties usually come at the very end of negotiations, during a time of demobilization and exodus of international funding agencies, and when the influence of civil groups and the human rights movement begins to wane. It may also be that there is no clear 'popular' position on the issue. In author discussions with over 150 victims of violations in 1995–8, a variety of perspectives on justice and reconciliation issues were encountered, ranging from blanket 'Christian' forgiveness and the abandonment of prosecutions in the interests of wider democratic stability, to a deep need for retribution, including the death penalty, for perpetrators. Further, while victims were not tightly organized into a social movement that could effectively campaign to prevent amnesty, it is also likely that no amount of pressure would have dissuaded the main political parties from agreeing an indemnity.

A mandate for an amnesty was established in the epilogue, or post-amble, as it is referred to, of the 1993 interim constitution. The post-amble, National Unity and Reconciliation, was agreed to after all other bargaining had ceased, after a last minute technical committee meeting between lawyers from the two main political parties.[3] It rejected retribution and called for past injustices to be addressed 'on the basis that there is a need for understanding but not for vengeance, a need for reparation but not for retaliation'. It was clear that the central mechanism for 'reconciliation' would be an amnesty, rather than the later formulations of the concept promoted by the Truth and Reconciliation Commission (TRC) (whose motto was 'Reconciliation through Truth' and not 'Reconciliation through Indemnity', which would have been closer to the constitutional accord).

Although human rights organizations (HROs) could not forestall an amnesty, they were able to shape the form that the amnesty would take, to prevent a blanket amnesty, and to push for its integration with the institution of the truth commission. HROs did a great deal of lobbying between the passage of the interim constitution and the National Unity and Reconciliation Act (NURA) in 1995, which established the TRC as a body to investigate gross human rights violations, as well as to oversee reparations and the amnesty process. Some HROs sought to work with the ANC-dominated government to create a truth commission with legal 'teeth'. The citizenship rights group Justice in Transition, headed

[3] The writing of the post-amble was entrusted to the technical committee of Mac Maharaj (ANC) and Fanie van der Merwe (National Party).

by Alex Boraine, who was later the manager of the TRC, played an important role in framing the terms of the commission. The Centre for the Study of Violence and Reconciliation (CSVR) also intervened. When it seemed that congressional deputies would balk at 'naming names' in the final report, the organization flew a number of victims' family members to Cape Town, where they successfully demanded the right to know the names of the killers of their kin. Thus, once the political deal was struck between the two main political parties, civil groups had a limited but important impact on negotiating the terms and functions of the truth commission and amnesty mechanism.

The TRC as a Liminal Institution

Truth commissions are now standard post-conflict structures which have been set up in over seventeen countries in the last twenty years to investigate unresolved cases arising from past human rights violations (Hayner, 1994; Cassell, 1993; Stanley Cohen, 1995; Diamond, 1994; Ensalaco, 1994). They are also one of the main mechanisms whereby transitional regimes seek to create legitimacy for state institutions still tainted by the legacy of authoritarian rule. Despite the holding of elections and the apparently radical reform of the laws and the structure of government in the new South Africa, there was an inevitable degree of continuity of state institutions in structure, organization, and personnel. A lingering institutional memory impeded the development of citizens' trust in, and allegiance to, the new political dispensation. Since negotiated settlements usually ensure an ongoing role for the outgoing political elite, a truth commission has become one of the main ways to say that the new government is different and is committed to protecting and respecting the rights of citizens. By asserting discontinuity with the past, it is claimed that such commissions can re-establish the basis of citizenship and even deter state-sponsored violence in the future.

How do truth commissions manufacture legitimacy, and in what ways can the political constraints actually encourage a culture of impunity? Truth commissions are associated with wider attempts to overhaul the image of the criminal justice system. The importance of legitimate legal institutions and an independent judiciary is very significant in South Africa because the country has invested so much historical political capital in constitutional sovereignty. If Hannah Arendt was justified in writing that the first act of totalitarianism is to kill the legal impulse in citizens, then part of the role of transitional bodies such as truth commissions is to revive that juridical impulse. An important impediment to the resuscitation of the legal person has been the historical inability of the justice system to carry out prosecutions of human rights violations.

Lack of faith in the courts was therefore one of the strongest arguments in favour of a truth commission in South Africa; it was widely perceived that apartheid crimes could not be handed over to the old criminal justice system. The whole edifice of a culture of human rights and equal citizenship rests upon the existence of a 'state of right', which involves an end to the arbitrariness and irrationality of a repressive juridical apparatus and the establishment of due process and fairness. This has not been easy in South Africa. However hard new justice ministries have worked towards judicial reform, the transition of the criminal justice system has lagged behind reforms to political institutions. It has been much easier for the ANC government to replace political posts in the public sector than to replace bureaucratic and technical staff. This has forced it to rely, in part, upon an apartheid legal infrastructure, as so many magistrates and senior police officers from the old order are still in place.

The way in which human rights violations are documented and brought before the courts (or not) has a direct bearing upon the complexion of human rights in the post-conflict period. During the peace talks, despite all the evidence of police involvement and government training and the arming of hit squads in the press, the ANC could not make the charges of government involvement in random violence stick. This was partly because of the way in which violence was organized, with some central support and direction for the training, arming, and selection of types of target, but also a decentralized form of operations that was not always evenly controlled by the centre. There is still a great deal of debate about the degree of state involvement in informal repression. As opponents of the Third Force thesis insist, the relationship between de Klerk and the security forces had become increasingly strained. None the less, it appears that the President was kept informed of major covert initiatives. The evidence that has emerged at criminal trials indicates that the highest levels of the de Klerk regime were aware of the links between the state security apparatus and other Third Force elements such as the IFP and the white far right. Since such networks were covert, it was often very difficult for local HROs with limited resources to monitor, much less mediate, violent conflicts.[4]

Thus, the task of debunking official myths and exposing police and political party involvement fell to national commissions of enquiry such as the Harms, Goldstone, and Waddington commissions, the latter an offshoot of the Goldstone Commission set up investigate the 1992 Boipatong massacre. All of these commissions had insufficient resources, were overly legalistic in the search for prima facie evidence, were misled by police and political party cover-ups, and were disappointing in their results. Had they wielded a wider political analysis they would have revealed more about state involvement in informal repression. National peace monitors largely convinced the international community of the existence of a policy of informal state violence, but few mechanisms existed to bring external pressure to bear on political actors to negotiate in good faith. The Goldstone Commission finally confirmed the involvement of the police in equipping and training IFP hit squads, but only in March 1994, a month before all-party elections when the violence of the transition had decreased. Thus, inquiries and national monitoring played little part in diminishing violence during the talks themselves. The work of these inquiries would have been greatly aided by an international verification mission, which might have revealed more about Third Force activities earlier and therefore possibly forestalled the government's strategy of destabilization. Above all, the commissions demonstrated the limitations of using existing structures and personnel to unearth past violations.

The Harms and Goldstone Commissions resulted only in one significant prosecution: that of the former commander of a security police unit at Vlakplass, Colonel Eugene de Kock. In late 1996, in the most important criminal trial in post-apartheid history, de Kock was sentenced to 212 years, having been convicted of dozens of offences including eight murders, numerous counts of attempted murder, and supplying arms and bombs to the IFP to wage war against anti-apartheid activists. The criminal courts proved more conclusive than governmental commissions of inquiry in establishing evidence of NP participation in the structures of terror. Despite rogue elements and the decentralized nature of repression, irrefutable evidence emerged that the government, the right wing, security forces and the IFP were allied in a strategy of covert violence during the negotiation process.

[4] For a discussion of the local peace committees set up under the National Peace Accord, see Shaw (1993).

Many of the unverified allegations of the human rights movement during the early 1990s were confirmed in the de Kock trial. The defendant confirmed that security forces trained IFP hit squads in Natal and Namibia, in order to destabilize the position of the ANC. He also claimed that high-ranking cabinet ministers, including Minister of Law and Order, Adriaan Vlok, Minister Louis Le Grange, Foreign Minister Pik Botha, and Defence Minister Magnus Malan, all had knowledge of dirty tricks operations (*The Star*, 16 and 18 September 1996). A month later, Attorney-General McNally of KwaZulu–Natal issued arrest warrants against former defence minister General Magnus Malan and ten other high ranking officials in connection with a massacre of thirteen people in KwaZulu–Natal in 1987. The judge accepted that IFP agents had committed the killings after training with the South African Defence Force (SADF), but found no evidence to connect the perpetrators of the killings to the military top brass. As the verdict was read out, an anguished relative of one victim cried out 'they must have committed suicide!' (*Sunday Independent*, 27 October 1996).

These were potentially the most extensive and far-reaching prosecutions since the demise of apartheid. However, the case against Malan was dismissed in October 1996, demonstrating the weaknesses of the judicial system. The state prosecution was a procedural nightmare: it called unreliable state witnesses and neglected to call others who could have corroborated its case. The kind of investigative process necessary for successful prosecution —producing evidence through sophisticated forensic work and then arguing it cogently in court—did not occur. This was the legacy of apartheid legality. In the decades before 1994, state prosecutors could rely upon brutal police methods, forced confessions by suspects, and rigged 'state security trials'. Officials such as McNally did not have the disposition to develop the prosecuting skills necessary under a democratic legal order. The rapid and effective prosecution of police officers in the new political dispensation has also been hampered by repeated accusations that some attorneys-general failed to prosecute for political reasons. In September 1995 McNally was closely questioned by the parliamentary select committee on justice for his reticence to prosecute political cases. During his seven-year stewardship of the justice system in KwaZulu-Natal, he had not followed through on a single prosecution of those responsible for the 12,000 political killings in the province since 1984.

One must understand the significance of the TRC in this judicial and political context. TRC Chairperson Archbishop Desmond

Tutu highlighted the difference between the approach of the commission and that of the legal system to evidence and guilt. In his words, 'the court acquits because the evidence is not sufficient to prove beyond a reasonable doubt. But you know as you walk free out of the court that people know that you did this. You still have to face your God.' For Tutu, the TRC offered 'a better prospect of establishing the truth about our past than criminal trials'. Because the criminal justice system simply could not cope with all the violations committed over a thirty-four-year period, the TRC was easily justified. Prosecuting each and every offender would have been too lengthy, costly, and destabilizing, especially in a context where there was little public demand for prosecutions. The legal system could not handle the backlog of past abuses it had once ignored, and thus could not be expected to handle its own rehabilitation singlehandedly, by reversing its attitude to state crimes.

National legal systems and truth commissions are to an extent complementary and work in tandem, with the latter compensating for the limitations and deficiencies of the former. The de Kock prosecution was relevant for the TRC process since it persuaded some wavering lower-ranking security force officials to testify in the hope of gaining amnesty. The two may also work against each other, however. The TRC amnesty mechanism provided an escape route for some security policemen under investigation by state prosecutors, such as Brigadier Cronje and four other policemen under investigation by Transvaal Attorney-General Jan D'Oliveira in 1996. Perpetrators were also emboldened by the weakness of the judiciary, as exemplified by the collapse of the Malan trial, and thus failed to approach the TRC for amnesty. Whatever the nature of the relationship, criminal prosecutions and truth commissions clearly have a direct bearing on the work each carries out. They are never autonomous, unrelated processes.

Thus, truth commissions occupy a liminal space between existing institutions, with the hope that their aura of benevolence may infect surrounding state structures. In anthropological parlance, liminality is associated with mediation, and in the case of the TRC it refers to how the Commission mediates between different branches of government. The Commission exhibited a number of liminal characteristics that made it neither a legal, a political, nor a religious institution. It was a transitory and fleeting statutory body, which functioned for no longer than two years. It was not the product of any single government branch; rather, it was nominally independent, but positioned somewhere in between all three major branches of government.

The TRC was formally beholden to the executive. The seventeen Commissioners were selected and could be removed solely by President Nelson Mandela. It made recommendations to the President regarding reparations and 'the institutional, administrative and legislative measures which should be introduced in order to prevent the commission of violations of human rights'. It had an ambivalent relationship to the legal order: it was not exclusively a legal institution, as hearings on human rights violations could not lead to prosecutions or sentencing. In fact, the TRC bypassed the legal process by naming perpetrators before they had been convicted in a court of law and granting amnesty before a perpetrator had been through the trial process and been convicted. The amnesty hearings were an unusual kind of inversion of the law, as was pointed out in an interview by Judge Bernard Ngoepe: The NURA 'does not encapsulate the principles of common law; therefore we don't find guidance for legal precedent. I can tell you that I find it strange that I as a judge should listen to the gory details of someone [who] killed, cut the throat of another person, and then asks that I let him go. Normally, I should punish him instead of grant *political* immunity.'[5]

The amnesty hearings, in contrast to the hearings about human rights violations, were constituted as court hearings with legal consequences. They could lead either to a refusal of immunity from prosecution or to amnesty. Procedurally, the amnesty process mimicked a court. Thus, the TRC sought to establish truth according to rules of evidence, based primarily upon testimony and information proposed by a TRC 'evidence leader', who attempted to ensure in amnesty cases that 'full disclosure' had in fact occurred. At the same time, many TRC functions were overseen and administered by Minister of Justice Dullah Omar. Among other things, he was in charge of negotiating pay and employment terms with the commissioners, mediating between the TRC and the witness protection programme, gathering information from foreign countries, and dealing with applications for amnesty from persons in custody. Further, the Act had established all kinds of interdependencies between the TRC and the formal justice system. It required that a judge should be the chairperson of the amnesty committee, that procedures for investigation

[5] Author interview in Cape Town, 17 December 1996. Ngoepe uses 'political' instead of 'legal' immunity, seeking to distance the law from the amnesty process.

should require a search warrant from a judge, a magistrate, or the Supreme Court, and that people should be compelled to testify only after consultation with an attorney-general.

The intermediary position of the TRC between the justice system and the executive and parliament served to create a set of distinctions between those branches of government. This defining of boundaries is part of the system of checks and balances, which is one of the hallmarks of a liberal democratic order. Under authoritarian rule, it was precisely this lack of boundaries that allowed the judiciary to act largely as the oppressive legal arm of the executive. Truth commissions are liberal state structures *par excellence*, and their position attests to their democratic credentials. The liminal nature of the TRC, which stood between state institutions, granted it a certain freedom from both the strictures of legal discourse and the institutional legacy of apartheid. It allowed the commission to generate new forms of authority for the post-apartheid regime. The amnesty hearings were a theatrical representation of the power of the new state, which compelled representatives of the former order to confess, when they would rather have maintained silence. Perpetrators were compelled to speak in the language of human rights and thus to recognize the moral legitimacy of the new government, as well as its power to admonish and punish. This theatrical representation of power gives us a clue as to why democratizing governments set up truth commissions rather than relying upon the existing legal system. Truth commissions are transient politico-religious-legal institutions with much greater symbolic potential than dry, rule-bound, and technicality-obsessed courts of law. The position of the TRC as a quasi-judicial institution allowed it to mix genres of law, politics, and religion in particularly rich ways. Hence it is an interesting case study for understanding how human rights issues interact with wider moral and ethical discourses.

The work of the TRC began in December 1995.[6] It was divided into three committees: on Human Rights Violations (HRC), Reparations and Rehabilitation (RRC), and Amnesty (AC). Throughout 1996 and early 1997, the HRC held fifty hearings in town halls, hospitals, and churches all around the country, where thousands of citizens came and testified about past abuses. The process received wide national media coverage and brought ordinary, mostly black, experiences of the apartheid era into the national

[6] On the TRC, see Krog (1998), Lyons (1997), Nuttall and Coetzee (1998), Price (1997), Werle (1996), and R. A. Wilson (1995, 1996, 1997).

public arena in a remarkable way. It took more statements than any previous truth commission in history—over 21,000. It then faced the daunting task of corroborating the veracity of each testimony, choosing which would be retold at public hearings, and passing along verified cases to the RRC. The TRC also adopted an investigative role, building a wide-ranging view of the past by issuing subpoenas and taking evidence in camera. In its final report, published in October 1998, the TRC produced findings on the majority of the 21,298 cases brought before it. Further, unlike its Argentine and Chilean counterparts, it named perpetrators in hundreds of cases.

The South African TRC had the widest remit of any truth commission so far. In contrast with most other cases, it investigated gross human rights violations between 1 March 1960 and 10 May 1994. This included the killing, abduction, torture, or severe ill treatment of any person, as well as any attempt, conspiracy, incitement, instigation, command, or procurement to commit an act referred to in the Act. However, the mandate was limited in so far as it included only cases that exceeded the wide latitude of abuse permitted by apartheid laws. Detention without trial, forced removals, and the 'Bantu' education policy were legal under apartheid, and were not included under the terms of the Act. The TRC explicitly stated that racist attacks by persons who were not members of a political organization were beyond its mandate. Routine abuses under the apartheid legal order were thus often excluded from the category of human rights violations. Judging the past on its own terms contaminated the new democratic conception of justice. The exclusion of crimes that were legal under apartheid created a false distinction between the normative aspects of a racial authoritarian order and illegal forms of violent coercion, when in fact one implied the other. In essence, the TRC focused primarily on extreme cases, not on the normal, everyday, banal and mundane violent reality of apartheid. It therefore excluded the land dispossession, the pass laws, and the policy of segregation, among others, a point made by Mahmood Mamdani (1996). Because of its narrow, individual and legalistic view, the TRC actually obstructed a wider search for 'social justice', by which Mamdani means redistribution for the majority of Africans. Further, the TRC adopted an instrumental conception of violence, when it is known that regimes of terror thrive upon uncertainty, mystery, and disguised violence in order to cultivate a 'culture of terror' (Taussig, 1986; Bourdieu, 1991). An overemphasis on visible, quantifiable acts of violence failed to take into account levels of symbolic violence embedded in everyday life, which cannot be expunged as easily since they are located in that amorphous domain of habitual practice, where the impact of state policy is indeterminate. The pervasive social nature of violence, as opposed to its formalized state dimensions, was perhaps one of the greatest limitations on the ability of the TRC to articulate a clear break with the past.

The TRC, however, was cognisant of these limitations and took measures to address them through the 'event hearings', which focused on assessing the degree to which different social sectors provided an environment in which human rights violations could thrive. Institutional hearings were held for the 'business and labour', religious, legal, health, media, and prison communities. The TRC report was damning. Business was involved in 'state security initiatives . . . specifically designed to sustain apartheid rule . . . Business in turn benefited directly from their involvement in the complex web that constituted the military industry' (*Guardian*, 30 October 1998).

The judiciary was blamed for upholding apartheid legislation, unquestioningly granting police search warrants, and turning a blind eye to causes of death in police custody. Some Christian churches were condemned for giving their blessing to the apartheid system. Doctors and surgeons were accused of regularly misrepresenting forensic evidence, and the media was savaged for being a docile tool of the NP government. Through these hearings, the TRC transcended some of the limitations of its narrow human rights mandate and addressed the social context and routine everyday nature of a structural system of violence.

The efforts of the RRC to facilitate 'reconciliation' were the weakest of the three committees' activities. Part of the problem was structural and was the result of the fact that the TRC had no money of its own to disburse to survivors; instead, it could only make unbinding recommendations to the President's Fund with regard to monetary compensation, the building of symbolic memorials, and medical expenses. The TRC made it abundantly clear that victims should expect little from the process, only a fraction of what they might have expected had they prosecuted for damages through the courts. Such pronouncements were internalized by victims, many of whom have severe material needs. At the human rights violation hearings, for instance, it was common to hear accounts of the murder of family members followed by requests for a tombstone as compensation. In the end, the TRC recommended that designated 'victims' should receive approximately US$3,500 a year over a six-year period. In January 2000, the Mbeki government stated its intention to offer only token compensation of several hundred US dollars in total to victims, instead of the US$21,000 recommended in the TRC report of 1998. The reparations process, a key element in 'reconciliation', did not even begin to address the needs and expectations (however lowered) of survivors.

The RRC squandered or ignored other opportunities to pursue 'reconciliation'. In South Africa there is a large community of conflict mediation and HROs. Twenty-two of these came together in 1996 along with the South African Police Service to create a victim–offender mediation network, which would bring victims face-to-face with perpetrators and allow the two parties to confront past traumas. Their proposal would have created very concrete 'reconciliation' mechanisms, which the TRC was not envisaging. After an initial interest, however, the commissioners refused to endorse the proposal formally. This was seen by critics as indicative of the inability of the TRC to either take firm policy decisions or fully include civil groups within them.

The South African TRC was unique in linking the amnesty process with the truth commission, as in other countries the former has been a separate juridical mechanism. The TRC was overwhelmed by over 7,000 applications for amnesty. At the time of writing, around 568 people had been granted amnesty and 5,287 denied it. In order to be granted amnesty, the applicant must fulfil a number of legal criteria. For example, the crime must fall within the period 1 May 1960–10 May 1994, and the panel must be convinced that the crime was political and was not committed for personal gain, or out of malice and spite. Crucially, the applicant has to fully disclose all that is known about the crime and its political context, including the chain of command that led to the crime. Perpetrators are not required to express remorse. If a perpetrator is facing legal proceedings at the time, these are suspended until the appeal for amnesty is heard. If amnesty is refused because, for example, it is found that the applicant has not fully disclosed all information, the applicant can face future criminal or civil prosecution. Inextricably linked to this individualizing of responsibility was the less publicized programme of indemnifying the state itself. The TRC did not give citizens the right to make claims for civil damages. If the AC grants amnesty to a former government agent, then the state is automatically indemnified. The state has become a silent partner in the amnesty process, benefiting when an amnesty request is successful. The state can consider what reparations it wishes to make to survivors in the wake of a successful amnesty petition. Thus, the slate is wiped clean, and ministries such as the Ministry of Safety and Security no longer bear responsibility for the actions of the past.

Perpetrators did not come forward in great numbers, showing their faith in the unlikelihood of future prosecutions. Applications from the former SADF and IFP were particularly low. In some cases, as with the November 1998 hearings on the Boipatong massacre, the seventeen IFP applicants clearly did not reveal the full story. They protected superiors such as Themba Khoza, the youth leader of the IFP, whom former security policeman de Kock had confirmed as a part of the Third Force operation. There were some breakthroughs, however. In the case of Brigadier Cronje and four other former members of the security police, new information was divulged about the existence of a hitherto covert body called Trewits. This consisted of a group with military police and civilian government representation, which drew up lists of enemies of the state as well as erstwhile allies such as KwaNdebele leader Piet Ntuli, to be 'eliminated'. At these hearings, former police commissioner General van der Merwe admitted that in 1989 President Botha had ordered the bombing of Khotso House, the head office of the South African Council of Churches (SACC), and the unofficial ANC headquarters in the country at the time. The revelation led to ten amnesty applications in January 1997 and further insights into the apartheid security apparatus.

Despite many evasions on the part of perpetrators, a great deal of new information emerged from the amnesty hearings. Importantly, victims' lawyers were given an opportunity to cross-examine violators, and often to challenge rationalizations and the reformulation of events, which contributed to the contesting of impunity. Further, the amnesty process allowed victims greater access to information than the failed prosecutions of Malan and his cronies, or prosecution that might have occurred for most 'ordinary' cases of violations.

Although there were benefits to linking the amnesty process to the TRC, as information could be pooled, this created a number of strategic and ethical problems, which might have been avoided if amnesty had been a separate legal mechanism. There was a large gap between survivors' expectations of justice and the reality, for example, as they saw perpetrators being granted amnesty immediately while they had to wait up to two years to receive meagre reparations. Popular principles of justice were violated when perpetrators obtained amnesty without even expressing regret, which was not called for by the Act. Indeed, perpetrators were sometimes even proud of what they had done. Many repeated ideological justifications for their acts with little self-reflection and analysis. The 'truth' of amnesty hearings, therefore, was often the truth of unrepentant serial murderers who still felt that their war had been a just one.

Although by and large it has not met victims' expectations, the amnesty process does have the most stringent legal requirements of any recent amnesty, and will probably be seen as model for other countries. Rather than a blanket amnesty, it is an individualized process in which applicants must prove that the violation in question had a political objective and occurred within a specific time period, and must also fully disclose the nature and context of their actions. In a context in which the judicial system is inconsistent in its application of justice, this kind of process is probably the best suited to ensure that a majority of ordinary survivors and their families to come to know more about their cases.

Thus, although truth commissions aim to legitimate a new regime, it is not clear that they actually can or do legitimate state institutions. In many Latin American countries, the political constraints posed by a negotiated settlement have led to an attenuated search for truth and justice and ultimately to the erosion of legitimacy. Whether a truth commission promotes or challenges impunity and thereby generates legitimacy for the legal system depends on its contribution to an ongoing process of legal reform and on the enhancement of the capacity of the criminal justice system to carry out prosecutions. Naming names is the first step in breaking the silence in public spaces required by impunity. The TRC report (SATRC, 1998) named 400 perpetrators, many of whom had applied for amnesty and confessed to apartheid-era violations. The report was remarkable not so much for establishing new lines of investigation and making new revelations as for confirming what was already known by some and suspected by others. Individual experiences of thousands of historically marginal South Africans were made part of the official history of the country. Their voices come through in long quotes from human rights hearings that permeate the report. The latter is a remarkable document, impossible to reduce to a single reading, written by dozens of authors, and pasted together by numerous editors.

The five volumes, with 3,500 pages and almost a million words, read like a nineteenth-century social realist novel by Dickens or Hugo in scope and ambition. The relentless barrage of tragic cases produces the effect of ensuring that South Africans and others could no longer deny the veracity of the crimes of the apartheid regime. According to NP revisionists, apartheid was a well-meaning policy to enable races live harmoniously together that just went wrong. The report confirms instead that apartheid was a crime against humanity. It incorporates into national history the view that the system was based on a vicious ideology justifying economic and social privilege, which had enormous and unjustifiable human costs. Of the 21,298 statements, Africans made the overwhelming majority (76 per cent), alleging 38,000 instances of gross human rights violations, of which 10,000 were killings. There is a surprising amount of clarification of ordinary cases, which, because they were not high-profile ones like the Steve Biko or Griffiths Mxenge cases, might never have been investigated by a prosecutor. Because it charts the political darkness of South African history that the country never wishes to return to, the report is a more of a 'founding document' for the new South Africa than that utopian charter, the 1996 Constitution Bill of Rights. The knowledge imparted by the report, then, has direct implications for the context of impunity from which South Africa has slowly emerged, because it provides a further impetus to transform state institutions more quickly and thoroughly.

In places, however, the truth in the report is limited and tepid, and lacks the rigour of a criminal court prosecution. This resulted partly from the low level of applications from the military and other parts of the security services. There were, for instance, no applications from members of the National Intelligence Service (NIS). In the vast majority of cases where there were no amnesty applications, the approximately sixty investigators could do little other than 'corroborate' that violations had indeed occurred, by consulting death certificates, inquest documents, or police dockets. In addition, there were poor investigations and serious errors of analysis, as in the chapter on political violence in the era of negotiations and transition (1990–4) in the second volume. In that period, 14,000 people died—more than in the previous ten years.

Despite strong evidence about the existence of a Third Force in the de Kock trial and with the Goldstone Commission, involving senior NP officials, the security forces, the intelligence forces (Stratcom), and the SADF, the TRC report made little progress in that area. The report states that,

> while there is little evidence of a centrally directed, coherent or formally constituted 'Third Force', a network of security and ex-security force operatives, acting frequently in conjunction with right wing elements and/or sectors of the IFP were involved in actions that could be construed as fomenting violence and which resulted in gross violations of human rights, including random and targeted killings. (SATRC, 1998: ii.270).

The link to higher levels of government, it argued, was unproven. Instead of blaming the NP regime, it ends up blaming 'high levels of political intolerance' (ii.710). The most widely publicised omission at the time of its release resulted from the successful court injunction obtained by former state president de Klerk.[7] The former head of the last apartheid government had been accused of contributing to a culture of impunity and being an accessory to the SACC bombing in the mid-1980s. However, the report merely stated that de Klerk had been present at a meeting of the State Security Council, in which former state President Botha had congratulated Police Minister Adriaan Vlok for the successful bombing. De Klerk's successful block on the allegations meant that a page of the report had to be blacked out before release. One journalist referred to that page as 'an ironic memorial to apartheid censorship in the TRC report' (*Electronic Mail and Guardian*, 2 October 1998).

As is often the case when the report of a truth commission is finally released, there was an immediate clamour from some political sectors for a blanket amnesty. As was to be expected, the NP and far right parties such as the Freedom Front (FF) adopted this position. It was perplexing, however, to see Archbishop Tutu give some credence to the idea. He suggested that there should be a time limit of six years on prosecutions for political crimes. Others argued for a blanket amnesty in the hope that a fall-back position such as an amnesty would be agreed to only for the war-torn province of KwaZulu–Natal. This region produced more TRC human rights abuse statements than any other did, comprising 44 per cent of the total for the thirty-four-year period. At the time of writing, there seems to be no political will at the top level of the ANC to introduce a blanket amnesty, which would make a mockery of the process so far. There was, most importantly, opposition from Minister of Justice Omar, and from President Mandela's successor, Thabo Mbeki.

As argued above, criminal prosecutions and truth commissions must be seen as a part of a single process dealing with impunity, and not as separate expressions of either a 'political logic' or 'ethical logic'. In the South African case, the investigating functions of the TRC meshed quite closely with the parallel legal process, contributing to the investigative process. There is no legislation

[7] Sensitive to criticism on human rights abuses, particularly torture, in special camps such as Quatro, the ANC also attempted to block the release of the report, but failed.

that prevents TRC information from being used by prosecuting attorneys, with archives formally sent to the National Archives in Pretoria. In this, the South African case differs from other truth commissions such as the Guatemalan, where legislation prohibits the use of information gathered by the truth commission by the justice ministry, which is responsible for bringing criminal proceedings.

What are the concrete possibilities for prosecutions of apartheid-era abuses? Director of prosecutions for the Transvaal, D'Oliveira, stated in late 1998 that his office was 'a long way down the road' (*The Star*, 10 November 1998), preparing cases against some of the people named as responsible for gross human rights violations. D'Oliveira reported that 'two former generals' could face prosecution as a result of de Kock's testimony to the TRC. He also indicated that he was waiting for the amnesty process to end in order to proceed with prosecution. The South African weekly, *Mail and Guardian* (13 November 1998) learned that one of the generals is General Engelbrecht, who could be charged with obstructing justice for his alleged role in tampering with evidence from the plane crash that killed former Mozambican president, Samora Machel. De Kock is the main state witness against Engelbrecht, who is also likely to stand trial for allegedly misleading the Harms Commission.[8] Other high-profile prosecutions may occur as a result of TRC revelations. Former police commissioner Coetzee was implicated by his successor, General van der Merwe, who applied for amnesty in connection with a case of a booby-trapped hand grenade in the East Rand. Coetzee, who did not apply for amnesty, is subject to prosecution. Winnie Madikizela-Mandela, convicted for the death of Stompie Seipei, was found by the TRC to have been involved in number of other violations, including assault and covering up violations committed by the Mandela United Football Club. She too may face criminal prosecution.

The release of the TRC report led to various positive developments and a shake-up of prosecution services. In November 1998 Bulelani Ngcuka was appointed to the newly created post of national director of public prosecutions, which will oversee all attorneys-general. This 'super attorney-general' was created to establish a clearer line of command between the prosecutions service and the Ministry of Justice, as well as to prevent the emergence of 'enclaves of impunity', exemplified by McNally in KwaZulu–Natal.

[8] Engelbrecht was appointed to investigate the existence of hit squads in the early 1990s and was the Harms Commission's main investigator.

It also aimed to centralize and promote further prosecutions of apartheid-era atrocities. This event heralded significant reforms of the ailing criminal justice system, which are essential if it is ever to take over from the TRC in dealing with the legacy of past abuses. Ngcuka toured the country in 1998 appointing new justice officials with 'an alacrity generally unheard of in the civil service' (editorial, *Mail and Guardian*, 6 November 1998). In the ensuing reshuffling came the widely appreciated dismissal of McNally. A new head of prosecutions in the province of Gauteng, Silas Ramaite, also replaced the Transvaal attorney-general. Jan D'Oliveira, who is seen as one of the most effective in promoting criminal prosecutions in cases of political violence, became Ngcuka's deputy. There has also been a redrawing of the jurisdictional boundaries to replace the old apartheid provincial boundaries. Further, two former TRC commissioners, Denzil Poitgeiter and Sisi Khampepe, have been seconded to Ngcuka's office, providing some continuity between the two institutions. After the end of the TRC amnesty process in December 1999, and as time passes it will become much clearer whether the criminal justice system has been able to use effectively the information that the Commission generated to pursue pending issues linked with the legacy of violence.

Concluding Remarks

According to the doctrinal orthodoxy of international human rights covenants and the language of transnational organizations such as Amnesty International, those responsible for human rights violations must be brought before a court of law.[9] International human rights law and practice advances retributive justice—punishment for offenders and just compensation for victims. Countries emerging from authoritarian rule exalt a 'culture of human rights' when establishing of the rule of law and engaging in political transformation. In these contexts, human rights comes to mean the reverse of the international orthodoxy: it means amnesty for perpetrators, selective prosecutions of others who do not submit to the established process, and a limited 'truth-finding' operation as a parallel compromise solution. Amnesty and truth findings

[9] See the Convention on the Prevention and Punishment of the Crime of Genocide (UNCPPG), the UN Convention against Torture and other Cruel, Inhuman or Degrading Treatment or Punishment (UNCAT), the Universal Declaration of Human Rights (Article 8), and the International Covenant on Civil and Political Rights (ICCPR).

disrupt but also feed into and strengthen criminal prosecution. In the context of a 'justice in transition' away from a deformed authoritarian legality, justice is not available through widespread judicial redress; rather, justice is achieved through human rights sanctioned indemnities, glossed as 'restorative justice'. In this context, human rights language becomes less that of principle and more that of pragmatic political compromises.

This is the main obstacle to popular acceptance of human rights as a new language for the constitutional state. Constitutionalism purports to be about absolute rights protecting the citizen, rights that cannot be abrogated. But the implementation of 'human rights' in South Africa is shaped by political deals where everything is negotiable, where cut-off dates for amnesty can be extended endlessly, and seemingly resolved issues constantly find their way back to the negotiating table. In making these criticisms, it must be recognized that post-authoritarian institutions in South Africa have pursued a more extensive project of investigation and prosecution than any other post-conflict context produced by a political settlement. The TRC has been the biggest, best funded, and most productive truth commission ever, and high-ranking apartheid-era perpetrators have been and will continue to be tried for past atrocities in way that has not happened in other countries.

Justice in post-1994 South Africa was shaped by prior political constraints. More specifically, it was shaped by the fact that the liberation movement was much stronger politically than opposition movements elsewhere. No Latin American opposition, for example, was able to marshal the kind of mass action that the ANC was able to when talks broke down in 1992. Because of this, the ANC could exact greater compromises from the outgoing political elite, and go after top officials of the security apparatus with greater vigour. Its motivation was to create legitimacy for the new regime, and to forestall the hegemonic crisis that has apparently faced all post-colonial regimes in Africa. The TRC and prosecutions service must be seen in relation to one another, as single projects to establish legitimacy for judicial institutions, and as products of a process that is historically constituted during the conflict period itself. Transitional societies do not, as some have argued, face two abstract and competing forms of logic, one political the other ethical. It would be an anaemic and minimal kind of liberalism indeed that relied upon human rights for an ethical code. In questions of post-war justice, there is only the political.

This is not to say simply that expediency is supreme. Moral decisions are certainly made within the context of political struggle and negotiation. Moreover, in the case of South Africa, such decisions have stemmed less from universal principles of rights and duties and more from within a vision of a free, self-governing community of citizens seeking to build a different kind of *res publica*. Indeed, one of the aims of this chapter has been to chart how the political tradition of the liberation movement has sought to reformulate the meaning of 'justice' in South Africa, even working within the battered shell of an authoritarian and delegitimized state.

7

De-communization and Political Justice in Central and Eastern Europe

Carmen González-Enríquez

Introduction

The varying international and political conditions in which new democracies are born makes it difficult to isolate the 'settling accounts with the past' variable, and to ascertain its links to democratization. Eastern Europe offers an exceptionally homogeneous field of study, with contiguous countries and similar institutional and economic systems, all engaging in a transition to democracy. These countries undertook their transitions simultaneously, which means they had similar opportunities for learning from other cases. The Spanish experience and the post-1990 German model—the latter because of secret services and collaborators—were important examples. Thus, Eastern Europe presents a special opportunity for the analysis of the impact of political justice and administrative purges and for the study of why some democracies opt for judicial processes to deal with past repressors and 'cleanse' state institutions, while others opt for pardon or amnesia.

This chapter explores the nature and scope of de-communization and political justice in Poland, the Czech Republic, Slovakia, Hungary, Romania, Bulgaria, and Albania. The term 'political justice' is ambiguous and has negative connotations, reminding one of the political uses of justice. Here, however, it is meant to refer to proceedings held to try crimes committed by outgoing regimes. Such crimes are generally related to political repression, although they

I wish to thank Alexandra Barahona de Brito and Rudolf Tökés for their comments on this chapter. An earlier version of it was published in the *Revue D'Etudes Compartives Est–Ouest*, 29 (December 1998), 23–54.

can include economic corruption or other activities having deep social repercussions, such as ecological crimes. Political justice does not always have to mean punishment. Often it consists of an attempt to provide some form of symbolic or economic compensation for those who suffered past injustice. This second aspect, however, is not studied in this chapter.

With the exception of Albania, transitions in these countries were initiated in 1989. In all cases, great political tensions arose from demands for the punishment of former communist authorities and those responsible for political repression. These demands formed part of a wider political and cultural process, namely the reworking of public discourse on the nature of the communist regime. The nature and result of these demands, however, varied considerably from country to country. Only two—the former Czechoslovakia and Albania—actually carried out purges that affected large numbers of people. This chapter attempts to answer to two main questions: (1) what explains the differences in the scope and nature of the policies adopted, and (2) what impact have they had on the process of democratization. Rather than focusing on the moral and legal debates surrounding the issue, I focus on the rationality of the political actors or the role that anti-communist campaigns had in shaping political competition.

The scope of de-communization in Eastern Europe was narrower than that of de-nazification in postwar Germany or of German de-communization after the unification. Judicial proceedings or public opinion 'trials' have been comparatively scarce. Hardly any former communist leaders are serving prison sentences, and many that were condemned were subsequently released for humanitarian reasons. Some anti-communist parties called for measures to expel former communist leaders and political police agents from the public administration posts and democratic institutions. They also demanded the trial of political crimes. In most cases, however, these demands have not met with great public support.

A cause of popular indifference is the relatively 'soft' nature of political repression during the final decades of the communist regimes and the reduced number of victims in the 1980s.[1] The worst period of violence in these countries took place during the consolidation of the communist system with the repression of opposition

[1] The biggest group of victims of political repression in all countries were young people who refused to do the military service for ethical or religious reasons, but even this group was small. Albania may be an exception, not so much because of the existence of strong political opposition but because of the repression of attempts to flee the country, for which people were killed until 1991.

groups, mostly between 1947 and 1950, and was particularly bad in 1953 in the case of Germany and Czechoslovakia, 1956 in Hungary, and 1970 in Poland. The invasion of Czechoslovakia in 1968 by Warsaw Pact troops caused very few deaths, because it encountered mostly passive resistance.[2] The absence of violent repression after 1970 was not so much a product of liberalization, which was non-existent in some cases, as of the absence of political opposition. Indeed, Poland was the only country where the government faced an active popular opposition. Even here, repression occurred only on a minor scale in the latter years of the regime and political arrests ceased after the 1986 amnesty. The absence of opposition and repression contributed greatly to the peaceful handing over of power by the communist elite. Unlike Latin American dictators, they seemed to have little cause to fear acts of revenge. Lack of interest in de-communization was also due to the size of the communist parties. They were huge, and included an average of 10 per cent of the total population in Eastern Europe, or 15 per cent if one takes into account only the working population. If the relatives of communist party members (parents, children, and spouses) are considered, between 30 and 40 per cent of the population were either members or closely related to members. This leads one to assume that there was a diffuse sense of social complicity with the party. Complicity does not mean consent, but does imply effective collaboration.

Economic crisis also explains popular indifference to political justice. Most East Europeans endure harsh daily lives under democracy, lives dedicated to work, moonlighting, and finding monetary or non-monetary resources (Rose and Haerpfer, 1992–6). They have little time and energy left to take an interest in politics, particularly when it is not related to the material problems of the present and focuses on settling accounts with the past (Holmes, 1994: 33–36). In addition, the population of these countries is apparently aware that de-communization is a political weapon used by competing elite groups, so that it mistrusts its social use (Stewart and Stewart, 1995: 904–906; Walicki, 1997: 187, 194–205). Suspicions regarding de-communization are also a result of memories of the major purges undertaken by the Communists after 1945. At that time, collaboration with the Nazis led to the expulsion from

[2] It is unclear whether this list should include 1987 in terms of the repression of worker protest in Brasov, when some people may have died. Fejtö (1992: 214) talks of 'dozens of dead' and Veiga (1995: 193) of two dead, but Amnesty International annual reports mention only a few arrests.

the administration of people opposed to communist parties. Now social and cultural changes that have accompanied the political transition process, with new values affirmed by politicians and the mass media, have favoured a climate of moral relativism, which is not compatible with the moral debates surrounding political justice.

Finally, because the 1989 crisis was caused by international and economic rather than internal political factors, there is a problem in terms of 'national conscience': widespread rejection of the communist model co-exists in most countries with the recollection that society failed to act against it. Soviet domination also allowed Eastern Europeans to blame a foreign power for their dictatorial experience, exonerating their own societies and elites to some extent. This need for exoneration is less where rejection of the communist past is weaker, as in Bulgaria, Romania, or the former Soviet republics.

Despite lack of widespread popular interest, de-communization occupied an important place on parliamentary agendas and in public debates during the first years of democracy. Indeed, it fuelled heated moral, legal, and political discussion about its suitability, feasibility, utility, and legitimacy. The political elite tended to promote de-communization as symbolic compensation for widespread feelings of economic injustice. The industrial and budgetary crisis as well as economic transition have created a new class of losers, and the privatization process and the influx of foreign capital have made part of the former nomenklatura wealthy entrepreneurs. Feelings of economic injustice grow where living conditions worsen and new inequalities have sometimes provoked new desire for retaliation against newly rich, former communists.

The political elites have also found retribution a useful way to signal its intention to break with the past, and their need to mark such a break is stronger wherever they are the same old elites. Thus, Bulgaria and Romania, where the communist elite remained in power after the crisis of 1989, undertook spectacular gestures of breaking with the past. Hence the execution of the Ceausescus broadcast by television, or the gaoling in Bulgaria of Zhivkov, secretary-general of the Communist Party, and former national leader (1954–89). Moreover, de-communization manufactures new political identities for the anti-communist opposition. In Poland and Czechoslovakia (Stewart and Stewart, 1995: 902–903) as well as Hungary, many of the instigators of de-communization were groups or individuals who were not famous for their anti-regime stance in the past or for their sufferings caused by political repression. By calling for punishment, such individuals quickly created an anti-communist identity (Siklova, 1996: 60–61). As the chairman of the Polish Democratic Union, Frasyniuk, pointed out in 1993, 'you will notice that groups that have in their ranks genuine victims of persecution never engage in these debates. It is invariably others who remind the deputies that Mr X or Ms Y were physically abused but, somehow neither X nor Y want to take the floor and demand retribution, even though they are attending the meeting' (Stewart and Stewart, 1995: 903).

New political parties in Eastern Europe have encountered many difficulties in conveying a clear image to the electorate. Indeed, during the first years of democracy party systems were rather shapeless, lacking clear-cut programmes or ideological cleavages. In the struggle to define a party image and to mark the differences between one party from another, anti-communist gestures and calls for de-communization were useful. At a time of improvised structures, and an absence of programmes to tackle the main problems of each country, being a 'radical' anti-communist was an easy way for a party to define its position in the political arena. As party systems became gradually consolidated, anti-communist identities have declined. Members of parliaments and party leaders have gained political experience and can project their views on issues that are more interesting for the populations of their countries. De-communization, and accusations of collaboration with former secret police forces in particular, was used as a weapon to disqualify opponents and eliminate them from electoral competition. The most notorious case was Albania, but throughout the whole of Eastern Europe accusations of collaboration with the former secret services became a method of political disqualification.

The fact that the secret police were singled out as the main scapegoats has aroused little debate in Eastern Europe, but it is relevant to ask why this group and not another? Why not lay the blame on all finance ministers? Or on all senior officials who encouraged disastrous experiments with state-run economies? Or on all interior ministers and attorney-generals who protected the 'socialist order'? Or on all the foreign affairs ministers and ambassadors who sustained foreign policies subordinated to the Soviet Union? As Claus Offe points out, the results of some of these policies, especially in the economic arena, are more permanent and structural than the violation of the human rights (Offe, 1993: 18). The sizes of the secret services and the numbers of informers on their payrolls reached huge proportions in most East European countries. The secret services also attained a level of social penetration far higher than that of their southern Europe or Latin American counterparts, with the possible exception of Socialist Cuba. The East German Stasi, for example, had about 95,000 agents and 100,000 informers, in a country of 16 million. In Romania, with 23 million, the Securitate had fewer members (38,000), but many more informers (400,000), 2 per cent of the total population. Informers became the top targets of de-communization. They are blamed more than the officials who recruited them and the leaders who used the information they collected. This may be partly because informers were one's work colleagues, relatives, and friends; to 'discover' them provoked feelings of betrayal, humiliation, and rage. It may also be because punishing the large number of informers is more appropriate when seeking catharsis through political justice; punishing a handful of leaders lacks the political effect of punishing 10,000 persons. Furthermore, targeting one group seems to produce the psychological and political effect of removing blame from oneself, or from the rest of the population. Using secret police files to uncover the identity of informers posed serious practical difficulties, however. Many of the files were destroyed or hidden in 1989, and the information they contained was often false or highly implausible.

Police services have been reformed all over the region to ensure compatibility with democratic governance. Except for the Czech Republic, reform has excluded purges and consisted of new appointments at the top, the dissolution of the political secret services, and cosmetic changes, such as the renaming of departments. Broadly speaking, in Poland, the Czech Republic, and Hungary adaptation to democracy has been soft and easy and, along with every other state institution, police services have learnt new behaviour patterns. In Slovakia and Romania, however, the secret police largely continued to be at the service of authoritarian governing parties during most of the 1990s.

The scope and nature of retroactive justice also varied owing to the role of the judiciary. This body played a moderating and non-partisan role in Poland, Hungary, the Czech Republic, and Slovakia, where the existence of constitutional courts prevented the implementation of ill-defined laws of retroactive justice or administrative purging. In these countries the judicial system was reformed to guarantee independence and professionalism, although purges were not used. It should be remembered that the judiciary was not involved in political trials in the final decade of communism, so it had a relatively clean slate when democracy arrived. During the 1970s and 1980s, political criteria lost weight in shaping a judicial career, so by the 1990s judicial personnel were fairly prepared for democracy. This picture is different in south-eastern Europe, where a merit-based society has not developed and where political, clientelist, and nepotistic criteria have had a far stronger hold. The independence of the judicial systems in these countries is still an aim to be achieved, and the partisan use of justice has been a tool for governments seeking retribution and political power.

The Cases

Czechoslovakia

Czechoslovakia was the first country of the region whose new democratic institutions solemnly condemned the previous regime. On 23 May 1991 the federal parliament declared the communist regime 'illegal and condemnable' and detailed the evils it had caused. In July 1993 the parliament passed the Law on Illegitimacy and Resistance to the Communist Regime. It declared that Communist Party (KSC) militants, responsible for national government in 1948–89, were guilty of the systematic destruction of the values of European civilization, human rights violations, and economic decline. The law also morally justified and rendered homage to those who had resisted the old regime.

The debate on de-communization in Czechoslovakia (and after 1993, in the Czech Republic) was dominated by what to do about secret police collaborators (Bren, 1993: 16–22). The Ministry of the Interior listed some 140,000 people, 1 per cent of the total population. About 70,000 of these were marked as 'candidates for collaboration' and the rest were supposedly actual informers. From the inauguration of democratic rule in 1990, this issue clouded administrative and political life. That year, a purge of the administration was undertaken in the absence of any legal framework. Lists of purported informers were leaked to the press, and several government ministers, as well as prominent politicians from all parties, were accused of having collaborated with the state police.

Aware of the dangers that the climate of accusations entailed for the prestige of new political groups and democratic institutions, the political parties decided voluntarily to present lists of electoral candidates to the Ministry of the Interior. The aim was to allow it to check whether any of the candidates appeared in secret police files. Most parties did present their lists of candidates, although the KSC did not. The results were transmitted confidentially to party leaders, who were under no obligation to exclude candidates mentioned in the files.

But it soon became apparent that the files were none too reliable. In June 1990, the federal and two state interior ministers issued a communiqué. It stated that 15,000 files had disappeared after November 1989, that the most valuable informers were missing from them, and that many remaining files pertained to persons who were targets rather than collaborators of the secret police. The ministers recommended the immediate banning of access to the files to avoid further destabilizing accusations, but their proposals fell on stony ground. Instead, parliament set up an all-party commission to investigate the past of its members, as well as of the government and the President's office. The commission replaced a previous one formed to investigate the events of November 1989 in Prague; two of its members had resigned when it was revealed that they were members of the secret police. During a parliamentary session broadcast live on television on 22 March 1991, the new commission read out the names of ten parliamentarians who had been secret police collaborators. They came from all the parties but mostly from the KSC. Two other parliamentarians were denounced later, one of whom had spent twelve years in prison on political charges (1951–63) and had been an informer for five years (1963–8). The commission also discovered fourteen informers among high-ranking ministerial officials, thirty-three in the Prime Minister's office, twenty-five parliamentary employees (eleven of whom were still on the police payroll) and ten in the President's office. Parliament passed a resolution calling for their resignation, but to no avail. Instead, several of the accused filed lawsuits alleging slander, which some won (Orbman, 1991: 8–9; Stewart and Stewart, 1995: 887–893).

The findings of the commission did nothing to improve the image of political parties and new institutions. On the contrary, most of the population did not believe them and parliament was tarnished.[3] The case of Jan Kavan, one of the twelve deputies singled out by the commission, further discredited the whole process. Kavan, a famous dissident, exiled in London since 1969 where he worked as a journalist, was accused of having collaborated with the secret services of the Czechoslovakian embassy. He was backed by numerous English and American journalists, who

[3] Only 20% of Slovaks and 40% of Czechs considered the scrutiny system reliable (Orbman, 1991: 9).

protested to the Prague government. An open letter written to the parliament by a former secret police official, stating that he had forged the signature of one of the deputies accused, in exchange for a recruitment bonus, also caused a scandal, as the signature had been the evidence used to incriminate him.

None the less, the findings revealed the widespread presence of former informants in all the institutions. In October 1991, parliament passed the Lustration Law. Its aim was to remove five kinds of people from elected or appointed high-ranking office (Pehe, 1991: 6–7). First, it aimed to exclude agents and collaborators of the political police, the StB, which amounted to around 70,000 people. Second, it affected leaders of the KSC between 1948 and 1989 at the central or district level, which covered approximately 200 posts, but excluded leaders of 1968–9. Third, it covered members of the Working Militia, a paramilitary organization created to 'defend socialism', with about 100,000 people. Fourth, it affected anyone who had studied at one of three high-level police schools in the Soviet Union, or agents of the Soviet secret police, the KGB, in Czechoslovakia. Finally, it covered members of the Action Committee of the National Front of 1948, which consisted of fifteen people responsible for the coup that initiated the Stalinist era in February 1948.

The law was passed soon after the failed coup attempt in the Soviet Union in August 1991, and its wording was toughened in reaction to the coup. It should be borne in mind that the KSC was very close to the Soviet Communist Party, and that up until the last moment it hoped to see Gorbachov deposed and replaced by a more orthodox figure. Hence the Soviet coup reinforced fears about local communists and the desire to have them removed from state institutions. The original version of the law included three categories of secret agent: professional police employees, regular collaborators who were paid for their work, and 'voluntary' collaborators. The third category, which included about 70,000 people, was challenged by the constitutional court and annulled because the burden of proof fell upon the defendants. The Council of Europe also protested against the inclusion of this category. Other international organizations, such as the International Labour Organisation (ILO) and the International Committee of Helsinki, objected to the law, arguing that it gave rise to politically based labour discrimination and that it presupposed collective guilt. As was to be expected, the successors of the Communist Party also opposed the law, as well as the 1993 law on the illegitimacy and resistance to the communist regime for the presumption of collective guilt and the lack of differentiation between Stalinists and reformists such as Dubcek. In doing so, they implicitly accepted the core of the disqualification debates for the period of 1948–89.

There are no statistics on the number of people forced to give up jobs or political posts because of the law. According to the Ministry of the Interior, however, by July 1996 approximately 300,000 certificates had been issued, 9,000 of which indicated that the individual concerned belonged to one of the five categories. The law was to remain in force between 1 January 1992 and 1 January 1996. In 1995, however, over the opposition of President Vaclav Havel, parliament extended it to January 2001. Consequently, it also affected candidates to parliament in the elections of 1996 and 1998.

The main political effect of the law was to de-legitimate left-wing Marxists and the heirs of the liberalizing socialist movement of 1968. These socialists with a 'human face' had been the core of the dissident movement in the 1970s and 1980s and therefore suffered most pressures from the secret police (Kusin, 1979: 60–112). They were, ironically, the group most affected by accusations of collaboration with the StB (Stewart and Stewart, 1995: 888; Dvorakova and Kunc, 1997: 286–287). In short, many of those who ran risks and suffered reprisals for doing so have been excluded from political life. On the other hand, the large numbers of people who accepted the regime without opposition or who actively supported the KSC as rank-and-file members were not targeted by the StB and had nothing to fear. Many people who forged careers under the communist regime survived and became a significant part of the new post-communist elite. For example, Vaclav Klaus, finance minister in 1990 and prime minister until 1997, had headed an economic research institute in the 1980s, which required the blessing of the KSC. Moreover, as pointed out by the sociologist Jirina Siklova (1996: 61), many of those who advocated lustration were masking their lack of opposition or their active collaboration with the communist regime. Thus, several journalists who favoured lustration had written in the past praising the regime and had signed a manifesto against Charter 77, an organization that grouped the dissident movement since 1977. Similarly, many who had not been admitted to the KSC, and therefore had less of a chance to climb the professional ladder, wanted in the 1990s to punish the leaders of the party. The 'outlawing' of dissidents was one of the unexpected effects of lustration, although the punishment of KSC leaders achieved the intended result of discrediting the party and its successors.

In addition to lustration, political justice took the form of a small number of court cases. Vasil Bilak, secretary of the KSC Central Committee in 1968, was found guilty of calling for the invasion by Soviet troops in 1968. Former head of the StB, Alojz Lorenc, was convicted of 'abuse of power' in the repression of dissidents in the 1970s and 1980s. Secretary of the Prague KSC, Miroslav Stepan, was found guilty of repressing the 1989 street demonstrations in that city. They were all paroled for good behaviour after serving half their prison terms. In 1994 two former police officers were convicted of abuses of power when repressing student demonstrations in November 1989. The Office for Documentation and Investigation of the Crimes of Communism, which reports to the Ministry of the Interior and is headed by a radical anti-communist, Vaclav Benda (*Transitions*, 1 (16), 1995: 30) sought to take to court five communist leaders in 1995. The latter were accused of treason for trying to form a new government in 1968 under the aegis of the Warsaw Pact invaders. One of the accused was Milos Jakes, general secretary of the KSC in 1987–9. Magistrates dismissed the case for lack of evidence, but after several judicial battles the case against Jakes was opened again, in accordance with a Supreme Court decision of January 1998, and is now being investigated further by the prosecutor.

In Slovakia the Lustration Law ceased to be in force when the Federation broke up on 1 January 1993. It was not formally repealed, but administrative mechanisms required to enforce it were not activated. The Slovak elite has retained stronger ideological and personal affinity with the KSC and has therefore shown less enthusiasm for enforcing the law. On 21 March 1996, probably influenced by the Czech experience, parliament passed a law on the 'Immorality and Illegitimacy of the Communist Regime'. It was a peculiar decision, as 92 of the 110 deputies present were former KSC members. The first version of the law, which condemned the KSC as a 'criminal organization', was modified to read, more mildly, '. . . a party that did not prevent its members from committing crimes' (*EECR*, Winter 1996: 26). The law does not include measures against former Communists, secret police agents or individuals responsible for particular repressive acts, but it cancels the statute of limitations covering crimes committed under communist rule that were not prosecuted for political reasons. To date, this measure has not had any significant effect.

Albania

The Albanian communist–Maoist regime was perhaps the most repressive in Eastern Europe. Its borders were the most tightly sealed and its policy towards social and cultural customs the most repressive. It was the only regime that banned religious practice altogether, outlawing a good part of the population.

The weight of past repression and the scant respect for rule of law today help to explain why Albania carried out the most wide-ranging process of de-communization and is the place where the partisan use of justice has been most notorious. The old Communist Party, now the Labour Party (PPS), won the first democratic elections in 1991, thus excluding any attempt by the opposition to incriminate former authorities. Political justice and administrative purges began in 1992, when the Democratic Party (PDSH) won the elections, and remained in force until 1996, when the party won the election again. In 1992 two paragraphs were added to the Labour Code, purportedly to reform the administration and state-run enterprises; this addendum allowed any senior official to replace any employee (with no right of appeal) considered guilty of having excessively supported the previous regime (Imholz, 1995a: 58–59; Abrahams, 1996: 52). This provision was used to undertake a wide-ranging purge and replace former employees with PDSH supporters. There are no official figures regarding the scope of the purge, but sources suggest that around 10,000 people were thrown out of government or state enterprise jobs (Imholz, 1995: 58). For example, 90 per cent of diplomatic personnel was sacked and replaced.[4]

A further provision affected judges and public prosecutors, two-thirds of whom were replaced after 1992 by new, rapidly trained judges and 'assistant judges', who completed their law studies in the record time of a year and a half (Abrahams, 1996: 52). This raises strong doubts regarding judicial autonomy. The law was abolished in 1996 before the general elections, officially because it had already served its purpose, but most probably to prevent it from being used by the PPS if it won the elections.

In 1995 parliament passed the Law on Genocide and Crimes against Humanity. This made it possible to bar from administrative positions and parliament, for a period of six years, former high-level leaders of the PPS, members of governments before 1991, or

[4] Data supplied by diplomatic sources to the author.

former members of or collaborators with the secret police. The law was justified by the need to punish those responsible for setting up concentration camps and shooting anyone trying to leave the country. Although there are no reliable figures, data supplied by Albanian diplomatic sources indicate a high level of physical repression and thus widespread desire for revenge. An estimated 5,000 Albanians died trying to cross the border illegally and 100,000 were sent to concentration camps during the communist period. To enforce the law, a commission examined the records of all candidates for the 1996 parliamentary elections and passed sentences against 136 people, the great majority of them members of the PPS or former dissidents who had left the PDSH (*Transition*, 31 May 1996: 63). The PDSH government appointed all commission members, thus fuelling major doubts as to its impartiality and independence.

The partisan use of political justice was even more evident in the three death sentences and two sentences of life imprisonment for PPS leaders made public two days before the May 1996 elections. Convicted under the new penal code, which includes the crime of genocide, the defendants sentenced to death were the former attorney-general, the deputy minister of the interior who had headed the police, and the president of the Supreme Court. Ramiz Alia, former president of the Republic and successor of Enver Hoxa as head of the PPS, and the former deputy prime minister were sentenced to life imprisonment. These three death sentences are, with the exception of the Ceausescu executions, the only instances of the use of capital punishment for political reasons in post-communist Eastern Europe. Alia was acquitted in 1997, after having escaped from prison that year during the March riots.

The use of the judicial system to discredit PPS leaders caused international protest in 1994. The European Parliament and the Council of Europe protested when Fatos Nano, leader of the Socialist Party (PSSH, formerly PPS) and prime minister in 1991, was sentenced to twelve years in prison for embezzlement and forging public records, after very dubious trial proceedings (Imholz, 1995: 57). During the 1997 savings fund crisis,[5] the intervention of the Organization for Security and Co-operation in Europe (OSCE) promoted the signature of a 'political contract' that included the

[5] In the 1990s, hundreds of thousands Albanian families invested their money in a fraudulent savings fund, which went bankrupt in 1997. Most of the families lost their money. The crisis fuelled riots and escalated into a chaotic situation during which the Albanian state almost collapsed.

abrogation of parts of the genocide law. Under the reformed law, the scope of categories of people excluded from competition for parliament was reduced to former members of the PPS Politburo, secret police agents, foreign intelligence agents, and persons convicted of crimes against humanity. This allowed Nano to run in the elections and become the new prime minister. Furthermore, none of the death sentences signed in 1996 was acted upon. Each was derogated, and during the 1997 riots the convicts escaped from gaol like every other prisoner.

Bulgaria

During the period of regime liberalization before the first democratic elections in June 1990, the press discovered and published figures on the bloody repression that had followed the communist seizure of power in Bulgaria in 1944. It also revealed facts about concentration camps used until 1962, where more than 1,000 prisoners arrested for political reasons had perished. In 1990, mass graves containing the remains of those murdered since 1944 were discovered in several towns. The same year saw the publication for the first time of official figures on the scope of the show trials in the 1940s, in which 2,730 people had been sentenced to death and 1,305 to life imprisonment (Engelbrekt, 1990: 5–9).

These revelations about the scope of communist repression in the 1940s and its continuation in the post-Stalinist period shocked Bulgarian society and contributed to the discrediting of the former members of the Communist Party (BKP), newly organized as the Socialist Party (BSP). None the less, in the minds of many Bulgarians, the horrors of the communist repression were 'offset' by the horrors of right-wing repression before 1944. Moreover, a split within the BSP between conservatives and reformers enabled the latter to blame the former for what had happened and thereby to reinforce their image of change.

The renewal of the party leadership in 1989 and the arrest of Todor Zhivkov, who had led the party since 1954 and been accused in 1990 by his comrades of cultivating a 'personality cult' and nepotism,[6] helped forge an image of transformation in the party. Revelations about the harshness of repression in the past did not stop the BSP

[6] Zhivkov and Milko Balev, the former secretary of the Central Committee, remained under arrest for several months without being charged formally. Party reformists feared a confrontation with conservatives if any charges were made. In the end, both men were released from prison and put under house arrest, still without being formally charged.

from winning the first democratic elections in June 1990. Political trials began in 1992, after the triumph of the anti-communist Union of Democratic Forces (SDS), the main opposition party, in the autumn 1991 elections, and the formation of a coalition government with the party representing the Turkish minority, the Movement for Rights and Freedom (DPS). The trials aimed to investigate responsibility for economic deterioration and corruption, the decline in environmental and public health standards, and excesses in political repression (Engelbrekt, 1992: 6–10). As far as economic deterioration is concerned, prosecutors sought to find out to what use Western loans worth US$11 billion had been put in the 1970s. The answer was felt to be the corruption of high-ranking officials and the diversion of funds to Third World communist parties. Former prime ministers Atanasov and Ovcharov were sentenced to seven and nine years' imprisonment respectively for 'theft'. Atanasov was later released because of his advanced age and health problems. Zhivkov too was tried and sentenced to seven years for embezzlement and abuse of power, but in 1996 he was acquitted by the Supreme Court. Another forty-seven high-ranking officials were investigated, but no incriminating evidence was found.

The government's attempt to carry out de-communization in the economic sector took the form of a law that barred former communists from holding top posts in banks and financial companies, but the constitutional court rejected the law (Engelbrekt, 1993: 81–82). In 1992, another law was passed to purge bodies governing the university. The constitutional court upheld it 1994, but the BSP-dominated parliament repealed it in 1995.

In comparison with other East European countries, Bulgaria suffered the worst ecological degradation, which led to serious public health problems. This explains the importance given to this problem by the Public Prosecutor's office—a judicial relevance unique in the region. The Chernobyl accident in 1986 particularly affected Bulgaria, but government authorities silenced any efforts to inform the public of the effect of the radioactive leak, making it impossible to adopt precautionary measures. The then Deputy Minister of Health and the Vice-President were sentenced in 1992 to three and two years' imprisonment for this cover-up. In addition, thirty-seven companies were investigated for chemical pollution, but the case was closed for lack of evidence.

Trials for past political crimes focused on the ill-treatment of prisoners in forced labour camps (1959–62) and the confinement of the Turkish population to improvised concentration camps during the forced assimilation campaign (1984–9). In neither case was a final sentence passed. In 1992 and 1993, several trials were promoted by Attorney-General Ivan Tatrchev, but the new BSP majority in parliament of 1994 removed him from his post by passing a new law on the judicature that required judges and prosecutors to have five years' legal experience before holding high offices. The purpose of the law was to expel from office the attorney-general and the president of the Supreme Court Ivan Grigorov, as well as expelling from office other anti-communist judges and public prosecutors who did not meet the requirements when appointed. Those accused of mistreating work-camp internees included Zhivkov, this time charged with ordering the creation of two camps, Lovech and Skravena (1959–62), where 149 detainees had died from abuse. The then minister of interior Spasov and three officials directly involved in running the camps were also charged, as were five former state security officials, for the Turks' confinement.

Most of the files of the Bulgarian police secret services, which employed about 8,000 people and had some 100,000 informers, were destroyed in 1990.[7] Nevertheless, in 1990–1 the names of politicians who supposedly appeared in the files were leaked to the press. Many were members of the SDS, whose leader had to resign when his ties to the secret police were revealed; he did so after admitting to part of the accusations. In 1991 a newspaper published a list of thirty-two members of parliament who were named as informers, most of them from the SDS. Parliament reacted to the scandal by passing a law that allowed members of parliament to consult the secret police files in the presence of the leader of their parliamentary group. However, the new government formed after the BSP electoral victory of 1994 banned the access to the files to everyone but the president of the republic and the director of the information services (Engelbrekt, 1994: 21–27).

The April 1997 elections, held in a climate of social unrest and public distrust of a BSP involved in scandals of corruption, gave control of the parliament and government to the SDS. This change reopened the issue of the files. In July 1997 parliament passed a law on disclosure of secret police files, which made mandatory the disclosure of files for all deputies, members of government, the

[7] The secret police showed a strong degree of subordination to the KGB, unknown in the other cases studied. The secret service of the political police was closed down in 1990 and all other secret services were abolished in 1991 and replaced by new ones (Engelbrekt, 1991: 5–9).

president and vice-president, judges from the constitutional, supreme, and supreme administrative courts, the Supreme Judicial Council, and prosecutors and investigative officers (*EECR*, Fall 1997: 8–9). The only sanction against former agents provided for by the law was public disclosure of their files. The commission in charge of the process revealed the names of sixteen politicians, judges or officers, but only two politicians resigned. The DPS was especially affected by this disclosure, as four of the sixteen listed were members of the group, including the chairman, Ahmed Dogan. The Turkish population was a top target of the secret services in the 1980s, when an aggressive assimilation campaign was carried out.

Thus, as with the Czechoslovakian dissidents, the group most affected by repression under the communist regime was also the one most affected under democracy, because of secret file disclosures. In October 1998 the SDS government passed a law on the civil service that included a ban on former secret police agents and leading communists from top state posts for five years. The law was not very precise regarding posts or the level of leadership to be affected, so SDS President Petar Stonayov and the BSP rejected it. It was presented to the constitutional court, which in January 1999 decided against it on grounds that it violated equality before the law and the right to work (*EECR*, Fall 1998: 8; Spring 1999: 7).

To summarize, during first years of democracy in Bulgaria (1990–1) revelations about the nature of political repression fuelled attempts to make a clear break with the communist regime. None the less, the continuity of the political elite meant that only symbolic measures were adopted, the main one being the expulsion from the party and the arrest of Zhivkov. The anti-communist opposition, which won the elections in 1992, did not accept that the blame should be laid solely on Zhivkov and pressed for an inquiry into responsibility for the worst of the communist heritage. It also sought to open secret police files to the public and have those responsible for political crimes brought to trial. Proceedings were hindered from 1993 onwards, after the SDS lost control of the government. They came to a provisional end after the 1994 elections, when the new BSP majority managed to replace the attorney-general and president of the Supreme Court, after long months of confrontation between the judiciary and the executive. Even the Zhivkov case, the most symbolic, collapsed when the Supreme Court acquitted him, in February 1996, of all charges of abuse of power and embezzlement. He died in August 1998 (*EECR*, Winter 1996: 7). In 1997, after the victory of the SDS in the general elections, this time with a greater majority than in 1992, the new parliament approved the law on disclosure of secret police files and attempted to purge the civil service.

Thus, electoral results have marked the evolution and rhythm of political justice and lustration in Bulgaria, but until 1997 anti-communist forces lacked sufficient popular and parliamentary support to launch a wide-ranging lustration campaign. Even then, political justice was hindered by the weakness of the judicial system, which was seriously corrupted at all levels and permanently in conflict with the government and parliament (*EECR*, Winter 1998: 6–8; Spring 1998: 5–6). The rule of law is still feeble in Bulgaria, and this weakness has rendered impossible the implementation of lustration measures in a legal and non-arbitrary way.

Romania

Despite signs of 'revolutionary violence' and the events of December 1989—the mass demonstrations, bloody repression and the execution of the tyrants—subsequent political developments in Romania have revealed the resilience of the ruling elite. The National Salvation Front (FSN), three of whose four founding members were former high-ranking officials in the Ceausescu governments, was literally set up overnight, on 22–23 December, to take over after the flight of the Ceausescus. Despite rhetorical advocacy of democracy and a market economy, it violently hounded opposition parties, opposed liberalization or privatization measures, and either confirmed many high-ranking communist civil servants in their posts or promoted them.

Romania is the only East European country where the Communist Party (PCR) vanished. Moreover, it had had the largest communist party in the region, with nearly 4 million militants (3,800,000), out of a population of 23 million. The party ceased to exist in December 1989 but was not formally dissolved. In November 1990 the Socialist Labour Party (PSM) was formed, led by former top members of the communist nomenklatura. The party won 3 per cent of votes in the elections of 1992. The FSN, which won the first election by an ample margin with 66 per cent of the vote, picked up the post-communist vote. FSN President Ion Iliescu had been, during the Ceausescu era, minister for youth, secretary of the Central Committee responsible for ideology, and a member of the Executive Political Committee of the PCR. In 1990–6 he was president of Romania, elected with 85 per cent of votes.

In sum, the so-called Romanian revolution was more of an act of tyrannicide accompanied by the persistence of an entrenched elite. The swift trial of the Ceausescus was held without legal guarantees. They were even accused by the counsel for the defence. The speed of the trial and execution, both of which took place on 25 December 1989, may have a 'revolutionary' explanation—to avoid any attempts by the army or the Securitate to free the dictator—but a 'continuity' explanation is at least as credible as the former—i.e. to prevent the judicial process from turning the trial into a judgement of the regime and not just of the Ceausescus. The two explanations do not contradict each other, and could both be true.

From the outset, the FSN government revealed its intent to limit political justice to the small circle around the Ceausescu family. Under popular pressure, the government also promoted the trial of those responsible for the massacres in December 1989. The Ceausescus's son Nicu, famous for his abuses of power and life of luxury, was imprisoned and sentenced to over twenty years, but was later freed because of a serious liver ailment. His sister Zoë was also gaoled, but was later freed without charges. Four members of the PCR executive political committee, one of them the interior minister, were charged with responsibility for massacres in Timisoara and Bucharest in December 1989, in which about 1,200 people had died. The court-martial/trial was broadcast live, and the four defendants constantly incriminated themselves, declaring that they had been 'idiots'—in the best style of the show trials of the 1940s (Ionescu, 1990: 46). The initial charge was 'complicity in genocide', and when the prosecution tried to strengthen this to 'shared responsibility in genocide' the four defended themselves by stating that only Ceausescu and his wife had given the order to fire on the demonstrators. The charge of 'complicity in genocide' was also levelled against twenty-one Securitate and army officers for the Timisoara events. Altogether, seventeen former high-ranking PCR officials were convicted in different trials in 1990 for 'complicity in genocide' in December 1989; all were later freed for 'health problems' and were then pardoned by President Iliescu. In 1993 seven members of the Securitate and two senior officials from the Interior Ministry were convicted for the murder of three detainees who had tried to hijack a bus in order to leave Romania in 1981. This has been the only trial related to pre-1989 political repression.

The Securitate, which had about 38,000 members and 400,000 informers, was officially dissolved in January 1990. However, it was set up again under a new name soon after the violent confrontation between the Hungarian and Romanian communities of

Tirgu Mures in March 1990. These events became a justification for a powerful intelligence service. The new intelligence service recruited 60 per cent of former Securitate members and immediately adopted a markedly partisan role, harassing opposition groups, attacking their headquarters, and organizing the attack by miners on opposition protestors in Bucharest during 1991. That year, thousands of intelligence documents, which proved these partisan activities and which the service had tried to bury, were unearthed accidentally in a ravine (Sturdza, 1991: 23). To discredit opposition parties in 1991, the intelligence services leaked to the government-controlled press files that purported to show that leading members of the opposition had co-operated with the Securitate (Ionescu, 1992: 9–15). In 1992 Securitate files were declared secret for forty years, thus preventing any attempt to enforce laws similar to the Czech Lustration Law.

The peculiar nature of Romanian political culture was revealed in 1993 by the success of a novel about the Securitate, which was portrayed as a patriotic force. This best-selling series of novels were written by Pavel Corut, a former senior official of the Securitate, who then became a member of the Romanian National Unity Party (PUNR), a nationalist, pro-communist party. The text was openly pro-Ceausescu and denounced the overthrow of the regime as an international conspiracy (Shafir, 1993: 14–18). It was only after the 1996 elections, which gave power to the opposition Democratic Convention (CDR), that proposals to open the files were acceded to. According to the law, passed on June 1998, people holding high positions in the state apparatus and religious leaders should be scrutinized for past connections with the Securitate. As in Hungary or Bulgaria, the only punishment contemplated by the law is the publicizing of names of those who have collaborated with the Securitate and do not resign voluntarily. The law also created the Council for Studying Former Security Archives, but it allowed the intelligence agencies to deny people access to files on national security grounds.

Overall, the resilience of the Romanian elite has prevented any form of political justice. Instead, it has used the execution of the Ceausescus and a few perfunctory prosecutions of officers involved in the December 1989 massacres to symbolize the break with its past and its intention to turn over a new leaf.

Poland

Poland did not undergo de-communization, but the issue has been one of the most divisive in political life under democracy. Intellectuals and politicians are profoundly divided about the memory of the past, and the success of post-communists in the market economy and in open electoral competition has generated frustration and a desire of revenge among the heirs of Solidarity (Walicki, 1997: 193–196, 204, 218–219). The first democratic Polish government (September 1989–January 1991), led by Tadeusz Mazowiecki, a long-time Solidarity adviser and a Catholic intellectual, showed no interest in political justice and announced that a 'thick line' would be drawn between the past and present. Many Solidarity leaders, such as Jacek Kuron, Adam Michnik, and Bronislaw Gemerek, were of Marxist origin and had began their political life in the communist Polish Unified Workers Party (PZPR), where they sought to combine socialism with personal and public freedom. Even Prime Minister Mazowiecki had been a youth activist in the Catholic movement Pax, controlled by the PZPR, and a member of parliament in the 1960s representing a Catholic group. Many PZPR militants joined Solidarity, and many Solidarity members entered parliament in the 1980s. In other words, the incumbent political elite and the opposition were more closely related than allowed for by the 'society against the state' stereotype of 1980s Poland.

Calls for de-communization began only in 1991, when the economic crisis started to undermine the legitimacy of the new regime and confidence in the government's capacity. The demand came from sectors of Solidarity that had been excluded from the government and high-ranking posts, and complained that they were not being rewarded for the sacrifices they made as underground militants while the nomenklatura had managed to remain in power and accumulate wealth. The more anti-communist right-of-centre government formed in 1992 and led by Jan Olszewski enjoyed very little room for manoeuvre in the economic arena. That is probably why it focused its attention on launching attacks on the former nomenklatura who had become successful in business or remained in power in municipalities and counties. The government accused President Walesa himself of succumbing to communist influence.

The Olszewski government was also responsible for opening the 'Pandora's box' of lists of secret police collaborators. In May 1992 parliament approved a Lustration Law. It obliged the Ministry of the Interior to provide information about candidates for parliament, state administration, local government, and administration of justice posts, regarding connections with the secret police in 1945–90. The government set up a bureau of investigation to compile a list of such collaborators (Sabbat-Swidlicka, 1993: 103; Vinton, 1992; 16–20; Walicki, 1997: 197–198). The non-post-communist opposition, the Democratic Union (UD), also an heir to Solidarity, opposed the initiative, claiming that it was a breach of state secrets and that it pursued partisan and even personal aims.

The bureau presented parliament with a list of sixty-four police informers, which included numerous leading Solidarity politicians, not least Walesa and other notorious advocates of anti-communist measures. The list was published in the press and was so hard to believe that it sparked off a scandal. Soon afterwards, the Minister of the Interior admitted that the list was a mixture of actual and would-be informants that the police had tried to recruit without success. In view of this event, even the parliamentarians who had advocated lustration began to reconsider. Days later, the constitutional court ruled against the Lustration Law. However, the publication of the list and the scandal it caused forced the government and parliament to adopt a resolution to settle the affair.

During the second half of 1992, parliament debated various draft bills on how to deal with former police informers, but none advanced. President Walesa opposed any 'cleansing' of the secret services and armed forces, arguing that it would weaken national security by depriving the country of necessary skilled professionals. Gradually the matter was forgotten, having little weight during the government of Suchocka (July 1992–May 1993), which was based on a coalition between the two biggest post-Solidarity parties, the centre–right Christian Democratic Union (DChN) and the centre–left UD and focused on economic matters. Decommunization was hardly mentioned at all during the election campaign of 1993, and when an alliance of post-communist forces formed the new government in the wake of that election the issue provisionally disappeared from parliamentary life. It did not disappear from public life, however, as anti-communist intellectuals and politicians continued to complain about 'the stealing of the revolution' and to deplore the lack of an official historic review condemning the old regime, as had occurred in the Czech Republic. As a consequence of the electoral success of the post-communist Democratic Left Alliance (SLD) in 1993, Solidarity's heirs moved to the right and many of them began to criticize the Roundtable Agreements of 1989 and Mazowiecki's 'thick line'. The words of Kwasniewski, the leader of the SLD, in parliament apologizing to 'all those who had experienced injustices and wickedness of the authorities and the system before 1989' (Walicki, 1997: 200), were considered insufficient by the anti-communist right. The triumph of Kwasniewski over Walesa in the 1995 presidential elections added more fuel to anti-communist complaints about the 'stolen revolution'.

During 1996 and the first months of 1997, the issue of secret police collaboration re-emerged, probably because of the vicinity of the parliamentary elections held in September 1997. In April 1997 the Peasant Party (PSL), a populist, left-wing group devoted to the defence of peasant interests that was allied to the PZPR under communism, and a member of the government coalition, supported an opposition draft, and the Congress passed the lustration or 'screening' law. According to it, all deputies, senators, judges, high-ranking civil servants and candidates to these positions had to issue a statement declaring whether they had collaborated with or worked in the secret services in 1944–90. A screening court formed by twenty-one judges was to check these statements, and only those making false statements would be banned from every high-ranking position for ten years and their names would be published in the state gazette. The screening law should have applied to candidates in the 1997 elections, but it did not because the court in charge of the process was not constituted (*EECR*, Winter 1997: 22). In any case, eleven candidates for the 1997 election acknowledged in their statements that they had been former secret police agents.

The 1997 elections gave power to the heirs of Solidarity and the issue of de-communization was raised again. On 18 June 1998 parliament passed a law with the opposition of the SLD, condemning the 'communist dictatorship imposed in Poland with force and against the will of the nation by the Soviet Union and Joseph Stalin'. It blamed the PZPR for the 'many crimes and offences' of the regime, which 'was maintained by means of force, lies and the threat of Soviet intervention and served to secure foreign interests' (*Radio Free Europe/Radio Liberty*, Internet, 11 June 1998). This was the first time that a state institution issued a condemnatory appraisal of the former regime, and it constituted an important moral triumph for anti-communist groups. In December 1998 parliament passed a law stating that judges serving in 1944–89 could be brought before a disciplinary court and removed from service if was proved that they had issued unjust sentences or obstructed the defendant's right to a defence (*EECR*, Fall 1998: 25–26; Winter–Spring 1999: 26–27). Judges have regarded the passage of this law as a revenge gesture, responding to their lack of co-operation with the Lustration Court.

The courts had not dealt with the events leading to 1981 *coup d'état*. In 1992 parliament declared illegal the 1981 introduction of martial law and created a Committee on Constitutional Responsibility. It had to determine whether the State Court should judge General Jaruzelski, members of Military Council of

National Salvation who implemented martial law, and members of the State Council who had endorsed the 1981 decision. After four years, the Committee voted to end its investigation and recommended that parliament should drop the case (Walicki, 1997: 205–217). The decision did not calm the most radical anti-communist right-wing groups, which continued to campaign against Jaruzelski. The version put forward by Jaruzelski—that the coup had been necessary to forestall the imminent Soviet invasion and avoid chaos and economic collapse—has apparently been accepted by the majority of Poles. None the less, Jaruzelski was tried on other grounds, for responsibility for the deaths caused by repression of strikes in 1970. He was finally acquitted. Attempts have been made to deal with repressive episodes of the Stalinist period (1944–56), but most of the accused were too old and sick, and only one of the ninety-five cases presented to the state attorney resulted in a public trial. It lasted two years and was regarded as a trial of the whole Stalinist period. The defendant, Adam Humer, was accused of cruelty towards political prisoners in 1944–54, and was sentenced to nine years' imprisonment. In addition, eleven former security police agents working with Humer in those years were sentenced to from two to eight years (Walicki, 1997: 220–221).

Hungary

The first democratic government in Hungary (1990–4) was a coalition led by the Christian and nationalist Hungarian Democratic Forum (MDF). Under the leadership of Jozsef Antall, it made various attempts to denounce those responsible for crimes committed in the 1940s and 1950s, the period of communist bloody political repression (Bence, 1990: 85–86). The Zeteny–Takacs bill, named after the two MDF parliamentarians who sponsored it and approved by parliament in November 1991, was passed with the opposition of the Socialist Party (MSzP) and the liberal Alliance of Free Democrats (SzDSz). This law aimed to bring to trial those perpetrators of the crimes of treason, voluntary manslaughter, and mistreatment resulting in death, committed in 1944–90 who had escaped justice for political reasons. President Arpad Göncz (1990–), a former dissident and member of the SzDSz, rejected the law and took it to the constitutional court, which ruled against it in the spring of 1992 on the grounds that it contradicted the statute of limitations on crimes.

The main supporter of the law, the MDF, had been a moderate opposition group during the final years of communist rule, very close to the 'national popular' sectors of the then ruling party, the Hungarian Socialist Workers Party (MSzMP). The MDF was thus distinct from the more radically anti-communist SzDSz. Many MDF activists had been in the MSzMP or belonged to small-town elites, while a large part of its leaders had held middle-ranking posts that required the MSzMP blessing. Jozsef Antall, for example, who was prime minister in 1990–3, had been the director of a small museum in Budapest in the 1980s. In other words, the MDF was neither socially nor politically a radical opposition force. Indeed, members of SzDSz had suffered more political repression, although it is true that political repression in Hungary under Kádár rule (1956–88) was less severe than in most communist countries. MDF plans to encourage political justice were part of its efforts to forge a distinct image and were an ingredient of its policy of gestures and symbols, which it used widely throughout its mandate.

To overcome the stumbling block posed by the constitutional court rejection of the Zeteny–Takacs law, the government submitted a new bill in which the crimes committed during the repression of the 1956 rebellion were deemed crimes of war and crimes against humanity, and therefore were not affected by statute of limitations. The parliamentary historic commission investigating the events of 1956 had already concluded that about 1,000 people had been killed in the conflict, most of them civilians. This time the constitutional court approved the law, only striking down some articles; but the absence of witnesses, the lack of evidence, and the health problems of the few people arrested prevented its enforcement (Oltay, 1993: 6–10). Only two trials were held under the law. In one, the court ruled that the crimes were not war crimes or crimes against humanity and that the domestic statute of limitations was applicable. The case was closed. The second trial found only two of the twelve defendants guilty and condemned them to five years in prison (Halmai and Scheppele, 1997: 169). In September 1996 the constitutional court responded to a petition from the Supreme Court and public prosecutor, again putting an end to the law. It ruled that the law lacked procedural norms and that the criminal procedure code could not remedy the situation. Parliament then had to provide new procedural norms before new trials could be held. To date, it has not done so.

The most ambitious attempt to promote an administrative purge was the screening law which the government passed through parliament two months before the 1994 elections. The MSzP voted against it and the SzDSz abstained. Approval of the law was linked to a short-term political calculation; it was meant to hamper the electoral chances of the MSzP, which polls had forecast would be the winner of the forthcoming elections. The screening law affected about 10,000 positions, including members of parliament, ministers, deans and heads of university departments, judges, and editors of leading newspapers. Its stated purpose was to prevent anyone who had collaborated with the III/III Department of the Interior Ministry (the political police) from holding such posts. It also affected those who had been members of the 'law and order' squads in 1956 (involved in counter-insurgency), or had belonged to the Crossed Arrow Nazi party, which ruled during the German occupation in 1944, the era of the 'final solution' for Hungarian Jews.

Under the law, if a person belonged to one of the aforementioned categories and did not resign voluntarily, their name and relationship with these organizations would be published in the official gazette. The state news agency would then disseminate the information. Supporters of the law argued that it prevented the blackmail of anyone holding important posts and, as it was being passed before the elections, ensured that such people would be stopped from having a seat in parliament. Thus, the law did not advocate a real purge, because it was left to the accused to decide whether or not to remain as candidates or in public office. The law provided for the creation of two groups of three judges, which would examine the records and look for files on anyone holding relevant posts. The process was set to last from July 1994 to June 2000. In 2030, the list of agents of the III/III Department will be made public (Oltay, 1994: 13–15).

Gyula Horn, the leader of the MSzP, should have felt the full force of the law, because in 1956 he had been a member of the 'law and order' squads. However, this fact is widely known and Horn had publicly regretted his 'youthful sin,' so the penalty provided for by the law cannot hurt him. MSzP members were not the only ones affected by the law, however. As in Czechoslovakia, police informants are more likely to include former dissidents. Thus, Istvan Csurka, a prominent dissident in the 1980s and currently leader of a radical anti-Semitic minority party, the Hungarian Justice and Life Party (MIEP), was accused during 1993 of having been a police informer. Csurka publicly acknowledged that he had signed a collaboration agreement with the secret police, but claimed that he never gave them information. Jozsef Torgyan, leader of the radical and populist Smallholders Party (FKgP), was also accused of having been an informer.

After the MSzP took power in 1994, it showed little interest in enforcing the screening law. The new Interior Minister set up a Committee of Experts to examine the files of the III/III

Department, which reported to parliament that many of the files had disappeared or been destroyed in 1989. Moreover, although agents were listed, the files did not state their functions or the information they had provided. It was thus impossible to distinguish between people who only agreed to co-operate because they were forced to do so and 'real' collaborators. The secret services in Hungary were relatively small in comparison to neighbouring countries. It is calculated that approximately 30,000 people worked for the III/III Department as agents or informers. In view of the difficulties, the MSzP proposed that the scope of the law should be limited to officials sworn into office or taking an oath before parliament or the president. The reduction was approved by parliament in 1996, limiting the number of people under examination to 540 posts (*Népszabadság*, 6 July 1996). This is in line with a prior recommendation by the constitutional court (*Heti Világgazdaság*, 815, 7 January 1995; Halmai and Scheppele, 1997: 175).

The general public, intellectuals, and the majority of Hungarian politicians are not overly interested in political justice or de-communization. Unlike Poland, there have been no protests about a 'betrayed revolution'. Broadly speaking, the Hungarian elite and the population as a whole seem to accept the fact that the country did not undergo a revolution, in the heroic sense of the term, but rather a general crisis and an uphill new start.

Conclusions

De-communization has followed different paths in the countries examined in this chapter, and only in the Czech Republic and Albania has it led to a large-scale replacement of public administration officials. Three important factors explain these differences.

First, they are a result of the nature of the agreement arrived at during the transition. In countries where the government and the opposition negotiated a transition, as in Poland and Hungary, political justice or purges did not occur. The screening laws approved in both cases have not prevented the old political elite from holding high office, as the case of Hungarian Prime Minister Horn shows. Although there is no evidence of this, the agreements hammered out at the negotiating table may have included a renunciation of any type of 'revenge' measure. This does not mean that de-communization was not a significant part of intellectual and parliamentary debates. In Poland, where a popular anti-communist opposition, led by Solidarity, confronted governments in the 1980s, many of its members or sympathizers are now calling for punishment to vent their frustration with the economic success of the old nomenklatura and the return to government of the PZPR heirs (1993–7). Expressions such as 'the expropriated revolution' or 'the lost revolution' are used every day by anti-communist politicians and intellectuals. In Hungary, by contrast, the return of the successors of former communists to government (1994–8) and the economic triumph of the nomenklatura is widely accepted as unavoidable.

Second, the strength of the rule of law in political culture is a key factor. It marks a striking difference between the solutions adopted in the Czech Republic and in Albania, for example. The Czech Republic has established a norm of lustration that seeks to offer guarantees of universality, impartiality, and objectivity, whereas Albania passed laws that accepted arbitrariness. Romania and Bulgaria have also shown little respect for legality in some political justice proceedings, although in both cases very few people have been affected. Closely linked to this factor is the level of independence of the judiciary and shortcomings in the separation of powers, allowing the partisan use of the legal system in the case of south-eastern Europe. The different political traditions and histories in the region are strongly related to the political cultures of today; countries that have experienced democracy and a rule of law in the past, like Czech Republic, now enjoy a deeper democratic culture and a more firmly rooted respect for the separation of powers.

Third, the electoral success or failure of the former communist elite is of vital importance. Wherever groups succeeding former communist parties have remained in power after the first democratic elections, as in Bulgaria, Romania, and Albania, de-communization has been limited to symbolic gestures with great public impact, such as the execution of the Ceausescus or the arrest of Zhivkov.[8] Attempts to undertake more thorough purges began only after the second round of elections, when opposition parties were victorious. In Romania the second elections gave a second term of office to the FSN. It ruled in coalition with several left-wing and nationalist parties, and did not promote lustration. In Central Europe, after the electoral victory of the Polish and Hungarian former communists in 1993 and 1994 respectively, the public relevance of debates on the issue died down and the screening law passed by

[8] The weight of symbolic measures in Romania is also evident in the creation of a special legal status for the 'Revolutionaries of' 89, which gives more than 8,000 individuals free public transport, income tax exemptions, and other privileges.

TABLE 7.1 *De-communization and Transition in Central and Eastern Europe*

De-communization	Negotiated transition	Failed elite change	Elite replacement
Failed	Hungary/Poland	Slovakia	
Symbolic		Bulgaria/Romania	
Successful			Czech Republic/Albania

the previous Hungarian parliament was amended and whittled down. The breakup of Czechoslovakia led in Slovakia to the replacement of a liberal government under Klaus with a populist–nationalist government that had much stronger personal and ideological ties to the former KSC. For this reason, Slovakia suspended enforcement of the lustration law that the Czechs continued to apply.

In assessing the political effects of de-communization or political justice, it is helpful to use these cases as a political laboratory to validate or deny the hypotheses that settling accounts by new democracies contributes to democratic consolidation. This set of cases shows that there is no link between the level of democratic consolidation attained and the accomplishment of de-communization measures. Hungary, for example, where political justice or de-communization did not take place, has achieved a level of political stability and a consolidation of democratic institutions that is comparable to the Czech Republic, where de-communization measures were broadly implemented. Albania, a well-known example of state dissolution, chaos, and violence, undertook wide-ranging purges and numerous political trials.

On the other hand, although this 'political laboratory' does not provide proof that political justice improves democratic life, nor does it not prove the contrary—that purges and 'cleansing' are negative. Rather, it appears not to matter one way or the other where democratic consolidation in the region is concerned. The main reason for its 'irrelevance' is the previous destruction of the power of the old elite in the new democracies. The demise of communism was complete in 1989–90 (or 1991 in Albania), and new governments have not had to protect democracy against military or civilian threats. Domestic military forces were never a threat to society in the communist countries studied here. The Soviet Red Army was the instrument for securing the socialist order, while domestic armed forces (barring Poland) were not involved in internal repression

(Barany, 1992: 2–7). Indeed, the new democracies were born in a power vacuum of sorts, in societies where the old power structure, based upon the absolute control by a communist party over social and economic life, collapsed when the parties crumbled.

Thus, in Eastern Europe political justice and purges could be undertaken when non-anti-communist parties met with electoral success because the old elite had no power to impede them. At the same time, however, neither political justice nor purges were necessary to secure democracy and the rule of law, precisely because they had no power and there was no other authoritarian threat to contend with. Furthermore, in contrast with Central America or South Africa, these countries were not socially fragmented; on the contrary, one of the heritages of the communist system was a homogeneous society.[9] Thus, political justice was not necessary to reconcile social groups. The only exception here is the Bulgarian Turks, given the racial persecution of the forceful assimilation campaign of the 1980s.

On the other hand, the persistence over the years of debates around the issue, as in the case of Poland, is an element of continued instability that arguably weakens the political system. Thus, administrative purges and measure of retroactive justice, if undertaken, should be implemented quickly or not at all. Clearly, this does not exhaust the debate about the legal and moral convenience of such political measures in new democracies, but it may contribute to clarify the more political aspects of the issue.

[9] The former Yugoslavia, ethnically and economically fragmented, falls beyond the scope of this chapter. Romania also has important national minorities (gypsies and Hungarians), but this does not influence the issues analysed here.

8

East Germany: Incorporation, Tainted Truth, and the Double Division

Jan-Werner Müller

Introduction

The East German case of transitional justice is unique in more ways than one: whereas in other Central and Eastern European countries dictatorships disappeared, in East Germany the country disappeared along with the dictatorship.[1] Where in other countries economic transition was precarious and often provoked the return of communist parties to power, in united Germany institutional stability and social safety were guaranteed by the fact that East Germany was absorbed into what was then one of Europe's strongest economies and, arguably, most stable democracies. Thus, the ascendancy of a socialist successor party to national power was effectively impossible. Moreover, where other countries felt their way towards an appropriate way of dealing with a difficult past, the West Germans had already been through a more or less successful experience with 'overcoming the past' (*Vergangenheitsbewältigung*). Given these idiosyncratic characteristics, can the East German case hold any 'lessons' for its neighbours?

After spring 1990, when the German Democratic Republic (DDR) revolutionaries negotiated a 'transition by transaction' with the old regime, the evolution towards democracy by 'incorporation' into West Germany was never at risk, and consequently old elites could be tried and purged (Glaessner, 1992: 55). Because of this

Thanks to Jonathan Allen, Alexandra Barahona de Brito, Claudia Bull, Claus Offe, and Peter E. Quint.

[1] For other 'transitology' studies focusing on the exceptional nature of the East German case, see Pickel and Wiesenthal (1997) and Wiesenthal (1996).

'inner security' and large financial resources, united Germany could also afford a vast and expensive bureaucracy to investigate the past thoroughly. In that sense, East Germany might at least serve as a 'laboratory case' or even a 'most favourable case analysis' (Offe, 1996: 87).

At the same time, the complete incorporation of East Germany has produced unique problems, and policies to deal with the past were arguably contaminated by what many observers have seen as a 'colonialism in one country' of sorts. Achieving 'inner unity' between former East and West Germany was superimposed on the objectives of achieving justice and establishing secure foundations for democracy. Thus, while many commentators have deemed the policy of openly dealing with the past a success, they have also claimed that the problem of the double division between East and West and within East Germany has probably been exacerbated by this very policy and remains to be solved. The East German case, then, poses special problems and holds special answers, but it also presents particularly stark choices, given the dilemmas that are common to democratic transitions.

East Germany: Red Prussia or Totalitarian Unrechtsstaat?[2]

The nature of the East German regime remains the subject of much historical and, inevitably, moral, controversy. After 1989 there was a succession of 'historians' disputes' about questions such as whether the DDR had always lacked legitimacy, whether the DDR could and should be compared to the Third Reich, and whether outside historians had a right to judge life in the DDR at all.[3] Nevertheless, there is a minimal consensus that East Germany, at least in its final years, had reverted to a kind of neo-feudalism, in which the threat of repression was coupled with consumerism as a means of social integration. Socialism used privilege as a tool of governance, and relied on an implicit social contract, in which the government traded 'bread and circuses' for a kind of quietism

[2] The notion of the *Unrechtsstaat* as the opposite of the German *Rechtsstaat* is a highly charged one in this context. It refers to a state that not only perpetrates systematic injustice through its laws, but also breaks its own laws. What makes the notion so charged is that all too often the concept of *Unrechtsstaat* has served to lump together the Third Reich and the DDR.

[3] For an overview of controversies and different approaches to GDR history after 1989, see Schroeder (1998).

among the population. It was a Faustian bargain of freedom for security in the form of generous health care, housing, and jobs for life (Maier, 1997: 45; Rosenberg, 1995a: 227). While the public sphere became subject to negotiated bargains and was corrupted through privilege as well as pervasive policing, the private sphere was corrupted through surveillance, secrecy, and distrust (Maier, 1997: 45).

The Stasi, the secret police, in particular provided the regime with its *arcana imperii*, but was also able to contaminate dissent and independent initiatives through a wide network of 'corrupting complicity' (Maier, 1997: 47). After the army East Germany's largest employer, the Stasi directly or indirectly employed up to 2 per cent of the population. It kept files on roughly half the adult population, and was the largest political police organization in human history. In retrospect, it seems to have been demonic in its relentless terror against individual dissidents, as well as its limitless power to corrupt, and yet comic in its equally relentless accumulation of useless information.

Timothy Garton Ash has characterized this culture as 'the routine, bureaucratic forms of infiltration, intimidation and collaboration, which characterised the German communist dictatorship: the quieter corruption of mature totalitarianism' (Garton Ash, 1997b: 12). However, rather than totalitarian, East Germany might better be described as a repressive authoritarian state, much in the tradition of the nineteenth-century German police state (*Polizeystaat*), run by paranoid petty bourgeois, which is not to deny that in some respects it made total claims on its citizens. The regime engaged in torture, harassment, and murder, even, as it recently turned out, causing cancer through hidden radiation in prisons. None the less, oppression was largely broad and shallow, rather than concentrated and deep, as it was in Latin America. The majority of citizens retreated into 'niches' of private happiness, engaging in day-to-day negotiations with the authorities that were neither morally untainted nor truly reprehensible.[4] The line of division between accommodating the regime and keeping one's distance ran through most subjects, and often led to an inconsistent stance of half-truths and half-hearted acts of complicity that characterized everyday life in the DDR (Wolle, 1998: 336).

Only a minority achieved a kind of 'living in truth' and paid the price for it. Until the 1980s, when the Protestant Church afforded an umbrella for opposition groups, dissent remained extremely

[4] Günter Gaus's concept of the 'niche society' still captures an important aspect of DDR society (Gaus, 1983).

fragmented (Fulbrook, 1995). However, even those opposed to the regime were not necessarily opposed to socialism, and invested the DDR with some legitimacy as the 'better' German state, because of its anti-fascist foundation myth.[5] In turn, the regime could easily diffuse dissent by essentially 'dumping' or even selling opposition members across the border in West Germany. For the rest of the population, suffering was at most diffuse; but, as Tina Rosenberg has put it, all lived smaller lives as a consequence of a criminal regime, in which loyalty measured all things (Rosenberg, 1995a: 400).

In the end, quietism was more important in propping up the DDR than the threat of outright force, which was nevertheless frequently and ruthlessly used. Even the East German dissidents for the most part aimed not to overthrow the system altogether but rather to reform it from within and to move closer to an environmentally sound and peaceful democratic socialism (Torpey, 1995). In sum, 'under communism, the lines of complicity ran like veins and arteries inside the human body' (Rosenberg, 1995a: 399). By mixing the dreary daily oppression of 'really existing socialism' with older German authoritarian traditions, the DDR achieved extraordinary medium-term stability; but it also undermined itself in the long run.

The Transition: From the Round Table to an Executed Unification

The East German transition took place in three distinct phases. The first was an 'exit' phase, during which hundreds of East Germans fled across the newly opened Hungarian border. In the second, the opposition groups and demonstrators within East Germany expressed their 'voice' of protest. The third phase consisted of a 'pacted transition' between the East German government and opposition politicians at the Round Table, with West Germany weighing in on the process ever more heavily.

When Gorbachev initiated his policies of *glasnost* and *perestroika* in the Soviet Union, the East German leadership remained inflexible in social and economic matters and resisted any liberalization of the public sphere. Despite mounting debts and the threat of bankruptcy looming ever larger, East Germany continued on its special path to socialism and economic disaster. The same

[5] On legitimacy, see Meuschel (1992).

sort of neo-feudalism and implicit social contract that had lent the system stability in the 1970s and 1980s was now undermining it. The fact that the leadership of the Socialist Unity Party (SED) had no intention of initiating either *perestroika* or *glasnost* was made painfully obvious by the DDR-wide local elections in May 1989, in which the overwhelming victory of the SED was seen as a manifest fraud. When Hungary opened its borders in the summer of 1989, ever more East Germans chose the 'exit' option and circumvented the Wall altogether, especially since they were granted automatic citizenship upon arrival in West Germany. The massive exit in turn encouraged DDR reform groups such as the New Forum, which wanted to change the system from within, and aimed at the establishment of true democratic socialism in the DDR, rather than unification. Unlike in other Eastern European countries, East German dissidents were explicitly anti-nationalist, and still saw some legitimacy in the DDR's anti-fascist foundation myth (Joppke, 1995). As on many previous occasions, the regime initially reacted with repression. However, as ever greater numbers fled across the border, and as ever more citizens took to the streets demanding reform and defiantly announcing 'We are staying' and 'We are the people', the party leadership decided against a 'Chinese solution' and attempted a belated reform from within the Politburo. Head of government Erich Honecker was toppled, and his successor Egon Krenz struggled to retain a grip on a rapidly changing situation by making tactical concessions, while holding on to the leading role of the party under socialism. When the Wall was opened (more or less accidentally), the dynamic of exit and 'voice' escalated, prompting the West German government to take the first decisive steps in the direction of what was then seen as the rather daring plan of a confederation (Korte, 1998: 438–77).

It has sometimes been argued that 1989 was no genuine revolution at all, but a mere decolonization, a dissolution or implosion, especially since the events have passed into language as a mere 'turn' (*Wende*). According to such interpretations, the SED leadership essentially lost its will to power and was then swiftly replaced by the Kohl government as the decisive factor in the transition. Opposition groups gave the DDR the last push and inadvertently contributed to the end of the very state they wished to transform in the direction of a 'true socialism'. Certainly there were two distinct languages in the revolution. One was a 'language of social functionalism shared by the Stasi and the protesters, the regime and the new reform groups', which still hoped for a reformed socialism, and which aimed at social harmony and took account of social complexity. The other was an almost Protestant language of 'simplicity and emancipation', which in the eyes of many observers was equally 'apolitical' (Maier, 1997: 133).

These revolutionaries, like so many others in German history, were unprepared to take power and largely unwilling to form a counter-elite. They refused to form 'normal' parties and organizations until the West German parties began to establish alliances with the East German 'bloc' parties, especially the Christian Democrat and Liberal parties, which had always been subordinate to the SED. In general, they were afraid to lose their moral authority, but also their particular identity, as social movements like the Greens in the West had supposedly done when they had become a party (Glaessner, 1992: 70). Rather than concentrating on building institutions, these reluctant revolutionaries sought to re-educate hearts and minds, starting with the values of dialogue, transparency, and consensus (Sa'adah, 1998: 67). Thus, grass-roots democracy and dealing with the so-called 'cancer' of the Stasi, particularly through the confrontation and reconciliation of victims and perpetrators, became priorities. But the dissidents were also unable to appeal to the rural population and industrial workers, most of whom sought better living standards and an economic reorganization of the DDR by West German elites, rather than a reformed socialism. By now, the 'We are the people' slogan shouted out in 1989 had been replaced by the unification slogan, 'We are one people'. For the opposition movement, however, those clamouring for Western consumer goods were selling out the 'material and moral values' of the DDR.[6]

In December 1989, a Round Table, modelled on Polish and Hungarian precedents, was formed with the more reform-minded sections of the old SED elite to fill the power vacuum that had opened up after the collapse of the Wall. Under another new leadership, the SED renamed itself, but struggled to hold on to parts of the old system. The Stasi was also renamed, and continued to operate into 1990. When protesters began to demand the right to see their files ('freedom for my file'), Stasi employees began to destroy as many files as possible. They were slowed down in this attempt only because many East German shredding machines began to break down under the sheer workload, after which files were simply torn apart or archives were flooded (Carstens, *Frankfurter Allgemeine Zeitung*, 5 October 1996). The Modrow government refused to disband the renamed Office for National Security, and finally an

[6] See also Philipsen (1993).

angry crowd stormed the central office of the Stasi in Berlin–Lichtenberg, in an effort to salvage as much as possible from the archives.[7] Citizens' 'committees' were formed to secure the files. Nevertheless, parts of the Stasi were left to dissolve themselves and destroy their archives, in particular the section concerned with foreign espionage headed by famous 'spy master' Markus Wolf.[8] The Round Table instructed the government to destroy the central hard disks of the Stasi, lest the West German foreign services or the US Central Intelligence Agency (CIA) should use the information.

In an increasingly volatile situation, representatives of the Round Table agreed to establish a 'government of responsibility', bringing thirteen parties together. These drafted a new constitution, and arranged for the first free elections in March 1990. Still, the basic fact remained that there was no rationale for a separate East German state if it had no socialist society or a political system sufficiently distinct from that of West Germany. This, together with the East German demand for West German consumer goods, the aggressive intervention of West German parties in the March elections, and the manoeuvring of Helmut Kohl towards economic and monetary union (Grosser, 1998) of the two Germanys, made unification seem increasingly likely. This trend was confirmed when the pro-unification Alliance for Germany, and particularly the former 'bloc' party, the Christian Democratic Union (CDU), won the March general elections. Moreover, just before and after the elections a number of party leaders were exposed as unofficial Stasi collaborators, revealing for the first time the sheer depth and pervasive nature of the social infiltration of Stasi activity among opposition groups. When the Soviet Union finally gave its consent to a united Germany within the North Atlantic Treaty Organisation (NATO) Alliance and the Currency Union was successfully implemented, the Unification Treaty was negotiated between Wolfgang Schäuble, the representative of the West German government, and Günter Krause, his East German counterpart. The Treaty was a contract between two unequal partners, the weaker of which ceased to exist after its conclusion, and was therefore unable to enforce it. For the most part, the Treaty stipulated the wholesale adoption of Western institutions by the DDR.

[7] There is some evidence that the Stasi partly engineered the occupation.

[8] To this day, there are theories that the Stasi in fact organized the entire peaceful dissolution of the DDR. For a refutation of such theories, see Richter (1996) and Wolle (1998: 339).

During the first half of 1990, the appropriate procedure for unification was hotly debated. Should it be undertaken according to Article 23 of the West German Basic Law, which allowed individual German states to accede to the federation whenever they chose, or Article 146, which invalidated the Basic Law upon unification and required the drafting and ratification of a new Constitution?[9] At the time, left–liberal intellectuals such as Jürgen Habermas argued that the democratic consciousness of the new Germany would be damaged if what he called a mere annexation (*Anschluß*) took place through Article 23. Others felt that the socialist achievements of the DDR should somehow be recognized in a new common constitution, so as to ensure the recognition and dignity of DDR citizens. At the heart of the discussion was the question of how to achieve social integration, or 'macro-integration', between East and West Germany, as well as democratic consolidation in East Germany. Should it be on the basis of nationalism, the promise of economic prosperity, or the meting out of justice? Or could it be accomplished on the basis of political principles, and in particular the West German conception of 'constitutional patriotism', which required citizens to have a primary allegiance to the democratic constitution, rather than the nation?

The Kohl government essentially opted for social integration on the basis of prosperity and, to some extent, justice. There was also a degree of instrumental elite nationalism to appeal to national solidarity between West and East Germans; but popular nationalism played almost no role during the unification process. During the summer of 1990 'the strategy of the West German government was based on creating irreversible conditions quickly by executive decision and international contracts, while pushing the costs of the rapid transition into the future or leaving them to the markets to absorb' (Offe, 1996: 17).

With East Germany having no more bargaining power, West German elites were now entirely in control of the unification process, including the instant transfer of Western institutions to the East. After implementation of the Currency Union, the East German economy collapsed in a way that was unprecedented in world economic history, with the West Germans left to cushion the free fall of East German industry. Massive transfers of both financial resources and West German civil service and business personnel began immediately and, in the absence of an economic

[9] The former Article was intended mainly for the Saarland, while the latter underlined the provisional nature of the Basic Law.

miracle in the East for which the Kohl government had hoped, continued throughout the 1990s. In that sense, social integration through prosperity proved to be an at least somewhat miscalculated strategy, which exacted its price in that East Germans, lacking civic pride and pride in their own past, fell back on an ethnonationalist German identity (Kurthen *et al.*, 1997).

After Dictatorship: Cultural and Institutional Strategies

From the outset, there was a consensus that somehow the past of the dictatorship had to be confronted.[10] The mistakes of the previous *Vergangenheitsbewältigung*, when the Nazi past had been largely repressed in the 1950s, were not to be repeated. Instead, the new slogan, *Aufarbeitung*, was adopted. This was a 'working through the past', which implied liberation from the past. A 'preemptive forgiveness' and *de facto* amnesty as advocated by Vaclav Havel was out of the question. East German dissidents in particular sought a comprehensive reckoning with the perpetrators. Only a minority agreed with philosopher Hermann Lübbe's controversial view that a 'communicative silence' would best serve to consolidate democracy and integrate former perpetrators into the new polity. According to Lübbe, this had happened in the 1950s when a silence had covered the activities of former Nazis in order to integrate them into the Federal Republic (*Frankfurter Allgemeine Zeitung*, 24 January 1983).

Although there was broad agreement on the need to do 'something about the past' and an availability of resources to do it, there remained the question of concrete strategies to promote truth, justice, and civic trust in the public sphere. Anne Sa'dah has usefully distinguished between two different strategies of building democracy, institutional and cultural (Sa'adah, 1998: 3). Institutional or procedural strategies occur in a top-down manner and define political trust in terms of outward reliability, rather than in terms of true convictions or trust-as-trustworthiness. They are essentially Hobbesian: if the right institutions and incentives are in place, undemocratic inclinations will be kept in check and eventually overcome as the behaviour and the political values of citizens are

[10] Indeed, some felt that during the revolution, when power was 'up for grabs', an opportunity for retribution or 'informal justice' had already been missed. This was seen as yet another manifestation of a German tradition of being 'apolitical' and insufficiently radical. See Leggewie and Meier (1993: 51), and Bohrer (1992).

reshaped. Cultural strategies adopt a bottom-up perspective and focus on the justice for the victims of a dictatorship as well as the formation of genuine democratic convictions, where institutional strategies put order first.

After 1990 Germany pursued a largely institutional strategy, as West Germany had done after 1945. But because at least its Western institutions were secure, it could also incorporate important elements of cultural strategies, which aimed at transparency regarding the past and the recognition of past crimes. However, institutional strategies tend to disappoint those who have fought a previous, unjust regime and now seek comprehensive justice for the victims. Rather than remobilizing citizens on democratic terms, institutional strategies demobilize what is seen as a mobilized and over-politicized population (Sa'adah, 1998: 57). East Germany was arguably no exception.

The Trials, or Retribution

The trials arguably constituted the greatest failure of efforts to deal with the DDR past. The trials of the East German border guards who had shot DDR citizens fleeing to the West, the *Mauerschützenprozesse*, attracted much attention, but from the start were riddled with controversy. The trials were intended to strengthen the case against Honecker and others who had been ultimately responsible for the policy of firing on East Germans crossing the border, but also to put the Wall as a whole on symbolic trial (Rosenberg, 1995a: 265). None the less, the first trial of the four border guards involved in killing the last East German citizen trying to cross the Wall confronted all the familiar legal-cum-moral dilemmas surrounding institutionalized violence, particularly the question of whether the guards had simply been following orders and the moral status of following such orders.

The trials also had to negotiate the conflict between two basic legal principles: on the one hand the notion that grave human rights violations should be appropriately punished, on the other hand the principle of non-retroactivity (*nullum crimen nulla poena sine lege*), whereby acts can be tried only if they were illegal at the time they were committed.[11] While there was a clear sense that

[11] Additional legal problems were caused by the vagueness of the Border Law and the so-called *Republikflucht* paragraph dealing with 'fleeing' from the DDR.

someone had to be accountable for making the East Germans prisoners in their own country, punishing the border guards and other East German officials risked substituting morality for law and thereby undermining the very *Rechtsstaat* that the trials were supposed to foster. Article 103 (2) incorporates the *nullum crimen sine lege* principle into the Basic Law, but Nuremberg and the punishment of Nazi officials by German courts in the postwar period set a precedent for punishment despite *nullum crimen*. At that time the courts had followed the Radbruch formula, named after legal theorist Gustav Radbruch. Radbruch had argued that positive law takes precedence, even if its content is unjust and ineffective, except when the contradiction between positive law and justice is such that, as 'wrongful law', it must yield to justice.

After 1945 there had been a brief flowering of natural law thinking, subsequently superseded again by traditional German positivism. West German politicians were eager to stress that they did not want to hold political trials and that the proceedings should not damage the self-understanding of the Federal Republic as a *Rechtsstaat* (McAdams, 1997: 241). Consequently, the Unification Treaty stipulated that all acts committed before 3 October 1990 should be judged according to DDR law, except when West German law was milder. This was a beautiful legal rendering of *nullum crimen sine lege*, but morally it immediately raised the question of how the laws of an *Unrechtsstaat* could be used to judge human rights violations. Such a policy could endow DDR law, which had been purely instrumental in propping up the dictatorship, with retroactive legitimacy.

The first trial of the border guards, which resulted in the conviction of two of the defendants, was surrounded by much media frenzy and arguably erred on the side of substituting morality for law. When convicting two of the defendants, Judge Seidel argued very much in terms of natural law, and was widely criticized for it. In the second trial, therefore, the judges went out of their way to remain within codified DDR law, and based their conclusions on the fact that the use of firearms had been 'disproportionate'. They also immediately suspended the sentences. Overall, the trials opted for an uneasy compromise between *nullum crimen sine lege* and a strong underlying strand of natural law thinking.

In subsequent appeals, the highest civil and criminal Federal Court held that under DDR law the actions of border guards and their superiors had actually been illegal, thereby circumventing the prohibition on retroactivity altogether. However, in a further ruling the Constitutional Court essentially reverted to natural law thinking, arguing that the undemocratic nature of the DDR and its failure to protect human rights made DDR law less reliable. Shooting at the border constituted an 'extreme injustice', although the political indoctrination of the guards also had to be taken into account. Consequently, the Court suggested a compromise in that only suspended sentences would be handed down. In the end, most border guards were convicted, but were given suspended sentences: although thirty-five soldiers were convicted, only one has actually been imprisoned.

The trials of DDR leaders had similarly mixed results. In the first major trial, members of the National Defence Council were indicted for ordering the 'shoot to kill' policy at the border. The prosecution tried to pinpoint the meeting of the Council at which the fateful policy had been decided, and sought to establish a direct link between the discussion of the Council and the charge of 'collective manslaughter'. The trial against Honecker and his colleagues, however, was ill fated from the start. It was overshadowed by the embarrassing fact that only four years earlier the West German government had rolled out the red carpet for Honecker on his only visit to Bonn. Honecker returned from Moscow, where he had fled in 1990, and, ironically, was held in the very same prison where the Nazis had incarcerated him. The trials of DDR President Willi Stoph and head of the Stasi Erich Mielke had to be suspended almost immediately because of ill health. After much macabre debate about the state of Honecker's liver, the Berlin Constitutional Court of Appeals stopped his trial in 1993, alleging that a long trial violated the human dignity of the defendant, which was guaranteed by Article 1 of the Basic Law. Honecker subsequently flew to Chile as a free man, where he died later that year.

The trials caused outrage among the population and strengthened the suspicion that some of the leaders had been let off, while the small fry were being sent to gaol. However, the healthy leaders of the National Defence Council were eventually convicted for 'co-responsibility' in the shoot-to-kill policy and other acts of government criminality (*Regierungskriminalität*). The judges acknowledged the dangers of creating an impression of victors' justice and took into account the circumstances of the Cold War to justify milder sentences than demanded by the prosecution. Subsequently, however, the Constitutional Court not only upheld the sentences, but also made them harsher in one case to drive home the point that even in dictatorships individuals had moral and political choices. Subsequently, four of the military leaders of the DDR were convicted. In a second major trial, mainly of members of the

Politburo, Krenz and others were convicted for breaching DDR and international law. At the time, a majority of West and East Germans found the judgment fair or demanded a higher sentence. East and West Germans also opposed an amnesty for the DDR leadership, including a majority among voters of the former communist party, the Democratic Socialist Party (PDS). Furthermore, they overwhelmingly rejected the suggestion that the trials were an instance of victors' justice, except for PDS voters, of which 88 per cent saw the trials in this light (*Der Spiegel*, 1 September 1997).

In general, regime criminality was investigated by a special office, the Central Office for the Investigation of Government and Unification Criminality (ZERV), and the Berlin state prosecutor's office, known as St II. Regime criminality included crimes such as election rigging, fraud, violation of mail privacy, and manslaughter through judicial organs.[12] The ZERV was understaffed and poorly funded. The *Länder* were supposed to have made police officers available for it, but in many cases failed to do so. The head of St II, Christoph Schaefgen, also complained that the *Rechtsstaat* and the content of the Unification Treaty made successful prosecution extremely difficult. He concluded that the fight of the *Rechtsstaat* 'against Stasi terror had been a failure' (Schmelz, *Die Welt*, 12 November 1998).

It was particularly hard to make a coherent case against perpetrators of low-level harassment and terror (*Zersetzungsmaßnahmen*), which went mostly unpunished despite the fact that they had been especially effective in destroying people's life chances. Moreover, the scattershot approach of St II, which combined cultural and institutional strategies, ultimately led to an absurdly low ratio of convictions to investigations—of 21,360 investigations, 20,502 never even produced indictments, and only 157 of the 629 defendants were convicted. As some pointed out, this result amounted to a *de facto* amnesty. The legal system had been able only to attribute responsibility but not to mete out retribution (Körting, 1999: 1–4). Ultimately, because success in prosecuting remained elusive, the media and the public lost interest in ZERV activities. As public interest waned, financial resources were withdrawn and prosecution became even more difficult. In short, a vicious circle of prosecution failure was established.

[12] In addition, there were the 'unification crimes', or *Vereinigungskriminalität*—in particular, fraud—committed by both East and West Germans during and after 1990. These crimes were also investigated by ZERV, whose work was to be completed in 2000. On ZERV see Borneman, (1997: 59–79).

The trials arguably went some way towards giving justice to the victims of border shootings and of the regime more generally. However, the legal and historical contortions of Western officials, instead of shoring up the notions of legality and legitimacy, sometimes gave the impression of legally veiled victors' justice, not because the wrong people were convicted, but because of how and why they were convicted. Mielke for instance, was eventually convicted for having shot a policeman in 1931, and border guards were admonished that they should have known, from the Western media that what they were doing was wrong. Alternatively, judges argued that DDR law should have been interpreted in the way it might have been interpreted in a *Rechtsstaat*, in the way most favourable to human rights, when in fact the law was regularly instrumentalized for political purposes in East Germany. Consequently, it is hard to sustain the view that any of these trials strengthened respect for the rule of law.

Rather than a ritual purification necessary to prevent cycles of retributive violence, they were often seen as instances of revenge, especially in the case of Markus Wolf.[13] DDR judges who were accused of perverting the course of justice seemed to receive much lighter sentences than the border guards. In the case of the judges, the context of DDR law and politics was taken into account far more than in the case of the guards, who were expected to know about international human rights standards. The selection of the accused seemed in the eyes of many East Germans political and arbitrary, a fact that was unlikely to increase their respect for the principle of equality before the law: the 'German authorities were almost too eager to bring *somebody* to trial' (McAdams, 1997: 241). The seeming violation of *nulla poena sine lege* in at least some of the early trials also seemed to undermine the *Rechtsstaat*, rather than strengthen it. There seems to be a basic paradox here: the *Rechtsstaat* will always first benefit those who opposed it in the past, which might damage respect for its principles; yet violating its principles by suspending *nulla poena sine lege* in favour of natural law thinking, for example, will also damage it (Leggewie and Meier, 1993: 60).

Moreover, there is the added problem that systemic injustice cannot be dealt with through the law at all, or only very selectively. Unlike in Nuremberg, no organizations as such were declared

[13] Eventually, however, the Constitutional Court ruled that members of the DDR intelligence service who had spied on West Germany were not criminals. West German spies who had betrayed their own government, however, could still be prosecuted.

criminal and put on trial. This certainly promoted an actor-centred view of history and a sense of personal responsibility, but could hardly do justice to the complexities of the DDR. Law as a means of *Aufarbeitung* thus reached its limits. The task of establishing transparency and what Claus Offe has called the 'politics of knowledge' had to be shouldered by agencies such as the Gauck Authority and the Study Commission (EK), analysed below.[14] Given the limitations of law in *Aufarbeitung*, it is not surprising that former dissident Bärbel Bohley, in what is probably the most famous expression of dissident disappointment, stated that 'we wanted justice, and we got the rule of law'.

The trials also hardly added much to public knowledge about the past or the nature of day-to-day repression, despite the fact that the prosecution often took painstaking care to link the inner workings of the DDR leadership with crimes at the border. If anything, the trials were sensationalized. Nor did they have any effect in deterring future crimes by the military or the old nomenclature, since, unlike in other post-transitional situations, no such threat existed. In that sense, while they brought justice for some, they failed in their 'expressive function' (Joel Feinberg) or in the goal of expressing a certain moral sentiment and redefining political common sense (Sa'adah, 1998: 144). And yet, it is far from obvious what might have been done differently. There had simply been no time for the DDR in its last days to put its own leaders on trial. The newly democratic legislature *had* wanted to bring the DDR leaders to trial, however, and East German officials had actually started prosecuting Honecker and others for high treason in 1990, which should have weakened the perception of victors' justice. But the problem remained that West German judges were now carrying out the wishes of East German opposition members. Moreover, some of the worst DDR crimes had actually taken place in the 1950s, and it was hard to disentangle what had been done because of Moscow, and what was DDR-generated crime. Finally, most of the perpetrators of these crimes were dead in any case.

Rehabilitation and Purges

Purges in East Germany were swift, thorough and arguably more just than in most East–Central European countries.[15] The speed

[14] For these limits of law, see also Battis *et al.* (1992) and Schlink (1998).

[15] For the legal details of rehabilitation, restitution, and disqualification, see the contributions in Isensee and Kirchhof (1997).

and, as some argued, the ruthlessness that favoured West German elites taking over arguably had something to do with the fact that there had already been a 'militant democracy' tradition in West Germany. Under it, it was acceptable to ban parties and exclude citizens with affiliations to 'extremist' parties from public jobs.[16] Those who did not support the 'free democratic basic order' of the Federal Republic could be rejected for positions in the civil service.

The Treaty of Unification had stipulated that East German government employees should be excluded from employment if they failed to satisfy the usual West German requirements, including the need to support the 'free democratic basic order'. The procedure was simple: employees filled out a questionnaire, which would be discussed by a committee, which also heard the employee, and then took a decision on the case. As initially envisaged, former party and Stasi members would have failed the West German 'loyalty test'. However, in a 1995 decision the Constitutional Court held that the West German 'Radicals Decree' could not be applied retroactively to the DDR public service. It also noted that the behaviour of state employees since 1990, or their willingness and ability to adapt to a 'free democratic basic order', should be taken into account. Thus, the Court sought to mediate between the principles of a militant democracy and the need for inner unity and reconciliation (Quint, n.d.).

The purges were hardly flawless, but they were fairer than those in comparable cases, such as the Czech lustration. Employers could request their employees' Stasi files and make decisions on an individual basis. Also, most of those assessed negatively by the Gauck Authority have nevertheless retained their jobs, while those dismissed at least had recourse to the labour courts. On the other hand, the peculiar dynamic of West German elites doing the purging both helped and contaminated the process.

The dismissal of 'incompetent' personnel, expressly authorized by the Treaty, 'helped to take care of many of those cases in an implicit way which in other countries would have had to be processed on the basis of explicit charges of involvement with the previous regime and its political police' (Offe, 1996: 94). Finally, those who were deemed to have been closely associated with the state (*systemnah*), such as employees of the Stasi, military, and academics, had the generous special pensions that the regime had granted them

[16] On militant democracy, see also Kommers (1997a).

cut. However, in a stunning decision in the spring of 1999, the Constitutional Court ruled that such cuts were unconstitutional, because they violated the principle of equality enshrined in the basic law. Again, it seemed that the Court gave priority to the goal of 'inner unity' over immediate claims for justice. East German former dissidents were predictably outraged by this decision, and argued that the perpetrators were now considerably better off than most of their victims.

Disqualification found its logical counterpart in rehabilitation. The East German legislature had been particularly concerned to draft a rehabilitation law, and wanted it to be carried out immediately. However, it was only in 1992 that the first law was promulgated; it aimed mainly at the rehabilitation of politically persecuted persons. Two years later, a law rehabilitating those adversely affected by administrative and employment decisions followed. Financial compensation for injustice (mostly time served in prison) was generally seen as meagre and significantly widened only in July 1999. In general, however, according to Articles 18 and 19 of the Treaty, verdicts by DDR courts and administrative decisions remained in force. In other words, there was no 'total revision' of DDR law through a retroactive validity of the *Rechtsstaat*. Nevertheless, any decision not compatible with the free democratic order of the Federal Republic could now be challenged, and would be decided by special senates and chambers at the district and *Land* level. Legal and administrative rehabilitation was complemented by a policy of returning property expropriated by the state, which was guided by the principle of 'restitution before compensation'. This effectively led to a large degree of legal indeterminacy and insecurity among the East Germans, and to a massive transfer of wealth from East to West Germany, since the victims of expropriation had in many cases moved to West Germany.

By delaying the rehabilitation laws, Germany arguably missed a chance to send a strong signal to the victims of the old regime early on that their claims would now be put first. Many of these grievances, such as life chances destroyed by the regime and long-term psychological damage, could not be dealt with by the judicial system at all. Moreover, the property legislation proved a major hindrance to speedy investment in East Germany, and led to a massive subsidy to West German lawyers as so many conflicting claims had to be adjudicated. Further, it led to resentment and a sense of injustice among the East Germans, who now had to give up their houses and felt expropriated in turn.

Truth and Openness: The Politics of Knowledge

The Federal Authority for the Records of the State Security Service of the Former German Democratic Republic, or *Gauck Authority*, has arguably been the outstanding feature of the German 'politics of memory' after 1989. In June 1990 the East German legislature formed a special commission for the Stasi files, and put Joachim Gauck, a dissident pastor, in charge. Gauck persistently advocated a tripartite strategy of legal, political, and historical *Aufarbeitung*, and was generally critical of any premature amnesty (Gauck, 1991). He co-authored a law which gave individual citizens access to their files, and which the West German government at first refused to incorporate into the Treaty, despite the fact that at the time 86 per cent of East Germans were in favour of giving Stasi victims access to their files (*Der Spiegel*, 23 April 1990). Instead, the leave as was sought to move the files to West Germany, and to make them available only to the West German secret service. After vigorous protests and even hunger strikes by East German dissidents, provisions to open the files were included. In the end, the Bundestag modified the East German law to the extent that the intelligence service could request material from Gauck, and that the press could publish the files of Stasi informers. With the Stasi law of autumn 1991, passed after nearly a year of heated public debate, Gauck was appointed head of the Federal Authority, soon known simply as the Gauck Authority, which was accountable to neither parliament nor particular ministries.[17]

The Authority was essentially a bureaucracy of openness built directly on top of a bureaucracy of secrecy, or a 'ministry of truth now occupying the former ministry of fear' (Garton Ash, 1997b: 17). Above all, it showed that Germany had a financial edge to carry out truth and reconciliation strategies: the Authority has around 3,100 employees, and costs US$110 million. It allowed a systematic opening of the files and an unprecedented act of thoroughness in archiving and accessing the past, for both historians and individual citizens. The Authority classifies the files, which stretch to more than 180 kilometres, with each metre containing around 10,000 pages and around 6 million filing cards. Authority employees are also busy piecing together the files shredded in 1990, and recovering information that had been erased from hard disks. But what do dusty files mean for democratization?

[17] On the debate, see Schumann (1997) and Henke (1993).

Opening the files was an unprecedented act of civic empowerment and of what was already known in West German constitutional jurisprudence as 'informational self-determination'. It reflected the wishes of the overwhelming majority of DDR citizens, and allowed them to make a choice to whether or not they wanted to see their files and to find out who had spied on them. By May 1999, the Gauck Authority had received around 1.6 million applications from individual citizens, of which 1.4 million had been dealt with.[18] Files could actually be found for roughly only a third of all applications. The number of applications has been consistently higher than expected, and calls for closing the files, often voiced by the PDS, have repeatedly been rejected.[19] While the general notion of 'drawing a line' became more popular among East Germans in the 1990s, a majority have remained opposed to closure (*Der Spiegel*, 3 July 1995). At the same time, 1.5 million requests about employees in the civil service have been received, almost all of which have been dealt with; and around 300,000 requests relating to rehabilitation and trials have been processed. In other words, in addition to 'informational self-determination', the Authority made an important contribution to the turnover of elites, rehabilitation cases, and prosecutions. Moreover, 90 per cent of those who had access to their files viewed the experience as positive, although they dealt with it in mostly personal, rather than political, terms.[20]

The truth has often been painful, of course. Most famous is the case of peace activist Vera Wollenberger, who discovered that her own husband had informed on her. There are enough cases to caution against any facile connections between truth and reconciliation. Moreover, a sensationalist media revealed the Stasi connections of famous East Germans, arousing suspicion that the Authority had leaked information. An obsession with unmasking individuals often seemed to replace a concern with more profound questions of collective responsibility. Others criticized the Authority for ultimately contributing to a distorted picture of the DDR past. The Stasi was now solely blamed for any evil, when in fact other institutions, particularly the SED, had been often just as

[18] See the *Vierter Tätigkeitsbericht des Bundesbeauftragten für die Unterlagen des Staatssicherheitsdienstes der ehemaligen Deutschen Demokratischen Republik*, issued in July 1999.

[19] In 1997 a majority among East and West Germans also opposed closing the files. PDS voters were the exception, with 79% in favour of doing so.

[20] See the survey of citizens who had access to their files in the *Vierter Tätigkeitsbericht*.

brutal (R. Schneider, *Die Woche*, 4 August 1995). In other words, de-stasification became too closely identified with de-communization. In addition, the Stasi was also wrongly viewed as being entirely an East German problem, when it had also deeply penetrated parts of West German society. In that sense, the fixation on the Stasi deepened the division between East and West (Knabe, 1997).

Still others criticized the Authority for being far too bureaucratic and for its failed attempt to 'institutionalize' the Revolution of 1989 (Fuchs, 1998). It has also often been asserted that the files, being the record of an *Unrechtsstaat*, are inherently tainted and unreliable. This seems hardly credible, however, as the Stasi did not produce its files to dupe researchers after the end of the DDR. Stasi documents will remain indispensable to an understanding of the inner workings of the dictatorship, and, if the usual precautions are employed, can be relied upon. While truth was often painful, opening the files allowed many citizens to gain a new dignity and to re-appropriate their own lives. It is plausible to argue that such recovered dignity and private knowledge about the past made better citizens and thereby contributed to the consolidation of a democratic political culture. The Gauck law treated the 'victims of the Stasi as thinking citizens and owners of their own dossiers' (Rosenberg, 1995a: 296).

Moreover, by checking the past of politicians and applicants for jobs in public service, the Authority contributed to a diminution of the widespread suspicion among Easterners that the old elites were still running the government and administration in post-socialist East Germany. In that sense, the Authority furthered a sense of trust in democratic institutions.

Finally, predictions of revenge, bloodshed, and even civil war, often heard not least from West German politicians before the opening of the files, have simply turned out to be false. Instead, allowing a form of contained conflict, by releasing information and then leaving victim and perpetrator to bring the past into the open if they so wished, may have contributed significantly to democratization. After all, democracy *is* a kind of contained conflict. Moreover, the Authority itself was accountable, as its actions and decisions could be appealed in ordinary administrative courts. Its activities sparked numerous lively debates which, despite their (sometimes) vituperative nature, contributed to a kind of moral and political self-clarification in the public sphere. Moreover, Authority representatives never failed to stress that its democratic legitimacy was directly derived not only from a parliamentary decision but also from the revolutionary actions of East Germans. Arguably, this civic empowerment through openness has had a beneficial effect on political culture, and frequently the Authority has been called a 'source of democracy' (T. Reitzschel, *Frankfurter Allgemeine Zeitung*, 14 July 1999). However, there is simply no way of assessing empirically whether the opening of the Stasi files in particular contributed to democratic consolidation.

Truth and National Memory

After unification, many Eastern dissidents also demanded a truth commission or tribunal with the power to summon witnesses but not impose punishment. Gauck and others argued that only such a comprehensive reckoning with the past could lead to a national catharsis, and proposed different institutional mechanisms to bring about 'healing' through truth. Dissidents, on the other hand, advocated a parliamentary committee of inquiry, in which members from all parties would be represented, and which would investigate the workings of the dictatorship, particularly systematic injustice that was beyond the scope of individual trials. All parties, including the PDS, favoured this option, and the EK began its work in 1992, under the chairmanship of East German pastor Rainer Eppelmann. It held hearings and conducted research, and five years after unification it produced a comprehensive report running to an impressive 15,378 pages (Deutscher Bundestag, 1995). The EK tried its best to produce a 'didactic public history', but for the most part was able to offer only contending narratives and selective memories organized along party lines (Maier, 1997: 326). Precisely because nothing was at stake (as amnesty was in the paradigmatic South African case), the German truth commission often amounted to a rehearsing of well-known positions. No obvious catharsis resulted from the process and no new information was produced, but the report did provide important historical documentation. For 'students of the East German dictatorship this may yet be what the records of the Nuremberg trials are for the students of the Third Reich' (Garton Ash, 1999: 308).

The EK drew explicitly political and historical lessons, by stressing the need for an 'anti-totalitarian consensus' in Germany, and by pointing to National Socialism as the root cause of the Soviet occupation and thus of the establishment of a second 'German dictatorship'. In that sense, it sought to pre-empt the playing off of Nazis against Communists, and the mutual moral relativization that often went with it. Finally, it made a conscious effort not to reduce the history of the DDR to the Stasi, but to understand it as a part of a common German history. In that sense, its findings had the explicit second-order goal of overcoming the division (Wilke, 1997). The first EK was immediately followed by a second charged specifically with furthering *Aufarbeitung* and developing 'all-German' forms of remembering the two dictatorships. The focus shifted increasingly to coping with the consequences of the DDR. Parliamentary investigative commissions were also set up at the Land level. Mecklenburg-Vorpommern, for instance, produced a report running to three volumes of documentation and testimony (Lndtag Mecklenburg-Vorpommern, 1998). Again, the public response to these efforts was mute.

Today, *Aufarbeitung* has become more differentiated and decentralized. An official foundation for *Aufarbeitung* was formed in the wake of the second EK, and civil society groups adopted countless initiatives. Although these have often had financial difficulties and have had to resort to official sources for additional funding, the presence of many dense networks of dissidents and victims has been beneficial in a state-centred society such as Germany's. Such initiatives were complemented by symbolic acts of public and state-led acknowledgement. The Constitution of Saxony, for instance, refers to the 'painful experience of National Socialist and Communist domination through violence (*Gewaltherrschaft*)'. Further, Article 117 stipulates that the *Land* must contribute to 'reduce the causes of individual and societal failure in the past, the consequences of violations of human dignity and to increase the capacity for self-determined and responsible conduct of one's life'.[21] Other constitutions in the new *Länder*, with the exception of Saxony-Anhalt, also include such references.[22] In addition, monuments have been erected all over the DDR. Particular care has been taken with monuments in spaces also associated with National Socialism, such as Buchenwald and Sachsenhausen, to avoid a mutual relativization of sorts. In former concentration camps where the Soviets also interned and killed Germans after the war, smaller monuments were erected for postwar victims.

Finally, in 1992 East Germans tried to form Committees for Justice, to investigate the past from within civil society (Fieber and Reichmann, 1995). Eventually, they were supposed to have been

[21] See also Saxony Constitution at: http://www.sachsen.de/deutsch/buerger/landtag/4/.

[22] On *Vergangenheitsbewältigung* through constitutional changes, see also Stein (1998).

extended to the West. Arguably, these committees were intended to provide East Germany with a body through which to express grievances. However, despite a lot of fanfare, the committee movement fizzled out rather quickly. West German leaders felt that the committees were unnecessary, since the institutions of the *Rechtsstaat* and the EK were sufficient to deal with the past. For Easterners, this lack of support was further evidence that Westerners felt no need to revise their own approach and institutions.

From Dissolution to Dissatisfaction

Ten years after the fall of the Wall, East Germany was by any standard a consolidated democracy. Political actors in East Germany were making decisions according to accepted constitutional rules, and were respecting a horizontal differentiation of social, economic, and political spheres.[23] But then, how could East Germany not be 'consolidated'—at least on paper—given the wholesale adoption of the 'ready-made' democratic institutions and personnel of the West, financed and guaranteed by the West? As Offe has put it, while other Eastern European countries had to repair their sinking ships at sea, the DDR was retrofitted into the dry dock of the Federal Republic (Offe, 1996: 151).

To be sure, the repair took longer than expected and at points seems to have been botched altogether. There are alarming signs of anomie and democratic distrust. There is violence by young neo-Nazis against foreigners, and more than 10 per cent of votes were given to a far-right-wing party, the German People's Union (DVU), in the Saxony–Anhalt *Land* elections of March 1998. The PDS has established itself as a regional protest party, or, as Gauck put it, as a party of 'institutionalized resentment'. Despite its ambivalence towards its own past and the value of Western democracy, in 1998 the party finally participated in a coalition government in Mecklenburg–Vorpommern. Germany pursued an 'institutional strategy' towards communist successor parties. Rather than wait for the party to work through the past alone, it was hoped that inclusion in democratic institutions would transform trust as democratic conformist behaviour into trust as trustworthiness.

The consolidation of the PDS, however, was only one sign of a still somewhat shaky democratic culture in the East. While East Germans voted overwhelmingly for Western parties, around 50 per

[23] For these criteria of 'consolidation', see Elster *et al.* (1998).

cent could not identify with any Western party (Staab, 1998: 157). Satisfaction with the way democracy worked fell as low as 30 per cent in 1997. Democracy is accepted in the abstract, but the numbers decline significantly as soon as democracy 'like the one we have in the Federal Republic' is put to the test in polls (Gensicke, 1998: 181). Also, Easterners still cling to socialist and plebiscitarian ideals, and judge the performance of institutions in unified Germany accordingly (Rohrschneider, 1999: 104). A more centralized, collectivist, and welfare-state oriented notion of democracy persisted throughout the 1990s, while values such as tolerance, pluralism, and democratic self-restraint have spread far more slowly (Rohrschneider, 1999: 104; Gensicke, 1998: 176). East Germans have also been dissatisfied with interest representation at the national level, and have often seemed to feel that yet another alien political system has been imposed on them. Moreover, there has been markedly less trust in the executive, the judiciary, and the police in East Germany than in West Germany (Gensicke, 1998: 184).

This evidence needs to be put into perspective, however. Violence against foreigners is almost as common in West Germany as in East Germany. The fact that a party like the DVU received a significant share of the vote in state (but not in national) elections arguably shows that the East Germans have learnt a democratic lesson from the West, namely to confine their protest vote to the sub-federal level. As Rohrschneider has pointed out, values such as tolerance and willingness to compromise are developed by practice rather than by watching, and such 'institutional learning' takes time (1999: 137). Moreover, participation in the federal election of 1998 actually increased, and civil society participation is on the rise. Finally, East Germany compares favourably with postwar West Germany when, ten years after the war, acceptance of democracy in the abstract was significantly lower. By comparison, East Germans are model democrats (Rohrschneider, 1999: 236).

And yet, there remains a high level of what is known in political science jargon as 'PUD' or post-unification dissatisfaction (Wiesenthal, 1996). This dissatisfaction arguably has less to do with a shaky democratic political culture than with the legacy of the unification process. There was excessive hope that prosperity would allow social integration, whereas truth and justice were 'tainted' because they were perceived as imposed by the West. In addition, *Aufarbeitung* seemed contaminated by the fact that so much of it, from the work of the EK to the reassessments of Ostpolitik, got caught up in West German party politics.

Where the Allies had forced de-nazification on the West Germans, the West Germans forced de-Stasification on the East Germans—even though the East Germans had wanted de-stasification where the West Germans had not wanted de-nazification. In both cases the imposition of justice and truth from outside bred resentment, even among those who had little to fear from either.[24] The social market economy made East Germans better off across the board, but did not eradicate the prosperity gap between East and West and made many East Germans feel like second-class citizens or even immigrants in the unified country. The old West Germany remained the reference point for most East Germans, so the fact that they were so much better off than other East–Central European countries did not make a difference. Given the rate at which productivity levels are catching up with the West, this relative deprivation is set to continue for decades. Moreover, there is now a two-tier society in the former DDR, with those who have jobs at the top and those who do not at the bottom. Easterners have been exposed at times to the worst aspects of capitalism, and have increasingly seen Western government and business representatives as arrogant and paternalist colonizers.

In other words, instead of adopting an identity as the carriers of a new economic miracle, many East Germans, feeling overwhelmed by economic dislocation and a *Vergangenheitsbewältigung* imposed by the West, have retreated to an old DDR identity, in which social solidarity and egalitarianism are upheld as specifically Eastern values. This identity, born of escapism and nostalgia, mandated a certain level of identification with the past of dictatorship. Nevertheless, the fundamental problem is not so much one of genuine nostalgia, as has so often been asserted, but of disillusionment and disappointment. Most East Germans do not want a return to a socialist past, but rather wish to salvage their identity and their dignity, and thus cast a melancholic (and selective) eye on the past. Post-unification dissatisfaction is not therefore a threat to democracy, but the expression of unease about the speed and nature of a profound socioeconomic transformation. Nostalgia is a form of psychological self-defence, a reversion to a cultural cluster that promises some security against a perceived Western superiority and capitalist streamlining.

In light of these feelings, calls for a final amnesty, for drawing a thick line under the past, have increased in recent years,

[24] On West German resistance to de-nazification, and amnesty policies in particular, see Frei (1996).

although the majority of crimes cannot in any case be prosecuted after 2000. Some have argued that, where there was not enough *Vergangenheitsbewältigung* after 1945, there has been too much after 1989. Supposedly, Westerners were too harsh, and placed too much trust in judicial proceedings. Such feelings and arguments leave the question of whether the East would have dismantled old Stasi networks by itself, whether border guards would have been brought to justice effectively, and whether the dissidents would not have had even less of an influence than they have now in unified Germany. Calls for amnesty, it seems, are often veiled demands for recognizing the dignity of the East German experience at a symbolic level or, in the case of the PDS, demands to recognize the legitimacy of the old communist party, among whose clientele are many SED functionaries.

Moreover, it is not clear whether it was really justice, rather than capitalism, that deepened the division between East and West and exacerbated the problem that, in the words of Friedrich Schorlemmer, East and West Germans talk more *about* each other than *with* each other. Finally, the simple fact remains that consolidating democracy in the East through building a civil society will take time. To say that it will take a generation is an optimistic forecast, given the quality of both the institutional 'hardware' and the social 'software' that East Germans started out with (Offe, 1996; Mushaben, 1998).

On the other hand, it is clear that most dissidents have ended up being deeply disappointed with the institutional strategies pursued, and with their own influence which has waned steadily since 1989 (Offe, n.d). They remain a minority not only in Germany as a whole, but also within East Germany. West Germans take little interest in their claims. The dissidents lacked charismatic leaders such as Havel or Tutu, and did not find a clear party-political home after 1989. With recent developments such as the reinstatement of extra pensions for *Systemnahe*, they often feel like the real losers of the democratization process. However, such claims are often countered by the argument, made by the last DDR prime minister, Lothar de Maizière, that the feelings of the victims cannot be the criterion for either justice or democratization (*Freitag*, 29 January 1999).

At the same time, it is important to question the goal of 'inner unity' or 'inner peace', which appears in so many German debates to be normatively self-evident, as an appropriate goal for institutional strategies. There are many kinds of social unity, and only a democratic consensus, rather than some elusive notion of a thick, unmediated consensus, is compatible with the notion of democratic consolidation and with a *principled* trade-off with justice (Allen, 1999). Arguably, in an immobile and conflict-averse society such as the German there is a danger of never arriving at the kind of conflict-free 'inner unity' that East and West German politicians and intellectuals often evoke. Instead, if one understands democracy as a form of contained conflict, an exaggerated search for 'inner unity' might actually work against the acceptance of democracy.

In the end, then, the fact remains that Germany did it all, and in a most systematic way, but that sometimes arrogant Westerners, and East Germans' feeling of being colonized by the West, significantly distorted the politics of memory. What could have been a model of widespread and generously financed 'working through the past' was contaminated by the identification of supposedly besieged East Germans with their own past. In addition, German ethnic identity came to be one of the last bastions of East German self-esteem (Staab, 1998: 159). Nevertheless, incorporation afforded Germany the chance of a comprehensive reckoning with the past through the *Rechtsstaat* and the creation of an 'institutionalized memory', where other former dictatorships had to opt for institutionalized amnesia. Civic empowerment through the Gauck Authority and the trust it inspired in institutions arguably made the greatest contribution to strengthen democratic values, and in that sense it was the politics of knowledge, rather than the politics of memory or of retribution, that turned out to be crucial in Germany. Indeed, the fact that Poles and Hungarians, who had initially erred on the side of amnesia, have changed course and followed a number of German practices suggests that the East German case holds some lessons after all.

9

In Search of Identity: The Collapse of the Soviet Union and the Recreation of Russia

Nanci Adler

Introduction

Throughout much of its history, the Soviet Union practised the politics of forgetting. Those who fell out of official favour simply disappeared from the scene. They were expelled, incarcerated in prisons and camps, or executed. These well-known political actors, 'the Party's children', were airbrushed out of photographs (King, 1997) or excised from encyclopaedias and history books, as if they had never existed.[1] Millions of ordinary, non-political, innocent citizens also disappeared. They were arrested for 'counter-revolutionary activities' and dispatched to the barely habitable regions of the North and Far East to mine nickel, chop wood, excavate gold, or build railroads leading nowhere—to waste away through hard labour and hunger. They were not expected to survive. As the poet Anna Akhmatova, whose husband and son were imprisoned during the Stalinist terror, said: 'the whole calculation was that no one would return'. But a number of victims somehow managed to survive and did return. Many of them were broken in mind, spirit, and body. Most maintained a public, and often private, silence about their

I owe a special thanks to Jonathan Sanders for his helpful comments and suggestions.

[1] The rewriting of history was sometimes almost comical. In the post-Beria era, subscribers to the Great Soviet Encyclopaedia were instructed to cut out and dispose of the section on the notorious secret police chief, subsequently executed as a British spy, and to replace it with the new section on the Bering Strait that accompanied the instruction.

experiences for decades, for fear of being arrested again. Their fears were well grounded, because terror and repression were the Soviet government's key instruments for maintaining authority.

Repression abated after Stalin's death in March 1953. Those closest to the great dictator who survived and then seized power initiated the first period of 'de-Stalinization.' Under Khrushchev there were broad-scale releases from the camps and selective efforts at truth-telling. In typical Russian fashion, this was a 'reform' ordered from above that went into 'remission' when the rulers became fearful or were themselves replaced. The first campaign of reconciliation with the past ended in the early 1960s. Nearly twenty-five years of official amnesia and re-Stalinization followed. The silence from above was broken in 1987 on the seventieth anniversary of the October Revolution, when the reform-minded Mikhail Gorbachev admitted that mass repression of Party members and others had taken place under Stalin,[2] and announced that it was time to fill in the blanks of Soviet history. Thus began the second period of de-Stalinization. What ensued was an explosion of revelations about the camps and ultimately about the nature of the Soviet system itself. The effect was numbing. As one Russian put it, 'it's easy to talk about the future and the present, but the past keeps changing every day' (*International Herald Tribune*, 27 July 1990). As it turned out, when the past became unpredictable, so too did the future.

The agonizing examination of Soviet history produced political tremors. David Remnick observes that, 'under this avalanche of remembering, people protested weariness, even boredom, after a while. But really, it was the pain of remembering, the shock of recognition, that persecuted them' (1993: 7). Russian philosopher Grigory Pomerants describes it thus: 'imagine being an adult and nearly all the truth you know about the world around you . . . has to be absorbed in a matter of a year or two or three' (Remnick, 1993: 7). He considered that the country suffered from 'mass disorientation'. But it was more than being politically lost: it was the shock of finding out and being found out. There were confrontations between victims and victimizers. As in the Khrushchev era, 'two

[2] Characteristically, Gorbachev refrained from revealing how his own family was repressed until after he fell from power on 25 December 1991. Only then did he feel safe enough to tell two curious American reporters, Jonathan Sanders and David Remnick, about members of his and Raisa Maksimovna's family who had been arrested as 'kulaks' and exiled to Siberia.

Russias [were once again] eyeball to eyeball—those who were imprisoned and those who put them there' (Anna Akhamatova in Stephen Cohen, 1985: 99–100).

Revelations of the past further wounded the pride of an already economically failing nation, fast losing its Eastern European empire. Society and the state suddenly had to deal with feelings of guilt, shame, and disgrace as well as the dismaying culture shock of learning a dreadful political truth. Even so, the political tide continued to drift, however unsteadily, away from repression. This endangered the stability of the Soviet regime. As a system that was adapted to repression, the Soviet structure was both rigid and fragile. Apparently, evidenced by its fate, it had trouble bending without breaking. As we shall see, many of the same kinds of barriers that were confronted during Gorbachev's liberalization campaign plagued post-Soviet efforts at democratization.

This chapter explores Russia's attempts to come to terms with its Stalinist past in an endeavour to build a civil society based on the rule of law. It begins by examining the nature of Stalinist repression and the legacy of Soviet terror. It then focuses on halted official efforts at truth-telling and persistent unofficial efforts, led by the organization Memorial, at remembering and commemorating. This provides insight into the issues that daunted the quest for moral recovery. The chapter then looks at post-Soviet efforts to come to terms with the Stalinist past, and finally it assesses the impact of the discussion of past injustices, or the politics of memory, on Russia's subsequent process of democratization.

The information presented and the conclusions drawn in this chapter are necessarily based on a number of scattered sources, including memoirs, interviews, and official archives. Russia's experience is unique, and difficult to compare with other post-authoritarian political systems, especially as democracy has not taken substantial hold. As the Russian transition is so new, questions of accountability are only beginning to be addressed. The researcher is hard-pressed to find sufficient answers in the existing literature. They need to be sought elsewhere. Official censors, self-censure, and poor or inaccurate memory influenced the Soviet politics of memory, while in the post-Soviet period collective memory proved an additional challenge to efforts at truth-telling. A critical exploration of 'bottom-up' history, which looks not *at* but *through* events, individuals, and informal organizations, is the best way to reconstruct and determine the Soviet and Russian experiences.

The Stalinist Past: The Gulag of the Mind

Terror and forced labour were integral means of preserving Soviet state power from mid-1918, when Lenin legalized a decree sanctioning the existence of work camps (Conquest, 1990: 310). It was a state born in civil war and imperialist invasion, determined to have power at any price. By 1922 there were sixty-five work or concentration camps (Conquest, 1990: 310). A year later, the first 'correctional labour camps' were opened in the Solovetsky island monasteries in the far north (Bacon, 1994: 44). Terror, along with bureaucratization, ruthless leadership, and loyal executors and believers, formed an essential component of Stalin's rule and of Stalinism in general (Adler, 1993: 39).

The term 'Stalinism' has a number of definitions, of course. Some define it as the personal evil of Stalin the person, while others view it as a larger phenomenon, describing a system. The beginning of Stalinist repression has been variously attributed to the 1934 murder of Sergey Kirov, first secretary of the Leningrad Party, or to the collectivization in 1930. There are even those who regard Lenin's 'Red Terror' in the early days of the Soviet state as the starting point. Nobel Prize winner Andrey Sakharov, the revered dissident often referred to as 'Russia's secular saint', defined Stalinism as 'illegal and terroristic methods of governing,' applicable to the entire period of Soviet rule, as its effects persisted (Adler, 1993: 3).

While repression was, indeed, an integral part of the Soviet system from its early days, 1926 seems to have marked the actual birth of large-scale forced labour as a 'method of re-education' (Bacon, 1994: 45). The camps of the 1920s, especially Solovki or the Solovetsky monasteries, were populated by, among others, Social-Revolutionaries, Mensheviks, White Guards, anarchists, and other political opponents (Jansen, 1982: 175). Stalinist terror was a constant threat. It varied in its intensity with waves of arrests and releases in different periods. In 1929, in the midst of the forced collectivization and de-kulakization campaigns, the idea of colonizing the northern regions with prisoners who had terms longer than three years was proposed and accepted. This was as much practical as ideological, because the prisons and prison camps could no longer accommodate so many people. Prisoners were used to exploit resources and build such infrastructures as railways, roads, and canals. By mid-1930 the camps had expanded to hold 41,000 people in the northern camps and 15,000 in the far eastern camps, while the Siberian and Solovetsky camps confined another 84,000 prisoners (Bacon, 1994: 46–47).

Peasants were those mostly arrested in the countryside in the years 1930–2, while those arrested in the cities were mostly engineers, scientists, and the 'bourgeois' intelligentsia. The terror gained new momentum after the 1934 murder of Kirov, and 1935–6 saw arrests of members of the opposition, mostly professional revolutionaries, as well as Party and Soviet workers. The 'Great Trials' began in 1936 and were followed by the great purges of 'Yezhovshchina' in 1937–8, a campaign of terror named after Stalin's secret police chief Yezhov. It 'renewed' the whole state and Party apparatus, military cadres, whose leadership was decapitated, the diplomatic corps, and the managers on all levels.[3] Many victims were Party members, but millions of ordinary citizens, workers, and peasants who were not Party members were affected. The Yezhov terror machine destroyed its creator, as blame for excesses with the purges was deflected to Yezhov, who was replaced by Beria at the end of 1938.

The releases of the late 1930s 'liberated' some victims of collectivization as well as 'Trotskyites' and other opposition groups, but the system of repression remained, and the Gulag and prisons were constantly replenished. As the circle of suspicion widened, 'Article 58', which defined 'counter-revolutionary crimes', was applied liberally. It listed fourteen different kinds of 'counter-revolutionary' crimes. According to the Russian and Soviet Criminal Code, offences included 'any action directed toward the overthrow, undermining or weakening of the authority of the worker-peasant soviets . . . espionage . . . terrorist acts . . . [anti-Soviet] propaganda or agitation . . .' (Russian Criminal Code, *Ugolovny Kodeks RSFSR*, 1950: 35–43). In essence, almost any type of action—or inaction—made one vulnerable to arrest. Likely suspects came to include active members of the Church and religious sects, rebels, or anyone who in the past had, however remotely, been involved in an anti-Soviet uprising. Active members of student organizations, the National Guard, anyone who had fought against the Reds in the Civil War, and anyone who had contact with foreign countries, including businessmen, hotel or restaurant owners, shopkeepers, bankers, clergy, and the former Red Cross, were suspect. Even a veterinarian who had treated consular dogs, a woman who had supplied the German consul's milk, or her brother were subject to arrest (Conquest, 1990: 257, 271).

By 1940, offences such as arriving at work twenty-one minutes late were criminally punishable (Bacon, 1994: 51; Solomon, 1996:

[3] Roy Aleksandrovich Medvedev, in response to a questionnaire in a letter written to Stephen Cohen, 10 September 1980.

301–305). In 1942–5 political repression was carried out according to nationality. There were also 'national operations' in 1937–8 directed against various ethnic groups for alleged collaboration, as well as repressive measures against Poles and Balts after August 1939. Kalmyks, Chechens, Tatars, Balkars, Volga Germans, and others 'suspected of collaboration' were deported *en masse* to Kazakhstan and other remote regions. After the Second World War returning POWs were arrested, coming back from incarceration in German camps only to enter the 'verification–filtration points' of the Main Administration of Labour Camps (Gulag). They often received ten- to twenty-five-year sentences on charges of spying or treason (Craveri, 1994: 16). Not surprisingly, some former officers went on to lead camp revolts in the late 1940s and early 1950s (Graziosi, 1992). In 1947–8, many of those who had survived the arrest and incarceration of the Great Terror were released. The next arrest wave, in 1949–52, struck 'cosmopolitans', that is, the Jewish intelligentsia, with notorious episodes such as the 'Doctors' Plot' and the 'Leningrad Affair' (Conquest, 1990).

The scope of Stalinist terror has been the subject of heated debates both before and since the Russian government opened the archives. Was the terror a historical pinprick, or was it a holocaust-like scourge that should never be forgotten? A number of historians contend that 8–12 million prisoners were victimized in the 1930s and 1940s (Bacon, 1994: 16–35; Nove, 1993). Various Russian estimates are even higher. Dmitry Volkogonov, a historian with access to official archives, asserted that 21.5 million individuals were repressed from 1929 to 1953 (*Nezavisimaya Gazeta*, 4 March 1993; *Times Literary Supplement*, 24 February 1995: 8). Aleksandr Yakovlev, one of the architects of *perestroika* and head of Gorbachev's and later Yeltsin's Rehabilitation Commission, suggests that around 15 million Soviet citizens fell victim to man-made famine, de-kulakization, deportation, and terror.[4]

Other scholars, however, have arrived at different conclusions. According to official Soviet reports culled by 'revisionist' historians, approximately three-quarters of a million people were executed for 'counter-revolutionary' crimes between 1930 and 1953, most at the height of the Soviet terror in 1937–8 (Getty *et al.*, 1993: 1017–1049; Thurston, 1996). Some historians who support the low-range figures argue that the terror had no profound, long-term effects on everyday life, but the evidence points to millions of

[4] 'Staraya Komnata', Russian television broadcast, May 1996.

victims of Soviet terror.[5] Repression was pervasive. It affected not only those arrested, but also their families, friends, and acquaintances, whose relationship to the victims often became a threat to their own safety. We are looking at systemic terror on a massive scale. Dealing with this fact proved to be one of the greatest challenges to Soviet society and the Soviet political system.

The Post-Stalin Era

Stalin's death on 5 March 1953, 'a biological event' that constituted 'the first act of de-Stalinisation' (Stephen Cohen, 1985: 103; 1983: 7), led to an amnesty on 27 March that released 1.2 million ordinary criminals, out of an official Gulag population estimated at 2.5 million.[6] The amnesty explicitly did *not* apply to 'Article 58ers'. Moreover, approximately 600,000 new arrivals were added to the camp population that year.[7] In 1953–5 a 'silent de-Stalinization' took place, during which some non-publicized 'rehabilitations', or exonerations, occurred (Van Goudoever, 1986: 11). The release of those convicted for 'counter-revolutionary crimes' was sanctioned by a decree of the General Procuracy of the Soviet Union of 19 May 1954.[8] Until 1956 this led to tens of thousands of releases. However, there was movement into as well as out of the Gulag. Khrushchev's Secret Speech at the XX Party Congress on 25 February 1956 led to the liberation of a majority—indeed, millions—of surviving prisoners and their families in exile in 1956–7. It also allowed for the return of some of the 'deported peoples'. Further, some of those who had not survived incarceration were granted posthumous rehabilitation (Medvedev and Medvedev, 1977: 20). The pace of rehabilitation of 'returnees' was slow and tedious. The struggle of these ordinary citizens, formerly labelled 'enemies of the people', to re-enter society, and the Soviet system's

[5] To the victims we must add exiled family members and deported ethnic groups. Thus defined, it is likely that the number of victims who survived the terror to return to society was not less than 7 million.

[6] State Archive of the Russian Federation (GARF), f. 9401, op. 2, d. 450, l. 471. See also Craveri and Khlevnyuk (1995: 182).

[7] GARF, 464.

[8] *Prikaz Generalnogo Prokurora Soyuza SSR*, 96ss/oo16/00397/00252, 19/5/54. See also GARF, f. 8131, op. 32, d. 3284, 40–41. The Soviet Procuracy is like the Public Prosecutor, theoretically responsible for monitoring public law, conducting pre-trial investigations, and verifying citizens' complaints. It was the main institution processing the legal return of prisoners and deportees to society.

efforts to avoid prima facie evidence of its criminal nature, began in these years.

The vicissitudes of the liberalization and repression of the Khrushchev era are beyond the scope of this work. The co-existence of both forces does, however, lead one to ask to what extent the Communist structure could adapt to de-Stalinization without destabilization. Brezhnev apparently felt that the tolerable limit of liberalization had been exceeded under Khrushchev. Under his regime, a process of re-Stalinization took place in the 1960s and 1970s. By and large, the Soviet political system of these years did not tolerate dissidents, a group that sometimes overlapped, but was not synonymous with, the 'Article 58ers' of the Stalin era; it incarcerated them, placed them in psychiatric hospitals, or expelled them. It stands to reason that in this political climate the problems of re-assimilation of the 1950s camp returnees were ignored.

The Legacy of Terror

For decades after Khrushchev, the traumatic experience of Gulag victims was at variance with both accepted morality and official description. It was once again risky to attempt to gain social validation for the camp experience. Openly recalling events of Stalinist repression was not seen as helpful to the new regime, which resorted to similar techniques for silencing opposition and dissent. Official social memory was systematically imposed from above through schooling, newspapers, books, and radio and television. There are officials and others who insist that the victims of Stalinism were received as heroes upon their return. In fact, on the whole, victims were not welcomed back into society. Their status as former prisoners was a source of 'eternal instability'.[9] They encountered obstacles in their search for housing, work, and in reuniting with their families because of who they were and where they had been. Moreover, they always feared that repression was an event waiting to repeat itself: when asked if they felt a continuing sense

[9] Arseny Roginsky, in an interview held at Memorial headquarters, Moscow, 26 April 1996. Roginsky, a historian, chair of Memorial's Scientific Research Centre, and general director of Memorial, was active in the dissident movement and incarcerated in 1981–5 for allegedly forging papers to gain access to an archive for historical research. He is also the son of a Stalin-era political prisoner who did not survive his second arrest. Roginsky's views are confirmed by numerous ex-prisoners' oral and written accounts.

of injustice after release, one former victim answered 'always' in 1995.[10] For another, 'Yes, in my contact with people I was a white raven.'[11] Zoya Marchenko, at age 88, arrested three times and having spent twelve years in the harshest of labour camps, as well as eight years in 'eternal exile', recounted the following: 'I always lived with the sense of being a "second class citizen". I was always prepared for any trouble. I understood that my life and fate did not depend on my personal qualities, but on the forces that governed the country and I simply had to somehow try to survive.'[12]

In the 1980s and 1990s, Marchenko became an active force in the organization 'The Return' (Vozvrashchenie). This historical–literary society was established in 1989 under the chairmanship of former Kolyma prisoner Semyon Vilensky. It publishes the memoirs of camp survivors as well as of those who did not survive. Its headquarters house a few hundred unpublished manuscripts. Vozvrashchenie also runs a journal, *Freedom*, and provides moral and other assistance to its dwindling elderly constituency.

Finally, the feeling of one survivor before and after Gorbachev provides a poignant example of the depth of the legacy of Soviet terror. This former prisoner, who remained in Norilsk, Siberia, after her release in 1954, did not discuss her camp experience until 1985. Indeed, in the post-Soviet Russia of 1995, this former 'enemy of the people' was still hesitant to disclose details of the Stalinist terror, so deeply ingrained was her fear that the Soviet *system* might somehow have survived the dissolution of the Soviet *state*. Reflecting on the post-camp decades, she told an interviewer: 'the whole time we were silent, careful not to say anything anywhere, so that we were not sent back to where we had been. And now I'm talking to you, and maybe I'll say something wrong and be punished again and I'll sit [in prison camp] again. So you're afraid your whole life.'[13]

[10] Lev Razgon, in an interview held at his Moscow home, 16 April 1995. Razgon, a writer, was in the camps in 1938–55. Unlike many others, after rehabilitation he returned to work at the same publishing house, to his old communal apartment, and into the party. He did, however, sustain irremediable loss; while he managed to survive, his wife died during transit in 1938. Razgon became a member of Memorial and was still active until his death in 1999 at age 92.

[11] E. Repa, spring 1995 response to a questionnaire developed for a project on returnees. This survey was conducted on a small scale in Moscow, St Petersburg, and Magadan. Evidence supporting such claims is both abundant and consistent with corroborating data.

[12] Zoya Dmitrievna Marchenko, in interviews held at her Moscow home on 6 and 13 April 1995.

[13] 'Gijzelaren van de Goelag', RTL5 (Dutch television), 3 July 1995.

'Perestroika', 'Glasnost', and the End of the Soviet Regime

Gorbachev did not view himself as a transitional leader, nor as a force that would ultimately influence the collapse of the Soviet Union. He aimed his reforms at strengthening, rather than weakening, the failing Soviet system, which clearly was not able to compete with the Western democracies. Liberalization, however, was problematic, because the Soviet system had always maintained its authority through repression. As one analyst pointed out, 'Gorbachev's delusion was that a benign form of communism would be popular in a more pluralist system, and he took away the coercion. But when you take away the coercion, people want the real thing, which is freedom' (*International Herald Tribune*, 7 July 1998: 4).

Moreover, with the rediscovery of history under Gorbachev, the truth about the criminal nature of Soviet communism could no longer be denied. This served to weaken the legitimacy of the Soviet socialism that Gorbachev strove to keep intact. In his public speech on 2 November 1987, the seventieth anniversary of the October Revolution, Gorbachev declared that 'thousands' of party members and other Soviet citizens had been repressed under Stalin. This was a gross understatement, but it was the first public admission of state terror since Khrushchev. It opened the door for people to investigate the real numbers. Rather than taking responsibility for some of the jarring disclosures, the leadership would let the numbers speak for themselves. There would also be some efforts at backward-looking accountability from the top down. Gorbachev announced in this speech that a Politburo commission had been set up to study the crimes of the past (*Izvestiya TsK KPSS*, 1, 1989: 109–110). The commission was set up on 28 September 1987 in accordance with a decision by the Central Committee Plenum of October 1987. It continued the rehabilitation process begun under Khrushchev. Not surprisingly, the initial focus of the commission was on the mostly posthumous exoneration of prominent Bolsheviks and other party members, effectively helping to legitimate 'other paths to socialism'.

From August 1987, an eleven-person group, Memorial, had begun to conduct a campaign on the streets of Moscow to gather signatures in support of the creation of a monument to victims of Stalinist repression. Its mandate and constituency grew rapidly. By mid-1988 the group had gathered 30,000 signatures (Adler, 1993: 46) and had expanded its goals to encompass the establishment of a research centre in Moscow with an open archive containing information about the victims of Stalinism, a museum, a reception room, and a library. The political potential of an organization with such professed goals apparently did not escape Gorbachev. At the time, Memorial suspected that some of the impediments they encountered were, in fact, attempts on the part of the government to curtail its growth. These included excessive bureaucratic obstacles to official registration, without which Memorial could not have a bank account, and co-option of the monument plan by putting it into the hands of the Ministry of Culture, thus making it appear that the honourable initiative had been taken by the Party (Adler, 1993: 56–57). In this sense it would almost seem as if the regime felt some rivalry with Memorial. But in fact, the ruling elite was concerned for its political safety.

The opening of the archives confirmed Memorial's suspicions. At a 1988 Politburo session, the agenda item 'Memorial' was up for discussion. Apparently apprehensions about the political potential of the organization, whose efforts were already revealing numbers much higher than the 'thousands' referred to by Gorbachev, led him to adopt the path of caution. He suggested limiting Memorial to the regional level under Party supervision.[14] This would ensure that the investigation of the Soviet past would remain in the hands of the Party. A full-blown exposure of the truth of the crimes committed under the Soviet regime would have been too great a threat to the system's legitimacy. Moreover, many of the political elite had come up through the ranks of the Communist Party of the Soviet Union (KPSS), and as its representatives would have been implicated directly or indirectly.

Despite numerous obstacles, Memorial eventually achieved its aims. In 1990 it erected its monument 'to victims of the totalitarian regime', an uncut stone from the Solovetsky island labour camps that stands on former Dzerzhinsky Square, right across from the notorious Lubyanka, headquarters of the secret police, the Committee for State Security or KGB. It also established a public scientific research and information centre in Moscow, complete with a museum, library, and human rights centre. By 1998 the Memorial archive contained over 50,000 dossiers on those victimized by Soviet terror. The collection includes unpublished camp memoirs as well as questionnaires, victims' letters, documents on rehabilitation, and other testimonials to repression.[15]

[14] *Zasedanie Politbyuro TsK KPSS*, 24/11/88, TsKhSD, f. 89, op. 42, d. 23, 1–5.

[15] The International Institute of Social History, Amsterdam, Netherlands, microfilmed the collection.

With all the remembrance of repression released, the government needed a mechanism for damage control. Public relations efforts were made to polish the KGB's image, and discussions were even set up between victims and henchmen. These did not always occur without incident. In Karaganda in Kazakhstan, for example, former employees of the Karlag camp held a meeting with former prisoners of the camp. In it, former Ministry of Internal Affairs (MVD) officials demanded a stop to the publication of a number of articles on the camp that had been appearing in a regional newspaper. They claimed that it was turning people against the Party. The discussion got so heated that a former MVD official said he would have shot the journalist responsible, if he 'had only had a gun' (Adler, 1993: 84). Some angry victims called for trials of Stalinist henchmen and stiff sentences, including capital punishment, for those found guilty of repression. Others disagreed, among them authoritative figures like Andrey Sakharov, honorary chairman of Memorial, and the politician and historian Yuri Afanasyev. The former contended that the moral recovery of the nation could not be achieved by revenge, and that organizations like Memorial should not play prosecutor; the latter argued that Stalinism was so deep-rooted that there were too many Stalinists to try (Adler, 1993: 76, 79, 127). The trials never took place.

Under Gorbachev, some significant legislative steps were taken. In 1989 and 1990, the Politburo commission issued directives to clear the way for the rehabilitation of individuals who had undergone Stalinist repression as well as that of ethnic groups, or deported peoples, exiled for 'collaboration' during the war.[16] Another important transition was that a select number of individuals who had been victims had risen to the top. Among the former dissident–prisoners elected to legislative positions were Sergey Kovalyov, who would later become Yeltsin's Commissioner for Human Rights, and Andrey Sakharov. Even though their views were often met with considerable resistance—we need only recall that Gorbachev switched off the microphone once while Andrey Sakharov was speaking in parliament—the fact that they could become 'People's Deputies' at all was an important symbolic step toward a reconciliation with the past. But it was not enough to save the system.

The re-emergence of camp returnees and the circulation of their tales of Soviet repression considerably discredited the Soviet system. But it was not former prisoners of the Stalin era or dis-

[16] See e.g. 'Deklaratsiya Verkhovnogo Soveta SSSR', 14 November 1989; 'Ukaz Prezidenta SSSR', 13 August 1990.

sidents who ultimately brought about major changes in, and later the downfall of, the Soviet system. It was rather the nomenclatura. Faced with economic crisis and international isolation, the Soviet leadership implemented changes to serve their own interest, namely to strengthen their position nationally and internationally. But this was not to be the long-term result. Once public discussion of the camps and returnee themes had emerged, overt and covert efforts at minimizing the damage (like Gorbachev's low-range public estimates of the number of victims and his subsequent limitation of Memorial) did little to stem the tidal wave of revelations. Massive evidence of the systemic and systematic repression that came to characterize Soviet governance presented a serious challenge to its legitimacy. The newly reformed leadership was not well equipped to deal with the question, because it wanted to maintain the Soviet regime. Hence the KPSS did not assume moral responsibility for the repression under Soviet rule. Worse still, it implicitly denied serious responsibility. Thus, issues of responsibility lingered long after the collapse of the Soviet Union. Indeed, the unresolved question of culpability was also to dog Russia's efforts at building a civil society.

The Post-Soviet Era: The Ambivalent Struggle to Come to Terms with the Past

The Yeltsin administration's attempts to rectify past injustices began almost immediately after the fall of the Soviet Union. On 18 October 1991 a law was passed 'on the rehabilitation of victims of political repression' that paved the way for the systematic review of rehabilitation requests. An official of the Rehabilitation Commission reports that, in the two-year period following the dissolution of the Soviet Union, two million people filed applications for juridical rehabilitation, of which one million were examined. Half a million of these applicants were granted rehabilitated status, while another half million were still under review in 1995.[17] Officials expected several million additional applications, because a 1994 law rendered the restoration of property and compensation contingent

[17] Vladimir Pavlovich Naumov, a historian and member of the rehabilitation commission, in an interview in Moscow, 21 April 1995. Many millions did not obtain rehabilitation in the years immediately following their return, and now are trying to do so. We can infer from this backlog the state's ambivalent attitude towards this group of former political prisoners, both during Khrushchev's de-Stalinization period and in ensuing years.

upon the status of 'rehabilitated' (*Rossiskaya Gazeta*, 20 May 1994: 1). In 1995 the government expanded the definition of who was eligible for rehabilitated status. In November of that year Yeltsin signed a law declaring that 'children who were together with their parents in places of detention, in exile, or special settlement are considered to have undergone political repression and are subject to rehabilitation.' The Constitutional Court of the Russian Federation went even further and changed the official status of those labelled *postradavshy*, a term applied to children of victims, who were not themselves incarcerated but were 'suffering' by virtue of their family status, to 'repressed', or those who had suffered directly (*Rossiskaya Gazeta*, 20 June 1996: 3). Individuals categorized as 'repressed' were eligible for rehabilitation.

Rehabilitation provided, in addition to an exonerated status, compensation for confiscated property, privileges such as free medicine and public transportation, and financial restitution to the sum of three-quarters of the legal minimum wage for each month of loss of liberty up to 100 months (Memorial, 1994). This differed from the Khrushchev 1955 compensation, which allotted a one-time compensation in the amount of two months of the victim's last salary. Also in 1995, Yeltsin issued a decree 'on measures for the realization of territorial rehabilitation of the repressed peoples'. This decree not only recognized the problem, but also recommended the broad use of regional and local self-governance with the support of the federal government (*Rossiskaya Gazeta*, 19 September 1995: 4). These changes in the legislative realm were symbolic of a changing attitude about the past.[18] But changes in mindset were still limited.

Many complicated issues surround exoneration and restitution, which Stephen Cohen aptly defined as the 'official admission of colossal official crimes' (Cohen, 1985: 97). Indeed, the grudging and contradictory nature of rehabilitation was directly related to this. To date, the problem of culpability has not been resolved adequately. It stands to reason that the omission of admission of guilt in the rehabilitation process has not escaped the victims. Witness the sentiments of the son of an executed 'enemy of the people', who spent years in various state orphanages. After expressing regret that the culprits could no longer be punished, he argued that they could and should be exposed, as should the malfeasance of the system itself.

[18] Yeltsin's actions also served an immediate, practical purpose: to discredit the Communists, his rivals for power and authority. In a rapidly changing and deteriorating economic situation, nostalgia for the Soviet Union's glorious past naturally arose. Reminding the populace of the horrific costs of Stalin cost Yeltsin little.

'They did that in Germany and they are doing it in South Africa . . . how can someone be [considered] a victim of a regime that has not been officially declared criminal?' (*Algemeen Dagblad*, 1 November 1997: 1–2). The answer to this question is indeed complex. Soviet Russia could not condemn its own system of governance, because in many instances people would be judging themselves. What about post-Soviet Russia, however?

An opportunity presented itself a year after the dissolution of the Soviet Union. On 7 July 1992, a hearing was held to determine the constitutionality of a ban on the KPSS. It attracted old Communists defending the system and new democrats representing the victims of that same system. A number of human rights activists hoped that it would eventually lead to juridical condemnation of the Party for 'crimes against humanity' (*International Herald Tribune*, 8 July 1992). It did not. The legal forum that could have examined the communist system itself did not venture beyond constitutional issues.

This outcome was assessed by Sergey Kovalyov, an activist who had been a dissident and later co-chair of Memorial, a parliamentarian, and finally a government official as Commissioner for Human Rights. He commented regretfully that, had there been national or international legal proceedings in 1992, conducted by unbiased officials to try the KPSS, the equivalent of a Nuremberg Trial could have been achieved. The Party 'would have been declared a criminal organization, and any activity, under any possible past or present name, would have been forbidden.' He maintained that it would have been very healthy for a young democracy to do so.[19] Kovalyov lamented the fact that the court had ruled inadmissible incriminating documents from the Party archives that 'unambiguously showed the Party to be the main organizer of large-scale terrorist activity against its own people' at the 1992 trial, because it was not a 'historical trial'. Kovalyov was called as a witness at these proceedings. In his testimony he accused the Party of gross transgressions of the law. He also added that a part of the responsibility lay with each individual. Much to his dismay, his testimony about everyone's complicity apparently made the Party seem less culpable. Kovalyov was even thanked afterwards by a Communist official for his honest statement.

The Constitutional Court partially revoked the ban on the KPSS, and in the ensuing years the Party re-invigorated itself, and

[19] Sergey Adamovich Kovalyov, in an interview at Memorial headquarters, Moscow, 14 April 1998.

even thrived, as worsening economic conditions turned public attitude away from its Gorbachev-era anti-Stalinist orientation. Gennady Zyuganov's candidacy as the leader of the Russian Communist Party in later presidential elections was no surprise to Kovalyov. Zyuganov dismissed past repression as having little to do with him or his Party: 'We are a new generation. We can't answer for the mistakes of the past.' Some of those who challenged that attitude held up a poster in the December 1995 parliamentary elections that read '50,000,000 victims of civil war, collectivisation and repression would not vote for Zyuganov' (*Newsweek*, 19 February 1996: 18). The Communists ended up doing well in the elections and the liberals did not.

It is interesting to reflect upon the fact that the Russian Communist Party was able to gain support despite public knowledge of the abuses committed under its predecessor, the KPSS, in the past. The question of belief in the Party is indeed perplexing. This is all the more so when considering that a number of ex-prisoners requested reinstatement in the KPSS, not just on practical but on ideological grounds. For many, it was the only belief system they had known for much of their lives, and it had come to occupy their need for meaning, provided by religion in other societies. Furthermore, a lot of Russians led more stable, even predictable, lives under the communist system and are more preoccupied with re-establishing that stability than with backward-looking truth and justice. As Kovalyov points out, disregarding past injustices is not the way to build a civil society. However, such inquiries may be to some extent the luxury of a stable democracy, a luxury that many Russians feel they cannot afford. Pro-communism also at times gave way to pro-Stalinism. In a 1998 poll taken by *Argumenty i Fakty*, 34 per cent of the 6,000 respondents gave Stalin a positive assessment (vol. 10, 1998). Russians often use the expression 'Stalin died yesterday' to describe the continued presence of Stalinist sympathies. But one 90-year-old ex-prisoner, Lev Razgon, begged to differ with this assessment: 'Stalin didn't die yesterday . . . he's still alive' (*Novye Izvestiya*, 1 April 1998).

A number of Sergey Kovalyov's experiences in Russian government provide an insight into the nation's attempts to come to terms with its past. The reform of the security services is a particularly telling illustration. In 1994 Kovalyov participated in the work of a commission set up to ascertain whether officials were qualified for higher posts in the state security service (FSB, formerly KGB). Other members of the commission included the President's National Security Adviser, the Secretary of the Security Council, and the Director of the Federal Security Service. The commission's mandate could have demonstrated the Russian government's 'democratic' efforts to reform itself. However, Kovalyov discovered that it was not willing to recognize that the crimes must be exposed and distance itself from the system that had perpetrated them. Kovalyov's criterion for the advancement of officials to supervisory functions was quite simple. He would not recommend candidates who had served in the fifth division (those responsible for interrogating dissidents and waging the battle against 'ideological diversion'), because of their tainted past. Kovalyov distinguishes between the practice of a mere freezing-out and lustration. For him, lustration as practised in East Germany and the Czech Republic (Garton Ash, 1998: 37–38; Bronkhorst, 1995: 78) amounted to the exposure and the subsequent banning from public service jobs of officials, and a wide range of others, who had collaborated with the state security services. Kovalyov made this distinction, because the commission's aim was not to forbid individuals from working in the state services, but rather simply to prevent them from fulfilling important functions or working in sensitive divisions.

Kovalyov was against lustration in Russia because he believed that a democratic state should not begin its existence with a witch-hunt, and that it was even a morally dubious and dangerous undertaking for a young democracy. He voiced this opinion in public discussions on the theme in 1991–2. Later, as he drove past the ruins of houses in Grozny on his way back to Moscow in 1995, Kovalyov began to wonder if his rejection of lustration had been so justified (Kowaljow, 1997: 222). Initially, he had been convinced that Yeltsin was, indeed, determined to clean up his security services. As it turned out, all kinds of reasons were found (e.g. that someone was close to retirement age) to allow candidates with a dubious record to stay on, and even move up the ranks. Many of the best and brightest who had not participated in 'evil deeds' moved on to work in the private sector, leaving behind seasoned thugs, hacks, and other misfits. Kovalyov remarked that, according to the candidates' testimonies and the subsequent official approval, 'it seems that none of them played any part in the Soviet repressive apparatus—except for the fact that I knew some of them personally.' Kovalyov's own principled stance was not surprising for a man who has been called 'the conscience of Russia'. In his view, 'a person who committed repressive acts has no place in an organization that claims that it no longer intends to commit repression.'[20]

[20] Ibid.

Kovalyov's attempts to foster change were consistently met with stubborn resistance. 'I was a fool,' he regretfully admitted. 'I . . . thought Boris Nikolaevich wanted to make decisive changes in these special services . . . when in fact he just wanted to remain surrounded by the trusted KGB people with whom he had maintained a close relationship since he was first secretary of the Moscow Provincial Committee.' Kovalyov ended up disappointed by the commission's cosmetic purges and disillusioned with Yeltsin. On an ironic note, in 1994 Kovalyov's KGB interrogator became chief of the Federal Security Service for the city and district of Moscow (Kowaljow, 1997: 90).

Financial assistance and privileges, however inadequate, are among the only means of the state to compensate former victims for their suffering in the camps and for their years of living with a stigmatized status. Such services are clearly extremely significant in today's Russia. In February 1998 the amount of compensation due to victims of Stalinism was up for discussion in the Russian Chamber of Deputies (the Duma). At issue was the latter's decision to reduce by half the compensation that was planned by the government 'for the defence of the rights of those who suffered illegal repression'. Witness the mad ravings of the (un)Liberal (un)Democratic Party's Vladimir Zhirinovsky in support of reducing or eliminating restitution to deported peoples: 'Comrade Stalin, head of our government, did not just deport people. When the KGB informed him that thousands of Kalmyks organized brigades, joined the ranks of the Red Army, and destroyed thousands of Soviet fighters, yes, then he naturally deported those who were still alive.'[21] In addition to justifying the deportations, Zhirinovsky also went on to declare that there were no 'victims of repression', and that all of Russia was repressed in the twentieth century. Although this performance barely merited a response, Memorial objected to the fact that Zhirinovsky's 'scandalous' behaviour did not summon indignation or condemnation among the majority of deputies. In fact, despite Zhirinovsky's outburst—or perhaps because of it—the Duma still voted in favour of the reduction in compensation, for which he had in fact argued. More significant and worrisome for democratic reformers, however, was what Memorial called the 'gradual rehabilitation of Stalinism', a trend actively supported by some, and passively observed by others.

Compensation, the acknowledgement of past injustices and the restoration of rights or rehabilitation constitute concrete efforts on the part of the Russian government to come to terms with the past.

[21] *Informatsionny Byulleten*, vypusk 1, February 1998.

Organizations like Memorial and Vozvrashchenie have attempted to further promote the moral–ethical, non-material expression of rehabilitation (Golovkova, 1997: 5–30; *Russkaya Mysl*, 25–31 December 1997; *Trouw*, 9 February 1998: 2). Semyon Vilensky, the ever-vigilant chairman of Vozvrashchenie, points out that Magadan, the Far Eastern capital of the notorious Kolyma labour camp region, has the dubious honour of being the only city in the world to erect a monument to a former labour camp supervisor, Edvard Berzin. The construction of Magadan began in 1932 under the supervision of Berzin, who was the first person to head the forced labour camp division of the predecessor to the KGB, the People's Commissariat for Internal Affairs (NKVD), called Dalstroy. Vilensky recounts that Berzin was considered a 'liberal' even though he commanded that 'thousands of new prisoners' be taken to Magadan in the 1930s. A number of these subsequently died of illness or exhaustion from forced labour or execution. Like many others before and after him, Berzin himself eventually became one of the victims of the terror, since he too was arrested and executed. Ironically, on 12 June 1996 the Mask of Sorrow, a monument to the victims of Stalinism, was also erected in Magadan. Vilensky notes how these two monuments 'look at each other, like the [Memorial] Solovetsky stone and the Lubyanka in Moscow' (Vilensky, 1997: 9–14). Indeed, one sees the 'two Russias' all over again. Anna Akhmatova's description of Russia as being made up of the imprisoned and the gaolers is most useful when we look at Russian efforts to come to terms with the past, as the dividing line is very unclear. The pathology of the Soviet system extended to all its components—victims, victimizers, and informants alike. People had strong inducements to turn in neighbours, friends, and even family members, and this had lingering consequences. Sometimes victims had subsequent dealings with their informants. Sometimes informants and secret policemen became victims. In the camps, some prisoners cooperated with the camp administration in an attempt to survive their incarceration and experienced heavy moral suffering as a result of that survival. In short, with so many implicated, efforts at truth-telling, remembrance, and accountability have to be considered against this background.

What we choose to remember publicly and to commemorate is largely determined by the direction in which the political wind is blowing. In a gesture marking continuity with the Soviet past, at the end of 1995, Yeltsin decreed that 20 December would be officially recognised as the 'Day of Secret Service Workers' (*Sobranie Zakonodatelstva Rossiskoy Federatsii* 52, 25 December 1995: 9350; *Het Parool*, 3 October 1996; *Het Parool*, 6 January 1996).

It was on this day in 1917 that Lenin's dreaded secret police organization, the Cheka, was established. Why would Yeltsin go that far in placating the contemporary secret service, full of old-time KGB agents, when he also professed concern for the victims of the terror? Did he in 1995 need the support of the secret services so much that he had to cater to their ignominious past? That a president who claimed to pursue democratization should celebrate such a bloody organization is remarkable. The Yeltsin of 1989 would not have made such a gesture. Power corrupts in a corrupt society, and hanging on to power often means counting on the most effective, or corrupt, forces. On another ironic note, in December 1998 a large majority of the Russian parliament voted in favour of resurrecting the statue of Feliks Dzerzhinsky, founder of the Cheka. Only one parliamentary faction voted against the motion. Demonstrators had removed 'Iron' Feliks from his perch in front of the Lubyanka after the aborted putsch of August 1991, an act that constituted '*the* visual metaphor for the Soviet regime's collapse' (Jonathan Sanders in Adler, 1993: ix). The gesture on the part of the post-Soviet Russian parliament leaves little to the imagination as to its democratic spirit. The Day of the Revolution, 7 November, is a public holiday in Russia still. Soviet leaders traditionally used the October Revolution commemorations to legitimize their government (Naarden, 1997: 587–592). In an apparent attempt to do just that, on the eightieth anniversary of the Revolution in 1997, Yeltsin proposed that the day henceforth be the 'Day of Agreement and Reconciliation' (*Rossiskaya Gazeta*, 10 November 1997). This raises interesting questions, considering that Stalin is still buried beside the Kremlin wall, and that Lenin's mummy still lies in the mausoleum on Red Square. Aleksandr Yakovlev, one of the architects of *perestroika* and later head of the rehabilitation commission, remarked:

> with whom should we reconcile, with whom should we agree? [Should we] reconcile with people who still adore Lenin and honour Stalin? The state should make it clear that the country suffered under a criminal regime from 1917 on. [It should state] that Lenin was a murderer and Stalin was a mass-murderer. I can imagine 7 November as a day of mourning and repentance. (*Algemeen Dagblad*, 1 November 1997: 1–2; *Rossiskaya Gazeta*, 29 May 1997)

Yeltsin's proposal never got off the ground, and the meaning of this day has remained officially unclear.

A highly controversial issue presented itself in 1998 when the Russian Supreme Court pronounced itself in favour of a re-evaluation of the cases of Stalin's henchmen. This could potentially lead to their posthumous rehabilitation, or at least partial rehabilitation.[22] Yagoda, Yezhov, Beria, and Abakumov were all Stalinist state security chiefs who were subsequently arrested, tried, and executed under the same types of trumped-up charges that they themselves had used against many innocent victims. The charges included espionage, sabotage, Trotskyism, treason, and other 'anti-Soviet' activities. The four under discussion were guilty of a host of other crimes, but not these. According to the Court, some of the key figures implementing Soviet terror should have received twenty-five-year prison camp terms rather than the death penalty (*De Volkskrant*, 6 May 1998). Each of the men in question had sowed such 'immeasurable evil' that new words like *Yezhovshchina* had to be invented to describe the phenomenon (*Izvestiya*, 28 April 1998). The posthumous rehabilitation of these men, who had personally committed and/or ordered atrocious criminal acts, but who were indeed not guilty of the crimes with which they were charged, raises a tricky legal question in Russia's quest to be a country that respects the rule of law. Though human rights advocates in Russia argue that injustice cannot be rectified with injustice, the rehabilitation laws of the 1990s did not envisage benefits for former henchmen. They were established in order to restore the honour of innocent people who had suffered the consequences of Stalinist repression for crimes that they did not commit. Considering all the crimes that can be attributed to these Stalinist executioners, exoneration would be an affront to their victims. Yezhov was ultimately denied posthumous rehabilitation, but the very contemplation of even partial exoneration raised considerable ire among those striving to build a civil society. The Supreme Court ruled that Yezhov could not be considered a victim of the terror, which he himself had organized. Abakumov, minister of state security from 1946 to 1951, was partially rehabilitated (*Izvestiya*, 28 April 1998; 4–5 June 1998; *Kommersant-Daily*, 28 February 1998). Beria was not recognized as a victim of political repression (*Izvestiya*, 8 September 1998). To date, Yagoda's case is still open.

An article in the influential anti-communist Russian daily *Izvestiya* analyses the problem further. It points out that it is incumbent upon society to be aware of the political and moral consequences of the fact that, according to the Soviet Criminal Code of the 1930s to 1950s, i.e. the legislation that must guide the re-evaluation of

[22] For revealing portraits and profiles of some of Stalin's executioners, who are not in line for rehabilitation, see Boris Sopelnyak, *Novye Izvestiya*, 18 April 1998, and Peter d'Hamecourt, *Algemeen Dagblad*, 9 May 1998.

cases, these four men were not guilty of state crimes. However, the article goes on to argue that 'common sense, conscience, memory, and historic responsibility to the past and the future' dictate against such reasoning because the consequences are too great. If the culpability of the Lubyanka henchmen was to be minimized, then, by extension, the blood would also be removed from the 'generalissimo's' hands. A Russian Nuremberg trial was therefore necessary, as a tribunal could pass judgement on Stalinism and determine 'the personal culpability of the main inspirer and organizer of genocide against his own people, the personal culpability of his comrades in arms . . . as well as those who carried out orders'. For the author of the article, the expression 'Stalin died yesterday' means that the system 'invented by him was not yanked out by its roots . . .' It meant that 'the people did not condemn it' and 'a [cancer grew] in our society . . .' Thus, 'signs at demonstrations like "Glory to the Soviet state", portraits of the "leader of all peoples", and the nostalgic longing for a "firm hand" prove that society did not recover from its ailment.' Finally, the author cautions that the threat of a return to a repressive regime is not unrealistic (Boris Pilyatskin, *Izvestiya*, 28 April 1998).

Judgement criteria for rehabilitation raise complicated questions in a country that is striving for democratization. Memorial has criticized rehabilitation procedures for legitimizing Stalinist laws by focusing on whether the sentences were appropriate to the laws that existed at the time. Rendering judgement on those laws means that those who committed acts against the Soviet system are not eligible for rehabilitation,[23] and that those who did not commit acts against the Soviet system are eligible for rehabilitation. Until there is a wholesale condemnation of that system, these issues will remain unsolved.

In post-Soviet Russia there seems to be both an official and a public tendency towards forgetting, or at least towards not being reminded of, the Soviet past. In some instances this amnesia reflects ignorance. In 1995, only 34 per cent of the pupils surveyed in top Moscow schools knew the meaning of the word 'Gulag', compared with 82 per cent in 1992 (Davies, 1997: 116). There are a number of explanations for this trend. On a political level, keeping open old wounds could undermine, rather than strengthen, a new democracy and the building of a civil society. The question,

[23] Consider e.g. the cases of disaffected East Europeans or Russians who had spied on the Soviet government for the Americans. Rehabilitation and compensation is still denied to many of them, even though in hindsight, the anti-Soviet stance proved to be largely legitimate (*New York Times*, 22 January 1998: 22).

then, arises as to the ends to be served by practising a 'politics of memory'. While Russians have knowledge of other national processes of transitional truth and justice, these models cannot be well applied to the post-Soviet condition. A trial in Russia at this stage would be complicated. Many of the victims and perpetrators are already dead, the totalitarian mechanism was so pervasive that a number of victims were also implicated at some level, and the scope and duration of the Soviet Communist dictatorship would make the reach of the trial enormous (Garton Ash, 1998: 35–40; Ignatow, 1997; Varoli, 1997: 35–41). On a societal level as well remembrance is complicated. In the words of Lev Razgon, writer and former political prisoner, 'people wish to avoid spiritual discomfort' and to develop anew a sense of national pride (*Novye Izvestiye*, 1 April 1998). In an already divided society, the truth about the criminal nature of a regime that represented the only belief system that many people knew for much of their lives could prove even more divisive.

Regardless of the problems associated with dredging up an onerous past, however, understanding past mistakes may well help to prevent their repetition. Memorial is well recognized for its efforts at chronicling the history of Soviet terror. The organization has succeeded in documenting tens of thousands of individual cases of repression through its questionnaires, and has also examined the bases for mass repression by ascertaining official policy and practice through research into the KGB and KPSS archives. A French publisher with an anti-left agenda timed the publication of the reference work, *The Black Book of Communism* (Courtois *et al.*, 1997) to coincide with the eightieth anniversary of the Bolshevik Revolution. Lest there be any doubt as to the criminal nature of communism as it has been practised, this 800-page volume documents the crimes of the regimes of the Soviet Union, Eastern Europe, Communist China, Cambodia, North Korea, Vietnam, and others. Mass murder to enforce conformity, as a prophylaxis for potential opposition, or simply to sow fear and obedience was a common denominator to all of these governments (*International Herald Tribune*, 23 December 1997; *Forward*, 5 December 1997: 1). The book has not been translated into Russian, and, with the exception of a review essay in a Russian newspaper, has received no attention in Russia.

As a rule, under Gorbachev and later books about the past and memoirs sold out quickly. Today those interested in the historical record on Stalinism constitute a more limited readership. Growing public apathy towards past injustices can also be observed in the mass media. In the late 1980s and early 1990s, television programmes on past repression enjoyed considerable popularity. The theme returned briefly in the summer of 1996 when the *perestroika*-era film, *Burnt by the Sun*, was rebroadcast on the state television. This popular film about a high-ranking military man who became a victim of the Great Terror was presumably aired to help Yeltsin in his election victory over the Communists. Today the subject no longer has political priority. Perhaps in an effort to escape what many perceive as an endless, weary, and painful discussion, Western-style talk shows and soap operas have become viewers' preferred fare. This can be taken as a reflection of wider public sentiment.

None the less, history is once again being re-thought in Russia. As in the past, this liberalizing process has been followed by the re-emergence of old, questionable practices. In this regard, a number of archives that were once declassified have become reclassified. The quest for freedom of information is an ongoing part of the battle against forgetting. After August 1991, many of the archives documenting the terror became accessible to researchers and family members of victims. The entrenched Soviet tradition of providing as little documentation as possible was replaced by new procedures,[24] which made stacks of inventories and their corresponding documents available upon request. However, this trend has now been reversed. Memorial researchers noticed this and wrote articles commenting that since 1996 they had encountered problems in working in the archives. One Memorial chairman laments that certain documents are being withheld on 'legal' grounds:

> the joke is that the 'Law on archives' is formulated very cleverly. The preamble is marvellous; [it basically reads that] any Russian citizen or foreigner for that matter may become acquainted with the materials that are preserved in the archive. But then the 'buts' begin. Access to personal files is prohibited. This is motivated by the fact that materials on individuals can be used for ignoble ends . . . [T]here is no mechanism for contesting the rules.

He goes on to say that access to the former Party archive is particularly blocked. The director examines all the documents, and if they mention the repression 'they are immediately treated as personal files, to which access is prohibited' (*Nezavisimaya Gazeta*, 24 March 1998). Furthermore, only with great difficulty did these researchers manage to obtain declassified documents on the camps from the former KGB archive. Another author with similar

[24] For early discussions on the declassification of archives see Kozlov (1994: 43–50).

experiences concludes that this may be attributable to the increasing mid-level and perhaps high-level influence of the Communist Party (*Izvestiya*, 6 September 1997). Access to archives has always been an important indicator of which way the political winds are blowing.

On the other hand, there were some encouraging developments on the archival front. In April 1998 Yeltsin ordered the transfer of documents on Soviet repression from the largely closed Presidential Archive to the Rehabilitation Commission for further examination (*New York Times*, 1 April 1998: 4). Archives are a powerful weapon—presumably this action was part of Yeltsin's battle against Zyuganov and others. The documents consist of lists of victims, letters of individuals who were arrested and convicted, and transcripts of hearings, among other testimonials of terror. Open to question was how immediately the transfer would take place. As Memorial researchers warned then, 'at present it is only a promise'.[25] Nor is it clear how broad access to the materials will be.

Finally, it is important to mention another unofficial, 'bottom-up' effort at remembrance, as some Russians looked to the post-Holocaust European example. Postwar Europe made the concentration camps an important theme in its efforts to expose the ideology and practices of fascism (Ivanova, 1997: 213). Post-Soviet Russia has the potential to do the same thing. The beginnings are evident: the camp in the Urals, approximately 950 miles east of Moscow and 130 miles north-east of the city of Perm, is now a historical site. The physical structure of the Gulag itself, a 'visible trace of [Russia's] recent, harrowing past', serves to condemn the nature of the Soviet system. Thus, Memorial is currently transforming the partially bulldozed ruins of the notorious Perm 36, which was opened in 1946 and closed in December 1987, from a labour camp into a living museum of Russia's past. It is to be called the Memorial Museum of the History of Political Repression and Totalitarianism in the USSR, Perm 36, or simply, the Museum of Totalitarianism. It will constitute a memorial to those who perished as a result of Soviet repressive practises. As one journalist wrote in 1997, 'in a nation bent on forgetting, the museum is the most tangible attempt to illustrate the darkest corners of the Communist system' (*International Herald Tribune*, 30 October 1997; *NRC Handelsblad*, 20 September 1997: 1–2).

[25] Nikita Petrov, vice-chairman of the Memorial Scientific Research Centre, in a discussion at Memorial headquarters, Moscow, 14 April 1998.

The Perm camps housed such dissident-era political prisoners as Josef Begun, Vladimir Bukovsky, Sergey Kovalyov, Natan Sharansky, Gleb Yakunin, and two famous prisoners of conscience, Anatoly Marchenko and Vasily Stus, both of whom died during incarceration. Visitors will be able to see their dismal barracks and cells and their prisoners' uniforms, to feel the flimsiness of the blankets allotted to them in sub-zero temperatures, and to view the so-called 'exercise blocks' (essentially steel cages), the punishment cells, and the holes in the floor that functioned as latrines (*Daily Telegraph*, 15 November 1997: 14). Perm seems as good a site, and maybe better than most, for the museum. In 1995 the city had not yet changed its Soviet street names. Witness the ironic circumstance conveyed by one former prisoner who received his rehabilitation document in 1994: 'I was rehabilitated in the Dzerzhinsky [head of the Cheka] district of the city of Perm, on Communist Street. That says it all' (*Newsweek*, 25 September 1995: 46–48). In addition to subsidies provided by the local government and local businesses, this project was funded by start-up grants from the Ford Foundation and other international organizations. These institutions have provided organizational and special project support to Memorial from its early days, but Memorial has maintained its independence in all further aspects of its functioning.

Conclusion

At the end of the violent twentieth century, the Russian government and people are struggling with the challenge of how to cope with the past, to move forward, and perhaps even to build a civil society on the way towards democracy. They yearn to prosper in the aftermath of over seven decades of Soviet rule. The freedoms that have been gained since the fall of the Soviet regime are fragile, but none the less detectable. Liberal reformers, despite their loss of influence, still have access to the political scene, and the government is liberally mocked in the newspapers and on television (*International Herald Tribune*, 24 February 1999). Moreover, Russians have the opportunity to choose their own president in a democratically oriented electoral process. All this notwithstanding, Russia has not yet achieved democracy. Lev Razgon in 1998 pointed to a dilemma: the mentality and political traditions of Russia had been formed over a long period of time. Yet when change occurred, Russians wanted improvements to happen then and there, fast. The changes that Russians noted were too few and were too slow in coming. Razgon went on to point out that a deeply ingrained element of that mentality and political tradition was that it suppressed the dignity of the individual. This is the element that he believes must first be eradicated. Real changes can take place only with a new generation. At age 90, Razgon concluded, 'my hope rests on those who are entering the first class [of school] today' (Gokhman, 1998; *Izvestiya*, 1 April 1998: 4). Indeed, these 6 and 7-year-olds were born in Russia, not the Soviet Union.

Still unanswered is the question of whether the 'politics of memory' will remain as contentious an issue for the new generation as it has been for the previous two generations. Or can remembrance of past repression aid the consolidation of democracy in a land ruled for most of the century by a ruthless system, with a rigid hierarchy, only top-down accountability, and no feedback mechanisms to respond to the needs of the population? What effect will knowledge of the repression of the Soviet past have on the formation of the consciousness of the new generation of Russians who were not socialized by the Soviet system? Part of the answer lies in the place that is accorded to that ignominious past. Thus far, no institutional way has been found to judge the crimes of Soviet rule. Nor do the Russians have a concept like the German *Vergangenheitsbewältigung* to describe the process of coming to terms with the (national) past. Though a far cry from the official amnesia that was practised throughout much of the Soviet period, state-sponsored acknowledgement of past repression is still limited in Russia. Not only were individual perpetrators not brought to justice, but also, the system itself in which they operated was not brought to justice. The fact remains that the KPSS was never condemned. Since it was also never banned, the Party faithful do not even have to regroup under another name.

Apparently, as other concerns abound, knowledge of past injustices is not contributing greatly at this stage to the process of democratization. The military, once the pride of the Soviet Union, has become a demoralized institution. Old people with old attitudes staff the intelligence services. The courts are struggling with the legacy of a lack of judicial dependence and the institutional self-interest of former Soviet agencies (Fogelsong, 1997: 282–324; Huskey, 1997). The police force is rampant with corruption. A continued practice of the politics of memory deals a great blow to an already greatly ailing sense of national pride, and has perhaps for this reason been relegated marginal status for the time being. A precise chronicle of Soviet repression is nevertheless still being pieced together, as researchers doggedly pursue information in the archives. But the return of repressed history, like the return of repressed people in the Soviet period, is often a painful confrontation for individuals, society, and the state. The psychological, political, and moral impact of truth-telling, especially over a long period of time, can sometimes result in the opening of wounds, destabilization, and national shame. For this reason, it is regrettable that the opportunity was missed to pass definitive judgement on the Soviet Communist regime right after its fall. Russia's transition has yet to lead to a recognizable democracy. The ranks of Gulag survivors dwindle. Thus, it must be hoped that the continued chronicling of histories of repression at the hands of Soviet authorities, and the continued vigilance and remembrance by unofficial organizations such as Memorial, will serve as a safeguard against any return to that system under any name.

Conclusion

The main aim of this book has been to analyse what determines how new democracies face an authoritarian past, and human rights violations in particular, and in turn the way in which policies of truth and justice shape the process of democratization. Thus, eighteen cases are analysed in detail, covering a good part of the processes of democratization that have taken place since the beginning of the 1970s. Countries experiencing a political change that did not undergo a transition to democracy have been left out, as have countries in which truth and justice policies are the result of the end of a civil conflict where there is no accompanying movement towards democratization.

The key obstacle to theorizing about this topic is the enormous influence of the particular historical evolution of each country, and various factors emerging therefrom, on policies of truth and justice in transition. Some of these factors are very distant in time. Thus, there is a variability of cases and contexts that is truly wide-ranging and difficult to catalogue and categorize. In other words, what a new democracy does or does not do about past repression depends not only on factors linked with the recent past; the solutions adopted are also largely conditioned by the experience and memory of past events and developments, such as the Civil War in Spain or the anti-fascist purges in Eastern Europe after the Second World War. Such processes can be 'typified' and included within a theoretical framework, together with more recent elements. None the less, events in the distant past increase the problem of contingency to the point where it is almost impossible to present a logically exhaustive framework that takes all possibilities into account.

Thus, a general overview is immediately useful to categorize different experiences of transitions from dictatorial rule according to the balance of power between authoritarians and democrats. Yet, as soon as the researcher deepens his or her look at each particular case, it becomes more difficult to generalize and create a theoretical framework encompassing all cases. The aim of the editors of this book has been to keep sight of the peculiar nature of national experiences and yet to provide some kind of useful guidelines that may give readers a sensible way to approach this subject.

It is in this spirit that these conclusions offer a 'way of looking' at the issue of transitional truth and justice. Despite the difficulties outlined above, the growing literature on the subject as well as the work presented in this book permits one to draw a series of conclusions that approximate a theoretical framework about the issue. These conclusions can be divided into two sets. The first pertains to the probability that a new democracy will undertake policies of this kind. The second refers to the consequences that such policies may have for democratic life or democratization.

It is important to clarify at this point that truth policies are easier to implement, and have a 'softer' impact, than punitive policies involving trials or administrative purges. In many cases, new democracies can absorb the impact of the former without the threat of severe conflict or destabilization that arises from the latter. It may not look this way to an outside viewer, particularly with the benefit of hindsight; but the situation doubtless seems different from the perspective of decision-makers governing in transitional periods, which are usually fraught with uncertainty. Thus, it is difficult to make the same generalizations about the two processes—truth policies and punitive actions—given that they are clearly different. However, because they are often linked and intertwined, and because justice policies are often justified politically and morally following the revelations of a truth policy, both can be dealt with as a single set of policies.

On the Probability of Truth and Justice Policies under New Democracies

The first thing to keep in mind is the degree to which the general political and social context favours the implementation of truth and justice policies, both nationally and internationally. At the national level, the most important general factor to look at is the balance of forces between the elite of the old regime and groups favouring democratization. Others factors include the availability of resources and the degree to which a new elite is committed to notions of retroactive justice.

The balance of forces is the most self-evident variable and the one most often emphasized in studies of this topic, and is referred to as either a 'transition type' or 'correlation of forces'. Transitions are negotiated when there is a balance of power between opposition and regime forces. In transitions by 'collapse', the opposition is not obliged to negotiate because the balance of power is much more favourable. The concept of balance of forces, however, is more useful than that of 'transition type'. The former is a more flexible and dynamic concept, permitting variation over time, while the latter refers to a historical period that is more or less fixed. In other words, the balance of power during a transition does not remain unaltered with the passing of time. Indeed, even within what is, with hindsight, defined as the 'period of transition', the balance of power may shift, sometimes dramatically, in favour either of those pursuing justice or of those seeking to protect themselves from any punitive action. Argentina is a case in point. The military was defeated and demoralized during the first part of the transition period, but it subsequently recovered sufficiently to force the civilian government to backtrack and limit the scope of previously undertaken punitive policies. In Portugal, another transition by 'collapse', the purges ended when more moderate left and centre–right forces gained control of the political arena, sidelining the military and extreme left-wing groups that had dominated the process during the 'revolutionary' period of the transition.

It is less frequent to find cases of a reversal of the balance of power unfavourable to an outgoing authoritarian elite when the transition is negotiated. When the outgoing dictatorship was led by the military, the latter often retains the power of coercion as it can exert violence, often after years of 'democratic' education and subordination to civilian authority. The institutional legacy of the dictatorial period often remains intact, even if it apparently contradicts the gradual absorption of new values. And in ethnically divided societies such as Guatemala and South Africa, the social and economic domination of a 'white' minority resistant to truth and justice may persist for years to come, however efficient the implementation of equal opportunities policies under the new democracy.

However, even in these more restricted settings, policies of truth and justice that are put aside during the early years of a transition process can be taken up years later, either because of a shift in the balance of power or as a result of international factors. Thus, there seems to be no democracy that can definitively put an 'end to a repressive past'. The issue remains ever present and may erupt again and again, demanding new investigations, more compensation policies, and new punishments years after the dictatorship has passed.

The balance of power not only shapes the probability of a new democracy undertaking—or not—policies of truth and justice; it also substantially affects the way in which such policies are undertaken and evolve. The more unfavourable the balance of power for the elite of the old regime, the more probable that trials and administrative purges will be arbitrary. On the other hand, the more balanced the balance of forces, the more probable that the rule of law will be strictly observed. Indeed, in such cases it is likely that there will already be either an explicit or an implicit understanding regarding the scope of such policies. This understanding is more likely when the new elites are not deeply concerned with constitutional legality or the rule of law.

The East German purge, for example, affected about 500,000 people, or 3 per cent of the population, in the largest administrative purge in the history of new democracies. It was only possible given the complete defeat of the communist forces and the absorption of East Germany by West Germany. The German case is example of the most unfavourable balance of forces for the old elite, when a country is absorbed by another and a completely new political structure is adopted at once. The decision of the German authorities as to who should have their contracts renewed and who should be purged was adopted according to the judgement of new bureaucratic chiefs regarding the ability of the individual at stake to adapt to the new exigencies of a civil service post. In the Czech Republic, by contrast, although inspired by the German example, the number of people affected was 10,000, or about 0.1 per cent of the population, thirty times fewer than those purged in the German case. It was so because the margin for discretionary action was much lower, and only people about whom there was documentary evidence of involvement in certain specific actions were purged. The purge of economic enterprises in Portugal during the revolutionary period is a good example of a lack of concern for due process and the rule of law by 'winners', when the balance of power favours them overwhelmingly.

The availability of institutional, human, and financial resources fundamentally shapes the capacity to carry out a truth and justice policy as well as its quality. Unlike Germany, the Czech Republic did not have the arsenal of technical and administrative personnel, trained outside the communist mould, available to take on vacated administrative posts in universities, courts, or other civil service posts. It lacked alternative human resources. Nor did it have sufficient resources to offer those purged a satisfactory unemployment pension and thereby to carry out a purge without provoking excessive social tension. It lacked sufficient financial resources. In the German case, both personnel and funds were provided to the East by the West of the country. The impact of institutional resources, understood as the availability of developed and well functioning institutions, is also a key issue. As some African cases show, the trial of suspects by ill equipped and understaffed judiciaries leads to the violation of minimum guarantees of due process.

The nature of the ideological preferences and commitments of the new democratic forces and leadership is crucial. It is theoretically possible to have a transitional situation or a balance of power that is imminently favourable to the new forces but in which these will not feel under any pressure to carry out measures of retroactive truth or justice. Similarly, there can be difficult balance of power situations that do not discourage some leaders and parties to continue to press for truth and justice, even against the odds. This partly explains why Chile and South Africa, two of the most constrained negotiated transitions, have produced the most wide-ranging truth telling processes or, in Chile, put the greatest number of military officers in gaol for human rights violations of all the cases described in this book.

It should not be forgotten that elite attitudes are not the only ones that matter. As most of the cases in this book show, an important element conditioning elite responses to the issue of truth and justice policies is the degree to which there are social groups or civil society organizations pressing for them. The more pressure a new democratizing elite is under from mobilized human rights organizations or other bodies, such as opposition parties and churches and even from public opinion, the more likely it is to adopt some sort of policy to deal with the past.

In addition to the above, the impact of the international context cannot be underestimated and must be understood historically. The *zeitgeist* regarding issues of justice, rights, and the nature of 'truth' in the political sphere are crucially important. As noted in the Introduction, transitional justice was conceived of differently in the Cold War climate that still predominated in the 1970s. It was also shaped by the polarization of positions between left and right in the national sphere as a result of that conflict, and by the absence of a fully fledged human rights discourse and practice. This means not only that early democratizing elites had different aims and different ways of framing the dilemma, but also that the policies adopted differed in nature from those found in the later transitions. At the same time, the actual intervening power of international institutions has increased over the half century and, most particularly, since the 1970s. Thus, it is not just the 'ideological climate' or *zeitgeist* that matters, but the capacity of international organizations or transnational groups to act. Were it not for international intervention, in some countries there would have been either a much more limited accountability policy or none at all of truth and justice.

The most notorious case is the arrest of General Pinochet in London, which, despite its final outcome, has led to a new understanding of evolving international human rights jurisprudence, the limits of national sovereignty, and the legitimacy of external intervention by new actors such as foreign courts and transnational human rights coalitions. The case not only affected the dictator himself, but also shifted the balance of forces in favour of those seeking justice for past human rights violations in Chile. It led to a questioning of the 1978 Amnesty Law and of the limits imposed on popular sovereignty in the new democracy. It is unlikely that such a shift would have occurred purely as a result of the dynamic of Chilean political life on its own. Another example is Guatemala, where the Clarification Commission, which produced a wide-ranging report on human rights violations during the prolonged period of civil conflict, was the result of a UN-sponsored initiative, an organization that also played a central role in the peace process.

Another element to remember is the *contagion-learning* effect, since the elite in any given country will act according to inherited 'knowledge' or 'know-how' gathered from the accumulated experience of previous transitions. Thus, government-sponsored truth commissions spread throughout Latin America and travelled to South Africa, following the Chilean example. Unofficial truth-telling exercises took the Brazilian *Nunca Mais* (Never Again) report as their model. In Eastern Europe the German model has been emulated, promoting the removal from office of former collaborators of the political police. First, and most harshly, applied in Czechoslovakia and Albania, it was then taken up in a softened form in Poland, Hungary, Romania, and Bulgaria.

Understanding the immediate transitional context, be it national or international, is just the first step towards establishing the various conditions that shape, and increase or decrease the probability of, truth and justice policies. The impact of a number of authoritarian legacies is also vital. The duration and degree of institutionalization of the dictatorship, the nature and extension of repressive practices, and the institutional and legal–constitutional framework inherited from the dictatorial period are important elements to take into account.

There is no dictatorship that can sustain itself for a long period of time without gaining some form of popular acceptance or support and some degree of institutionalization. Violent repression, detentions, and executions serve to ensure domination in the first moments after the coming to power of dictatorial forces. Over the long term, however, such a regime must garner a minimum level of consensus among a significant part of the population and must succeed in establishing more routinized mechanisms for social control. In doing so, it will permeate the state bureaucracy and the court system, and may even transform the productive or socioeconomic system, creating new elites favoured by the regime's economic policies.

During the transition, the groups favoured by the old regime, as well as the institutions contaminated by it, will constitute obstacles to truth and justice policies. Such measures will not only attack the *raison d'être* or legitimacy of the outgoing regime but will also discredit its supporters and upset the status quo and inherited, often entrenched, institutional practises. Thus, the more prolonged and institutionalized a dictatorship, the more difficult a new democracy will find it to carry out truth and justice policies, because these would stigmatize social groups and institutions that supported the dictatorship.

A durably institutionalized dictatorship also means the socialization of a class of civil servants in the values that sustained it and its repressive activities. Judges, magistrates, and military and police officers will have developed the greater part of their careers under the dictatorship and will have had to act with some loyalty towards it in order to be promoted. In the absence of thorough purges, these very same civil servants are often those that are responsible for implementing policies of truth and justice. Although the overturning of a regime can lead former supporters to 'turn' quickly and co-operate with a new regime in order to survive, it will be difficult to ensure their active enthusiasm for implementing policies of this kind. At the same time, a long-lasting and well institutionalized dictatorship usually has a higher level of residual legitimacy. (This does not apply to dictatorships that were sustained mainly by external support, such as the communist regimes of Eastern Europe.) In addition, this legitimacy will increase if the regime managed to pacify serious civil conflicts or introduce a period of economic growth and stability. In sum, durability coupled with institutional penetration, as well as perceptions of 'success' in resolving past conflicts, work against the application of truth and justice policies in the democratic period.

The nature and extension of repression against opposition forces is also important. The key words here are 'magnitude', 'methods', and 'complicity'. The greater the magnitude of repression, the greater the need for truth and justice policies. Paradoxically, however, a great magnitude of repression usually means that such policies will be harder to design and implement, as the universe of victims to be compensated and of repressors to be punished is concomitantly greater. Method matters in so far as it shapes the kinds of policies called for. New democracies that emerge after a regime that used *intensive* methods of repression—torture, assassination, and disappearances—will face different solutions from those faced by democracies coming to power after *extensive* methods of repression. Repressive methods that are clandestine and involve official denial, as in Central and South America and South Africa, produce a very particular kind of legacy. Social demands for truth and acknowledgement will be particularly powerful and a need to clarify what happened is more likely to lead to the establishment of truth commissions. Furthermore, disappearances require different responses from mass and prolonged detainment and torture. They involve a search for bodies or the confirmation of death by the state to solve pending legal problems for relatives, both of which require co-operation from repressors which is difficult to obtain. Conversely, when repression is 'open', this kind of exigency may not be as common. The victims of repression of Solidarity in Poland or against opposition forces in Spain were tried in courts and gaoled in state prisons after the application of legal norms, although these norms were not always respected by police and authorities. Regardless of the fairness of the sentences, therefore, repression required very few subsequent investigations as most repressive activity is registered in official archives. Social demands will more likely focus on the opening of such files to the public, although full access is often denied and it may be difficult to gain an overall vision of the repressive universe by reference to them.

This brings us to the issue of complicity. Where repression has been based on widespread social complicity, devising the limits of legal culpability and implementing a justice policy is a more complex matter. Finally, as far as repression is concerned, the time that has gone by since the worst period of abuse is also important in conditioning responses in the transitional period. In Spain or Eastern Europe there were few people killed in the last 20 years of dictatorial rule. Further, with the exception of Poland, there were few political prisoners in Eastern Europe at the time of the collapse of communist rule. The violent action exerted by these dictatorial regimes to consolidate themselves was in the distant past and is therefore less likely to raise passions and demands for punitive measures. The people that were the victims of long-past repression are often very old or even dead, they are not organized and do not constitute a political pressure group; while younger generations leading the transition may not feel a commitment to deal with a past they have no personal experience of. Hence in durable dictatorships, where the worst period of repression is long past, social demands for justice have not been as powerful as in other cases. The same is true when violence is the responsibility of regime authorities and also of some opposition forces, as in the case of terrorism in Spain. Besides, the existence of civil war before the establishment of dictatorial rule may reduce the desire of a democratizing elite to pursue punishment for human rights violations, particularly when the dictatorship is perceived to have put an end to a period of violence and chaos. An adequate response to that would require the thorough revision of responsibilities of winners and losers alike for the former period of violence and political instability.

In addition to the global transitional context and specific legacies of authoritarianism, older historical conditions will also shape transitional justice and truth measures. The nature and power of the dominant church or churches is an example. In some instances they can play a powerful role in favour of policies of truth and justice, or in promoting a form of dealing with the past that emphasizes a reconciliation with truth rather than trials; Chile and South Africa are cases in point. In other settings, they may be the only force working with civil society groups to pursue truth or justice, as in Brazil. And in yet others they can play a negative role, backing up the forces of repression or at least not indicting them, as in Argentina.

Societies historically accustomed to high levels of violence may not attach such importance to punishing authoritarian violators. The social acceptance of violence under a new democracy as a 'normal' part of daily life may lead to a deadening of responses to past repression and may lower demands for punishment and accountability; the case of Brazil is exemplary of this. Social 'acceptance' of violence is more common in countries where poverty is extended in fragmented and ethnically divided societies, such as South Africa, Guatemala, or Brazil, where conditions of life are very different for white or black and indigenous populations.

The weakness of a political culture of respect for the rule of law which is favourable to the peaceful resolution of conflicts is also linked to lower demands for truth and justice. This is frequently the case in countries without successful previous experiences with democracy. Conversely, the stronger a past experience with democracy has been, the more likely is the demand for truth and justice policies, as expectations for justice are historically embedded and are higher. This presents us with another paradox. The more democratic a country's past and the less violent its social coexistence, the more likely it is that truth and justice will gain a hearing. And it is those that most need an accounting for the past—those with the most violent traumatic histories—that often achieve less in the realm of transitional justice.

The above does not exhaust the kind of elements one needs to consider when assessing what shapes truth and justice policies in the transition to democracy. As noted above, there are myriad, country-specific conditions that are too numerous to list here. However, the above are some of the most important, in that they seem to cut across national specificities and to affect the experience of various countries assessed in this book.

On the Effects of Truth and Justice Policies on New Democracies

These conclusions have not concentrated on the moral dimension of policies of truth and justice. The aim has been to focus on the more empirically observable links between truth telling, punishment, and democratization, and in this realm some of the links that are commonly expected have not been found. It would appear to be the case that trials and truth commissions do not have a determining impact on the quality of the new democracy, when observed some years after transition. Democracy is just as strong and deep in Spain, Hungary, and Uruguay, where there was no punishment or truth telling, as it is in Portugal, the Czech Republic, or Argentina, which did experience purges and trials. It seems that truth commissions and trials may not be strictly necessary to improve democratic prospects, but that forward-looking institutional reform is, especially of the police, military, and judiciary. None the less, while purge policies that affect such institutions, and sideline individuals linked to repressive activities or carriers of authoritarian values of a previous dictatorship, may help to ensure a better-quality democracy, there is no indication that this reform process cannot occur in the absence of purges. Other slower, more discreet, and less conflictive measures can obtain the same results. The inconvenience of delay can be compensated, moreover, by the fact that gradualist reform measures do not raise the spectre of a conflict that may threaten a new democracy.

We did not find any direct correlation between the implementation of policies of backward looking truth and justice and the global functioning of democracies, in the sense that those are neither necessary nor sufficient for a democratic regime to take root. None the less, it is also true that, when policies of truth, justice, and rehabilitation have been undertaken with regard for due process and all the legal guarantees, these have had an exemplary impact on the way people perceive the new regime, which might help to strengthen its legitimacy. On the other hand, finding a cause–effect mechanism of the impact of certain measures in the quality of the functioning of specific institutions should require further analysis, with a cross-country approach, establishing more strict distinctions among different truth and justice policies, and focusing on particular institutions.

There seems to be a positive link between the social and political integration dimension of policies of backward-looking accountability and democratic legitimacy. If a new democracy makes no effort publicly to recognize the victims of repression, particularly when the victims are numerous or well organized, it will encounter difficulties in obtaining support from these social groups, which may feel that 'democracy has failed them'. The moral satisfaction derived from the public recognition of atrocities, measures of economic or symbolic compensation, and the trial of those guilty of repressive acts all contribute to integrating previously persecuted social groups into the social and political fabric. Again, however, truth telling and justice as well as compensation are of themselves insufficient to ensure political integration, which usually requires a response to wider categories of economic, social, and in some cases ethnic exclusion.

Truth and justice policies may also have the effect of depriving an old dictatorial elite of its legitimacy and prestige, as well as of discrediting the ideology that sustained the old regime. Institutional declarations condemning the authoritarian past, such as those proffered in some Eastern European countries, in Germany, or in South Africa, can reduce the residual legitimacy of the authoritarian regime. This effect has been observed through electoral results. However, while the discredit produced by truth reports or court findings diminish social support and identification with an old authoritarian elite, they do not destroy it. Furthermore, the discrediting effect is lessened when policies of truth and justice are arbitrary or violate due process, as in Albania, or when they are perceived as externally imposed, as in the case of East Germany or with the arrest of General Pinochet in London. Thus, Fatos Nano, who was tried by an anti-communist government in Albania, later was elected prime minister of the country. In the former East Germany, the successor party of the Communists has maintained a stable electoral base that is sometimes higher than that of the Social Democratic party. In the Czech Republic, the Communist Party, which obtained very low voting results in the first years of the transition, has become the second-largest electoral force in the country. And in Chile support for Pinochet is still significant, based on the view held by wide sectors of the population that the dictatorship saved the country from communism, and civil conflict.

In sum, there is no single answer to how truth and justice policies affect democracy or democratization, as this depends on starting conditions, as well as on the historical and more recent institutional, social, and political legacies that are peculiar to each country. What one can say is that the effects of such policies are the least noticeable where their implementation is easiest.

This brings us to *the paradox of the probable and the unnecessary*. The impact of truth and justice policies on a new democracy depends on starting conditions or the initial balance of power; in other words, the more likely the implementation of such policies is because of a favourable balance of forces, the less necessary they are to ensure a process of democratization. When the balance of forces favours democratizing groups, as in transitions by collapse or through 'rupture', nothing prevents such reforms from being undertaken to benefit democratic governance. The weakness of the forces of the old regime makes it unnecessary to implement policies to remove them from the state apparatus or to put them on trial. If the new democracy faces no threats, such policies are not strictly necessary because democratic aims can be obtained without them. By contrast, when old regime forces are still a threat and continue to have veto power, a common scenario in post-military dictatorial contexts, the policies required to punish or remove them from their posts are more likely to produce conflicts that are threatening to the new order.

The foregoing is not meant in any way to act as an argument *against* policies of truth and justice. It merely attempts to highlight some of the aspects of their links to democratization. Indeed, whatever their effect on democratization, such policies are crucially important moral and political demands which are, even if imperceptibly, part of a changing climate that places respect for human rights at the forefront within and between national communities.

Bibliographical Survey[1]

Introduction

Just fifteen years ago, the literature on transitional truth and justice was very limited. With the exception of works on transitional justice in the wake of the Second World War, the vast body of legal literature on the Nuremberg trials, and, to a lesser extent, on the Tokyo Tribunal, the phenomenon of transitional trials, truth commissions, purges, and policies of resitution or compensation was not an object of study by social scientists and the wider academic community until the mid-1980s. This was the result of various interrelated factors. Until the beginning of the transitions to democracy in Latin America, which gave rise to the 'first wave' of transitional truth and justice since the Second World War, such experiments were not common. The cumulative effect of the human rights revolution, which made human rights part of the political vocabulary of transitional elites and societies, gave renewed impetus to human rights causes in domestic politics. Related to the above, the emergence of political and legal strategies to combat human rights violations in Latin America led to writing on the issue, published mostly in legal journals or by human rights organizations, with some of the earliest work produced by organizations like Amnesty International and Human Rights Watch. Within the political science community, the new interest in transitional truth and justice was reflected in early 'transitology' studies, or work on transitions from authoritarian rule, initiated by Linz (1968) and taken up by Huntington (1991), who referred to the issue as the 'torturer problem' in his classic study of the 'third wave' of worldwide democratization processes, and in the edited three four-volume series on transitions by O'Donnell *et al.* (1986a, b, c), which mention the issue

[1] The book *chapters* referred to in this bibliographical survey from Boraine and Levy (1995), Boraine *et al.* (1994), Henkin (1989; 1998), McAdams (1997), Roht-Arriaza (1995), Sieder (1995a; 1998), Deák *et al.* (2000) and Farer (1996) are not included individually in the bibliography at the end of the book: rather, only the books themselves are included, and page numbers are given here. Such chapter references are included in the bibliography only when they are referred to in the individual chapters of this book.

in passing as one with a strong capacity to destabilize a process of transition from authoritarian rule (1986a: 131–133; 1986b: 28–32; 1986c: 28–29).

The first book to concentrate specifically on the topic of transitional justice, analysing it in a systematic comparative way, was edited by Herz (1982). It concentrated on various postwar European cases, as well as those of southern Europe in the 1970s. In 1989 the Aspen Institute for Peace in the USA produced the first edited volume that looks primarly at Latin America and addressed the issue from a more 'modern' perspective, using the language of human rights, truth, and justice rather than more classic references to 'political justice' (Henkin, 1989). Since then, hundreds of articles have been written on the subject, as well as a growing number of edited books. Indeed, literature has followed life, with work appearing as countries have undertaken truth and justice processes. Interdisciplinary conferences, seminars, and projects in the United States, Latin America, South Africa, and Europe have furthered work on the issue from the mid-1980s onwards, leading to the publication of various edited works of a comparative nature resulting from international conferences, such as Henkin (1989) already mentioned above, ICJ (1993), Boraine and Levy (1995), Boraine *et al.* (1994) (both of these arising from conferences organized in South Africa), and McAdams (1997).[2]

The most valuable single book source is the three-volume compilation published by the United States Institute for Peace, which includes extracts of books and articles as well as original documents and laws (Kritz, 1995). A fourth volume is currently being prepared

[2] To mention only some international academic conferences: State Crimes Conference, Aspen Institute, Maryland (1988), which produced the Henkin (1989) volume; Truth and Justice, the Delicate Balance, Budapest (1990); Reconciliation in Times of Transition, San Salvador (1991); Justice in Times of Transition, Salzburg (1992); Dealing with the Past, Capetown (1994); Truth and Reconciliation, Capetown (1995), the latter two of which produced the Boraine volumes (Boraine and Levy, 1995; Boraine *et al.*, 1994); Political Justice and the Transition to Democracy, University of Notre Dame, North Carolina (1995), which produced the McAdams (1997) volume. There have also been a number of longer-term study projects. To name the most important, there was the Project on Justice in Times of Transition of the Foundation for a Civil Society (Charter 77 and Soros Foundation), with five conferences over 1992–4; the project on Memory in Latin America, US Social Sciences Research Council (1998); and the project on Justice in Times of Transition, led by Jon Elster at the University of Columbia (1999–). The New York University School of Law also initiated a project on Transitional Justice in 1999. The ICJ (1993) publication arose from a conference held in Geneva on Impunity of Perpetrators in Gross Human Rights Violations, 2–5 November 1993.

on the cases of Guatemala, South Africa, and Bosnia, which were not included in the first three volumes. This sums up the main books produced on the subject that constitute useful introductory and comparative readings.

Apart from the volumes mentioned above, there are a few cross-continental comparative books. The book edited by Roht-Arriaza (1995) not only examines a variety of specific cases but also has a very useful introduction on international law and its relevance of transitional justice. The forthcoming books by Biggar (2000) and Hayner (2000) examine transitional justice in post-conflict societies, and official truth commissions established in Latin America, Europe, Africa, and Asia, respectively. In addition, there are comparative studies that focus on a single region. For Latin America there is Weschler (1990), which provides an excellent journalistic account of the truth telling projects in Brazil and Uruguay, Barahona de Brito (1997), which compares the Chilean and Uruguayan processes, and includes in its introduction a survey of various cases and general issues, and Roniger and Sznazjder (1999) on Argentina, Chile, and Uruguay. Henke and Woller (1991) and Deák *et al.* (2000) give an account of the purge process in postwar Europe,[3] while Borneman (1997) and Rosenberg (1995a) look at accountability processes in post-communist Eastern Europe. Other books that look at the dilemmas of transitional truth and justice more widely, be they legal, moral, or political, are Kirscheimer (1961), the classic study of transitional and political justice; Crelinsten (1993), Christenson (1986), and Teitel (2000), which examine political trials and transitional justice, respectively, from a legal perspective; Osiel (1997), which argues in favour of transitional trials as political theatre that can educate societies about values of democracy and the rule of law; Bronkhorst (1995), which provides an empirical overveiw of various instances of transitional accountability processes; and Minow (1998), a more journalistic account that discusses the trade-off between truth and justice and argues that truth is not a second-best option. The edited volume by Rotberg and Thompson (2000) looks at the more moral philosophical and political–theoretical aspects of truth commissions, while Shriver (1995) examines the general question of forgiveness in politics. In addition, Henkin (1998) looks at a variety of peace processes directed by the United Nations, with a section dedicated in each

[3] Although not specifically about transitional justice, the edited volume by Larsen *et al.* (1998) is another good comparative source on the postwar European cases.

case to truth and justice-seeking policies. Although not dedicated to truth and justice *per se*, its combined analysis of the transition, domestic, and international actors in the peace process and its integration of the concern with truth and justice makes it a valuable contribution.

Some journals have edited special issues on the topic of transitional accountability, providing a good source of the main debates about the issue and various case studies. The 1990 issue of the *American University Journal of International Law and Policy* (5, 4) looks at civil military relations and human rights in Latin America during the transition to democracy. The *Hamline Law Review* issue of the same year (13, 3) and the 1997 issue of *Law and Contemporary Problems* (59, 4) examine the moral and political dilemmas involved in transitional truth and justice policies more widely, as does the 1992 issue of the *New York Law School Human Rights Journal* (9, 3). The 1995 issue of *Law and Social Inquiry* (20, 1) on 'Accountability for International Crimes and Serious Violations of Fundamental Rights', and that of the *Journal of International Affairs* (5, 2) focus on the more legal and international human rights law dimensions of the problem. The special issue of *Index on Censorship* in 1997 (25, 5), entitled on *Wounded Nations, Wounded Lives*, offers some insights into the issue in countries that have undergone or are still suffering from armed conflict.

As far as single journal articles are concerned, the most useful for a general assessment of truth commissions on a comparative basis are Hayner (1994; 1996a,b), the Harvard Law School Human Rights Programme and the World Peace Foundation report (1997), Roht-Arriaza (1998b), Popkin and Roht-Arriaza (1995), Shey, Shelton and Roht-Arriaza (1997). Moore (1989) and Barcroft (1993), offer general discussions of pardons, while Shey *et al.* (1997), Popkin (1999) and Popkin and Bhuta (1999) look at amnesties from a comparative perspective.

Good overviews of transitional justice issues are offered by Elster (1998), José Zalaquett in Henkin (1989), and Zalaquett (1990; 1992), which focus mostly on Chile; Pion-Berlin (1994; 1997), Pion-Berlin and Arcenaux (1998), Nino (1991; 1996), Jaime Malamud-Goti in Henkin (1989: 71–87); and Malamud-Goti (1990; 1991; 1998a,b), all of which look primarly at the Argentine case; and Offe (1992) on Germany and Eastern Europe. Kritz (1996), Little (1999), Balint (1997), Landsman (1996), Benomar (1993), Van Dyke and Berkley (1992), and Teitel (1997) offer general overviews from a legal and political perspective.

Finally, there are a growing number of web sites with information about transitional truth and justice. The US Institute for Peace site at http://www.usip.org contains the Kritz volumes (1995) mentioned above as well as various other valuable materials on truth commissions. The Internet Bibliography on Transitional Justice at http://userpage.fuberlin.de/~theissen/biblio/index.html contains citations of about 2,000 monographs, book chapters, and periodical articles in English or German, with special emphasis on South Africa, Germany after 1945 and 1989, and international criminal law, including the international criminal tribunals. The bibliography is compiled by the Transitional Justice Project run jointly by the Law Faculties of the University of the Western Cape and the Humboldt University in Berlin.

Other useful sites, while not directly focused on transitional justice, are the Human Rights Watch site at http://www.hrw.org and the Amnesty International site at http://www.amnesty.org. Both are excellent sources and the most regularly updated, covering human rights issues in general. The press releases and reports published by Amnesty International, many of which refer to this topic, are found at http://www.amnesty.org/news/index.html. The International Commission of Jurists at http://www.icj.org, as well as the Lawyers' Committee for Human Rights, at http://www.lchr.org, are also both good sources.

For Latin America the best sites are http://www.derechos.org, which offers a wealth of material, including documents, rulings, and full articles on various countries and aspects of human rights and accountability, and http://www.derechos.org/nizkor. This latter site has links to various human rights organizations, many of which publish updates and newsletters on human rights cases. Another useful general site for Latin America is found at http://www.derechos.org/cejil, which publishes a gazette with updated information on human rights cases. For official decisions by the Inter-American Human Rights Systems, the appropriate site is that of the Organisation of American States (OAS), at http://www.oas.org. There are various HRO sources that are useful for an analysis of the human rights issue. The most important are the Mothers and the Grandmothers of the Plaza de Mayo at http://www.madres.org and http://www.wamani.apc.org/abuelas, respectively. The Children of the Disappeared have a new site, at http://www.hijos.org. The Argentine Forensic Anthropology Team has a site with useful information about the work of that organization at http://www.eaaf.org. For Chile, the Foundation for Social Assistance of the Christian Churches (FASIC), which publishes a regularly updated chronology on the evolution of the human rights situation, has a site at http:/www.fasic.org. The archives of the Vicariate of Solidarity of the Catholic Church at http://www.iglesia.cl/santiago/solidaridad, and of the Chilean Commission for Human Rights at http://www.cdhc.cl, are also useful. The ODHAG web site at http://www.guateconnect.com/odhagua is a good source of information on Guatemala.

For Eastern Europe, updated information can be found the Radio Free Europe/Radio Liberty site at http://www.rferl.org. The Irish site at http://www.incore.ulst.ac.uk contains some very useful papers presented at the 'Dealing with the Past: Reconciliation Processes and Peace-Building' conference of 8–9 June 1998, as well as links to other relevant sites. Similarly, the South African Centre for the Study of Violence and Reconciliation site at http://www.wits.ac.za has various articles, conference papers, and other materials on the South African Truth Commission as well as other examples of transitional truth and justice. The South African Truth and Reconciliation Commission site at http://www.truth.org.za holds the full text of the South African Commission and background information as well as links to other relevant sites. Finally, Carter and Davidson (1997) offer a good overview of the Internet resources on human rights in general, many of them useful for research on transitional truth and justice.

The Main Debates

Conditions Shaping Transitional Truth and Justice

José Zalaquett in Henkin (1989) and Zalaquett (1990; 1992), a member of the Chilean Truth Commission, was the first to create a framework of transition types and transitional justice policies. He focuses especially on the tension between the ethics of responsibility and the ethics of conviction emerging in restricted transitional contexts. He outlines six basic transition types. First, there are those where there are few constraints due to victory by occupying forces. The second type occurs when the regime loses legitimacy but retains military power. The third is when the military allows a civilian government to come to power after negotiations on its own terms. The fourth involves a gradual transition followed by popular forgiveness. The fifth results when the new government represents a realignment of forces in a situation of armed conflict. And the sixth takes place when ethnic, national, or religious divisions remain in the way of pacification. The main weakness of this approach is that the types of transition seem to be more descriptive of actual cases than to represent a complete list of all the 'ideal type' situations, each with a predictably different transitional justice solution. Indeed, most analysts have come up against this problem, as the number of variables shaping transitional truth and justice policies is so great that any attempt to create an overarching framework inevitably oversimplifies reality or reduces it to a list of descriptions of cases and 'probabilities'.

Barahona de Brito (1997) bases her work on that of Zalaquett, but modifies his approach. Although she uses a similar list of transitional situations, her book sees the 'mode of transition' merely as the starting point of 'enabling' or 'disabling' conditions for the implementation of truth or justice policies. She argues that the nature of repression and various legal, political and institutional legacies of authoritarian rule are also very relevant. Similarly, the nature of the opposition to authoritarian rule and its attitude to the human rights issue is crucial. This approach combines the behavioural with the 'transitology' focus of the Zalaquett study.

Sriram (2000) adopts a slightly different angle. She too takes transition types as a starting point of 'conditions favourable for' transitional justice, using Huntington's transition types (1991) as the basis for her framework. She then argues that the balance of forces between pro-justice civilians and recalcitrant militaries, international factors, and the duration, intensity, and nature of the repressive legacy being dealt with are the most important conditioning factors. The legacy of repression is also emphasized in Huyse (1998), Rosenberg (1995a), who all argue that each legacy requires a different 'truth' and 'justice' response. Like Sririam, Barahona de Brito (1997), Huyse (1998), Brysk (1993), and Sikkink in Farer (1996: 150–168) also attach importance to the role of international actors in shaping transitional justice perspectives.

Tucker (1999) focuses on three types of transition: democratic restoration, as in Athens, and Western Europe; post-authoritarian transition after a longer period of authoritarian rule and a weak or non-existent prior democracy, as in Spain, Portugal, Latin America, and Greece; and post-totalitarian transitions, where there is a weak civil society and fragile alternative elites. However, Tucker's approach has the virtue of combining an assessment of transition type with past legacies—more specifically, with a prior experience with democracy. For him, the nature of prior experience with democracy is crucial in shaping the nature of the transitional justice policies adopted. Welsh (1996) and Morgan (1994) undertake a similar exploration of the elements that come into play to shape a policy, particularly the focus on legacies of the past and transitional type and context, this time for the Eastern European cases.

Pion-Berlin (1997) adopts a more institutional and less path-dependent focus compared with some of the studies mentioned above. Looking at the case of Argentina, he shows how important institutions are in shaping policy, as they acquire an autonomous life and give continuity to initiatives, even when political actors are either opposed to or no longer particularly interested in an issue. In another study (1994) he combines the institutional focus with an look at the role of the presidency, showing how the attitude of the presidency explains different outcomes in Chile, Argentina, and Uruguay, although he emphasizes that no one factor can account for policy outcomes.

Elster (1998) makes perhaps the most sophisticated attempt yet. However, he rejects a search for an overarching theory, and calls for the identification of recurring causal patterns or mechanisms. His approach is behavioural rather than focusing on the type of transition. First, he lists six dependent variables that shape that policy: the decision to engage in a process of transitional justice by a new regime; the identification of wrongdoers; the decision about how to deal with the wrongdoers; the identification of the victims; the decision about how to deal with the victims; and the procedural decisions adopted regarding implementation. He goes on to discuss the independent variables, which are the political actors involved, and the real or perceived constraints on their decisions, their motivations, and beliefs, and the mechanisms whereby conflicting individual preferences are aggregated into a collective decision. Nino (1996) offers perhaps the best analysis of the motivations that guide actors in their decisions regarding transitional justice. The 1998 Mellon Seminar organized by Elster produced a series of papers in which the same framework was loosely adopted by various authors looking at different cases. Acuña (1998), Dahl (1998), du Toit (1998a), and Huyse (1998) loosely use this framework to analyse the cases of Argentina and Chile, Denmark and Norway, and South Africa and the Netherlands, respectively.

Peace v. Justice

One of the most important debates on transitional justice has discussed the trade-off between democratic stability and justice in particular. This debate emerged primarily in reference to the difficulties of undertaking a full accountability process after negotiated transitions. The most important between the late Emilio Mignone, the head of one of the most important HROs in Argentina, and two legal scholars (Mignone *et al.*, 1984) and the late Santiago Nino (1985), former adviser to Argentine president Alfonsín on truth and trials in that country; this debate was repeated between Nino (1991) and legal scholar Orentlicher (1991a,b). Nino essentially argued that it was necessary to take into consideration political constrainst on justice, while Mignone and Orentlicher emphasized the moral and legal duty to punish, above and beyond political context. This has been one of the main dividing lines in the literature on transitional justice.

Other important writings on the duty to prosecute or the obligation of states to punish gross human rights violations are Human Rights Watch (1989d), which outlines a policy statement on how to deal with past repression in terms of truth and justice, and the more legal studies by Roht-Arriaza (1990), Orentlicher (1991a, b), Edelenbosch (1994), Juan Méndez in McAdams (1997: 1–26), Méndez (1997), and Neier (1998). On the other side stand José Zalaquett, a member of the Chilean Truth and Reconciliation Commission (CNVR) (in Henkin, 1989; Zalaquett, 1990, 1992), and Argentine President Alfonsín, who outlines the difficulties he faced when confronting this dilemma (1993). Others that have focused specifically on the stability and justice dilemma are de Grieff (1996), which looks at the problem from a philosphical perspective and points out the insufficiencies of both punishment and pardon, and Sieff and Vinjamuri Wright (1999).

Law v. Lustration

Transitional justice can be fraught with legal problems with difficult political implications. These problems arise because, on the one hand, there is a need to punish as many of the guilty as possible, but on the other hand, for this to be done, due process may be violated. The assumption of collective guilt, reversing the equation 'innocent until proved guilty', and the retroactive application of laws are two examples. This can debilitate the rule of law and, by extension, the values that are at the basis of democratic life. The best literature on these problems has emerged from an analysis of the postwar European cases and the Eastern and Central European transitions, precisely because such problems have been most severe in these cases. In addition, there is some literature that addresses the problems of justice from a wider angle, looking at the legal, political, and ethical challenges they pose.

Waldron (1992) offers a good account of the ethical problems posed by trials, while chapters by Villa-Vicencio and Verwoerd (pp. 449–473) and Levinson (pp. 339–377), both in Rotberg and Thompson (2000), discuss similar problems facing truth commissions. Walzer (1997) offers a short but sharp insight into the dilemmas of transitional justice, while Boed (1999), Borneman (1997), and Walsh (1996) offer interesting perspectives on the dilemmas of justice and lustration in Eastern Europe.

One of the limitations on prosecutions is the due obedience criteria, whereby lower ranking officers may not be prosecuted if they were merely 'obeying orders'. L. C. Green (1976) provides a good outline of the problem of superior orders, and Bakker (1989) looks at the *mens rea* principle, whereby one cannot be punished for acts having consequences that one was not aware of. Crawford (1990) and Osiel (1998) look at the limitations posed by due obedience criteria with reference to the Argentine case. This issue has also been the subject of much legal and political debate in Germany, due to the prosecution of the border guards. K. A. Adams (1993) and M. Goodman (1996) discuss these trials, the former showing how natural law traditions offer different answers regarding the meaning of justice from those offered by the rule of law, with a concomitant impact on how we assess the fairness of trials of 'little fish'. Schulhofer *et al.* (1992) examine the due process problems caused by lustration.

The Aims of Truth and Justice

One of the other important debates on transitional truth and justice regards its aims. The best general study for the moral aims of truth telling is Rotberg and Thompson (2000), particularly the chapters by Rotberg (pp. 1–32), Minow (pp. 378–418), Gutmann and Thompson (pp. 133–168), Bhargava (pp. 70–106), Kiss (pp. 107–153), Croker (pp. 154–187), du Toit (pp. 189–220), and Greenawalt (pp. 301–337). The presentation by Juan Méndez in Boraine *et al.* (1994: 88–93) also summarizes key arguments in favour of truth. Truth as a form of justice has been discussed by Hayner (1994), Benomar (1993), Minow (1998), Roht-Arriaza (1995), and Popkin and Roht-Arriaza (1995), the latter developing a victim-centred approach to justice, rather than a punitive or retributive perspective. Allen (1999), André du Toit in Rotberg and Thompson (2000: 189–220), and Minow (1998) examine justice as recognition (1999). Mamdani (1996) and Verwoerd (1996) focus on justice as a form of compensation and the problems with focusing particularly on abherrant crimes rather than the everyday violence of apartheid in this case. The political theory or moral side of this legal debate is that which has taken place between those who defend justice as retribution. The best work to consult for this is Neier (1998), Rychlak (1990) who argue in favour of a more retributive form of justice. Zalaquett (in Henkin, 1989; Zalaquett, 1990, 1992) offers a more moderate vision, where the need for retribution is balanced by a search for stability. In Boraine *et al.* (1994), Neier (pp. 2–8), Méndez (pp. 35–40, 88–93), and Rosenberg (pp. 66–68, 93–99) debate the aims of justice in a short but informative discussion reflecting mostly on the Latin American experience. In addition, the value of trials has been well discussed by Osiel (1997). A growing literature, especially centred on the South African case, has focused on the link between truth commissions and reconciliation or national unity. One of the best analyses of this issue is Allen (1999), assessing the claims of national unity and justice made for the commission in South Africa. Other works that focus on this issue are Dyzenhaus (1999) and Goldstone (1996). Also strong in the South African literature has been the idea of truth as a form of restorative rather than retributive justice, a good example of which is Llewellyn and House (1999). Popkin and Roht-Arriaza (1995) discuss more widely how truth is a form of justice.

Related to the above argument, another key debate in the literature has been whether truth is preferable to punishment or whether it is a second-best option chosen only when punishment it not politically feasible. The accounts most favourable to trials are given by Osiel (1995a, 1997), which both note the value of trials as a form of political theatre through which the values of human rights can be transmitted and learnt. Most other analyses are less sanguine. Although looking at the Touvier trial in France only, Wexler (1995) provides a very good analysis of how trials can become law in action and political theatre, but still largely fail to transmit wider lessons about the nature of atrocity. A stronger argument about the failure of trials to provide a picture of the total 'universe', which gets lost in the morass of legal detail, is given by Finkielkraut (1992), who assesses the Klaus Barbie trial. Minow (1998) looks at both truth commissions and trials and argues that truth is not a second-best option but a form of justice in itself, one that often supersedes criminal justice efforts in that it provides precisely a clearer picture of blame and responsibility and victimization. Other works that have assessed the value of truth, justice, and trade-offs are Crocker (1999), Rotberg and Thompson (2000), Landsman

(1996), and Malamud-Goti (1991), who assesses the complex relationship between rights under a democracy and punishment.

Compensation and Restitution

Although this issue is not analysed in detail in the chapters of this book, it is worth pointing out the importance of policies of compensation and restitution. United Nations Commission on Human Rights (1993) offers a wide-ranging overview of the general problem of restitution and compensation. The articles by Barkan (1996), Rosenfeld (1996), and Shapland (1990) present useful analyses of the general issues involved in compensation and restitution policies.

The first wave of property restitution after the Second World War is covered in a growing literature on the topic. The *American University International Law Review* issue of 1998 (14, 1) is dedicated to the question of neutrality during the war and the location and restitution of assets robbed by the Nazis. Similarly, the *Cardozo Law Review* of 1998 (20, 2) looks at the problem of the restitution of loot associated with the Holocaust. The *Journal of Israeli History* (18, 2–3) of 1998 also has a special number dedicated to 'Restitution, Reparation and Indemnity: Germany and the Jewish World'. Borer (1999), which focuses on Swiss holding of looted assets, Blum (1998), and Bindnagel (1999) also focus on the process of the loot, postwar restitution, and the problems associated with it.

For the post-communist restitution and compensation question, the debate by Offe *et al.* (1993) is a good starting point. Elster (1992) and Orban (1991) offer a negative opinion of restitution efforts, while Neff (1992), Tucker (1995), Kozminski (1997), and Platt *et al.* in Kritz (1995, ii: 571, 578, 751) offer an overview of compensation policies in post-communist Europe, highlighting general problems and challenges. As for individual country studies, Youngblood (1995) offers a view of the Polish case; while Jezovica (1992), Burger (1992), Cepl (1991), and Jelinek (1994) look at the Czech and Slovak Republics, with the latter focusing on Jewish property in particular. Hughes (1995) looks at restitution in Germany after each world war, and Southern (1993) examines the specific issue of the restitution of land in Germany. Von Rundstedt (1997) does a comparative study of the issue in Poland, Germany, and the Czech Republic. Takacs (1992) and Comisso (1995) look at restitution in Hungary, and Pogany (1998) looks at the postwar restitution of Jewish property in that country. Grimsted (1997) deals with Russian restitution of assets looted in the immediate postwar period, and Fischer (1999) examines restitution in Romania. Finally, Kiuranov in Kritz (1995, ii: 715–721) examines the case of Bulgaria. There is also a very new emerging literatue on Japanese postwar compensation, related to the case of the comfort women, which is covered in a very good article by Parker and Chew (1994). Although not specifically dedicated to the issue, Lutz *et al.* (1989) also contains a useful general discussion of compensation policy issues.

The International Dimension

The literature on the international dimension of transitional truth and justice is of two basic kinds—legal and political—with the former clearly dominant. One of the best comparative works, which takes on both dimensions, is Roht-Arriaza (1995). The volumes by Ratner and Abrams (1997) and Jokic and Ellis (2000) present a good introduction to the state and evolution of international law and mechanisms to deal with mass violations since 1945. V. Morris and Scharf (1995) and J. Jones (1998) are valuable source books on the international criminal tribunals for the former Yugoslavia and Rwanda.

In terms of journal issues, there are the 1997 issue of the *Whittier Law Review* (19, 2), which looks at transitional justice, impunity, and the international dimension; the 1997 issue of *Duke Journal of Comparative and International Law* (7 (2)), which examines 'Criminal Trials in the Wake of Mass Violence'; and the *Connecticut Journal of International Affairs* of 1997 (12, 2), which focuses on 'Law, War and Human Rights: International Courts and the Legacy of Nuremberg'. Other articles that examine international law on redress for human rights violations are Osofsky (1997) and Klug (1998), which focus on the international obligation to prosecute mass human rights violations, and Nanda (1998), which describes the mechanisms available in international law to address human rights violations. Ratner (1998a, b) and M. Ellis *et al.* (1998) look more specifically at how international law helps societies to deal with violations in transition. Harris and Livingstone (1998) provide an overall introduction to the Inter-American system, which has played a key role in the human rights struggle in Latin America, and Tesón in Farer (1996: 29–51) analyses how that system has gained in strength and jurisdictional powers.

Various legal scholars have addressed the links, compatibility, contradictions as well as obligations established between international or regional human rights law and amnesty or accountability. R. Goldman (1988), Cassell (1997), Roht-Arriaza and Gibson (1998), Joyner (1996; 1998), and Pasqualucci (1994b) look at amnesties and their compatibility with regional and international human rights law. Pasqualucci (1995) also examines reparations and Standaert (1999), 'friendly settlements' between the Inter-American system and regional governments. Disappearances and legal obligations thereto related are examined by Egeland (1982), Méndez and Vivanco (1990), Medina Quiroga (1988), Kaplan (1980), Grossman (1992), and Brody and González (1997), and truth commissions by Pasqualucci (1994a) and Cassell (1993).

The literature on transnational prosecutions is still small. Most are articles in legal journals, concentrating above all on civil suits in the US and ATCA cases, as described in the chapter by Roht-Arriaza in this book (Chapter 1), or on the more recent trials in the wake of the Yugoslavian war. Einhorn *et al.* (1997) look at the prosecution of war criminals in the USA; Drinian and Kuo (1993) assess the impact of the US Torture Victim Protection Act; Gibney (1996a), Gibney *et al.* (1997), Roht-Arriaza (1998a), Simon (1993), Claude (1983), and Rickard (1981) all examine one of the first cases in the USA involving a Paraguayan torturer, in Filártiga *v.* Peña-Irala. Steinhardt (1995) and Stephens *et al.* (1993; 1996) examine more recent cases, including the Marcos litigation, while Gibney (1996b) looks at the case of former Argentine General Suárez Masón. Crocker (n.d., 1998; and in Rotberg and Thompson, 2000: 154–187) provides insight into the contribution of international civil society to such processes.

The Pinochet case has produced many articles. R. J. Wilson (1999) and Boyle (1998) examine how Spanish domestic law frames the prosecution effort. Barahona de Brito (2000a), Bhuta (1999), and E. Bradley (1998) all assess the implication of the case in terms of an evolving 'universal jurisdiction'. Bracegirdle (1999), Bradley and Goldsmith (1999), and Fox (1999a,b) also offer useful political and legal assessments of the case. Finally, HRW (1999a) has the best account of the case, both in terms of its impact on domestic politics in Chile and internationally.

There is an enormous body of legal–political literature on the tribunals for the former Yugoslavia and Rwanda. Bassiouni and Manikas (1996) undertake an assessment of the legal issues of the Yugoslavian Tribunal; useful articles are Akhavan (1998), as well as Álvarez (1996; 1998) and Greenwood (1996), which both examine the trial of war criminal Tadic. Human Rights Watch, Amnesty International, and the Commission on Security and Cooperation in Europe at http://www.house.gov/csce/ are the best sources for updated information on the work of this tribunal. There is somewhat less work on the Rwandan case. Boutros Ghali (1996) is a good sourcebook from the UN regarding its activity in Rwanda. Cisse (1998) and Álvarez (1999) provide a good introduction to the work of this tribunal, while Martin in Henkin (1998: 97–132) looks at the actual peace process In Rwanda. Finally, Cisse (1997), E. Bradley (1998), J. Jones (1998), USIP (1997), and Teitel (1995) undertake a comparative assessment of the two tribunals.

The literature on human rights organizations and their growing influence as transnational actors is immense. To offer just some examples, Keck and Sikkink (1998) give an excellent study of the transnationalization of normative activism. The special issue of the *Columbia Human Rights Law Review* of 1997 (28, 2) gives a good overview of various dimensions of and perspectives on the promotion of human rights and transnational associations. Farer (1996) also provides a series of chapters on how external actors have become important in the promotion of democracy and human rights in the Americas, while Buergenthal *et al.* (1986) constitutes a good source book on the Inter-American Human Rights system. Otto (1996) gives a view of the increasing importance of non-governmental organizations in national and international human rights practice and law, particularly in the United Nations. Barahona de Brito (1999) shows how the human rights movement in Latin America has become increasingly influential in national as well as transnational politics. For an account of perhaps the most famous transnational human rights organization, formed in response to torture by the first case studied in this book, Portugal, see Larson's (1979) and Power's (1981) books on the formation and early work of Amnesty International. Finally, Guest (1990) gives an excellent account about how a human rights lobby developed in the United Nations and was combated by the Argentine dictatorship.

Transitional Justice and the Politics of Memory

The literature on the politics of memory is immense, and it is not the place of this book to make an in-depth analysis of this body of work. Memory literature that focused on the social and political dimensions first emerged in the 1960s, although Halbwachs (1980), considered one of the 'fathers' of memory studies, began work on the issue as early as the 1930s. In the 1970s, critiques of older studies of institutionalized memory emerged which questioned the objectivity of linear, official histories, paying new to the social historical and anthropological construction of memory and spreading the idea that there is no single memory but a multiplicity of memories. At the same time, scholars began to assess the nature of memory itself and to compare it with real events. The volume by Gillis (1994) provides a good introduction to the study of collective memory in historical and anthropological scholarship. It assesses the problematic use of terms such as 'identity' and 'memory' and looks at commemorations in order to gain an understanding of the complex links between the two. Connerton (1989) and Bond and Gittiam (1994) also give accounts of the problems and multiple manifestations of 'memory politics'. Boyarin (1994), another edited volume, looks at the reconstruction of different national memories. The edited volume by Antze and Lambek (1996) also provides a very good overview of the importance of memory in contemporary culture. The essays in their book look at how the idea of memory comes into play in society and culture and at the uses of memory in collective and individual arenas. The book pays special attention to role that trauma and victimization play within the politics of memory. Nora (1982–92; 1989), Terdiman (1993), and H. White (1973) offer an examination of memory in the nineteenth century. B. Anderson (1991) argues that it is a question not of whether memories are false or real, but of understanding the ways in which people 'imagine' their 'communities'. He argues that narrative comes into play exactly when there is a loss of memory, and he links systematized forgetting or 'collective amnesia' with imagined community.

Mosse (1990), together with Young (1992) look at the politics of commemorations, memorials, and monuments in the postwar period. There is also a good study in the introduction to the spring 1989 special issue of *Representations* on memory and counter-memory, showing how a new politics of monuments has arisen that aims to be more democratic and to represent new notions of remembering and multiple social memories. Johnston (1991) provides a good account of how anniversaries and commemorations are now part of popular culture in the USA and Europe. Judt (1992; 2000) provides a general assessment of memory in postwar Europe and its impact on current politics. Bodei (1995) presents a challenging argument that lack of political direction in the West is due to a loss of memories about the conflicts of the past, while current developments in the East are related to a reawakening of memories of war and old tensions of the past.

The literature on Germany is immense for obvious reasons. Maier's famous book (1988) on how the past is never past is a key reader, as is Jaspers's (1947) classic study of German guilt. Kramer (1996) gives an excellent journalistic account of how the two Germanys are now dealing with the double legacy of Nazism and Communism, a topic also covered by Karstedt (1998), Carnes *et al.* (1995), and Marcuse (1992). Buruma (1994) gives a good account of the very different ways in which memory making and guilt have been processed in Germany and Japan, while Schwan (1998) concentrates on guilt in Germany and its political impact, an issue also dealt with by Webb *et al.* (1995). Santner (1990) looks at the link between film and memory in postwar Germany, and Herf (1997) looks at how memory of the Nazi past has been constructed differently in East and West to serve different political ends and create different founding myths. Ludtke (1993) examines how memory is just as much about selective forgetting as remembering, when talking about the Nazi past in West Germany. Kellner (1994) looks at shifting paradigms of Holocaust memory and shows how it is impossible to restrict interpretations of the Holocaust to ensure that they are 'proper'. Historians are constantly revising the past and reconstructing it; hence his contention that 'never again is always in the here and now'. Vidal-Naquet (1992) provides a look at those now denying the Holocaust, while Piper (1993) looks at the controversy among historians regarding the interpretations of the Holocaust in what was known as the *Historikerstreit*. Young (1988; 1993) provides another good account of attempts to rewrite the Holocaust, and on the politics of memorials for the Holocaust. Finally, Amis's (1991) fictional account of how an escaped Nazi war criminal living in the United States is forced to live his life backward is an excellent study in the complex nature of memory. The man starts out ignorant of what he is and ends up cognisant of the fact that he was a doctor at Auschwitz, and his life ends as he is born.

Production on French memory is perhaps as prolific as that on Germany. Perhaps the best known study is by Nora (1982–92), a seven-volume work on cultural history of France in the *anales* tradition. The Spring 1989 issue of the journal *Representations* explores French memory politics, as does the 1995 issue of *Contemporary French Civilisation* (19, 2), which focuses on the French memory of the Second World War, the 'Vichy Syndrome', and its impact on current politics. Rousso (1991) provides an excellent account of the Vichy Syndrome. Ruscio *et al.* (1994) look at amnesia in French politics, while Haegel (1990) looks at the memory of those shaped by the historical experiences of the Resistance and the war in Algeria.

For Eastern Europe, a wide-ranging study is provided by Brossat *et al.* (1990). Irwin-Zarecka (1993) shows how the collapse of Communism did not produce a single truth, but the search for true history competes with other pressures for social harmony, moral justice, and political practice, such that the future of the past is uncertain. Among others, Irwin-Zarecka (1994) assesses the memory of Communism and its impact on politics in the countries or the people that bear those memories, while Mostov (1998) shows how political elites in Eastern Europe have manipulated history to support ethnocentric nation building projects. Although not covered in the present book, it is important to note that much of the writing on the East has been about the countries where ethnic conflict has emerged. Various authors have argued that memory of a glorious past and ethic myths of 'a chosen people' have played a key role in fomenting renewed war and conflict. Among the best writing is Norfolk *et al.* (1999), Ignatieff (1998), A. Smith (1996), and Vujacic (1996), which assesses how a collective memory of ethnic victimization is one of the key elements leading to nationalist mobilization in Serbia. Judah (1997) shows how the use and abuse of historical memory was used by the Milosevic regime to prepare the Serbs for war. Ignatieff (1996; 1998) does not so much examine transitional justice *per se* as offer very interesting insights into the politics of memory and history, particularly in the case of Serbia. Finally, Szacka (1997) makes an analysis of the Polish case, outlining the changes in collective memory in Poland after the fall of Communism.

For Russia, Hochschild (1994) provides a good view of memories of past terror in interviews with those involved, both victimizers and victims, while K. Smith (1996) looks at the memory of the victims of Stalinism. King (1997) provides an excellent account of how photographs were doctored under the Soviet regime to reshape memory according to political needs. Ferretti (1995) shows how, with *perestroika* and the doubts cast over the October Revolution, the memory of Stalinism was repressed around a new myth-making about pre-revolutionary Russia to reaffirm new values of liberal democracy and to banish feelings of guilt. The edited volume by Passerini (1992) assesses memory and totalitarianism and is particularly relevant for the study of Russia considered in this book. The essays offer some insightful contributions on oral history and memory in the post-*glasnost* Soviet Union. Russian oral historians trying to reconstruct the victims' experience of repression were confronted with numerous obstacles. Among these was the fact that public remembering had been virtually forbidden for decades. Once victims were free to speak, their long suppressed memories sometimes merged with the recollections of others that they picked up in the media. It was thus difficult to determine accurately individual experiences of trauma in this wave of collective remembrance.

There is not much literature on the subject in the cases of southern Europe and Latin America. For Spain, the most comprehensive work is by Aguilar (1995a,b; 1996a,b,c,d; 1997a,b,c; 1998a,b,c,d; 1999a,b,c,d, 2000). Watson (1996) provides an interesting account of how folklore and myth have been used adeptly by the Basque Nationalist movement to articulate a Basque rather than a Spanish identity. The volume by Passerini (1987) looks at popular memories of Fascism in Europe in general.

There is a dearth of writing on Africa. Hobsbawn and Ranger (1993), who argue that the relationship between memory and identity is historically constructed, provide some insights into the Africa case during the colonial period, but more from the colonial European perspective. Soyinka (1999) provides a series of reflections on the burden of the past and the meaning of reconciliation in African politics today, with a focus on the South African case.

For Latin America, NACLA (1998) provides a good overview of the politics of memory of post-military repression. Argentina and Chile have had the most work on memory. For Argentina, Feitlowitz (1998) looks at the impact of the legacy of repression on language and offers very good accounts of the struggle over sites of memory. Jelin (1994, in Acuña *et al.*, 1995: 101–146; 1998), and Dussel *et al.* (1997) focus on memory making, and Perelli (1992) assesses the impact of memory and fear in that country, while Izaguirre (1998) similarly looks at how memory shapes current politics in Argentina. For Chile, Dorfman's play (1991) dramatizes the problem of guilt and retribution on an individual basis. Moulián (1997) looks at memory more widely and at how it affects cultural practices as a whole, with the experience of dictatorship transforming attitudes and social expectations. Wilde (1999) provides an excellent analysis of what he calls 'irruptions of memory', whereby repressed memories come back to haunt current politics. For Uruguay, Roniger and Snazjer (1997) look at the formation of collective identities after repression in Uruguay, while Sosnowski and Popkin (1993), as well as Bergero and Reati (1997), focus on popular resistance and memory politics in Argentina and Uruguay. An excellent discussion of modern truth commissions and the making of history or historical memory is found in Maier (in Rotberg and Thompson, 2000: 419–447).

Country Studies

Each region has contributed to the literature on transitional justice in different ways. The first wave in Europe gave rise to the first literature on international human rights law, stemming from the Nuremberg precedent. The third wave in Eastern Europe has contributed to the body of work primarily on the problems of collective guilt and individual legal guilt, on how justice can often lead to new injustices and the violation of the rule of law; in short, it generated the *law* v. *lustration* debate. The literature on Latin America, on the other hand, has added to our knowledge of the conditions prevailing during transitional periods and of the tension between the need for stability and for justice and truth; in sum, it gave rise to the *peace* v. *justice* debate. Similarly, the South African case, the most successful in Africa, has made a unique contribution to the literature on the link between truth and reconciliation and national unity. The following section provides an overview of the main literature on each of the four continents in which transitional justice efforts have been undertaken.

Africa

The literature on Africa is relatively undeveloped compared with that for Latin America or Eastern Europe, but there are some useful sources. For an account of the truth commissions that have been established in Africa, Hayner (1994; 2000) should be consulted. The only general account on African transitional truth and justice is Carver (1990). A good general source of information is *Track Two*, the quarterly publication of the Centre for Conflict Resolution and the Media Peace Centre, which focuses predominantly on South Africa but also provides information about other countries in the region.

On a country-by-country basis, AI (1996) covers the case of Angola. Clapham and Martin in Henkin (1998: 97–132) cover Burundi and Congo. The truth report for Burundi is published by international HROs in FIDH (1993). HRW (1994d) and Mayfield (1992) look at the trials in Eritreia. The Mozambican case is discussed in Matonse (1992), while HRW (1992e) describes truth telling in Namibia. Oder, the chief justice who led the Commission of Inquiry into Human Rights Violations (in Kritz, 1995: ii.521–531, ii.513–519), looks at the case of Uganda. Brickhill (1995), Carver (1989; 1993; also in Roht-Arriaza 1995: 252–266), De Waal (1990), and García Bochenek (1995) discuss the case of Zimbabwe. As noted above, Rwanda is covered by Cisse (1998; 1997), E. Bradley (1998), Álvarez (1999), J. Jones (1998), Teitel (1995), USIP (1997), and Boutros Ghali (1996), which examine the ICTR and the wider transitional justice and human rights issue in the country. Sarkin (1999) assesses truth telling in the country, whose truth report is provided by FIDH (1994).

The South African is one of the most explored of all recent transitional truth and justice processes and certainly the most discussed African case. The books written on the subject are already numerous. Frost (1998), Hamber and Kibble (1998), and Nuttal and Coetzee (1998) make an overall assessment of the evolution of the government's truth policy, while Chipasula and Chilivumbo (1993) examine the transition process and the dilemmas it generated, among them how to deal with the past. Jeffery (1999); and Miering (1999), J. Taylor (1999), and Meredith (1999) look at the working of the Truth Commission itself and its impact on the transition and society as a whole. Krog (1998) provides an engrossing semi-fictionalized account of the TRC hearings. Comparative studies are undertaken by HRW (1992f), Gravil (1995), Boraine *et al.* (1994), and Hamber (1997b), which all draw lessons from the South American cases, while Boraine and Levy (1995) explore comparatively the kinds of policies that will help the country to overcome its past in a positive way. Rwelamira and Werle (1996) provide another good comparative study that looks at the cases of Germany and South Africa and compare the political and legal strategies adopted in each case. Asmal *et al.* (1996) explore the links between truth and the reconciliation process chosen by the Mandela government. Dyzenhaus (1998) assesses the TRC legal hearings in an excellent study that looks more widely at the role that a judiciary can play in processes of political change. Cochrane *et al.* (1999) look at the relationship between the Truth Commission process and religious communities in South Africa, one of the most important civil society links between the government's policy of coming to terms with the past.

There are numerous articles on the South African case, more so than on any other case of transitional truth and justice. For an excellent overall look at how the transition shaped the policy adopted, producing truth without justice, Berat and Shain (1995) is a must. The best articles exploring the peculiarities of the South African process and the benefits and drawbacks of this specific approach are Garton Ash (1997c) and D. Goodman (1999), which provide perhaps the most favourable view of the amnesty truth-linked process. Boraine (pp. 221–246) and Slye (pp. 267–300), in Rotberg and Thomspon (2000), and Lyons (1997) explore the unique link between truth and confession and amnesty/indemnity. Du Toit (1998a) examines the dilemmas of undertaking perpetrator findings, Keightley (1993) and Sarkin (1996) look at the indemnity process, and Dyzenhaus (1998) assesses the TRC legal hearings and, along with Klaaren (1998), gives a special view of the judiciary in the process of truth telling. Natrass (1999) looks at the TRC on business and its role in sustaining apartheid. In addition, general analyses of the TRC process are offered by du Toit in Boraine and Levy (1995: 94–98), and by Dullah (pp. 2–8), Sachs (pp. 126–130), and Burton (pp. 120–124) in Boraine *et al.* (1994); Berat in Roht-Arriaza (1995: 267–280); Hayner (2000); Berat (1993); Edelstein (1999); Saino (1998); Sarkin (1996); Simpson (1994; 1998); Van Zyl and Simpson (1997); Van der Merwe *et al.* (1998); and Verwoerd (1996; 1997).

Bird and Garda (1997) examine press coverage of the TRC. Braude (1996), Hamber *et al.* (1998), Van Zyl and Simpson (1997), Wilson (1997), Crocker (n.d., 1998; in Rotberg and Thompson, 2000) focus more on the civil society dimension, looking as popular participation in the TRC process, while Gibson and Gouws (1999) assess public opinion responses to the TRC. For an analysis of the moral claims of truth, justice, reconciliation, and nation building, as well as the political foundations of the TRC and their implications, the best studies are Allen (1999), du Toit in Rotberg and Thompson (2000: 189–220), and Dyzenhaus (1999). These, together with Llewellyn and House (1999), also examine truth as a form of 'restorative justice'. Others exploring reconciliation are Hamber (1995; 1997a), Dwyer (1999), Wilson (1995, 1996), and Mamdani (1996, 1998). Hamber (1998a,b, 1997c), Hamber and Lewis (1997), Lansing and King (1998), Norval (1998), Werle (1996), and Statman (1995) cover the more psychological aspects of the truth process and overcoming victim trauma. Two other excellent sources that give a good view of the victim's perspective on the TRC victims' hearings are the video films *Speak Out* (Khulumani) of 1995 and *We Are Still Speaking Out* (Sisakhuluma) of 1997. Graybill (1998a, b) undertakes a moral theological assessment of the TRC. In addition to the above books, some articles look at the relationship between the TRC and different social groups, such as Bozzoli (1998) and Marx (1998). Finally, Braude (1996), Nina (1997), Wylie (1995), and Foner (1995) examine various aspects of the creation of public memory, history making and myth building and the TRC process.

Asia

Asia is the least written about region. The first books were are about postwar Japan, with Brackman (1987), Minear (1971), and Piccigallo (1979) offering assessments of the Toyko Tribunal. Nakasone (1995), and Senzaburo and Itakashi (1995) provide more recent assessments of how Japan has processed its past, while Parker and Chew (1994) take a legal–political look at the issue of compensation for Japanese war rape victims (the so-called 'comfort women'), which has only recently been activated.

The case of the Philippines has produced three main articles and reports, by Aquino in Roht-Arriaza (1995: 231–242), S. Jones (1989), and the Lawyers Committee for Human Rights (1991), although Hayner also mentions the case in her study of truth commissions (1994). Sri Lanka has received slightly more attention, with the main publications being HRW (1992g), AI (1995b), Gómez (1998), Kois in Rotberg and Thompson (2000), and an unpublished doctoral dissertation by Sriram (2000), which makes an original comparative study of the Argentine, Salvadorean, Honduran, South African, and Sri Lankan experiences. Adams, as well as Adamson, both in Henkin (1998), Vickery and Roht-Arriaza in Roht-Arriaza (1995: 243–251), Marks (1994), and HRW (1999b) provide an overview of how the issue is playing out in Cambodia, while Klosterman in Henkin (1998) discusses the possibility of establishing a truth commission for that country. Finally, although the South Korean case has not produced a 'typical' truth-telling exercise and only a symbolic trial, this case is the only other in which any kind of effort has been made to carry out a policy of this sort. Han covers the 1960–1961 period, and the period following the fall of General Chun Doo Hwan (1995: 238–240).

Europe

The literature on the European cases is quite prolific, especially if one takes into account both the postwar and the post-Communist experiences. For transitional justice and postwar political justice in Europe, as a general introduction, the best readers are Herz

(1982), and the Henke–Wolle (1991) and Deák *et al.* (2000) studies on the purge process and retribution in Europe after the war. On a country-by-country basis, Stiefel (1981), Pellinka and Weinzierl (1987), Garscha and Kuritsidis-Heider (1995), and Garscha (1993) cover Austria. Zinner (1985), Deák (1995) and Deák *et al.* (2000: 39–73 and 233–251) give accounts of the Hungarian process. Huyse (1991), Huyse and Dhont (1993), and Deák *et al.* (2000: 133–156; 157–172) cover Belgium. Belinfante (1978), Hirschfeld (1988), and Romijn (1989; in Deák *et al.* 2000: 173–193) look at the case of the Netherlands. For Denmark and Norway, Dahl (1998), Givskov (1948), and Tam (1989) are good reference papers. Deák *et al.* (2000) also covers Greece (pp. 212–232) and Czechoslovakia (pp. 252–290). The French case has produced many studies of the response to the Vichy regime in the postwar period, in part because of the evolution of memory studies in the country. A good introductory reading is offered by Macridis in Herz (1982: 161–178), although the main books on the subject are by Conan and Rousso (1994), Lottman (1986), Novick (1968), and Ruscio *et al.* (1994), which describe the purge process and other punitive measures adopted in that case. Deák *et al.* (2000: 194–211) examines postwar justice measures in Bordeaux.

For Germany, there is a vast literature. For the Nuremberg Tribunal, the texts by B. Smith (1977), Woetzal (1962), and Conot (1983) provide a solid background. For the trials within Germany, good introductory readings are offered by Herz (1982: 15–38) and in the preface to the European section of the book by Roht-Arriaza (1995). In a more general account of how the past was dealt with after 1945, Reuter and Durr (1990) offer a wide-ranging overview and a comparative perspective with Austria. There are some very interesting accounts of the trials of Nazi war criminals long after the immediate postwar period—of the Klaus Barbie trial (Finkielkraut, 1992) and that of Paul Touvier, a Nazi collaborator under the Vichy regime (Wexler, 1995). Each gives a quite different account of the value of trials as 'political education' or as a way of generating a comprehensive picture of the past. Gordon (1995) makes a comparative assessment of the Touvier, Bousquet, and Papon cases; and Froment (1994) tells the Bousquet story in detail. Finally, Italy is covered by the chapter by di Palma in Herz (1982: 107–134), which looks at the nature of the Fascist legacy, and by Domenico (1991), which looks more specifically at the trials and policies adopted to deal with past repressors.

Very little work has been done on the southern European cases in the 1970s. On Greece, the first study was undertaken by AI (1975a), followed by Psomiades (in Herz, 1982: 251–273), Danopoulos (1991), Woodhouse (1985), and Alivizatos and Diamandouros (in McAdams, 1997: 27–60). On Portugal, the only writing on the subject has been done by Costa Pinto (1991, 1995, 1998); the first and third of these publications have only a small section on the subject, so that Chapter 2 above is effectively the second study on the topic for this country. Similarly, there is not much about the Spanish case. Aguilar, author of Chapter 3 above, has worked most extensively on the issue, with a book (1996a) and articles (1997b; 1998c) on the topic. In addition, there is a study by Malefakis (in Herz, 1982: 216–230) that focuses on the legacies of Francoism and other longer-term legacies and their impact on Spanish democracy.

By contrast, there is a wealth of writing on the Eastern European cases, even though it is very recent. The best general studies or accounts are by Rosenberg (1995a), which gives a journalistic account of transitional justice in Eastern Europe, with some insights that are simply put but quite profound. Although it is devoted mainly to East Germany, it also provides useful information about and a deep look at Poland and Czechoslovakia. In terms of articles, the main sources of information are the *East European Constitutional Review* and the review edited by Radio Free Europe/Radio Liberty, the *RFE/RL Research Report* (previously called *Report on Eastern Europe*), and *Transition* (later renamed *Transitions*), which published its last issue in February 1999. Each of these has published numerous short articles on purges, trials, and other political justice measures.[4] The *FBIS Daily Reports* are also a good source of information. In addition, the Commission on Security and Cooperation in Europe (CSCE) has produced a series of reports (1993a, 3b, 1994), on Germany, Bulgaria, and Albania, which offer an overview of the challenges faced by these countries in their search for justice.

The best overview has been that by M. Ellis (1997), who provides an overview of lustration laws and the political process leading to their passage in the Czech and Slovak Republics, Hungary, Albania, Bulgaria, the Baltic states (Lithuania, Latvia, and Estonia), Poland, Romania, Russia, and the Ukraine. Also useful is the panel discussion in the *Boston College Third World Law Journal* (1992, 12(2)), which also discusses the Soviet Union. Offe (1992; 1993; n.d.) provides the best analytical account of the

[4] For the most part, the articles in these journals or newsletters will not be listed, as they are too short and numerous, even if they are valuable research tools.

dilemmas of transitional justice. Borneman (1997) also gives an overall view of the process of accountability, as does Gibney (1994; 1997). Garton Ash has published shorter articles that outline the dilemmas of transitional truth and justice very well (1995; 1997a; 1998). His book *The File* (1997b), while focused on the opening of the Stasi file in Germany, raises many issues about 'truth telling' that are universal to the East European setting. C. González (1998), Smith (in Roht-Arriaza, 1995: 82–98), Siegelman (1995), Los (1995), Morgan (1994), Pomorski (1996), Darski (1993a), Schwartz (1994), Walsh (1996), Rosenfeld (1996), Cepl and Gillis (1994), Tanfa (1996), Torpey (1993), with his distinction between the weight of the past and the politics of the present as competing for attention, Tucker (1995; 1998; 1999), Weigel (1992), and Stewart and Stewart (1995) all offer good insights into the general process of and problems with lustration and democratization. The only article that focuses specifically on prosecutions is by Quill (1996), which compares trials in Germany and Czechoslovakia. The novel by Barnes (1992) makes a satire of the trial of 'Stoyo Petkanov' (Zhivkov in Bulgaria), cleverly revealing the ambiguity of the kind of truth that emerged from trials of this kind in the region. Sklar (1995) and Groceva and Krassmir (1994) examine the ill-effects of lustration and screening laws on scientific and academic freedom, the former in Bulgaria, the Czech Republic, and Germany and the latter in Bulgaria. Finally, Schwartz (1992) looks at the important role that constitutional courts have played in politics in these countries, with an assessment of the issue of accountability and compensation policies.

There are few accounts of the Bulgarian case. In addition to the work on scientific freedom referred to above, readers must refer to CSCE (1993b), Petrova in Boraine *et al*. (1994: 73–80), a short piece on the opening of secret police files and the political conflicts around it. HRW (1993c) offers a full account of the de-communization process to that date. Krause (1995) examines the purges, and Engelbrekt (1990; 1991; 1992; 1993; 1994) the various issues relating to settling accounts with the past in that country. Bertschi (1995) compares the lustration efforts in Bulgaria and Poland, linking the nature of policies with the transition process, and Dimitrov (1999) assesses the role of the Constitutional Court.

The most complete study on Poland is by Walicki in McAdams (1997: 185–238), which is rather critical of lustration as a whole. Other good analyses are offered by Klich (1996), Stewart and Stewart (1995) and Bertschi (1995). Misztal (1999) gives a more favourable view of the process, and Ostianski (1992; 1994) and

Sustrova (1992), more journalistic accounts of phases in the process. Karpinski (1991; 1993) looks at the issue of secret police files in this country.

For Hungary, Halmai and Scheppele in McAdams (1997: 155–184) is the best account. Bence (1990), Fahidi (1994), and Paczolay (1992) are also useful, the latter two looking at the problem of compensation. Kiuranov in Kritz (1995: ii. 715–721) looks at restitution, and Halmai *et al*. (1995) and Solyom (1994) at the role of the Constitutional Court in the lustration process, a topic also covered by Morvai (1994).

In the Czechoslovakian case, Weschler (1992) gives a great account of the Jan Kavan case, highlighting the pitfalls of a process that ends up targeting dissidents. Laber (1992) also offers a journalistic account of the trials. HRW (1992d) provides a legal and policy-oriented critique of lustration, while Schwarzenberg in Boraine *et al*. (1994: 81–85) makes a short but insightful critical discussion of the opening of files, a subject also covered by Devaty (1991). Wolchik (1993) as well as Stewart and Stewart (1995) combines an assessment of political justice measures with a focus on the transition and democratization process. Former dissident and president Vaclav Havel has been one of the most important democratic critics of lustration; his views are expressed in Michnik and Havel (1993). Cepl (1992b) looks at restitution, Siklova (1996) at screening, and Quill (1996) assesses the dilemma prosecution *v*. pardon.

The only significant studies of the Romanian case are by HRW (1990c), Rekosh in Roht-Arriaza (1995), which looks at impunity and the absence of a culture of the rule of law and truth, and Gurvita (1998) and Ionescu (1990, 1992), who highlight the problems of dealing with the Securitate.

The Albanian case has been examined only by CSCE (1994) and HRW (1996b), although the short articles by Imholz (1993; 1995a, b), who has written on Albania, undertakes an assessment of the trials of former Communist officials in the country.

M. Ellis (1997) covers some of the Baltic states, Estonia, Latvia and Lithuania, the only article that includes a survey of these countries, and Taras (1998) and Darski (1992; 1993b) look at the Soviet legacy in Lithuania alone and at how the KGB was dealt with and de-communization implemented.

For the German case after reunification, the single richest source is the Study Commission report by Deutscher Bundestag (1995), full of documentation and opinions. Volume ix offers a view of the process of 'working through' (*aufarbeitung*) the two dictatorships, and thus gives a particularly relevant view of the politics of memory. It is also worth looking at the anecdotal but interesting view by the chief of the Gauck authority (Gauck, 1991; 1994; and in Boraine *et al.* 1994: 71–74). Rosenberg (1995a) and Garton Ash (1999) provide excellent accounts, as does Sa'adah (1998), who creates a conceptual framework of transitional justice, which usefully distinguishes between cultural and institutional strategies to deal with the past, and the different impact and outcomes of each. Other good discussions of the German process are found in found in CSCE (1993a), Rwelamira and Werle (1996), Werle (1995; 1996), Offe (1992; 1994; n.d.), Kommers (1997b), McAdams in McAdams (1997: 239–267), Welsh (1995), Hassemer and Starzacher (1993), and Quill (1996). Childs and Popplewell (1996) give the best account of the Stasi in English, but better materials are available in German from the Gauck authority. On this authority, the short piece by Muller (1992) is good. There is much writing on the impact of opening the Stasi files from various perspectives. Gauck (1991; 1994) offers an insider view, while J. Miller (1998) offers an overall view of the how the Stasi was dealt with, and Hassemer and Starzacher (1993) examine the problems arising from the use of the files to deal with the past. B. Miller (1997), Marcuse (1993), Siegert (1993), Lemke (1992), Wolle (1992), Hartwig (1992), and Burgess (1992a,b) all examine the more social aspects of the Stasi legacy, its impact on politics, social trauma and identities, and (in the case of the last two authors) on the Church. In addition, there are articles that deal with specific aspects of the policy of accounting for past violations. Adams (1993), Walther in Roht-Arriaza (1995: 99–112), and M. Goodman (1996) discuss the famous border guards case. The first of these shows that natural law traditions offer different answers regarding the meaning of justice than the rule of law, with a concomitant impact on how we assess the fairness of trials of 'little fish'. Finally, Markovits (1996) and Blankenburg (1995) examine the fate of East German lawyers in the wake of reunification.

There are very few books that deal exclusively with the issue of dealing with the past in Russia, although Smith in Roht-Arriaza (1995: 113–128) provides a good comparative analysis of attempts to ensure accountability in Russia and Eastern Europe. There is abundant literature on the transitional process, and some works, or parts thereof, address the issues of truth and justice. Adler (1993) and A. White (1995) provide the fullest account of the Memorial Society and its efforts to remember and commemorate those who were repressed under the Soviet system; they also fill in the blank spots in Soviet history, showing how many obstacles there are to democratization. In addition, A. White (1995) looks at the experience of Memorial in the Russian provinces, highlighting the 'memory work' the organization has undertaken, but also its isolation. Hochschild (1994) gives a well researched journalistic account of the legacy of the terror through interviews with former prisoners, historians, camp guards, and relatives of 'enemies of the people'. It deals with key issues, such as the meaning of rehabilitation in the Soviet Union and the continued belief in the Communist Party among victims, and includes a vivid account of the 'voyage to the land of the dead', the notorious Kolyma labour camps. Goudoever (1996) provides a thorough early (pre-Gorbachev) account of political rehabilitations in the Soviet Union. Kowaljow (1997) describes his experience as Commissioner for Human Rights under Yeltsin, a post from which he was eventually compelled to resign for his opposition to Russian military intervention in Chechnya; he discusses the search for justice, as well as the questions surrounding establishment of the rule of law and the development of a civil society in Russia. Remnick (1997) gives an eloquent account of the rediscovery of Soviet history in the *perestroika* years, while Löwenhardt (1995) explores, among other issues, the burden of the past, the undemocratic nature of Russia's political culture, and the challenges that both present for democratization. Yasmann (1993) and Podrabinek (1993) give the only two existing accounts dedicated to the attempt to pass a screening law in Russia, while Sharlet (1993) looks specifically at the role of the Constitutional Court in the post-communist era, with reference to the issue of accountability. Additional information on the Russian case is also to be found in the *RFE/RL Research Report* and the other newsletters and journals with information on the East European cases, as well as in the *Report on the USSR*, which occasionally contains short articles on the issue.

Finally, some work has recently emerged on the Bosnian and Northern Irish post-conflict cases. D'Amato (1994) discusses the stability and peace *v.* accountability dilemma as it plays out in this case. Kritz and Stuebner (1998) and Gisvold (1998) discuss the possibility of a truth commission for Bosnia Herzegovina, while O'Flaherty in Henkin (1998: 71–96) examines the peace process as whole and the Rules of the Road of February 1996 that unsuccessfully framed prosecution efforts in that region. In addition, although this case is not yet one of 'transitional truth and justice', Northern Ireland has become the subject of some recent studies on the subject, as various people are calling for at least a truth-telling process (Rolston, 1996). While not a classic truth report, the

Bloomfield (1998) report does perform the task of giving dignity to the victims. Smyth (1998) looks at the problem from a victim-centered perspective, and Hamber (1998d) considers the possibility of a truth commission for Northern Ireland, as well as generally discussing how to deal with the past in a transitional context, with reflections for the Northern Irish case (1998c). This latter paper can be found at the Initiative on Conflict Resolution and Ethnicity (INCORE) web site at http://www.incore.ulster.co, along with various other articles on trauma, truth telling, reconciliation, and other related matters pertaining to the Northern Irish case.

Latin America

The only comparative single-author books on transitional truth and justice in Latin America are Barahona de Brito (1997), which assesses the cases of Uruguay and Chile, the excellent account by Weschler (1990) on Uruguay and Brazil, and Roniger and Snazjder (1999), which looks at Argentina, Chile, and Uruguay. The edited volumes by Roht-Arriaza (1995) and McAdams (1997) contain chapters on Latin American cases. Cleary (1997) looks at the issue as part of a wider assessment of the struggle for human rights in the region.

There are also some comparative articles that view more than one country experience. Rosenberg in Boraine *et al.* (1994), Rosenberg (1995b), Harper (1996), and Mattarollo (1992) provide short but excellent overviews of the key issues in Latin America. Acuña (1998) gives an excellent comparative account of the Argentine and Chilean processes. Popkin (1999), Popkin and Bhuta (1999), and Roht-Arriaza (1998b) give assessments of the amnesties the region, discussing whether they contribute to reconciliation. J. Moore (1991) examines the amnesty in Nicaragua and El Salvador as negotiated parts of peace accords. In addition, Hayner (2000) undertakes the most comprehensive comparative analysis of truth commissions, concentrating on the cases of Argentina, Chile, El Salvador, and Guatemala. Other assessment of truth commission are Hayner (1994); Popkin and Roht-Arriaza (1995), which examines the truth commissions in Chile, Honduras, El Salvador, and Guatemala; Kaye (1997), which looks at truth telling in El Salvador and Honduras; Ensalaco (1994), which compares Chile with El Salvador; Barahona de Brito (1993), comparing Uruguay with Chile; and Whitfield (1997), comparing El Salvador with Guatemala. Cuya (1997) provides an assessment of various truth-telling reports in South and Central America, while Barahona de Brito (1991) looks at the truth reports of Brazil, Argentina, Uruguay, and Chile. García Laguardia (1997) comparatively assesses transitional accountability and peace accords in Central America as a whole.

As mentioned, writing on Latin America has been characterized by a development of the stability *v.* justice dilemma, given the high incidence of negotiated transitions and concomitant limited scope for action. The main debates to refer to are those between Nino (1985; 1991) and Orentlicher (1991a, b) and Mignone *et al.*, (1984) in Argentina, and between Zalaquett (in Henkin, 1989; 1990; 1991; 1992) and Neier (in Boraine *et al.*, 1994; also Neier, 1998) from Human Rights Watch. At the same time, in light of the unique role played by the military in these cases, a number of studies have assessed the impact of military power on accountability, and the other way around. Pion-Berlin (1994) assesses the dilemma between prosecution and pardon in the Southern Cone cases. Pion-Berlin and Arceneaux (1998) look at how key institutions such as the judiciary have pushed back the power of the military to control this issue over time. B. Loveman (1994), McSherry (1997b), and the special issue of the American University *Journal of International Law and Policy* (1990), on civil military relations and human rights in Latin America during the transition to democracy, all examine the limits imposed by continued military power in the region on democratization and human rights policies. Panizza (1995) provides a general overview of the issue of justice and truth in transition, linking this up with democratization and the protection of human rights more generally. Finally, Idelber (1999) offers a more general discussion of the issue from the point of view of victims and their need for compensation of various kinds.

In addition, there are comparative articles examining the impact of the human rights accountability issue on civil society and citizenship in Uruguay and Argentina (Roniger, 1997), and on the work of HROs in pushing for accountability in Argentina, Chile, and Uruguay (M. Loveman, 1998). The role of the courts is being increasingly examined, given their greater role in the accountability process with the passage of time. Another article that pays particular attention to this dimension is Quinn (1994), and to a lesser extent Mera in Roht-Arriaza (1995: 171–184), which assesses the Chilean case. Acuña and Smulovitz in McAdams (1997: 93–122) and Malamud-Goti (1996) look at the new judicial dynamic in Argentina since Menem, while Acuña (1998) examines the cases of Argentina and Chile comparatively.

For Argentina, good overall accounts are provided in HRW (1987; 1991a) and AI (1987; 1991; 1995a). Acuña and Smulovitz

(1991; in McAdams, 1997: 93–122), Smulovitz in Boraine and Levy (1995: 56–65), and Acuña *et al.* (1995) look at the evolution of the issue from a balance of forces perspective, particularly between civilians and the military. Malamud-Goti (in Roht-Arriaza, 1995: 160–170; also 1996; 1998a, b) proffers a provocative argument that morality and the politics of justice in Argentina has served to reinforce an authoritarian morality by scapegoating the military, making it responsible for the breakdown of democracy and violations and letting civil and political society off the hook. Ledesma (1995) offers a clear view of military culpability. Osiel (1997) has also produced some very interesting work that examines the wider political meaning of trials, and (1987) on the conflict between the courts and the Alfonsín administration, which places particular emphasis on the presidency, the HROs, and the military as key actors in the drama. The other major account is by Brysk (1994a), who focuses more on the HRO movement and democratization. Gravil (1995) provides an assessment of the period highlighting the legal and political mechanisms that serve as guidelines for South Africa.

One of the most prolific writers is the late Santiago Nino. His main work on this case (1996) looks at how key political–ideological tendencies in Argentine history, such as corporatism, anomie, and the concentration of power, explain the advent of massive and systematic human rights violations. He offers a political and philosophical analysis of the morality of prosecution. In this and other articles in which he engaged in a legal and political debate with other scholars, he defended the position of the Alfonsín government (Nino, 1985; 1991), and engaged in a debate with Orentlicher (1991a, b) and Mignone *et al.* (1984). There are many legal studies on the Argentine case. Crawford (1990) looks at the problem of due obedience and Rogers (1990) and Latchman (1989) at the duty to punish. Garro and Dahl (1987) combine a legal and political assessment of the process, and Groisman (1985) focuses on the judicial system in the wake of dictatorship.

Díaz Coludrero and Abella (1987), Smulovitz in Boraine and Levy (1995: 56–65), and Hayner (2000) provide a good account of the work of the CONADEP (1984), and Osiel (1987) covers the early Alfonsín period and transitional justice policy-making in that period. The trial of the juntas is assessed by Sancinetti (1988) and the Asociación Americana de Juristas (1988), which provide some of the legal as well as documentary background. Ciancaglini and Granovsky (1995) also examine the repression and military politics during the dictatorship. Calloni (1999) and D'Andrea Mohr (1999), which look at the repression, are worth reading as they have had an impact on the issue as it has unfolded under the Menem presidency, becoming part of the politics of memory. The first is on Operation Condor, which is under investigation by Spanish Judge Garzón, while the latter was used as part of evidence by an Argentine judge in a case of the kidnapping of minors.

On more specific issues, Brysk (1993) has assessed the social aspects of the struggle for truth and justice, as well as the influence of international actors in that process. Similarly, Roniger (1997) looks comparatively at the links between accountability for past violations and citizenship in Argentina and Uruguay. Like Brysk, Weissbrodt and Bartolomei (1991) assess the significance of international pressures. Brysk has also written an interesting account of the conflicts that have emerged over the counting of the disappeared, between the government and HROs (Brysk, 1994b). For the social, memory, and psychological aspects of the issue, Perelli (1992) argues that a 'culture of fear' and the nature of the transition process in Argentina shaped what were ultimately inadequate policies to deal with the past. Jelin (1994), on the other hand, argues that veneration of the victims and their memory can become a paralysing mechanism for those who did not experience state terror. Suárez Orozco (1991) looks more closely at the impact of trauma, while Izaguirre also explores memory.

On the human rights movement in particular, there are few general works on the movement a whole, although Leis (1989) gives an overall view. By contrast, there are many books on the Mothers of the Plaza de Mayo. To mention just a few, the books by Guzmán Bouvard (1994; 1998) give an overall account of the political trajectory of the Mothers and the Grandmothers, respectively. Malin (1994) focuses on the more recent events, arguing that their declining prestige is a sign of the decreased relevance of the issue under the Menemato, while Arditti and Brinton Lykes (1992) assess the work of the Grandmothers. M. Loveman (1998) provides a more analytical comparative analysis of the work of human rights activists in Argentina, Chile, and Uruguay.

On the Menemato in particular, the best accounts are by Feitlowitz (1998), which looks closely at language and the politics of memory in the cultural arena. Acuña and Smulovitz in McAdams (1997: 93–122) focuses on the new role of the courts, Pion-Berlin and Arcenaux (1998) looks at the shifting balance of forces in favour of human rights and away from military power, and González Bombal in Acuña *et al.* (1995: 193–216) examines the pursuit of justice beyond the trial of the century. Verbitsky (1995) contains the whole interview with Captain Scilingo that put human rights back on the high-profile political agenda in 1995. Together, these provide an excellent overview of changing conditions of the human rights issue in the country. In addition, McSherry (1997a) undertakes an interesting analysis of the close alliance between Menem and the military, more pessimistic than that offered by Pion-Berlin. Langan (1991) looks at the way the media portrayed the Menem pardons. For a presidential view, see Alfonsín (1993) and his somehow moving account of his inability to 'go further'. For an account of victim trauma and recovery, the work by Kordon (1995) is a useful starting point, while Izaguirre (1994) and Stener Carlson (1996) offer a view of the disappeared and from the perspective of the victims, respectively. Finally, Quevedo and Vacchieri, in Acuña *et al*. (1995: 217–269), have prepared a full bibliography of Spanish publications on the Argentine case up to 1990.

Chile, like Argentina, is one of the cases best covered by the literature. For basic information, the best sources are HRW (1988; 1989a; 1991b; 1992b; 1994a; 1999a), WOLA (1991), and the journal *Mensaje*, published by the Vicariate of Solidarity of the Catholic Church in Chile. The summer 1991 issues of *Estudios Públicos* (nos. 41 and 42) contain good accounts of the responses of the Armed Forces and the Supreme Court to the findings of the truth report in that country. Brett (1992) for the International Commission of Jurists, Barahona de Brito (1997; 2000b), Zalaquett (in Henkin 1989; also Zalaquett, 1990; 1991; 1992) and Correa (1992; in McAdams 1997: 123–154) provide the most favourable accounts of the accountability process in Chile. The best critical assessments of the process are by López Dawson (1994), Mera in Roht-Arriaza (1995: 171–184), Pearce in Sieder (1995a: 45–56), Garretón (1994, 1996), and L. Taylor's study (1998).

Popkin and Roht-Arriaza (1995), Ensalaco (1994), Weissbrodt and Fraser (1992), L. Taylor (1993), and Hayner (2000) all provide assessments of the truth commission and the report. A good source of information is the final report of the Commission for Reparations and Reconciliation, CNRR (1996). The work by Quinn (1994) offers an interesting view of the legal strategies adopted to wear down the boundaries of impunity. Lowden (1996) offers a valuable insight into the role of the Catholic Church Vicariate of Solidarity, while M. Loveman (1998) gives a more up-to-date view of human rights activism as a whole. For the civil military dimension of the issue, the best articles are those by Pion-Berlin and Arceneaux (1998), B. Loveman (1991; 1994), and Oppenheim (1991). The best work on the psychosocial aspects of trauma has been done by Agger (1996), Lira (1989; 1990), and Lira *et al.* (1987; 1996). For a presidential view, Aylwin in Boraine and Levy (1995: 38–43) highlights the strengths of the 'Chilean path' to offer lessons for South Africa.

Finally, work that focuses more on the internal impact in Chile of the Pinochet case includes that by Barahona de Brito (2000a), NACLA (1998), and Lagos and Muñoz (1999), who assess the dilemmas that the case has presented for the Chilean government, as well as by Moulián (1999), Brody (1999), and Valenzuela (1999). J. Anderson (1998) offers a very interesting profile of General Pinochet just before he was arrested, showing how radically the image of the dictator changed after his arrest. Finally, HRW (1999a) offers an excellent account of the international legal as well as domestic political implications of the case.

Literature on the remaining cases of the Southern Cone is sparse. The best sources of information on the Bolivian case are HRW (1992a; 1993a), Escobar (1987), Albarracín (1996), CAJ (1993: 114–117), Mayorga in McAdams (1997: 61–92), and the *Nunca Más* report for that country in Aguiló (1993). There is a dearth of work on Brazil. The first foreign piece was a short article by Dassin (1986a, b) on the impact of the Nunca Mais report (1985). Since then, the only other work done abroad on this case is Weschler (1990), which gives an excellent account of the preparations for the report. Less substantially, the Brazilian case is also assessed in Barahona de Brito (1991), Hamber (1997b), and, in more depth, in the first article looking at the case of a Brazilian *desaparecido* in an English-language journal (Serbin, 1998). More recently, with the resurgence of the matter in 1995, some Brazilians have written about the subject, including Mierelles Neto (1996) and Tavares de Almeida e Silva (n.d.), although these are in the form of unpublished working papers found on the Internet. HRW (1991d) also provides a report on the search for the bodies of the disappeared.

Similarly, the Paraguayan and Uruguayan cases have been largely ignored. For basic background information on Pargauay, there is HRW (1992c) and AI (1990). For Uruguay, the most complete analyses are the Weschler (1990) book, Barahona de Brito (1997), Roniger and Snazjder (1999). In Uruguay, there is a very partisan but interesting personal account by Araújo (1989), and the more scholarly analysis by Perelli (1987) on amnesties in Uruguayan political life. HRW (1989c), Burt (1989), and Varela (1989) provide good analyses of the amnesty law and the referendum campaign specifically. CUI (1989) examines the handling of the issue by the Sanguinetti administration, and Rial (1986) as well as Ramírez

(1989) look at civil–military relations in the early transitional period, with references to the issue of transitional justice and truth. The only study of a lawsuit is HRW (1991c), and, aside from Barahona de Brito, the only published work on the role of HROs is M. Loveman (1998). R. Goldman (1992) writes about the international legality of the amnesty law. Perhaps the best work on Uruguay has been done on the more social or psychosocial aspects of the question, as in the works by Roniger (1997), Sosnowski and Popkin (1993), and Bergero and Riati (1997).

Central America is better covered. An excellent general source for Central America is the journal *Estudios Centroamericanos*, which has regularly published articles on the subject. The only work on Honduras has been HRW (1989b; 1990b; 1994b), which look at the work of the Inter American Court in the country, impunity, and the truth report issued by the National Commissioner for the Protection of Human Rights, and AI (1992a). Grossman (1992) has done a detailed legal study of human rights litigation in Honduras, which reflects the historical importance of the IAHRC decision on the country. The HROs CODEHUCA and COFADEH both publish newsletters and working papers that offer useful updated information on accountability and other related issues.

The Salvadorean case has been dealt with quite thoroughly, given the unprecedented involvement of the United Nations. As usual, the best background accounts are by HRW (1990a; 1993b), although AI also has regular updates on the issue (1992a; 1993a). Popkin (2000) has written the most complete account of the peace and transitional justice processes. Tappatá de Valdéz in Boraine and Levy (1995: 66–79), Buergenthal (1994), Cardenal (1992) and Ensalaco (1994), who compares Chile with El Salvador, as well as Whitfield in Henkin (1998: 163–188) and Whitfield (1997), have focused on the truth commission and the report, published by the United Nations Security Council (1993). Like Whitfield (1997), Hayner (2000) offers an analysis of the Salvadorean and Guatemalan commissions. Dodson and Jackson (1997) look at how the peace process has affected the re-establishment or affirmation of the rule of law in the country. For more wide-ranging analyses that look at the transition process and the peace accords, there are the books by Johnstone (1995), and the articles by Bar-Yaacov (1995), Brody (1995), and Popkin in Roht-Arriaza (1995: 198–217). In addition, J. Moore (1991) does an interesting comparison and legal–political assessment of the amnesties granted as part of peace processes in Nicaragua and El Salvador. The weekly *El Salvador Proceso* is a useful source of background up-to-date information, and can be found at the website for the Central American University at http://www.uca.edu.sv/publica.

For Guatemala, there are the AI (1993b) and HRW (1994c; 1995a) reports, with the latter examining the IAHRC decision on a Guatemalan disappeared person, which, along with the Honduras decision, has been one of the most important in hemispheric human rights jurisprudential developments. Alvarado (1998), Franco and Kotler in Henkin (1998: 39–70), Whitfield (1997), and Wilson (1998) provide a good account of the transition process and accountability, Altoaguirre (1998) and Hayner (2000) analyse the truth commission's work, and La Rue in Sieder (1998: 173–180) argues for the 'right to truth' in Guatemala. CIEPRODH (1994) outlines the struggle to establish the truth, found in the report of the Human Rights Office of the Archbishop of Guatemala (ODHAG) (1998), the unofficial truth report, and the United Nations Security Council (1999), the official truth report. An account of the repression and responses to it is found in LAB (1999). EPICA/CHRLA (1996) provides an account of the efforts to locate and exhume the bodies of the disappeared by national and international HROs and forensic anthropologists. The books by Zur (1998) and L. Green (1999) on war widows provide accounts of trauma and the politics of memory among women of Mayan and rural origins. Finally, the attempt to implement truth and justice in Haiti is assessed by HRW (1995b; 1996a), as well as in Andreu in Sieder (1995a: 33–43), Bar-Yaacov (1995), Martin (1999), and Granderson in Henkin (1998: 227–256).

References

ABRAHAMS, FRED (1996). 'A Tenuous Separation of Powers', *Transition*, 2 (3): 51–53.

ACUÑA, CARLOS (1998). 'Transitional Justice in Argentina and Chile: A Never Ending Story?' Paper presented at the Mellon Seminar on Transitional Justice, Columbia University, 15 December.

—— and SMULOVITZ, CATARINA (1991). *¿Ni olvido ni perdón? Derechos humanos y tensiones cívico-militares en la transición argentina* (Buenos Aires: CEDES).

—— *et al.* (1995). *Juicio, castigos y memorias: derechos humanos y justicia en la política argentina* (Buenos Aires: Nueva Visión).

ADAM, HERBERT, and MOODLEY, KOGILA (1993). 'Political Violence, "Tribalism" and Inkatha', *Journal of Modern African Studies*, 30 (3): 485–497.

ADAMS, KIF AUGUSTINE (1993). 'What is Just? The Rule of Law and Natural Law in the Trial of Former East German Border Guards', *Stanford Journal of International Law*, 29 (2): 271–314.

ADELL, RAMÓN (1997). 'Manifestations et transition démocratique en Espagne', *Les Cahiers de la Sécurité Intérieure*, 27: 203–222.

ADLER, NANCI (1993). *Victims of Soviet Terror: The Story of the Memorial Movement* (Westport, Conn.: Praeger).

AGGER, INGER (1996). *Trauma and Healing under State Terrorism* (London: Zed Books).

AGÜERO, FELIPE (1995). *Militares, civiles y democracia* (Madrid: Alianza Editorial).

AGUILAR, PALOMA (1993). 'Los lugares de la memoria de la Guerra Civil en el franquismo. El Valle de los Caídos: la ambigüedad calculada', in Javier Tusell *et al.* (eds.), *El régimen de Franco, 1936–1975* (Madrid: UNED), 485–498.

—— (1995a). 'La amnistía y la memoria histórica de la Guerra Civil en la transición', in Javier Tusell *et al.* (eds.), *Historia de la transición y consolidación democrática en España* (Madrid: UNED), 3–13.

—— (1995b). 'Aproximaciones teóricas y analíticas al concepto de memoria histórica: breves reflexiones sobre la memoria histórica de la Guerra Civil española (1936–1939)', in Carlos Barros (ed.), *La Historia a Debate/Historia a Debate* (Santiago de Compostela: La Historia a Debate/Historia a Debate), 129–142.

—— (1996a). *Memoria y olvido de la Guerra Civil española* (Madrid: Alianza Editorial).

—— (1996b). 'La memòria de la guerra civil en la transició espanyola', *L'Avenç*, 207: 44–47.

—— (1996c). *Collective Memory of the Spanish Civil War: The Case of Political Amnesty in the Spanish Transition to Democracy*, Working Paper 85 (Madrid: Centro de Estudios Avanzados en Ciencias Sociales del Instituto Juan March de Estudios e Investigaciones).

—— (1996d). *Aproximaciones teóricas y analíticas al concepto de memoria histórica: la memoria histórica de la Guerra Civil española (1936–1939)*, Working Paper 196 (Madrid: Fundación Ortega y Gasset).

—— (1997a). 'La amnesia y la memoria: las movilizaciones por la amnistía en la transición a la democracia', in Rafael Pérez Ledesma and Rafael Cruz (eds.), *Cultura y acción colectiva en la España contemporánea* (Madrid: Alianza Editorial), 327–357.

—— (1997b). 'Collective Memory of the Spanish Civil War: The Case of the Political Amnesty in the Spanish Transition to Democracy', *Democratization*, 4 (4): 88–109.

—— (1997c). 'Consensos y controversias de la Guerra Civil y su memoria', *Libre Pensamiento*, 23: 28–30.

—— (1998a). 'La memoria, el olvido y la tergiversación histórica en el discurso nacionalista', in Javier Ugarte (ed.), *La transición en el País Vasco y España* (Vitoria: Universidad del País Vasco), 121–154.

—— (1998b). 'La peculiar evocación de la guerra civil por el nacionalismo vasco', *Cuadernos de Alzate*, 18: 21–39.

—— (1998c). 'The Memory of the Civil War in the Transition to Democracy: The Peculiarity of the Basque Case', *West European Politics*, 21 (4): 5–25.

—— (1998d). *La guerra civil española en el discurso nacionalista vasco: memorias peculiares para un aprendizaje político diferente*, Working Paper 397 (Madrid: Fundación Ortega y Gasset).

—— (1999a). 'The Memory of the Civil War in the Transition to Democracy: The Peculiarity of the Basque Case', in Paul Heywood (ed.), *Politics and Policy in Democratic Spain: No Longer Different?* (London: Frank Cass), 2–25.

—— (1999b). 'Agents of Memory: Spanish Civil War Veterans and Disabled Soldiers', in Jay Winter and Emmanuel Sivan (eds.), *War and Rememberance in the Twentieth Century* (Cambridge: Cambridge University Press), 84–103.

—— (1999c). *Institutional Legacies and Collective Memories: Stateness Problems in the Spanish Transition to Democracy*, Working Paper 7 (New York: Columbia University Institute of Latin American and Iberian Studies).

—— (1999d). 'La cultura política del País Vasco en el contexto español: legados institucionales y culturales de los procesos de cambio político', unpublished paper.

—— (2000). 'Memoria histórica y legados institucionales en los procesos de cambio político', *Revista Internacional de Filosofía Política*, 14: 31–46.

AGUILÓ, FEDERICO (1993). *Nunca Más para Bolívia* (Cochabamba: Asamblea Permanente de Derechos Humanos de Bolivia).

Ahumada, Eugenio, *et al.* (1989). *La memoria prohibida: las violaciones de los derechos humanos en Chile, 1973–1988* (Santiago: Pehuén).

AI (Amnesty International) (1975a). *Torture in Greece: The First Torturers' Trial* (London: AI).

—— (1975b). *Amnesty International Report. Mission to Spain* (London: AI).

—— (1977). *Amnesty International Report* (London: AI).

—— (1978). *Amnesty International Report* (London: AI).

—— (1979). *Amnesty International Report: The Death Penalty* (London: AI).

—— (1984). *Amnesty International Report: Torture* (London: AI).

—— (1985). *Spain: The Issue of Torture* (London: AI).

—— (1987). *Argentina: The Military Juntas and Human Rights, Report of the Trial of the Former Junta Members* (London: AI).

—— (1990). *Paraguay: Investigations into Past Human Rights Violations* (London: AI).

—— (1991). *Argentina: Presidential Pardon to Military Officers before Trial* (London: AI).

—— (1992a). *El Salvador Army Officers Sentenced to 30 Years for Killing Jesuit Priests* (London: AI).

—— (1992b). *Honduras: Disappearance in Honduras: A Wall of Silence and Indifference* (London: AI).

—— (1993a). *El Salvador: Peace without Justice* (London: AI-Index AMR 29/12/93).

—— (1993b). *Guatemala: Impunity a Question of Political Will* (London: AI).

—— (1995a). *Argentina: The Right to the Full Truth* (London: AI).

—— (1995b). *Sri Lanka: Time For Truth and Justice, Observations and Recommendations regarding the Commission Investigating Past Human Rights Violations* (London: AI-Index ASA 31/04/95).

—— (1996). *Angola: From War to What? No Reconciliation without Accountability* (London: AI).

—— (1999a). *East Timor: Justice and Accountability are Long Overdue* (London: AI).

—— (1999b). *Asian NGOs Call for Justice and Respect for Human Rights in Indonesia and East Timor* (London: AI).

—— (1999c). *East Timor: Amnesty International Calls for a Thorough, Independent and Effective Inquiry* (London: AI).

Akhavan, Payam (1998). 'Justice in the Hague, Peace in the Former Yugoslavia? A Commentary on the United Nations War Crimes Tribunal', *Human Rights Quarterly*, 20: 737–816.

Albarracín, Waldo (1996). 'La impunidad en Bolivia: los regímenes democráticos en Latinoamérica y la impunidad', paper presented at the Conference on Impunity and its Effects on Democratic Processes, Santiago, 14 December (www.derechos.org/koaga/xi/2/albarracin.html).

Alfonsín, Raul (1993). 'Never Again in Argentina', *Journal of Democracy*, 4 (1): 15–19.

Alizivatos, Nicos, and Diamandoros, P. Nikiforos (1997). 'Politics and the Judiciary in the Greek Transition to Democracy', in James McAdams (ed.), *Transitional Justice and the Rule of Law in New Democracies* (South Bend, Ind.: University of Notre Dame Press), 27–60.

ALLEN, JONATHAN (1999). 'Balancing Justice and Social Unity: Political Theory and the Idea of a Truth and Reconciliation Commission', *University of Toronto Law Journal*, 49 (4): 315–353.

ALMEIDA, DINIS DE (1978). *Ascensão, apogeu e queda do MFA* (Lisbon: Edições Sociais).

ALMEIDA, JOÃO FERREIRA DE (1998). 'Society and Values', in António Costa Pinto (ed.), *Modern Portugal* (Palo Alto: SPOSS), 146–161.

ALMOND, GABRIEL A., and GENKO, STEPHEN J. (1977). 'Clouds, Clocks, and the Study of Politics', *World Politics*, 29 (4): 489–522.

ALTOLAGUIRRE, M. (1998). 'Alcances y limitaciones de la Comisión para el Esclarecimiento Histórico de las Violaciones a los Derechos Humanos y los Hechos de Violencia que han Causado Sufrimiento a la Población Guatemalteca', in Rachel Sieder (ed.), *Guatemala after the Peace Accords* (London: Institute of Latin American Studies), 153–172.

ALVARADO, RICARDO (1998). *4 años de vigencia del acuerdo global sobre derechos humanos: ¿cumplimiento y/o transgresión?* (Guatemala: Fundación Friedrich Ebert).

ÁLVAREZ, JOSÉ E. (1996). 'Trial of the Century? Assessing the Case of Tadic before the International Criminal Tribunal of the Former Yugoslavia', *ILSA Journal of International and Comparative Law*, 3 (2): 613–662.

—— (1998). 'Rush to Closure: Lessons of the Tadic Judgement', *Michigan Law Journal*, 96 (7): 2031–2112.

—— (1999). 'Crimes of State, Crimes of Hate: Lessons from Rwanda', *Yale Journal of International Law*, 24 (2): 365–485.

AMERICAN UNIVERSITY JOURNAL OF INTERNATIONAL LAW AND POLICY (1990). 'Symposium: Transitions to Democracy and the Rule of Law', *American University Journal of International Law and Policy*, 5 (4): 498–1018.

AMIS, MARTIN (1991). *Time's Arrow* (New York: Vintage).

ANDERSON, BENEDICT (1991). *Imagined Communities: Reflections on the Origin and Spread of Nationalism* (London: Verso).

ANDERSON, JON LEE (1998). 'A Profile: The Dictator', *New Yorker*, 74 (19 October): 44–57.

ANDERSON, THOMAS P. (1971). *Matanza: El Salvador's Communist Revolt of 1932* (Nebraska: Lincoln Press).

ANDREU, FEDERICO (1995). 'The International Community in Haiti: Evidence of the New World Order', in Rachel Sieder (ed.), *Impunity in Latin America* (London: Institute of Latin American Studies), 33–43.

ANTZE, PAUL, and LAMBEK, MICHAEL (eds.) (1996). *Tense Past: Cultural Essays in Trauma and Memory* (New York: Routlege).

ARAÚJO, GERMÁN (1989). *Impunidad: Y sé todos los cuentos. Diálogo con Chury Iribarne* (Montevideo: Talleres Gráficos Coopren).

ARDITTI, RITA, and BRINTON LYKES, M. (1992). 'Recovering Identity: The Work of the Grandmothers of the Plaza de Mayo', *Women's Studies International Forum*, 15 (4): 461–471.

ARMONY, ARIEL C. (1997). *Argentina, the United States, and the Anti-Communist Crusade in Central America, 1977–1984* (Athens, Ohio: Ohio University Centre for International Studies).

ASMAL, KADER, ASMAL, LOUISE, and SURESH ROBERTS, RONALD (1996). *Reconciliation through Truth: A Reckoning of Apartheid's Criminal Governance* (Capetown: David Philip Publishers).

ASOCIACIÓN AMERICANAE DE JURISTAS (1988). *Argentina: Juicio a los militares, documentos secretos, decretos leyes y jurisprudencia* (Buenos Aires: Rama Argentina de la AAJ).

ATKINSON, DOREEN, and FRIEDMAN, STEVEN (1994). *The Small Miracle: South Africa's Negotiated Settlement* (Johannesburg: Ravan Press).

BACON, EDWIN (1994). *The Gulag at War: Stalin's Forced Labour System in the Light of Archives* (London: Macmillan).

BAENA DEL ALCÁZAR, MARIANO, and GARCÍA MADARIA, JOSÉ MARÍA (1982). *Normas políticas y administrativas de la transición, 1975–1978* (Madrid: Servicio Central de Publicaciones de Presidencia del Gobierno).

BAKKER, JEANNE L. (1989). 'The Defence of Obedience to Superior Orders: The Mens Rea Requirement', *American Journal of Criminal Law*, 17 (1): 55–71.

BALINT, JENNIFER L. (1997). 'Conflict, Conflict Victimisation and Legal Redress, 1945–1996', *Law and Contemporary Problems*, 59 (4): 231–247.

BALL, PATRICK, KOBRAK, PAUL, and SPIRER, HERBERT F. (1999). *State Violence in Guatemala, 1990–1996: A Quantitative Reflection* (Washington DC: AAAS/CIIDH).

BALLBÉ, MANUEL (1983). *Orden público y militarismo en la España constitucional (1812–1983)* (Madrid: Alianza Editorial).

BALOYRA, ENRIQUE (1982). *El Salvador in Transition* (Chapel Hill, NC: University of North Carolina Press).

BARAHONA DE BRITO, ALEXANDRA (1991). 'The Nunca Más Reports of Brazil, Argentina, Uruguay and Chile', unpublished paper.

—— (1993). 'Truth and Justice in the Transition to Democracy in Uruguay and Chile', *Parliamentary Affairs*, 46 (4).

—— (1997). *Human Rights and Democratization in Latin America: Uruguay and Chile* (Oxford: Oxford University Press).

—— (1999). 'The Human Rights Movement and Democratisation in Latin America', in Nicola Phillips and Nicola Burton (eds.), *Contemporary Latin American Politics*, i (Manchester: Manchester University Press).

—— (2000a). 'The Europeans, the Chileans and their General: An Unfinished Tale', *Revista Estratégia*, forthcoming.

—— (2000b). 'Passion, Constraint, Law and *Fortuna*: the Human Rights Challenge to Chilean Democracy', in Nigel Biggar (ed.), *Burying the Past: Making Peace and Doing Justice After Civil Conflict* (Washington DC: Georgetown University Press), forthcoming.

—— and PANIZZA, FRANCISCO (1998). 'Human Rights in Democratic Brazil: "A Lei Não Pega"', *Democratization*, 5 (4): 20–51.

BARANY, ZOLTAN (1992). 'East European Forces in Transitions and Beyond', *East European Quarterly*, 24 (1): 1–30.

BARCROFT, PETER A. (1993). 'The Presidential Pardon: A Flawed Solution', *Human Rights Law Journal*, 14 (11–12): 361–394.

BARKAN, ELAZAR (1996). 'Payback Time: Restitution and the Moral Economy of Nations', *Tikkun*, 1 (5): 52–57.

BARNES, JULIAN (1992). *The Porcupine* (London: Picador).

BARRETO, ANTÓNIO (1999). 'Portugal: Democracy through Europe', in Jeffrey J. Anderson (ed.), *Regional Integration and Democracy: Expanding on the European Experience* (Lanham, Md: Rowman & Littlefield), 95–122.

BAR-YAACOV, NOMI (1995). 'Diplomacy and Human Rights: The Role of Human Rights in Conflict Resolution in El Salvador and Haiti', *Fletcher Forum of International Affairs*, 19 (2): 47–64.

BASSIOUNI, CHERIF (1998). *The Statute of the International Criminal Court* (Ardsley, NY: Transnational Publishers).

—— and MANIKAS, PETER (1996). *The Law of the International Criminal Tribunal for the Former Yugoslavia* (Ardsley, NY: Transnational Publishers).

BASTIDA, FRANCISCO J. (1986). *Jueces y franquismo: el pensamiento político del Tribunal Supremo en la Dictadura* (Barcelona: Ariel).

BATISTA, ANTONI (1995). *Brigada Social* (Barcelona: Empúries).

BATTIS, ULRICH *et al.* (1992). *Vergangenheitsbewältigung durch Recht* (Berlin: Duncker & Humblot).

BELINFANTE, A. (1978). *In plaats van bijltjesdag: de geschiedenis van de Bijzondere Rechtspleging na de Tweede Wereldoorlog* (The History of the Purge in Postwar Holland) (Assen: Van Gorcum).

BELTRÁN, MIGUEL (1985). *Los funcionarios ante la reforma de la administración* (Madrid: Centro de Investigaciones Sociológicas/Siglo XXI).

—— (1994). *Política y administración bajo el Franquismo: la reforma administrativa y los Planes de Desarrollo*, Working Paper 53 (Madrid: Instituto Juan March).

BENCE, GYORGY (1990). 'Political Justice in Postcommunist Societies: The Case of Hungary', *Praxis International*, 10 (2): 80–89.

BENET, JUAN (1976). *Qué fue la Guerra Civil* (Barcelona: La Gaya Ciencia).

BENOMAR, JAMAL (1993). 'Confronting the Past: Justice after Transitions', *Journal of Democracy*, 4 (1): 3–14.

BERAT, LYNN (1993). 'Prosecuting Human Rights Violators from a Predecessor Regime: Guidelines for a Transformed South Africa', *Boston College Third World Law Journal*, 13 (2): 199–232.

—— and YOSSI SHAIN (1995). 'Retribution or Truth Telling in South Africa: Legacies of the Transitional Phase', *Law and Social Inquiry*, 20 (1): 163–189.

BERGERO, ADRIANA J., and REATI, FERNANDO (eds.) (1997). *Memoria colectiva y políticas de olvido: Argentina y Uruguay, 1970–1990* (Rosario, Argentina: Viterbo Editora).

BERMEO, NANCY (1997). 'Myths of Moderation: Confrontation and Conflict during Democratic Transitions', *Comparative Politics*, 29 (3): 305–322.

BERTSCHI, CHARLES C. (1995). 'Lustration and the Transition to Democracy: The Cases of Poland and Bulgaria', *East European Quarterly*, 2 (4): 435–452.

BHUTA, NEHAL (1999). 'Justice without Borders? Prosecuting General Pinochet', *Melbourne University Law Review*, 23 (2): 499–512.

BIGGAR, NIGEL (ed.) (2000). *Burying the Past: Making Peace and Doing Justice after Civil Conflict* (Washington DC: Georgetown University Press), forthcoming.

BINDNAGEL, J. D. (ed.) (1999). *Washington Conference on Holocaust Era Assets* (Washington DC: US Department of State and United States Holocaust Memorial).

BIRD, EDWARD, and GARDA, ZUREIDA (1997). 'Reporting the Truth Commission: Analysis of the Media Coverage of the Truth and Reconciliation Commission of South Africa', *Gazette*, 59 (4–5): 331–343.

BLACK, GEORGE (1984). *Garrison Guatemala* (London: Zed Books).

BLANKENBURG, ERHARD (1995). 'The Purge of Lawyers after the Breakdown of the East German Communist Regime', *Law and Social Inquiry*, 20 (1): 223–245.

BLOOMFIELD, SIR KENNETH (1998). *We Will Remember Them: Report of the Northern Ireland Victims Commissioner* (Belfast: HMSO Stationery Office).

BLUM, YEHUDA Z. (1998). 'Restitution of Jewish Cultural Property Looted in World War Two: To Whom?', *Leiden Journal of International Law*, 11 (2): 257–274.

BODEI, REMO (1993). 'Farewell to the Past: Historical Memory, Oblivion and Collective Identity', *Philosophy and Social Criticism*, 18 (4): 251–265.

—— (1995). 'Historical Memory and European Identity', *Philosophy and Social Criticism*, 21 (4): 1–13.

BOED, ROMAN A. (1999). 'An Evaluation of the Legality and Efficacy of Lustration as a Tool of Transitional Justice', *Colombia Journal of Transnational Law*, 37 (2): 357–402.

BOHRER, KARL HEINZ (1992). 'Deutsche Revolution und protestantische Mentalität', *Merkur*, 46: 958–64.

BOND, G. C. and A. GITTIAM (eds.) (1994). *Social Construction of the Past: Representation as Power* (London: Routledge).

BORAINE, ALEX, and LEVY, JANET (eds.) (1995). *The Healing of a Nation* (Capetown: Justice in Transition).

—— LEVY, JANET, and SCHEFFER, RONEL (eds.) (1994). *Dealing with the Past: Truth and Reconciliation in South Africa* (Capetown: Institute for Democracy in South Africa).

BORER, THOMAS G. (1999). 'The Assets of the Holocaust: The Swiss Perspective', *Whittier Law Review*, 20 (3): 649–658.

BORNEMAN, JOHN (1997). *Settling Accounts: Violence, Justice, and Accountability in Postsocialist Europe* (Princeton: Princeton University Press).

BORÓN, ATILIO (1991). 'Los axiomas de Anillaco: la visión de la política en el pensamiento y en la acción de Carlos Saúl Menem', in Oscar

Martínez *et al. El Menemato: Radiografía de dos años de gobierno de Carlos Menem* (Buenos Aires: Ediciones Buena Letra), 49–83.

Boston College Third World Law Journal (1992). 'Accountability for State Sponsored Human Rights Abuses in Eastern Europe and the Soviet Union: Panel Discussion'. *Boston College Third World Law Journal*, 12 (2).

Bourdieu, Pierre (1991). *Language and Symbolic Power* (Cambridge: Polity Press).

Boutros Ghali, Boutros (1996). *The United Nations and Rwanda, 1993–1996* (Ardsley, NY: Transnational Publishers).

Boyarin, Jonathan (1994). *Remapping Memory: The Politics of Time Space* (Minneapolis: University of Minnesota Press).

Boyle, Julia K. (1998). 'The International Obligation to Prosecute Human Rights Violations: Spain's Jurisdiction over Argentina's Dirty War Participants', *Hastings International and Comparative Law Review*, 22 (1): 187–195.

Bozzoli, Belinda (1998). 'Public Ritual and Private Transition: The Truth Commission in Alexandra Township', *African Studies*, 57 (2): 167–196.

Bracegirdle, Alan (1999). 'Re: Pinochet', *New Zealand Law Journal*, 1: 272–296.

Brackman, A. C. (1987). *The Other Nuremberg: The Untold Story of the Tokyo War Crimes Trials* (Westport, CT: Greenwood Press).

Bradley, Curtis, and Goldsmith, Jack L. (1999). 'Pinochet and International Human Rights Litigation', *Michigan Law Review*, 97 (7): 2129–2184.

Bradley, Evelyn (1998). 'In Search for Justice: A Truth and Reconciliation Commission for Rwanda', *Journal of International Law and Practise*, 7 (2): 129–158.

Branco, Jorge Freitas, and Oliveira, Luísa Tiago (1993). *Ao encontro do povo: 1-A missão* (Oeiras: Celta).

Braude, Claudia (1996). 'The Archbishop, the Private Detective and the Angel of History: The Production of South African Public Memory and the Truth and Reconciliation Commission', *Current Writing*, 8 (2): 39–65.

Bren, Paulina (1993). 'Lustration in the Czech and Slovak Republics', *RFE/RL Research Report*, 2 (29): 16–22.

Brett, Sebastian (1992). *Chile. A Time of Reckoning: Human Rights and the Judiciary* (Geneva: International Commission of Jurists).

Brickhill, Jeremy (1995). 'Making Peace with the Past: War Victims and the Work of the Mafela Trust', in Nawaki Bebe and Terrence Ranger (eds.), *Soldiers in Zimbabwe's Liberation War* (Harare: Zimbabwe University Publications), 163–173.

Brody, Reed (1995). 'The United Nations and Human Rights in El Salvador's "Negotiated Revolution"', *Harvard Human Rights Journal*, 8: 153–178.

—— (1999). 'The Pinochet Precedent: Changing the Equation of Repression', *NACLA Report on the Americas*, 32 (6): 16–30.

Brody, Reed, and González, Felipe (1997). 'Nunca Más: An Analysis of International Instruments on Disappearances', *Human Rights Quarterly*, 19 (2): 365–405.

Bromke, Adam (1993). 'Postcommunist Countries: Challenges and Problems', in Regina Cowen Karp (ed.), *Central and Eastern Europe* (Oxford: Oxford University Press), 17–44.

Bronkhorst, Daan (1995). *Truth and Reconciliation: Obstacles and Opportunities for Human Rights* (Amsterdam: Amnesty International Dutch Section).

Brossat, Alain, Sonia Combe, Jean-Ives Potel, and Jean-Charles Szurek (eds.) (1990). *A l'Est la memoire retrouveé* (Paris: La Découverte).

Bruneau, Thomas, and Macleod, A. (1986). *Parties in Contemporary Portugal: Parties and the Consolidation of Democracy* (Boulder, Colo.: Lynne Rienner).

Brysk, Alison (1993). 'From Above and Below: Social Movements, the International System and Human Rights in Argentina', *Comparative Political Studies*, 26 (3): 259–285.

—— (1994a). *The Politics of Human Rights in Argentina: Protest, Change and Democratization* (Stanford: Stanford University Press).

—— (1994b). 'The Politics of Measurement: The Contested Count of the Disappeared in Argentina', *Human Rights Quarterly*, 16 (4): 676–692.

Buck, Marcus (1998). 'The Exemplary Transition from Authoritarianism: Some Notes on the Legacy of Undemocratic Decision-making in Spain', in Stein Ugelvik Larsen (ed.), *Modern Europe after Fascism, 1943–1980s* (Boulder, Colo.: Social Science, East European Monographs), 1607–1635.

Buergenthal, Thomas (1994). 'The United Nations Truth Commission for El Salvador', *Vanderbilt Journal of Transnational Law*, 27 (3): 497–544.

—— Norris, Robert, and Shelton, Dinah (1986). *Protecting Human Rights in the Americas: Selected Problems* (Arlington, Va: N. P. Engel).

Burger, Josef (1992). 'Politics of Restitution in Czechoslovakia', *East European Quarterly*, 26 (4): 485–498.

Burgess, John P. (1992a). 'Coming to Terms with the East German Past', *First Things*, 21: 27–35.

—— (1992b). 'Notes from East Berlin: Coming to Terms with the Past', *Occasional Papers on Religion in Eastern Europe*, 12 (5): 19–30.

Burt, Jo Marie (1989). *El Pueblo Decide: A Brief History of the Referendum against Impunity In Uruguay* (Montevideo: Servicio de Paz y Justicia).

Buruma, Ian (1994). *The Wages of Guilt: Memories of War in Germany and Japan* (London: Jonathan Cape).

Byrne, Hugh (1996). *El Salvador's Civil War: A Study of Revolution* (Boulder, Colo.: Westview Press).

CAJ (Comisión Andina de Juristas) (1993). *Administración de justicia y derechos humanos* (Lima, Perú: CAJ).

Calloni, Stella (1999). *Los Años del lobo: Operación Cóndor* (Buenos Aires: Ediciones Continente).

Cardenal, Rodolfo (1992). 'Justice in Post-Cold War El Salvador: The Role of the Truth Commission', *Journal of Third World Studies*, 9 (2): 313–338.

Carmack, Robert (1988). *Harvest of Violence: The Mayan Indians and the Guatemalan Crisis* (London: University of Oklahoma Press).

Carnes, Lord, Hollander, Paul, and Tamas, Gaspar M. (1995). 'How Can We Reconcile Communist and Nazi Legacies? Conflicting Moral Reassessments of Nazism and Communism. The Nazi Past of the Two Germanies. Recent German Nationalism', *Partisan Review*, 62 (4): 579–606.

Carrillo, Santiago, and Sánchez-Montero, Simón (1977). *Partido Comunista de España* (Bilbao: Albia).

Carter, Christina E., and Davidson, Rus (1997). 'Human Rights on the Internet: A Select Bibliography of Web Resources', *References Services Review*, 25 (1): 51–60.

Carver, Richard (1989). *Zimbabwe: A Break with the Past? Human Rights and Political Unity* (New York: Human Rights Watch).

—— (1990). 'Called to Account: How African Governments Investigate Human Rights Violations', *African Affairs*, 89 (3): 391–415.

—— (1993). 'Zimbabwe: Drawing a Line through the Past', *Journal of African Law*, 37 (1): 69–81.

Casals, Xavier (1998). *La tentación neofascista en España* (Barcelona: Plaza & Janés).

Cassell, Douglass (1993). 'International Truth Commissions and Justice', *Aspen Institute Quarterly*, 5 (3): 69–90.

—— (1996). 'Lessons from the Americas: Guidelines for International Response to Amnesties for Atrocities', *Law and Contemporary Problems*, 59 (4): 197–230.

Castells, Miguel *et al.* (1978). *Democracia: sí, no* (San Sebastián: Ediciones Vascas).

CCCF (Cámara de lo Criminal y Correccional Federal) (1997). *Privaciones ilegales de libertad en el centro clandestino de detención Club Atlético* (Buenos Aires: CCCF).

CEIPRODH (Centro de Investigación, Estudio y Promoción de los Derechos Humanos en Guatemala) (1994). *La búsqueda de la verdad* (Guatemala City: Editorial Tucur).

Cepl, Vojtech (1991). 'A Note on the Restitution of Property in Postcommunist Czechoslovakia', *Journal of Communist Studies*, 7 (3): 368–375.

—— (1992a). 'Ritual Sacrifices', *East European Constitutional Review*, 1 (1): 24–26.

—— (1992b). 'Retribution and Restitution in Czechoslovakia', *Archives Europeénnes de Sociologie*, 33 (1): 202–214.

—— and Gillis, Mark (1994). 'Making Amends after Communism', *Journal of Democracy*, 7 (4): 118–124.

CHAO, RAMÓN (1976). *Después de Franco, España* (Madrid: Felmar).

CHILDS, DAVID, and POPPLEWELL, RICHARD (1996). *The Stasi: The East German Intelligence and Security Service* (New York: New York University Press).

CHIPASULA, JAMES, and CHILIVUMBO, ALIFEYO (eds.) (1993). *South Africa's Dilemmas in the Post-Apartheid Era* (Lanham, Md: University Press of America).

CHRISTENSON, RON (1986). *Political Trials: Gordian Knots in the Law* (New Brunswick, NJ: Transaction Books).

CIANCAGLINI, SERGIO, and GRANOVSKY, MARTÍN (1995). *Nada más que la verdad: el juicio a las juntas. La guerra sucia desde el golpe hasta las autocríticas militares* (Buenos Aires: Planeta).

CIIR (Catholic Institute of International Relations) (1996). *South Africa: Breaking New Ground* (London: CIIR).

CISSE, CATHERINE (1997). 'The International Tribunals for the Former Yugoslavia and Rwanda: Some Elements for Comparison', *Transnational Law and Contemporary Problems*, 7 (1): 103–128.

—— (1998). 'The End of a Culture of Impunity in Rwanda? Prosecution of Genocide and War Crimes Before Rwandan Courts and the International Criminal Tribunal for Rwanda', *Yearbook of International Humanitarian Law*, 1: 161–204.

CLAPHAM, ANDREW, and MARTIN, FLORENCE (1998). 'Smaller Missions, Bigger Problems', in Alice Henkin (ed.), *Honoring Human Rights: From Peace to Justice* (New York: Aspen Institute), 133–149.

CLAUDE, RICHARD (1983). 'Torture on Trial: The Case of Joelito Filártiga and the "Clinic of Hope"', *Human Rights Quarterly*, 5 (3): 275–295.

CLEARY, EDWARD L. (1997). *The Struggle for Human Rights in Latin America* (Westport, Conn.: Praeger).

CNRR (Comisión Nacional de Reparación y Reconciliación) (1996). *Informe sobre calificación de víctimas de violaciones de derechos humanos y de la violencia política* (Santiago: CNRR).

CNVR (Comisión Nacional de la Verdad y la Reconciliación) (1991). *Informe de la Comisión Nacional de la Verdad y la Reconciliación* (Santiago: Ediciones del Ornitorrinco).

COCHRANE, JAMES, DE GRUCHY, JOHN, and MARTIN, STEPHEN (eds.) (1999). *Facing the Truth: South African Faith Communities and the Truth and Reconciliation Commission* (Athens, Ohio: Ohio University Press).

COHEN, STANLEY (1995). 'State Crimes of Previous Regimes: Knowledge, Accountability and the Policing of the Past', *Law and Social Inquiry*, 20 (1): 7–50.

COHEN, STEPHEN (1983). 'The Victims Return: Gulag Survivors of the Soviet Union after Stalin', unpublished paper.

—— (1985). *Rethinking the Soviet Experience: Politics and History Since 1917* (New York: Oxford University Press).

COLOMER, JOSEP MARÍA (1990). *El arte de la manipulación política* (Barcelona: Anagrama).

—— (1996). 'Venganza democrática o reconciliación', *Claves*, 60: 22–30.

—— (1998). *La transición a la democracia: el modelo español* (Barcelona: Anagrama).

COMISSO, ELLEN (1995). 'Legacies of the Past or New Institutions? The Struggle over Restitution in Hungary', *Comparative Political Studies*, 28 (2): 200–238.

CONADEP (Comisión Nacional sobre la Desaparición de Personas) (1984). *Nunca Más Argentina: informe sobre la desaparición forzada de personas* (Buenos Aires: CONADEP).

CONAN, ERIC, and ROUSSO, HENRY (1994). *Vichy: un passé que ne passe pas* (Paris: Fayard).

CONNERTON, PAUL (1989). *How Societies Remember* (New York: Cambridge University Press).

CONOT, ROBERT (1983). *Justice at Nuremberg* (London: Weidenfield & Nicholson).

CONQUEST, ROBERT (1990). *The Great Terror: A Reassessment* (London: Pimlico).

CORRADI, JUAN E., WEISS, PATRICIA, and GARRETÓN, MANUEL ANTONIO (1992). *Fear at the Edge: State Terror and Resistance in Latin America* (Berkeley: University of California Press).

CORREA SUTIL, JORGE (1887). '"No Victorious Army Has Ever Been Prosecuted . . .": The Unsettled Story of Transitional Justice in Chile', in James McAdams (ed.), *Transitional Justice and the Rule of Law in New Democracies* (South Bend, Ind.: Notre Dame University Press), 123–154.

—— (1992). 'Dealing with Past Human Rights Violations: The Chilean Case after Dictatorship', *Notre Dame Law Review*, 67 (5): 1455–1485.

COTARELO, RAMÓN (ed.) (1992). *Transición política y consolidación democrática: España, 1975–1986* (Madrid: Centro de Investigaciones Sociológicas).

COURTOIS, STÉPHANE *et al.* (1997). *Le livre noir du communisme: crimes, terreur et répression* (Paris: Robert Laffont).

CRAVERI, MARTA (*c.* 1994). 'The Strikes of Norilsk and Vorkuta Camps and their Role in the Breakdown of the Stalinist Forced Labour System', unpublished paper.

—— and KHLEVNYUK, OLEG (1995). 'Krizis Ekonomiki MVD konets 1940–1950 gody', *Cahiers du Monde russe*, 34 (1–2): 179–90.

CRAWFORD, KATHRYN LEE (1990). 'Due Obedience and the Rights of Victims: Argentina's Transition to Democracy', *Human Rights Quarterly*, 12 (1): 17–52.

CRELINSTEN, RONALD D. (1993). *After the Fall: Prosecuting Perpetrators of Gross Human Rights Violations*, Pioom Report (Leiden: Leiden University Press).

CROCKER, DAVID A. (n.d). *Transitional Justice and International Civil Society*, Working Paper 13 (College Park, Md: National Commission on Civic Renewal).

—— (1998). 'Transitional Justice and International Civil Society: Toward a Normative Framework', *Constellations*, 5 (4): 492–517.

CROCKER, DAVID A. (1999). 'Reckoning with Past Wrongs: A Normative Framework', *Ethics and International Affairs*, 13: 43–64.

CRUZADO, MIGUEL A. (1977). *Partidos políticos y economía: 22 alternativas para el futuro* (Madrid: Akal).

CSCE (Commission on Security and Co-operation in Europe) (1993a). *Human Rights and Democratization in Unified Germany* (Washington DC: CSCE).

—— (1993b). *Human Rights and Democratization in Bulgaria* (Washington DC: CSCE).

—— (1994). *Human Rights and Democratization in Albania* (Washington DC: CSCE).

CUI (Centro Uruguayo Independiente) (1989). *1985–1989: Impulso democrático, bloqueo conservador* (Montevideo: CUI).

CUYA, ESTEBAN (1997). 'Las comisiones de verdad en América Latina', *América Indígena*, 57 (2): 167–212.

DAHL, HANS FREDRIK (1998). 'The Purges in Denmark and Norway after World War II', paper presented at the Mellon Seminar on Transitional Justice, Columbia University, 17 November.

D'AMATO, ANTHONY A. (1994). 'Peace vs. Accountability in Bosnia', *American Journal of International Law*, 88 (3): 500–505.

D'ANDREA MOHR, JOSÉ LUIS (1999). *Memoria debida* (Buenos Aires: Colihue).

DANNER, MARK (1993). *The Massacre at El Mozote* (New York: Vintage Books).

DANOPOULOS, CONSTANTINE P. (1991). 'Democratizing the Military: Lessons from Mediterranean Europe', *West European Politics*, 14 (4): 25–41.

DARSKI, JOZEF (1992). 'Police Agents in the Transition Period', *Uncaptive Minds*, 4 (4): 15–28.

—— (1993a). 'Decommunization in Eastern Europe', *Uncaptive Minds*, 6 (1): 73–82.

—— (1993b). 'Decommunization: The Case of Lithuania', *Uncaptive Minds*, 4 (1): 78–81.

DASSIN, JOAN (1986a). 'Time up for Torturers: A Human Rights Dilemma for Brazil', *NACLA Report on the Americas*, 20 (2): 2–6.

—— (1986b). 'Introduction to the Brazilian Edition', in *Torture in Brazil: A Report by the Archdiocese of Sao Paulo* (Petrópolis: Editora Vozes), 3–9.

DAVIES, R. W. (1997). *Soviet History in the Yeltsin Era* (London: Macmillan).

DEÁK, ISTVAN (1995). 'A Fatal Compromise? Debate over Collaboration and Resistance in Hungary', *East European Politics and Societies*, 9 (2): 209–233.

—— GROSS, JAN T., and JUDT, TONY (eds.) (2000). *The Politics of Retribution in Europe: World War II and its Aftermath* (Princeton, NJ: Princeton University Press).

DE GREIFF, PABLO (1996). 'Trial and Punishment, Pardon and Oblivion: On Two Inadequate Policies for the Treatment of Former Human Rights Abusers', *Philosophy and Social Criticism*, 22: 93–111.

Del Águila, Rafael, and Montoro, Ricardo (1984). *El discurso político de la transición española* (Madrid: Centro de Investigaciones Sociológicas).

Delgado, Julián (1996). *Prietas las filas: recuerdos de un capitán de los grises* (Barcelona: Editorial Libros PM).

Deutscher Bundestag (ed.) (1995). *Materialien der Enquete-Kommission 'Aufarbeitung von Geschichte und Folgen der SED-Diktatur in Deutschland*, i–ix (Frankfurt/Main: Suhrkamp).

Devaty, Stanslav (1991). 'The Files Weren't Destroyed', *Uncaptive Minds*, 4 (1): 56–69.

De Waal, Victor (1990). *The Politics of Reconciliation: Zimbabwe's First Decade* (London: Hurst).

Diamond, Larry (1994). 'Toward Democratic Consolidation', *Journal of Democracy* 5 (3): 4–17.

Díaz Coludrero, José Luis, and Abella, Mónica (1987). *Punto final: amnistía o voluntad popular* (Buenos Aires: Puntosur).

Dimitrov, Hristo D. (1999). 'The Bulgarian Constitutional Court and its Interpretative Jurisdiction', *Columbia Journal of Transnational Law*, 37 (2): 459–506.

Dodson, Michael J., and Jackson, Donald W. (1997). 'Re-inventing the Rule of Law: Human Rights in El Salvador', *Democratization*, 4 (4): 110–134.

Domenico, Roy Palmer (1991). *Italian Fascists on Trial, 1943–1948* (Chapel Hill, NC: North Carolina University Press).

Dorfman, Ariel (1991). *Death and the Maiden* (New York: Penguin).

Downs, Charles (1989). *Revolution at the Grassroots: Community Organisations in the Portuguese Revolution* (Albany, NY: State University of New York Press).

Drinian, Robert, and Teresa T. Kuo (1993). 'Putting the World's Oppressors on Trial: The Torture Victim Protection Act', *Human Rights Quarterly*, 15 (3): 605–624.

Dubow, Saul (1995). *Scientific Racism in Modern South Africa*. (Cambridge: Cambridge University Press).

Dugard, John (1978). *Human Rights and the South African Legal Order*. (Princeton: Princeton University Press).

Dullah, Omar (1994). 'Building a New Future', in Alex Boraine and Janet Levy (eds.), *The Healing of a Nation* (Capetown: Justice in Transition), 2–8.

Dunkerley, James (1994). *The Pacification of Central America* (London: Verso).

Durán Muñoz, Rafael (1997). *Acciones colectivas y transiciones a la democracia: España y Portugal, 1974–1977* (Madrid: Instituto Juan March de Estudios e Investigaciones).

Dussel, Inés, Finocchio, Silvia, and Gojman, Silvia (1997). *Haciendo memoria en el país del nunca más*. (Buenos Aires: Eudeba).

du Toit, André (1998a). 'Perpetrator Findings as Artificial Evenhandedness? The TRC's Contested Judgements of Moral and Political Accountability for Gross Human Rights Violations', unpublished paper.

du Toit, André (1998b). 'Transitional Justice in South Africa', paper presented at the Mellon Seminar on Transitional Justice, Columbia University.

Dvorakova, Vladimira, and Kunc, Jiri (1997). 'Los desafíos de la transición checoslovaca', *Revista de Estudios Políticos*, 95: 271–293.

Dwyer, Susan (1999). 'Reconciliation for Realists', *Ethics and International Affairs*, 13: 65–81.

Dyzenhaus, David (1998). *Judging the Judges, Judging Ourselves: Truth, Reconciliation and the Apartheid Legal Order* (Oxford: Hart Publishing).

—— (1999). 'Balancing Justice and Social Unity: Political Theory and the Idea of a Truth and Reconciliation Commission', *University of Toronto Law Journal*, 49 (3): 315–353.

EAAF (Equipo Argentino de Antropología Forense) (nd). *Brazil: An Investigation into the Causes of Death and Identities of Disappeared Persons*. (at: http://www.eaaf.org.ar/brazil eng.htm).

EAFG (Equipo de Antropología Forense de Guatemala) (1995). *Las masacres en Rabinal: Estudio histórico antropológico de las masacres de Plan de Sánchez, Chichupac y Río Negro* (Guatemala: EAFG).

Edelenbosch, Carla (1994). 'Human Rights Violations: A Duty to Prosecute?' *Leiden Journal of International Law*, 7 (2): 5–22.

Edelstein, Jillian (1999). 'The Truth Commission', *Granta*, 66: 107–146.

Egeland, J. (1982). *Humanitarian Initiatives against Political 'Disappearances': A Study of the Status and Potential of International Humanitarian and Human Rights Instruments and the Role of the International Red Cross in Protecting against the Practise of Disappearances* (Geneva: Henry Dunant Institute).

Einhorn, Bruce J., Sinai, Arthur, Felde, Kitty (1997). 'The Prosecution of War Criminals and Violators of Human Rights in the US', *Whittier Law Review*, 19 (2): 281–978.

Ellis, Mark S. (1997). 'Purging the Past: The Current State of Lustration Laws in the Former Communist Bloc', *Law and Contemporary Problems*, 59 (4): 182–196.

—— Morris, Madeline, and Schlunk, Angelika (1998). 'Accountability and Redress: Guidelines for the Handling of Genocide, War Crimes, Crimes against Humanity and other Serious Human Rights Violations', *ILSA Journal of International and Comparative Law*, 4 (2): 407–422.

Ellis, Stephen (1998). 'The Historical Significance of South Africa's Third Force', *Journal of South African Studies*, 24 (2): 261–299.

Elster, Jon (1992). 'On Doing What One Can: An Argument against Postcommunist Restitution and Retribution', *Eastern European Constitutional Review*, 1 (2): 15–16.

—— (1995). 'On Doing What One Can: An Argument against Postcommunist Restitution and Retribution', in Niel J. Kritz (ed.), *Transitional Justice: How Emerging Democracies Reckon with Former Regimes*, i (Washington DC: US Institute of Peace Press), 566–568.

—— (1998). 'Coming to Terms with the Past: A Framework for the Study of Justice in the Transition to Democracy', *Archives Europeénes de Sociologie*, 39 (1): 7–48.

—— Offe, Claus, and Preuss, Ulrich K. (1998). *Institutional Design in Postcommunist Societies: Rebuilding the Ship at Sea* (New York: Cambridge University Press).

Engelbrekt, Kjell (1990). 'Uncovering Communist Atrocities', *Report on Eastern Europe*, 1 (25): 5–9.

—— (1991). 'The Lasting Influence of the Secret Services', *Report on Eastern Europe*, 2 (29): 5–9.

—— (1992). 'Bulgaria's Communist Legacy: Settling Old Scores', *RFE/RL Research Report*, 1 (28): 6–10.

—— (1993). 'Bulgaria: The Weakening of Postcommunist Illusions', *RFE/RL Research Report*, 2 (1): 78–83.

—— (1994). 'Bulgaria's State Security Archives: Toward a Compromise?' *RFE/RL Research Report*, 3 (5): 21–27.

Ensalaco, Mark (1994). 'Truth Commissions for Chile and El Salvador: A Report and Assessment', *Human Rights Quarterly*, 16 (4): 656–675.

EPICA/CHRLA (1996). *Unearthing the Truth: Exhuming a Decade of Terror in Guatemala* (Washington DC: EPICA).

Escobar, Carlos (1987). 'El rol de las fuerzas armadas en el proceso democratico', in René Mayorga (ed.), *Democracia a la deriva: dilemas de la participación y concertación social en Bolivia* (La Paz: CLACSO/CERES), 317–354.

Esteve, Francisco (1977). *Manual del elector* (Barcelona: Ediciones Mayler).

Fahidi, Gergely (1994). 'Paying for the Past: The Politics and Economics of Compensation', *Hungarian Quarterly*, 35 (136): 54–62.

Falla, Ricardo (1994). *Massacres in the Jungle: Ixcán, Guatemala, 1975–1982* (Boulder, Colo.: Westview Press).

Farer, Tom (ed.) (1996). *Beyond Sovereignty: Collectively Defending Democracy in the Americas* (Baltimore: Johns Hopkins University Press).

Feitlowitz, Marguerite (1998). *A Lexicon of Terror: Argentina and the Legacies of Torture* (Oxford: Oxford University Press).

Fejtö, François (1992). *La findes démocraties populaires* (Paris: Seuil).

FIDH (Federation Internationale des Ligues des Droits de l'Homme and Human Rights Watch) (1993). *Violations massives et systematiques des droits de l'homme despuis le 1er Octobre 1990* (Paris: FIDH).

—— (1994). *Comission Internationale d'Enquête sur les Violations des Droits de l'homme depuis de 21 Octobre 1983* (Paris: FIDH).

Fieber, Hans-Joachim, and Reichmann, Johannes (eds.) (1995). *'Komitess für Gerechtigkeit': Erwartungen, Meinungen, Dokumente* (Frankfurt/Main: Verlag für Interkulturelle Kommunikation).

Ferretti, Maria (1995). 'La Memoire refouleé: la Russie devant le passé Stalinien', *Annals*, 50 (6): 1237–1257.

Figuero, Javier *et al.* (1976). *Las reformas urgentes* (Madrid: Taller Ediciones Josefina Betancor).

Finkielkraut, Alain (1992). *Remembering in Vain: The Klaus Barbie Trial and Crimes against Humanity* (New York: Columbia University Press).

Fischer, Barry A. (1999). 'No Roads Lead to Rome: The Fate of the Romani People under the Nazis and in Postwar Restitution', *Whittier Law Review*, 20 (3): 513–546.

Fogelsong, Todd (1997). 'The Reform of Criminal Justice and Evolution of Judicial Dependence in Late Soviet Russia', in Solomon, Peter H. (ed.), *Reforming Justice in Russia, 1864–1996* (Armonk, NY: M. E. Sharpe), 282–324.

Foner, Eric (1995). 'We Must Forget the Past: History in the New South Africa', *Yale Review*, 83 (2): 1–17.

Forest, Eva (1978). 'Nuevas formas de represión en la democracia', in Miguel de Castells *et al.*, *Democracia. Sí/No* (San Sebastián: Ediciones Vascas).

Fox, Hazel (1999a). 'The Pinochet Case #3', *International and Comparative Law Quarterly*, 48 (3): 687–702.

—— (1999b). 'The First Pinochet Case: Immunity of a Former Head of State', *International and Comparative Law Quarterly*, 48 (1): 207–228.

Frei, Norbert (1996). *Vergangenheitspolitik: Die Anfänge der Bundesrepublik und die NS-Vergangenheit* (Munich: C. H. Beck).

Friedman, Steven (1993). *The Long Journey: South Africa's Quest for a Negotiated Settlement* (Johannesburg: Ravan Press).

Froment, Pascale (1994). *Réné Bousquet* (Paris: Stock).

Frost, Brian (1998). *Struggling to Forgive: Nelson Mandela and South Africa's Search for Reconciliation* (London: Harper Collins).

Fuchs, Jürgen (1998). *Magdalena: MfSMemfisblues Stasi Die Firma VEB Horch & Gauck—ein Roman* (Berlin: Rowohlt Berlin).

Fulbrook, Mary (1995). *Anatomy of a Dictatorship: Inside the GDR 1949–1989* (Oxford: Oxford University Press).

García Bochenek, Michael (1995). 'Compensation for Human Rights Abuses in Zimbabwe', *Colombia Human Rights Law Review*, 26 (2): 483–548.

García Laguardia, Jorge Mario (1997). 'Derechos humanos y acuerdos de paz', *América Indígena*, 57 (2): 77–87.

Garretón, Manuel Antonio (1994). 'Human Rights and Processes of Democratisation.' *Journal of Latin American Studies*, 26 (1): 221–234.

—— (1996). 'Human Rights in Processes of Democratisation', in Elizabeth Jelin and Eric Hirschberg (eds), *Constructing Democracy: Human Rights, Citizenship and Society in Latin America* (Boulder, Colo.: Westview Press), 39–56.

Garro, Alejandro, and Dahl, Henry (1987). 'Legal Accountability for Human Rights Violations in Argentina: One Step Forward and Two Steps Backward', *Human Rights Law Journal*, 4 (3): 287–294.

GARSCHA, WINFRIED R. (1993). *Die Verfahren vor dem Volksgerischt Wein (1945–1955) als Geschichtsquelle* (Vienna: Dokumentationarchiv des Osterreichischen Widerstandes).

—— and KURITSIDIS-HEIDER, CLAUDIA (1995). *Die Nachkriegsjustiz als nichburokratische Form der Entnazifizierung: Osterreichische Justizakten im europaischen Vergleich* (Vienna: Dokumentationarchiv des Osterreichischen Widerstandes).

GARST, RACHEL (1997). *The New Guatemalan National Civilian Police: A Problematic Beginning*, Briefing Series on the Guatemalan Peace Process (Washington DC: WOLA).

GARTON ASH, TIMOTHY (1995). 'Central Europe: The Present Past', *New York Review of Books* (13 July).

—— (1997a). 'True Confessions', *New York Review of Books* (17 June): 33–38.

—— (1997b). *The File: A Personal History* (London: HarperCollins).

—— (1997c). 'The Truth and Reconciliation Commission in South Africa', *Esprit*, 238: 44–62.

—— (1998). 'The Truth about Dictatorship', *New York Review of Books* (19 February): 35–40.

—— (1999). *History of the Present: Essays, Sketches and Despatches from Europe in the 1990s* (London: Allen Lane).

GATTO, HERBERTO (1997). 'Nuestras responsabilidades ante los desaparecidos', *Cuadernos de Marcha*, 11 (126): 29–32.

GAUCK, JOACHIM (1991). *Die Stasi-Akten: Das unheimliche Erbe der DDR* (Reinbek: Rowohlt).

—— (1994). 'Dealing with a Stasi Past', *Daedalus*, 123 (1): 277–289.

GAUS, GÜNTER (1983). *Wo Deutschland liegt: eine Ortsbestimmung* (Hamburg: Hoffmann und Campe).

GENSICKE, THOMAS (1998). *Die neuen Bundesbürger: Eine Transformation ohne Integration* (Opladen: Westdeutscher Verlag).

GETTY, J. ARCH, RITTERSPORN, GABOR T., and ZEMSKOV, VIKTOR (1993). 'Victims of the Soviet Penal System in the Pre-war Years: A First Approach on the Basis of Archival Evidence', *American Historical Review*, 98 (4): 1017–49.

GIBNEY, MARK (1994). 'Decommunisation: Human Rights Lessons from Past and Present and Prospects for the Future', *Denver Journal of International Law*, 23 (1): 87–134.

—— (1996a). 'Human Rights Litigation in US Courts: A Hypocritical Approach', *Buffalo Journal of International Law*, 3 (2): 261–288.

—— (1996b). 'The Implementation of Human Rights as an International Concern: The Case of Argentine General Suárez Mason and Lessons for the World Community', *Case Western Reserve Journal of International Law*, 24 (2): 165–198.

—— (1997). 'Prosecuting Human Rights Violations from a Previous Regime: The East European Experience', *East European Quarterly*, 31 (1): 93–110.

GIBNEY, MARK, TOMASEVSKI, KATARINA, and VEDSTED-HANSEN, JENS (1997). 'Transnational Responsibility for the Violation of Human Rights', *Harvard Human Rights Journal*, 12: 267–296.

GIBSON, JAMES L., and GOUWS, AMANDA (1999). 'Truth and Reconciliation in South Africa: Attributions of Blame and the Struggle over Apartheid', *American Political Science Review*, 93 (3): 501–517.

GILLIS, JOHN R. (ed.) (1994). *Commemorations: The Politics of National Identity* (Princeton: Princeton University Press).

GILLS BARRY, ROCAMORA, JOEL, and WILSON, RICHARD (eds.) (1993). *Low Intensity Democracy: Political Power in the New World Order* (London: Pluto Press).

GISVOLD, G. (1998). 'A Truth Commission for Bosnia–Herzegovina: Anticipating the Debate', in M. O. Flaherty and G. Gisvold (eds.), *Postwar Protection of Human Rights* (London: Dordrecht).

GIVSKOV, CARL CHRISTIAN (1948). 'The Danish Purge Laws', *Journal of Criminal Law and Criminology*, 39 (4): 447–460.

GLAESSNER, GERT-JOACHIM (1992). *The Unification Process in Germany* (New York: St Martin's Press).

GLEIJESIS, PIERO (1991). *Shattered Hope: The Guatemalan Revolution and the United States, 1944–54* (Princeton: Princeton University Press).

GOKHMAN, MIKHAIL (1998). 'Yubiley L'vy Razgony: pisatelyu, obshchestvennoy deyatelyu, avtoru i drugu "MN"-ispolnyaetsya 90 let', *Moskovskie Novosti*, 12 (29 March–5 April).

GOLDMAN, FRANCISCO (1999). 'Murder Comes for the Bishop', *New Yorker*, 15 March: 60–77.

GOLDMAN, ROBERT KOGOD (1988). 'International Law and Amnesty Laws', *Human Rights Internet Reporter*, 12 (2): 9–11.

—— (1992). 'Uruguay: Amnesty Law in Violation of the Human Rights Convention', *Review of the International Commission of Jurists*, 49: 37–45.

GOLDSTONE, RICHARD J. (1996). 'Exposing Human Rights Abuses: A Help or Hindrance to Reconciliation?' *Hastings Constitutional Law Quarterly*, 22 (3): 607–770.

GOLOVKOVA, LIDIYA (1997). 'Introduction', in Butovsky Poligon, *Kniga Pamiati zhertv politicheskikh repessii* (Moscow: Moskovskii Antifashistiskii Tsentr), 5–30.

GÓMEZ, MARIO (1998). 'Sri Lanka's New Human Rights Commission', *Human Rights Quarterly*, 20 (2): 281–302.

GONZÁLEZ, CARMEN (1998). 'Elites and Decommunisation in Eastern Europe', in John Higley, Jan Pakulski, and Wlodzimierz Wesolowski (eds.), *Postcommunist Elites and Democracy in Eastern Europe* (London: Macmillan), 277–295.

GONZÁLEZ, FELIPE, and GUERRA, ALFONSO (1977). *Partido Socialista Obrero Español* (Bilbao: Albia).

GOODMAN, DAVID (1999). 'Why Killers Should Go Free: Lessons from South Africa', *Washington Quarterly*, 22 (2): 169–182.

GOODMAN, MICAH (1996). 'After the War: The Legal Ramifications of the East German Border Guards Trials in Unified Germany', *Cornell International Law Journal*, 29 (3): 727–766.

GORDON, BERTAM M. (1995). 'Collaboration, Retribution and Crimes Against Humanity: The Touvier, Bousquet and Papon Affairs', *Contemporary French Civilisation*, 19 (2): 250–274.

GOUDOEVER, ALBERT P. (1996). *The Limits of Destalinization in the Soviet Union: Rehabilitations in the Soviet Union since Stalin* (New York: St Martin's Press).

GRAHAM, LAWRENCE (1992). 'Redefining the Portuguese Transition to Democracy', in John Higley and Richard Gunther (eds.), *Elites and Democratic Consolidation in Latin America and Southern Europe* (Cambridge: Cambridge University Press), 282–299.

GRAVIL, ROGER (1995). *Wrestling with the Past: Human Rights and Stability in Alfonsín's Experience. Can South Africa Learn from the Experience?* (Pretoria: University of South Africa).

GRAYBILL, LYN S. (1998a). 'South Africa's Truth and Reconciliation Commission: Ethical and Theological Perspectives', *Ethics and International Affairs*, 12: 43–62.

—— (1998b). 'The Pursuit of Truth and Reconciliation in South Africa', *Africa Today*, 45 (1): 103–130.

GRAZIOSI, ANDREA (1992). 'The Great Strikes of 1953 in Soviet Labour Camps in the Accounts of their Participants: A Review', *Cahiers du Monde Russe et sovietique*, 33 (4): 419–446.

GREEN, L. C. (ed.) (1976). *Superior Orders in National and International Law* (Leiden, Netherlands: A. W. Sijthoff).

GREEN, LINDA (1999). *Fear as a Way of Life: War Widows in Rural Guatemala* (New York: Columbia University Press).

GREENWOOD, CHRISTOPH (1996). 'International Human Rights Law and the Tadic Case', *European Journal of International Law*, 7 (2): 265–283.

GRIMSTED, PATRICIA KENNEDY (1997). 'Displaced Archives and Restitution Problems on the Eastern Front in the Aftermath of the Second World War', *Contemporary European History*, 6 (1): 27–74.

GROCEVA, DENITSA, and KRASSMIR, KANEV (1994). *The Effects of the Panev Law on the Development of Science in Bulgaria* (New York: Bulgaria Helsinki Committee).

GROISMAN, ENRIQUE I. (1985). 'El sistema jurídico frente a las secuelas del Proceso de Reorganización Nacional', in Alain Rouquié, Bolívar Lamounier, and Jorge Schvarzer (eds.), *Como renacen las democracias* (Buenos Aires: Emecé), 197–210.

GROSSER, DIETER (1998). *Das Wagnis der Währungs-, Wirtschafts- und Sozialunion: Politische Zwänge im Konflikt mit ökonomischen Regeln* (Stuttgart: DVA).

GROSSMAN, CLAUDIO (1992). Disappearances in Honduras: The Need for Direct Victim Representation in Human Rights Litigation', *Hastings International and Comparative Law Review*, 15 (3): 363–391.

GRUPO DE ENSEÑANZA SFCM (1992). *Historia de la Aeronáutica. Resumen cronológico* (Armilla: SFCM).

GUEST, IAIN (1990). *Behind the Disappearances: Argentina's Dirty War against Human Rights and the United Nations* (Philadelphia: University of Pennsylvania Press).

GUNTHER, RICHARD, SANI, GIACOMO, and SHABAD, GOLDIE (1986). *El sistema de partidos políticos en España. Génesis y evolución* (Madrid: Centro de Investigaciones Sociológicas).

GURVITA, BIANCA (1998). 'In the Shadow of Securitate', *Transitions*, 5 (9): 38–46.

GUZMÁN BOUVARD, MARGUERITE (1994). *Revolutionising Motherhood: The Mothers of the Plaza de Mayo* (Wilmington, Del.: Scholarly Resources).

—— (1998). *Grandmothers: Granddaughters Remember* (Syracuse: Syracuse University Press).

HAEGEL, FLORENCE (1990). 'Mémoire, héritage, filiation: dire le gaullisme est se dire gaulliste au RPR', *Revue Française de Science Politique*, 40 (6): 864–879.

HAGOPIAN, FRANCES (1990). 'Democracy by Undemocratic Means? Elites, Political Pacts and Regime Transition in Brazil', *Comparative Political Studies*, 23 (2): 147–170.

Halbwachs, Maurice (1980). *The Collective Memory* (New York: Harper & Row).

HALMAL, GÁBOR, and SCHEPPELE, KIM LANE (1997). 'Living Well is the Best Revenge: The Hungarian Approach to Judging the Past', in James A. McAdams (ed.), *Transitional Justice and the Rule of Law in New Democracies* (South Bend, Ind.: University of Notre Dame Press), 155–184.

—— MAJTENYL, LASZLO, and SCHEPPELE, KIM LANE (1995). 'Confronting the Past: The Hungarian Constitutional Court's Lustration Decision of 1994', *East European Human Rights Review*, 1 (1): 111–128.

HAMBER, BRENDON (1995). 'Dealing with the Past and the Psychology of Reconciliation: The TRC a Psychological Perspective', paper presented at the Fourth International Symposium on The Contributions of Psychology to Peace, Cape Town, June.

—— (1997a). *Do Sleeping Dogs Lie? The Psychological Implications of the TRC in South Africa*, Occasional Paper (Johannesburg: Centre for the Study of Violence and Reconciliation).

—— (1997b). 'Living with the Legacy of Impunity: Lessons for South Africa about Truth, Justice and Crime in Brazil', *Unisa Latin American Report*, 13 (2): 4–16.

—— (1997c). 'When Should Society Tire of the Voice of the Past?' *Mail and Guardian*, 13 (2): 17–23 (at: http://www.disappearances.org/othdoc/other1.html).

—— (1998a). 'Dr Jekyll and Mr Hyde: Problems of Violence Prevention and Reconciliation in South Africa's Transition to Democracy', in E. Bornman *et al.* (eds.), *Violence in South Africa* (Pretoria: Human Sciences and Research Council), 349–370.

—— (1998b). *The Burdens of Truth: An Evaluation of Psychological Support Services and Initiatives undertaken by the South African Truth and Reconciliation Commission*, Working Paper (Johannesburg: Centre for the Study of Violence and Reconciliation).

—— (1998c). *Past Imperfect: Dealing with the Past in Northern Ireland and Societies in Transition* (Londonderry: Incore).

—— (1998d). 'How Should We Remember? Issues to Consider when Establishing Commissions and Structures for Dealing with the Past', paper presented at conference on Dealing with the Past: Reconciliation Processes and Peace-building, Belfast, 9 June (at: http://www.incore.ulst.ac.uk/publications/conference/thepast/hamber.html).

——, and KIBBLE, STEVE (1998). *From Truth to Transformation: South Africa's Truth and Reconciliation Commission*, Briefing Paper (London: Catholic Institute for International Relations).

——, and LEWIS, SHARON (1997). *An Overview of the Consequences of Violence and Trauma in South Africa*, Working Paper (Johannesburg: Centre for the Study of Violence and Reconciliation).

—— MOFOKENG, TLHOKI, and SIMPSON, GRAEME (1998). *Evaluating the Role and Function of Civil Society in a Changing South Africa*, Working Paper (Johannesburg: Centre for the Study of Violence and Reconciliation).

HAMMOND, JOHN L. (1988). *Building Popular Power: Workers' and Neighbourhood Movements in the Portuguese Revolution* (New York: Monthly Review Press).

HAN, SUNG-JOO (1974). *The Failure of Democracy in South Korea* (Berkeley: University of California Press).

—— (1995). 'The Experiment with Democracy', in: Korea Briefing. (Boulder, Colorado: Westview Press).

HANDY, JIM (1984). *Gift of the Devil: A History of Guatemala* (Toronto: Between the Lines).

HARPER, CHARLES (ed.) (1996). *Impunity: An Ethical Perspective. Six Case Studies from Latin America* (Geneva: World Council of Churches).

HARRIS, DAVID J., and LIVINGSTONE, STEPHEN (eds.) (1998). *The Inter American System of Human Rights* (Oxford: Clarendon Press).

HARTWIG, HANNA (1992). 'The Shock of the Past', *Uncaptive Minds*, 5 (1): 102–104.

HARVARD LAW SCHOOL HUMAN RIGHTS PROGRAM and WORLD PEACE FOUNDATION (1997). *Truth Commissions: A Comparative Assessment* (Cambridge: Harvard Law School Human Rights Program).

HASSEMER, WINFRED, and STARZACHER, KARL (eds.) (1993). *Data Protection and Stasi Documents: Push the Issue Aside or Overcome Them?* (Baden-Baden: Nomos).

HAYNER, PRISCILLA B. (1994). 'Fifteen Truth Commissions, 1974 to 1994: A Comparative Study', *Human Rights Quarterly*, 16 (4): 597–655.

—— (1996a). 'Commissioning the Truth: Further Research Questions', *Third World Quarterly*, 17 (1): 19–29.

HAYNER, PRISCILLA B. (1996b). 'International Guidelines for the Creation and Operation of Truth Commissions: A Preliminary Proposal', *Law and Contemporary Problems*, 59 (4): 173–180.

—— (2000). *Unspeakable Truths: Confronting State Terror and Atrocities* (New York: Routledge).

HENKE, KLAUS-DIETMAR (ed.) (1993). *Wann bricht schon mal ein Staat zusammen! Die Debatte über die Stasi-Akten auf dem 39. Historikertag 1992* (Munich: DTV).

—— and HANS WOLLER (eds.) (1991). *Politische Säuberung in Europa: Die Abrechnung mit Faschismus und Kollaboration nach dem Zweiten Weltkrieg* (Munich: Deutscher Taschenbuch Verlag).

HENKIN, ALICE (ed.) (1989). *State Crimes: Punishment or Pardon* (Wye Centre, Md: Aspen Institute for Peace).

—— (ed.) (1998). *Honouring Human Rights: From Justice to Peace* (Wye Centre, Md: Aspen Institute for Peace).

HERF, JEFFREY (1997). *Divided Memory: The Nazi Past in the Two Germanys* (Cambridge, Mass.: Harvard University Press).

HERZ, JOHN H. (ed.) (1982). *From Dictatorship to Democracy: Coping with the Legacies of Authoritarianism and Totalitarianism* (Westport, Conn.: Greenwood Press).

HIRSCHFELD, GERHARD (1988). *Nazi Rule and Dutch Collaboration: The Netherlands and the German Occupation, 1940–1945* (Oxford: Berg).

HOBSBAWN, ERIC, and RANGER, TERRENCE (1993). *The Invention of Tradition* (Cambridge: Cambridge University Press).

HOCHSCHILD, ADAM (1994). *The Unquiet Ghost: Russians Remember Stalin* (New York: Penguin Books).

HOLMES, STEPHEN (1994). 'The End of Decommunisation', *East European Constitutional Review*, 3 (4): 33–36.

HRW (Human Rights Watch) (1987). *Truth and Partial Justice in Argentina* (New York: Human Rights Watch).

—— (1988). *Chile: Human Rights and the Plebiscite* (New York: Human Rights Watch).

—— (1989a). *Chile in Transition: Human Rights and the Plebiscite 1988–1989* (New York: Human Rights Watch).

—— (1989b). *Honduras: Without the Will* (New York: Human Rights Watch).

—— (1989c). *Challenging Impunity: The Ley de Caducidad and the Referendum Campaign in Uruguay* (New York: Human Rights Watch).

—— (1989d). *Accountability for Past Human Rights Abuse* (New York: Human Rights Watch).

—— (1990a). *A Year of Reckoning: El Salvador a Decade after the Assassination of Archbishop Romero* (New York: Human Rights Watch).

—— (1990b). *Honduras: The Inter American Court of Human Rights Wraps Up its First Adversarial Case* (New York: Human Rights Watch).

—— (1990c). *Trials in Romania: A Rush to Appease . . . and to Conceal* (New York: Human Rights Watch).

—— (1991a). *Truth and Partial Justice in Argentina: An Update* (New York: Human Rights Watch).

—— (1991b). *Human Rights and the 'Politics of Agreements': Chile during President Aylwin's First Year* (New York: Human Rights Watch).

—— (1991c). *Judiciary Bars Step to Identify Child Kidnapped during Military Regime* (New York: Human Rights Watch).

—— (1991d). *Search for Brazil's Disappeared: The Mass Graves at Dom Bosco Cemetery* (New York: Human Rights Watch).

—— (1992a). *Bolivia: Trial of Responsibilities. Nine Years and no Verdict* (New York: Human Rights Watch).

—— (1992b). *Chile: The Struggle for Truth and Justice for Past Human Rights Violations* (New York: Human Rights Watch).

—— (1992c). *Paraguay: An Encouraging Victory in the Search for Truth and Justice* (New York: Human Rights Watch).

—— (1992d). *Czechoslovakia: Decommunisation Measures Violate Freedom of Expression and Due Process Standards* (New York: Human Rights Watch).

—— (1992e). *Accountability in Namibia: Human Rights and the Transition to Democracy* (New York: Human Rights Watch).

—— (1992f). *Accounting for the Past: The Lessons for South Africa from Latin America* (New York: Human Rights Watch).

—— (1992g). *Human Rights Accountability in Sri Lanka* (New York: Human Rights Watch).

—— (1993a). *Bolivia: The Trial of Responsibilities: The García Meza Tejada Trial* (New York: Human Rights Watch).

—— (1993b). *Accountability and Human Rights: The Report of the UN Commission on the Truth in El Salvador* (New York: Human Rights Watch).

—— (1993c). *Decommunisation in Bulgaria* (New York: Human Rights Watch).

—— (1994a). *Chile: Unsettled Business: Human Rights at the Start of the Frei Presidency* (New York: Human Rights Watch).

—— (1994b). *The Facts Speak for Themselves: The Preliminary Report on Disappearances of the National Commissioner for the Protection of Human Rights in Honduras* (New York: Human Rights Watch).

—— (1994c). *Human Rights in Guatemala during President De León Carpio's First Year* (New York: Human Rights Watch).

—— (1994d). *Reckoning under Law* (New York: Human Rights Watch).

—— (1995a). *Disappeared in Guatemala: The Case of Efraín Bamaca Velásquez* (New York: Human Rights Watch).

—— (1995b). *Human Rights after President Aristide's Return* (New York: Human Rights Watch).

—— (1996a). *Thirst for Justice: A Decade of Impunity in Haiti* (New York: Human Rights Watch).

—— (1996b). *Human Rights in Postcommunist Albania* (New York: Human Rights Watch).

HRW (Human Rights Watch) (1999a). *When Tyrants Tremble: The Pinochet Case* (New York: Human Rights Watch).

—— (1999b). *Impunity in Cambodia: How Human Rights Offenders Escape Justice* (New York: Human Rights Watch).

HUGHES, MICHAEL L. (1995). 'Restitution and Democracy in Germany after Two World Wars', *Contemporary European History*, 4 (1): 1–18.

HUNTER, WENDY (1997). 'Civil Military Relations in Argentina, Chile and Peru', *Political Science Quarterly*, 112 (3): 453–475.

HUNTINGTON, SAMUEL P. (1991). *The Third Wave: Democratization in the Late Twentieth Century*. (Norman: University of Oklahoma Press).

HUSKEY, EUGENE (1997). 'Russian Judicial Reform', in Peter H. Solomon (ed.), *Reforming Justice in Russia, 1864–1996* (Armonk, NY: M. E. Sharpe), 325–347.

HUYSE, LUC (1991). 'The Criminal Justice System as a Political Actor in Regime Transitions: The Case of Belgium, 1940–1950', *Recht der Werkelijkheid*, 12: 87–96.

—— (1995). 'Justice after Transition: On the Choice Successor Elites Make in Dealing with the Past', *Law and Social Inquiry*, 20 (2): 51–78.

—— (1998). 'Dutch and Belgian War Trials after World War II Compared', paper presented at the Mellon Seminar on Transitional Justice, Columbia University.

HUYSE, LUC, and DHONT, STEVE (1993). *La répresion des collaborations 1942–1952: un passé toujours présent* (Brussels: Crisp).

IBARZÁBAL, EUGENIO (1977). *Euskadi: Diálogos en torno a las elecciones* (Zarauz: Erein).

ICJ (International Commission of Jurists) (1993). *Justice not Impunity* (Geneva: International ICJ).

IDELBER, AVELAR (1999). 'Restitution and Mourning in Latin American Postdictatorship', *Boundary 2*, 26 (3): 201–224.

IGNATIEFF, MICHAEL (1996). 'Articles of Faith', *Index on Censorship: Wounded Nations, Wounded Lives*, 25 (5): 110–122.

—— (1998). *The Warrior's Honour: Ethnic War and the Modern Conscience* (London: Chatto & Windus).

IGNATOW, ASSEN (1997). 'Vergangenheitsaufarbeitung in der Russische Föderation', *Berichte des Bundesinstituts für ostwissentschaftliche und internationale Studien*, 42: 3–28.

IMHOLZ, KATHLEEN (1993). 'A Landmark Constitutional Court Decision in Albania', *East European Constitutional Review*, 2 (3): 23–25.

—— (1995). 'Can Albania Break the Chain? The 1993–94 Trials of Former High Communist Officials', *East European Constitutional Review*, 4 (3): 54–60.

IONESCU, DAN (1990). 'Old Practices Persist in Romanian Justice', *Report on Eastern Europe*, 1 (10): 44–48.

—— (1992). 'Romania's Public War over Secret Police Files', *RFE/RL Research Report*, 1 (29): 9–15.

IPSEN, JÖRN (1995). 'Die rechtliche Bewältigung von Unrechtsfolgen des DDR-Regimes', in Jörn Ipsen *et al.* (eds.), *Verfassungsrecht im Wandel* (Cologne: Heymanns), 65–74.

IRWIN-ZARECKA, IWONA (1993). 'In Search of Usable Pasts', *Society*, 30 (2): 32–36.

—— (1994). *Frames of Remembrance: The Dynamics of Collective Memory* (New Brunswick, NJ: Transaction Publishers).

ISENSEE, JOSEF (1992). *Vergangheitsbewaltigung durch Recht?* (Berlin: Duncker & Humblot).

—— and KIRCHHOF, PAUL (eds.) (1997), *Handbuch des deutschen Staatsrechts*, x, *Die Einheit Deutschlands: Festigung und Übergang* (Heidelberg: Müller Juristischer Verlag).

IVANOVA, G. M. (1997). *GULAG v sisteme totalitarnogo gosudarstva* (Moscow: Moskovsky Obshchestvenny Nauchny Fond).

IZAGUIRRE, INÉS (1994). *Los desaparecidos: recuperación de una identidad expropriada* (Buenos Aires: Centro de América Latina).

—— (1998). 'Recapturing the Memory of Politics', *NACLA Report on the Americas*, 31 (6): 28–35.

JAIME-JIMÉNEZ, ÓSCAR, and REINARES, FERNANDO (1998). 'The Policing of Mass Demonstrations in Spain: From Dictatorship to Democracy', in Donatella della Porta and Herbert Reiter (eds.), *Policing Protest: The Control of Mass Demonstrations in Western Democracies* (Minneapolis: University of Minnesota Press), 166–187.

JANSEN, MARC (1982). *A Show Trial under Lenin: The Trial of the Socialist Revolutionaries, Moscow 1922* (The Hague: Martinus Nijhoff).

JASPERS, KARL (1947). *The Question of German Guilt* (New York: Dial Press).

JAÚREGUI, FERNANDO, and MENÉNDEZ, MANUEL ÁNGEL (1995). *Lo que nos queda de Franco: símbolos, personajes, leyes y costumbres veinte años después* (Madrid: Temas de Hoy).

JEFFERY, ANTHEA (1999). *The Truth About the Truth Commission* (Johannesburg: SAIRR).

JELIN, ELIZABETH (1994). 'The Politics of Memory: The Human Rights Movement and the Construction of Democracy in Argentina', *Latin American Perspectives*, 21 (2): 38–58.

—— (1995) 'Building Citizenship: A Balance Between Solidarity and Responsibility', in Joseph S. Tulchin and Bernice Romero (eds.), *The Consolidation of Democracy in Latin America* (Boulder, Colo.: Lynne Rienner), 83–97.

—— (1998). 'Minefields of Memory', *NACLA Report on the Americas*, 32 (2): 23–29.

JELINEK, YESHAYAHU A. (1994). 'Restitution of Jewish Property in the Czech and Slovak Republics: An Interim Report', *East European Jewish Affairs*, 24 (2): 73–88.

JERVIS, ROBERT (1976). *Perception and Misperception in International Politics* (Princeton: Princeton University Press).

JEZOVICA, MILAN (1992). 'Restitution of Property in the Czech and Slovak Republics', *Comparative Juridical Review*, 29: 49–60.

JOHNSTON, WILLIAM M. (1991). *Celebrations: The Cult of Anniversaries in Europe and the United States* (New Brunswick, NJ: Transaction Publishers).

JOHNSTONE, IAN (1995). *Rights and Reconciliation: UN Strategies in El Salvador* (Boulder, Colo.: Lynne Rienner).

JOKIC, ALEXANDAR, and ELLIS, ANTHONY (eds.) (2000). *War Crimes Revisited* (Cambridge: Cambridge University Press).

JONES, J. R. W. D. (1998). *The Practice of the International Criminal Tribunals for the Former Yugoslavia and Rwanda* (Ardsley, NY: Transnational Publishers).

JONES, SIDNEY (1989). *Will to Prosecute Past Offenders Lost in the Philippines* (New York: Human Rights Watch).

JOPPKE, CHRISTIAN (1995). *East German Dissidents and the Revolution of 1989: Social Movement in a Leninist Regime* (New York: New York University Press).

JOYNER, CHRISTOPHER C. (1996). 'Arresting Impunity: The Case for Universal Jurisdiction in Bringing War Criminals to Accountability', *Law and Contemporary Problems*, 59 (4): 153–172.

—— (1998). 'Redressing Impunity for Human Rights Violations: The Universal Declaration and the Search for Accountability', *Duke Journal of Comparative and International Law*, 26 (4): 591–264.

JUDAH, TI (1997). 'The Serbs: The Sweet and Rotten Smell of History', *Daedalus*, 126 (3): 23–45.

JUDT, TONY (1992). 'The Past is Another Country: Myth and Memory in Postwar Europe', *Daedalus*, 121 (4): 83–118.

JULIÁ, SANTOS (ed.) (1999). *Víctimas de la guerra civil* (Madrid: Temas de Hoy).

JUSTICIA DEMOCRÁTICA (1978). *Los jueces contra la dictadura: justicia y política en el franquismo* (Madrid: Túcar Ediciones).

KANE-BURMAN, JOHN (1993). *Political Violence in South Africa* (Johannesburg: South African Institute of Race Relations).

KAPLAN, SUSAN (1980). *The Legal Response to Disappearances: Habeas Corpus and Amparo* (New York: Lawyers Committee for International Human Rights).

KARL, TERRY L. (1992). 'El Salvador's Negotiated Revolution', *Foreign Affairs*, 71 (2): 147–64.

KARPINSKI, JAKUB (1991). 'Files into Ashes', *Uncaptive Minds*, 4 (1): 5–7.

—— (1993). 'Politicians and the Past', *Uncaptive Minds*, 5 (3): 99–106.

KARSTEDT, SUSANNE (1998). 'Coming to Terms with the Past in Germany after 1945 and 1989: Public Judgements on Procedures and Justice', *Law and Policy*, 20 (1): 15–56.

KAUR, KULDIP (1998). 'The Reconstruction of Mayan Female Identity through the Politics of Loss and Retrieval', unpublished MA thesis, Institute of Latin American Studies, University of London.

KAYE, MIKE (1997). 'The Role of Truth Commissions in the Search for Justice, Reconciliation and Democratisation: The Salvadorean and Honduran Cases', *Journal of Latin American Studies*, 29 (3): 693–716.

KECK, MARGERET E., and SIKKINK, KATHRYN (1998). *Activists beyond Borders: Advocacy Networks in International Politics* (Ithaca, NY: Cornell University Press).

KEIGHTLEY, RAYLENE (1993). 'Political Offences and Indemnity in South Africa', *South African Journal of Human Rights*, 9 (3): 334–357.

KELLNER, HANS (1994). 'Never Again is Now', *History and Theory*, 33 (2): 127–144.

KING, DAVID (1997). *The Commissar Vanishes: The Falsification of Photographs and Art in Stalin's Russia* (New York: Henry Holt).

KIRCHEIMER, OTTO (1961). *Political Justice: The Use of Legal Procedure for Political Ends* (Princeton: Princeton University Press).

KIURANOV, DEYAN (1995). 'Assessment of the Public Debate on the Legal Remedies for the Reinstatement of Former Owners and the Realisation of Liability for Damages Inflicted by the Totalitarian Regime', in Niel J. Kritz (ed.), *Transitional Justice: How Emerging Democracies Reckon with Former Regimes*, ü (Washington DC: United States Institute for Peace), 715–721.

KLAAREN, JONATHAN (1998). 'The Truth and Reconciliation Commission, the South African Judiciary and Constitutionalism', *African Studies*, 57 (2): 197–208.

KLICH, AGNIESZKA (1996). 'Human Rights in Poland: The Role of the Constitutional Tribunal and the Commissioner for Citizens' Rights', *Saint Louis School of Law Transatlantic Journal*, 33–64.

KLOSTERMAN, THERESA (1998). 'The Feasibility and Propriety of a Truth Commission in Cambodia: Too Little? Too Late?' *Arizona Journal of International and Comparative Law*, 15 (3): 833–870.

KLUG, HEINZ (1998). 'Amnesty, Amnesia and Remembrance: International Obligations and the Need to Prevent the Repetition of Gross Violations of Human Rights', *Proceedings of the American Society of International Law*, 92: 316–321.

KNABE, HURBERTUS (1997). 'Die Stasi als Problem des Westens: Zur Tätigkeit des MfS im "Operationsgebiet"', *Aus Politik und Zeitgeschichte* (5 December): 3–16.

KOMMERS, DONALD P. (1997a). *The Constitutional Jurisprudence of the Federal Republic of Germany* (Durham, NC: Duke University Press).

—— (1997b). 'Transitional Justice in Eastern Germany', *Law and Social Inquiry*, 22 (3): 829–848.

KORDON, DIANA (1995). *La impunidad: una perspectiva clínica y psicosocial* (Buenos Aires: Editorial Sudamericana).

KORTE, KARL-RUDOLPH (1998). *Deutschlandpolitik in Helmut Kohls Kanzlerschaft: Regierungsstil und Entscheidungen 1982–1989* (Stuttgart: DVA).

KÖRTING, EHRHART (1999). 'Ist (Straf-)Recht ein geeignetes Mittel zur Aufarbeitung der Geschichte? Rechtliche Aufarbeitung oder Amnestie?' *Neue Justiz*, 53 (1): 1–4.

KOWALJOW, SERGEY (1997). *Der Flug des weissen Raben: Von Siberien nach Tschetschenien: Eine Lebensreise* (Berlin: Rowohlt).

KOZLOV, V. P. (1994). 'Publichnost rossiskikh arkhivov i problema rassekrechivaniya arkhivnikh dokumentov', *Vestnik arkhivista*, 1: 43–50.

KOZMINSKI, ADRZEJ K. (1997). 'Restitution of Private Property and Reprivatisation in Central and East Europe', *Communist and Postcommunist Studies*, 30 (1): 5–22.

KRAMER, JANE (1996). *The Politics of Memory: Looking for Germany in the New Germany* (New York: Random House).

KRAUSE, STEFAN (1995). 'Purges and Progress in Bulgaria', *Transitions*, 1 (18): 46–51.

KRITZ, NEIL J. (ed.) (1995). *Transitional Justice: How Emerging Democracies Reckon with Former Regimes*, i–iii (Washington DC: United States Institute for Peace).

—— (1996). 'Coming to Terms with Atrocities: A Review of Accountability Mechanisms for Mass Violation of Human Rights', *Law and Contemporary Problems*, 59 (4): 127–152.

—— and STUEBNER, WILLIAM A. (1998). 'A Truth and Reconciliation Commission for Bosnia and Herzegovina: Why, How and When?' paper presented at the Victimology Symposium, Sarajevo, Bosnia, 9–11 May 1998.

KROG, ANTJE (1998). *Country of my Skull* (Johannesburg: Random House).

KURTHEN, HERMANN, BERGMANN, WERNER and ERB, RAINER (eds.) (1997). *Antisemitism and Xenophobia in Germany after Unification* (New York: Oxford University Press).

KUSIN, VLADIVIR V. (1979). 'Challenge to Normalcy: Political Opposition in Czechoslovakia, 1968–1977', in Rudolf Tökés (ed.), *Opposition in Eastern Europe* (London: Macmillan), 60–112.

LAB (Latin American Bureau) (1999). *Nunca Más Guatemala* (London: Latin American Bureau).

LABER, JERRI (1992). 'Witch Hunt in Prague', *New York Review of Books* (23 April): 5–8.

LAGOS, RICARDO and MUÑOZ, HERALDO (1999). 'The Pinochet Dilemma', *Foreign Policy*, 144: 26–39.

LAIZ, CONSUELO (1995). *La lucha final: los partidos de la izquierda radical durante la transición española* (Madrid: Libros de La Catarata).

LANDSBERG, CHRIS (1994). 'Directing from the Stalls? The International Community and the South African Negotiating Forum', in Doreen Atkinson and Steven Friedman (eds.), *The Small Miracle: South Africa's Negotiated Settlement* (Johannesburg: Ravan Press), 276–300.

LANDSMAN, STEPHAN (1996). 'Alternative Responses to Serious Human Rights Abuses: Prosecution and Truth Commissions', *Law and Contemporary Problems*, 59 (4): 81–92.

LANERO, MÓNICA (1996). *Una milicia de la justicia: la política judicial del franquismo (1936–1945)*. Madrid: Centro de Estudios Constitucionales.

LANGAN, MICHAEL (1991). 'Argentine President Menem's First Pardons: A Comparative Analysis of Coverage by Buenos Aires' Leading Dailies', *Canadian Journal of Latin American and Caribbean Studies*, 16 (31): 145–156.

LANSING, PAUL, and KING, JULIE C. (1998). 'South Africa's Truth and Reconciliation Commission: The Conflict between Individual Justice and

National Healing in the Post-Apartheid Age', *Arizona Journal of International and Comparative Law*, 15 (3): 753–790.

LARKINS, CHRISTOPHER (1998). 'The Judiciary and Delegative Democracy in Argentina', *Comparative Politics*, 30 (4): 423–442.

LARSEN, STEIN UGELVIK (1998). 'The Democratic Latecomers: Transition to Democracy in Portugal, Spain and Greece', in Stein Ugelvik Larsen (ed.), *Modern Europe after Fascism, 1943–1980s* (Boulder, Colo.: Social Science East European Monographs), 1565–1579.

—— *et al.* (eds.). (1998). *Modern Europe After Fascism, 1945–1980* (New York: SSM-Columbia University Press).

LARSON, EGON (1979). *The Flame in Barbed Wire: The Story of Amnesty International* (New York: W. W. Norton).

LATCHMAN, ANNE MARIE (1989). 'Duty to Punish: International Law and the Human Rights Policy of Argentina', *Boston University International Law Journal*, 7 (2): 355–378.

LAWYERS COMMITTEE FOR HUMAN RIGHTS (1991). *Impunity: Prosecutions of Human Rights Violations in the Philippines* (New York: LCHR).

LEDESMA, GUILLERMO A. C. (1995). 'La responsabilidad de los comandantes militares por las violaciones a los derechos humanos', in Leonardo Senkman and Mario Sznajder (eds.), *El legado del autoritarismo: derechos humanos y antisemitismo en la Argentina contemporánea* (Buenos Aires: Grupo Editor Latinoamericano), 121–142.

LEGGEWIE, CLAUS, and MEIER, HORST (1993). 'Zum Auftakt ein Schlußstrich?' in Cora Stephan, (ed.), *Wir Kollaborateure* (Reinbek: Rowohlt), 51–79.

LEIS, HÉCTOR (1989). *El movimiento por los derechos humanos y la política argentina* (Buenos Aires: Centro Editor de América Latina).

LEMKE, CHRISTIANE (1992). 'Trials and Tribulations: The Stasi Legacy in Contemporary German Politics', *German Politics and Society*, 26: 43–53.

LEVY, JACK S. (1992). 'An Introduction to Prospect Theory', *Political Psychology*, 13 (2): 171–186.

LEYES FUNDAMENTALES DEL ESTADO (1967). *La Constitución Española* (Madrid: Servicio Informativo Español).

LINZ, JUAN J. (1986). *Conflicto en Euskadi* (Madrid: Espasa-Calpe).

—— and STEPAN, ALFRED (1997). *Problems of Democratic Transition and Consolidation: Southern Europe, South America, and Postcommunist Europe* (Baltimore: University of Baltimore Press).

LIPTON, MERLE (1985). *Capitalism and Apartheid: South Africa, 1910–1986* (London: Wildwood House).

LIRA, ELIZABETH (1990). 'Subjetividad y política: Los derechos humanos en la transición a la democracia'. *Persona y Sociedad*, 4 (2–3): 101–110.

—— and BECKER, DAVID (ed.) (1989). *Derechos humanos: Todo es según el dolor con que se mira* (Santiago: Ediciones Sur).

—— WEINSTEIN, ELIZABETH, and ROJAS, M. E. (1987). *Trauma, duelo y reparación* (Santiago: Editorial Interamericana).

—— PIPER, ISABEL, and ARENSBURG CASTELL, SVENKA (1996). *Reparación, derechos humanos y salud mental* (Santiago: Ediciones Chile América).

Little, David (1999). 'A Different Kind of Justice: Dealing with Human Rights Violations in Transitional Societies', *Ethics and International Affairs*, 13: 65–80.

Llewellyn, Jennifer, and House, Robert (1999). 'Institutions for Restorative Justice: The South African Truth and Reconciliation Commission', *University of Toronto Law Journal*, 49 (3): 355–388.

Lndtag Mecklenburg-Vorpommern (ed.) (1998). *Aufarbeitung und Versöhnung: Leben in der DDR, Leben nach 1989* (Schwerin: Stiller & Balewski).

López Dawson, Carlos (1994). *Las deudas de la transición: balance de derechos humanos* (Santiago: Comisión Chilena de Derechos Humanos).

López Garrido, Diego (1987) *El aparato policial en España: historia, sociología e ideología* (Barcelona: Ariel).

Los, Maria (1995). 'Lustration and Truth Claims: Unfinished Revolutions in Central Europe', *Law and Social Inquiry*, 20 (2): 117–162.

Lottman, Herbert R. (1986). *The Purge: The Purification of French Collaborators after WWII* (Paris: Fayard).

Loveman, Brian (1991). 'Misión cumplida? Civil Military Relations and the Chilean Political Transition', *Journal of Inter-American Studies and World Affairs*, 33 (3): 35–74.

—— (1994). 'Protected Democracies and Military Guardianship: Political Transitions in Latin America', *Journal of Inter-American Studies and World Affairs*, 36 (2): 105–175.

Loveman, Mara (1998). 'High Risk Collective Action: Defending Human Rights in Chile, Uruguay and Argentina', *American Journal of Sociology*, 104 (2): 477–492.

Lowden, Pamela (1996). *Moral Opposition to Authoritarian Rule in Chile* (1973–1990) (Basingstoke, Hants: Macmillan).

Löwenhardt, John (1995). *The Reincarnation of Russia: Struggling with the Legacy of Communism, 1990–1994* (Harlow, Essex: Longman).

Ludtke, Alf (1993). 'Coming to Terms with the Past: Illusions of Remembering, Ways of Forgetting Nazism in West Germany', *Journal of Modern History*, 65 (3): 542–569.

Lutz, Ellen, Hannum, Hurst, and Burke, K. (1989). *New Directions in Human Rights* (Philadelphia: University of Pennsylvania Press).

Lyons, Beth. S. (1997). 'Between Nuremberg and Amnesia: the TRC in South Africa', *Monthly Review*, 19 (4): 5–22.

McAdams, James A. (ed.) (1997). *Transitional Justice and the Rule of Law in New Democracies* (South Bend, Ind.: University of Notre Dame Press).

MacQueen, Norrie (1997). *The Decolonisation of Portuguese Africa: Metropolitan Revolution and the Dissolution of Empire* (London and New York: Longman).

McSherry, Patrice (1997a), 'Strategic Alliance: Menem and the Military–Security Forces in Argentina', *Latin American Perspectives*, 24 (6): 63–92.

—— (1997b). *Incomplete Transition: Military Power and Guardian Structures in Latin America* (New York: St Martin's Press).

MAIER, CHARLES S. (1988). *The Unmasterable Past: History, Holocaust and German National Identity* (Cambridge, Mass.: Harvard University Press).

—— (1997). *Dissolution: The Crisis of Communism and the End of East Germany* (Princeton: Princeton University Press).

MAINWARING, SCOTT, O'DONNELL, GUILLERMO, and VALENZUELA, SAMUEL J. (1992). *Issues in Democratic Consolidation* (South Bend, Ind.: University of Notre Dame Press).

MALAMUD-GOTI, JAIME (1990). 'Transitional Governments in the Breach: Why Punish State Criminals?' *Human Rights Quarterly*, 12 (1): 1–16.

—— (1991). 'Punishment and Rights Based Democracy', *Criminal Justice Ethics*, 10 (3): 1–13.

—— (1996). *Game without End: State Terror and the Politics of Justice* (Norman, Okla.: University of Oklahoma Press).

—— (1998a). 'Dignity, Vengeance and Fostering Democracy', *University of Miami Inter-American Law Review*, 29 (3): 417–450.

—— (1998b). 'State Terror and Memory of What', *University of Arkansas at Little Rock Law Review*, 21 (1): 107–118.

MALEFAKIS, EDWARD (1982). 'Spain and its Francoist Heritage', in John H. Herz (ed.), *From Dictatorship to Democracy: Coping with the Legacies of Authoritarianism and Totalitarianism* (Westport, Conn.: Greenwood Press), 216–230.

—— (1995). 'The Political and Socio-economic Contours of Southern European History', in Richard Gunther, P. Nikiforos Diamandouros and Hans-Jürgen Puhle (eds.), *The Politics of Democratic Consolidation: Southern Europe in Comparative Perspective* (Baltimore and London: Johns Hopkins University Press), 33–76.

MALIN, ANDREA (1994). 'Mother Who Won't Disappear', *Human Rights Quarterly*, 16 (1): 187–213.

MAMDANI, MAHMOOD (1996). 'Reconciliation without Justice', *Southern African Review of Books*, 45.

—— (1998) 'When Does Reconciliation Turn into Denial of Justice?' HSRC Lecture, Capetown University, Centre for African Studies, 18 February.

MANBY, BRONWEN (1992). 'South Africa: The Impact of Sanctions', *Journal of International Affairs*, 46 (1): 193–217.

MANIN, BERNARD, STOKES, SUSAN, and PRZEWORSKI, ADAM (eds.) (1999). *Democracy, Accountability and Representation* (Cambridge: Cambridge University Press).

MANZ, BEATRIZ (1988). *Refugees of a Hidden War: The Aftermath of Counterinsurgency in Guatemala* (Albany, NY: State University of New York Press).

MARAVALL, JOSÉ MARÍA (1978). *Dictadura y disentimiento político* (Madrid: Alfaguara).

MARAVALL, JOSÉ MARÍA (1996). *Accountability and Manipulation*, Working Paper 62 (Madrid: Instituto Juan March).

MARCUSE, PETER (1992). 'Repeating History: Denazification, Destalinisation and the Reworking of the Past', *Socialism and Democracy*, 8 (4): 43–58.

—— (1993). 'Moral Indignation and Politics: The Debate Over the Stasi', *New Political Science*, 24: 9–18.

MARKOVITS, INGA (1995). *Imperfect Justice* (Oxford: Clarendon Press).

—— (1996). 'Children of a Lesser God: GDR Lawyers in Post-Socialist Germany', *Michigan Law Review*, 94 (7): 2270–2308.

MARKS, STEPHEN P. (1994). 'Forgetting the Policies and Practises of the Past: Impunity in Cambodia', *Fletcher Journal of World Affairs*, 18 (2): 17–42.

MARTIN, IAN (1999). 'Haiti: International Force or National Compromise?' *Journal of Latin American Studies*, 31 (3): 711–734.

MARTÍNEZ INGLÉS, AMADEO (1994). *La transición vigilada: del sábado santo 'rojo' al 23-F* (Madrid: Temas de Hoy).

MARX, ANTHONY (1992). *Lessons of the Struggle: South African Internal Opposition, 1960–1990* (Oxford: Oxford University Press).

MARX, LESLEY (1998). 'Slouching towards Bethlehem: Ubu and the Truth Commission', *African Studies*, 57 (2): 209–220.

MATA LÓPEZ, JOSÉ MANUEL (1993). *El nacionalismo vasco radical: discurso, organización y expresiones* (Bilbao: Universidad del País Vasco).

MATEUS, RUI (1997). *Memórias de um PS desconhecido* (Lisboa: D. Quixote).

MATONSE, ANTONIO (1992). 'Mozambique: A Painful Reconciliation', *Africa Today*, 39 (1–2): 29–34.

MATTAROLLO, RODOLFO (1992). 'Proceso a la impunidad de crímenes de lesa humanidad en América Latina, 1989–1991', *Estudios Centroamericanos*, 47: 867–882.

MAXWELL, KENNETH (1982). 'The Emergence of Portuguese Democracy', in John H. Herz (ed.), *From Dictatorship to Democracy: Coping with the Legacies of Authoritarianism and Totalitarianism* (Westport, Conn., and London: Greenwood Press), 231–250.

—— (1983). *The Press and the Rebirth of Iberian Democracy* (Westport, Conn., and London: Greenwood Press).

—— (1995). *The Making of Portuguese Democracy* (Cambridge: Cambridge University Press).

MAYFIELD, JULIE V. (1992). 'The Prosecution of War Crimes and Respect for Human Rights: Ethiopia's Balancing Act', *Emory International Law Review*, 9 (2).

MAYORGA, RENÉ ANTONIO (1997). 'Democracy Dignified and an End to Impunity: Bolivia's Military Dictatorship on Trial', in James McAdams (ed.), *Transitional Justice and the Rule of Law in New Democracies* (South Bend, Ind.: Notre Dame University Press), 61–92.

MAZRUS, MICHAEL R. (1995). 'Coming to Terms with Vichy', *Holocaust and Genocide Studies*, 9 (1): 23–41.

MEDINA, FRANCISCO (1995). *Las sombras del poder: los servicios secretos de Carrero a Roldán* (Madrid: Espasa-Calpe).

MEDINA QUIROGA, CECILIA (1988). *The Battle for Human Rights: Gross Systematic Violations and the Inter-American System* (Utrecht: Netherlands Institute for Social and Economic Law Research).

MEDVEDEV, ROY A., and MEDVEDEV, ZHORES A. (1977). *Khrushchev: The Years in Power* (New York: Columbia University Press).

MEMORIAL (1994), 'Polozhenie o poryadke vyplaty denezhnoy kompensatsii litsam, reabilitirovannym v sootvetstvii s zakonom Rossiskoy Federatsii "O reabilitatsii zhertv politicheskikh repressii"', *Memorial Aspekt*, October.

MÉNDEZ, JUAN E. (1997a). 'Accountability for Past Abuses', *Human Rights Quarterly*, 19 (2): 255–282.

—— (1997b). 'In Defense of Transitional Justice', in James McAdams (ed.), *Transitional Justice and the Rule of Law in New Democracies* (South Bend, Ind.: University of Notre Dame Press), 1–26.

—— and VIVANCO, JOSÉ MIGUEL (1990). 'International Human Rights Symposium: Disappearances and the Inter-American Court: Reflections in a Litigation Experience', *Hamline Law Review*, 13 (3): 507–577.

—— O'DONNELL, GUILLERMO, and SÉRGIO PINHEIRO, PAULO (eds.) (1999). *The (Un)rule of Law and the Underprivileged in Latin America* (South Bend, Ind.: University of Notre Dame Press, 1999).

MEREDITH, MARTIN (1999). *Coming to Terms: South Africa's Search for the Truth* (New York: Public Affairs).

MEUSCHEL, SIGRID (1992). *Legitimation und Parteiherrschaft in der DDR* (Frankfurt am Main: Suhrkamp).

MICHNIK, ADAM, and HAVEL, VACLAV (1993). 'Justice or Revenge?' *Journal of Democracy*, 4 (1): 20–27.

MIERELLES NETO, TOGO (1996). 'Rescatando la memoria brasileira', paper presented to conference on Impunity and its Effects on Democratic Processes, Santiago, 14 December (at: http://www.derechos.org/koaga/xi/2/meirelles.html).

MIERING, PIET (1999). *Chronicle of the Truth Commission: A Journey through Past and Present into the Future of South Africa* (Vanderbijlpark: Carpe Diem Books).

MIGNONE, EMILIO, ESTLUND, CYNTHIA C., and ISSACHAROFF, SAMUEL (1984). 'Dictatorship on Trial: Prosecution of Human Rights Violations in Argentina', *Yale Journal of International Law*, 10 (1): 118–149.

MILLER, BARBARA (1997). 'Wiederaneignung der Eigenen Biographie: The Significance of the Opening of Stasi Files', *German Life and Letters*, 50 (3): 369–381.

MILLER, JOHN (1998). 'Settling Accounts with a Secret Police: The German Law on the Stasi Records', *Europe-Asia Studies*, 50 (2): 305–330.

MINEAR, RICHARD H. (1971). *Victors' Justice: The Tokyo War Crimes Trial* (Princeton: Princeton University Press).

MINOW, MARTHA (1998). *Between Vengeance and Forgiveness: Facing History after Genocide and Mass Violence* (Boston: Beacon Press).

MISZTAL, BARBBRA A. (1999). 'How Not to Deal with the Past: Lustration in Poland', *Archives Europeénes de Sociologie*, 40 (1): 31–55.

MONTERO, JOSÉ RAMÓN, GUNTHER, RICHARD, and TORCAL, MARIANO (1998). 'Actitudes hacia la democracia en España: legitimidad, descontento y desafección', *Revista Española de Investigaciones Sociológicas*, 83: 9–49.

MOORE, JOHN J. JR (1991). 'Problems with Forgiveness: Granting Amnesty under the Arias Plan in Nicaragua and El Salvador', *Stanford Law Review*, 43 (3): 733–777.

MOORE, KATHLEEN DEAN (1989). *Pardons: Justice, Mercy and the Public Interest* (New York: Oxford University Press).

MORALES, JOSÉ LUIS, and JUAN CELADA (1981). *La alternativa militar: el golpismo después de Franco* (Madrid: Editorial Revolución).

MORÁN, GREGORIO (1991). *El precio de la transición* (Barcelona: Planeta).

MORGAN, JOHN P. (1994). 'The Communist Torturers of Eastern Europe: Prosecute or Punish or Forgive and Forget', *Communist and Post Communist Studies*, 27 (1): 95–109.

MORLINO, LEONARDO (1998). *Democracy between Consolidation and Crisis: Parties, Groups, and Citizens in Southern Europe* (Oxford: Oxford University Press).

—— and HITE, KATHERINE (1999). 'Problematising Authoritarian Legacies and Good Democracy', paper presented to the Authoritarian Legacies Group, Summer Workshop, August 26–27, Arrábida, Portugal.

—— and MATTEI, FRANCO (1998). 'Old and New Authoritarianism in Southern Europe', in Stein Ugelvik, Larsen (ed.), *Modern Europe after Fascism, 1943–1980s* (Boulder, Colo.: Social Science East European Monographs), 1752–1774.

—— and MONTERO, JOSÉ RAMÓN (1995). 'Legitimacy and Democracy in Southern Europe', in Richard Gunther, P. Nikiforos Diamandouros, and Hans-Jürgen Puhle (eds.), *The Politics of Democratic Consolidation: Southern Europe in Comparative Perspective* (Baltimore and London: Johns Hopkins University Press), 33–76.

MORRIS, JAMES A. (1984). *Honduras: Caudillo Politics and Military Rulers* (Boulder, Colo.: Westview Press).

MORRIS, MADELEINE (1999). 'The Perils of Complementarity', unpublished paper.

MORRIS, VIRGINIA, and SCHARF, MICHAEL P. (1995). *An Insider's Guide to the International Criminal Tribunal for the Former Yugoslavia* (Ardsley, NY: Transnational Publishers).

MORROW, JAMES D. (1994). *Game Theory for Political Scientists* (Princeton: Princeton University Press).

MORVAI, KRISZTINA (1994). 'Retroactive Justice based on International Law: A Recent Decision of the Hungarian Constitutional Court', *East European Constitutional Review*, 2 (4): 32–35.

MOSKOVSKY, ANTIFASHISTSKY TSENTR (1997). *Butovsky Poligon: Kniga pamyati zhertv politicheskikh repressii* (Moscow: MATs), 5–30.

Mosse, George (1990). *Fallen Soldiers: Reshaping Memory of the World Wars* (New York: Oxford University Press).

Mostov, July (1998). 'The Use and Abuse of History in Eastern Europe: A Challenge for the 1990s', *Constellations*, 4 (3): 376–386.

Moulián, Tomás (1997). *Chile: Anatomía de un mito* (Santiago: Lom Ediciones).

—— (1999). 'The Arrest and its Aftermath', *NACLA Report on the Americas*, 32 (6): 12–16.

Mozzicafredo, Juan (1991). *Gestão local e legitimidade no sistema político local* (Lisbon: Escher).

Muller, Pawel (1992). 'The Gauck Commission', *Uncaptive Minds*, 5 (1): 95–98.

Muñoz Alonso, Alejandro (1982). *El terrorismo en España* (Barcelona: Círculo de Lectores).

Mushaben, Joyce Marie (1998). *From Postwar to Post-Wall Generations: Changing Attitudes toward the National Question and NATO in the Federal Republic of Germany* (Boulder, Colo.: Westview Press).

Naarden, Bruno (1997). 'Het geloof en geweld van Oktober', *Internationale Spectator*, 51 (11): 587–592.

NACLA (North American Congress on Latin America) (1998). 'Unearthing *Memory*: The Present Struggle over the Past', *NACLA Report on the Americas*, 32 (2).

Nakasone, Yasuhiro (1995). 'Reflections on Japan's Past', *Asia-Pacific Review*, pp. 53–71.

Nanda, Ved P. (1998). 'Civil and Political Sanctions as an Accountability Mechanism for Massive Violations of Human Rights', *Denver Journal of International Law and Policy*, 26 (3): 389–398.

Natrass, Nicol (1999). 'The Truth and Reconciliation Commission on Business and Apartheid: A Critical Evaluation', *African Affairs*, 98: 373–392.

Neff, Michael L. (1992). 'East Europe's Policy of Restitution of Property in the 1990s', *Dickinson Journal of International Law*, 10 (2): 357–382.

New York Law School Human Rights Journal (1992). *Truth and Justice: The Question of Accountability*, special issue, *New York Law School Human Rights Journal*, 9 (3).

Neyer, Arich (1998). *War Crimes: Brutality, Genocide, Terror and the Struggle for Justice* (New York: Random House).

Nikolaev, Rada (1991). 'Between Hope and Hunger', *Report on Eastern Europe*, 2 (1): 5–10.

Nina, Daniel (1997). 'Panel Beating for the Smashed Nation? The Truth and Reconciliation Commission, Nation Building and Construction of a Privileged History in South Africa', *Australian Journal of Law and Society*, 13: 55–72.

Nino, Carlos Santiago (1985). 'The Human Rights Policy of the Argentine Constitutional Government: A Reply to Mignone, Estlund and Issacharoff', *Yale Journal of International Law*, 11: 217–230.

—— (1991). 'The Duty to Punish past Abuses of Human Rights Put into Context: The Case of Argentina'. *Yale Journal of International Law*, 100 (8): 2619–2643.

—— (1996). *Radical Evil on Trial* (New Haven, Conn.: Yale University Press).

NOGUEIRA DA SILVA, PAULO NAPOLEÃO (1988). *Autoritarismo e impunidade: um perfil do democratismo brasileiro* (São Paulo: Edicões Alfa-Omega).

NORA, PIERRE (1982–92). *Lieux de mémoire*, i–vii (Paris: Gallimard).

—— (1989). 'Between Memory and History: Les Lieux de Mémoire', *Representations*, 26: 7–25.

NORDEN, DEBORAH L. (1996). *Military Rebellion in Argentina: Between Coups and Consolidation* (Lincoln, Neb.: University of Nebraska Press).

NORFOLK, SIMON, BERGER, HARVEY, and IGNATIEFF, MICHAEL (1999). *For Most of It I Have No Words: Genocide, Memory and Landscape* (New York: Dewi Louis).

NORVAL, ALETTA J. (1998). 'Memory, Identity and the (Im)possibility of Reconciliation: The Work of the Truth and Reconciliation Commission in South Africa', *Constellations*, 5 (2): 250–265.

NOVE, ALEC (1993). 'Victims of Stalinism: How Many? in J. Arch Getty and R. T. Manning (eds.), *Stalinist Terror: New Perspectives* (Cambridge: Cambridge University Press), 261–274.

NOVICK, PETER (1968). *The Resistance Versus Vichy: The Purge of Collaborators in Liberated France* (New York: Columbia University Press).

NUNCA MAIS (1985). *Nunca Mais: A tortura no Brasil* (Petrópolis: Editora Vozes).

NUTTAL, SARAH and COETZEE, CARLI (eds.) (1998). *Negotiating the Past: The Making of Memory in South Africa* (Cape Town: Oxford University Press).

ODER, ARTHUR H. (1990). 'Comments by Four Members of the Commission of Inquiry', excerpts from remarks by Justice Arthur H. Oder at a seminar organised by the Commission, 14–17 February, in Neil J. Kritz (ed.), *Transitional Justice: How Emerging Democracies Reckon with Former Regimes*, ii (Washington DC: USIP), 520–531.

—— (1991). The Role of the Commission of Inquiry into Violations of Human Rights Promotion in Uganda, in Neil J. Kritz (ed.), *Transitional Justice: How Emerging Democracies Reckon with Former Regimes*, ii (Washington DC: USIP), 513–519.

ODHAG (Oficina de Derechos Humanos del Arzobispado de Guatemala) (1998). *Guatemala Nunca Más: Informe del proyecto interdiocesano de recuperación de la memoria histórica*, i–iv (Guatemala City: ODHAG).

O'DONNELL, GUILLERMO (1992). *Delegative Democracy?* Working Paper 172. (South Bend, Ind.: Helen Kellog Institute for International Studies).

—— (1996). 'Illusions about Consolidation', *Journal of Democracy*, 7 (2): 34–51.

—— Schmitter, Philippe, and Whitehead, Laurence (eds.) (1986a). *Transitions from Authoritarian Rule: Comparative Perspectives* (Baltimore: Johns Hopkins University Press).

—— —— (1986b). *Tentative Conclusions about Uncertain Democracies* (Baltimore: Johns Hopkins University Press).

—— —— (1986c). *Transitions from Authoritarian Rule: Latin America* (Baltimore: Johns Hopkins University Press).

Offe, Claus (1992). 'Coming to Terms with Past Injustices', *Archives Europeénnes de Sociologie*, 33 (1): 195–201.

—— (1993). 'Disqualification, Retribution, Restitution: Dilemmas of Justice in Postcommunist Transitions', *Journal of Political Philosophy*, 1 (1): 17–44.

—— (1996). *Varieties of Transition: The East European and East German Experience* (Cambridge, Mass.: MIT Press).

—— (n.d.). 'Notes on Transitional justice in the German Democratic Republic/New *Länder*', unpublished paper.

—— Bonker, Frank, and Holmes, Stephen (1993). 'Forum on Restitution', *East European Constitutional Review*, 2 (3): 30–42.

Oltay, Edith (1993). 'Hungary's Attempts to Deal with its Past', *RFE/RL Research Report*, 2 (18): 6–10.

—— (1994). 'Hungary's Screening Law', *RFE/RL Research Report*, 3 (15): 13–15.

Opello, Walter C. Jr (1991). 'Portugal: A Case Study of International Determinants of Regime Transition', in Geoffrey Pridham, *Encouraging Democracy: The International Context of Regime Transition in Southern Europe* (Leicester: Leicester University Press), 84–102.

Oppenheim, Lois Hecht (1991). 'Redemocratisation in Latin America: Civilian Agenda and Military Legacy in Chile', *Review of Latin American Studies*, 4 (2): 184–206.

Oquaye, M. (1995). 'Human Rights and the Transition to Democracy under the PNDC in Ghana', *Human Rights Quarterly*, 17 (3): 556–573.

Orban, Viktor (1991). 'The Case against Compensation', *Uncaptive Minds*, 4 (2): 33–39.

Orbman, Jan (1991). 'Laying the Ghosts of the Past', *Report on Eastern Europe*, 2 (24): 4–11.

Orentlicher, Diane F. (1991a). 'Settling Accounts: The Duty to Prosecute Human Rights Violations of a Prior Regime', *Yale Law Journal*, 100 (8): 2537–2615.

—— (1991b). 'A Reply to Professor Nino', *Yale Law Journal*, 100: 2641–2643.

Ortzi (1979). *El no vasco a la reforma*, 2 vols. (San Sebastián: Txertoa).

Osiel, Mark (1987). 'The Making of Human Rights Policy in Argentina: The Impact of Ideas and Interests on a Legal Conflict', *Journal of Latin American Studies*, 18 (1): 135–178.

OSIEL, MARK (1995a). 'Ever Again: Legal Remembrance of Administrative Massacre', *University of Pennsylvania Law Review*, 144 (2): 463–704.

—— (1995b). 'Dialogue with Dictators: Judicial Resistance in Argentina and Brazil', *Law and Social Inquiry*, 20 (2): 481–560.

—— (1997). *Mass Atrocity, Collective Memory, and the Law* (New Brunswick, NJ: Transaction Publishers).

—— (1998). 'Obeying Orders: Atrocity, Military Discipline and the Law of War', *California Law Review*, 86 (5): 939–1121.

OSOFSKY, HARI M. (1997). 'Domesticating Humanitarian International Law: Bringing Human Rights Violators to Justice', *Yale Law Journal*, 107 (1): 191–260.

OSTIANSKY, WIKTOR (1992). 'Agent Walesa? Lustration Leads to a Grand Scale Political Provocation in Poland', *East European Constitutional Review*, 40 (1): 56–102.

—— (1994). 'Ostiansky on the End of Decommunisation', *East European Constitutional Review*, 3 (3–4): 26.

OTTO, DIANNE (1996). 'Non-governmental Organisations in the United Nations System: The Emerging Role of International Civil Society', *Human Rights Quarterly*, 18 (1): 107–141.

PACZOLAY, PETER (1992). 'Judicial Review of Compensation Law in Hungary', *Michigan Journal of International Law*, 13 (3): 806–831.

PALENCIA, TANIA (1997). 'Advocates and Guarantors: Establishing Participative Democracy in Post-war Guatemala', in J. Armon, Rachel Sieder, and Richard Wilson (eds.), *Negotiating Rights: the Guatemalan Peace Process, 1987–1996* (London: Conciliation Resources), 28–35.

PANIZZA, FRANCISCO (1995). 'Human Rights in the Transition and Consolidation of Democracy in Latin America', *Political Studies*, Special Issue, 43 (4): 168–188.

PARKER, KAREN, and CHEW, JENNIFER F. (1994). 'Compensation for Japan's World War II War-Rape Victims', *Hastings International and Comparative Law Review*, 17 (3): 497–558.

PASQUALUCCI, JO M. (1994a). 'The Whole Truth and Nothing but the Truth: Truth Commissions, Impunity and the Inter-American System', *Boston University International Law Journal*, 12 (2): 321–370.

—— (1994b). 'The Inter-American Human Rights System: Establishing Precedents and Procedure in Human Rights Law', *University of Miami Inter-American Law Review*, 26 (2): 297–362.

—— (1995). 'Victim Reparations and the Inter-American Human Rights System: A Critical Assessment of Current Practise and Procedure', *Michigan Journal of International Law*, 18 (1): 1–58.

PASSERINI, LUISA (1987). *Fascism in Popular Memory* (Cambridge: Cambrige University Press).

—— (ed.) (1992). *Memory and Totalitarianism: International Yearbook of Oral History and Life Stories*, i (Oxford: Oxford University Press).

Patriarca, Fátima (1999) 'A revolução e a questão social: que justiça social', in Fernando Rosas (ed.), *Portugal e a transição para a democracia, 1974–1976* (Lisbon: Colibri), 137–160.

Payne, Stanley (1993). *Spain's First Democracy: The Second Republic, 1931–1936* (Madison, Wis.: University of Wisconsin Press).

PDH (Procurador de los Derechos Humanos) (1994). *Las patrullas de autodefensa civil* (Guatemala City: PDH).

Pearce, Jenny (1995). 'Impunity and Democracy: The Case of Chile', in Rachel Sieder (ed.), *Impunity in Latin America* (London: Institute of Latin American Studies), 45–56.

—— (1996). 'How Useful is Civil Society as a Conceptualisation of the Process of Democratisation with Reference to Latin America?' in Lee-Ann Broadhead (ed.), *Issues in Peace Studies* (Bradford: Bradford University Peace Studies).

Pehe, Jiri (1991). 'Parliament Passes Controversial Law on Vetting Officials', *Report on Eastern Europe*, 2: 4–8.

Pellinka, Anton, and Weinzierl, Erika (eds.) (1987). *Das grosse tabu: Osterreichs Umgang mit siener Vergangenheit* (Vienna: Verlag der Österreichischen Staatsdruckerei).

Perelli, Carina (1987). *Amnistía no, amnistía sí, amnistía puede ser: la constitución histórica de un tema político del Uruguay en la transición* (Montevideo: Ediciones de la Banda Oriental).

—— (1992). 'Settling Accounts with Blood Memory: The Case of Argentina', *Social Research*, 59 (2): 415–451.

Philipsen, Dirk (ed.) (1993). *We Were the People: Voices from East Germany's Revolutionary Autumn of 1989* (Durham, NC: Duke University Press).

Piccigallo, Philip R. (1979). *The Japanese on Trial: Allied War Crimes Operations in the East, 1945–1951* (Austin, Tx: University of Texas Press).

Pickel, Andreas, and Wiesenthal, Helmut (1997). *The Grand Experiment: Debating Shock Therapy, Transition Theory, and the East German Experience* (Boulder, Colo.: Westview Press).

Pinto, António Costa (1991). 'The Radical Right in Contemporary Portugal', in Luciano Cheles, Ronnie Ferguson, and Michalina Vaughn (eds.), *Neo Fascism in Europe* (London: Longman), 108–128.

—— (1995). *The Salazar Dictatorship and European Fascism* (New York: SSM–Columbia University Press).

—— (1998). 'Dealing with the Legacy of Authoritarianism: Political Purges and Radical Right Wing Movements in Portugal's Transition to Democracy 1974–1980s', in Stein Ugelvik Larsen *et al.* (eds.), *Modern Europe after Fascism, 1943–1980s* (Boulder, Colo.: Social Science East European Monographs), 1679–1717.

—— (1999). 'A guerra colonial e o fim do império português', in Francisco Bethencourt and Kirti Chaudhury (eds.), *História da expansão portuguesa*, v (Lisbon: Círculo de Leitores), 65–98.

PINTO, ANTÓNIO COSTA, and TAVARES DE ALMEIDA, PEDRO (1999). 'The Legacies of the Past and Democratic Consolidation in Portugal', paper presented to the Authoritarian Legacies Group, Summer Workshop, 26–27 August, Arrábida, Portugal.

PION-BERLIN, DAVID (1994). 'To Prosecute or to Pardon: Human Rights Decisions in the Latin American Southern Cone', *Human Rights Quarterly*, 16 (1): 105–130.

—— (1997). *Through Corridors of Power: Institutions and Civil Military Relations in Argentina* (Philadelphia: University of Pennsylvania Press).

—— and ARCENEAUX, CRAIG (1998). 'Tipping the Civil Military Balance: Institutions and Human Rights in Democratic Argentina and Chile', *Comparative Political Studies*, 31 (5): 633–651.

PIPER, ERNST (ed.) (1993). *Forever in the Shadow of Hitler: Original Documents of the Historikerstreit, the Controversy Concerning the Singularity of the Holocaust* (Atlantic Highlands, NJ: Humanities Press).

PLATT, ALEXANDER *et al.* (1992). 'Compensating Former Political Prisoners: An Overview of Developments in Central and Eastern Europe', in: Neil J. Kritz, (ed.), *Transitional Justice: How Emerging Democracies Reckon with Former Regimes* (Washington DC: USIP), 571, 578, 751.

PODRABINEK, ALEXANDER (1993). 'Who Will Judge the Party?' *Uncaptive Minds*, 5 (3): 23–26.

POGANY, ISTVAN (1998). 'The Restitution of Former Jewish Owned Property and Related Schemes of Compensation in Hungary', *European Public Law*, 4 (2): 211–232.

POMORSKY, STANISLAW (1996). 'Meanings of Decommunisation by Legal Means', *Review of Central and East European Law*, 22 (3): 331–345.

PONS PRADES, EDUARDO (1987). *Crónica negra de la transición española (1976–1985)* (Barcelona: Plaza & Janés).

POPKIN, MARGARET L. (1996). *The Civil Patrols in Guatemala: Overcoming Militarisation and Polarisation in the Guatemalan Countryside* (Washington DC: Robert Kennedy Memorial Centre for Human Rights).

—— (2000). *Peace without Justice: Obstacles to Building the Rule of Law in El Salvador* (Philadelphia: Pennsylvania State University Press).

—— and BHUTA, NEHAL (1999). 'Latin American Amnesties in Comparative Perspective: Can the Past be Buried?' *Ethics and International Affairs*, 13: 99–122.

—— and ROHT-ARRIAZA, NAOMI (1995). 'Truth as Justice: Investigatory Commissions in Latin America', *Law and Social Inquiry*, 20 (1): 79–116.

POWER, JONATHAN (1981). *Against Oblivion: Amnesty International's Fight for Human Rights* (London: Fontana).

PRICE, ROBERT (1991). *The Apartheid State in Crisis: Political Transformation in South Africa, 1975–1990* (Oxford: Oxford University Press).

—— (1997) 'Race and Reconciliation in the New South Africa', *Politics and Society*, 25 (2): 147–178.

PRIDHAM, GEOFFREY (1991). *Encouraging Democracy: The International Context of Regime Transition in Southern Europe* (Leicester: Leicester University Press).

PRZEWORKSI, ADAM (1988). 'Algunos problemas en el estudio de la transición hacia la democracia', in Guillermo O'Donnell *et al.* (eds.), *Perspectivas comparadas*, iii (Buenos Aires: Paidós), 79–104.

—— (1991). *Democracy and the Market: Political and Economic Reforms in Eastern Europe and Latin America* (New York: Cambridge University Press).

—— (1995). 'Presentación', in Carlos H. Acuña *et al.*, *Juicio, castigos y memorias* (Buenos Aires: Nueva Visión), 13–18.

QUILL, ADRIENNE (1996). 'Comment. To Prosecute or not to Prosecute: Problems Encountered in the Prosecution of Former Communist Regimes in German, Czechoslovakia, and the Czech Republic', *Indiana University International and Comparative Law Review*, 7: 165–183.

QUINN, ROBERT J. (1994). 'Will the Rule of Law End? Challenging Grants of Amnesty for the Human Rights Violations of a Prior Regime: Chile's New Model', *Fordham Law Review*, 62 (4): 905–960.

QUINT, PETER E. (1997). *The Imperfect Union: Constitutional Structures of German Unification* (Princeton: Princeton University Press).

—— (n.d.). 'German Unification and the Jurisprudence of the Basic Law', unpublished paper.

RAMÍREZ, GABRIEL (1989). *La cuestión militar: democracia tutelada o democracia asociativa?* (Montevideo: Arca).

RATNER, STEVEN R. (1998a). 'New Democracies, Old Atrocities: An Inquiry in International Law', *Georgetown Law Journal*, 87 (3): 707–748.

—— (1998b). 'Judging the Past: State Practise and the Law of Accountability', *European Journal of International Law*, 9 (2): 412–246.

—— and ABRAMS, JASON S. (1997). *Accountability for Human Rights Atrocities in International Law: Beyond the Nuremberg Legacy* (Oxford: Clarendon Press).

REINARES, FERNANDO (1990). 'Sociogénesis y evolución del terrorismo en España.' In Salvador Giner (ed.), *España: sociedad y política*, i (Madrid: Espasa-Calpe).

REMNICK, DAVID (1993). *Lenin's Tomb: The Last Days of the Soviet Empire* (New York: Random House).

REUTER, LUTZ R., and DURR, VÖLKER (1990). *Coping with the Past: Germany and Austria after 1945* (Madison, Wis.: University of Wisconsin Press).

RIAL, JUAN (1986). *Las Fuerzas Armadas: ¿soldados políticos garantes de la democracia?* (Montevideo: CIESU).

RICHTER, MICHAEL (1996). *Die Staatssicherheit im letzten Jahr der DDR* (Weimar: Böhlau).

RICKARD, LISA (1981). 'Filártiga vs. Peña-Irala: A New Forum For Violations of International Human Rights', *American University Law Review*, 30: 807–833.

RIVERA, ANTONIO (1998). 'La transición en el País Vasco: un caso particular', in Javier Ugarte (ed.), *La transición en el País Vasco y España: historia y memoria* (Bilbao: Universidad del País Vasco), 79–92.

RODRÍGUEZ IBÁÑEZ, JOSÉ ENRIQUE (1987). *Después de una dictadura: cultura autoritaria y transición política en España* (Madrid: Centro de Estudios Constitucionales).

RODRÍGUEZ, JOSÉ LUIS (1997). *La extrema derecha española en el siglo XX* (Madrid: Alianza Editorial).

ROGERS, GEORGE (1990). *Argentina y la tortura: obligación de juzgar a los responsables*, Working Paper 2 (Buenos Aires: Centro de Estudios Legales y Sociales).

ROHRSCHNEIDER, ROBERT (1999). *Learning Democracy: Democratic and Economic Values in Unified Germany* (Oxford: Clarendon).

ROHT-ARRIAZA, NAOMI (1990). 'State Responsibility to Investigate and Prosecute Grave Human Rights Violations in International Law', *California Law Review* 78 (2): 451–513.

—— (1995). *Impunity and Human Rights in International Law and Practice* (Oxford: Oxford University Press).

—— (1998a). 'Foreign Sovereign Immunities Act and Human Rights Violations: One Step Forward, Two Steps Back?' *Berkeley Journal of International Law*, 16 (1): 71–84.

—— (1998b). 'Truth Commissions and Amnesties in Latin America: The Second Generation', *Proceedings of the American Society of International Law*, 92: 313–316.

—— and GIBSON, LAUREN (1998). 'The Developing Jurisprudence on Amnesty', *Human Rights Quarterly*, 20 (4): 843–885.

ROLSTON, B. (1996). *Turning the Page without Closing the Book: The Right to Truth in the Irish Context* (Dublin: Irish Reporter Publications).

ROMIJN, PETER (1989). *Snel, streng en rechtvaardig: politiek belied inzake de bestraffing en reclassering van 'foute' Nederlanders, 1945–1955* (Swift, Severe and Fair Justice: Dutch Politics and the Purge of Collaborators, 1945–1955) (Amsterdam: De Haan).

RONIGER, LUIS (1997). 'Patterns of Citizenship and the Legacy of Human Rights Violations: The Cases of Redemocratised Argentina and Uruguay', *Journal of Historical Sociology*, 10 (3): 270–310.

—— and SNAZJDER, MARIO (1997). 'The Legacy of Human Rights Violations and the Collective Identity of Redemocratised Uruguay', *Human Rights Quarterly*, 19 (1): 55–77.

—— —— (1999). *The Legacy of Human Rights Violations in the Southern Cone: Argentina, Chile and Uruguay* (Oxford: Oxford University Press).

ROSE, RICHARD, and HAERPFER, CHRISTIAN (1992–6). *New Democracies Barometer* (Glasgow: Strathclyde University).

ROSENBERG, TINA (1995a). *The Haunted Land: Facing Europe's Ghosts after Communism* (London: Random House).

—— (1995b). 'Overcoming the Legacies of Dictatorship', *Foreign Affairs*, 74 (3): 134–153.

Rosenfeld, Michel (1996). 'Restitution, Retribution, Political Justice and the Rule of Law', *Constellations*, 2 (3): 309–428.

Rotberg, Robert I., and Thompson, Dennis (eds.) (2000). *Truth vs. Justice: The Moral Efficacy of Truth Commissions in South Africa and Beyond* (Princeton: Princeton University Press).

Rousso, Henry (1991). *The Vichy Syndrome: History and Memory in France since 1944* (Cambridge, Mass.: Harvard University Press).

Ruscio, Alain, *et al.* (1994). *Oublier nos crimes: l'amnésie nationale, une specificité française?* (Paris: Editions Audemont).

Rwelamira, M. R., and Werle, Gerhard (1996). *Confronting Past Injustices: Approaches to Amnesty, Punishment, Reparation and Restitution in South Africa and Germany* (Durban: Butterworth).

Rychlak, Ronald J. (1990). 'Society's Moral Right to Punish: A Further Exploration of the Denunciation Theory of Punishment', *Tulane Law Review*, 65 (2): 299–338.

Rzeplinski, Andrzy (1992). 'A Lesser Evil?' *East European Constitutional Review*, 1 (3): 33–38.

Sa'adah, Anne (1998). *Germany's Second Chance: Trust, Justice, and Democratization* (Cambridge, Mass.: Harvard University Press).

Sabbat-Swidlicka, Anna (1993). 'Poland: A Year of Three Governments', *RFL/RL Research Report*, 2 (1): 102–107.

Saino, Maria (1998). *Gone Fishing: An Initial Evaluation of the South African TRC's Amnesty Process*, Working Paper (Johannesburg: Centre for the Study of Violence and Reconciliation).

Sánchez-Cuenca, Ignacio (1995). *Las negociaciones agrícolas entre la Comunidad Europea y los Estados Unidos en la Ronda Uruguay: un análisis desde la lógica de la elección racional* (Madrid: Instituto Juan March).

Sánchez Navarro, Ángel J. (1998). *La transición española en sus documentos* (Madrid: Centro de Estudios Políticos y Constitucionales/ Boletín Oficial del Estado).

Sancinetti, Marcelo A. (1988). *Derechos humanos en la argentina post-dictatorial: juicio a los ex-comandantes* (Buenos Aires: Lerner Editores Asociados).

Santner, Eric (1990). *Stranded Objects: Mourning, Memory and Film in Postwar Germany* (Ithaca, NY: Cornell University Press).

Sarkin, Jeremy (1996). 'The Trials and Tribulations of South Africa's Truth and Reconciliation Commission', *South African Journal of Human Rights*, 12 (4): 617–640.

—— (1999). 'The Necessity and Challenges of Establishing a Truth Commission for Rwanda', *Human Rights Quarterly*, 21 (3): 767–823.

SATRC (South African Truth and Reconciliation Commission) (1998). *Report of the South African Truth and Reconciliation Commission*, i–v (Cape Town: TRC).

SCHIRMER, JENNIFER (1998) 'Prospects for Compliance: The Guatemalan Military and the Peace Accords', in Rachel Sieder (ed.), *Guatemala after the Peace Accords* (London: Institute of Latin American Studies).

SCHLESINGER, STEPHEN, and KINZER, STEPHEN (1992). *Bitter Fruit: The Untold Story of the American Coup in Guatemala* (New York: Doubleday).

SCHLINK, BERNHARD (1998). 'Die Bewältigung von Vergangenheit durch Recht', in Helmut König, Michael Kohlstruck, and Andreas Wöll (eds.), *Vergangenheitsbewältigung am Ende des zwanzigsten Jahrhunderts* (Opladen: Westdeutscher Verlag), 433–451.

SCHMITTER, PHILIPPE C. (1995). 'Public Opinion and the "Quality of Democracy" in Portugal', in H. E. Chehabi and Alfred Stepan (eds.), *Politics, Society, and Democracy: Comparative Studies (Essays in Honour of Juan J. Linz)* (Boulder, Colo.: Westview Press), 345–359.

—— (ed.) (1996). *The Consolidation of Democracy* (Washington DC: Woodrow Wilson Centre).

—— (1999a). 'The Democratisation of Portugal in its Comparative Perspective', in Fernando Rosas (ed.), *Portugal e a transição para a democracia, 1974–1976* (Lisbon: Colibri), 337–363.

—— (1999b). *Portugal: do autoritarismo à democracia* (Lisbon: Instituto de Ciências Sociais).

SCHROEDER, KLAUS (1998). *Der SED-Staat: Partei, Staat und Gesellschaft 1949–1990* (Munich: Hanser).

SCHULHOFER, STEPHEN J., ROSENFELD, MICHEL, TEITEL, RUTI, and ERRERA, ROGER (1992). 'Dilemmas of Justice', *East European Constitutional Review*, 1 (2): 17–21.

SCHULTZ, DONALD, and SUNDLOFF-SCHULTZ, DEBORAH (1996). *The United States and the Crisis in Honduras* (Boulder, Colo.: Westview Press).

SCHUMANN, SILKE (1997). *Vernichten oder Offenlegen? Zur Entstehung des Stasi-Unterlagen-Gesetzes: Eine Dokumentation der öffentlichen Debatte 1990/91* (Berlin: Der Bundesbeauftragte für die Unterlagen des Staatssicherheitsdienstes der ehemaligen Deutschen Demokratischen Republik).

SCHWAN, GESINE (1998). 'Political Consequences of Silenced Guilt', *Constellations*, 5 (4): 472–491.

SCHWARTZ, HERMAN (1992). 'The New East European Constitutional Courts', *Michigan Journal of International Law*, 13 (3): 741–785.

—— (1994). 'Lustration in Eastern Europe', *Parker School Journal of East European Law*, 1 (2): 141–171.

SCPPG (Servicio Central de Publicaciones de Presidencia del Gobierno) (1977). *Pactos de la Moncloa: texto completo del acuerdo económico y del acuerdo político, Madrid, 8–27 October 1977* (Madrid: SCPPG).

SEEKINGS, JEREMY (1996). 'Civic Organisations during South Africa's Transition to Democracy, 1990–1996', paper presented at the conference of the Political Sociology section of the International Sociology Association and the South African Sociological Association in Durban, July.

Senzaburo, Sato, and Itakashi, Ito (1995). 'Coming to Terms with the War', *Japan Echo*, 22 (1): 58–67.

Serbin, Kenneth P. (1998). 'The Anatomy of a Death: Repression, Human Rights and the Case of Alexandre Vannuchi Leme in Authoritarian Brazil', *Journal of Latin American Studies*, 30 (1): 1–34.

SERPAJ (Servicio de Paz y Justicia) (1992). *Uruguay Nunca Más: Human Rights Violations 1972–1985* (Philadelphia: Temple University Press).

Shabad, Goldie, and Llera, Francisco J. (1995). 'Political Violence in a Democratic State: Basque Terrorism in Spain', in Martha Crenshaw (ed.), *Terrorism in Context* (Philadelphia: Pennsylvania State University Press), 410–469.

Shafir, Michael (1993). 'Best-Selling Spy Novels Seek to Rehabilitate Romanian Securitate', *RFE/RL Research Report*, 2 (45): 14–18.

Shapiro, Ian (1996). *Democracy's Place* (Ithaca, NY: Cornell University Press).

Shapland, Joanna (1990). *Guide for Practitioners Regarding the Implementation of the Declaration of Basic Principles of Justice for Victims of Crime and Abuses of Power* (United Nations A/Conf. 144/20 June).

Sharlet, Robert (1993). 'The Russian Constitutional Court: The First Term', *Post-Soviet Affairs*, 9 (1): 1–40.

Shaw, Mark (1993). *Crying Peace Where There Is None? The Functioning and Future of Local Peace Committees under the National Peace Accord*, Research Report 31 (Johannesburg: Centre for Policy Studies).

—— (1994). 'The Bloody Backdrop: Negotiating Violence', in Doreen Atkinson and Steven Friedman (eds.), *The Small Miracle: South Africa's Negotiated Settlement* (Johannesburg: Ravan Press), 182–203.

Shelton, Dinah (1992). 'The Inter-American Human Rights System', in Hurst Hannum (ed.), *Guide to International Human Rights Practice* (Philadelphia: Pennsylvania University Press), 119–134.

Shey, Peter A., Shelton, Dinah, and Roht-Arriaza, Naomi (1997). 'Addressing Human Rights Abuses: Truth Commissions and the Value of Amnesty', *Whittier Law Review*, 19 (2): 325–347.

Shriver, Donald (1995). An Ethic for Enemies: Forgiveness in Politics (New York: Oxford University Press).

Shubane, Khela, and Madiba, P. (1992). *The Struggle Continues? Civic Associations in the Transition*, Research Report 25 (Johannesburg: Centre for Policy Studies).

—— and Shaw, Mark (1993). *Tomorrow's Foundations? Forums as the Second Level of a Negotiated Transition in South Africa*, Research Report 33 (Johannesburg: Centre for Policy Studies).

Sieder, Rachel (ed.) (1995a). *Impunity in Latin America* (London: Institute of Latin American Studies).

—— (1995b) 'Honduras: The Politics of Exception and Military Reformism, 1972–78', *Journal of Latin American Studies*, 27 (1): 99–127.

—— (ed.) (1998). *Guatemala after the Peace Accords* (London: Institute of Latin American Studies).

SIEDER, RACHEL and COSTELLO, PATRICK (1996). 'Judicial Reform in Central America: Prospects for the Rule of Law', in Rachel Sieder (ed.), *Central America: Fragile Transition* (London: Macmillan), 169–211.

SIEFF, MICHELLE, and VINJAMURI WRIGHT, LESLIE (1999). 'Reconciling Order and Justice? New Institutional Solutions in Post-Conflict States', *Journal of International Affairs*, 2: 757–779.

SIEGELMAN, PETER (1995). 'The Problems of Lustration: Righting the Wrongs of the Past', *Law and Social Inquiry*, 20 (1): 1–6.

SIEGERT, DIETER (1993). 'The State, the Stasi and the People: The Debate about the Past and the Difficulties in Reformulating Collective Identities', *Journal of Communist Studies*, 9 (3): 202–215.

SIKLOVA, JIRINA (1996). 'Lustration or the Czech Way of Screening', *East European Constitutional Review*, 5 (1): 57–62.

SIMON, JEAN-MARIE (1993). 'The Alien Tort Convention Act: Justice or Show Trials?' *Boston University International Law Journal*, 11 (1): 1–76.

SIMPSON, GRAEME (1994). *Truth Recovery or McCarthysim Revisited: An Evaluation of the Stasi Records Act with Reference to the South African Experience*, Working Paper (Johannesburg: Centre for the Study of Violence and Reconciliation).

—— (1998). *A Brief Evaluation of South Africa's Truth and Reconciliation Commission: Some Lessons for Societies in Transition*, Working Paper (Johannesburg: Centre for the Study of Violence and Reconciliation).

—— and VAN ZYL, PAUL (1997). *Witch Hunt or Whitewash? Problems of Justice in Transition in South Africa*, Working Paper (Johannesburg: Centre for the Study of Violence and Reconciliation).

SINOVA, JUSTINO (ed.) (1984). *Historia de la transición: diez años que cambiaron España (1973–1983)*, i–ii (Madrid: Grupo 16).

SKLAR, MORTON H. (1995). *Decommunisation: A New Threat to Scientific and Academic Freedom in Central and Eastern Europe*, Report of the Science and Human Rights Programme of the American Association for the Advancement of Science (Washington DC: AAAS).

SMITH, ANTHONY D. (1996). 'The Resurgence of Nationalism? Myth and Memory in the Renewal of Nations', *British Journal of Sociology*, 47 (4): 575–598.

SMITH, B. (1977). *Reaching Judgement at Nuremberg* (New York: Basic Books).

SMITH, KATHLEEN E. (1996). *Remembering Stalin's Victims: Popular Memory and the End of the USSR* (Ithaca, NY: Cornell University Press).

SMYTH, MARIE (1998). 'Remembering in Northern Ireland: Victims, Perpetrators and Hierarchies of Pain and Responsibility', paper presented at the Conference on Dealing with the Past: Reconciliation Processes and Peace Building, Initiative on Conflict Resolution and Ethnicity (INCORE), Belfast, 8–9 June.

SOLOMON, PETER H. (1996). *Soviet Criminal Justice under Stalin* (Cambridge: Cambridge University Press).

SOLYOM, LASZLO (1994). 'The Hungarian Constitutional Court and Social Change', *Yale Journal of International Law*, 19 (1): 223–237.

SOSNOWSKI, SAUL, and POPKIN, LOUISE (eds.) (1993). *Repression, Exile and Democracy: Uruguayan Culture* (Durham: Duke University Press).

SOTO, ÁLVARO (1996). 'Conflictividad social y transición sindical', in Javier Tusell and Álvaro Soto (eds.), *Historia de la transición: 1975–1986* (Madrid: Alianza Editorial), 363–408.

SOUTHERN, DAVID B. (1993). 'Restitution or Compensation? The Land Question in East Germany', *International and Comparative Law Quarterly*, 42 (3): 690–696.

SOYINKA, WOLE (1999). *The Burden of Memory, The Muse of Forgiveness* (Oxford: Oxford University Press).

SPARKS, ALISTAIR (1996). *Tomorrow is Another Country: The Inside Story of South Africa's Negotiated Revolution* (London: Mandarin).

SPENCE, JACK, *et al.* (1998). *Promise and Reality: Implementation of the Guatemalan Peace Accords* (Cambridge, Mass.: Hemisphere Initiatives).

SRIRAM, CHANDRA LEKHA (2000). *Truth, Justice, and Accountability: The Way that Transitional Regimes Address the Human Rights Violations of the Past* (Ph.D. dissertation, Princeton University, January).

STAAB, ANDREAS (1998). *National Identity in Eastern Germany: Inner Unification or Continued Separation?* (Westport, Conn.: Praeger).

STAHLER-SHOLK, RICHARD (1994). 'El Salvador's Negotiated Transition: From Low Intensity Conflict to Low Intensity Democracy', *Journal of Interamerican Studies and World Affairs*, 36 (4): 1–61.

STANDAERT, PATRICIA E. (1999). 'The Friendly Settlement of Human Rights Abuses in the Americas', *Duke Journal of Comparative and International Law*, 9 (2): 519–532.

STANLEY, WILLIAM (1995). *The Protection Racket State* (Philadelphia: Temple University Press).

STANLEY, WILLIAM, and HOLIDAY, DAVID (1999). 'Everyone Participates, No One is Responsible: Peace Implementation in Guztemala', Draft Paper for the Stanford CISAC/International Project on Peace Plan Implementation, unpublished.

STATMAN, J. M. (1995). 'Exorcising the Ghosts of Apartheid: Memory, Identity and Trauma in the New South Africa', paper presented at the Annual Meeting of the International Society of Political Psychology, Washington DC.

STEIN, TINE (1998). 'Vergangenheitspolitik im Medium der Verfassungspolitik?' in Helmut Konig *et al.*, *Vergangenheitsbewältigung am Ende des swanzigsten Jahrhunderts* (Opladen: Wetdeutscher Verlag), 136–66.

STEINHARDT, RALPH G. (1995). 'Fulfilling the Promise of Filártiga: Litigating Human Rights Claims against the Estate of Ferdinand Marcos', *Yale Journal of International Law*, 20 (1): 65–87.

STENER CARLSON, ERIC (1996). *I Remember Julia: Voices of the Disappeared* (Philadelphia: Temple University Press).

STEPHENS, BETH, *et al.* (1993). *Suing for Torture and other Human Rights Abuses in Federal Court: A Litigation Manual* (Ardsley, NY: Transnational Publishers).

STEPHENS, BETH, *et al.* (1996). *International Human Rights Litigation in US Courts* (Hudson, NY: Transnational Publishers).

STEWART, DEBRA, and STEWART, CYNTHIA (1995). 'Lustration in Poland and the Former Czechoslovakia: A Study in Decommunisation', *International Journal of Public Administration*, 18 (6): 879–914.

STIEFEL, DIETER (1981). *Entnazifizierung in Osterreich* (Vienna: Europaverlag).

STOLL, DAVID (1993). *Between Two Fires in the Ixil Towns of Guatemala* (New York: Columbia University Press).

STOLLE, UTA (1997). 'Traumhafte Quellen: Vom Nutzen der Stasi-Akten für die Geschichtsschreibung', *Deutschland-Archiv*, 30: 209–21.

STOTZKY, IRWIN P. (ed.) (1993). *Transition to Democracy in Latin America: The Role of the Judiciary* (Boulder, Colo.: Westview Press).

STURDZA, MIHAI (1991). 'The Files of the State Security Police', *Report on Eastern Europe*, 2: 22–31.

SUÁREZ OROZCO, M. (1991). 'The Heritage of Enduring a Dirty War: Psychosocial Aspects of Terror in Argentina, 1976–1988', *Journal of Psychohistory*, 18 (4): 469–505.

SUSTROVA, PETRUSKA (1992). 'The Lustration Controversy', *Uncaptive Minds*, 5 (2).

SZACKA, BARBARA (1997). 'Systemic Transformation and Memory of the Past', *Polish Sociological Review*, 118: 119–131.

TAKACS, LASZLO (1992). 'Objectives of Property Indemnisation in Post-Cold War Hungary', *Comparative Juridical Review*, 29: 61–68.

TAM, DITLIV (1989). 'The Trial of Collaborators in Denmark after the Second World War', in H. Takala and H. Tham (eds.), *Scandinavian Studies in Criminology* (Oslo: Norwegian University Press).

TANFA, FATOS (1996). 'Overcoming the Past: Decommunisation and Reconstruction of Postcommunist Societies', *Studies in Comparative International Development*, 30 (4): 63–78.

TARAS, KUSIO (1998). 'Ukraine: Coming to Terms with the Soviet Legacy', *Journal of Communist Studies and Transition*, 14 (4): 1–27.

TAUSSIG, MICK (1986). *Shamanism, Colonialism and the Wild Man: A Study in Terror and Healing* (Chicago: University of Chicago Press).

TAVARES DE ALMEIDA E SILVA, CELMA FERNANDA (n.d.). 'Mortos e desaparecidos políticos sob a visão da imprensa: uma análise de posicionamento dos jornais impressos, Junho-Agosto 1995', *Tortura Nunca Mais-Pernambuco* (at: http://www.ecologica.com.br/humanrights/tortura/teoria1.htm.)

TAYLOR, JANE (1999). *The Ubu and the Truth Commission* (Capetown: University of Capetown Press).

TAYLOR, LUCY (1993). *Human Rights in the Processes of Democratization: Chile's Rettig Report*, Occasional Paper 55 (University of Glasgow: Institute of Latin American Studies).

—— (1998). *Citizenship, Participation and Democracy: Changing Dynamics in Chile and Argentina* (London: Macmillan).

TEITEL, RUTI (1995). 'Panel III. Identifying and Processing War Crimes: Two Case Studies, the former Yugoslavia and Rwanda', *New York Law School Journal of International and Comparative Law*, 12 (3): 631–686.

—— (1997). 'Transitional Jurisprudence: The Role of Law in Political Transformation', *Yale Law Journal*, 106 (6): 2009–2082.

—— (2000). *Transitional Justice* (Oxford: Oxford University Press).

TERDIMAN, RICHARD (1993). *Present Past: Modernity and the Memory Crisis* (Ithaca, NY: Cornell University Press).

THORNTON, ROBERT (1990). 'The Shooting at Uitenhage, South Africa, 1985: The Context and Interpretation of Violence', *American Ethnologist*, 17 (2): 217–236.

THURSTON, ROBERT W. (1996). *Life and Terror in Stalin's Russia 1934–1941* (New Haven: Yale University Press).

TIMMERMAN, JACOBO (1981). *Prisoner without a Name, Cell without a Number* (New York: Random Press).

TORCAL, MARIANO (1995). 'Actitudes políticas y participación política en España: pautas de cambio y continuidad', unpublished doctoral thesis, Universidad Autónoma de Madrid.

TORPEY, JOHN (1993). 'Coming to Terms with the Communist Past: East Germany in Comparative Perspective', *German Politics*, 2 (3): 415–435.

—— (1995). *Intellectuals, Socialism and Dissent: The East German Opposition and its Legacy* (Minneapolis: University of Minnesota Press).

TORRE, HIPÓLITO DE LA (ed.) (1996). *Fuerzas Armadas y poder político en el siglo XX de Portugal y España* (Mérida: UNED Centro Regional de Extremadura).

TROUILLOT, MICHEL-ROLPH (1995). *Silencing the Past: Power and the Production of History* (Boston: Beacon Press).

TUCKER, AVIEZER (1995). 'Privatisation, Restitution, Property Rights and Justice', *Public Affairs Quarterly*, 9 (4): 345–361.

—— (1998). 'Lustration in Czechoslovakia and the Czech Republic', paper presented at the Mellon Seminar on Transitional Justice, Columbia University.

—— (1999). 'Paranoids may be Prosecuted: Post-Totalitarian Retroactive Justice', *Archives Européenes de Sociologie*, 40 (1): 56–1–2.

TULCHIN, JOSEPH S., and ROMERO, BERNICE (eds.) (1995). *The Consolidation of Democracy in Latin America* (Boulder, Colo.: Lynne Rienner).

UNITED NATIONS COMMISSION on HUMAN RIGHTS (1993). *Study Concerning the Right to Restitution, Compensation and Rehabilitation for Gross Violations of Human Rights and Fundamental Freedoms: Final Report by Mr Theo van Boven* (Geneva: UN Doc. E/CN.4/Sub.2/1993/8).

UNITED NATIONS SECURITY COUNCIL (1993). *From Madness to Hope: The 12-Year War in El Salvador*, Report of the United Nations Commission on the Truth for El Salvador (New York: UN Doc. S/25500, 1 April).

—— (1999). *Guatemala: Memory of Silence Tz'inil Na'tab'al*. New York: UN.

USDS (United States Department of State) (1985–1998). US Department of State *Annual Reports on Human Rights Violations in the World* (Washington DC: USDS).

USIP (United States Institute for Peace) (1997). *Rwanda: Accountability for War Crimes and Genocide.* (Washington DC: USIP).

VALENZUELA, ARTURO (1999). 'Judging the General: Pinochet's Past and Chile's Future', *Current History*, 98: 99–104.

VAN DER MERWE, HUGO, DEWHIRST, POLLY, and HAMBER, BRANDON (1998). *The Relationship between Peace/Conflict Resolution Organizations and the TRC: An Impact Assessment* (Johannesburg: Aspen Institute International Study of Peace Organisations Paper).

VAN DYKE, JON M., and BERKLEY, GERAND W. (1992). 'Redressing Human Rights Abuses', *Denver Journal of International Law and Policy*, 20 (2): 243–268.

VAN GOUDOEVER, ALBERT P. (1986). *The Limits of Destalinisation in the Soviet Union: Political Rehabilitations in the Soviet Union since Stalin* (New York: St Martin's Press).

VAN ZYL, PAUL, and GRAEME SIMPSON (1997). *Reconciliation. From Rhetoric to Reality: The Contribution of Civil Society to the Truth and Reconciliation Commission*, Working Paper (Johannesburg: Centre for the Study of Violence and Reconciliation).

VARELA, CARLOS (1989). 'The Referendum Campaign in Uruguay: An Unprecedented Challenge to Impunity', *Human Rights International Reporter*, 13 (1): 16–18.

VARGA, CSABA (ed.) (1994). *Coming to Terms with the Past under the Rule of Law: The German and Czech Models* (Budapest: Windsor Klub).

VAROLI, JOHN (1997). 'Russia Prefers to Forget', *Transitions* (July): 35–41.

VEIGA, FRANCISCO (1995). *La trampa balcánica* (Barcelona: Grijalbo).

VERBITSKY, HORACIO (1995). *El vuelo* (Buenos Aires: Planeta).

VERWOERD, W. (1996). 'Continuing the Discussion: Reflections from within the Truth and Reconciliation Commission', *Current Writing*, 8 (2): 66–85.

—— (1997) 'Justice after Apartheid? Reflections on the South African Truth and Reconciliation Commission', paper presented at the International Conference on Ethics and Development, Globalisation, Self-determination and Justice in Development, Madras, India, 2–9 January.

VIDAL-BENEYTO, JOSÉ (1981). *Diario de una ocasión perdida* (Barcelona: Kairós).

VIDAL-NAQUET, PIERRE (1992). *Assassins of Memory: Essays on the Denial of the Holocaust* (New York: Columbia University Press).

VILENSKY, SEYMON (1997) 'Maska Skorbi', in *Volya: Zhurnal Uznikov totalitarnogo sistema,* 6–7 (Moscow: Vozvrashchenie), 9–14.

VINTON, LOUISA (1992). 'Poland's Government Crisis: An End in Sight?' *RFL/RL Research Report*, 1 (30): 15–25.

VON RUNSTEDT, SOPHIA (1997). 'The Restitution of Property after Communism: Germany, the Czech Republic and Poland', *Parker School Journal of East European Law*, 4 (3): 261–278.

Vujacic, Veljko (1996). 'Historical Legacies, Nationalist Mobilization and Political Outcomes in Russia and Serbia: A Weberian View', *Theory and Society*, 25 (6): 736–801.

Waldron, Jeremy (1992). 'Superseding Historic Injustice', *Ethics*, 103: 4–28.

Walicki, Andrzej (1997). 'Transitional Justice and the Political Struggles of Post-Communist Poland', in James A. McAdams (ed.), *Transitional Justice and the Rule of Law in New Democracies* (South Bend, Ind.: University of Notre Dame Press), 185–237.

Walsh, Brian (1996). 'Resolving the Human Rights Violations of a Previous Regime', *World Affairs*, 158 (3): 111–121.

Walzer, Michael (1997). 'The Hard Questions: Judgement Days', *New Republic* (15 December): 13–15.

Watson, Cameron (1996). 'Folklore and Basque Nationalism: Language, Myth, Reality', *Nations and Nationalism*, 2 (1): 17–34.

Webb, Igor, Mitscherlick, Margarete, and Kochi, Burkhard (1995). 'Former West Germans and their Past: How do Germans Face their Guilt? East Germans' Nazi and Communist Legacies', *Partisan Review*, 62 (4): 579–605.

Weigel, George (1992). 'Their Lustration—and Ours', *Commentary*, 94 (4): 34–39.

Weissbrodt, David S., and Bartolomei, María Luisa (1991). 'The Effectiveness of International Human Rights Pressures: The Case of Argentina', *Minnesota Law Review*, 75 (3): 1009–1035.

—— and Fraser, Paul W. (1992). 'Review of the Report of the Chilean National Commission on Truth and Reconciliation', *Human Rights Quarterly*, 14 (4): 601–622.

Welsh, Helga A. (1995). 'Shadows of the Past: Germany and the Legacy of SED Rule', in Peter H. Merkl (ed.), *The Federal Republic of Germany at Forty-Five: Union without Unity* (New York: New York University Press), 113–127.

—— (1996). 'Dealing with the Communist Past: Central and Eastern European Experiences after 1990', *Europe-Asia Studies*, 47 (3): 413–428.

Werle, Gerhard (1995). 'We Asked for Justice and We Got the Rule of Law: German Courts and the Totalitarian Past', *South African Journal on Human Rights*, 11 (1): 70–83.

—— (1996). 'Without Truth no Reconciliation: The South African Rechstaat and the Apartheid Past', *Law and Politics in Africa, Asia and Latin America*, 29 (1): 58–72.

Weschler, Laurence (1990). *A Miracle a Universe: Settling Accounts with Past Torturers* (New York: Pantheon Books).

—— (1992). 'The Velvet Purge: The Trials of Jan Kavan', *New Yorker* (19 October): 66–96.

Wexler, Leila Sadat (1995). 'Reflections on the Trial of Vichy Collaborator Paul Touvier for Crimes against Humanity in France', *Law and Social Inquiry*, 20 (1): 191–222.

White, Anne (1995). 'The Memorial Society in the Russian Provinces', *Europe–Asia Studies*, 47 (8): 1343–1366.

White, Hayden (1973). *Metahistory: The Historical Imagination in the Nineteenth Century in Central Europe* (Baltimore: Johns Hopkins University Press).

Whitfield, Teresa (1997). 'The Role of the United Nations in El Salvador and Guatemala: A Preliminary Comparison', paper presented at the Conference on Comparative Peace Processes in Latin America, Woodrow Wilson International Centre for Scholars, 13–14 March.

Wiesenthal, Helmut (ed.) (1996). *Einheit als Privileg: Vergleichende Perspektiven auf die Transformation Ostdeutschlands* (Frankfurt/Main: Campus).

—— (1998). 'Post-Unification Dissatisfaction, or Why Are So Many East Germans Unhappy with the New Political System?' *German Politics*, 7 (2): 1–30.

Wilde, Alex (1999). 'Irruptions of Memory: Expressive Politics in Chile's Transition to Democracy', *Journal of Latin American Studies*, 31 (2): 473–500.

Wilke, Manfred (1997). 'Die deutsche Einheit und die Geschichtspolitik des Bundestages', *Deutschland-Archiv*, 30: 607–13.

Williams, Philip J. and Walters, Knut (1997). *Militarisation and Demilitarisation in El Salvador's Transition to Democracy* (Pittsburgh: University of Pittsburgh Press).

Wilson, Richard A. (1995). 'Manufacturing Legitimacy: The Truth and Reconciliation Commission and the Rule of Law', *Indicator South Africa* (December): 41–46.

—— (1996). 'The Sizwe Will Not Go Away: The Truth and Reconciliation Commission, Human Rights and Nation-Building in South Africa', *African Studies*, 55 (2): 1–20.

—— (1997). *The People's Conscience? Civil Groups, Peace and Justice in the South African and Guatemalan Transitions*, Briefing Paper (London: Catholic Institute for International Relations).

—— (1998). 'The Politics of Remembering and Forgetting in Guatemala', in Rachel Sieder (ed.), *Guatemala after the Peace Accords* (London: Institute of Latin American Studies), 196–204.

Wilson, Richard J. (1999). 'Prosecuting Pinochet: International Crimes in Spanish Domestic Law', *Human Rights Quarterly*, 21 (4): 927–979.

Woetzal, Robert (1962). *The Nuremberg Trials in International Law* (New York: Praeger).

WOLA (Washington Office on Latin America) (1991). *Human Rights and Reconciliation in Chile* (Washington DC: WOLA).

—— (1998). *La reforma judicial en Guatemala, 1997–1998: una guía básica sobre los problemas, procesos y actores* (Guatemala: WOLA).

Wolchik, Sharon L. (1993). 'The Repluralisation of Politics in Czechoslovakia', *Communist and Postcommunist Studies*, 26 (4): 412–431.

Wolle, Stefan (1992). 'The Poisoned Society: The Stasi File Syndrome in the Former GDR', *History Workshop*, 33: 138–144.

—— (1998). *Die heile Welt der Diktatur: Alltag und Herrschaft in der DDR 1971–1989* (Berlin: Ch. Links).

WOODHOUSE, C. M. (1985). *The Rise and Fall of the Greek Colonels* (London: Granada).

WYLIE, DIANA (1995). 'Dealing with the Past: History in the New South Africa', *Yale Review*, 83 (2): 18–34.

WYNIA, GARY (1992). *Argentina: Illusions and Realities* (New York: Holmes & Meier).

YASHAR, DEBORAH (1997). 'The Quetzal is Red: Military States, Popular Movements, and Political Violence in Guatemala', in Douglas Chalmers *et al.* (eds.), *The New Politics of Inequality in Latin America: Rethinking Participation and Representation* (Oxford: Oxford University Press), 239–260.

YASMANN, VICTOR (1993). 'Legislation on Screening and State Security in Russia', *RFL/RL Research Report*, 2 (32): 11–16.

YOUNG, JAMES E. (1988). *Writing and Rewriting the Holocaust: Narrative and the Consequences of Interpretation* (Bloomington, Ind.: Indiana University Press).

—— (1992). 'The Counter Movement: Memory against Itself in Germany Today', *Critical Inquiry*, 18 (2): 267–296

—— (1993). *The Texture of Memory: Holocaust Memorials and Meaning* (New Haven, Conn.: Yale University Press).

YOUNGBLOOD, WILLIAM R. (1995). 'Poland's Struggle for a Restitution Policy in the 1990s', *Emory International Law Review*, 9 (2): 645–678.

ZAKARIA, FAREED (1998). 'The Rise of Illiberal Democracy', *Foreign Affairs*, 76 (6): 22–43.

ZALAQUETT, JOSÉ (1990). 'International Human Rights Symposium: Confronting Human Rights Violations Committed by Previous Regimes', *Hamline Law Review*, 13 (3): 623–660.

—— (1991). *The Ethics of Responsibility. Human Rights: Truth and Reconciliation in Chile*, Issues on Human Rights Paper 2 (Washington DC: WOLA).

—— (1992). 'Balancing Ethical Imperatives and Political Constraints: The Dilemma of New Democracies Confronting Past Human Rights Violations', *Hastings Law Journal*, 43 (6): 1425–1438.

ZINNER, TIBOR (1985). 'The Trials of War Criminals: Internments, Resettlements and Screening Processes 1945–1949', *Tortenelmi Szemle*, 23 (1): 118–137.

ZUR, JUDITH (1998). *Violent Memories: Mayan War Widows in Guatemala* (Boulder, Colo.: Westview Press).

Index